Irish poetry since 1950

MANCHESTER
UNIVERSITY PRESS

Irish poetry since 1950

From stillness into history

JOHN GOODBY

MANCHESTER UNIVERSITY PRESS

Manchester and New York

distributed exclusively in the USA by St. Martin's Press

Published by Manchester University Press
Oxford Road, Manchester M13 9NR, UK
and Room 400, 175 Fifth Avenue, New York, NY 10010, USA
http://www.man.ac.uk/mup

Distributed exclusively in the USA by
St. Martin's Press, Inc., 175 Fifth Avenue, New York, NY 10010, USA

Distributed exclusively in Canada by
UBC Press, University of British Columbia, 2029 West Mall, Vancouver, BC,
Canada V6T 1Z2

British Library Cataloguing-in-Publication Data
A catalogue record for this book is available from the British Library

Library of Congress Cataloging-in-Publication Data applied for

ISBN 0 7190 2996 1 *hardback*   0 7190 2997 X *paperback*

First published 2000

07 06 05 04 03 02 01 00   10 9 8 7 6 5 4 3 2 1

The author and publishers wish to thank the following: Paul Durcan for permission to quote 'Ireland, 1972', 'They Say the Butterfly is the Hardest Stroke' and 'For the Lord Tennyson I Will Lay Down My Life' from *A Snail in My Prime*, first published in Great Britain in 1993 by Harvill, copyright © Paul Durcan, 1993 and reproduced by permission of the Harvill Press; Faber and Faber Limited, for permission to quote from 'The Strange Museum' by Tom Paulin, 1980; Faber and Faber Limited, Farrar, Straus & Giroux and Wake Forest Press for permission to quote from 'Bog Oak' and 'Broagh' from *Wintering Out* (1972), 'Widgeon' and 'The First Kingdom' from *Station Island* (1984) by Seamus Heaney, 'Hedgehog' from *New Weather* (1973), 'Mules' from *Mules* (1977), 'October, 1950', 'Ireland' and 'Why Brownlee Left' from *Why Brownlee Left* (1980), and 'The Right Arm' from *Quoof* (1983) by Paul Muldoon; The Gallery Press for permission to quote from John Montague, *The Rough Field* (1989), Eiléan Ní Chuilleanáin, *The Second Voyage* (1986), Ciaran Carson, *The Irish For No* (1987), Derek Mahon, *Collected Poems* (1999), James Simmons, *Poems 1956–1986* (1986), Medbh McGuckian, *The Flower Master and Other Poems* (1993) and Michael Hartnett, *Selected and New Poems* (1994); Bloodaxe Press for permission to quote from 'Fundamentals' from *The Bradford Count* (1991) by Ian Duhig, 1991; Peter Fallon for permission to quote 'Canal Bank Walk' by Patrick Kavanagh; Thomas McCarthy for permission to quote from 'State Funeral'; and Anthony Farrell of Lilliput Press and R. Dardis Clarke, 21 Pleasants Street, Dublin 8, Ireland, for permission to quote 'Mother and Child' by Austin Clarke, 1955. Every effort has been made to secure all necessary clearances and permissions. Both the author and publishers will be glad to recognise any holders of copyright who have not been acknowledged above.

Typeset in Meridien with Gill Sans display
by Best-set Typesetter Ltd., Hong Kong
Printed in Great Britain
by Bell & Bain Ltd, Glasgow

Contents

Acknowledgements

Earlier versions of parts of Chapters 1 and 4 have appeared as: '"The Prouder Counsel of Her Throat": Towards a Feminist Reading of Austin Clarke' in the *Irish University Review*, Autumn 1999; and 'Hermeneutic Hermeticism: Paul Muldoon and the Northern Irish Poetic', in *In Black and Gold: Contiguous Traditions in Post-War British and Irish Poetry*, edited by C. C. Barfoot (Atlanta/Amsterdam: Rodopi Press, 1994), 137–68.

This book has been long in the making and substantial debts of gratitude have been incurred in the process. So too have debts of an opposite nature, since the first draft was destroyed by oversight – together with 80 kilograms of books and research material – on arrival at Swansea in October 1994. As tends to be the case in these buck-passing times, blame for this loss circulated for months, like the proverbial signifier in search of its signified, until at last it became clear that nobody had actually *done* anything at all; the boxes had effectively self-destructed; and if this recalls Krook's fate in *Bleak House*, I did consider at one stage giving the book, if I ever had the heart to rewrite it, Dickens's original title for *Little Dorrit*, *Nobody's Fault*. Thanks go to the only person in authority at that time who turned his shock into practical action, Professor Gino Bedani of the Italian Department at Swansea, and I thank him here for his help in winning more generous compensation as well as for raising morale when it was at its lowest low ebb. For their support and encouragement throughout I'd like to thank my colleagues Rob Penhallurick, Caroline Franklin, Steve Vine, Glyn Pursglove, Tom Cheesman and Marie Gillespie, and Alex Davis of UCC, who made useful suggestions at a formative stage. I thank Simon Jenner for a timely phone call following a panic attack and, of the poets treated in the book, I am grateful to Eiléan Ní Chuilleanáin, Ian Duhig and Peter Sirr for their generous assistance. Among my students, thanks go to Jo Furber who helped me get the show back on the road, and – most of all – to Chris Wigginton, whose tireless efforts in reading and editing the typescript were absolutely crucial. Tribute must also be paid to Manchester University Press who persisted in their faith that I could finish the book, beyond all reasonable expectation; in particular I'd like to thank John Banks, who commissioned it, and Lauren McAllister and Matthew Frost, who saw it to its conclusion. Nor would these acknowledgements be complete without a record of my thanks to my copy editor, Monica Kendall, who rooted out innumerable errors. The shortcomings of this book, despite the efforts of box-destroyers and their apologists are, of course, entirely my own responsibility. Finally, the biggest thanks of all go to Nicola, Katie and George, whose generosity, love and patience over the years made this book possible.

Introduction: 'from stillness into history . . .'

It is a fact of modern literary history that Irish poetry has, since the early 1960s, flourished as never before. From a mid-century largely characterised by inertia and isolation, it has moved, to adapt Tom Paulin's phrase, 'from stillness into history', with Seamus Heaney's Nobel Prize in 1995 only the most obvious sign of international recognition (Paulin, 1980: 30). By 1960, poets from the Republic – John Montague, Thomas Kinsella and Richard Murphy – had already become the first Irish poets to attract significant attention in the USA and Britain since the time of Denis Devlin in the 1940s, and Yeats before him, and were about to be caught up in the rapid economic and social modernisation of the country which began in 1959. But it has been Northern Irish poetry which, since the end of the 1960s, has attracted the lion's share of praise from readers and critics and which has been most influential on poetic practice beyond the island. In this sense, the Troubles after 1968/69, which this poetry mediated, and which drew attention to all aspects of Northern Irish life, have been arguably 'the most single influential factor on the subsequent history not only of Britain and Ireland, but also of contemporary "English" poetry' (Corcoran, 1993: 136). As a result it often seems that modernisation and violence have been the twin stars guiding the destinies of recent Irish poetry. Yet the terms of consideration – as reflected in my own vocabulary ('recognition', 'status', 'influential') – are all too often the potentially dangerous ones which are applied to small nation literatures whose largest audiences are located beyond their boundaries in more powerful states. The problem is that, seen from outside Ireland, the effects of modernisation and the Troubles can encourage the exaggeration and confirmation of existing stereotypes – tradition versus modernity, for example, or the centrality of violence – and assumptions about the kind of poetry being dealt with. Accordingly, Irish poetry is often presumed to be conservative (by comparison with US poetry) and anomalous (by comparison with British poetry), to be concerned with identity (but content to accept the stability of the self in philosophical terms), to be obsessed with the past and discursively realist (Northern Irish poetry 'serving up the horror of [the Troubles] hot', for example).[1]

This is not to say that Irish poetry is *not*, generally speaking, anomalous or conservative in comparison with Anglo-American, or general Western norms. Nor is it to deny that these factors have made it unique, at least in European/US terms, and given it something of its peculiar interest. Rather, in

highlighting the fact, I merely wish to note the tendency to circular, predetermined quality of much critical engagement, which encourages sweeping
generalisations (Irish poetry as 'postcolonial', Northern Irish poetry as a haven
of true poetic values in a world of parasitic metadiscourses) and exclusivity
(Northern Irish 'Protestant' or neo-modernist poetry as 'un-Irish'). At almost
every point in any discussion, I would argue, the complex explanation of the
circumstances of the poetry is more satisfactory than the simple one. Northern Irish poetry, for example, had undergone its crucial formative period before
the outbreak of violence, while the roots of the 1960s' poetry of the Republic
lie in the tortuously involuted cultural scene of the pre-modernisation period
of the 1940s and 1950s. Similarly, modernist experimentalism cannot be
limited to Joyce and Beckett and presumed to have no current existence or
contemporary relevance. A criticism tempted by quick-fix critical solutions
risks exoticising and simplifying the range and complexity of Irish poetry
(something the best of the poetry itself resists).

This book starts from the premise that not only is there a need for a more
detailed history than already exists, but that there are very good reasons why
more inclusive accounts have hitherto failed to materialise. One reason for
the lack of inclusivity is the obvious political one of the two Irelands, the
Republic and Northern Ireland. Criticism, and to a lesser extent poetry, still
suffers from the continuing effects of Partition, which copper-fastened the
isolation and conservatism of the two states, locking literary exchange into
the conditions of sectarianised misunderstanding which limited poetry on
both sides of the border, and confirmed the most inward-looking and stultify-
ing aspects of each. There is a belief still held in some quarters in the Republic, that Northern Irish poetry is a 'journalistic invention', a localised blip
ultimately to be subsumed within a larger, unitary 'Irish' tradition stretching
back over a thousand years. This claim, all but useless for contemporary critical purposes, finds its reflection in an assertion of the validity of an English-
oriented poetic which can show indifference to poetry in the Republic. What
has been most notable in recent years, however, has not been this particular
debate but the emergence of newer theoretical approaches – feminist, Marxist,
post-structuralist, postcolonial – which have been applied fruitfully to Irish
literature.

However, in breaking with older models, these approaches have so far
failed to yield a more inclusivist account of the poetry due to their reliance on
the traditional canon. Failure to broaden (or break with) the established canon
stems only in part from an understanding that a more general critical scepticism towards metanarratives is enhanced by the limited applicability of
Enlightenment-derived notions of progress and rationality (and hence of totalising, causal histories) to the Irish experience. More influential in certain other
accounts is the rather narrow fixation on identity which clearly obsesses
traditional critical discourse. In other words it is the very applicability of
newer forms of criticism to the deconstruction of traditionalist paradigms

which has on occasion acted to limit its potential for acknowledging the variousness of the poetry and hence open up broader lines of enquiry. There is, in the sensitivity of such criticism concerning its outsider status, a tendency to dismissively pre-empt the notion of a more inclusive account before an idea of what it might look like can form, both for ideological reasons and because its external location prevents a more thorough acquaintance.[2]

This is more than merely a thematic issue, or a question of simply filling in a few gaps and lost reputations for the sake of a smoother narrative schema. There are fundamental aesthetic and cultural issues at stake in extending the critical franchise. To overlook, for example, Anthony Cronin, Eugene Watters, Padraic Fallon, Denis Devlin, Brian Coffey, Austin Clarke, Eiléan Ní Chuilleanáin, Thomas McCarthy, Michael Longley or Catherine Walsh is not only to collude in a self-selecting mainstream (and hence reinforce a dubious notion of 'major' and 'minor' writing), but also to limit an understanding of better-known figures by suppressing awareness of the literary dynamic, the range of alternatives, from which they made their (more approved) stylistic and thematic choices.[3] Such a simplification of the corpus can lead to what are arguably far more improper 'totalising' narratives, ranging from the rejection of modernism as 'parasitic' and essentially un-Irish, to the claim that the mere fact of modernisation in Ireland has made Irish poetry modern*ist*, or that historical discontinuity produces a literature which is modernist *avant la lettre*. Put another way, there is a danger of generalising too easily from the 'unevenness' or lopsidedness characteristic of the Irish historical experience to either a merely empirical 'pluralism' or a radical theoreticism limited by its agreement on the canon under dispute. The lack of an inclusive account of recent poetry, then, flows from the narrowness of bilateral canonical agreements and that lack further reveals a set of critical discourses which work to reify the recent achievements in the field, yet steadfastly prevent a sense of its scope and the relationship between its parts emerging.

After Yeats or since Joyce?

Two related issues can be seen here, both bearing sharply on the most inclusive histories to have appeared to date, Dillon Johnston's *Irish Poetry after Joyce* (1985, revised 1995) and Robert Garratt's *Modern Irish Poetry: Tradition and Continuity from Yeats to Heaney* (1986, revised 1989), namely tradition and identity. While Garratt is strong on poetry between the 1920s and the 1950s, Johnston covers developments in the 1960s and 1970s thoroughly and illuminatingly. Each book has signal virtues, but both are innocent of recent critical theory and neither ranges beyond a handful of major figures (Garratt's are Clarke, Kavanagh, Kinsella, Montague and Heaney; Johnston adds to these MacNeice, Devlin and Mahon). The omission of Protestant-background and modernist poets permits Garratt's thesis that there is a single legitimate Irish poetic tradition which is Catholic-Nationalist and conservative.[4] Johnston's approach is more pluralistic, and his introductory chapter takes its title from the 1983 New Ireland Forum ('Towards a broader, more comprehensive definition . . .'). Again, though, the number of poets discussed is small and they are paired Tweedledum–Tweedledee fashion (Kavanagh/Heaney, Clarke/Kinsella, Devlin/Montague, Mahon/MacNeice – a schema which has been extended by Seamus Deane to include Muldoon/Paulin) (Deane, 1986). If this allows some interesting comparisons, its schematism tends to reduce poetry to a personalised oedipal struggle. Not only is poetry locked off from consideration of its mediation of social contexts, but the separation of poetry from its conditions of production and consumption is also upheld. As a result Johnston, like Garratt, ultimately reinforces the idea that there is a unitary national Irish poetic tradition, broadly characterised by a concern with identity in the process of separating poetry from its contexts. Praise for the 'Waterford-clear' qualities of Paul Muldoon's poetry – contextualising a Northern poet by reference to a factory in the Republic – thus seems both irritatingly knowing and bizarrely totalising, as it blithely erases cultural difference within single-nation assumptions and an anecdotal stylistics.

Behind both studies lies a disabling pseudo-argument or myth, perhaps the most pervasive in Irish criticism, one summed up in Patrick Crotty's observation that 'it might be said that Irish writers make poetry less out of the quarrel with themselves than with the founder of the Literary Revival'[5] (Crotty, 1995: 1). For Crotty, as for many critics, the story of modern Irish poetry is that of poets turning to Joyce to escape the 'menacing and deadly' mythologies of Yeats, with 'the Joycean tenor of post-Yeatsian poetry correct[ing] the tendency of the Revival to idealise Irish life by converting a poetry of feeling into a poetry of thought'[6] (Garratt, 1989: 269). This book takes issue not with the status of Yeats and Joyce or their 'influence' (exaggerated though this has been) so much as with what might be called After Yeats Or Since Joyce Syndrome, the tendency to relate all subsequent Irish poetry to a pair of founding fathers (Tweedledum and Tweedledee again). The division of Irish poetry into what John Wilson Foster has called the 'Romantic' and the 'pluralist' is deeply unsatisfactory in many ways.[7] It requires, for one thing, the conflation of (Protestant) Yeatsian Revivalism with 'myth' and (Catholic) Joyce with 'reality', effecting a progress from myth to realism which requires us to overlook Yeats's all-too-realist 1930s' interests in eugenics and fascism, as well as the myth-saturated methods of *Ulysses* and *Finnegans Wake*. (The fact that Kavanagh – upon whom, as the exorcist of Yeats, so many rely – read *Ulysses* as 'a transcription of reality', is insufficient critical sanction in the 1990s, and defining the poetry of the 1940s and 1950s in such terms tells us more about his counter-Revivalism than Yeats, Joyce or their significance for modern poetry.[8]) Furthermore, it assumes a prolonged intimidation by Yeats of later poets, although the actual evidence for this is thin. As Michael

O'Loughlin puts it, 'The problem is that *to the external eye* he seems to be the dominant figure . . . the label "After Yeats" . . . tends to yoke modern Irish poets into a discourse they do not belong to'[9] (O'Loughlin, 1985b: 18) (my emphasis). If this paradigm continues to flourish it is largely because the polarised critical debate in Irish cultural politics requires it. Yeats and Joyce are conscripted to set positions, although in reality the status of both subverts these. (Is Yeats Nationalist, imperialist and/or the upholder of the 'well-made' tradition in Irish poetry? Is Joyce anti-colonialist, escapist émigré and/or irresponsibly ludic?)[10]

The Yeats versus Joyce myth of origin has been influential both because it provides a 'tradition' which can pass over material contexts and because it figures a long-standing debate concerning Irish identity in its colonial and post-colonial forms. While this debate has been constant for nearly two centuries, the apotheosis of a pure Irish identity – one uncontaminated by the modern, the corruptly cosmopolitan, the linguistically and ethnically Anglo-Saxon – is summed up in the unstably tautologous phrase 'Irish Ireland', coined by D. P. Moran in the 1900s. Moran's policy was the logical terminus of an anti-colonial discourse of Irish identity which originated in nineteenth-century Romanticism and Nationalism.[11] Its instabilities (or ideological contradictions) had surfaced during the Revival period as the leadership of cultural national-ism passed from the Protestant middle-class/Anglo-Irish Ascendancy intelli-gentsia to one drawn from the Catholic middle classes, and centred on the question of how a new, decolonised Irish identity might be forged. While Douglas Hyde, the Protestant founder of the Gaelic League, had claimed in 1892 that Irish national consciousness could be decolonised by making Irish the national language again, Moran's programme went beyond Hyde's language-based inclusivism to the exclusivist goal of total national cultural self-sufficiency and a complete cultural, even ethnic, restoration of a 'pure' pre-colonial Irishness. This became the programme of the Catholic intelli-gentsia which ousted the likes of Yeats from leadership of the Revival project, and became the basis of the ideology of the Free State, underpinned by con-servative Catholicism and enforced through rigid censorship. Yet if censorship was effective in isolating Ireland, Gaelicisation proved a failure.[12]

In poetry, the neo-Revivalists who more or less accepted Irish Ireland – Higgins, Gibbon, Clarke, Fallon, Farren, Colum – sought to translate its ideas into stylistic terms via an application of its literary equivalent, the 'Irish mode'. The term, coined by Thomas MacDonagh in 1916, refers to a poetic style inflected by Hiberno-English and was seen as offering a writing distinct from metropolitan literary modes, a means by which Irish poets might avoid becom-ing 'John Bull's Other Rhymers'.[13] Effectively, it was an anti-colonial mode of writing intended to supplement the dominant Irish-language literature which it was assumed would emerge in the transition to a fully re-Gaelicised Ireland. MacDonagh's work, however, lent itself to a definition of Irish writing founded in ethnic identity, one which valorised the lyric and ruralism (the speech/ poetry of the rural areas – less distant from dying Irish – being deemed less corrupt than that of the urban population caught in 'the net of the crooked town'),[14] and his most influential follower, Daniel Corkery, elaborated in the 1920s and 1930s a literary litmus test by which Irish writing was to be judged according to the degree to which it reflected '(1) The Religious Consciousness of the People; (2) Irish Nationalism; and (3) The Land.'[15] Corkery's thoughts were shaped by the nature of the conservative state, even as they acted to shape it and its policies, which included approved literary representations. Neo-Revivalist poets were not merely influenced by official Nationalist ideology, official Nationalism *was* a form of poetry, an aestheticised mode of the anti-imperial struggle based on an inversion of colonial discourses which tended to mirror their categories. Poetry's idealisation of the rural and the peasant offered 'essentially a literary trope' as 'a cornerstone for cultural and economic policy' and was 'complicit with the essentialist ideologies deployed by the nationalist bourgeoisie to dominate the postcolonial state'[16] (Cairns and Richards, 1988: 133; Smyth, 1998: 133). In this way, the 'Irish mode', an interim tactic for asserting literary-cultural identity, became a long-term strategy which embodied linguistic-cultural schism and bound poetry to conservative forms of expression, acting as a figleaf for Revival idealism and symbolic of the quixotic hopelessness of recovering lost linguistic plenitude. An early form of cultural decolonisation, it was linked to a state whose illiberalism was emblematised in the flight abroad of many of its leading writers after 1922.

While the Yeats-versus-Joyce debate presents itself as a way beyond the Irish mode and Corkery, its function in critical debate shows that in many significant ways it merely continues the presuppositions of Irish mode poetics. The appeal to either author reflects a need for a point of re-origination for Irish poetry, drawing on the coincidence of the deaths of Yeats (1939) and Joyce (1941) and the publication of Patrick Kavanagh's *The Great Hunger* (1942), the first major break with Irish mode poetics – after Yeats himself – within Ireland (the 1930s' modernist poets broke with it, but lived abroad and had little influence in Ireland itself). The suggestiveness of these dates (which conveniently run epochal finality into the apotheosis of counter-Revivalism) is used to sanction a notion of overcoming past discontinuity which elides the severity of the hiatus of the 1940s and much of the 1950s. (Kavanagh's victory in *The Great Hunger* was a pyrrhic one, containing within it as it did a forecast of the limitations of a sociological critique even as it made its devastating case.) There was no singular moment of crisis and recovery in the Republic. Limited political thaw began between 1948 and 1951, but the crisis generated by mass emigration was not tackled until 1958/59. If anything, isolation increased in Northern Ireland in the 1950s. Poetry's response to and mediation of these processes was necessarily haphazard and contradictory, productive of generational and stylistic confusion.

All is changed . . . ?

In the 1960s the frozen relationship between the two Irish states and between them and the outside world was transformed. Tentativeness was replaced in some cases by a quasi-epic ambition in the young poets of the Republic, and by a regionalist self-assertion in Northern Ireland owing much to the shift in Britain from an authoritarian to a libertarian culture, and towards a more decentralised cultural production (the change in British culture also partly exposed the datedness of the terms in which poets in the Republic saw their relationship to it). Alex Callinicos has claimed that long-delayed industrialisation in France in the 1950s and 1960s resulted in a recrudescence of modernism in French culture, and something of the same effect can be traced in the Republic (Callinicos, 1989: 71). Limited deployment of modernist technique can be seen in Montague's *The Rough Field*, while Kinsella was to embrace US poetic modernism more wholeheartedly as a way of figuring Irish culture as radically discontinuous. By the end of the 1960s, however, the neo-modernist undercurrent in Irish poetry which had largely been displaced into exile writing had re-established itself in Ireland, drawing on even more radical poetic practice than those of Montague or Kinsella. The example of the New Writers' Press group serves as a warning that it would be misleading to claim all poetry of the period as somehow 'modernist' simply because it was produced by a society in the throes of modernisation. At the same time, other voices denied by the mid-century dispensation – of youth and popular culture, of women, of an urban and socialist consciousness – were developing alternatives to epic poetic synthesis and formal experimentalism.

It has been argued by Fredric Jameson that the 1960s saw 'the last surviving zones of precapitalism – the last vestiges of noncommodified or traditional space within and outside the advanced world – . . . penetrated and colonized in their turn' by multinational capital. This is roughly what happened in the Republic under Lemass as traditionalist autarky was dispensed with; 'roughly', because it makes little sense to view the Republic as 'Third World'. Jameson further argues that 'a First World 60s owed much to Third Worldism in terms of politico-cultural models', and that the 'most important First World political movement of all – the new black politics and Civil Rights movement [in the USA] . . . dated from . . . 1960'; it was thus the independence movements in Africa and the emergence of new 'subjects of history' – blacks, students, Third World peoples – which triggered what are usually thought of as First World 1960s' radical phenomena. Third World revolt thus needs to be seen in the context of political reaction of the 1950s in the West, to which it was a response, for, as metropolitan political paralysis provoked external revolution, this led in turn to a radicalisation of metropolitan politics. This is immensely suggestive in the Irish context(s), and not only because of the link between black and Northern Irish Civil Rights movements, or the re-involvement of the Republic in international politics. What Jameson refers to as 'a crisis in the institutions through which a real class politics had, however imperfectly, been able to express itself' applies to Fianna Fáil and the Unionist Party in the 1950s as much as to his more celebrated examples (Jameson, 1988: 206, 180, 181). But while in Jameson's schema radical movements in the US and France were linked to, but ultimately separate from, their Third World occasions – Algeria, Cuba/Vietnam – in Ireland, because of its dual metropolitan and colonial history, its advanced yet peripheral economy, both kinds of development were at work at once. A series of complexly linked processes can be seen in which there is a simultaneous sense of liberation and domination in a single geographical (and in some senses cultural) but politically divided territory.

Having Troubles

It was at this point, however, in 1968/69, that modernisation and the decolonising processes collapsed into the 'Troubles'. The poets at the heart of these events – the Belfast Group – display few similarities, as critics have pointed out. What does link them is the shared moment of historic opportunity of the early and mid-1960s which – while it was squandered at the political level – lent a sense of a collective destiny and formal conservatism to their work which survives even today. There is, also, a collective belief that the Troubles violate a pre-existing decorum – social, aesthetic, political – which requires poetry to represent it (lurking within this are the attendant urges, particularly marked in Heaney, that a poet needs to act as a spokesperson for a community). For all their differences, Heaney, Mahon and Michael Longley can be viewed as products of the 1947 Education Act, the British Welfare State and of a stable post-war society who regarded the events after 1968/69 as fundamentally abnormal.

Perhaps the most coherent expression of this feeling, and of the Northern 1960s' poetic generally, is to be found in the criticism of Edna Longley, whose writings consistently espouse a belief in the autonomy of the poetic artefact of New Criticism together with a Leavisite vitalism and faith in the primacy of the local and communal knowledge. Like the poets of her generation whose work she championed, her writing – asserting the power of the 'singing line', well-crafted stanza and discursive-symbolic modes – has both a radical and a conservative edge, insisting on poetry's ability, through auratic transcendence, to rise above its context.[17] This was to prove crucial after the outbreak of the Troubles, since for Longley the separation of the political and the poetic spheres was imperative if the aesthetic and formal values of the latter were not to be distorted by the demands of the former. As she has memorably expressed it, 'Poetry and politics, like church and state, should be separated' (E. Longley, 1986: 185). On the other hand, Longley's commitment to Northern Irish poetry as a hybrid, albeit in a rather limited formalist sense, makes her more tolerant to the idea of North–South exchange (she claims that 'there is no fixed barrier' between Northern and Southern poetries).

If Longley's commitment to the 'well-made' has a political subtext,[18] it may be that in her animus against modernism – seen as parasitically self-involved, 'literary' in a footling sense, hieratic and elitist – it is also possible to detect more than purely literary prejudice against the Republic (the terms used suggest sectarian transposition from religion to art, priestly modernism opposed by the puritan authentic witnessing of the empirical lyric). Against Longley's implicitly Unionist stance, an explicitly Nationalist case was made in Seamus Deane's essay 'Irish Poetry and Irish Nationalism' of 1975, which offered a four-phase model for the development of Irish poetry through its relationship to Irish nationalism (Deane, 1975: 16–17). Accordingly, the first phase is constituted by Yeats; the second by Devlin, Clarke and Kinsella; the third by Kavanagh and Montague; and the fourth by the 1960s' Northern poets.[19] But while this is not the place to fully discuss the inadequacies of each canon, it can be noted that, despite some very basic differences in content, Deane shares with Longley the commitment to a basically representative, non- (or anti-) modernist naturalistic poetic called upon either to transcend or reflect the violence (following Heaney's *North* in particular, this would take the form of a focus on the legitimacy of the use of myth as a way of accessing the historical sense of the opposing 'communities' of Northern Ireland).

Plurabilities

One way in which the poetic generation which appeared in the 1970s in the North may be distinguished from their predecessors is by their different sense of the relationship of the self to the Troubles. Appearing in print after violence had begun, their sense of a division between the 'abnormal' and the 'normal' has consistently been more permeable. Another way of putting this would be to say that in the work of Muldoon and Paulin,' the Troubles seem more constitutive of the self than in that of their predecessors, which is not to say that they are in any way more blasé or accepting of violence. It is, rather, more insistently part of their mental furniture, less to be deplored in a simply moral sense than incorporated and worked out within the poetry itself. In this sense, there is a shift from the idea of the poem as container for a given content, and both the younger poets (like Carson and McGuckian later) take liberties with received poetic form, while preserving a distance from modernist or neo-modernist procedures. Indeed, a general challenging of the boundaries of what is proper or acceptable lies behind much of the best Irish poetry from the late 1970s onwards. In the Republic this was most evident in the emergence of a distinct and powerful women's voice in poetry.

Irish literature (and 'Irishness' generally) has from the time of Thomas Moore, been intensely aware of, and has to a varying degree thematised, an awareness of these peculiarities, which stem from Ireland's interstitial geo graphical position between the two most powerful Anglophone cultures and a (frequently) violent history of colonisation, plantation, settlement and emigration. This interstitial nature has produced the possibility of a radical misreading of Irish culture of the kind I have tried to expose. It is in the light of the complicating of the simpler Nationalist versions of this history (and in some cases of its sanitisation) by 'revisionist' historiography that the concern with Irish writing as postcolonial, which has dominated critical discourse in the 1990s and earlier, has to be seen.[20] In my final chapter, which covers the period from the Anglo-Irish Agreement of 1985 through to the (still shaky) ceasefire and Good Friday Agreement in the North, and the so-called 'Celtic Tiger' boom in the 1990s' Republic, I am concerned above all else to explore the new ways in which 'Irish poetry' has been redefined in an era of globalisation, and its relationship both to the postcolonial debate and to the processes which lie behind it.

In discussing the poetry and critical developments outlined above, I have not neglected institutional, social and historical contexts, attempting at all times to show how the poetry engaged with and intervened within these to shape them to their advantage. I argue that the unevenness of the mapping of Irish poetry is a function – albeit complexly mediated – of the general uneven development of Irish society(ies) as a whole, attempting to trace connections and interactions between Northern, Southern and non-Irish-based poetries.[21] I have also tried to give a comprehensive overview in the sense of returning to the different phases of poets' work in successive chapters; there is a danger of repetition here, but there is little point in defining Heaney, say, according to the moment of *North*, and passing over the evolution which leads to *The Spirit Level*. My main point, however, is the urgent need for a much broader understanding of the variety of Irish poetic practice. Without this an increasingly sophisticated criticism will continue to increase, rather than decrease, the 'yawning gap in critical coverage between the brief and topical reviews afforded the living and the lightweight and the large tomes devoted to our dear, dead heroes'.[22]

Notes

1 Montague, 1979: 165.
2 In this sense, Edna Longley, Seamus Deane and Steven Matthews – to take one recent non-Irish theory-driven account – while displaying disagreements on *how* Irish poetry should be read, are in almost complete agreement of *which* poets (and even *which* poems) deserve attention. It takes no great insight to see that agreement in the second of these areas raises questions about how serious are the disagreements in the first.
3 It is doubly dubious in Irish literature, where the concept of 'minor' literature generally – as David Lloyd has shown – has functioned as a means whereby geographically and socially peripheral writings have been policed and marginalised in

order to maintain the authority of a metropolitan, self-defined literary 'mainstream' (Lloyd, 1987).

4 As McDonald points out, Garratt is not interested in the contradictions of poems but in the way 'the Irish literary tradition' leads to 'the question of identity', his criticism as a result reading as 'a series of roots proclaimed, allegiances declared and set gestures rehearsed' (McDonald, 1997: 6).

5 This remains the dominant paradigm, as indicated by the title of Maurice Harmon's *Irish Poetry After Yeats* (1979). Fallon and Mahon speak of Yeats as the 'Everest' of modern Irish poetry – a metaphor which surely says something about the monolithic quality of their claim (Fallon and Mahon, 1990: xvi).

6 Thomas Kinsella's 'The Irish Writer' (Kinsella, 1967) makes this suggestion in more qualified form, arguing that 'an Irish writer . . . *might find* that Yeats stands for the Irish tradition as broken, and Joyce stands for it as healed – *or healing* – from its mutilation' (my emphasis).

7 See Foster, 1991: 217.

8 Though the tactical usefulness of casting Joyce as a realist is not denied. A reading of Joyce as a realist writer was helped by the publication of *Stephen Hero* in 1940; Kavanagh's reading of *Ulysses* as a realist text can be considered in this context. My point here, however, is that the tactical and creative misreadings of Joyce of the 1940s cannot to be made the basis for a general interpretation of post-Yeatsian poetry.

9 A perfect, if touching, instance of an inability to grasp this appears in Garratt's naively baffled observation that 'Curiously, Clarke seems to be a more imposing figure for Kinsella than the great Yeats' (Garratt, 1989: 194). If O'Loughlin simplifies – he omits Yeats's influence on traditionalist metrics, as well as (thematically) on a host of later poets, from Fallon to Boland, including Kinsella himself – his basic claim is clearly accurate enough.

10 In the 1980s, Field Day writers drew heavily on it as 'a key model by which they could define the predicaments of the aesthetic-social polarity' in which they felt they were caught (Kirkland, 1996: 34, fn. 31).

11 Although there are roots in the Celticism of the eighteenth century, most critics date the emergence of cultural nationalism as a programme in the 1840s with the Young Ireland movement and its concern with authoring the nation as a politico-cultural entity. From the first, however, cultural nationalism was riven by its reliance on Romanticism (largely English-derived in its literary strategies), the tendency of caste/class divisions to be ethnicised and sectarianised at times of social crisis, and the loss of the Irish language as a resource for reconstituting Irish identity. Ireland thus offers a classic example of the European cultural nationalist movements of the period, through which, in Gramsci's terms, organic intellectuals attempted to forge links with the 'people-nation' (Gramsci, 1971: 418). Literary Romanticism offered a heady blend of retrospective-conservative and radical-revolutionary tropes, a flexible but double-edged cultural politics. Such was the success of this paradigm of cultural preparation for political renewal that the Ulster Regionalist movement of the 1940s adopted certain Irish Ireland criteria – racial expressivity, ruralism, identitarianism – to serve its own more limited territorial needs. Howard Sergeant defined Regionalism in 1953 as 'a movement towards a future in which a balanced life in every community . . . [arising] out of a particular affection for or an attachment, conscious or unconscious, to a particular environment, and [finding] expression through a language, outlook and manner of life . . . adapted to the intellectual and emotional experience of the individual' (Sergeant, 1953). Yet just as Regionalism marked itself off, to an extent, from Englishness, the quasi-national distinctness of the 'region' was also asserted in

order that it could be distinguished the more easily from the Free State; Sergeant adds that 'while regionalism offers its contribution to the whole culture of a nation or comity of nations, nationalism is more conducive to cultural isolation'. Here the conservative content of Regionalism is apparent in the evasion of the issue of which 'nation' to which the 'whole culture' of an undefined 'Ulster' (the pre-1922 nine counties? Northern Ireland's six?) might belong (the Free State? Britain?). The choice of 'comity' suggests open-mindedness on the issue of national affiliation, even as it sidesteps the question of existing territorial partition. In a tentative manner, and taking its cue from the Agrarians of the Southern USA, Regionalism grounded itself in the 'Anglo-Irish' tradition from Swift to Yeats which now had no institutional expression in the Republic.

12 The gap between Irish as a shibboleth of the new nation and the actual numbers who spoke it as a first language widened, and by mid-century the failure of the language policy, long blamed on the after-effects of colonialism, was being increasingly attributed to the cultural purism which drove it (Lee, 1989: 134–5).

13 If the poets of the Free State, many of whom had learned Irish and supported the language policy, nevertheless remained committed to its advancement, the irony was that they wrote in English. Despite the suspicion by extreme political Nationalists that an Irish literature in English was a contradiction in terms, the linguistic facts could not be helped. The gap between an English-speaking Ireland and the Irish-Ireland ideal had been ingeniously bridged during the Revival by the identification of a distinctive quality in Anglo-Irish literature. Thus, in 1894 William Larminie advanced the notion that the prosody and 'music' of Irish poetry written in English could be deemed uniquely Irish. This idea was taken up by Thomas MacDonagh, who – like Yeats – also drew on Whitman's use of non-standard English. In an attempt to avoid Matthew Arnold's racial stereotype of the 'Celtic note' he coined the phrase the 'Irish Mode' for Irish writing in English in which elements of the recently extinguished Irish language had been retained. Not merely linguistic, for MacDonagh the 'Irish Mode' had an ideological charge, pertaining as it did to a people for whom 'the ideal, the spiritual, the mystic are the true' in opposition to 'Anglo-Saxon' materialism.

14 See P. Colum, *The Poet's Circuits: Collected Poems of Ireland* (Dublin, Dolmen Press, 1985), 124. Thus it would be possible to write of 'The spiritual greatness of a people on whom no materialistic gods have smiled', an identity often underwritten by an implicitly racist terminology (Loftus, 1964: 182, 246; Cairns and Richards, 1988: 133). Although it has been claimed that MacDonagh modified the extremism of Irish Ireland ideology in the concept of an Irish mode, he undoubtedly made more systematic a historic and linguistic construct, raising it to the order of an essential difference between two ethnic expressivities, to '[replicate] Arnold in a specifically Gaelic context' (Welch, 1996: 333).

15 Corkery, 1931: 19.

16 It has been argued that the failure of Gaelicisation inserted a 'productive but troublesome disturbance into what might otherwise have become the complacent self-congratulation of a successful political revolution', but the reality was complacent enough (S. Smith in Kenneally, 1995: 61). The exceptions to 'self-congratulation' in the 1930s – Joycean modernism, MacNeice and Yeats – were ruled out of consideration *per se* by Corkery's terms of reference.

17 In Longley, Leavisite ideology and New Critical close reading techniques combined in an insurgent critical formation (thus, attacks on Longley's practice which see only her valorisation of an organicist and autonomous model of lyric poetry miss the radical potential of Leavisism translated to non-English locations). Longley's criticism opposed a tough-minded apolitical stringency to what was perceived as a

dilettantish Dublin-based practice, insisting on the inescapability and validity of the English poetic tradition to both Yeats and Northern poetry, and the inadmissibility of excluding either from consideration on the grounds of insufficient Irishness. For Longley, poetry overcomes history by acting on its own behalf and on its own terms – internal balance, verbal music, a marriage of form and content effecting closure through the transcendent symbol, with form 'the binding force of poetry's wholeness . . . the last ditch of its aesthetic immunity' (though in practice Longley has championed poetry lacking such formal wholeness if it is critical of Nationalism). This is a criticism which limits its function to determining excellence; having found it (and Longley's canon is more narrowly drawn than that of any other critic), its role becomes more or less the reflection of the structure of the poetic artefact, bearing witness to its perfect interiority. In this way a reading community 'above present schismatic discourses' and 'the partitioned aesthetic' may be established (Kirkland, 1996: 90). However laudable the intention of attempting to separate 'poetry and politics' in an effort to maintain a sense of alternatives, the dangers are of sliding into a reactionary valorisation of poetry as a numinous realm, on its guard against 'selling out to sociological surfaces' even as it presumes, in Leavisite fashion, to pass judgement on society's fallenness, subordinating history to the transcendent signifier which is the achieved or 'settled' poem.

18 As McCormack has pointed out, the suspicion inevitably lurks that the bounded, self-contained nature of poetry as defined in this way bears more than a passing resemblance to the artificially established but 'autonomous' and self-contained state(let) of Northern Ireland; aesthetic criteria reflect a political agenda as distinct as that of her opponents (McCormack, 1986: 66).

19 In Deane's narrative, modernism is acknowledged, but not in a way which troubles a dominant Nationalist narrative. Indeed, the achronological, thematic nature of Deane's groups (Clarke with Kinsella, born thirty-five years after him, but not with Kavanagh; Kavanagh with Montague, twenty-five years younger, but not with his contemporary Devlin) – reinforces the effect of history being overridden to produce a tale of evolution away from Anglo-Irish Yeats, through eccentricity and isolationism, into a more 'natural', representative contemporary sense of Irishness. This raises the issues noted earlier about exclusion and complexity and is troubled by the recognition that the latest 'phase' of Northern poets are 'remarkably without political conviction'. This is related to the formally conservative aspects of the poetry, but in a merely gestural manner; thus, the lyric concerns of the fourth-phase poets – Heaney, Longley and Mahon – bespeak an individualistic, rather than a communal concern. In his 1977 *Crane Bag* interview with Heaney, Deane made the issue of form ideological, associating use of the 'well-made' conservative form derived from the English tradition with a 'happy acceptance' of conservative political limits. As before, his idea of radical form remains undefined and its relationship to the 'well-made' remains unassessed (Deane, 1977).

20 Revisionism poses a more stringent challenge than Field Day to the idea of Irish history as the seven-hundred-year-long struggle against England. It is now over thirty years since Grattan Freyer, in 1967, wrote that 'in the last 15 years there has been a revolution in Irish historiography . . . C. C. O'Brien, Desmond Williams and F. S. L. Lyons have set new critical standards in examining what really happened' (G. Freyer, review of Calton Younger's *Ireland's Civil War*, *Eire-Ireland* (Spring 1969), 5:1, 155). All the best historical work of the last thirty years – Lee, Lyons, the marxisant history of Bew, Patterson, Gibbon, women's history – has indeed set new standards and served to make more complex our understanding of Irish history, whether or not 'revisionism' is seen as the new orthodoxy. In Freyer's phrasing 'what really happened', however, can be seen as the chief weakness of much of what goes under the heading of revisionist historiography; against this claim, since all history relies ultimately on texts, it can be argued that no history can claim *absolutely* to represent 'what really happened'.

21 Northern Ireland, however, had enjoyed the establishment of a tightly focused poetic and critical cadre as a result of academic activity in the Belfast Group from as early as 1963. Here, however, the late moment of establishing a more modern criticism, and its association with the flourishing poetic scene of the late 1960s and after, meant that the province would remain, into the 1970s and 1980s, a place where the Leavisite legacy 'lingered . . . more stubbornly than in other parts of the United Kingdom' (Kirkland, 1996: 88). Its pervasiveness meant that it thoroughly informed the criticism of even nominal opponents such as Tom Paulin and Edna Longley, and was at some remove from that in the Republic which, like its poetry, remained without a homogeneous tone or a coherent tradition.

22 T. Clyde, The Teeming Pond, *Irish Review*, 6, 1989, 157.

Nation and stagnation

[The] best silent indictment of the whole situation is the stream of exiles ... The serious young writer will inevitably have to face the problem of exile, for as Anthony Cronin argues he may be quite justified in taking his possible gifts away with him; it is difficult to feel that Ireland, in her present state, has any claim on him. (Montague, 1989: 171)

The mid-century hiatus

For Irish poetry the mid-century was a time of tentative beginnings and very definite endings. The energies of neo-Revivalism – kindled by enthusiasm for the new Free State in the 1920s – had turned inward during the 1930s, the tendency to introversion exacerbated by partition, wartime neutrality, isolation and rigid censorship (Brown, 1985: 211–38). Although the extent of this puritan philistinism may, to some extent, have been exaggerated by those who suffered from it, it was distinctive in being extended into the post-World War II period and confirmed the continuing self-exile of older poets who had emigrated in the 1930s, among them Brian Coffey. (Denis Devlin's various sojourns abroad, on the other hand, were the accidents of a successful career in the diplomatic corps rather than the result of alienation) (B. Fallon, 1998). It had a particularly negative effect on poets who chose to remain in the country, notably Patrick Kavanagh, whose masterpiece *The Great Hunger* fell 'stillborn' from the press in 1942, when its author was cautioned by the Garda Siochána about his poem's 'immorality'.[1] Austin Clarke's reputation as the leading post-Yeatsian poet was based on work produced in the 1920s and 1930s; in 1950 he had not published a collection for twelve years, and another five would pass before *Ancient Lights*, a pamphlet collection, in 1955. The fading neo-Revivalist mode – ruralist, sentimental, centred on Irish Ireland modes – was still seen, in Ireland and abroad, as constituting the only legitimate Irish poetic tradition. The critic John Jordan, looking back in 1962, would rightly see the 1940s as a low point, 'the bad old days when Yeats was in his Mediterranean grave and the singing-birds of AE and their progeny were accepted as the chief representatives of indigenous Irish verse' (Kinsella and Montague, 1962: 107). This introverted self-sufficiency was summed up by Robert Farren in *The Course of Irish Verse in English*, which assumed an Irish poetry so wholly defined in terms of a Nationalist-Catholic, rural 'Irishness' that it could be claimed, with no sense of the circularity of the argument, that 'Irish poetry on the whole and certainly in its better parts, is decidedly Irish' (Farren, 1948: 167). In the North a Presbyterian version of the Catholic puritanism of the South held sway, compounded by sectarianism; John Hewitt, the province's leading poet, was forced to leave to work in England in 1957 after his career was blocked owing to his friendship with 'communists, Catholics and stage people'. W. R. Rodgers and Roy McFadden were also silenced, partly by the onset of the little-Englandism of the Movement and by the contradictions of Regionalism.[2] Only Louis MacNeice of living Northern Irish poets – domiciled in England since the 1930s – seemed, by 1950, to have realised his potential.

With established poets choosing or forced to find work outside Ireland (MacNeice, Hewitt, Denis Devlin and Brian Coffey), or sidelined and held back within it (Clarke, Fallon and Kavanagh), their natural successors, born in the 1910s and early 1920s, faced yet greater difficulties. In their case, for once, the use of the over-used phrase 'lost generation' is completely justified. As one of them, Valentin Iremonger, claimed just before giving up poetry in 1950, there was

> . . . between me and the hostile, hard
> Ground of society, nothing . . .
> > nothing at all
> Now to prevent the damp and the needling chill
> Eating into my bones and burrowing to my heart.[3]

This disillusion at the lack of a context, of support, of an audience, can be seen even more starkly in Northern poetry precisely because in the 1940s it had been part of the Regionalist movement. So it was that the more established poets published nothing in book form after 1951, although, as in the South it was younger poets – Robert Greacen, Maurice Craig and Sam Harrison as well as Roy McFadden – who suffered most. By 1950 Regionalism was in decline, and on both sides of the border literary stagnation was reflected in the fact that there had been no Irish publisher of poetry since 1928 (the Dolmen Press was founded in 1951, but was alone until the late 1960s), with journals few and far between. The material deprivation grew out of, and reinforced, the long-standing Irish dependence on the literary markets of the UK and the US.[4] The second issue of *Envoy*, a short-lived if lively Dublin literary journal (1949–51), marked the century's midpoint by noting the large number of books by living Irish authors out of print, and a continued 'humiliating' dependence on English publishers.[5] In more general terms, as the Bodkin Report of 1949 noted, 'it has become justifiable to say of Ireland [the Republic] that no other country of Western Europe cared less, or gave less, for the cultivation of the arts'.[6]

Out of interregnum

Yet the few years separating the generation of poets which included Iremonger and McFadden from that born around 1930 – John Montague, Richard

Murphy, Thomas Kinsella – would see a reversal of this situation, and the identification of a 'new' Irish poetry in the 1960s. For although the depressed
Dublin literary scene of the early 1950s led Montague to describe it as a place
of 'acrimony and insult' where 'the begrudgers ruled' in 'an ingrown, dis-
couraging climate', like others of his generation he was to ultimately benefit
from the post-war stirrings which began at this time (Montague, 1989: 53–4).
These stirrings – which also helped the re-emergence of Clarke and the influential final phase of Kavanagh's achievement – were a series of political and
social shifts which laid the basis for a thaw in the seemingly frozen post-
Partition relationship between Britain, Northern Ireland and the Republic. The
first signs of this were hardly propitious. In 1948 the British government, pro-
Unionist in the aftermath of World War II, gave Stormont the loyalty bonus it
had requested by reaffirming the special status of Northern Ireland. The government of Éire responded by declaring a Republic. This broke the last links
with the Crown, and was seemingly entirely in keeping with inherited stereotypes. But, while anti-Partitionist rhetoric flowed freely in the early 1950s and
the constitutional claim on the North was maintained, it was a double-edged
gesture. To proclaim a 'Republic of Ireland' signalled postcolonial defiance, but
also implied that the Southern state now regarded itself as an integral territory without the return of the North. Unusually, it was not de Valera's Fianna
Fáil party which was responsible for the change; it had been ousted in the
1948 elections after ruling since 1932. The coalition which had replaced it,
despite the ambivalent republican gesture, had dealt a blow to Fianna Fáil
hegemony which inaugurated the pendulum politics characteristic of liberal
democracies elsewhere, and in 1955 international isolation ended with the
Republic's admission to the UN (Thornley, 1964: 8). According to Thornley, it
is 'in the period 1948 to 1951 [that] we can see the first clear suggestion that
the frame in which the immediately post-revolutionary society had set was
beginning to crack', although these developments did not mark a clear change,
since 'it is difficult to detect any coherent direction to such change as occurred
[in 1948–51]' (Thornley, 1964: 16; Lee, 1989: 320). Rather, these developments ushered in a climate of uncertainty in which the national mood was
dominated by conflicting rhetorics of a modestly proposed advance towards
modernisation and of actual economic retrenchment at a time of visible expansion elsewhere. This contrasted with the rigid certainties of the immediate past,
and with the confidence of the North (boosted by the Welfare State), but did
not necessarily guarantee any fresh departure. Thus, the state of the nation in
1951 could be described as 'in the awkward semi-stage between provincialism
and urbanisation . . . the writing that will best serve it should deal with the
problems of the individual against this uneasy, semi-urban setting' (Montague,
1989: 168–9). The results of such 'awkwardness' can be traced in the dissatisfaction and tonal instability of the work of the emergent poets; in Kinsella's
filigree mixture of gothic, Eliot and early Yeats, or in the more accessible Audenesque ironies of Montague's sequence 'The Sheltered Edge'. It is typical of

the ambiguous stasis of the time that the same facts about it have generated both optimistic and pessimistic interpretations among critics (Brown, 1985: 227; Deane, 1986: 229). In this light the new poetry of the 1960s, too often read as a triumphant response to the modernisation which started in 1958/59, can more accurately be regarded as the wary exploitation of unexpected possibilities.

This needs stressing, since experience of stagnation marked the post-war poets deeply. Economistic bias overlooks the fact that the crisis which forced the pace of reform – continued population decline and social stasis – was the result of prolonged *political* inactivity, as well as the extent to which the attempted solution was also politically motivated. One way in which this was signalled was the increasing failure of the language policy; by the late 1940s teachers were complaining about the demands made of schools to carry the revival policy alone. Mass emigration had returned, tellingly in the 1940s, and rose alarmingly during the 1950s (Lee, 1989: 334–5, 373–86; Lyons, 1973: 625). Before World War II it had been regarded as an unavoidable evil (certainly the prosperity of the elite required social stability, which in turn required the export of those who were surplus to requirements). But in a period of boom elsewhere, the 1956 census – showing a drop in population to 2,895,822, the lowest ever recorded – crystallised a shaming awareness that *laissez-faire* approaches were inadequate (Bew and Patterson, 1982: 80; Lee, 1989: 373). A sense of crisis was summed up in the title of an essay collection, *The Vanishing Irish*, published in 1954, in which it was calculated that the Republic's population would fall to two million by the end of the century and that the end of the nation as a viable entity was in sight. A Fianna Fáil government was forced to consider ways of jettisoning de Valera's 'antique Carlylean dream' and of responding to 'the increasingly violent frustration that lies under the surface of young Ireland' (Montague, 1957: 71). Reformists in Fianna Fáil, most notably Seán Lemass, took the chance to renew the party's weakened hegemony by extending its traditional rural base into the urban working class.

The Church and *The Bell*

The search for a new ideology of modernisation tacitly conceded the failure of the existing traditionalist discourse of Irishness which had, literally, failed to reproduce itself, throwing the values of ruralism and self-sufficiency into question; if the de Valeran state had attempted to embody the principles of neo-Revivalism, these were now seen as near-bankrupt. But failure also implicated the most powerful organisation within the state, the Catholic Church. On the one hand the Church was implicated through its direct influence on government. On the other it was indirectly associated with demographic crisis through the puritanical discourse of sexuality it had promulgated since the late nineteenth century. The Church's stress on unregulated fertility and opposition to sex education, abortion and contraception impelled a population growth which could only be dealt with through emigration, and with it the misery of divided families and exile.[7] As has been noted, the Irish Church was staffed by 'strong farmers in cassocks', 'the sons and daughters of the rural bourgeoisie [who] sanctified an economic and social order, the preservation of which depended upon the continuous emigration of those whom an agrarian system dominated by cattle production could not employ' (Lee, 1989: 159; Bew, Hazelkorn and Patterson, 1989: 209). To some degree, then, it shared the blame; a study like Michael Sheehy's *Is Ireland Dying?* would conclude that 'the great barrier to Irish development in the twentieth century was not British imperialism but Irish puritanism', an inversion of Irish Ireland ideology anticipated extensively in 1950s' poetry by Clarke and Kavanagh and the younger poets Anthony Cronin, John Montague, Desmond O'Grady and Pearse Hutchinson (Sheehy, 1968: 242).

In 1950 the liberal social and cultural journal *The Bell* was the main focus of radical and humanist intellectual opposition to Church and the de Valeran political dispensation. In its first editorial in 1940, its founder Seán O'Faolain had clearly identified the strength of these elements with a (largely literary) Gaelicist discourse, claiming that the 'old symbolic words' of Revivalism were now 'as dead as Brian Boru, Granuile, the Shan Van Vocht . . . These belonged to the time when we growled in defeat and dreamed of the future. The future has arrived and, with its arrival, killed them. All our symbols have to be created afresh' (Cairns and Richards, 1988: 137). He identified the problem in Irish society's 'thinness', its lack of a middle class sizeable and mature enough to support a developed literature, which he in turn associated with the realist novel. This marked the start of a strenuous attempt to rethink 'Irishness' from within, to challenge a chauvinist and ethnicist focus on identity. During its lifetime (1940–46 and 1950–54), *The Bell* consistently advanced a social critique which forcefully opposed censorship, and aired issues either ignored or taken for granted (transport, welfare, housing, sport, employment, language policy, the North – MacNeice was briefly poetry editor), promoting debate and dissent at a time of near-supine conformism. Its opposition to censorship was particularly strong. Since the Censorship of Publications Act of 1929 the works of most leading twentieth-century novelists had been banned in part or in total, and Irish writers using anything but the most innocuous material had had to publish abroad. The anomalies this produced were many and glaring; the *Decameron* was banned along with pulp fiction titles such as *She Died Without Nylons* and *Hot Dames on Cold Slabs* (Carlson, 1990: vii, 144). Despite some modification after the Emergency (the Republic's euphemism for World War II), 1953 saw a record number of books being banned, since 'by the 1950s the state's laws had degenerated into witch-hunting and anti-intellectualism of the worst kind' (Smyth, 1998: 96). Abetted by the Catholic Truth Society, bookshops and libraries were regularly vetted and, while poetry was rarely a target, the experience of censorship was deeply demoralising, even intellectually infantilising (library holdings, for example, could be reduced to 'an Irish stew of imported westerns, sloppy romances, blood-and-murders bearing the *nihil obstat* of fifty-two vigilantes') (Brown, 1985: 77). In keeping with the centrality of literature to national self-identity, and hence as a form of privileged self-knowledge in Irish society – the nation as a *literary* creation – The Bell fought constraints by fostering a literary counter-current, which included Iremonger, Behan, Kavanagh and Cronin. Richard Kearney has argued that these writers 'wiped the domestic slate clean. They served as a middle generation who cut through the lush vegetation of the Celtic Twilight and created spaces where new voices might be heard' (Kearney, 1992: 46). Yet the 'symbolic words' proved hard to dislodge. The *Bell's* own gapped career is evidence of just how hard – as is the fact that even when it closed, in 1954, lack of cultural nerve remained so profound that many thought it signalled the end of Irish literary life. As Kavanagh observed, in 1952, 'the great wet blanket of Fianna Fáil smothers the imaginative life of this country' (Warner, 1973: 80). What Kearney fails to account for is the agonising slowness and unevenness of change and its limited effects on writers, effects which can be traced in the poverty-stricken and alcohol-ravaged lives of his 'demythologising set'.[8] The evidence points to more fitful recovery and a more dispiriting actuality than 'wiping the slate clean' suggests, belying the idea of a continual, if gradual, improvement from the 1940s to the 1960s.

The spirit of change haunted the 1950s, then, but without taking concrete form, and in a way reminiscent of Gramsci's characterisation of an 'interregnum' period, whose crisis 'consists precisely in the fact that the old is dying and the new cannot be born; in this [period] a great variety of morbid symptoms appear' (Gramsci, 1971: 276). Young poets had emerged, North and South, but in a situation which allowed a challenge to traditional identitarian and ethnicist concerns to be mounted only sporadically, and only after mid-decade. The frustrations of the immediate post-war period saw the poets who persevered in Ireland forced towards extremes, often satiric ones. The revival of Clarke's and Kavanagh's careers shows them filling the vacuum left by a lost middle generation of poets between them and the much younger generation to which Montague and Kinsella belonged. The low level of literary activity in the 1940s and 1950s, the close alignment of literary and political Nationalist ideologies, meant that without a challenge to moribund Nationalist (and Unionist) ideologies on a broad social scale – and hence to the relationship between the poet and literary tradition – new styles and careers could only cohere with great difficulty. The fragmentary, embittered nature of the literary society in which the young post-war poets were shaped would prevent coterie formation such as occurred in Northern Ireland in the 1960s (a consistent feature of post-war poetry in the Republic has been a stress on isolation and the lack of collective purpose of the Revival or neo-Revival writers). Any developments that did take place reflected this in their one-step-forward-two-steps-back nature; in 1951, for example, the Irish Arts Council was established, but *Envoy* folded.[9] Nevertheless there existed by the middle of the 1950s an emerging sense of literary change, as Kinsella noted:

> Up to 1955 or so the feeling is one of isolation – isolation from War and then from the dynamic post-War phenomenon in literature, economics and everything else: an Ireland hardly aware of what modern men and nations were demanding of themselves. The poets and writers who liked to call themselves Literary Dublin survived Yeats in a closed world, writing Georgian verse for each other but giving it a 'sweet, wild Gaelic twist'. (Kinsella, 1965: 106)

Against the usual patterns of literary revolt – with young poets demoralised or in flight and their middle-aged predecessors largely silent – the lead in offering an alternative to the remnants of the 'sweet, wild Gaelic twist' of shamrock Georgianism was to be taken by the older poets who had grown up within its embrace. Two main strategies for protest were available – within the established Irish mode, and from outside it. The former was that adopted by Clarke and Fallon, the latter – more spectacularly – was that taken by Kavanagh.

Opposition in an Irish mode: Austin Clarke and Padraic Fallon

In the late 1930s F. R. Higgins had warned of censorship threatening to turn Ireland into an 'Easter Island of the Western sea' (Loftus, 1964: 256–7). Higgins – who died in 1941 – never looked like acting on his insight, but his comment shows a dawning awareness from within of the dead-end of neo-Revivalism, one pushed to the point of rupture by Clarke and Fallon by the 1940s. Both had made their reputations in celebrating an eroticised, pagan version of the idealised West beloved by Irish Ireland, a congery of green islands, grey skies and fiery sunsets set to a tin-whistle soundtrack, its landscapes peopled by obliging peasant girls, merry cattle-drovers and sage turf-cutters. This poetry was at once mildly subversive of the status quo and in thrall to 'buckleppery', to use the term Kavanagh had applied to Higgins's work. Even given a satirical edge, as in Clarke's Celto-Romanesque, its critique was limited to 'thinking . . . how wild blossom, bole and root / Was broken under a cleric's heavy foot' (P. Fallon, 1990: 23). With *Night and Morning* (1938) Clarke had discovered a poetry of religious doubt and anguish in which his complex style was harnessed to new, more urgently personal purposes. Yet although its confessionalism would later provide a means of breaking new ground in *Mnemosyne Lay in Dust* (1966) its potential was not exploited for many years. Fallon would develop in greater isolation and in some ways more radically, but for both poets the difficulty of escape from first allegiances is inscribed in the tortuous syntax, impasto textures and broken rhythms of their later poetry, their work and careers gapped and fissured by the difficulty of deconstructing the Irish mode from within. This has meant that their work has been easy to depict as wilfully obscure, clumsy and provincial.

Thomas Kinsella has noted that 'In those flat years at the beginning of the nineteen fifties, depressed so thoroughly that one scarcely noticed it, the uneasy silence of Austin Clarke added a certain emphasis' (Kinsella, 1974: 128). By this date, Clarke had for some years been trying to harness the intensities of *Night and Morning* to a similarly dense but less personal and agonised poetry, as occasional poems for journals showed.[10] Clarke's attitude to a critique of his Gaelicism was ambivalent; on the one hand, he had identified with what he called the 'hopeful' future of 'our new State' in the 1920s and 1930s;[11] on the other he had conceded as early as 1931 that despite independence 'the freedom of the artistic conscience is still ungranted [in Ireland], and every succeeding writer of originality must fight his own cause' (Schirmer, 1995: xviii). This 'fight' had almost silenced him, his occasional journal-published poems evidence of the developing critical, contemporary engagement with society required to break from the impasse. The partial and incomplete nature of this, and the potential for contradiction, is clear in other critical writings of the period. In 'Poetry in Ireland To-Day' of 1946, Clarke claimed that 'Far from being in decline, our poetry is both vigorous and lively' (Schirmer, 1995: 105). 'Decline' is dismissed as only apparent, the perception of it being attributable to a lack of Irish publishers and the decline in the English demand for Irish writing. His complaint that English critics have adopted 'a Sinn Féin policy' towards Irish poetry is ironic in a way he did not intend, suggesting as it does that an English readership should support Irish writing despite its anti-English basis.[12] Clarke's essay reflects a classic postcolonial double-bind; indigenous literature defines itself in its rejection of the former imperial power while requiring its markets in order to survive, even demanding access to them as a right.[13] His solution can thus only be rhetorical; he asserts that the Irish poet, 'far from being provincial . . . must be the focal point of many influences', with 'must' having the force of 'is' rather than 'ought to become'. This sidesteps any discussion of cultural autonomy and the way lack of Irish publication created a crisis of confidence about the value of poetry being written, and the essay contains the admission that poetry is in reality 'neglected and despised in this country' (Coughlan and Davis, 1995: 218).

It took the crisis of the 1950s to finally flush Clarke's social critique out into the open. In *Ancient Lights* (1955), *Too Great a Vine* (1957) and *The Horse-Eaters* (1960) – all subtitled 'Poems and Satires' and republished in *Later Poems* (1961) – the dense, Swiftian vein which had been occasionally revealed earlier was made public, although as if to foreground his neglect Clarke published the pamphlets in small editions under the imprint of his own Bridge Press until the 1960s, when Dolmen took over. In his social critique, he put himself at the service of those minorities which, as Terence Brown has pointed out, had been excluded from national life and history after 1922 – women, the poor and unemployed, the working class, Protestants (Brown, 1985: 102–37). His method – generalising from detailed particulars – challenged Nationalist tele-ologies which saw in the present nation the fulfilment of the aspirations of 1916, and exposed the way in which Nationalism elided religious, class and gender distinctions in the interests of an 'inefficient and often complacent bourgeoisie' and Church (Bew, Hazelkorn and Patterson, 1989: 84). Clarke's stance is best summed up in the coinage 'Ill-fare state', which inverts Britain's Welfare State in a manner most likely to offend a narrow Nationalist *amour propre* (Clarke, 1991: 60). 'Mother and Child', published in the *Irish Times* in 1954, is a good example of the satires as public intervention. Its occasion was the Church's designation of 1954 as a year devoted to worship of the Virgin Mary and the subsequent issuing of a special commemorative stamp; however, its origin lay in the fate of the Mother and Child Bill, which had been pro-posed three years before by a radical young member of the coalition cabinet, the Health Minister Dr Noel Browne (Clarke, 1976: 193). Browne's Bill had been intended to give help to poor nursing mothers, but had been opposed by the Church and the medical profession, for grossly self-interested reasons, as 'socialistic', leading to Browne's abandonment by cabinet colleagues and his resignation. Yet after Fianna Fáil – who had called for Browne's head – were re-elected in 1953, they introduced legislation almost identical to that which he had proposed. Clarke's target, then, in this condensed, angrily compas-sionate poem, seems to be not so much the blocking of Bill, the abandonment of Browne by his colleagues, or even the Church, as this policy reversal and what it reveals about refusal to acknowledge error:

> Obedient keys rattled in locks,
> Bottles in old dispensaries
> Were shaken and the ballot boxes
> Hid politicians on their knees
> When pity showed us what we are.
> 'Why should we care', votes cried, 'for child
> Or mother? Common help is harmful
> And state-control must starve the soul.'
> One doctor spoke out. Bishops mitred.
> But now our caution has been mended,
> The side-door open, bill amended,
> We profit from God's love and pity,
> Sampling the world with good example.
> Before you damp it with your spit,
> Respect our newest postage stamp.
>   (Clarke, 1991: 76)

Typical of Clarke are the puns at crucial points: bishops 'mitred' – shook their 'mitred' heads and 'might have' done differently – embodying the blurring of Church and state institutions, as God's 'love and pity' are subordinated to 'profit'. Apparently contingent and merely topical, 'Mother and Child' is actu-ally concerned with the *representation* of power behind the specific abuse. What angers Clarke is that democracy's 'ballot-boxes' are being made to serve as a cover for a politics of the 'side-door' (as of a church), and he takes the stamp as an image of the state's subservience to the Hierarchy and the professional greed of the medical establishment. It is this process, for Clarke, which is the most revealing of the hypocrisy of post-Independence public life, and the poem mimics the simultaneous brazenness and secrecy it describes by being both belated and immediate, circumspect and offensive ('pity'/'spit').

Most of the satires, like this, are short and stylistically dense, relishing paradox and pun, frequently gnomic – qualities compounded for the non-Irish reader by their sources in contemporary events and allusions to historical ones. Despite this the difficulty of Clarke's later poetry has been too readily conceded; moreover, the very term 'satires' is something of a misnomer. Although critical, especially of collusion between Church and state, these poems avoid the misogyny which has traditionally been satire's stock-in-trade. Clarke's own likening of his later career to that of Swift is, in this sense, not to be taken too literally; rather, he adapts the tradition to suit his own anticlerical Christian, humanist and socialistic sensibility. In dramatising his slow, painful overcoming of negative conditioning, Clarke perforce links the private with public spheres and an understanding that his personal trauma coincides with (literally, embodies) that of the post-Independence Ireland, and does so by blurring the distinctions between Juvenalian and Horatian modes of satire. Missing this deliberate blurring of modes, critics have seen the satires either too sharp or not sharp enough, or read them in terms of the grotesque (Brown, 1988: 127–40). Likewise, to see a merely personal motivation in his anticlericalism is to miss the point; the Church is, in general, attacked in ideological terms for its thwarting and distortion of human potential. In *Too Great a Vine*, for example, it is seen as starving the soil of the nation, forgetting the spiritual priorities it observed in the past, crushing those it purports to serve: 'Fabulist, can an ill-state / Like ours, carry so great / A weight upon its back?' (Clarke, 1976: 32, 34). For Clarke, as for Marx, religion is 'the heart of the heartless world'; in its institutional form an agency creating and preying on passivity and deprivation, even as its core teachings remain, for those who can see through the encrustations of dogma, a potential source of spiritual renewal and solace. The two Martha Blake poems – from either side of the 1938–55 gap – show the way Clarke brings this search into line with his later 'satire'. The first, 'Martha Blake', though set in contemporary Dublin, refers to it hardly at all, and is an empathic consideration of the narrow, limited faith of the named figure in a rapt, almost abstract sense. The second, 'Martha Blake at Fifty-One', sets the attempt to maintain such detachment amid the distracting particulars of a realised city life and the obtrusive materiality of the body; 'the 15 tram', 'particles' of the host lodged behind dentures, the 'wamble, gurgle, squelch' of indigestion. In both cases Martha Blake is a form of alter ego for Clarke, her name combining piety and iconoclasm, but the later poem contextualises religion deflatingly, demystifying it while saving it from false transcendence. With Martha, 'disappointed', bleeding 'inwardly', dying to the sound of 'jazz' from a fairground, we get one of Clarke's anti-saintly saints appropriate to the modern age, one through whom he rescues the religious impulse for the purposes of social critique.

The Martha Blake poems are significant, too, in that they register not just the adoption of social themes and a critical stance but also the centrality to the later poetry of women, whose exclusion and maltreatment is constantly linked to the personal, social and historical levels of Clarke's own experience. He sees the 'Ill-fare state' as bearing with particular intensity on women, both individually and through the family. The 1916 Proclamation of Independence had famously promised that an independent state would 'cherish equally' every member of the nation, but de Valera's 1938 Constitution, sanctifying the family as the basis of the nation and idealising women as home-makers, effectively made them second-class citizens. Society's burdens fell more heavily on women precisely to the degree that they were rendered invisible, and it is to Clarke's credit that he saw that an effective critique of Irish Ireland required an attack on patriarchal structures and attitudes (interestingly, criticism of Clarke often reads like an attack on 'female' particularism). Almost alone among male Irish writers of the time, Clarke attacks the Church's discourse on sexuality and its assumptions – that married women of childbearing age should be continually pregnant, that contraception should be prohibited ('Marriage')[14] – and society's hypocritical neglect of children's welfare. This is reflected in poems on the separation of illegitimate children from their mothers ('Unmarried Mothers'), brutal corporal punishment, a fire in which thirty-five children perished in a badly run Church orphanage ('Three Poems about Children') and unemployed families driven to despair or emigration (Clarke, 1991: 64, 66, 74). The later 'The Subjection of Women' sets this in a historical framework. Although one of its targets (as in Kinsella's contemporary 'Nightwalker') is 1960s' greed, its chief concern is to 'rememorise' outstanding women of the past, from those who have been turned into icons (and dehistoricised) like Maud Gonne, to the less well known, like Dr Kathleen Lynn, who have simply been written out of the record altogether. Their sacrifices for the well-being of the nation are set against old historical amnesia and the newer form involved in marketing 'heroic' Ireland:

> Women, who cast off all we want,
> Are now despised, their names unwanted,
> For patriots in party statement
> And act make worse our Ill-fare State.
> The soul is profit. Money claims us.
> Heroes are valuable clay.
> (Clarke, 1976: 118)

Rehabilitating women's history, Clarke overturns these national histories that erase the radical and plural aspects of the state's origins. Likewise, he stresses the Protestant and working-class contribution to Irish freedom in 'Wolfe Tone' and 'Inscription for a Headstone', written on the death of James Larkin in 1947 (Clarke, 1991: 70, 76). These poems probe the fissures in the seamless official ideologies of the nation (although this can also mean passing over aspects of the republican legacy, such as the IRA's 1930s' shift into brigandage). The general tenor of this work, then, is liberating through its intimate, insider's patient deconstruction of the complacent myths of state, Church and (in *Mnemosyne Lay in Dust*) selfhood.

Mnemosyne prefigures the historical 'remembering' we find in other long, complex poems of the 1960s and early 1970s, notably 'Ancient Lights', 'Loss of Strength' and 'The Hippophagi' which complement the shorter satires. The last of these, from *The Horse-Eaters* (1960), takes as its target the shipping of Irish horses to Europe for human consumption. For Clarke, the horse symbolises a number of things – Pegasus/poetry, childhood, the human bond with nature, a creature-paced world before the domination of the machine. The poem makes the horse an indicator of the negative aspects of modernity, moving from childhood guilts through a critique of Christianity's insistence on sexual continence, the decline of Church authority, the rise of technology at the expense of the horse and a consideration of the human ability to both cherish individual animals and permit their reduction, in the mass, to meat. Ideology's function in naturalising contradiction might, through this poem, be seen as extending to Irish history – the betrayal of the horse's trust and willingness to serve (like Boxer in Orwell's *Animal Farm*) seen as a form of cannibalism, with Irish willingness to export them a reminder of the export of its human population. But Clarke goes far beyond this to question the basis of human thought and identity in a world stripped of creaturely existence: 'What dare we call / Our thought ... Unwanted void or really us?' (Clarke, 1974: 235). If thought is truly 'void', leading the 'unatomised' world (that is, threatened by atomic war) to destruction, then the attempt to oppose repression and mechanisation with a faith based on a belief in social justice falters.

Maurice Harmon has, understandably, seen the poem's pessimistic conclusion as a result of the way it 'raise[s] the issue of hippophagism to a different level, involving the nature of being, the purpose of existence, and the possibility of things, including thought, being meaningless' (Harmon, 1989: 180). Yet – perhaps ironically for so learned a poet – Clarke's negativity is opposed in the last work by an emphasis on the persistence of the physical and instinctual, the body against the purely cerebral. *Forget-Me-Not* of 1962, also treating the disappearance of the horse, links the process to a loss of the self, but restores both through the self-delighting qualities of language, triumphing over the depradations of modernity through style and anticipating the redemptive role of memory in *Mnemosyne*. Change, then, is welcomed to the extent that it represents an overcoming of reactionary ideologies and social structures, but regretted insofar as it subjects creaturely sensitivity to the market and the machine. The poetry's physicality allows the enactment of a struggle against obscurantism, guilt and fear while remaining aware of the encroachments of instrumental rationality. The right to this qualified optimism is won through increasing experimentation, mobility and emotional release (notably in *Flight to Africa* (1963), concluding with the metamorphic sexual narrative poems of the last years – *Orphide* (1970), *Tiresias* (1971) and *Collected Poems* (1974). Using classical myth, these can be seen as an attempt to rewrite Yeats, although to confine their significance to a Bloomian *agon* diminishes their radicalism. While frankly sensual, Clarke's last poems manage, in a way far removed from Yeats, to deflate the Romantic wild old wicked man persona; the title of 'Impotence', for example, speaks for itself.

This later work, then, moves from satire to materialistic, anti-transcendent transcendence; unlike Fallon's use of mythic female archetypes, Clarke's vision remains rooted in mundane narrative, social specifics and a relish of physical detail bordering on the grotesque. In the process, for the first time, Clarke offers anti-mythic forms of Irish history (rather than Kavanagh's non-mythic vision). Paradoxically, it is through an intensification of localism that parochial isolationism is to be overcome (Valentin Iremonger, reviewing *Later Poems*, drew a comparison between Clarke's use of history and that of Seferis). There is a price to pay, since this demands an attention to the detail of Irish history, in order to read it 'against the grain' of official versions; and ironically, given Clarke's own insistence on the viability of an Irish mode, it was an English critic, Donald Davie, who was one of the first to champion his work in the mid-1950s (Davie, 1975: 37–51). By the same token, Clarke's opposition to a utilitarian reductionism (seen as the flipside to bogus transcendentalism) requires a refusal of documentary realism, or naturalised utterance. This separates his satire from that of the *Bell* writers, and it is important to realise that style is part of what Clarke's poetry does, not a means towards an end. Refusal to grasp this is the result of an instrumental view of language, a refusal of the unavoidable *readerly* difficulty of remembering a painful national and personal past which allows the poems to emerge precisely in the gap between realism and myth. Hence their foregrounding of their constructedness, the 'tricksy' dropping of definite and indefinite articles, the use of pun, anagram, acrostic, alliteration and Gaelic-derived *deibidhe* rhyme (rhyming against stress, e.g. 'stick' with 'logic'). Most characteristic and blatant of all is *rime riche* (e.g. 'Voltaire' with 'volt tear'), the single device most aggravating to critics seeking a naturalised, authentic utterance. Clarke's own description of these procedures is well known; 'I load myself with chains and try to get out of them' (Clarke, 1974: 545). The enactment of the loading and the escape from psychic and social repression is part of the point.[15] Clarke's offsetting of his topical, contingent subjects with such an anti-authenticist poetic – its gnarled vocabulary, its parataxis, its refusal to shape material to discursive, prose or speech rhythms – raises questions about the mythology-to-realism trajectory of post-Yeatsian poetry, making the artificiality of writing clear, as well as disclosing the constructedness of its social contexts.[16]

By the early 1960s, after years of neglect, Clarke 'had suddenly a discerning, if tiny, public' (Clarke, 1976: xiv). There was even less than this 'public' for Padraic Fallon, however, whose first collection of poems, his *Collected*, appeared just a few months before his death in 1974. Fallon's dependence on journal publication – chiefly Seumas O'Sullivan's *The Dublin Magazine*, which ran from the 1920s to 1957 – was an extreme example of the fate in print (or rather out of it) of poets of his generation (Davie, 1975: 52). The critical neglect of his work since his death, however, has not been merely the result of its unavailability during his lifetime. More important has been the difficulty of relating Fallon's very eclectic work to that of Clarke and Kavanagh, and the potential disruption to the neat, binary schema of mid-century poetry which the pair represent. Although acknowledged, then – usually in accessible but not wholly representative lyrics, such as 'A Flask of Brandy' – Fallon has been excluded from serious consideration. The arguments used have little to do with his real achievement as a poet, and usually stem from his presumed subservience to Yeats. As the generally sympathetic Donald Davie puts it, 'Fallon stands in a curious relation to Yeats . . . his direct, unabashed dialogue with that overbearing predecessor is strikingly at odds with Austin Clarke's evasive obliquities . . . [he] has not kept his distance from Yeats . . . And [he] pays the price' (Davie, 1975: 54). For Seamus Heaney the stylistic consequences are a tendency to incoherence, a poetry insufficiently individuated and liable to tonal and linguistic instability. Yet the terms by which Fallon has been judged often miss the point. The assumption of a head-to-head Oedipal struggle with Yeats avoids the ways in which Fallon attempted to change the terms of the confrontation, while stable lyric self-utterance is clearly not the only legitimate course open to an Irish poet.

Fallon's *Collected Poems* shows a renunciation of the Irish mode more complete in some ways even than Clarke's. There are only eight poems in its 'Early Poems' section, which covers Fallon's neo-Revival phase (dated 1930–45), and the late 'For Paddy Mac' is more programmatic than any poem of Clarke's, more conscious (if less vehement) than any by Kavanagh. The poem recalls a poet-friend's past attempts to elicit from Fallon tales of his native West, 'The last ledge of original earth' when it was still felt that 'Ours were the metres / Of early waters'. The tales are now dismissed as

> Bunkum, Dear P. The thing was gone, or
> Never was. And we were the leftovers,
> Lord-ridden and pulpit-thumped for all our wild
> Cudgels of Gaelic. Ours was Lever's
> One-horse country; the bailiff at the bighouse door.
> (P. Fallon, 1990: 134)

Like Clarke's, Fallon's poetry from the 1940s explores some of the tensions within unitary concepts of 'the nation'. It is particularly damning of Revival idealisation of the West, given Fallon's own origins and upbringing in Athenry, Co. Galway; unlike the Dubliner Clarke or Monaghan-born Kavanagh he was therefore well placed to comment on a society which, for all its virtues, endured with a culture of 'rags and tatters', a place of 'beast, sky and anger'. In contrast to Revival and Free State myths of classless rural communities, this is a society riven by class, inequality and poverty, where landless labourers sold themselves on hiring days 'From penury to slavery' (P. Fallon, 1990: 134–5). Here history is a memory of the Penal Laws and hedge-schools, and there are no poets to be found, only the ghost of the dispossessed vagrant bard of Gaeldom, Raftery. If in his early poetry Fallon had avoided such material, his son has noted that 'he was always clearheaded about . . . [the War of Independence's] real roots and impetus; in essence he saw it as a land war and a class struggle, fought primarily against the Anglo-Irish landowning and ruling class rather than against England' (P. Fallon, 1990: 265). Thus, in the 1940s, Fallon brought resentment at such idealisation to his reassessment of Revivalism, and in drawing on modern poetry (particularly Pound) and internationally current mythological systems (as opposed to Irish ones), he became the one poet of his generation living in the Republic to embrace international influences.

It is this turn which informs his treatment of Yeats, so often seen as limiting his work.[17] In what is perhaps Fallon's most direct address to him, 'Fin de Siècle', Yeats is presented as the last survivor of the 1890s' generation. Urged to 'Try the ride. / Old body, be / The most famous suicide', the aged poet '[rises] from his years to find / A great carnivorous creature under him' (P. Fallon, 1990: 102). The image of the 'carnivorous' Pegasus, part merry-go-round ride, part flesh-eating horse belonging to Diomedes of Thrace, perfectly captures the Nietzschean staginess of late Yeats. Yet this kind of elaborate challenge to Yeatsian monstrousness is untypical, and the Revival-assessing poems make more sense if read as a *refusal* of such struggles and as an attempt to create a more revisionary, fugitive practice. Fallon's poetic shift took some force from the non-Yeatsian, anti-authoritarian example of AE (George Russell), and, if he felt that AE's own poetry was a 'vague blue landscape', he also saw him as a valuable source of ideas on myth, philosophy and magic. For Yeats, of course, these things were types of arcane knowledge whose end was power; AE's emphasis, by contrast, was on non-masterful, renunciatory Eastern traditions. Fallon combines these with his other un-Irish influences – Baudelaire, Crane, Pound, Rimbaud and Rilke – and typical modernist themes.[18] For a poet who was best known in his lifetime for his version of O'Raftery's ballad 'Mary Hynes', these would seem unlikely sources; and if they did not lead to modernism *pur sang*, they certainly led to a more open-ended poetry of ragged verse forms, digressions and lists, which challenge the organic unity of the traditional lyric. The critique of the Revival this represents often takes as its location Fallon's own run-down, rural Athenry, juxtaposed, with mild provocation, beside Yeats's legendary ones, such as Ballylee, these two places being only a few miles apart.[19] Although contrasted, they are also permitted to overlap, Fallon's and Yeats's language and cadences running together.

In 'Yeats at Athenry Perhaps' Yeats is simply waiting for a train, 'an aimless / Straying gentleman' on his way to Ballylee, while 'Yeats's Tower at Ballylee', the first of these poems, begins with a 'pilgrimage' to Thoor Ballylee. Seeking the source of Yeats's achievement, the speaker finds his tower 'its passion spent / And wearied of its own brutality', unroofed and decaying for all its 'arty fireplace', the walls inside 'weeping / A peacock paint' (P. Fallon, 1990: 112, 42). Contemplating Yeats's attempt to overcome violence through art, however, the speaker is enabled to grasp a bleak understanding he has avoided hitherto, as the tower's militaristic origins connect it with the present, since its view of the desolate flooded plain gives on to 'a desolate and more desolate world', and 'the bloody vision' of civil war raging in Korea (thus aligning the poem with the contemporary 'J'accuse', an attack on General MacArthur) (P. Fallon, 1990: 39). From such a vantage point, Fallon claims, history is 'endless time in which things happen / In endless repetition'. This follows a tendency to see Irish history as cyclical, but set in a wider context. Similarly, the struggle for 'vision' is itself linked to more general violence, the product of increasing individualism and solipsism; 'The higher we climb up / Into ourselves the greater seems the danger' in a world where few effective forms of protest or resistance are left (P. Fallon, 1990: 43–4). Yeats's 'tower' is seen, then, as a tower of the self; and its rejection has a direct bearing on Fallon's use of myth.

Fallon's mythologising, like his incorporation of modernistic elements within the mid-century lyric, is what gives his work its unique significance. It is a form of rejection of the puritanism of the times but, as a version of compensatory spiritualism, it is far more heterogeneous than Clarke's radicalised Catholicism. The treatment of gender neatly highlights the distinction, since while Clarke demystifies the representation of women and makes them the heart of a social critique, Fallon draws on works such as Graves's *The White Goddess*, as well as more standard classical, religious and anthropological sources, even if social contexts do not entirely disappear.[20] As with Pound's use of numerous goddesses in *The Cantos*, Fallon's later poetry deploys a series of female figures or archetypes, including Athene, Danae, Penelope, Lakshmi and Mary, as well as Lady Gregory and Maud Gonne. All are forms of the Triple Goddess or Magna Mater, who features in her own right in the later poems. In one sense this echoes the Revival strategy for dealing with Catholicism by annexing it to pagan practice, sublimating Mariolatry within a plethora of goddesses and female intercessor-figures, and sets the work somewhere between Kavanagh's Marianism and Clarke's secularism. But it also forms a critique of Yeatsian phallocentrism, and can be related to the persistent drizzle of Yeatsian echoes. The autobiographical 'Yesterday's Man', for example, uses the phrase 'transfigured me' which occurs twice in Yeats, in 'The Lamentation of the Old Pensioner' and 'First Love'. The speaker of the poem is leafing through an old notebook, considering a lost almost-love and wondering 'is it really better / To rage than remain aloof . . . ?' Glancing at the quay below he sees 'the Frau / Of the Dutch Captain's hanging out her wash, / So young, so young, transfiguring me' (P. Fallon, 1990: 177). Yeats's phrase is used precisely to qualify a Yeatsian 'rage' that 'old men fall in love', their feeling that there is 'no decorum in the universe', though not before the poem has shared in and acknowledged that rage. 'Transfiguring me' '[Closes] the diary of yester-day's man', as sensual desire, regret and nostalgia are 'transfigured' in the balance between realistic and mythic aspects of the 'Frau'. The complexity of this minor usage – in what the poem calls 'Ambiguous territory for the halt and lame' – shows the subtlety with which Fallon can simultaneously adapt and resist his predecessor.

Similarly, in using Gonne and Gregory in his poetry, Fallon is making a point of modifying Yeatsian arrogance and aloofness, his phallic fixations, but he is also noting the increasingly androgynous element of Yeats's later work (as identified by Elizabeth Butler Cullingford, and discernible in the Crazy Jane lyrics).[21] The 'feminine' in Yeats is foregrounded to provide an alternative to the standard phallocentric readings of his work. Fallon follows a predictable enough line in this; woman is treated as essentially mysterious and in the abstract, as either to be revered or (rarely in his case) denigrated. In her positive aspects she is virgin maiden and/or lover, or muse, and ultimately mother or Magna Mater, the earth mother goddess. As goddess of death and birth she is ambiguous, and also embodies masculine castration anxiety (P. Fallon, 1990: 185, 189), and in the blatantly negative sense she is also the last item of 'Goddess, kitchenwoman, whore' (P. Fallon, 1990: 129). Women in Fallon's poetry hardly ever speak or have agency; in 'Poem for my Mother', for example, the mother's words are reported by the male poet (although the figure of the 'termagant' has her own characterful, abusive interjection). In this, Fallon is of his time and place, of course, although he qualifies his arche-typal terminology in 'The River Walk', which insists on the dual nature of the individual, her 'human business' 'not [to] be . . . a beautiful grotesque' repre-senting all nature:

Dangerous, dangerous
This mythology. . . .
Lover, go back no farther than your birth
A woman is a woman, not the earth.
(P. Fallon, 1990: 93)

This, however, is offset by the belief that the individual woman is 'just one face' of the goddess individualised, and therefore a means by which the male may achieve selfhood. Nevertheless, as I have argued, Fallon's mythic usages have, in their historical context, a mildly deconstructive and subversive force, challenging puritanism, asserting female erotic agency and subverting sub-Yeatsian rural discourses. The fascination with an *ewig weibliche* or feminine principle flows from the stifling circumstances of mid-century patriarchy, although subversive potential is limited by the absence of any critique of the exclusion of women from the cultural sphere. The idea that 'The higher we climb up / Into ourselves the greater seems the danger' can be referred to a poem like 'Women'. This presents the tower of phallogocentricity and modernity, up which the aspiring male climbs to do battle with the gods – the inevitable result of being divided from the 'first Oneness' of the mother, after which 'poetry is our apology' for the fall of birth:

> Rest says the earth. And a woman delicately
> Says 'It is here, it is in my arms somewhere'
> But a woman is a lie
> And I have a tower to climb, the tower of me,
> And a quarrel to settle with the sky
> But 'rest' says the woman. 'O lean back more
> I am a wife and a mother's knee,
> I am the end of every tower.'
>   (P. Fallon, 1990: 38)

Only merging with the feminine – returning to the earth, or mother – can prevent self-destruction; by comparison with the 'Great Goddess', 'Much is man and not enough' (P. Fallon, 1990: 90). On the other hand, of course, 'a woman is a lie' returns us to the de-individualised archetypes, and death itself is seen as return to the goddess (the Terrible Goddess or 'Mother Ogre and womb of all'), as Fallon makes clear in a poem of death and rebirth placed at the end of *Collected Poems*. 'To the Boy' speaks of rebirth to a new boyhood, the female goddess merely the medium for male self-individuation (P. Fallon, 1990: 189–90). Fallon's use of myth, then, can ultimately be said to rearrange, rather than destroy, the basic terms of a Catholic eschatology – the fall, the Virgin mother, the heaven-aspiring male, descent into the underworld, purgation, rebirth. Religious sensibility displaced into myth is a pattern to be found throughout Irish (male) poetry after Fallon, in Watters, Kinsella, Montague, Heaney and others. Fallon's origination of this pattern, at least, accrues some critical force from its mid-century circumstances.

Patrick Kavanagh: culchie authenticity and urban pastoral

> It is almost necessary for Irishmen to detonate themselves in the centre of the field of English literature before they are noticed. (Augustus Martin)[22]

'Bardic Dust', Kavanagh's poem of 1944, takes the form of a debate over the merits of Austin Clarke. It opens with 'The Public' announcing 'We hate verse plays, we hate verse plays, / We do not think there are worse plays', and continues with 'Clarke' – 'in the dusty robes of a medieval abbot' – described by 'Myself' as 'Always three removes from life'. The antagonism between Kavanagh and Clarke is well known and runs in predictable urban vs rural, learned vs uneducated, formal vs informal grooves. 'Bardic Dust', however, soon distinguishes between 'Clarke's consistent praisers' and the poet himself, allowing Clarke to state his dilemma: 'I know my limitations, I have died; / To come alive again how hard I've tried', his value acknowledged in the final lines by 'Myself' as 'a warm breath / Blowing in a room where once was death' (Kavanagh, 1992: 151–4). This significantly complicates the usual oppositional paradigm and the tendency to see the two as the yin and yang of post-Yeatsian poetry, pointing to a shared hostility towards puritanism (and modernism), mid-career neglect and reliance on hackwork to make a living. Nevertheless, if 'Bardic Dust' shows Kavanagh in unusually generous mood, it also defines the poet as 'twice / As much alive as any other man', a definition which fits the diffident Clarke only uneasily. Kavanagh's commitment to a capitalised 'Life' is insistent here as elsewhere, at least as much as his supposed creation of a vernacular Irish poetic voice in English, and helps explain his supplanting of the older poet in the 1960s as the most influential Irish poet, as well as his appeal over the heads of Murphy, Montague and Kinsella to the still younger Durcan, Kennelly and Hartnett (Behan's nickname for Kavanagh, 'the King of the Kids', captures this perfectly). His last collection, *Come Dance With Kitty Stobling* (1960), had gone through four editions by 1963, and although he wrote nothing of real note after 1960 before his death in 1967, it could be said that in his end was his beginning, his pre-eminence buoyed by the fact that the movement of his poetry tracks very closely the movement of Irish culture since Independence, but accelerated by 1960s' modernisation. Kavanagh's 'hegira', that is, from small-farm Monaghan to Dublin in 1938 to be the patronised, downtrodden and finally triumphant 'culchie', acquired national significance because it coincided with a general movement from the land to the town, making him an exemplary figure. Against this, of course, is the critical suspicion of Kavanagh as one who played the pub Irishman, one of those who Deane sees as having valorised failure and enshrined in Cronin's *Dead as Doornails*, John Ryan's *Remembering How We Stood* and J. P. Donleavy's *The Ginger Man* (Ryan, 1975: 95–126).

In a more purely poetic sense Kavanagh's importance lay in his delivery of the *coup de grâce* to neo-Revivalist and *Bell*-influenced poetic realism, his revision of the Yeatsian mage and 'smiling public man' as that of the poet as holy fool and holy show, and his erasure of myth-fixation in the socially blank pastorals of the Canal Bank poems. It was a task which as a Northerner (from Monaghan, one of the three excluded counties of historical Ulster), he was better equipped for than insiders such as Clarke or Fallon. The end of neo-Revivalism was accomplished with *The Great Hunger*, which marked a violent refusal of his initial complicity with the role of peasant poet the Dublin literati had marked out for him (Quinn, 1991: 255). What is remarkable about Kavanagh is the way he then turned against this achievement by breaking with his own satirical realism, most notably in the so-called 'Canal Bank' poems which feature in his last collection, *Come Dance With Kitty Stobling* (1960). These poems flow from a recognition of the impasse of the sociological response to neo-Revivalism. Reaching beyond realism and satire, these ten sonnets (beginning with 'The Hospital') and an equal number of lyrics, written between 1956 and 1959, develop the 'edgy, visionary subjectivity' which had always been present in the best of his work (Crotty, 1995: 31).

As this suggests, the positions Kavanagh had adopted in the debates of the 1940s had a strategic element as well as being merely reactive, and it should be noted that as late as 1945 Irishness was an aesthetic criterion for him. Yet just as *Tarry Flynn* (1948) reworks *The Green Fool* (1938), so the poetry of the late 1940s reads as an attempt to use his rural past, while acknowledging that a return to Monaghan was no longer an option. The result was the mixture of realism and nostalgia of *A Soul For Sale* (1948), whose poems consider the failure to move beyond oscillation between city and country, terms which increasingly seem to cancel each other out. Thus 'Temptation in Harvest' notes that 'clay could still seduce my heart/After five years of pavements raised to art', that he had idealised the 'City of Kings', but also that the inhabitants of the country threaten 'to lift their dim nostalgic arms' against the returnee (Kavanagh, 1992: 158). *A Soul For Sale* is unable to turn this dislocatedness to much advantage, as 'Pegasus', the poem which supplies the book's title, shows. In it 'an old horse/Offered for sales in twenty fairs' serves as a metaphor for the poetic gift, one rejected by 'the Church', 'the men of State', 'the crooked shopkeepers' and finally 'the/Tinkers'. Only in the poem's final lines, when the speaker finally accepts the gift for itself rather than as a commodity to trade, does it grow wings and become Pegasus (Kavanagh, 1992: 149–50). Allegorising his career, the poem makes a virtue of dire necessity, dramatising rejection as a form of negative authentication. Its weakness – as Kavanagh later acknowledged – lay in the basic sentimentality of the conception.

The final break with what Kavanagh called the 'anti-art' of Irishness-as-art had started in 1947 with a series of near-inchoate attacks against not just the neo-Revivalists but virtually all contemporary Irish writing, including many fellow-writers at *The Bell* (drawing from Hubert Butler the comment that Kavanagh's critical mind resembled 'a monkey house at feeding time', while O'Faolain complained of his 'narcissism' as a reviewer)[23] (Quinn, 1991: 265, 269). A lack of distance from his targets can be seen in the ramshackle quality of Kavanagh's criticism and satire, and he undoubtedly often invited the neglect which fuelled his outbursts.[24] Publicly, the mounting frustrations came to a head in the early 1950s, when a succession of literary and public indignities pushed him to the point of collapse – refusal of a visa for a visit to the USA in 1950, the collapse of *Envoy* and his uniquely fruitful relationship with its editor, John Ryan, in 1951, the quixotic fiasco of *Kavanagh's Weekly* in 1952[25] and the failed prosecution of *The Leader* for libel in 1954. Kavanagh's public performance ensured that the libel case was 'the climax of his career of histrionic self-promotion, his most notorious exhibition of the writer as public persona' in what was probably 'the worst year of his life', but it was immediately followed by a diagnosis of cancer of the lung and emergency surgery (Quinn, 1991: 334, 369). Nevertheless, despite all this,

Kavanagh's poetry had, since 1950, been pursuing a new self-critical introversion, as the titles of 'I Had a Future', 'To be Dead', 'Auditors In' indicate,
while his 'Diary' for *Envoy* marked a new direction with its stress on 'humility and love'. By 1955–56 this development was reinforced by the collapse of
the most histrionic aspects of public persona, and the Canal Bank poems which
flowed from it. 'Not caring', in the aftermath of the shocks of the early 1950s,
elevated his mask of the holy fool to that of the poet as seer. Kavanagh's model
for this positivity and self-abnegation was a religious one; stagnation is transcended in an act of renunciation, a subject position which might be located
in the 'placeless heaven', between town and country, of the earlier 'Temptation in Harvest'. It is both a definitive retreat from the attempt to be a Dublin
writer and, simultaneously, a complex pastoralisation of the city.

In this contradictory process Kavanagh moved beyond the simple negation of 'the English-bred lie' of neo-Revivalism by paradoxically adopting
Anglophile critical positions, as well as the sociologism of *The Bell*. His pastoralisation finds its most memorable critical justification, of course, in the
famous distinction between the 'provincial' – which is always looking over its
shoulder for metropolitan approval – and the 'parochial', secure in its sense of
self-worth and importance (Kavanagh, 1973: 281–3). Nevertheless, this should
not be taken as an outright valorisation of the rural, Kavanagh's 'parochial'
being both more and less than what has subsequently been made of it; his
contingent use of localism – shown in his claim that 'I have no belief in the
virtue of a place' (Kavanagh, 1973: 16) – needs to be distinguished from the
antiquarian, even fetishistic stance towards locality found in Heaney or Montague. At the same time, the intensely Catholic, sectarian nature of parochialism is often overlooked, and needs stressing (Butler, 1986: 153–62; Quinn,
1991: 203–4). Equally, given such contradictions, developments in the poetry
after *The Great Hunger* should not be seen teleologically and judged retrospectively in terms of the 'not-caring', 'comic' poise Kavanagh claimed. Rather they
demand consideration as a series of tactical shifts designed to avoid entrapment within stereotypes of Irishness; the 'wilfullness' of this is registered by
Bruce Stewart, when he notes that ' "parochial" and "provincial" are virtually
synonymous' in the cosmopolitan context towards which Kavanagh was
gesturing.[26] In this sense, the one consistent aspect of his career is the way
each phase of his writing rests on a denunciation of its predecessor. Kavanagh
savaged, in succession, *Ploughman and Other Poems* (1936), *The Green Fool*
(1938), *The Great Hunger* (1942), *A Soul For Sale* (1947), *Tarry Flynn* (1947) and
the satires. After *Come Dance With Kitty Stobling* (1960), physically and mentally
exhausted, there was no energy left for self-reinvention, as 'In Blinking Blank-
ness' sadly acknowledges (Kavanagh, 1992: 352–3).

What needs stressing, against the dominant view of Kavanagh struggling
for and finally achieving 'authenticity' and a return to some unproblematic
'real', is the unstable and heterogeneous nature of the 'noo poems' of 1956–59.
The notion that he finally arrived at a hard-won serenity – derived from

Kavanagh himself – is suspiciously homogenising and consoling (Heaney, 1989: 14; Brown, 1975: 220). Some critics, reacting to such a reception of the poems rather than the poems themselves, have, perhaps understandably, taken such notions at face value; and it has to be said that the poems' ambivalent tone does allow them to be used to naturalise a stereotypical association of Irishness with spontaneity, plain-speaking and so on. Declan Kiberd, for example, has accused Kavanagh of ruralising Dublin in a reactionary manner by '[recreating] Baggot Street as an urban pastoral, "my Pembrokeshire" [an] invented Ireland [which] proved far more attractive to poetry-readers among the new Dubliners than had Kavanagh's bitter indictment of rural torpor in *The Great Hunger*' (Kiberd, 1995: 492). But, without wishing to absolve Kavanagh completely, it is hard to see how this crudely literal and reflection-ist reading can be applied to the best of the later poems. How then do the Canal Bank poems differ from what went before? They are, to begin with, firmly of the present (unlike the earlier celebratory poems, which looked back-wards, and to the country). In this sense, strictly speaking, they are not 'parochial' according to Kavanagh's own definition. They are also frequently about poetry. As their often inconclusive conclusions suggest, they are rarely self-contained; 'they are preludes, poems to the next poem'. Moreover, unlike the earlier rural lyrics, they are self-effacing rather than self-asserting; 'I was not important', or ' "The self-slaved" advocates a programme of unselving', as Quinn puts it (Quinn, 1991: 401–2). But it is not that the consciousness of audience found in the satires has disappeared – on the contrary, it has been intensified. The difference, however, is that the problems of reception are turned to paradoxical advantage. In the final couplet of 'Come Dance With Kitty Stobling', the speaker claims 'I had a very pleasant journey, thank you sincerely/For giving me my madness back, or nearly' (Kavanagh, 1992: 292). Within (and between) the poems the position of the narrator, like the ma-terials used, shifts with disconcerting rapidity. 'Canal Bank Walk' is a case in point:

> Leafy-with-love banks and the green waters of the canal
> Pouring redemption for me, that I do
> The will of God, wallow in the habitual, the banal,
> Grow with nature again as before I grew.
> The bright stick trapped, the breeze adding a third
> Party to the couple kissing on an old seat,
> And a bird gathering materials for a nest for the Word
> Eloquently new and abandoned to its delirious beat.
> O unworn world enrapture me, encapture me in a web
> Of fabulous grass and eternal voices by a beech,
> Feed the gaping need of my senses, give me ad lib
> To pray unselfconsciously with overflowing speech
> For this soul needs to be honoured with a new dress woven
> From green and blue things and arguments that cannot be proven.
>
> (Kavanagh, 1992: 294)

Rather than Kiberd's thematic targets, it is the formal aspects of this sonnet which stand out most; tonal instability – wobble, even – is what first attracts a reader's attention. The main verb governing the opening clause, for example, is a present participle ('pouring'), which has the effect of reducing the distance between the object (the banks and water), and what they are doing (enacting the symbolic baptism which is a persistent theme). If this is disconcerting, the verb in the next sentence is even more so; 'the bright stick trapped', but 'trapped' what? We are forced to construct 'The bright stick which was trapped', but the sense of 'trapped' as intransitive remains to worry the rest of the sentence, which remains – whatever we do with 'trapped' – without a main verb at all. The poem seems blithely unaware of this kind of problem, indeed it indulges playfulness elsewhere with the compound opening phrase, 'Leafy-with-love', and the neologism 'encapture'. 'Encapture' is at one level merely a gratuitous echo of 'enrapture', but – like the compound and other features, such as the strained rhyme ('banal', 'canal') and hypermetrical lines – it contributes to the poem's effectiveness by enacting its subject of abandonment, casualness, the fortuitousness of spiritual grace. Take, for example, its mixture of tones; or, rather, its combination of a stress on the 'banal' with an exalted address ('O unworn world . . .'), its lumping together of everyday cliché ('a third/Party') and archaic-spiritual ('fabulous grass and eternal voices'). The poem is at once clumsily monosyllabic ('For this soul needs to be honoured . . .') and an example of the autodidact's relish of polysyllabic resonance. The 'overflowing speech' is contained, finally, within the form of a sonnet, albeit in such a way as to almost pull it apart.

Stylistic heterogeneity, a mixture of the visionary and the realist, but also the effective and the fustian, had been a characteristic of Kavanagh's poetry from the beginning – *The Great Hunger* can put a 'dead sparrow and an old waistcoat' together with early Yeatsian 'sunlight-woven cloaks', for example – but in the most effective of the Canal Bank poems this is made a stylistic principle (Kavanagh, 1992: 84–5). This tension between different registers, between eighteenth-century personification, romanticism, realism, ballad verse and 'high' art lyric, is what animates them. Rather than a factitious authenticity, or a display of integrity, the poems marginalise the speaking self in favour of creating an impression of spontaneity, improvisation, flow. The lyrical 'I' is rendered unstable, composed of a patchwork of different and conflicting kinds of poetic styles and discourses. This is not the 'integral', self-inventing but essentially Irish Kavanagh required by those who see identity as the chief concern of Irish poetry.[27] Seamus Heaney comments that 'Much of [Kavanagh's] authority and oddity derives from the fact that he wrestled his idiom out of a literary nowhere. At its most expressive his voice has the air of bursting a long battened-down silence' (Heaney, 1980: 116). However, as Michael O'Loughlin points out, although 'this is an apt description of Kavanagh's effect . . . the silence around [him] is only apparent'. He notes Kavanagh's fondness for the subculture represented by schoolbook poems, songs, newspaper verse and ballads which is 'an important part of the cultural background in Ireland' and related to the persistence of an oral culture; the unselfconscious and confident tone of English-language ballads and songs, whatever they lack in polish, bequeathed to Kavanagh 'an attitude to language that is both ludic and confident' (O'Loughlin, 1985b: 17).

This definition of oral – concrete and historically conditioned – is to be distinguished from the vague romantic valorisation usually invoked in support of the non-learned, primitive idea of Kavanagh, despite his own description of his work coming 'full circle'. On the contrary, these deliberately unstable poems exhibit an almost uncanny sense of balance and recovery from the collapses into the 'banal' they celebrate and which their mixed registers, discourses and tones risk. It is in this light that Kavanagh's legacy and his legend – in Barthes's term, the 'myth', or ideologically motivated naturalisation – needs to be considered (Barthes, 1989). Rather than achieving an organic fusion of realism and visionary transcendence, the best poetry is fundamentally unstable and heterogeneous, a risky juggling with (rather than blending of) a variety of contradictory elements, styles and traditions. It is precisely because of this risk and difficulty that there are so few wholly satisfying poems from this period. It is also why it proved so readily appropriable; hence the irony of the poet who proclaimed that 'Irishness is a form of anti-art' feeding not just a visionary and radical strain in Irish poetry, but also ruralist regressiveness (Kavanagh, 1973: 16). His own position is given in 'The Christmas Mummers', a satire of 1954. The closing lines (given to a 'Leading Editor'), in an echo of Clarke's 'Mother and Child', speak of 'The Liberal Opposition who complain of bishops' mitres' and of the 'New Statesmanism . . . essential to every well-run state' (Kavanagh, 1992: 269). In identifying co-opted dissent, Kavanagh reveals his reasons for continually attempting a more radical outflanking of its blandishments. But judging the necessary distance between himself and a liberal orthodoxy was difficult given a calculated philistinism conditioned by a tradition of 'inherited dissent', and the questioning of the normative grounds of 'authenticity' it would have involved was never carried out; sincerity could ultimately only be validated by the strength of its rejections.

John Hewitt and Ulster Regionalism

Austin Clarke is a fault-line in modern Irish poetry, his later work so specifically responsive to social failing, so stylistically gnarled, so thematically anti-traditional that Northern poets and critics have scarcely acknowledged it. Kavanagh, while critiquing the Free State, was – unlike Clarke – a countryman, his influence attributable to his refurbishing of a ruralism not based in Corkery's Munster or the 'Celtic' West but unprepossessing Monaghan. 'Ulster' in the original sense, Kavanagh's Catholic localism may well – as Edna Longley has claimed – 'shadow the larger, unstable Ulster regionalism conceived by

John Hewitt', the main poet of Clarke and Kavanagh's generation to write, for the greater part of his life at least, from Northern Ireland (E. Longley, 1994: 208). Things are more complicated than even Longley notes, since Hewitt and Clarke admired each other's work greatly (far more than Kavanagh's), suggesting links between Regionalism and Revivalism as common examples of cultural involution which have yet to be fully explored. If Clarke marks one 'fault-line', then, the opposed Nationalist critical camp sees Hewitt as marking another, viewing the Regionalist project as little more than cultural apologetics for Partitionism, of a piece with the claims for Ulster 'uniqueness' advanced in mid-century by figures like the social geographer Estyn Evans or Howard Sergeant.[28]

The question is the extent to which overcoming is merely ignoring; as McFadden noted, vagueness surrounded the whole concept of 'Ulster', a misnaming of Northern Ireland which overlooked the fact that it was not the organic, self-actualised, 'natural' territory of Mumford's and Geddes's writings on regionalism, but an artificially demarcated one riven by differences. Providing writers with an imaginary audience for their work, it was 'fatally flawed',[29] workable only if untested by political crisis (Smyth, 1998: 119). The more 'rootedness' was asserted under such circumstances, the greater the hostages to fortune: in the words of Hewitt's wife, Ruby Hewitt, 'Roots are all very well . . . until they rise up and strangle you.'[30] Ignoring such potential difficulties made Regionalism and its speaking subject unstable from the outset. Hewitt's main adumbration of Regionalism is in his poems and essays of the 1940s, although his faith in it, though waning, persisted into the 1950s, long after the international contexts which had enabled it had disappeared.[31] But it was at this time, nevertheless, during a period of mounting personal crisis (which concluded with his being 'sent to Coventry'), that Regionalism, ruralism and the identity politics of his poetry were tested, revealing and exploring this instability as never before.

According to Hewitt, 'The Colony' (dating from 1949/50 and published in *The Bell* in 1953) is 'the definitive statement of my realisation that I am an Ulsterman' (Hewitt, 1987: 154). The poem is a parabolic exploration of Unionist insecurity and claims to belonging, and thus of the characteristic negative terms of Hewitt's writing generally. In this sense, it is worth relating to Hewitt's other definitions of himself in terms of what sociologists refer to as 'nesting identities'. He identified himself (in 1974) as 'an Ulsterman, of Planter stock. I was born in the island of Ireland, so secondarily I'm an Irishman. I was born in the British archipelago and English is my native tongue, so I am British. The British archipelago consists of offshore islands to the continent of Europe, so I'm European. This is my hierarchy of values and so far as I'm concerned, anyone who omits one step in that sequence of values is falsifying the situation' (Hewitt, 1991: 6). 'The Colony' is an expression of this kind of interlocked allegiance, a monologue whose speaker is a colonist of a Roman province in a period of withdrawal by the legions. The poem articulates a sense of insecurity in the face of imperial retreat, establishing a link with Roman Britain in the fifth century and contemporary Britain and the dismantling of empire (Indian independence was granted in 1947). Hewitt's own ambiguities, as mirrored in the 1940s' regionalist work, are reflected in the ambiguity of the poem; while its arguments are not necessarily Hewitt's, they are clearly the dilemmas – of wanting to belong but with a guilty awareness of past usurpation – of Regionalism. This ambiguity and uncertainty of address and audience run through the poem.

It begins by demystifying the origins of the settlers/planters – 'camp-followers', 'rabble', some 'for conscience' sake the best of these', and the process of usurpation is hinted at in the next section of the poem, which begins 'We planted little towns to garrison/the heaving country' – 'heaving' presupposing violent expropriation along with the information that 'barbarian tribesmen' already live in guerrilla-like 'nests' on the higher ground (Hewitt, 1992: 76). Hewitt clearly ironises the speaker's language, and he matches allegory to history in some detail. Thus, the basic 'terror' of the colonists is located in a rebellion in a 'terrible year when . . . the dispossessed [lifted] their standards./There was great slaughter then, man, woman, child,/with fire and pillage . . . That terror dogs us; back of all our thought/the threat behind the dream . . . fear quickened by the memory of guilt/for we began the plunder' (Hewitt, 1992: 77). The 'year' is 1642, when the native Irish rose in Ulster against Scots and English settlers. At one point the speaker attempts to find a way out of the historical origins of the hatred which the dispossessed feel for the planters, by locating it in myth. He speculates that the 'creatures' of the lowland copses cleared by 'improvement' have hidden 'in thorny bushes' and become 'a crooked and malignant folk,/plotting and waiting for a bitter revenge'. But the speaker rejects this as a form of illness; 'So our troubled thought/is from enchantments of the old tree magic,/but I am not a sick and haunted man . . .' (Hewitt, 1992: 77–8). This kind of oscillation points to an interpretative difficulty concerning 'The Colony's' narrator, namely the extent to which he is the target of irony (as when he refers to 'barbarians'), a user of it, or a voice intended to be understood objectively. When, later in the poem, the persona calls the 'barbarians' the 'dispossessed', is this the voice of Hewitt himself offering a twentieth-century liberal judgement? Similarly, while the critique of the speaker's belief that the natives 'breed like flies' is obvious enough, the uncertainty of address with which the poem is riddled makes it more difficult to interpret a phrase like 'we made [the land] fat for human use', particularly given the positivism Hewitt endorses elsewhere in his writing. This is to say more than that the monologue is simply not consistently 'in character'; the speaker embodies the contradictions of a liberal pre-Civil Rights Protestant, both enlightened and 'haunted', healthy and 'sick' (Roulston, 1983: 105). Rejecting myth, the speaker nevertheless seems to unironically endorse the argument (by which imperialism has been commonly justified) that the colonisers 'improved' native agriculture and made the land more productive, a 'myth' in the Barthesian sense of naturalising ideology (what Richard Kirkland has called Hewitt's 'specious modernity') (Kirkland, 1996: 51). Speaking, sympathetically, of 'mak[ing] common cause with the natives, he admits that this is strategic, based on a hope 'to win a truce when the tribes assert/their ancient right' (Hewitt, 1992: 79). Yet 'The Colony' cannot be judged simply by whether it effectively presents the predicament of the liberal of Unionist background in a reflectionist sense; Hewitt's own problems of articulation are bound up in a general exploration of liberal Unionist impasse. For, by the end of the poem, despite its sweeping considerations, the distance characteristic of the poetry generally has been raised to an ontological level, the speaker's gestures of reparation pathetically circumscribed: 'I . . . would make amends/by . . . small friendly gestures'. As Hewitt himself said of it, this is 'a rather grudging plea' (Hewitt, 1987: 155). It is the inadequacy of this Wordsworthian credo which leads to the final balance of bluster and pessimism, the poem's – wholly negative – ineffable claims and self-assertion:

> for we have rights drawn from the soil and sky;
> we would be strangers in the Capitol;
> this is our country also, nowhere else,
> and we shall not be outcast on the world.
>   (Hewit, 1992: 79)

'The Colony', then, with its Regionalist-derived blindspots, cannot – because of Hewitt's adherence to the binary categories of racial–ethnic division, however guiltily framed, and despite his later disclaimers – be read as a wholly sustained exercise in irony. Neither, however, is it as fatally confused as some have argued. Although the temptation (here as elsewhere in Hewitt criticism) is to defend or deprecate the author, taken as a representative Protestant intellectual, the poem has its own life, and can be shown as critically considering its own strategies of evasion and representation, 'placing' myth and succumbing to it, relying on the most wooden ironies and subtly and urgently dramatising what postcolonial theory identifies as the coloniser's secret desire for the colonial Other, a desire which undermines the stereotypes with which Hewitt elsewhere works.

In this regard, however, it should be admitted that 'The Colony' is something of an exception. 'An Irishman in Coventry' of 1958 more glaringly reveals the mechanistic way in which Hewitt conceived of the opposition between progress and reaction, enlightenment and superstition and, ultimately, Protestantism (albeit in lower case) and Catholicism. (Most notoriously, in 'The Glens' of 1942, Catholicism is alluded to in the lines 'I fear their creed as we have always feared/The lifted hand between the mind and truth'.) In 'An Irishman in Coventry', the speaker (a version of Hewitt) is pleased to encounter an 'Irishman' (a Catholic), and claims kinship with him in order to gain the authority and critical distance in order to speak on his behalf. The context, crucial for Hewitt, is British post-war development embodied in 'the logic in the vast glass headlands,/the clockwork horse, the comprehensive school', which the fellow-countryman is shown as having failed to assimilate (Hewitt, 1992: 97). The speaker's feelings of superiority stem from this knowledge; difference is registered even as representation is assumed, but so too is puritan distaste ('the whiskey-tinctured breath, the pious buttons'). Protestant speaks, patronisingly, on behalf of Catholic; like 'The Colony', it is a study of well-intentioned but unstable ambivalence, and it is significant that Hewitt has to fall back in the final lines on mythology to unite speaker ('our') with the Irishman of the title, to overcome the difference the poem has stated but avoided analysing:

> Yet like Lir's children banished to the waters
> our hearts still listen for the landward bells.
>   (Hewitt, 1992: 98)

If Regionalism had faded as an organised literary force by the mid-1950s, its influence lingered. Later in life Hewitt attacked its nostrums more fully. He recognised the paradox at its heart, and its consequences – the forcing of a cultural unity on to an area deeply divided and only partially known by him. In 1984, for example, he noted 'the trouble was that I didn't realise there were several regions in the North of Ireland, and that the one region I thought it was, was heavily conditioned by a Protestant Planter background'.[32] Much of the later poetry is therefore palinodic, a labour of qualification and retraction. This can be seen in 'Cultra Manor: the Ulster Folk Museum', where a meliorist heritage industry presentation of the past is disturbed by the observation that what is lacking is 'a field for the faction fights' (Hewitt, 1992: 187). 'The Coasters', from *An Ulster Reckoning* (1971), attacks the fatally understated liberalism of some Protestants, who 'coasted along' while 'the sores suppurated and spread' (Hewitt, 1992: 137). This self-criticism – despite Hewitt's fine record of political activism – goes deep, while a poem such as 'A Local Poet' also casts doubt on the attempt to establish forebears among the Rhyming Weavers, finally turning on his own style and its silences:

> the pension which crippled his courage
> will keep him in daily bread,
> while he mourns for his mannerly verses
> that had left so much unsaid.
>   (Hewitt, 1992: 220)

What Hewitt acknowledges here are the limitations of the apparently smooth and often humdrum stylistic surfaces of his 'mannerly' writing, and – by implication – the way they are haunted by, and attempt to both explore and gloss over, ideological strain and threat. Arguably, it is this attempt which is the key to what Kirkland calls 'a long and uncertain writing career [spent] agonising over the politics of identity from a historical position which needed constant examination, constant rebeginning' (Kirkland, 1996: 28). Its characteristic negativity – for which socialism, ruralism and regionalism promised, but failed to deliver, expressive relief – reflects the plight of the 'protestant' Protestant attempting to free himself from social paralysis, but finding himself caught up in and elaborating a justification for it, making of its fixity an inevitability which the poetry projects as a fact of nature (typically, the subject of Hewitt's poetry is meditative, taciturn, watchful, negative, slow, decisive, 'basalt'-hard). This process of resistance and partial self-realisation, of ambivalence towards stereotypes, is at the heart of the much mentioned 'recognition of limits' or 'feeling for distances' of the work.

From the 1950s there is, then, a problematisation of some of the certainties of Regionalism. There is also a shift from generalising about 'Ulster' to family history, a rewriting of 'blood' and 'soil' belongingness at a domestic level (as in *Kites in Spring* of 1984). Clyde has claimed that Hewitt, by the time of his death, 'had long recognised the drawbacks, as well as the benefits, of the "two traditions" notion' (Clyde, 1988: 98–9). Yet, although Hewitt modified Regionalism thematically, he never rejected certain of the beliefs on which it was based – that is, the validity of the grounding of identity and a literary tradition in territory ('soil') and race ('ancestors', 'Planter stock'). For this reason he never quite relinquished the aspiration to be poet-as-vates, speaker for 'my people', no matter that an adequate definition of what that 'people' is, or the right by which the poet presumes to speak on their behalf, can barely be articulated.[33] These elements of an ideology we have seen at work in other poets of Hewitt's generation mean that neither his conversion into a figurehead, nor the argument that 'he revisit[ed] regionalism's grave, but only to pay [his] respects', nor yet the dismissal of the poetry as self-deluding, is quite satisfactory (McDonald, 1997: 22). Such claims involve a discounting of historical factors; as Miller has argued, the late 1950s and early 1960s were, in the North, a generally positive period: 'It is well to remember that the protracted crisis though which Northern Ireland has been passing had its origins in a partial rapprochement, not a growing alienation, between at least some elements in the two communities . . . The institutions which existed . . . were incapable of accommodating rapprochement' (Miller, 1978: 12–13). Hewitt was by no means alone in feeling that things were improving during the 1960s. His work, in all its self-contradiction, is that of a liberal Unionist caught up in the essentialist terms of a cultural Nationalism which could never fully apply to his chosen 'region', and constrained by his tacit acceptance of a set of binary terms – progressivism and conservatism, the rural and the city, unifying language and divisive dialect, individualism and collective voice, political radicalism and reaction – which his best poems problematise.[34]

Anthony Cronin and social realism

In the Republic, the struggle was to establish a critical realism against the Irish mode, the difficulties involved vividly illustrated by the fates of Valentin

Iremonger, noted earlier, and Anthony Cronin. It was Cronin who most consistently embodied the sociological ethos of *The Bell* in his poetry (he served
as its co-editor from 1952 to 1954).[35] Cronin's poetry was strongly influenced
by Kavanagh's maverick example, as his affectionate, if unsparing portrait in
Dead As Doornails shows (in 1962 he would be referred to by John Jordan as
'Mr Patrick Kavanagh's London representative', Cronin spending much of the
1950s and 1960s working as a freelance writer and critic there) (Kinsella and
Montague, 1962: 116). Jordan also describes Cronin as 'curious evidence of
how late Auden came to Ireland', and it is true that his style hovers somewhere between Auden and Kavanagh at its plainest. But Cronin – particularly
after the earliest work – displays a discursive, unadorned quality of his own,
an unillusioned stringency owing much to his Marxist and republican beliefs.
Like Iremonger's, then, his poetry represents an attempt to break out of the
impasse of the post-Yeatsian poetic by a limited use of foreign models to oppose
to the Irish mode. Unlike Iremonger, however, his work is distinctive in rejecting anything which could be remotely called 'stylishness'; consciously rebar-
bative, its style is unrhythmic, abstract and non-sensuous, opposed utterly to
Irish Ireland's sense of the necessary musicality of poetic language and the
blandishments of word-painting. In this it reflects a powerful urban-based urge
to attack ruralism, which Cronin views as a form of anachronistic kitsch, or
national regression.[36] 'The Man Who Went Absent From The Native Literature' – arguably the most thoroughgoing debunking of ruralist pieties in all of
Irish poetry – programatically rejects every element of the traditional Irish
poem – family, landscape, rural characters, place of birth, local or sectarian
allegiance – for the man of the title does not 'flog a line in identity whether
real or false, / Nor in the picturesque, / Whatever that is' (Cronin, 1982: 83).
Similarly, 'Homage to the Rural Writers, Past and Present, at Home and
Abroad', begins 'Country origins, country roots / Seduce long after our trans-
plantment', and ends with an attack on the notion that the rural is the 'real'
of Ireland:

> The realer seeming spade has struck,
> The realer seeming sod is turning.
> All lie in realer seeming muck
> While autumn leaves are really burning.
> (Cronin, 1982: 86)

Interestingly, although Cronin begins with the anti-'phony' stance of
Kavanagh, he ends up attacking the assumption of the rural as authentic (in
a sense anticipating the way Kavanagh's realism has been co-opted as a vehicle
for a revived neo-Revivalism since his death; this, as well as the 'unpoetic'
style, contributing to lack of critical recognition).[37] Nevertheless, like Kavanagh
Cronin does have an authenticist streak, valorising a world of outcast gurrier-
dom in which unsuccess is looked upon with favour.[38] His personal vision is
one which can only realise itself if its expressive aspects are pared back to a

bare minimum, the poem dominated by its concept, curbed by negativity, as if stripped of wit, artifice, play, music and metaphor for some enormous ground-clearing effort. As 'Lines for a Painter' puts it, 'Only inside the mind, / In the rubble of thought, / Were the pro-and-con, prose-growing, all-too-argumentative / Poems I sought' (Cronin, 1982: 48). Here, self-awareness of the dangers of negativity does not altogether offset them; if the poetry, then, refuses the reader the too easy consolations of subject matter and music, success rests almost entirely on the degree to which Cronin's intellectual struc-tures can maintain a genuinely dialectical argumentative complexity.

The extent of that success is best judged in Cronin's most impressive poetic work, the long (300-line) eleven-part *R.M.S. Titanic*, published in 1960. *R.M.S. Titanic* is set, like many of Cronin's poems of the time, in a context of Irish unemployment and mass emigration; the Afterword to the 1980 edition states that 'elements in [the poem] were the result of a prolonged acquaintance with members of the displaced and therefore demoralised section of the proletar-ian of my country in the doss-houses of London in the early 'fifties' (Cronin, 1980: 23). It opens in Liverpool, the traditional port of entry into Britain for emigrants, with the Mersey 'Trembling with engines, gulping oil', while 'in the doss the river fog is dawn'. The poem picks up the memories of an old man in the 'doss', with images of his Anglo-Irish boyhood in western Ireland. The social hierarchy of his world is established through a movement from 'black-thorn flowers', 'turf stacks' and 'turf smoke' that 'leaves a sweet, rich, poor man's smell in cloth', to 'rhododendrons' and 'chestnut blossom tops' around the demesne; it is a stable society, before the great shocks of World War I, Easter 1916, 1917 and the Irish civil war, in which a 'high, brass-bound De Dion coughing past . . . / Disturbs the dust but not the sleeping dogs' (Cronin, 1982: 54). But part two establishes the *Titanic* figuratively looming up, and the way its fate will anticipate historical upheaval: 'The west is not awake to where Titanic / Smokes in the morning, huge against the stars' (Cronin, 1982: 55). Cronin vividly realises the boy's surroundings on the Sunday of the disaster, his boredom and his absorption in an Edwardian world of imperial heroics – represented by R. M. Ballantyne and Fenimore Cooper – which will later lead him, it is suggested, 'like a romantic to the slaughter' of the Somme. His idealism is contrasted with the experience of the poor Catholic Irish emigrants bound for the US, 'battened now beside the pounding engines' in the *Titanic*'s steerage deck; here, as we know, most will perish when it sinks because the rich passengers will have been allowed into the lifeboats first. But the boy's idealism is shared by those who have designed, built and sail the *Titanic*. Cronin offers Lightoller, the ship's third officer, as the poem's representative English-man. He 'sees with pride the order of reasonable magnitude / Bulking and glis-tening around him'; and it is just possible, the poem allows, that there is such a 'schoolboy autumn order' as the boy has faith in 'with no rot at the core' (Cronin, 1982: 56–7). Nevertheless, crisis – of the liner, but also of empire, of world history – will show such an order to be fatally limited. While the limited man 'may act and judge', he must also 'prepare to incur some contempt'. As the 'Irish poor . . . [sing] / Their songs of Philadelphia in the morning', Cronin weaves echoes of emigrants' songs into his narrative, as well as the works of other poets. The general design of the poem is indebted to Goldsmith's *The Deserted Village*, while the opening of part six echoes Yeats's 'Meditations in Time of Civil War' ('Surely among the rich men's snowy linen / The dignified and decent can be found . . .'); a second section is more remotely modelled on Dr Johnson as well as Goldsmith and shows Cronin reaching for a psychological as well as political and material definition of class difference (Cronin, 1982: 57–9). This point is one of the most impressive in the poem:

> Sick in the bilboes of the world the poor
> Cling to each other, but the rich cling more
> Closely to the cruelty that prevents
> The dissolution of the modelled stance

Part seven, a meditation, claims that 'tragedy' is the final incident in a longer process, advancing a structural as opposed to an individually willed definition. Tragedy's historically contingent nature is stressed, although at the same time the idea fits Cronin's general tendency to take an objective stance towards his subject. This is emphasised in part eight, which notes that the *California* – another ship, which could have saved the passengers of the *Titanic* – was within rescue distance at the time of the sinking. In part nine, the *Titanic* finally sinks. As it does so, all moral judgements seem to be relativised – what do society's definitions of dishonour or weakness mean at such a moment? – as the narrative switches back to the west of Ireland and the knowledge that a form of naivety has died with the disaster. The penultimate section juxtaposes this knowledge with Irish politics ('The hot breath of the brass, the drum's insistence, / Tar-barrels flaming in the market square'), while part eleven takes us back to 'an April half a century on', and the waste of the lives of the old men in the dosshouse (Cronin, 1982: 62). Cronin's point is the way a form of decency becomes self-deluding weakness by being historically superseded. The poem's last lines, in effect, attempt to sum up the half century between 1912 and their present:

> A daily drudgery of approximate justice
> Is incumbent yet upon the brave who crouch
> Still over tasks on the drumming floor.
> But the eyes of survivors will ask both more and less.
> And no one now need ever fear a disgrace.
> The responses the night is listening to are aware
> Of the irrelevant ignobility of distress.
>   (Cronin, 1982: 64)

Read in the light of Cronin's Marxism, the 'daily drudgery of approximate justice' is the struggle to change society, the 'disgrace' of completely meaningless human tragedy having disappeared from a world where an alternative

– socialism – has been shown, at least to some degree, to provide an alternative. Unlike the *Titanic*'s signals 'The responses the night is listening to *are* aware / Of the irrelevant ignobility of distress' (my emphasis). The danger, however, is that describing distress as 'irrelevant' and ignoble might seem detached to the point of callousness.

Jeremy Hawthorn's *Cunning Passages* offers one of the best discussions of the *Titanic* in literature, attributing the endurance of the shock of the sinking in popular myth to the way in which the tragedy could be interpreted in multiple senses; the *Titanic* as society (from rich to poor), as the West on the eve of World War I, as technological hubris, as a rebuke for luxury and arrogance.[39] Drawing a distinction between the ideological and mythic uses of the event, Hawthorn points out that whereas ideological interpretations flourished in the immediate aftermath of disaster, the dominant interpretation became 'mythic' in the Barthesian sense. The fate of the *Titanic*, that is, came to be viewed ahistorically as a warning against human presumption and as a turning point in a naive belief in progress (Hawthorn, 1996: 87–157). Cronin's poem plays with some of the mythic interpretations that accrued around the disaster (that Protestant riveters in Harland & Wolff had chalked 'Down With The Pope!' on the ship; that the band on board played 'Nearer My God To Thee' as it sank; that a giant wave spread out as the *Titanic* sank; and so on). But it also re-ideologises the event. In particular it places it in the context of emigration, Northern Irish sectarian tensions (it was written at the time of the IRA border campaign) and of imperial hubris (the poem's anti-imperialist edge is sharpened, perhaps, by the recent debacle of Suez and anti-colonial struggles). The Irish dimensions of the *Titanic* 'myth' – the steerage passengers denied lifeboat places, the sectarianism of the Belfast shipbuilders, British pride humbled – suit it for Cronin's purposes. The purely nostalgic, mythic reading of the event – the end of a golden era, the end of an age of innocence, a foretaste of the decline of Britain – is rehistoricised, its ideological batteries recharged.

R.M.S. Titanic – partly as the result of its large ambition and the limitations of Cronin's sociological, relentlessly anti-poetic style – is only partly successful in avoiding the recurrent difficulty of his poetry, that of maintaining an intellectual interest sufficient to offset the denial of poetry as linguistic artefact. In the absence of a sensuous, material dimension, a lacklustre style courts banality; when the momentum of the thought breaks down little is left. In *R.M.S. Titanic* lack of verbal sensitivity and sententiousness are the result. Thus the poem foregrounds its attempts to see the British upper classes as victims of a system – of education, acculturation, feeling of imperial superiority – and to avoid sentimentalising the Irish in their 'drunken consociation', their self-pitying 'songs . . . always of misfortune'. To realise the contradictions within the system, and the systems of representation and self-representation, requires some notion of the complexity of their interaction. The poem's response to these demands is to withdraw from engagement. Yet a detached stance is only a legitimate response if something of the complexity of what is being withdrawn from has already been suggested; all too often, Cronin's anti-sensuous determinism has prevented this from occurring. All the human agents remain subordinated to their roles in an abstract way (this is even more the case in his longest work since *R.M.S. Titanic, The End of the Modern World*). As a result too much weight is thrown on the omniscient narrator, evident in the lapses into confused hectoring. Arguably such problems stem from Cronin's conception of ideology as more or less a conscious belief system, as 'false consciousness' rather than in the more pervasive sense of a set of lived experience and cultural practices; and, ultimately, *R.M.S. Titanic*'s ambitions require a more complex articulation of its parts than his simplified dialectic permits.

Ironically, it may be that the determination of Cronin's writing by the period in which his style was formed is at the root of these difficulties. Taking middle Auden (and the Eliot of *Four Quartets*), along with Kavanagh, as his models, Cronin was fixed in a style which had a limited range. Here the importance of a very few years – being born in 1925 rather than 1928 or 1930 – was crucial; a comparison of *R.M.S. Titanic* and, say, *The Rough Field*, shows an ability to animate complex material beyond Cronin, whose career coordinates were set by 1950 and whose influence has been greatest as a critic and catalyst in the arts. This raises the question of the form of *R.M.S. Titanic*. Cronin undoubtedly sees himself, in terms of poetic allegiance at least, as a modernist, and has written at length in favour of modernist writers and the modernist revolution in the arts. Yet the disruptive formal elements of *R.M.S. Titanic* – its dialogism, collage, quotation, dissolution of subject position – are tentative and insufficient to disturb its basically discursive drive. Impressive though it is in many ways, the poem also represents a fossilised, fatally sententious modernism; Cronin's radicalism, paradoxically, all too often has a fatally dated ring to it.

'Bitten by the T.S.E. fly': mid-century modernists

Cronin's poetry, for all the ambition of *R.M.S. Titanic* and his modernist sympathies, remains wedded to a formally non-experimental, realist–discursive aesthetic. The fact that this is so, even in the case of a poet radically at odds with the bulk of 1950s' Irish poetry, is a further reminder that – apart from Eugene Watters (considered in Chapter 2) – the neo-experimental current in Irish poetry was a wholly diasporic phenomenon from the 1930s to the late 1960s. Neo-Revivalists rejected it (although Clarke reviewed its products), returning with interest the attack on their 'flight from self-awareness' made in Irish poetic modernism's credo, Beckett's 'Recent Irish Poetry' of 1934.[40] Reviewing the *Oxford Book of Irish Verse* in 1958, for example, W. R. Rodgers observed that 'The Irish have never been bitten by the T.S.E. fly: they are not given to exploring the waste land of the spirit or the private condition of man.'[41] Most later critics have avoided discussing poetic modernism in detail by dismissing it as an example of the wish mistaken for the deed, criticising it in terms which preclude extended discussion (thus, Neil Corcoran refers to Devlin's *Lough Derg* as 'characteristically portentous and frenzied'), or ignoring it altogether (E. Longley, 1986: 15; Corcoran, 1986: 159). Like other silences or partial readings in Irish poetry, the lack of attention has only recently been addressed. As the editors of the critical text which has contributed most to a deeper understanding of the 1930s' modernists put it, exclusion reveals 'the greater ease of the critical establishment with work which can be more readily accommodated under the rubric of a more literalist and self-proclaimed Irishness'[42] (Coughlan and Davis, 1995: 7–8). Yet no account of Irish poetry since 1950 is complete which does not take into account not only these poets – Devlin, Coffey and the older MacGreevy – but also the way in which a modernist, or neo-modernist current persists in Irish poetry. Without a proper acknowledgement and assessment of this, not only is valuable poetry ignored, but precisely the kinds of binary opposition Longley and Corcoran deplore (Irish Nationalist versus Anglo-Irish/Protestant Northern Irish traditions) are reinforced, however unwittingly. What is at issue here is not an assertion of the alternative centrality of some 'experimental' tradition against an equally monolithically conceived dominant 'formalist' one, as Devlin and Coffey themselves would have done; this would be to take these poets' own conscious and self-willed peripheralisation as the whole story, and merely to invert the terms of the mainstream case. Rather, as has been argued, the point is to 'resist the whole logic of centres and peripheries and recognise in the 1930s, as today, a situation of complex and shifting assertions of difference', as a means for gaining a different perspective on the polarised models of Irish writing which dominate criticism (Coughlan and Davis, 1995: 10).

This is not to say that Devlin, Coffey or MacGreevy are themselves unaffected by such polarisation; all three notably accepted the Catholic-Nationalist parameters of Irish identity with which the later neo-modernists would break. These allegiances, however, may provide some clue to their re-emergence (most notably for Coffey) during the 1950s, since – as for Clarke and Kavanagh – a late burst of poetic activity roughly coincided with the crisis of the mid-1950s and the Lemassian response. Moreover, before discussing this work distinctions need to be drawn between the three poets in question, since their treatment as an undifferentiated group has been instrumental in the process of neglect. Like MacGreevy, Coffey and Devlin had aspired in the 1930s to create an Irish version of European Catholic poetic modernism. Rejected by, and rejecting, an anti-modernist Irish mainstream, their own conception of themselves is best seen in terms of the example of Joyce and of the European equivalents they translated so extensively, from Mallarmé to Jiménez and St-John Perse. Yet as Alex Davis has argued, using a distinction drawn by Marjorie Perloff in *The Poetics of Indeterminacy*, Coffey is more properly assigned to the exploratory, open-ended, tentative mode of modernist poetry associated with the Poundian 'wing' of modernist poetics, and developed in the writing of Williams, Zukovsky and the Objectivists, with its minimalism owing something to Beckett. Devlin by contrast (and in common with MacGreevy) belongs to the less formally experimental and dominant variant of modernism, drawn from Eliot's Symbolist–aestheticist poetic and developed in the work of Crane and Stevens.[43]

This link between poetry and the first stirrings of change in Ireland may seem most tenuous in the case of the oldest, MacGreevy.[44] Having written only one poem since 1934 (in 1950) MacGreevy produced his last three in a burst between 1959 and 1960, coinciding with his retirement as director of the National Gallery. Yet this may not merely be a case of having leisure for writing; as Tim Armstrong has noted, MacGreevy's major poems had always been 'written with a full consciousness of the pressures of history' (Coughlan and Davis, 1995: 55). The awareness of such pressures makes the last poems similar in all essential aspects to the early work. That is, they show how Mac-Greevy's modernism, powerfully inflected by the struggle for Independence and by his Catholicism, remained central to his writing (and just how fundamentally it differed from that of the rejectionist Joyce and Beckett). 'Moments Musicaux', 'Breton Oracles' and 'On the Death of Joseph Djugashvili *alias* Stalin' can arguably be read as rejections of modernisation cast as a reassertion of MacGreevy's earlier themes of imperialism, faith and Irishness (MacGreevy, 1991: 65–7, 68–70, 71). 'Moments Musicaux' (1961) records the return of 'She of the Second Gift'; in religious terms, the Holy Ghost's gift of understanding, but also – as Susan Schreibman argues (MacGreevy, 1991) – the return of the poetic gift which records the visitation. The poem stresses the speaker's belief that 'You thought she had left you alone' – this line being repeated five times – 'When, his piping over, / The shepherd waited / The silence that waited his silence'. Then, 'Across half a world / Across half a lifetime', 'movement', the vain strivings of existence, has 'ceased / And, blessedly, / Line found its direction'. The poem's second section rewrites the feeling of internal exile felt by MacGreevy on his return by turning its regard on those, like Beckett, who had remained abroad: 'How could they have the heart / To stay / With you gone.' What is extraordinary about the poem is the way in which it allows spiritual and literary narratives to be read equally into each other, in considering a broken writing career. The implicit opposition to the secular forces of modernity is more explicit in 'Breton Oracles'. As with the third of these pieces, 'Moments Musicaux', the poem's spare and fragmented modernist style resists attempts to interpret it in other than its own intensely religious terms. Nevertheless, the Gauls of 'Homage to Vercingetorix' (of 1950), are taken, in the course of a visit to Brittany, as contemporary figures not simply for the Irish but for a pan-Celtic culture. This, as Lee Jenkins has argued,[45] is the final, reduced form of MacGreevy's earlier desire for a European-style Irish modernism; the diminishment of the dream is embodied in a recognition of the momentary visitation of 'the Second Gift' which is at the same time an epitaph 'for a "lost tradition" of Celtic monasticism' and for MacGreevy's own poetry:

> The light green, touched with gold,
> Of clusters of grapes;
> And, crouching at the foot of a renaissance wall,
> A little cupid, of whitening stone,
> Weeping over a lost poetry.
>
> (MacGreevy, 1991: 70)

It is typical of MacGreevy that these last moving lines should so economically and unobtrusively bring together the major concerns of his poetry, from visual art ('renaissance') to Catholicism and modernist classicism ('A little cupid'), and – in the colours of the Irish tricolour ('dark green, touched with gold' and 'whitening stone') – Nationalism.

Brian Coffey

Like MacGreevy's, Coffey's return to poetry in the post-war period is marked by the Nationalist sentiment and religious piety which distinguished Joyce's successors from Joyce himself. His *Nine A Musing* (1961) and *Missouri Sequence* (1962) appeared after a gap of more than two decades, the second being a long and ambitious poem considering mid-career silence and the issues of exile and work (Coffey began it around 1954, conscious of his vulnerability after resigning from his post as philosophy lecturer at the University of St Louis). Much has been made of this relatively accessible poem, and it is significant for more than simply breaking a silence (Dawe, 1989: 121–3). As Davis points out, it exemplifies Coffey's poetic, which was heavily influenced by the work of the Neo-Thomist French Catholic philosopher Jacques Maritain under whom he had studied in Paris in the 1930s and 1940s. Maritain's teaching had reinforced Coffey's distrust of the aestheticist tendency of the modernist artwork to reify itself in pure form, a tendency both saw as abolishing the properly communal and craftsmanly aspect of art, usurping the structuring activity which belonged by right to God (Coughlan and Davis, 1995: 150–4). Nevertheless, it was felt, if the artwork succumbed too resignedly to its conditions of existence – the mere 'pathos of experience', in Poggioli's words, which lies behind surrealism – the result was what Maritain calls 'a flabby materialism'. Coffey therefore followed Maritain's view of the poet as '*artifex*, artist or artisan' rather than demiurge, as 'makar' in the Scots usage, poised between belief and modernism, the human, 'crafted' aspect of the work balancing the high modernist urge to the perfect work on the one hand, as typified by Mallarmé's *Le Livre*, and mere contingency and everydayness on the other. The tension between these aspects of Maritain's philosophy is a possible reason for Coffey's long poetic silence, as well as his isolation from Ireland; and both silence and exile are present structurally, as well as thematically, in *Missouri Sequence*.

With sections dedicated to MacGreevy and the memory of Devlin, the poem is clearly Coffey's bid to rejoin the modernist current. Its four sections follow the upward curve of the year, from winter, March and June to midsummer, and its tone is exploratory and meditative, showing its interaction with its surroundings in an attempt to illustrate Maritain's claim that 'poetry is ontology', that it has a human purpose and not a purely aesthetic one. It opens by foregrounding the act of writing, with Coffey sitting at his desk considering 'family cares and crises' and his children 'mak[ing] songs from room to room' but, worryingly, growing up to 'know nothing of Ireland, / they grow American' (Coffey, 1991: 70). The family's future is uncertain, and the first section considers the related ideas of home – 'Five miles away, at Byrnesville, / the cemetery is filled with Irish graves' – as well as unfulfilled poetic promise and the call of Ireland, criticising as it does so a Yeats-dominated poetic tradition (Coffey, 1991: 69–70, 72). The 'muse', however, does not visit those such as Coffey who have 'failed to choose / with loving-wise choice', although it 'permits the use of protest / as a second best'. The tone, as this suggests, is self-accusatory, resigned, the lack of 'wisdom' related to Coffey's anger in giving up his post ('a monument to celtic self-importance') (Coffey, 1991: 71, 73). In part two he distances himself from this by assuming the persona of the Chinese poet Su Tungpo, who also suffered exile, but who offers a model of equanimity. This section recalls the radical questioning of the self of 1930s' modernism: or, in Maritain's terms, the notion that desire for a 'perfect' or integral self should not be allowed to master the 'unthought-of change / love's way in unrestricted range', the 'here and now'. Caught in the cycle of the seasons, human beings are nevertheless created by culture; 'We face a testing / based on other grounds than nature's' (Coffey, 1991: 77). The third section presents the poet as hunter, opening with another domestic reference (the dinner-table at meal time, like the children running around the writer in part one, 'poetry as ontology'). The poet hunts a muse figure hidden in the June landscape, but his possession of her is delusory: 'What he fancied ended / she smiled at as begun / knowing him no freeman . . .' Unaware that it is he, not she, who is possessed, the poet is shown to be unselved and fragmented, 'his elements / scattered on shore and shore' (Coffey, 1991: 80). The subject position now shifts between first and third person, indicating a gradual realisation of the fact that the muse is not some perfect figure or stasis but 'the children shouting', 'a torment of oneself' which 'cannot be done without'. There is, as Davis argues, a final contradiction, or stasis, between fidelity to the muse and the (Devlinesque) search for beauty, and the contingent poetic process. The fourth part of *Missouri Sequence* tries to capitalise on the balance struck here, of poetry as a form of universal acceptance, 'for man' and 'at the service of our common culture': 'And poetry, what of poetry, / without which nothing exact is said? // Poetry becomes humankind. // Only it charms us / knowing in loving' (Coffey, 1991: 86). These, however, are large and vaguely phrased claims, and point to some of the problems of the poem: as Davis notes, the concluding pronouncements resolve the debate of the poem by shifting it on to a vatic plane. Moreover, there is, beneath the work's metapoetic concerns a more prosaic uncertainty, particularly in part one, in which a sentimental home-sickness and somewhat naive presentation of faith – against Coffey's stated aim of 'the elimination of the term irishness [sic] from the critical vocabulary' – cannot be absorbed within the larger argument (Coughlan and Davis, 1995: 282, fn. 3). A passage which runs 'I am charmed / by the hills behind Dublin, / . . . grass green as no other green is green' is dangerously close to the sac-charine landscapes of a John Hynde postcard, and ironically raises the spectre of Maritain's 'flabby materialism'. Billy Mills, one of Coffey's most committed champions, also considers the piece 'the least satisfactory of the long poems he was to write during the following 30 extraordinary years'. Nevertheless, *Missouri Sequence* is an important achievement; the tendency to cliché ('an eternal note of gladness') and poeticism ('whither') offset by the keen aware-ness of seasonal transience and the subtle verbal playfulness and luminous, spacious humility of Coffey's writing at its best:

> Watch the slender swallow flash its wings,
> dive, sheer sky in two,
> never before, never again,
> and such is poetry.

> It bears the truth of all,
> freely attends on who
> keeps constant watch,
> lives whenever everywhere
> awakens when our love
> says yes to all, accepts
> even the viper vibrant in the vine.
> (Coffey, 1991: 86)

Denis Devlin

Denis Devlin's poetry is generally far less concerned with the processes on which Coffey focuses than on poetry as finished, ritualised artefact, and deals largely with transpositions of Marianism, in which women act as ambivalent intermediaries between the speaker and an unattainable divine figure. Devlin, again unlike Coffey, suffered few interruptions to his writing and had a repu-tation in US New Critical circles sufficient to ensure publication. He wrote some of his best poetry in the 1950s, which was the decade of *The Colours of Love* and *The Heavenly Foreigner*, as well as of 'Memoirs of a Turcoman Diplo-mat' and 'The Passion of Christ'. The relative anomalousness of 'Memoirs' make it a way into Devlin's work which prevents easy dismissal of the work as a whole as 'portentous' and hints at what it has to offer serious critical con-sideration. That is, the projected world of the poem's speaker, in this case, pre-vents the poem from following the usual solipsistic course of an imagination endlessly projecting subjective fantasies on to the world, pursuing a love which is possibly self-love. The female figures habitually used by Devlin as the focus for his meditations on the crushing responsibility of self-creation in the face of the unspeaking Jansenist God are only fitfully present, and his taste for a language of negotiation is thematised; the speaker/subject of the poem is, like its author, a diplomat. This persona, however, is non-Irish and non-Catholic; as a result, some escape from the constraints which usually operate in Devlin's work become possible, enabling an oblique but highly imaginative critical meditation on Irish history and society to occur.

'Memoirs' is in eight short sections, framed by the setting of the narrator drinking, at evening, on the terrace of the 'Oteli Asia Palas, Inc.', and gazing over Istanbul. The opening strives for a form of imaginative imposition (reminiscent in some ways of Wallace Stevens), its terms at once both abstract and opulent:

> Evenings ever more willing lapse into my world's evening,
> Birds, like Imperial emblems, in their thin, abstract singing,
> Announce some lofty Majesty whose embassies are not understood . . .
>   . . . while sunlight falls
> Like thick Italian silks over square houses in the Bosporus.
> (Devlin, 1989: 295)

This meditation is prolonged in the second section, 'The Golden Horn', in which the diplomat elaborates on his 'magic kingdom' of the past, a country half-perceived which recurs throughout the poem in leitmotifs of women, 'warm colours in striking contrast, muted lights and shifting water, birdsong and horses and the wind' (Mays, 1999: 84). The tension between the concrete, external world and an ideal otherwhere is used to define Turkey against the West (the 'Franks') and the West's rationalism and modernity, striking a note of Keatsian negative capability: 'When a rare sunlight, a rare birdsong, / Compose the absolute kingdom far in the sky / The Franks must ask how it was known, how reached, how governed, how let die?' (Turkey is also defined against her bitterest enemy, the 'chatterbox Greeks', originators of rationalistic Western thought.) Yet the Turkish victor over them, 'our Westernising dictator' Kemal Ataturk, embodies, in his self-consciously modernising project, the fact that the struggle between the utilitarian and the magical also exists within Turkey. It is in dramatising these internal and external struggles that the poem signals its Irish dimension. Mays argues that

> it [is] helpful to recognise how Turkish history could be conceived as being cast in a mould similar to Irish history. Broad similarities cover the same indissoluble blend of religious and nationalist feeling, the same consciousness of being at the edge of European culture, the same traumatic and shabby beginnings as a modern state . . . The high barren plains of Anatolia, forgotten and intransigent, represent the same rallying-point of conscience for old-fashioned Turkish nationalism as the Gaeltacht

for republican Ireland. These could indeed be memoirs of a TD. (Mays, 1999: 83)

Stan Smith echoes this: 'Islam . . . seems almost a mirror image of Devlin's Catholicism, reconciling ascetic rigour with a worldly hedonism' (Coughlan and Davis, 1995: 240); or, if we ascribe it a more critical stance, we might say that the terms of the balance between spiritualism and sensuality in Irish Catholicism (overtly criticised in 'Lough Derg'), and between imperial and colonial mentalities, are deliberately shifted in the outlook of the diplomat, providing a new and tangentially challenging perspective.

Having established the ideal kingdom at the edge of consciousness and its critical rebuke to the kingdoms of the world, 'Golden Horn' is followed by a second 'movement' of three poems – 'Wars of Religion', 'Four Turkish Women' and 'Anatolia' – which explore what commitment to such a 'kingdom' entails; namely, Muslim fundamentalism, women as embodiment of racial purity, and the uncompromising nature of the national and imperial pride bred in Anatolia:

> In the high country, there is no food for ghosts,
> The dead stay underground, which is their place
> We had enough to do to keep the Arabs and the Bulgars in their place
> If the dead have bad dreams, they live in us, querulous and lost.
> (Devlin, 1989: 299)

The section does not, then, simply illustrate the first but counterpoints it by anatomising the varieties of absolutism which underlie the diplomat's wry detachment. Two separate quatrains sum this section up, restating the points about Turkey's enemies with clipped aggression ('they're lost and know not'). The third section of the poem, 'The White City', returns to the themes and images of the first. The city of the title – Belgrade – encapsulates the failed Ottoman imperial design on Europe, for which – at least implicitly – the 'magic kingdoms' of the first section are a compensation. For Mays, this setting up of 'The White City' is 'contrived', and he makes the point that the defeat of Suleiman the Magnificent at Belgrade 'was not quite the decisive turning-point in Turkish history the sense requires'. Similarly, Mays claims that the conceit in the opening line of the poem – 'The Sava and the Danube like two horses folded, mane on mane' – 'has more justification in the system of the poem's imagery than in reality'. Yet the appeal to 'reality' seems inappropriate given the modernist, non-realist nature of the poem, just as the insistence on the 'not quite' significant historical defeat of Suleiman rather pedantically over-looks its status as national myth. Nor does Mays note 'The White City's' organi-sation around the diplomat's experience as a post-World War II tourist in the Balkans:

> Only ten years ago the invaders came,
> The pretty guide talked on and showed our party –
> In which were former Nazis, former Fascists –

Photo-posters of men hanging like blotting paper,
Dirty blood on dirty children, dirty mothers
The willowy water of the Sava bathed . . .

(Devlin, 1989: 300)

In this sense 'Memoirs' – like work by Montague, Watters, Kinsella and Coffey – is part of a general Irish determination to encounter the worst of a recent, missed history, in this case the slaughter of 900,000 Serbs by the Nazis and their Croatian Ustase allies (there are also what might be references to the Turk's own massacre of Armenians in 'Anatolia'). Here Devlin – intensely of our own time, with its Bosnian and Kosovan bloodshed – refers to one of the least-known and dirtiest events of the war, one minimised in Ireland (as Hubert Butler noted) because of the Catholic Church's opposition to Tito.[46] Given this, it is disputable that the diplomat's turn from history to whiskey and women immediately afterwards is an 'anti-climax': 'A truce to talk of genocide, and nation and race!' is a life-affirming, if limited response to historical horror. The final lines, in which the speaker exclaims 'Johannes, my boy . . . we're all the rage now, whiskey-flushed men of our age, / The callow and the shallow and the fallow wiped off the page!', is a Browningesque conclusion which belies the meditative opening but is hardly 'pathetic'.[47] The gesture is of a piece with the ambivalent nature of the diplomat, whose initial wry resignation, Paris and Göttingen education, 'European' drink, and so on, place a question mark over his national representativeness and even over an essential 'Turkish' identity as such. There is, as Stan Smith points out, an irony in his attempt to endow place – or race – with any absolute value, given 'the nomadic ancestry of the Turks themselves, late inheritors of the residue of several empires – an experience crystallised in the title of the shortest piece in the sequence: "The Turkish for Greek is Roman"' (S. Smith in Coughlan and Davis, 1995: 242). The point is that – like the Oteli Asia Palas, Inc. – Nationalist authenticity is a sham and that at one level the diplomat knows this. But in showing this, the poem also hints that 'civilised' West Europeans who may feel above the appeal of 'primitive' nationalism were, in the last war, murderously in thrall to it; in this sense it reads as a critique of Nationalist essentialism, while reminding us that liberalism may serve to disguise similar beliefs.

'Memoirs', then, richly complicates any understanding of the way Irish poets were assessing their relationship to the state and to the dominant Nationalist tradition in poetry in the 1950s. Asia – here as in 'Ank'hor Vat' – is a zone in which Devlin gains a certain imaginative freedom from the constrictions demanded by Irish or other Christian territories; despite the obvious Orientalism in his outlook it is nevertheless a critical move. Above all, 'Memoirs' points to alternatives to the kinds of polarities found in *The Heavenly Foreigner*, another late work in which, as Armstrong has pointed out, religious meaning is so fixed that 'starting an argument about Bath vs. Chartres can stand for Protestantism in general' (Coughlan and Davis, 1995: 63). Turkey does not play the same role as the classical mythology of Clarke's later work or of Kavanagh's 'not-caring' philosophy in the Canal Bank poems, since its value lies in its liminality rather than as an outright oppositional space. Nevertheless like these poets, if more obliquely, Devlin negotiates between two potentially destructive extremes, of criticism of the Irish state and of the postcolonial legacy. The diplomat is both an essentialist Nationalist, the equivocating Devlin, and an exemplary colonialist: Turkey is both marginal 'Irish' *and* ex-imperial 'British'.

Louis MacNeice: cold war parables

Louis MacNeice – like Devlin in this, if in little else – remains one of the major unaccommodated facts of post-Yeatsian poetry. This is a problem of reception, one problematised by his adoption by post-1960s' Northern Irish poets and his palpable and profound influence on their work. Put another way, as McDonald has argued, MacNeice refuses to fit into either of the two dominant existing paradigms of post-Yeatsian poetry, the British and the Irish, to be an Irish pseudo-Auden, or reducible to the product of 'a colonial family in Northern Ireland' (Kinsella, 1995: 108). Complicating the issue is the fact that the 'rooted' qualification of Regionalism meant that MacNeice was never fully accepted as a Northern Irish, let alone as a fully 'English' or 'Irish' poet, during his lifetime.[48] For a time after the war this might have seemed a role which MacNeice himself fulfilled, since his poetry of the late 1940s and early 1950s is exactly of the kind which, to the suspicious glance of a Hewitt (or a Grigson or a Clarke) might have seemed to be vitiated by its author's inability to make the necessary, hard choices about where he belonged. *Ten Burnt Offerings* (1952) and *Autumn Sequel* (1954) seemed to show how 'slackening tensions are reflected in slackening poetry', despite the virtuosity of the latter; as MacNeice himself put it, 'This middle stretch / Of life is bad for poets' (Welch, 1996: 346). In his last three collections, by general critical agreement, MacNeice made a bold and successful move out of the impasse not by 'returning' to 'roots', but by developing a wholly new style of 'parable-poem' in *Visitations* (1957), *Solstices* (1961) and the posthumous *The Burning Perch* (1963).

It is interesting to consider the ways in which the parable-poems of MacNeice's last phase are, in their way, an attempt to use the material of a specifically Irish Anglican upbringing not only as a way of exploring 'sordor, disappointment, defeat, betrayal' but also as occasional (if unnerving) opportunities for renewal (MacNeice, 1979: 507). This dimension is clear in 'The truisms', for example, whose title refers to MacNeice's father's life as an Anglican cleric dispensing the 'truisms' of religion. The speaker returns to 'a house / He could not remember seeing before' only to find he can now 'bless' it as his early home, and accept 'the truisms' as 'a tall tree sprouted from his father's grave'. That this is not a straightforward tale of a prodigal's return is clear from the unnerving as well as redemptive quality of the final image, however; the poem critiques ancestor worship even as it accommodates the inevitability of a return to origins. Seemingly simple, and using a pared-down language, the later poems in this way comment on and inflect the issues of identity in which MacNeice's reputation has been entangled. (As McCormack has argued, he can be placed in the company of other marginalised twentieth-century Irish writers of (chiefly) Protestant extraction who deconstruct the integral self and betray Ascendancy claims to tradition McCormack, 1994: 18.) Identity is a central theme; as 'Visitations' asks, 'How can you prove your minds are single' (MacNeice, 1979: 464). More famously, in 'The Taxis', the different selves accumulated over a lifetime are visible to the taxi-driver while remaining invisible to the present self of the passenger:

> As for the fourth taxi, he was alone
> Tra-la when he hailed it but the cabby looked
> Through him and said: 'I can't tra-la well take
> So many people, not to speak of the dog.'
>   (MacNeice, 1979: 522)

The repeated 'tra-la' refrain appears to be nonsensical, or to stand in for deleted expletives, but becomes an increasingly sinister hiatus or blanking-out of meaning. Certainly, the concentration on surfaces and flux, once seen as proof of MacNeice's superficiality, demands to be read more as an obsession with mutability and the contingent self of modernity, the impossibility (and dangers) of essentialist identity (it is in this way, for example, that he serves the – albeit tendentious – argument of Muldoon's *Faber Book of Contemporary Irish Poetry* (1986), whose epigraph is taken from a 1938 radio interview in which MacNeice scrupulously defies F. R. Higgins's insistence on the 'racial' basis of Irish poetry). MacNeice recognised early in his career the ease with which Ireland could be fixed in stereotypical and binary thinking, pinning down the problem in his prose even as some of his own poetry about Ireland slipped into the too-easy dichotomies.[49] 'Prologue', completed in 1962 for the projected *The Character of Ireland* plainly states: 'Let us dump the rubbish / Of race and get straight to the point: what is a nation?', defining members of that 'nation' as the 'Inheritors of paradox and prism'.[50]

It would be something of an evasion, however, simply to say that MacNeice's poetry 'interrogates the self', and thus dissents from the identity-fixations of most Irish poetry of the period. A sense of the provisionality of the self is prominent in the early poetry too, but the scepticism it represents is qualitatively different from that found in the later verse. The difference lies in the shift from the interrogation of what is taken as the pre-given, existent self – however contingently determined – to that of the subject as such. Under the sign of modernity and purposeless movement, emblematised in taxis, cars and buses, there is an exploration in the later poetry of the limits of subject positioning, predicated on the lack of any monadic sense of identity or of a self engaging (in a more straightforward sense) with the flux of modernity. This is revealed in the consistent plight of the subjects of these poems, which generally involve a vain attempt to acquire agency. Loss of agency (and the sense of deterministic entrapment which results) leads to the adoption of parabolic procedures. Considered in this manner, the use of parable acquires a wider dimension than that simply of MacNeice's Irish–Northern Irish–English multilocatedness. This – taken with a consideration of the generic and historical-social contexts of the later work – should be seen as qualifying the recent tendency to read MacNeice as a father of modern Northern Irish poetry.

MacNeice's thinking on parable can be traced in his Clark Lectures of 1963, published after his death as *Varieties of Parable* (MacNeice, 1965). Drawing upon a wide range of literature, from Spenser and Bunyan to Kafka and Golding, the key contemporary figure for MacNeice is clearly Beckett, with whom he expresses kinship, with Beckett standing at the darkest end of a spectrum stretching from allegory to parable. Beckett, Kafka and Golding all suggest that MacNeice was attracted to a negative theology, and many of these poems elaborate the structure of a meaningful narrative – often, as in 'The Wiper' or 'Charon' – in journey form, but with only the ghostliest meaning-content. One constant preoccupation is the nearness of death and the simultaneous impossibility of knowing it; in 'Charon' the traveller is told 'If you want to die you will have to pay for it', while in 'After the Crash' the central figure has missed, or forgotten, the moment of his death as he looks up and knows 'in the dead, dead calm / It was too late to die'. It is tempting to claim that MacNeice saw endurance and salvation through trial as the ultimate 'message' of these poems. 'Round the Corner is – sooner or later – the sea', as 'Round the Corner' puts it, or – using the same marine image – 'Thalassa' implies (MacNeice, 1979: 504, 530, 524, 518, 546). To do so, however, would be to deny the darkness of the tone of most of these poems, which set their face against the consolations of an easy humanism, let alone religious consolation. Not only the confusions of MacNeice's personal life in his later years, but the socio-political context of these poems offer some possibility of aligning their procedures, and their lack of comfort, with larger issues. MacNeice himself in *Varieties of Parable* points to the cold war fear of nuclear annihilation as a factor behind the bleakness of contemporary uses of parable. In the wider post-war international contexts in which he was involved, a narrative of disenchantment can be discerned, from his coverage for the BBC of the communal bloodletting which accompanied Indian Partition, to his role as a British Council employee in Greece just after the 1943–49 civil war (in which British troops supported monarchist forces and the Right against communist partisans) and in South Africa in 1959 on the eve of Vorster and apartheid. There is also the formal question of the poems, which show a deliberate avoidance of the assured discursiveness of his earlier styles (and in the remarkable 'All Over Again' almost break with conventional syntax entirely). The combination of mythopoeic-allegorical mode with a 'penny-plain technique where fancy rhythms and rhymes would not obtrude too much', as Heuser puts it, and the 'high proportion of sombre pieces', may be linked with MacNeice's comment that many of the poems were 'trying to get out of the "iambic groove" we were all born into' (MacNeice, 1987: 224, 228). This is not to argue that MacNeice was veering towards experimentalism; the challenge to the poem as artefact resides in a numbed, almost null quality, which reveals someone for whom questions of expression are beside the point; an understanding that 'The lines of print are always sidelines / And all our games are funeral games' (MacNeice, 1979: 533).

The end of stagnation

The 1950s' poetry of Hewitt, MacGreevy, Devlin, MacNeice, Cronin and Coffey represents, in very different ways, the limits to which the horizons of Irish poetry could be expanded given the glacial effects of partition, isolation and exile. Perhaps revealingly, the year in which *R.M.S. Titanic* was published – 1960 – was also the same year of the appearance of Padraic Colum's *The Poet's Circuits*, the apotheosis of Irish Ireland lyricism. Ostensibly there is little to link these works; perhaps even less to link either with 'The Heavenly Foreigner', the Canal Bank poems, Clarke's satires or 'The Colony'. Yet what all of these works share is a sense of circumscribed conditions, a mirroring of the basic frozen tensions of the post-1922 settlement and of literary oppositions established long before it; between the mythical and the 'real', the rural and the urban, the Irish Ireland and the modernist. So fixed was the paradigm, so implicated in the ideologies on which the two states within the island of Ireland rested, that it could only be shattered by non-literary, even non-cultural shock of the first magnitude.

That shock occurred in 1958/59 with the triumph of the modernising wing of Fianna Fáil under Seán Lemass. Faced with a mounting demographic and economic crisis, the party took power in 1957. De Valera, now seventy-five, was eased out of the leadership and into the presidency, a largely ceremonial post. Lemass was able to draw on the work of T. K. Whitaker, the new Secretary of Finance, whose 1958 report on the state of the economy, *Economic Development*, opened with the words 'the greatest fault lies in pursuing a policy after it has proved to be unsuitable or ineffective' (Lee, 1989: 342–3). This became the basis for a White Paper published in November, *Programme for Economic Expansion*. Both documents signal a shift from protection towards free trade, and from discouragement to encouragement of foreign investment. A five-year investment programme was specified, and a 2 per cent annual growth rate was projected – modestly above the existing level. The emphasis was shifted from 'the economics of equilibrium' to the 'economics of growth'. Lemass's attempts to attract foreign capital in the short term were aimed at boosting indigenous Irish industry in the medium and long term, it having significantly having failed to expand after nearly forty years of protection from competition. Restraints on the repatriation of manufacturing profits were lifted, industrial growth was prioritised over agricultural, and tax holidays, grants and greenfield sites were offered to attract multinationals and inward investment. Aimed at creating jobs rather than merely balancing the budget, with the first Economic programme the Irish economy belatedly entered the Keynesian era of post-war boom.

The initiatives succeeded beyond the wildest expectations of the government. Jumping on the coat-tails of the final phase of the worldwide post-war capitalist boom, the Republic was caught up in the general massive increase in trade and production which characterised the world economy. The influx of capital began with Hallmark Cards, a US company, in 1958 and was followed by Burlington Textiles (1960), General Electric (1962) and a host of others; by 1983, foreign firms had invested £IR16 billion in the economy, £IR4,500 of which was from the USA, which supplanted the UK as the largest foreign economic presence. As Lemass's gamble paid off, national self-confidence and optimism was renewed (Brown, 1985: 241). Between 1958 and 1970 over 350 new industrial ventures were established and in the 1960s the Republic's GNP grew by 4 per cent per annum, well ahead of the 1 per cent of the de Valera years, the 2 per cent target figure, or growth rates in the UK. The decade also witnessed the sharpest ever rate of growth in Irish output, while living standards rose by 50 per cent. The cultural and literary consequences of expansion and modernisation, as I shall show in the next chapter, were far-ranging. In his Introduction to the 1984 edition of his brother Patrick's *Complete Poems*, Peter Kavanagh would begin by explaining, for the benefit of a younger generation, that 'Patrick lived in a period when Ireland, or at least the district in which we were born, was still largely medieval. In a very few years from about 1955 to 1970 Ireland jumped from the primitive ass-and-cart economy to that of the tractor-trailer' (Kavanagh, 1992: xviii). If this has its exaggeration – 'medieval' – the basic modesty of the claim should not blind us to the profound consequences of such a change, particularly for those who, like Kavanagh himself, saw Ireland in primarily rural terms.

Notes

1 *The Great Hunger* broke with both the lyric forms and the sentimental ruralism of most post-Independence Irish verse. Although its novelty was acknowledged, however, it failed at the time to inaugurate a new phase of Irish poetry, its untimeliness underlined by Kavanagh's failure to complete two similar critical-realist poems at this time, *Lough Derg* and *Why Sorrow?* (both 1941).

2 W. R. Rodgers's (1909–69) last collection was *Europa and the Bull and Other Poems* (1952), the subject of a scathing review by Kingsley Amis. After *The Heart's Townland* (1947), McFadden (1921–99) did not publish a full-length collection until *The Garryowen* in 1971; similarly, after *The Undying Day* (1948) Robert Greacen (1920–) did not publish again until *A Garland for Captain Fox* in 1975. Padraic Fiacc (1924–) had no early collection but nevertheless reveals a similar publishing history; his first collection, *By the Black Stream*, appeared only in 1969.

3 V. Iremonger 'Poem', *Envoy* 1:1 (1949), 22. Iremonger's small poetic output, marked by use of speech rhythms, slang, references to the war and jazz and

rejection of insularity, is strikingly different from other poetry of the Republic and reflects the influence of Auden, MacNeice and John Crowe Ransom (his role as a bridge between Northern and Southern poetries is also attested to in his co-editorship of anthologies with Greacen and Bruce Williamson). Unlike Kavanagh, Iremonger distinguished between the Irish mode and the Irish tradition in Gaelic, and claimed to have derived the metrical freedom of his loose colloquial line from the latter. Though operating within the *The Bell* milieu he oppposed its sociologism, and the confidence with which his poems reach out to a non-Irish audience is striking. By the late 1940s he would be seen as 'The main opposition to the neo-Gaelic lobby', while in a US-published anthology of 1948 he went on record as 'think[ing] it high time the Irish overseas stopped harping on the 700 years of persecution theme – "it's history, it's fact, but it's over"' (Montague, 1989: 217; Garrity, 1948: 205). The untenability of his position given mid-century circumstances is apparent in an article of 1951. Its terms are individualist; nobody is interested 'in the young writer as young writer only', whose true task lies in posing and answering 'the fundamental questions that present themselves to all humanity'. Vaguely humanist, this is a plea for non-provincial writing. But the claim that the young Irish writer 'often abandons writing in despair at the lack of . . . encouragement' underlines Iremonger's own silence after this date. Indeed, his earlier recourse to elegy and use of anti-hero or underdog figures (Hector, Dedalus) finally seems emblematic, an anticipation of his own fate. See V. Iremonger, The Young Writer and *The Bell*, 2, *The Bell*, 17: 7 (October 1951), 15.

4 Maunsell and Roberts closed in 1928, leaving only private publishers like the Yeats' Cuala Press. Most published poets had UK publishers (Kavanagh and Iremonger were with Macmillan; Greacen and Iremonger's *Contemporary Irish Poetry* was published by Faber and Faber), or published privately (Clarke's Bridge Press).

5 Foreword, *Envoy*, 1 : 2 (1950), 10.

6 T. Bodkin, *Report on the Arts in Ireland* (Dublin, The Stationery Office, 1949), 9.

7 The Church's position was the product not just of dogma, but of the specific set of material circumstances which had developed a century before in the aftermath of the Famine with the spread of familism, a system of inheritance designed to prevent the division of the land through inheritance, and which thus involved strict control of marriage and sexual activity. Its position, in other words, flowed from its provision of a rationale for an agonising economic and social reconfiguration, one which involved the definition of sin in almost wholly physical, sexual terms. The Church was able to accomplish this because of its deep roots in Nationalist ideology, roots put down in the Penal Era (although it distanced itself from radical Nationalism during the nineteenth century); in this period it had become synonymous with Gaelic identity and self-esteem because it provided almost the sole conduit for feelings of opposition to British rule. As a result it had powerfully shaped constitutional Nationalism as a Catholic middle class emerged in the nineteenth century, and went on to play a strongly conservative role in the new state. Its leading figures anticipated the potential threat of urbanisation and modernisation; under the leadership (until 1972) of the ultra-conservative Bishop of Dublin, John Charles McQuaid, it embarked on a mid-century building and expansion programme, maintaining a strong presence in family life and a high urban level of church attendance, bucking the secularising trends at work elsewhere in Europe. By eschewing overt political intervention, except on rare occasions, much of its grip on education and welfare provision, and considerable indirect influence, was preserved (Lee, 1989: 157–68).

8 Behan, Kavanagh and O'Brien are all prime examples of what Augustine Martin has identified as 'inherited dissent' and Seamus Deane – somewhat sourly –

describes as a cult of failure: '[T]alent, time and money could be wasted, drunkenness and unemployment could be given moral status and, finally, writing itself would be imbued with something of the spirit of subversive squalor' (Deane, 1986: 228). If Martin and Deane to some extent make these writers scapegoats for the more general failings of mid-century Ireland, they nevertheless underline the near-impossibility of individuals transcending a national malaise. Given the lack of a wider audience willing or even able to respond to its critique, the *Bell's* adversarial stance and commitment to realism was liberating but also limiting.

9 *The Envoy*, as Smyth points out, had been distinct from *The Bell* in its conception of nationality as incidental, as opposed to the *Bell's* progressive Nationalism, and also in its more outward-looking stance (Smyth, 1998: 113–19).

10 'Celebrations', a satirical account of the development of the Free State, was written in 1935 and published in 1941. See Cooney, 1967: 16–26.

11 See A. Clarke, *Later Poems* (Dublin, Dolmen Press, 1961), 89.

12 Clarke's periodic reviews of the state of Irish poetry – in 1935, 1951 and 1971 as well as 1946 – consistently display his belief in the centrality of Irish mode poets (conversely, he underrated the importance of Kavanagh).

13 According to Smyth, the critique of the past at the time was compromised by its continuing 'engagement with the comparative terms of traditional decolonising discourse', by which a recognised need to 'shut the door on the past' leads to the discovery that 'such a gesture is anticipated by an established structure of Irishness and non-Irishness received from the colonial period'. The rejection of the colonial past can thus only be conceptualised in terms which, by merely inverting these, remain within its intellectual framework (Smyth, 1998: 95–6). See also Deane's comment that writers of the time are 'caught between their alienation from, and commitment to, the new Ireland' (Deane, 1986: 376).

14 No other poet of Clarke's generation would have considered calling a collection *The Pill*, as he did in 1967 of the volume which became *Old Fashioned Pilgrimage*.

15 Terry Eagleton, discussing baroque echo-poems (a form Clarke uses in 'The Echo at Coole'), remarks that drawing attention to the 'empty' device undermines an empiricist poetics: 'No finer image of such constraint can be found than in the baroque echo-game, in which the echo, itself quite literally a free play of sound, is harnessed to dramatic meaning as answer, warning, prophecy or the like, violently subordinated to a domain of significance that its empty resonance nonetheless threatens to dissolve' (Eagleton, 1992: 5).

16 Again, this contrasts sharply with Kavanagh, who overthrew the Irish mode in part by removing its ideological content; in other words, Clarke turned the Irish mode against itself in a form of immanent self-criticism, though he did not abandon its rationale (as Denman says, Clarke retained his earlier style partly because it signified a necessary tradition; 'Clarke's anxieties centred on the *absence* of influence') (Denman, 1989: 74–5). Archaic elements in his work have made it much more difficult for later poets to assimilate and hence acknowledge him than Kavanagh (he is omitted from Muldoon's Faber anthology of 1985). Complex and contradictory, Clarke's can be seen as an example of a parochial or (to use a less loaded term) a localised modernism, like those of MacDiarmid or David Jones. Ironically, given his own opposition to high modernism, it would prove to be neo-modernists – Thomas Kinsella and Catherine Walsh – who would owe most to his work.

17 Another context for Fallon's revisionary readings was the growth of international academic interest in the Irish Literary Revival from the late 1940s onwards. Studies of Yeats, Joyce, O'Casey and Synge appeared and were paralleled by a concomitant growth in specialist publications, conferences, biographies and professional associations. The majority of the critics involved in these developments – Donald

Davie, Richard Ellmann, A. Norman Jeffares, Hugh Kenner, T. R. Henn, William York Tindall – were non-Irish or Irish critics based abroad (such as Vivian Mercier and Denis Donoghue). This was part of the broader challenge of professionalisation to the impressionistic and amateurish literary and critical scene in the Republic at the time. Smyth cites Bruce Arnold: 'Like many of their fellows since, Irish critics of the 1950s were caught between resentment at this usurpation . . . and flattery' (Bruce Arnold, *The Scandal* of Ulysses (London, Sinclair-Stevenson, 1991) 87–101) (Smyth, 1998: 97). Fallon's treatment of Yeats, however, counters the tendency of these writers to accept uncritically Yeats's mythicisation of the eighteenth century and the Anglo-Irish Ascendancy.

18 'The gynaeolatry of the Troubadours; elements from Frazer's *Golden Bough* and from Jung . . . Christian symbolism combined with a rather un-Christian pantheism; and finally, a very twentieth-century sense of "dread" and impending catastrophe, which sometimes is at war with a serene inner fatalism' (P. Fallon, 1990: 269–70).

19 The poems in question are from the 1945–60 period referring to Yeats, 'Yeats's Tower at Ballylee' and 'Johnstown Castle', and to Maud Gonne 'Maud Gonne'; from 1960–74, referring to Yeats, 'Fin de Siècle', 'Yeats at Athenry Perhaps', 'Letter from Ballylee' and 'Stop on the Road to Ballylee', to Lady Gregory 'Kiltartan Legend' and 'On the Tower Stairs' (which refers to the entire ménage). Gonne appears in section 2 of 'The Small Town of John Coan (2)'.

20 In a number of poems of the 1940s and 1950s, the archetypal representations of women Fallon uses in his poems – the muse-figures and lovers of 'The Small Town of John Coan' or the Mothers of Creation of 'The Mothers', for example – inflect his consideration of the relationships between Yeats, Lady Gregory and Maud Gonne, as Fallon remythologises the Revival in his own peculiar way. Mythicising the women – as aspects of the Triple Goddess empowering Yeats – and making them central to Yeats's creative endeavour clearly does not accord with the myth-to-realism trajectory approved by some critics, and is in part what lies behind the charge of anxiety of influence; that, in dealing with Yeats, 'the voice falters, the focus blurs, and the language loses its poetic quality'. Given its concern with female representations, it is surely ironic that this work provokes a gendered criticism blind to their significance, hinted at in Garratt's comment that 'the bulk of Fallon's work denies that he was his own man'. Judging poetry in terms of masculine self-possession, Garratt casts what he sees as Fallon's weaknesses as a form of 'feminine' surrender; 'he yielded to Yeats's shade, either by allowing the intrusion of the latter's voice or by loosening his own concentration upon the poem's design, permitting it to drift towards parody' (Garratt, 1989: 74–5). There is, of course, a sense in which Fallon's many returns to the Revival reveals the stalled dynamic of mid-century poetry, and hence of some element of 'imaginative stalemate' in his own work. But this does not explain why (feminine) lack of self-control is seen as producing generic and tonal impropriety ('parody'), a point repeated in Johnston's claim that 'what should be counterstatement [to Yeats]' in 'Johnstown Castle' 'results in burlesque' (Johnston, 1985: 40). Why precisely is 'parody' (or 'burlesque') an inappropriate way to deal with Yeats? In a different way, when Heaney celebrates Fallon's heterogeneity he does so in terms of his own poetry; Fallon's use of legend is asserted to be most successful when he 'keeps his grip on the actuality of his experience . . . the reeks and textures of known places'. He is in danger, for Heaney, when he tries 'to establish his own poetic and political freehold in a territory where Yeats is still demanding the ground rents' (P. Fallon, 1990: 15). Here the masculine/feminine equation becomes that of landlord and tenant and Fallon's rewriting of the imperious, masculine aspects of Yeats, and calculated disruptions of the troping of poetry as land, are missed. Heaney offers a generally positive reading of Fallon, but his claims beg the question of what 'actuality' is (that is, why experiences not concerned with being located in a specific 'place' are assumed to be less than fully actual – don't Buddhas and books have alluring 'reeks and textures' too, and particularly for poets?). While accepting Fallon's critique of Irish Ireland, then, Heaney resists it by valorising the rural, casting as exotic those elements which constitute Fallon's escape from the claims of instinctualism (hence the objection to Fallon's 'over-absorbed ratiocination' by which 'the poem's argument grows too intent and the suppleness of natural rhythm gets hampered') (P. Fallon, 1990: 13).

21 E. B. Cullingford, *Gender and History in Yeats's Love Poetry* (Cambridge, Cambridge University Press, 1993).

22 A. Martin, 'Brendan Behan', *Threshold*, 18 (1964), 22.

23 The critical assault paralleled Kavanagh's phase of verse satire which ran from the mid-1940s to the mid-1950s.

24 For example, he declined the opportunity to appear in the Faber anthology *Contemporary Irish Poets* (1949) (J. W. Foster, 1991: 78).

25 *Kavanagh's Weekly* was a weekly journal into which Kavanagh and his brother, attempting to fill the gap left by the demise of *Envoy* in 1951, had poured their small savings and large energies with signal lack of success (Kavanagh wrote virtually all of the twelve weekly broadsheet pages of material). For a rather over-positive assessment, see Smyth, 1998: 103–13.

26 Bruce Stewart, *IASIL Newsletter*, 5:1 (April 1999), 23.

27 The political implications of Kavanagh's stylistic heterogeneity are worth considering in the light of David Lloyd's comments on the functions of hybridity in nineteenth-century street ballads and *Ulysses*. Noting that 'the processes of hybridisation registered in the street ballads go far beyond the integration of Gaelic into English-language forms', Lloyd notes in such works a 'refusal to differentiate the burlesque from the serious' which corresponds to 'an indifference to cultural registers'. Subversive of Nationalist cultural requirements for monologic modes of expression these are 'recalcitrant' to its aesthetic politics 'and . . . to those of imperialism. Hybridisation and adulteration resist identification both in the sense that they cannot be subordinated to a narrative of representation and in the sense that they play out the unevenness of knowledge which, against assimilation, foregrounds the political and cultural positioning of the audience or reader. To each recipient, different elements in the work will seem self-evident or estranging' (Lloyd, 1993: 96–7, 114).

28 The problem with Regionalism is the (always latent) potential for cultural-geographical distinctiveness to slide into *post factum* justification for Partition. Sergeant brings this out in a way Hewitt usually avoids, or glosses over: it is a short step from 'while regionalism offers its contribution to the whole culture of a nation or comity of nations, nationalism is more conducive to cultural isolation' to geo-mythological obfuscation: 'Ulster is in a unique position. No other province in Ireland is so well defined, geographically, politically, or in its ancestry . . . Deirdre's flight to Scotland with the Sons of Usna seems to imply that from the earliest times there was a close connection with Scotland' (Sergeant, 1953: 4).

29 Peter McDonald, The Fate of 'Identity': John Hewitt, W. R. Rodgers and Louis MacNeice, *The Irish Review*, 12 (Spring/Summer 1992), 74. In collecting this essay as a chapter in his 1997 study, McDonald modifies the phrase to the more anodyne 'obviously flawed enough' (McDonald, 1997: 24).

30 Quoted in R. McFadden, No Dusty Pioneer, *Threshold*, 38 (Winter 1986/87), 6.

31 The crucial essays are 'The Bitter Gourd' (1945) and 'Regionalism: The Last Chance'

(1947), and the poems *Conacre* (1943), *Freehold* (1946) and 'Homestead' (1949) (Hewitt, 1987; 1992). The journals associated with Regionalism were *Lagan* (edited by Hewitt and John Boyd) which appeared between 1943 and 1946 and *Rann* (edited by McFadden and Barbara Hunter) which appeared between 1948 and 1953. *Threshold*, set up in 1957, was an intermittently published general cultural journal which, in its early years, conveyed little belief in the existence of any 'movement' in Northern writing.

32 Quoted in M. Mooney, 'A Native Mode': Language and Regionalism in the Poetry of John Hewitt, *The Irish Review*, 3 (1988), 73.

33 The belief that the poet should speak for a community meant that he has to find some other place than sectarian Belfast to 'represent', and produced Hewitt's turn to ruralism, with which he was never comfortable; the sense of overall failure can be seen in his comment that 'I . . . have written poems which are relevant to the political situation. Yet they are quoted in the *Irish Times* but not in the *Belfast Telegraph*. I am not speaking to my people . . . they are taken up by a more distant audience than that for which they were intended' (Hederman and Kearney, 1982: 728). An unexamined notion of collectivity and community is also behind Clyde's statement in 'An Ulster Twilight?' that 'The most important word in poetry is "we": as soon as it is uttered all thoughts, images and reflections click into place' (Clyde, 1988: 99).

34 In this sense Hewitt's socialism deserves more consideration than as a simple transference of energy to Regionalism; rather, it is overlaid by Regionalism, shaping it and outcropping within it. 1930s' socialism and Marxism worked with a mechanical materialist, economistic and deterministic concept of culture as a superstructure. National culture, like art, was in this scheme of things more or less epiphenomenal, and it is arguable that Hewitt's heavy-handedness in regard to internal cultural difference was partly due to this (as well as to his limited experience of Northern Ireland).

35 Chiefly known as a biographer, memoirist, novelist, journalist and general cultural force in the life of the Republic (it was at Cronin's instigation that Charles Haughey would create the national artists' bursary scheme, Aosdána, in 1980), Cronin is an intellectual with socialist affiliations and professional raiser of hackles; in 1955, his quasi-official visit to the Soviet Union in the company of a number of trade unionists and writers provoked 'a virtual smear campaign from the Catholic *Standard*' (B. Fallon, 1998: 258).

36 As Seamus Heaney has rather nervously noted, he sees 'the vogue for poetry based on images from a country background as a derogation of literary responsibility and some sort of negative Irish feedback' (Heaney, 1989: 9).

37 Asked to nominate the most underrated poet in Ireland in a *Poetry Ireland Review* poll in 1980, Cronin offered himself.

38 This can be seen in the article 'A Massacre of Authors' attacking the New Critics and Leavis in *Encounter*, 4:31 (January/June 1956), 25–32. Cronin labels New Criticism 'literary necrophily', identifying the characteristic evasiveness of Leavis's attempts to ground his literary judgements. The critic's role as an 'uncreative commentator' is viewed as the parasitical triumph of analytical orthodoxy over the supremely important 'personal vision' of the artist.

39 Hawthorn, 1996. For a critique of Hawthorn, and a thorough discussion of the *Titanic*'s specifically Protestant symbolism, see Fran Brearton, Dancing unto Death: Perceptions of the Somme, the *Titanic* and Ulster Protestantism, *The Irish Review*, 20 (Winter/Spring 1997), 89–103.

40 According to Montague, Clarke denounced modernism at a time when he was at his boldest in his own poetry, 'anything experimental being gloomily described

as "modernist"' (Montague, 1989: 217). *The Great Hunger* uses some modernist-derived free rhythms and Clarke's compressions and distortions can achieve quasi-modernist disruptive effects. Kavanagh, however, read *Ulysses* as a realist text, while Clarke could claim to find in *Finnegans Wake* the apotheosis of stage-Irishism and the excesses of the Celtic Twilight (Schirmer, 1995: 92).

41 W. R. Rodgers, *Threshold*, 2:4 (Winter 1958), 63.

42 Thus Edna Longley's assessment of the 1930s' modernists is that 'Derek Mahon's transmutation of Beckett is the most significant poetic legacy of that group [of the 1930s' modernists]', reducing a large, varied and in some ways impressive body of work to a mere footnote in literary history ('transmutation' here seeming to mean, in almost its original alchemical sense, a magical abolition of the need to consider experimental form). Longley's extensive polemics against modernism, in her Intro-duction to *Poetry in the Wars*, are based on the belief that modernism was a mistake and that criticism should pay more attention to 'the more traditional team' – 'Yeats . . . Hardy, Frost, Thomas, Owen, Graves, Auden, MacNeice, Douglas, Larkin, Heaney, Mahon', rather than to poetry deriving from the examples of Pound and Eliot. Although this position is rigorously and consistently argued in her work, its rigid division of monolithically defined 'modernist' and 'traditionalist' currents is untenable. While Longley is also a fierce critic of 'self-proclaimed Irishness', this is offset by a devotion to a localist, empiricist aesthetic and a belief in the autonomy of the poem as self-sufficient artefact (E. Longley, 1986: 9–21; 'The Irish Poem', *The Irish Review*, 8 (Spring 1990), 56.

43 Thus, MacGreevy corresponded with Stevens, and Devlin was taken up by the Southern Agrarians and New Critics who codified Symbolist-aesthetic modernism in their critical practice (Devlin's *Selected Poems* of 1963 was edited by Robert Penn Warren and Alan Tate). Such distinctions, of course, also complicate the usual accounts of Irish-US poetic traffic (Heaney/Muldoon–Frost, Montague–Snyder, Kinsella–Pound).

44 Because of the exile status of Devlin and Coffey, and the long silence of MacGreevy, it is difficult to determine the extent to which this activity was connected to the new mood of the 1950s. In a sense, this is unimportant, of course; what matters is the way in which the resultant publications in the early 1960s – of Devlin's *Selected* and *Collected Poems* (1963; 1964) and Coffey's *Missouri Sequence* (1962), together with the growing reputation of Beckett – made possible the renewal of the modernist current in Ireland around 1967.

45 Lee Jenkins, unpublished section of '"A Position Intermediate": The Modernism of Thomas MacGreevy' (Goodby and Scully, 1999: 61–6).

46 See 'The Sub-Prefect Should have Held His Tongue' and 'The Artukovitch File' in Butler, 1986: 270–305.

47 Mays's questions appear somewhat beside the point: 'Does the appeal to Johannes to "down this petty brace" convince us of an outward-turning invigorated rhap-sodist of life? Or does it appear rather pathetic, the half-mechanical lunge of an elderly roué on vacation?' It is by no means certain that, given the ambiguities and qualifications of the diplomat's beliefs which have been made that we are looking to be 'convinced' by some kind of stereotypical extrovert. Mays concedes this, but asserts – rather than convinces – that it must, nevertheless, be otherwise.

48 In his essay of 1945, 'The Bitter Gourd: Some Problems of the Ulster Writer', Hewitt allows that the 'Ulster' writer must seek 'some recognition outside his native place'; yet he adds 'I believe this had better not be achieved by his choosing materials and subjects outside or beyond his native environment. He must be a *rooted* man, must carry the native tang of his idiom like the native dust on his sleeve; otherwise he is an airy internationalist, thistledown, a twig in a stream' (Hewitt, 1987: 115).

There is little doubt that Hewitt intends MacNeice, and the strain of rejection shows ('native' repeated twice, the emphatic *'rooted'*).

49 As in the Irish section XVI in *Autumn Journal* (MacNeice, 1979: 131–4).
50 The poem is given in full in J. Stallworthy, *Louis MacNeice* (London, Faber and Faber, 1995), 488–91.

2
From Éire to modernity

The most important author of the contemporary Irish canon is T. K. Whitaker, secretary of the Department of Finance at the end of the fifties, and its seminal work is his First Programme of Economic Expansion. (O'Toole, 1988: 13–14)

Out of stasis

'In the late fifties', John Montague claimed in 1973, 'Irish poets began to write, without strain, a poetry that was indisputably Irish (in the sense that it was influenced by the country they came from, its climate, history and linguistic pecularities) but also modern' (Montague, 1989: 124). He concluded: 'An Irish poet seems to me to be in a richly ambiguous position, with the pressure of an incompletely discovered past behind him, and the whole modern world around him' claiming that, used to straddling different cultures, the contemporary Irish writer 'at his best, is a natural cosmopolitan'.[1] Montague's stance involved rejection not only of the English Movement poets, whose insularity was linked to British post-war decline, but also of the Americanised Auden who had previously served as the chief model for younger Irish poets (Montague, 1989: 198). In the same vein Thomas Kinsella noted in 1965 that the cutting edge of poetry was now in the USA. At the same time, the 1960s saw a renewed interest in the possibilities of the Gaelic tradition and translation from it, and in European poetry (O'Driscoll in Kenneally, 1995: 48–60). These varied interests reflected not simply a desire to 'break out from the English-speaking world or at least that part of it which is dominated by the Home Counties', but more significantly a desire to break out of Irish isolation by expressing cultural diversity (Ní Chuilleanáin, 1992: 38). Yet as the variousness of these interests and Montague's rather anxious parenthetical definition suggests, the smooth emergence of a 'modern' poetry 'without strain' is debatable. If the substitution of an insular Britain for an insular Ireland suggests a somewhat willed inversion of terms, 'modern' remains problematic, while a definition of what is 'Irish' may be anything but 'indisputable'.

Nevertheless, the onset of Lemassian modernisation, in boosting confidence and prosperity in the Republic (the years of the First Programme have become 'legendary'), had its effect on the emerging group of young poets of the late 1950s (Brown, 1985: 241). Together with Montague and Kinsella, Richard Murphy, Richard Weber, Pearse Hutchinson, Brendan Kennelly and Desmond O'Grady seemed to restore a poetic succession which had broken down in the 1940s and 1950s. They were part of a broader general renewal of Irish writing which found collective expression in Dolmen's *Miscellany of Irish Writing* of 1962, an anthology of new writing edited by Montague and Kinsella. This marked a generational coming of age, and confirmed links already made at a joint reading the year before and in a television documentary of Kinsella, Montague and Murphy as the leading triumvirate of young Irish poets. It is prefaced by a credo:

> In recent years a new generation of writers has begun to emerge in Ireland, probably the most interesting since the realists of the 1930's. While not forming any sort of movement, they do reflect a general change of sensibility . . . they are, in general, more literary than their predecessors . . . many of them are poets, and the prose writers seem to be working towards a more experimental form of story. The main link between them, however, is their obvious desire to avoid the forms of 'Irishism' (whether leprechaun or garrulous rebel) which have been so profitably exploited in the past. In such a context, a little solemnity may be a revolutionary gesture. (Kinsella and Montague, 1962)

Coloured by the 1950s – wariness,[2] the isolationism implicit in disclaiming membership of 'any sort of movement', the rejection of 'Irishism' – this nevertheless shows a calculated modesty, a measured embrace of change, a faith in alternatives to localism, the sociologism of *The Bell* and vestigial neo-Revivalism.[3] The key terms are 'more literary' and 'more experimental', pointing as they do to new stylistic allegiances. The rejection of obvious Irishness was in part a reflection of their career paths, since 'the typical movement in their work was an initial outward trend and then the return to Ireland' (Harmon, 1973: 205).[4] The three *Miscellany* poets (Montague, Kinsella and Murphy) had all been published by 1960.[5] Unlike the mid-century – when attempts to change the course of Irish poetry had been thwarted by limited horizons and a lack of interest – innovation and expansiveness were now confirmed by a wider sense of national awakening, catching the energies of poetry elsewhere. With this new confidence it became possible for the 1950s' poets to be assigned to the role of predecessors; editions of Kavanagh and Clarke, by Montague and Kinsella respectively, indicate a conscious settling of accounts in a move to create a modern, internationally recognised poetry.

Modernisation

The economic growth generated by the First Programme succeeded in its chief aim of arresting emigration and population decline.[6] As prosperity increased there was a closing of the gap between Irish social provision and that in the UK and Europe, while the subordination of Nationalist economic dogma to market forces also meant some loosening of political orthodoxy. Nevertheless Lemass justified reform in terms of achieving the original goals of Independence, with modernisation presented not as the abandonment of bankrupt policies, but rather as the final stage in the struggle to develop a modern state.[7] The implications of this ambivalence for ruralist and Gaelicist ideologies, as the drift from the land to the cities accelerated and rhetorics of national identity began to conform to the changed situation, were not at all clear-cut.[8] Similarly, although the effects of change can scarcely be exaggerated, the nature of that change was more complex than has sometimes been assumed, for although the Republic had missed out on the post-war boom, it was scarcely 'backward' in material terms and was well acclimatised to the industrial world.[9] A large proportion of its population had been going to live and work in the world's most advanced industrial economies for the previous century and a half, a process which allowed change to be absorbed without the level of social upheaval which accompanied modernisation elsewhere.[10]

Given its ideological centrality, change nevertheless made unavoidable the contesting of inherited images and myths in literature, even if writers were still caught in the complex frustrations of the 1950s. In political terms, the decade witnessed a leftward shift, the most visible sign of which was the gradual emergence of group politics in the late 1960s for the first time since the 1920s, notably in the Women's Movement (and in the North, the Civil Rights Movement), but also detectable in the unrest which accompanied industrial expansion and protests and enquiries into public housing, redevelopment and corruption scandals. A significant change in religious attitudes also followed the reforms of the Second Vatican Council (1962–65) and Pope John XXIII's *aggiornamento*, which tempered the ultramontane severities of the Irish Church, and was reflected in the abolition of much (though not all) of the apparatus of censorship in 1967.[11] Like Britain and the USA, Ireland also saw the rise of a youth culture, one which took specifically national as well as international forms, with the immense popularity of showbands and a traditional music revival.[12] Many of these changes were hastened by television, as RTE started broadcasting for the first time in 1962; programmes, bought in from the USA and UK because of the high costs of production, undermined isolationist attitudes (although, as Luke Gibbons has argued, certain Irish-made programmes, such as *The Late Late Show*, were probably even more influential) (Gibbons, 1996: 4).

Literature mediated the larger cultural, economic and political debates about national identity and the direction in which the nation was moving, partly because of the lack of official discourses assessing the implications of change (Cairns and Richards, 1988: 140–1). As has been argued, there was an undercurrent of unease about the lack of intellectual effort directed to coming to terms with modernisation. David Thornley's essay 'Ireland: The End of an Era?' of 1964 acknowledged that the Republic was 'at the threshold of a delayed, peaceful social revolution', but noted the dangers of the widespread notion that Ireland was a country 'which has somehow managed to combine uniquely a revolution in its attitudes to growth . . . with the preservation of the . . . virtues of a rural and deeply Catholic community' (Thornley, 1964: 2). For Thornley this suggested that attitudes to change were 'fundamentally flawed. They started from a semi-mythological concept of the past which may never have in fact existed – a kind of "Once upon a time, and a very good time it was"', in which change was conceived of 'as a struggle between religion and "materialism", between country and town, between . . . "national culture" and cosmopolitanism'. These antitheses were false, both because the continuity of change had been ignored and because assessment of the extent of change had been 'coloured by pessimism and wishful thinking' (Thornley, 1964: 7). The extent of the 'pessimism' was revealed two years later, in the year of the fiftieth anniversary of the Easter Rising, when *Studies* declined to publish a commissioned article by Francis Shaw which criticised Pearse and the cult of blood-sacrifice associated with 1916, attacking the republican view of Irish history – albeit from a Christian-pacifist viewpoint – as 'seven centuries of solid and unbroken military resistance' as a travesty of the actual Irish experience (the article did not finally appear until 1972) (Brown, 1985: 288). The unwillingness to confront such issues reflects the difficulty of dealing ideologically with change, although the decade was marked by the emergence of what has since become known as revisionist historiography (Brown, 1985: 287–8).[13] From the first this was a highly charged *political* issue, since it concerned the identity, even the validity, of the state, and it was made even more contentious when in the early 1970s Conor Cruise O'Brien, then a Labour minister in the coalition government, denounced traditional Nationalist narratives in the bluntest terms. One of O'Brien's points, crucially, was his call for history proper to be distinguished from what he saw as the essentially literary current in Irish history, and hence the extent to which explicitly historical poems of the period (such as 'Nightwalker', *The Battle of Aughrim* and *The Rough Field*) might be considered to draw upon the different versions of Irish history on offer.[14]

Lyric limitations: O'Grady, Galvin, Hutchinson

One difficulty in dealing with modernisation lay in the survival of a diasporic mode of literary production as a response to perceived backwardness, isolation and lack of opportunity.[15] If emigration was still common in the 1940s and 1950s for young poets such as Pearse Hutchinson, Patrick Galvin and Desmond O'Grady, it was now paradoxically a product of the greater opportunities for travel, and so lacked the full heroic, Joycean mystique attaching to the pre-war concept of 'exile'. At the same time, although in a sense enabled by modernisation, emigration also contributed to insulation from the modernisation process. Comprehension of what was happening in the Republic could therefore be partial, while internationalism did not necessarily make for a re-examination of inherited stereotypes. While emigration in one sense confirmed the confidence of a new poetry, and what Brown calls 'a new kind of iconoclasm distinct from the satiric, antagonistic bitterness that had characterized the work of an earlier generation of writers', these poets also reveal the problems inherent within it, such as lack of scrutiny by a writing community and the threat of arrested development as writers (Brown, 1985: 227). Hutchinson, Galvin and O'Grady show certain similarities in this sense, as also – to a limited degree – with the leading post-war poet to follow this career trajectory, John Montague. Their poetry registers the energy of their different host cultures – Italy, Greece, Spain, Egypt, England – but at the same time often treats Irish experience in the terms in which it was set at the time of their departure; that is, as straightforwardly negative, and therefore to be responded to with a mixture of rebelliousness and self-protective distancing. Because of this their oppositionalism can seem pre-programmed, their detachment disengagement, such that both the Irish and foreign aspects of the poetry can appear to be trapped in stereotypes, a condition identified in an essay of 1965 by the critic Augustine Martin as 'inherited dissent'.[16] These younger poets dealt with marginalisation by reinscribing, within the European 'exile' bohemian paradigm, the 1950s' valorisation of indigence and squalor. In doing so they gave new scope to Irish poetry, but arguably this was by simply changing the content, rather than challenging the form, of the subjective lyric still dominant in mid-century Irish poetry.[17]

O'Grady's work in particular illustrates the persistence of the 'garrulous rebel' stereotype of the *Miscellany* Introduction. While some of O'Grady's 1960s' poetry (notably in *The Dark Edge of Europe* of 1967) rises in a limited way above inchoate rebelliousness and posturing, *Reilly* (1961) is more representative of the bulk of his work in its assumption that the stance of poet as wild goose is its own justification. There is a tendency, here as elsewhere, to assume bardic authority through unembarrassed name-dropping and to present the artist as inspired scapegrace. This is clearest, perhaps, in the book's title sequence.[18] Written as part of the search, in Peter Fallon's words, 'to discover something to replace the old ways, some scheme of ritual or behaviour with modern relevance', it is both transparently autobiographical and shamelessly stereotypical (O'Grady, 1979: 9):

> One was a sailor come home from the sea unwilling to work;
> Another a dandy too good for the jobs he was offered;
> One a sister who mothered a poet and died in a madhouse;
> Then the spoiled priest who never recovered.
>
> (O'Grady, 1996: 43)

This 'devil's brood' of his family unwittingly serve not so much as foils to Reilly's artistic self-realisation as exempla of backwardness in the 'inherited dissent' mode, as O'Grady clumsily echoes Joyce; thus, 'Self Portrait of Reilly as a Young Man' claims, Dedalus-fashion, 'I must be priest poet layman to myself'. Although the work of a young writer, the limitations are clear; 'Reilly' reads as an intensification of the negativity of Cronin and the slipshodness of Kavanagh, veering from 'realistic' grimness to Synge-song ('great was the hate that was at her on him'), with all the problems of a poetry relying on 'Irishness' as an aesthetic writ large.[19]

In the poetry of Galvin and Hutchinson, awareness of these dangers is more marked, although both are also limited by a discourse of dissidence. Of the two, Galvin is closest to O'Grady and the oral traditions he invokes, to the point – for John Hewitt, reviewing Galvin's first book – of being 'revolting'.[20] Galvin's clearest allegiance, beside late Yeats and ballad and song, is to the Lorca of *Romancero Gitano* and the promise it holds of uniting folk energy with modernism and surrealism (a promise invoked, but more despairingly, by Michael Hartnett).[21] As Delanty and Welch note, Galvin's narratives and character sketches – like the well-known 'The Madwoman of Cork' – owe much to Spanish and Latin American models, 'enigmatic situations' often being 'evolved in a kind of skeletal folk tale' (Galvin, 1996: xv). The synthesis of the Irish and the Iberian is put to a variety of uses. In 'The White Monument', modelled on the Gaelic lament genre of the *caoine*, Galvin mourns Michael Collins, drawing on Lorca's great *Lament for Ignacio Sánchez Mejías*. The effect is a startling cultural hybrid in which Cork, Collins's city also, becomes half-Andalucian: 'The Great Bull of the city is dead. / The Civic Guards come down from Barrack Street / With iodine on their lips.' A translation from Irish ('An Caisideach Bán') and urban, socialist republicanism – in 'A Day of Rebellion', on the Easter Rising – also feature, and his international interests take a political aspect in 'Chicken Coop', critical of the communist takeover of Hungary in 1949. Political controversy is broached again in *Christ in London* (1960), which reflects cold war fears. More specifically, the fourth section of the title sequence attacks the racism suffered by West Indian immigrants in the Notting Hill riots of 1958. In the poem, the 'White Man' is ironically presented armed with the weapons of, and acting in the manner of, the 'savages' he beats up as 'the Law come out / And stand and stare'. In the wake of the Stephen Lawrence inquiry this is a poem whose compelling contemporary relevance has again been renewed, and it is worth noting that it was at first withheld from a scheduled broadcast on George MacBeth's BBC radio programme 'Poetry Now' for fear it would be too controversial (Delanty, 1994: 132). Galvin's authority rests on his own lowly status within his host society, a reminder of a time when notices hung in the windows of British boarding houses reading 'No Blacks, No Dogs, No Irish'. It is precisely this ability to be 'revolting' that produces Galvin's strongest effects, although it also lies behind a tension between the celebration of energy *per se* and a fiercely moral politics of the underdog. It may be an awareness of this, and of the generic constraints within which he works, which has limited his output and contributed in the later work to a distrust of linguistic display which can verge on banality (Galvin, 1996: xv). Whereas the earlier poetry problematised its simple dichotomies (black/white) and personifications ('the Great Bull') by an amoral, Blakean energy, the later poems rely too heavily on a plain-speaking suspicion of linguistic brio, and collude with, rather than attack, the instrumental language usages of a society with which it is ostensibly at odds.

While his Hispanic and Gaelic literary influences recall Galvin, Pearse Hutchinson shows the same *wanderlust* as O'Grady. Hutchinson, however, is a more substantial and varied poet than either, and a genuine linguist (he has translated from Catalan, Galaicoportuguese and other Iberian languages, and writes in Irish as well as translating from it). His response to mid-century stagnation is representative: 'To give joy free rein . . . I had to leave home. And not just home but homeland. Puritanism seemed to me the worst thing ever invented, it was my enemy, and with it I identified (not unnaturally, given that prevailing late-Forties atmosphere) Ireland itself' (Hutchinson, 1990: 14). 'Fleadh Cheoil' from the early *Expansions*, is set among returned emigrants at a music festival. It registers vividly the sense of freedom to be found for a gen-eration without prospects at home even in the 'scaffoldings and grim digs of England' for a 'boy about eighteen . . . convinced beyond / shaming or furtive-ness, a thousand preachers, / mothers and leader-writers wasting their breath' (Hutchinson, 1982: 25). Since the 1960s, Hutchinson has lived chiefly in Dublin – he was a founder of *Cyphers* magazine in 1975 – and, associated with members of the 1960s' generation of poets, has had influence without ever becoming an imposing presence. Hutchinson is particularly impressive as a love poet; 'Málaga', for example, movingly uses the otherness of a foreign culture to confirm the otherness of being in love:

> The tranquil unrushed wine drunk on the daytime beach.
> Or from an open window all that our sight could reach
> Was heat, sea, light, unending images of peace;
> And then at last the night brought jasmine's great release –
> Not images but calm uncovetous content,
> The wide-eyed heart alert at rest in June's own scent . . .
> (Hutchinson, 1982: 16)

Here, the alexandrines (unusually, for Hutchinson, rhymed) mimic the 'great release' of the scent, which symbolises love throughout the poem; yet the meditative reconsideration of the final couplet shows the speaker to be as lin-guistically 'alert' as the 'wide-eyed heart'. The other great theme of the poetry is cultural oppression, animated – although without a distrust of language or avoidance of cultural reference – by the same politics of sympathy for the underdog found in Galvin. With both it is possible to detect the transfer of anti-colonial sentiment out of the specifically anti-English discourses of the Free State – reflecting mid-century awareness of Irish sovereignty and self-responsibility – into other national contexts, although without necessarily erasing a Nationalist sense of grievance. Thus, Hutchinson is eloquent on the suppression of Catalan culture by Castilian state power, and mourns the decline of Gaelic culture in a way which anticipates the neo-Corkeryanism of the 1970s. Before Montague and Heaney, too, Hutchinson adumbrates the sense of cultural dispossession through linguistic dispossession: thus, 'To kill a language is to kill a people', but it is also 'to kill one's self' (Hutchinson, 1982: 76–7), while 'Gaelic names [beat] their wings madly / behind the mad cage of English' (Hutchinson, 1982: 74). If this form of language politics and public address lends itself less readily than theirs to contemporary critique it is for all that capable of a piercing historical compassion. This offsets an ingrained generational sense of outsiderness and the lyric limits imposed by an embattled, romantic and solitary conception of writing, as in 'Pibroch', a piece about emigrants from the Highland clearances insisting on taking their clan piper with them to 'the new land, the new planet' of Canada:

> So the people in their need scraped around in their poverty
> and mustered the pittance for the music to travel,
> and so the masters made a little more money,
> but the festering hold was dancing,
> lamentation swabbed the landless deck,
> the creaking, rotting boat was outraged and blest.
>
> (Hutchinson, 1982: 78)

Thomas Kinsella: gothic modernism

The isolation of the Irish writer is a leitmotif in the career of Kinsella, commonly seen as the leading poet of his generation until 1968; as he has said, 'The only semblance of escape – consonant with integrity – is into a greater isolation' (Kinsella, 1967: 11). Kinsella had established himself early as a poet, but a career in the Civil Service (in Whitaker's department in fact) meant that he developed as a poet within the Republic between 1946 and 1965, closely collaborating with Liam Miller of Dolmen Press (which he had co-founded) while most of his contemporaries were abroad. His early poems – which are Audenesque and stylised to a degree – established two concerns central to the rest of his work. One is the (lack of) continuity of Irish culture and poetic tradition, which led to a series of translations from Irish and which became a major preoccupation in the middle of the 1960s. The other is a fascination with order and disorder, flux and fixity (arguably, it is the convergence of the two which produces *Nightwalker*, where Kinsella's break with traditional form takes place). Indeed, his very first published poem – *The Starlit Eye* (1952) – uses a topos of Dublin, shore, sea and stars to explore these themes. Always, in the poems of the 1950s, there is the sense that an occasionally shaky virtuoso style is standing in for the absence of some sustaining narrative. Such tropes and locations are most systematically explored in his best-known early poem, 'Baggot Street Deserta' from *Another September* (1958):

> The window is wide
> On a crawling arch of stars, and the night
> Reacts faintly to the mathematic
> Passion of a cello suite . . .
>
> (Kinsella, 1996: 13)

The poem articulates the anxieties concerning the 'fairy bog' of the Revival 'double crossed / By pad of owl and hoot of dog', and exhumed by 'a swollen Burke' and 'decomposing Hare' in terms which establish the solipsistic, gothic obverse of Kinsella's uncertain stylistic brio. *Poems* (1956) and *Another September* reveal the tension between these terms, which point to a deep historical unease only imperfectly explained in terms of 'influence'. Marshalled within traditional form, these 'influences' produce poetry which seems simultaneously archly ironic and romantic to mainstream formalist criticism. Edna Longley identifies these as the mythological-decorative and 'cosmic', viewing the blend as 'confused', Audenesque but 'without an Audenesque intellectual grasp', over-emblematic, lacking a lodging in 'the colloquial and concrete', mythologising and moralising (E. Longley, 1975: 133). Although this is true in its own ('colloquial and concrete') Leavisite terms, it does not address the symptomatic nature of the stylistic and tonal instability, the extent to which the mythic material of many poems is less significant than the allegorical urge which lies behind its deployment. More satisfactory is Robin Skelton's claim that in *Poems* 'the theme of division and unity begins to take on the complexities which later attend all its reappearances in Kinsella's work'. For Skelton 'division' and 'unity' are aspects of the conflict between flux and fixity which generate the discontent which leads to a more experimental poetry, rather than being simply weaknesses which the poet ought to overcome in forging the 'colloquial and concrete' autonomous object (Skelton, 1969: 87).

Moralities (1960) shows Kinsella exploring his stylistic hybrid via the kind of compression which, as the examples of Eliot and Pound show, often precedes a modernist radicalisation of form. Thus, 'At the Heart's' Yeatsian trappings – 'Heraldic, hatched in gold, a sacred tree / Stands absorbed, tinkering with the slight / Thrumming of birds, the flicker of energy / Thrown' – are ironically governed by verbs associated with machinery, although the full consequences of the confrontation between the archaic and the modern are not yet enacted; 'disciplines proliferate', 'yet / Not one has sped direct as appetite' (Kinsella, 1996: 30). The gnomic compression shows Kinsella's indebtedness to Clarke (and similarities with the English poet Geoffrey Hill) yet, – as the book's title hints – in the light of the modernity he is about to confront, Kinsella will not be able to share Clarke's radical humanism, interpreting the contemporary in a more starkly moral way. Skelton's contention that Kinsella is 'a moralist, but not a humanist' is apposite here, indicating the consequences of his move towards exploring modern darkness in a specifically post-Catholic context; his moral concern, for Skelton, issues 'not from a concern for human order but from a belief in struggling towards the necessity of Divine Grace' (Skelton, 1969: 108). The theological terminology is inaccurate – 'significant form' should be substituted for 'Divine Grace' – but the insight accurately describes the way the 1960s' poetry moves away from Clarke's optimism; as Kinsella himself put it, 'In the poetic voice, once religion disappears, you're in trouble, you're out on your own and you're really forced back on your own depths' (Cadogan, 1997b: 5). The mediating force of the gothic in this situation is crucial; another *Moralities* poem, 'Handclasp at Euston', describes a returning emigrant in something like the sociological style of Cronin, but is transformed by gothic shock in its final line: 'Wales, / Wave and home; I close my eyes. The track / Swerves to a greener world: sea-rock, thigh-scales' (Kinsella, 1996: 30). Here, darkened by Kinsella's post-Holocaust historical awareness, satire is suddenly displaced into a darker, more ungovernable register, and moral judgement is invoked.[22]

Fred Botting has argued that the gothic as a genre acts to register distress, uncertainty, disturbance, subversive marginality; gothic is the 'signification of a writing of excess' which shadows the progress of modernity and enlightenment with a dark counter-narrative and not merely a question of 'colour' or thematics.[23] For a poet lacking a sure tradition its generic capacity for fusing disparate stylistic elements, operating with hybrid states and forms, can usefully convey a sense of simultaneous threat and freedom conferred by isolation and disruptive modernity. If Kinsella's early poetry gradually turns to engage with modern history, then, it does so precisely by facing backward to incorporate radical solitude, the archaic and mythic, within allegorical structures. *Downstream* (1962) illustrates the way loss of faith, under the burden of fresh historical understanding, leads towards allegory, suggesting the necessity of a moral worldview (though unable or unwilling to offer one) with gothic as its organising genre. Its trilogy – 'Downstream', 'A Country Walk' and 'Old Harry' – with their subjects of the bomb, the Holocaust, World War II and Irish history, as well as their use of allegorical journey tropes, confirm the trend.

In 'A Country Walk' the speaker traverses a landscape littered with emblematic ruins – well, aqueduct, asylum, railway – ending at a 'speckled ford', the legendary site of Cuchulainn's killing of his brother Ferdia. These meditations match thoughts on Irish history, from legend through to the civil war of 1922–23; and these are in turn matched by the 'endless debris' swept along by the river skirted by the speaker's route. 'Debris' signifies the external world's resistance to imposed order and, at the level of historical meditation, the poem subjects traditional Nationalist narratives to the larger debate between fixity and flux, ironising it but not wholly rejecting its terms. At its conclusion the debris of the poem achieves a brief coherence, flashing briefly and epiphanically from his scattered self-communing at the point where road and river meet: '*Venit Hesperus*. / In green and golden light. / Bringing sweet trade' (Kinsella, 1996: 48).

'Downstream' reconsiders Irish history, this time in the light of change which has broken down isolation to produce a recognition of twentieth-century atrocity[24] (Harmon, 1973: 185–6). The difficulty of aligning World War II and the Holocaust with Irish history is clear from the number of revisions of the poem; these reduced the Yeatsian rhetoric, but reflected a growing difficulty with formal closure. The poem's journey, involving the narrator and a companion drifting 'downstream' at night, invokes the boat-stealing scene in

The Prelude as well as echoing Conrad's *Heart of Darkness*, and with even fewer naturalistic details than 'A Country Walk' the potential for allegoric interpretation is increased. A historical meditation is triggered by a youthful memory of the discovery of a man's body in the woods beside the river; in the same summer, the speaker now realises, war and genocide raged in Europe as Ireland, itself 'through seven hundred years accurst', looked on

> The haunt of swinish man. Each day a spit
>
> That, turning, sweated war. Each night a fall
> Back to the evil dream where rodents ply,
> Man-rumped, sow-headed, busy with whip and maul
>
> Among nude herds of the damned. It seemed that I,
> Coming to conscience on that edge of dread,
> Still dreamed, impervious to calamity,
>
> Imagining a formal drift of the dead . . .
> (Kinsella, 1996: 49–50)

The speaker's 'impervious' gaze is neutral Ireland's, though the extent to which neutrality is seen as culpable, as opposed to being balanced out by its past suffering, is left unclear (the linkage of Irish and Jewish history long pre-dates World War II and should not necessarily be seen as self-aggrandising). Much of Kinsella's early work had concerned (and concealed) the struggle to find ritual order in the chaotic flux of contingency. In 'Downstream', however, ritual is now seen as an improperly aesthetic imposition, albeit the initial impulse is to 'imagine' the dead juxtaposed with a cosmic order to make sense of chaos and waste. This tendency is rebuked by the poem, which deprives the narrator of any sure footing, symbolised by a 'barrier of rock . . . blotting heaven' at the end which forces the travellers to '[Search] the darkness for a landing place' (Kinsella, 1996: 51).[25]

Gothic in Kinsella mediates the violence which is a feature of modern Irish poetry generally; it recurs, in Seamus Deane's words, because of the need 'to break, however reluctantly, out of a deep insulation from the actual, and to take on again the burden of history . . . Indeed, the attraction of violence for Irish poets is perhaps especially strong not merely on account of its pervasiveness but also because, as a theme, it provides an exit from provincialism' (Deane, 1985: 137). To return to the generic and allegorical framework is to discover a reading of Irish history which accords with what diaspora theorists call the 'traumatic' paradigm; that is, a sense of history as 'nightmarish burden of uncanny familiarity, repeating the dreary pattern of revolt and defeat over and over again, as in a neurosis', a tendency which is 'evinced by the tradition of Irish gothic which reaches from Maturin to Le Fanu to Kinsella . . . the idea that history in this country no longer progresses, but has become stuck like a needle in the groove of past recrimination' (Cohen, 1997: 181; Leerssen, 1998: 45).

Between *Downstream* and *Nightwalker* (1968) Kinsella tested his lyric forms to breaking point by confronting their decorum with a more violent content; thematics challenge form, foregrounding the disparity between Irish isolation and European history, between culture and nature (one danger for Kinsella – as for Deane – is thus of reinstating that violence, seen in earlier imperialistic discourse as essentially Irish, as a token of the authenticity of poetic utterance). In *Wormwood* (1966) the violence turns confessional, the central situation a couple and family caught in the banal 'hells of circumstance', the bitterness of which – looking forward to the use of Jungian and alchemical figures in *Notes From the Land of the Dead* (1973) – must be accepted and 'transmuted'. Again, the fatalism and notion of endurance might be traced back to a vestigially religious desire for structure, while the moralist's concern with violence – to qualify Deane – stems from the way atrocity exceeds the grasp of rational thought and the explanatory power of belief systems. A deracinated moralism and a suspicion of imposed structure generates the open-ended quest for it which dominates *Nightwalker* and the poetry which followed. For Kinsella it is increasingly the search itself rather than any goal (the poetic equivalent of which is formal closure) which is the point of writing. Reflecting this new awareness, but still bound by traditional form, the poetry of the mid-1960s centres on images of self-devouring and voracity.[26] This is also a hermeneutic obsession related to a vision of Irish history as cyclical and it led, inevitably, to the abandonment of a poetry of symbolic closure in favour of one of process. While it would not quite be true to compare the effect this had on most of his audience to that which would have been occasioned if, say Philip Larkin had suddenly started writing like Pound after *The Whitsun Weddings*, the shock was nevertheless substantial.[27]

Richard Murphy: last of the Anglo-Irish?

If Kinsella's considerations of modernisation before *Nightwalker* seem opaque, Richard Murphy's can at first appear downright escapist (one review of *Sailing to an Island* described it as 'mild, mellifluous and . . . about as modern as Jean Ingelow').[28] Yet Murphy's poetry preserves a distinct apartness from contemporary English poetic norms, as a *Listener* article of 1955 shows. Referring to Larkin's 'Poetry of Departures', Murphy declares himself 'bewildered' at 'the horror of reality, the treeless, grassless, waterless future of existence which continues where his apparantly ordinary words leave off, the deliberate suffering of a common way of life in which there will never be a spring or autumn. The poem leaves me asking a continual why' (R. Murphy, 1955: 373–4). Refusing a mundane modernity, it might be said that Murphy seeks precisely the 'audacious, purifying, / Elemental move' Larkin's poem finds 'so artificial'. In his work the elementalism of Ted Hughes is tempered by that of a Yeats democratised and filtered through a history of decades of cautious but largely uncontentious relations between Southern Protestants and the Irish state. A specifically Irish history of accommodation and Protestant decline rather than 'English' restraint underlies the constraint and self-discipline of the poetry, although the relative neglect it has suffered stems in part from a perception of 'Protestant' in terms of stereotypes of Anglo-Irishness or Englishness. In fact, Murphy's marginalised position, in terms of caste, culture and geography, complicates to some extent such stereotypes, and his split inheritance is not as neat as at first appears.

The 'elemental' activity detailed in the poems, while it echoes Revivalist idealisation of the West, nevertheless challenges certain dominant critical concepts of community, colonialism and tradition in its strenuously anomalous quality. Radicalism and anti-modernity produce a somewhat different form of the isolation common to other poets of his generation, one based on social rather than geographical or aesthetic marginality, and mixing escapism, affection, guilt and improving zeal in varying measure. For Murphy, family inheritance is figured indirectly by his grandmother, and its decay is emblematised in her decline in 'The Lady of the House'. Although affectionate, the poem records the way even a benign gentry were rooted in what they attempted to alleviate:

> She bandaged the wounds that poverty caused
> In the house that famine labourers built,
> Gave her hands to cure impossible wrong
> In a useless way, and was loved for it.
> (R. Murphy, 1985: 16)

Murphy's grandmother reappears in a brief but revealing prose memoir 'The Pleasure Ground' (R. Murphy, 1963: 237). The formal garden of her house, this was a place of childhood happiness; but it is seen in hindsight as having embodied the 'impossible wrong' of the Ascendancy, surrounded as it was 'by an Anglo-Irish wall . . . of pride and oppression'. Initially a prelapsarian site, it gives way to a tension in later life between a liberating (but dissolving) wildness/wilderness and a productive (but paralysing) discipline. The garden is, in any case, shown as gradually reverting to a state of nature and threatened (like Eden) by internal subversion. Its fecundity requires continuous vigilant discipline, threatened by the young Murphy or his brother, who 'kept a herd of goats in the woods' one of which '[lay] under the piano my mother played at our morning prayers' (R. Murphy, 1963: 237). The garden is seen to have taught him independence and husbandry, but of the hermit-poet rather than the diplomat his mother wanted him to become. 'The Pleasure Ground', then, reads as a variant on both the Planter/culture versus Native/nature argument, but one containing elements of Memmi's 'coloniser who refuses' in a belated, posthumous sense, and so transposed into an individualist and aesthetic rather than political mode.[29] For if the garden underwrites the culture–nature divide it is also seen as having taught guilt, with the dawning realisation that there exists another, deprived landscape 'on the far side of the Connemara mountains, on the harsh Atlantic coast', where the family also holds land. Privilege is rebuked by the juxtaposition, but introduces a set of values more removed and 'authentic'. Murphy can realign himself with these because Connemara is the place where his grandmother was raised; the discovery of the link between 'pleasure ground' and Connemara grants him an allegiance with a 'real' Ireland he comes to see as 'stark, wild, and simple . . . more beautiful than the deeply nurtured garden we had left'. The new 'ground' and its inhabitants are embraced in a move intended to erase the stigma of privilege, to 'cure' 'impossible wrong'. It is within this contradictory location, complicated by his father's post as a colonial administrator (and childhood residence in Ceylon) and an English education that Murphy's poetry maneouvres.[30]

Moving to Cleggan in Connemara in 1958, Murphy explored the themes of fixity and dissolution, of isolation, community and post-Ascendancy *tristesse* hinted at in his earliest work. *Sailing to an Island* (1963) draws on the landscapes of Connemara's islands and coasts and on the manual work in which he immersed himself, refurbishing the almost legendary *Ave Maria*, the last Galway hooker, and sailing her for tourists in the summer months. The title encapsulates the dual themes of isolation and labour, the tensions between poetry and purposive activity, between the fluid untameability of the sea and the self-contained 'clinker-built' quality the poems embody. Yet attachment to the West is balanced by opposition to its fatalism (which Murphy sees also in literary Dublin) with the energy of the self-dispossessed but exasperated improving landlord:

> Up to the 1960s this country was beladen with the sense that art isn't worth your while; it's been tried before and failed, you won't catch any fish or you'll get wrecked in a storm. Why bother going out, there are easier ways to live? In Dublin some of my predecessors impressed me poorly by the self-destructive nature of their lives, drinking themselves to death. This village, Cleggan, was synonymous with disaster . . . For two years I was the only person . . . who owned a boat that fished. (Haffenden, 1981: 146–7)

Murphy's 'improvement' comes through restoring the old, but also in facing down the past, in this case the long refusal to engage in fishing by Cleggan inhabitants after the Cleggan Disaster of 1927, in which thirteen men from the village were drowned. There is, then, something of the dualistic attitude to modernisation noted earlier in Murphy's stance, with change being evaded and advocated: Murphy 'seems less disapproving of modernization than Montague', but at the same time shares with him 'a patrimony of scatter and decay' at its hands (J. W. Foster, 1991: 160–1). In these poems – 'Sailing to an Island' and the long 'The Cleggan Disaster' – the sea is represented as a primal landscape whose threat allows the proving of a core self, free from the burden of a divided identity; poem and psyche, it is implied, are like boat and ocean (or poet and host community), the one traversing but never totally overcoming or knowing the other. 'Sailing to an Island' explores this self-division. Ostensibly an account of a failed attempt to sail to Clare Island, its initial impulse is a spurious desire for a romantic Ireland/island, 'its crags purpled by legend'. There is from the start something excessive about the trip, which is overblown rhetorically, and then literally by bad weather. This self-critical aspect is missed by Rosenthal, who follows a common critical line on Murphy when he claims that the poem '[serves] a timeless artistic purpose in the way [it] repossesses a particular kind of experience and life-style. Nostalgia for a lost and (sayeth the poet) a nobler past, as seen from the viewpoint of the Ascendancy, is heavy' (Rosenthal, 1967: 306–7). However, 'timeless' is exactly what the voyage is not: passengers get sick, the boat is driven back to unlegendary Inishbofin, the poet – forced to stay overnight – gets drunk, listens to an old man's ramblings, stumbles 'among stones and nettles' and falls asleep. Nostalgia is allowed, but in order to be undermined; it is clear that the speaker does not belong with the 'courteous fishermen' he drinks with towards the end and envies their more 'intimate' knowledge of the sea (R. Murphy, 1985: 5). Attempting to escape from it, he is returned to contemporary Ireland, with the poem's banal ending mocking the pretensions of his quest.

'The Cleggan Disaster', unlike 'Sailing to an Island', offers an exemplary figure for the poet, with Pat Concannon ensuring the survival of his boat and crew only by refusing to surrender to the elements or to collective resignation: 'The oarsmen were calling for Concannon to let go, / Take it easy for a while . . . // Concannon silenced them, and stiffened his hold' (R. Murphy, 1985: 35). The struggle dramatises the struggle between Murphy's own faith in rationality and his desire for community and release from a divided selfhood. There is also, in these poems, a gender dimension; the worlds presented are exclusively male with the sea typed as female and associated with origins (in 'The Pleasure Ground' the sea is contrasted with the garden as a product of 'masculine energy').[31] In a general sense the poetry exploits the contradictions of the ghost-life of Ascendancy culture, balancing the urges to test selfhood and to lock it into absolute security. Boats, sea, houses and islands become psychological states inflected by caste displacement, allowing risk, openness and the threat of dissolution to be juxtaposed against resistance and integrity. This in turn threatens petrifaction (the title of Murphy's penultimate collection, *The Price of Stone* (1985), suggests his awareness of the danger). These states are contextualised by labour which is the antithesis of Ascendancy absenteeism, and by identification with non-bourgeois, marginal elements of society (Murphy has been active on behalf of Ireland's nomadic tinker, or Traveller, population). Since self-mastery can never be absolute, however, it is always potentially at risk, and hints of 'excess' – bisexuality, narcissism and emotional miserliness – occur. These are more openly explored in later poems such as 'Seals at High Island' from *High Island* (1974), in which, as Brown puts it, 'male and female [seals] luxuriate in a hauntingly plangent, sexually explicit veneration of the powers of creativity, in which the sea's final erotic power is acknowledged' (Brown, 1988: 193). 'Anglo-Irish', far from being 'clinker-built', reveals itself to be a contradictory site whose speaker exists only through continual self-assertion, evidence that, in Alan Finlayson's words, 'identity is the result of a process of contingent and strategic political dispute [and] does not derive from abstract existential deliberation but from political and ideological operations'. [32]

This 'contingent and strategic' dispute is most explicitly 'political' in *The Battle of Aughrim* (1968), Murphy's most imposing work. [33] That the reader is invited to interpret the poem in this light is signalled by its companion poem in *The Battle of Aughrim* volume, 'The God Who Eats Corn'. Originally published in 1963 this second piece had been commissioned by *The Times* to mark the British handover of power in Southern Rhodesia, its title referring to the ambiguous perception Africans had of the first Europeans: godlike (because of their technology), but also human because having to 'eat corn' like themselves. Ironically, given the total absence of reference to Murphy in current critical debates on postcolonialism, 'The God Who Eats Corn' is perhaps the only poem by an Irish writer to deal first-hand with a post-war decolonisation event, revealing the narrowness of the field of discussion. Both it, and *The Battle of Aughrim*, ask to be read together as variations of the decolonising experience. *Aughrim* reveals the complex identities and allegiances which underlie so many apparently binary oppositions in Irish history. The battle, in 1691, saw William of Orange's forces, under Baron Ginkel, defeat those of Irish Jacobites, fighting under the French general St Ruth for James II, precipitating the flight of the 'wild geese' – remnants of the old Gaelic ruling class – and inaugurating the Penal Law era, the lowest ebb in the fortunes of the Catholic Irish. For Murphy, the significance of the battle lies in the fact that members of his family fought on both sides (hence the anomalous appearance of the name 'Richard Murphy'). *Aughrim* is an exemplary historical work which reflects on the new historiography as well as the growth in the popularity of local history which began in the 1960s (and to which it refers). Fulfilling one of the conditions of the modern epic – the exemplary nature of the narrator – it foregrounds a divided inheritance and disperses its narrative voice among a series of dramatic lyrics, divided into four abstractly titled sections ('Now', 'Before', 'During', 'After'). [34] Although Murphy's sympathies lie with defeated Gaeldom the schema allows a detachment from familial, mythic and racial categories which is lacking in parts of *The Rough Field*. In 'The God Who Eats Corn', however, the family predicament is separation across the starker divisions between 'native' and 'colonist'. Murphy's parents, retired to a Rhodesian farm and plantation (which they run on liberal lines) are set against a history which now threatens race war – the contemporary context is the Pass Laws and the Sharpeville Massacre – and, while sympathetic to their sense of disconnection, their naive belief in the White Man's Burden is viewed as dangerously outdated.

The question which opens *Aughrim* – 'Who owns the land . . . ? – is more complex in the Irish context than in the African one, although as Brown observes it is not one the dispossessed Irish would ask, 'or one that a planted occupant [would] dare ask as he validates possession by work and improvement' (Brown, 1988: 194). In Rhodesia the rawness of colonial expropriation makes the question far easier to answer; in Ireland, the narrator of 'Historical Society' can drink a 'republican toast' and be involved in the contemporary excavation of the past. Although this has its merely symbolic aspect, symbols of involvement and reconciliation in 'The God Who Eats Corn' remain merely that; chief among these is the estate's 'loyal garden', with trees given by visitors in whose shade, his father feels, 'indaba [counsel] could heal the blood feud . . . and [cool] the racial fever' (R. Murphy, 1968: 58). Idealism is ineffectual in a state whose 'roots' lie in recent imperial duplicity and where 'the white man [still] rides: the black man is his horse' (R. Murphy, 1968: 60). The scholar–diplomat father, poring over his Homer, may honourably attempt local improvement, but the extremity of the crisis means he is part of the problem he would solve. Indeed, the liberal paternalist is the most deluded figure of all; he 'upholds the manners of a dead empire', but only because 'Time has confused dead honour with dead guilt.' As the trees fail to be 'devoured by ants', other whites 'cling to their laagers, / Wire for a gun-boat . . . sneer at the Munts' (R. Murphy, 1968: 62–3). *Aughrim*'s first section 'Now', however, presents a figure who, despite marginalisation, is part of the life of his society if only because his caste no longer have power. This is not straightforward; the poisonous fall-out from Aughrim still lingers in Northern Orangeism and paramilitarism (in 'Orange March' and 'History'), and – in a more muted manner – the fusion of Irish Nationalism and religion (in 'Green Martyrs'). The situation of Ireland is best summed up in 'Casement's Funeral', in which the body of the patriot executed by the British is returned by the Wilson government for reburial. Casement is an ironic icon since his record of service for the British Empire and homosexuality (recorded as 'black diary deeds' and the 'chalk remains of once ambiguous bone') sit uncomfortably with the pieties of traditional Nationalism (R. Murphy, 1985: 49–50).

Aughrim mixes a universal 'pity of war' with its partisan sentiments (Murphy describes the Williamite War as 'an analogue of the Vietnam War' then raging) (Haffenden, 1981: 151). Thus, in 'Martial Law' 'A country woman and a country man' are hanged by 'soldiers' who suspect them of poisoning a well, but the side the soldiers belong to is not identified (although it follows 'St Ruth's Address to the Irish Army') (R. Murphy, 1985: 57–8). The juxtaposition of short poem and prose is typical of the poem's quasi-documentary procedure, which, while not as radically heterogeneous as *The Rough Field*'s, generates a mildly dialogic effect. Part three, 'During', more or less catalogues the misfortunes of the Irish Army – St Ruth's decapitation (echoing the description of John F. Kennedy's head on a memorial plate in 'Green Martyrs'), the treachery of Luttrell, who deserts the Irish Army in crisis – and the ruthlessness of the Williamite forces in victory. Here Murphy's habitual distance from his subject makes for over-schematism: 'Sarsfield rides a chestnut horse', one lyric begins, while another opens 'Luttrell on a black charger', as if the two represented pure principles of good and evil, and a corresponding sentimentalisation of Sarsfield. This is not excessive, but – in 'Patrick Sarsfield's Portrait' in part four of the poem, 'After' – may recall too insistently the soft focus of 'Lady of the House':

> Sarsfield, great-uncle in the portrait's grime,
> Your emigration built your fame at home.
> Landlord who never racked, you gave your rent
> To travel with your mounted regiment.
> (R. Murphy, 1989: 75)

Here, the antithesis of 'racked' and 'rent' is altogether too neat to be convincing, despite Sarsfield's heroism. Yet the image is offset by Sarsfield's ineffectuality, forcefully presented in 'Sarsfield': 'He hears cries, groans and shrieks. / Nothing he will do, or has done / Can stop this from happening', and even more disturbing in 'Patrick Sarsfield's Portrait':

> 'Change kings with us, and we will fight again,'
> You said, but sailed off with ten thousand men;
> While women clutched the hawsers in your wake,
> Drowning – it was too late when you looked back.
> (R. Murphy, 1989: 77)

In 'The God Who Eats Corn' the same solidarity with the oppressed Africans is – properly – not claimed, although their independence is seen, like that of the Irish, as damaged by colonialism. At the same time, it is hinted, return to a pristine, pre-colonial reality is impossible; 'the half-freed slaves are freed, / But not into a garden that anyone remembers' (R. Murphy, 1968: 63). At this point, the poem has exposed the complexity of colonial attitudes and also made links with Ireland through Murphy's father's memories; problematically, concluding images which conflate fire and flood with native Africans – as in the Connemara poems – succumb to the nature–culture division. They complete the prophetic logic of the poem, but risk stereotype (the transferred epithets of '*voodoo* climate' and 'tribes in their *idle* forest' are ironic, but queasily so). Nevertheless, 'The God Who Eats Corn', like *Aughrim*, combines critique with insider knowledge of imperial dependency and avoids mythicised history, guiltily and fruitfully inhabiting history as it attempts to detach itself from it, respecting history as history. The exorcism of the Williamite Anglo-Irish usurpation, like the decay of imperial service, continues the concerns of 'The Pleasure Ground' and the early poetry, while contradictory voices now complicate the fixation on the past of *Sailing To An Island*. Most criticism of *Aughrim* has damned Murphy with faint praise, and part of the problem is that even the poem's advocates accept the 'Two Traditions' interpretation of Irish history and its essentialist, ethnic premises, rather than challenging them. Yet *Aughrim* and 'The God Who Eats Corn', read together as poems which query, challenge and qualify each other's assumptions, offer a complex negotiation not only of Murphy's origins, but of postcolonial Irish identity; *Aughrim*'s effects are opposed, but the lesson of the poem is that history is fundamentally ironic. If, as Edna Longley claims, 'the determined confrontation of History must involve a certain exteriority', it is only in this way that Murphy resists being 'bogged down in provincialism and self-repetition', showing how the roots of the suffering which fuelled sectarianism arose in a period before modern nationalism as such (E. Longley, 1975: 130). To have done so without recourse to myth, and thus have acknowledged the scope of rational agency (if at the cost of a certain woodenness of style), is a not inconsiderable achievement. Historical myths feature in, but do not suffuse, Murphy's two poems. In his discussion of *Aughrim*, Seamus Heaney links St Ruth's decapitation to Kennedy's head proffered John the Baptist-like on a plate by a *cailleach* figure: 'we are invited to intuit some hermetic link between the beheading of St Ruth and the head of the murdered Kennedy', a comment deriving from the Celtic custom of decapitating enemies after battle (Harmon, 1978: 25). The point, however, is surely that such an 'invitation' is not at all clear. The transhistorical gesture is queried and ironised by Murphy; and if he locates Aughrim as the 'navel', geographically and historically, of Ireland, it is one very unlike the 'omphalos' of Heaney's Mossbawm.

John Montague: the erotics of Irishness

By contrast with Murphy, John Montague's origins are dislocated between a sense of *echt*-Irishness and the diaspora; son of a republican activist driven to New York by post-Partition harassment in the North, sent back to Co. Tyrone to be reared by aunts at the age of four (and deeply marked by maternal rejection), he was educated not in England but in Dublin, Europe and the USA. In the late 1950s Montague worked for the Irish Tourist Board in Dublin, from 1961 in Paris as a correspondent for the *Irish Times* and, after 1964, as a lecturer in the USA, settling in Cork in the 1970s. These facts delineate a tension which underwrites the roving, outsider–insider status of the most overtly political and cosmopolitan of the *Miscellany* poets, one able very early to cogently dissent from the 'argumentative complex' of *The Bell* – in the 'Young Writers' Symposium' of 1951 – and to show a greater ability than the young poets born in the Republic to identify and engage with 'the awkward semi-stage between provincialism and urbanization' in which the country found itself. Montague has spoken of Irish poets having been 'wiped off the map' by isolation and neutrality, and it has arguably been his chief aim to put them back on the map in international terms (Boland, 1973: 10). A collection of short stories, *The Death of a Chieftain* (1964), reads as an almost programmatic working-out of his prescriptions for the young *Bell* writers, and the need for internationalism was a theme of much subsequent criticism.[35] Thus, if like Cronin's, Montague's early poetry is engaged in coming to terms with emigration, stasis and ruralism – neutrality is glanced at in 'A Welcoming Party' which defines Irishness as being 'always at the periphery of incident', and the title of *Forms of Exile* (1958) speaks for itself – an ability to move beyond the rejectionism of *The Bell* and of Kavanagh's parish shows him to have more in common with Murphy and Kinsella (Montague, 1995: 342).

Montague's multiple outsiderness accounts for his political shrewdness as well as an ironic stylishness evident from the outset. 'The Sheltered Edge' of 1953 (later 'Rhetorical Meditations in Time of Peace') convincingly fuses a 1930s', Audenesque sense of malaise with apprehensions concerning the Irish future as viewed from the present's becalmed 'extraordinary hour of calm / And day of limitation'. Although 'The light that never was' still 'Enlarge[s] profile, gun and phrase' in the politics of the Republic, the poem rejects their paralysis to look variously at the 'doomed opulence' of the Anglo-Irish, belated slum clearance, emigration and, in 'Incantation in Time of Peace', the unnatural 'calm' which hints at disaster 'rising from the . . . webbed marshes of history'. This final section discloses a sporadic impulse to turn outwards and 'assist all those fearful, exiled, ailing', but concludes with an image of 'clouds . . . banking / For a yet more ominous day' (Montague, 1995: 199–202). There is a desire to encounter the future, but also a recognition of helplessness learned from the traumatic paradigm of Irish history, as the stylisation and scrupulous syntax of the poem trace the poet's feelings of hesitancy and entrapment. Its prescience is of the kind available only to a displaced Catholic Northerner, a cooly nervous ironic survey of the de Valeran nation. Less secure in his sense of the value of a given Irish identity than Kinsella, less aloof from its dominant strain than Murphy, in *Poisoned Lands* (1961) Montague bridges a gap between desired cosmopolitan sophistication and inescapable national identity, offering a critique of the stasis of the Irish 1950s as well as the plight of Northern Catholics (the title refers to land on which poisoned carrion has been left out by farmers to kill off predators, but has obvious political overtones). In a similar manner, in his best-known early poem 'Like Dolmens Round My Childhood, the Old People', Montague manages to mix symbolic and realist modes, sympathy and clear-sightedness, in evoking and then distancing, figures emblematic of the Tyrone of his childhood. 'Red Star' pulp fiction, a 'crumbling gatehouse', a mixed marriage, isolation, madness, generosity and malice, all contribute to a moving portrait of a background whose inadequacies must, *Great Hunger*-style, finally be judged in order to move on:

> Ancient Ireland indeed! I was reared by her bedside,
> The rune and the chant, evil eye and averted head,
> Formorian fierceness of family and local feud.
> Gaunt figures of fear and friendliness,
> For years they trespassed on my dreams,
> Until once, in a standing circle of stones,

I felt their shadows pass
Into that dark permanence of ancient forms.
(Montague, 1995: 13)

Unlike Kavanagh, Montague measures the present against past discourses of Irishness, implicitly rejecting the latter in the painstaking realism of the first two collections. By this stage his early Audenesque style had been put to school with US modes, its tact, poise and understatement made to serve an empirical fidelity. As Patrick Crotty notes, 'the enterprise of these early poems is more daring than their slightly tentative air might seem to indicate, as it involves nothing less than an attempt to internationalize the perspectives and procedures of Irish poetry', their style 'resistant to the iamb, distrustful of emotional directness, sparely lyrical but never songlike', at work on mainly Irish subject matter (Crotty, 1997: 137). There is the Cronin-style refusal of rural romanticism in a piece like 'A Drink of Milk', as a lone farmhand, preparing for bed, takes 'A last glance at a magazine, / . . . puts the mug to his head, / grunts and drains it clean'; but by contrast with the older poet, Montague's knowledge of rural life tempers judgement, preventing this from seeming merely jaundiced (Montague, 1995: 192). The same poem convincingly symbolises the balance between modernity and tradition in the countryside in its image of a blaring transistor radio and the statuette of the Virgin trembling (but undislodged) beside it on a kitchen shelf. Montague's critique is almost always an implicit one, reliant on accuracy of representation to generate readerly agreement, and the poems move in a self-questioning, tentative manner which enacts that struggle for accuracy. This patient, recording ideal and the poems' self-consciousness are often thematised, as in 'Tim', about a horse which was a childhood favourite, which concludes by praising the stoical animal for 'denying / rhetoric with your patience, / forcing me to drink / from the trough of reality' (Montague, 1995: 208). Similarly 'A Bright Day', from *A Chosen Light* (1967), makes explicit what attentiveness to the moment involves. Dedicated to John McGahern – who lost his teaching post when his novel *The Pornographer* was banned in 1965 – it speaks of 'The only way of saying something / Luminously as possible', 'Not the accumulated richness / Of an old historical language', but 'a slow exactness / Which recreates experience / By ritualizing its details – . . . till all / Takes on a witch-bright glow' (Montague, 1995: 225). Here 'ritualizing' is balanced against 'details' to suggest the poet's moral and artistic credo.

The doubleness in such poetry lies, then, in the way it seeks the present moment (and deliberately situates the past), and yet simultaneously tries to arrest, contemplate and 'ritualize' that very process. In this sense the poetry is both a labour of retrieval – anticipating the archaeological-rural aspect of subsequent Irish poetry – and a subtly transgressive alignment of the subject with modernity, the city, the quest for art and love. This tension between secularising and ritualistic aspects has a bearing on Montague's notion of the poet's social role, but more significantly on his love poetry, his chief contribution to Irish poetry in the 1960s. This differs from that of Clarke in setting sexual love in specifically private, modern contexts, a celebration conditioned by detachment and an awareness of the historical flux out of which any sexual encounter must be stolen. Seemingly incidental to the larger historical themes of *The Rough Field*, this vein of his work runs through *A Chosen Light* (1967), *Tides* (1971), *A Slow Dance* (1975) to *The Great Cloak* (1978). Typically, the lovers are isolated, thrown together almost accidentally before being parted by the centrifugal forces of the modern world surrounding them – its 'panelled skyline' is opposed to 'a blessing moon' – but in the knowledge that the city is the necessary site and precondition of such encounters, as in 'Talisman':

> Slant afternoon light
> on the bed, the unlatched
> window, the scattered sheets
> are part of a pattern
> hastening towards memory
>
> as you give yourself
> to me with a cry of
> joy, not hunger, while
> I receive the gift
>
> in ease, not raw desire
> (Montague, 1995: 92)

As Maurice Riordan has observed, 'this courteous exchange – a canonization of the flesh – is posited against the alien commercial energy of the city', with its 'superstructure' of 'twenty iron floors / of hotel . . . ['Talisman'] gainsays what could perhaps be seen as the carnal comedy: fearfully aware of predatory and phallic energies, it erects a strict code of the licit, designates a redemptive sanctuary of ideal love' (Riordan, 1985: 52). Yet if the poem is offered as a protection against 'Unease', one can also sense a certain fudging in this formula, both in its conscious qualifications ('what could perhaps'), as in its implicit acceptance of Montague's own 'phallic energies' and imperatives ('*erects* a strict code': my emphasis). The designation earlier in the poem of the act of love as a 'progress' denotes the hieratic conception of erotic love as a royal triumph (lover and beloved as king and consort in ritual performance); a courtly dance is opposed to the 'raw desire' of the besieging city to comment obliquely on 'progress' in its sense as the watchword of modernity.

Yet although 'accumulating . . . within the Irish context, a polemical insistence', erotic freedom in Montague depends heavily on fixed gender roles (Riordan, 1985: 53). This aspect of the sexual-political nexus is probably clearest in his eroticising of the Irish landscape, where there is an inevitable appeal to traditional tropes of Ireland gendered as female, as in 'Virgo Hibernica'. The two modes are not wholly distinct: 'Virgo Hibernica' is both goddess and a specific individual, whose chestnut hair falls in modern fashion 'over the stained / freedom of a raincoat'. Used together, the unassertively mythic and contemporary idioms can forestall extremes of mythicisation or confessionalism, as in Montague's most accomplished and sheerly beautiful lyric, 'All Legendary Obstacles':

> All legendary obstacles lay between
> Us, the long imaginary plain,
> The monstrous ruck of mountains
> And, swinging across the night,
> Flooding Sacramento, San Joaquin,
> The hissing drift of summer rain.
> (Montague, 1995: 217)

'Imaginary', Crotty argues, is a case of Montague wanting to have it both ways – the adjective containing 'imagined' within the resonance of myth and legend – but this is surely signalled in advance by 'legendary', hinting at the state of mind of the waiting speaker which magnifies the 'obstacles' between himself and his lover. Nevertheless, the problems which would arise with a more full-blooded use of myth, as Montague's poetry became more politicised in the late 1960s, are foreshadowed in 'The Siege of Mullingar' (dated 1963), which, while it famously asserts (rather prematurely) the end of repression, also nervously notes a more assertive female sexuality:

> At the Fleadh Cheoil in Mullingar
> There were two sounds, the breaking
> Of glass and the background pulse
> Of music. Young girls roamed
> The streets with eager faces
> Shoving for men. Bottles in
> Hand they rowed out a song:
> *Puritan Ireland's dead and gone,*
> *A myth of O'Connor and O'Faoláin.*
> (Montague, 1995: 67)

Acknowledging a central aspect of 1960s' liberation, the poem retreats from its insights in its final verse, where the ideal erotic relationship of the speaker is presented in Yeatsian terms in an image of 'two swans' gliding 'nobly' by. As this suggests, eroticism serves to bring together the realist-Irish and historic/mythic aspects of Montague's poetry, and gains its original force through its modern awareness of isolation as both alienation and liberating freedom from communal pressures. Sexuality is acknowledged as central to the construction of contemporary selfhood, although the effort required to do so generates a countervailing hieratic sense and quasi-'aristocratic' detachment, a carnal echo of Catholic ritualism. The erotic is celebrated, but its threat is kept under tight control. Increasingly, however, ritualism and its archaicising tropes structure the individualist urge. Whereas the early 'The Sean Bhean Bhocht', which also genders the nation as female, is speculative – 'What hidden queen lay dust?' – the later poetry would accept more wholeheartedly Gravesian notions of the 'triple goddess' – virgin, mother and crone – to tilt the balance in favour of myth. An ironic-erotic critique of an impoverished Irish scene thus moves towards a neo-Revival notion of Ireland as a potential site of pleasure, as a responsive, nourishing and fertile goddess, subordinating sexuality to myth. An ability to speak on behalf of the goddess's 'tribe' or 'race' of Northern Irish Catholics is denied in an individual sense in *The Rough Field*, while it is nevertheless increasingly seen as part of the poet's social function. Under the sign of gender, then, a Nationalist history is juxtaposed with, and in the last sections of the poem is subsumed in, a series of gender stereotypes. Increasingly, this would become the mystery presided over by the poet, as tribal bard or priest, in *A Chosen Light* (1967) and *Tides* (1970). In *A Slow Dance* (1975) and *The Great Cloak* (1978), as Patricia Coughlan has pointed out, 'mythical appropriations play an increasingly important role', such that women – acknowledged, to a limited extent, as partners in the quest for erotic liberation in the 1960s' poetry – become, increasingly, 'the silenced attendants of a masculine quest' to achieve selfhood (Coughlan, 1991: 93–9).

Anniversary and epic: 1966 and all that

In the full throes of modernisation, the fiftieth anniversary of the 1916 Easter Rising was 'commemorated with the full pomp of state ceremony', a reminder of the unassimilated nature of certain aspects of the Republic's history (F. Tobin, 1984: 144). Despite new attitudes to the past, it was marked in an old-fashioned, celebratory manner which verged on triumphalism.[36] Other groups used the anniversary for their own symbolism of protest. Misneach, a group of Irish-language writers which included Eoghan Ó Tuairisc (Eugene Watters), protested against the failure of government language policy (and its neglect of Gaeltacht areas) by holding public hunger-strikes and vigils in Easter Week (F. Tobin, 1984: 147–54); the IRA, opposed to celebrating an 'incomplete' national revolution, blew up Nelson's Pillar in O'Connell Street. In the North the most violent signs to date of a Loyalist backlash against even superficial modernisation and conciliatory gestures towards the Republic took the anniversary celebrations as a pretext for dissent. There were the first post-war sectarian murders, of three Catholics in Belfast.[37] The always frail possibility of a growth-driven convergence was, by this stage, beginning to crumble: events had recently revealed the limits of O'Neill's reforms, while Lemass's resignation as party leader in November 1966 and the fall of his government in that year has been seen as the result of a 'recrudescence of Irish irredentism' surrounding the Rising; certainly they provided excuse for those, like Paisley in the North, whom it suited to portray the Republic as bent on takeover (Barton, 1996: 122).

Before this, however, the 1960s would find their poetic culmination and characteristic expression in expansive long works which offered an overview of the nation in the confident spirit of the times. In their sweeping ambition, these poems – *The Rough Field* and *The Battle of Aughrim* – belong to a line of

Irish epics since Ferguson, but substitute history for mythic subject matter. The modern form of the epic idea in Irish poetry can be traced to Charles Gavan Duffy's claim that the history of Ireland, once fully known, would be found to have 'the unity and purpose of an epic poem',[38] a belief in accord with arguments that nation-creation is implicated 'with the exercise of narrative in general' (Connor, 1996: 44). If the lyric was the dominant form in Irish poetry between 1930 and 1960, witness to the withdrawal under the pressure of censorship and public indifference from an inauthentic collectivity, its hegemony had been sporadically broken by attempts 'to renegotiate [poetry's] entrance to the public domain' in long poems (Brown, 1988: 93, 113). In this sense, the 1960s' 'epics' attempt to assess modernisation in the light of older histories. Yet both were closer to lyric sequences than narrative epics in the nineteenth-century or Revival sense, reflecting the way the privatisation of experience the lyric represents is incorporated in twentieth-century long poems elsewhere (as in Crane's *The Bridge*, for example). The requirements of epic-as-national-destiny (a mythic history and pre-existent national identity – 'unity and purpose'), encounter contemporary experience, along with an insistent thematics of modernity (railways, bridges, mechanised warfare, etc.) to produce a disjunctive modernist style, although to a limited degree in the work of the Irish poets; the differences between the poems can be related to their different emphases on these traditionalist and modern elements. The distinctively Irish aspect of the efforts by the *Miscellany* poets lies in the degree to which they look backwards and their more critical attitude towards technology (Crane's quasi-Futurist worship of technology, for example, is absent). This is partly because they were writing at a point when the concept of progress, and hence of modernisation, had come under greater scrutiny, but there is, too, a specifically Irish sensitivity to what was seen as a threatened traditional culture; the enthusiastic embrace of modernisation held the danger of betraying values essential to national identity (although that identity is also one of the things being questioned). The dominance of 'the backward look' and its centrality to Nationalist narratives can be seen operating, and is revealed by the claim made by Seamus Deane in his discussion of *The Rough Field* that 'the lyric presupposes a culture which is broken; the epic one which is whole' (Deane, 1975: 17). In Montague's poem in particular, the escape from myth into a secularised historical narrative is at the expense of a certain mythicisation of history. Ironically, then, it was in two long poems of the 1960s, by older poets – Austin Clarke's *Mnemosyne Lay in Dust* (1966) and Eugene Watters's *The Week-End of Dermot and Grace* (1964) – where a mythic method is used more openly, that it is subject to greater critical scrutiny.[39]

Mnemosyne Lay in Dust

Mnemosyne Lay in Dust, its fourteen sections matching those of the stations of the cross, follows its central figure Maurice Devane from loss of self to gradual recovery under the aegis of Mnemosyne, the goddess of memory and the mother of the muses. The poem itself is, as Hugh Maxton claims, a sort of 'talking cure' (Clarke, 1991: 19). It opens with a Maurice in mortal 'terror', believing that 'Void would draw his spirit, / Unself him', entering the asylum. Here he is subject to its brutal, disorienting routine, undressed violently, 'plunged / Into a steaming bath', 'half-suffocated' by 'assailants gesticulating' as if in 'A Keystone reel gone crazier'. Visions, nightmares, encounters with other inmates, bedwetting, force-feeding and petty beatings follow, and Maurice's experiences are rendered with the full resources of Clarke's late style, from a jostling, compressed, energetic assonantal verse of part two, to the *Night and Morning* horrors of part eight ('The heavens opened. With a scream / The blackman at his night-prayers / Had disappeared in blasphemy'), the discursive, playfully knotted and sinuous reportage in parts four and ten and meditative lyricism of part three:

> Looking down from bars
>   With mournful eye
> Maurice could see them beckoning,
>   Some pointed, signed.
> Waving their arms and hands,
>   They wandered. Why
> Should they pretend they did not see him
>   Lost to mind?
>   (Clarke, 1991: 111)

The errant, 'wandering'/wondering and 'beyond the Pale' quality of Clarke's best work is evident throughout the poem, which spares us no physical or mental detail of Maurice's anguish, self-abasements and miseries. 'A great many substances visibly flow from [Maurice] in the early parts of the poem', Corcoran notes, suggesting the dissolution of the bounds of selfhood, as Clarke hints at both the ostensible causes for Maurice's fast – a hunger strike which parallels that of the Sinn Féin prisoners of the British at the time – and the psychic blockages that lie behind it, explored through dream imagery and verbal slips with which a Freudian analyst would be familiar (Corcoran, 1983: 44–6). Maurice, in fact, constructs a mythic dream-world of considerable beauty as compensation for the real world he has abandoned, and out of his thwarted sexual desire. Having heard the warders talk of a gate, garden and fountain, he elaborates on them; thus, in section five, he is harassed in a dream by 'a silent form', a 'policeman' and – a reminder of his crushed sexuality – pillars decked as 'holy ictyphalli' beneath which he abjectly 'worship[s], a tiny satyr, / Mere prick beneath those vast erections'. The mythic 'release' abruptly takes (oriental / fantastic) shape:

> Joyously through a gateway, came a running
> Of little Jewish boys, their faces pale
> As ivory or jasmine, from Lebanon

To Eden. Garlanded, caressing,
Little girls ran with skip and leap . .
                              . . .Love
Fathered him with their happiness.
                              (Clarke, 1991: 114)

In reality, as the vision shows when it recurs in part nine, the gate and 'the primal Garden' are, punningly, as 'guarded' as Eden, the 'leaping' of the children echoing the name of the 'tall, handsome, tweeded Dr Leeper'. Similarly, Maurice's fantasies of fighting for Ireland as a 'Daring Republican' lead to nothing but the doctor's reiterated appeal to ' "Think . . . Think" '. Nevertheless, in the 'top-room' of a very Yeatsian tower in the hospital – another, Bloomian, trauma being figured – Maurice still finds himself 'stumbling / Where Mnemosyne lay in dust'. Release – from delusion, self-loss and his fast – finally occurs in two forms, sexual and gustatory. Mnemosyne herself has not been able to help Maurice; but withdrawal to the sexual self-sufficiency of masturbation, in part ten, offers itself as one release and paradoxical affiliation with his fellow-sufferers:

Often in priestly robe on a
Night of full moon, out of the waste,
A solitary figure, self-wasted,
Stole from the encampments – Onan,
Consoler of the young, the timid,
The captive. Administering, he passed down
The ward. Balsam was in his hand.
The self-sufficer, the anonym.
                              (Clarke, 1991: 123)

It would be prudish to view Onan as merely 'eerie and destructive', a member of a 'perverse priesthood' whose relief is 'furtive, shameful and associated with madness' as does Harmon (Harmon, 1989: 217). As readers of 'Ancient Lights' and Clarke's memoir *Twice Round the Black Church* will know, masturbation figures in opposition to the 'shameful' 'confession' of 'tak[ing] pleasure, when alone' which, in real life, the terrified seven-year-old Clarke was bullied into making. Onan represents Maurice's abjection – both are 'anonyms' – but, as Corcoran finely observes, also fills the absence at the poem's centre 'with the presence of the conditioning circumstances which have provoked and produced that absence: the impossibility of a true sexual relation; the anxiety induced by a false, neurotic religion; the terror of living through a period of violent political upheaval' (Corcoran, 1983: 47–8). In spite of his mythopoeic and therefore illusory aspect ('Balsam' recalling the 'balsam' tree of Maurice's mythicising of the words 'gate', 'fountain' and 'garden' in part nine), Onan nevertheless grants a physical benediction, a release which causes the one fluid which has not yet flowed in the poem – semen – to do so. Unlike the 'unwanted' semen in Maurice's reliving of his sexually continent relationship with 'Margaret', an impossibly asexual 'romantic dream', this is very much desired, and liberatory; it is no coincidence that immediately following the acceptance of the 'Balsam', Maurice breaks his fast in part nine by eating straw-berries brought to him by his mother.

This is a Wordsworthian moment – 'Nature', as part twelve glosses it, 'Remembering a young believer' 'Gave him from the lovely hand / Of his despairing mother / A dish of strawberries'. But it is also, and more impor-tantly, a Keatsian one. This is not just because the urge to gratify the senses which sees Maurice reach out to take the fruit placed beside him 'so ripe, ruddy, delicious', and his quasi-deferral of the pleasure, recall the feast 'heaped' at Madeline's bedside in *The Eve of St Agnes*. It is also because Mnemosyne herself inevitably recalls the Mnemosyne of *Hyperion* who becomes the central figure (as Moneta, her Roman name) of *The Fall of Hype-rion*. She, like Onan, is a figure who is 'self-wasted', her 'wan face . . . bright-blanched / By an immortal sickness which kills not', a monitory but healing presence. Similarly, Moneta–Mnemosyne inspires the poet of *The Fall of Hype-rion* to successfully endure a trial which could turn him into 'dust'. 'Nature' helps save Maurice, but so too do his bodily appetites and memories; as Keats agonisingly put it, in a poem addressed to Fanny Brawne (in a relationship as sexually unconsummated as Maurice's with Margaret) '[t]ouch has a memory'.[40] Clarke's mother is related to Mnemosyne in her capacity of mother of the muses, the fruit of which is the poem itself. Led by 'nature', embody-ing Mnemosyne, the last six parts of the poem – which detail Maurice's growing objectivity and sense of selfhood as he is 'rememorised' – can be read as a making amends for the brutal opening line of the poem: 'Past the house where he was got'. In moving towards the loving recognition of the final lines, in which we learn of how at 'Number One Thomas Street / Shone . . . The house in which his mother was born', Clarke not only charts Maurice's, his own, and national recovery from trauma, but traces the course of his life as the overcoming both of sexuality as bestial ('got') at its female-inflected close and the Church's transcendent dismissal of the flesh.

Still Watters: *The Week-End of Dermot and Grace*

The writings of Eugene Watters underline the radical interruption of the ex-perimental poetic tradition in Ireland in the 1930s. While chronologically a member of the 'lost generation', an almost complete lack of critical attention has been compounded by the fact that Watters wrote in Irish (as Eoghan Ó Tuairisc) as well as English, and in many genres. Nevertheless, the main reason for neglect of his main work, *The Week-End of Dermot and Grace* (1,270 lines long, in three sections), is its unabashed modernism, which makes it unas-similable to standard accounts of Irish poetry. It is difficult to link Watters's work with that of his most obvious predecessors, the 1930s' modernists, given his residence in Ireland. Moreover, it lacks the religious or Nationalist interests of Devlin and MacGreevy, and its relish of demotic and exuberant verbal play mark it off from the minimalism of Coffey. Neither the *Miscellany* nor neo-modernist New Writers' Press poets of the late 1960s showed any awareness of Watters's work, and it found no champion until Maurice Scully, a later neo-modernist, began writing in the early 1980s. What the problem of establishing antecedents and successors serves to highlight, of course, are the issues of belatedness, of forgotten and ignored literary currents, of generational overlapping and gapping characteristic of the Irish poetic condition. For all that, however, *Week-End* is relatively simple to define, if not 'place', in terms of a tradition or chronology.

Week-End is an Irish equivalent of *The Waste Land*, and in many ways a more successful one than the usual candidate for the position, Kinsella's 'Nightwalker'. It is a wholly modernist, multi-layered work based primarily on the legend of Diarmaid and Grainne, but drawing on other death/rebirth myths – Christ, Adonis and Ra. Eliot's irony and pessimism are tempered by the comic and cyclical spirit of later Joyce (given that the ostensible narrative of the poem is a couple's attempt to escape from Dublin for a dirty weekend in the seaside town of Castlefinnerty, parallels might also be drawn with the use of female archetypes by Fallon and the sexual imperatives of Kavanagh and Clarke). This is reflected structurally in the poem's tripartite division (Friday, Saturday and Sunday) and its use of the legend of Diarmaid and Grainne, a Revival favourite; in it the two young lovers are pursued by the ageing Fionn McCumhail to whom Grainne has been promised from birth (despite reconciliation, Fionn is later responsible for Diarmaid's death). Their avatars in the poem's Ireland of August 1945 are Grace, Dermot and his employer Mr Finn. The poem opens with the couple catching a train from Dublin on Friday afternoon for the seaside village of Castlefinnerty:

> Amiens Street. I tipped the porter a shilling
> And walked the length of the platform, twinned
> In the reflective windows of the carriages,
> The I and the I shall be.
> I was the sunrise and its shadow in the evening
> I was the spring field and the stooked corn
> The alphabet and the Iliad,
> First kiss on a bench at startime,
> The last gag when candles are lit to sweeten the air.
> The engine wagged its grey beard and said,
> Vah! Himself he cannot save.
>   (Watters, 1985: 27)

These lines introduce the themes of the poem and its disorientating shifts of register, rhythm, mood and style; city life, the split self, vegetation myths, the threat of atomic weapons, death and rebirth are cast in language by turns discursive, biblical, demotic or discursive. The two lovers, pursued from Dublin by Finn, or versions of him, seem to arrive in Castlefinnerty where they spend

Saturday bathing, wandering the fields and canoodling on the golf links as they watch the rising moon. Sunday seems to be represented by a morning in bed which turns to lovemaking. 'Seems', in both cases, because while the poem contains substantial quantities of realist material, it is increasingly disrupted by interjections, liturgical responses, speculations, classical and Irish mythic references and variations on leitmotifs which, like the musical intertexts of the poem, recall the Sirens chapter of *Ulysses* ('Let us alone. The bright day is free'; 'Alalalone'; 'Alone, alone, old pal, the bright blood is free', 'Brethren pray that my sacrifice') (Watters, 1985).

The chief crux in this apparent conflict between realist and non-realist registers occurs early in the poem where, as Seán Lucy has argued (Watters, 1985: 77), the train carrying Dermot and Grace crashes in a tunnel, killing them:

> Alone.
> They have tunnelled the earth and laid us in a tomb.
> Aphrodite's lamp is out. Where have we laid
> Her clearcut image in this smuttering time?
> Grace.
>   (Watters, 1985: 30–1)

From this point on – in an extraordinary stroke – the poem, and the narrative, can be read as a projection of Dermot's dying brain. The poem becomes a debate between Dermot – a dying and then reborn Adonis–Christ figure at the comparative mythic level – and Grace and Finn. Dermot craves oblivion and an escape from rebirth; Grace and Finn attempt to persuade him to accept it. This makes sense of the allusions to fertility rituals, Grace's acquisition of divine attributes, Finn's final representation as a universal law of cyclical confinement. Neither mythic nor realist level is privileged in the poem, both flowing into and out of each other in the course of the psychodrama. Within this, the poem's events acquire further meanings; 'Saturday', with its dip in the sea, its view of the August fields 'Tipsy with fertilization', its shedding of individual identity under the rising moon, uses the idea of ontology as phylogeny; that is, the Darwinian thesis that human foetal development is a recapitulation of previous evolutionary history (although in this section, to begin with at least, Dermot is *de*-evolving, progressing towards non-being). Perhaps most important is the main reason Dermot offers for wishing to escape the 'dreaming wine' of existence, being 'crucified with bitter screws to the grain / Of our timbered world' (Watters, 1985: 49, 33). For, despite its use of mythical archetypes, *Week-End* is in fact crushingly aware of its historical moment, its Ireland-centred narratives set within the context of recent European and world history – those of the post-World War II dispensation and the nuclear balance of terror.

Crucial to its meaning is *Week-End*'s setting over the August weekend on which the Hiroshima bomb was dropped (Watters's most ambitious poem in Irish, *Aifreann na Marbh*, published on the same day as *Week-End*, is a nine-part requiem for the bomb's victims). Allusions to the birth of the atomic age saturate the poem – sometimes in the form of an intertext which thematises the West's brutality to the East through a sexual relationship, Puccini's *Madame Butterfly* – and these are offered as the main cause for Dermot's desire to escape rebirth. This concern with World War II and mass destruction recalls Kinsella's 'Downstream' and 'Old Harry', but Watters's radical syntactic dislocations and wordplay convey the shock of the historic rupture at the level of form – and incidentally point to the difference between modernist and modernistic poetic practice:

Hero.
He rose?
Hiroshima.

Hail hole in determinate night,
O round O,
By Jove, Leda's only easteregg.
X marks the out out damned spot.
Ah, my dear brethren,
Who would not give all the world for threep-
Ennyworth of beautiful sleep.
                    (Watters, 1985: 31)

Heroic pretension, from the militarist codes celebrated by traditional epic, fall under the shadow cast by the bomb ('He rose?' / Heroes is cast down by 'Hiroshima'; but 'rose', in a less excruciating pun, also refers to the rose-pattern on a girl's kimono which was shadowgraphed on to a wall by the bomb's explosion, such that 'a white rose against a brick wall in Drumcondra / Is simply a shattering thing'). This typically playful-serious passage uses the 'Huge humped hilarious hiroshima' as more than ironic-nostalgic contrast; it ruptures 'determinate' night, the Einsteinian universe making itself appallingly present in the Newtonian one, a 'hole' in what was 'whole'. It is 'O round O', the perfect (egg) figure, the X – as in some cosmic game of noughts and crosses – placing this origin under a sign of erasure ('O' is also zero). Dermot craves 'beautiful sleep' because the bomb ruptures for ever the continuum of past and future which rebirth represents. Hiroshima, for *Week-End*, represents a crisis not just for Dermot but of human self-understanding, with the socio-political crisis seen, in the best modernist manner, as a crisis of representation, of language.

Yet Dermot, as hero-victim, is brought to the point of acquiescing in rebirth. By Sunday morning he seems to be lying in an east-facing bedroom – where he would be if he was alive. Since he is dead/unborn, this is a tomb (similar to those of the Boyne Valley) and a womb, while Grace has been changed from a distinct individual into a goddess. Kelly, the old man who was with Dermot and Grace in their railway carriage in the Friday section, now explains the meaning of Finn as the principle of limitation, or finitude – mensuration, convention, ageing, repetition – to be followed by Finn himself explaining that all civilisation is the same as the sexual wheel. There is no escape from the basic processes; Dermot must drink another life. His undoing – his literal unselving, the precondition for rebirth – is Grace. The lyric 'I', under great pressure and disruption throughout the poem, here collapses, seduced into reincarnation by a beauty seen as an inescapable field of energies, a desire traversing the self, almost as Jacques Lacan would define it; selves are constituted and reconstituted by desire as part of the eternal physical process of the universe. In the very act of washing his hands of existence Dermot finds himself touching and inadvertently desiring, Grace

> Blind sailor in these straits, the I dispenses
> At least with its dreaming masks, shrinks,
> Unthinks itself into birth's wounds, a Friday moment . . .
> Here death and love are one. Strangled and alone . . .
> The I cries its whimpering negation,
> Drawing in the air to make blood and voice.
>
> Brethren pray that my sacrifice.
>
> (Watters, 1985: 70–1)

Self-exiled in the world of Irish-language writing, overshadowed by the emergence of the self-consciously modern Kinsella and Montague, detached from any alternative 'modernist tradition', what is remarkable about Watters's work is its exuberance, its embodiment of the self-reinventing capabilities of that 'tradition', even in isolation. Dermot is both a modernist everyman and, it should be noted, a risen Ireland, Watters – for all his scepticism concerning Nationalist shibboleths – ensuring the presence of the defining moment of modern Irish history (an Easter-recalling 'week-end' of sacrifice) within that of world history, in a manner both more contrived and less dubious than 'ourselves through seven hundred years accursed'.

Montague, epic and *The Rough Field*

The difference between the attitude of the *Miscellany* poets and Clarke and Watters to the long poem lies in their attraction to it for its potential for epic expression. While the latter offer representative narratives at extremes, the younger poets, under modernising pressures, were attracted to the idea of the epic as 'national form', embracing the long poem – particularly in Montague's case – as an ultimate test of the worth of a poet and poetry itself.[41] This aim is not encompassed simply by greater representativeness, and in modern epic there is inevitably a conflict between the poet's individualism and the collectivity espoused; Pound defined the genre as 'The speech of a nation through the mouth of one man' and this contradiction is the central tension animating twentieth-century examples. Typically 'modern epic attempts to identify and synthesize the various voices and details of a culture or "tribe"' but, unlike the traditional epic, finds itself 'in a society no longer unified by a single, generally accepted code of values' (Preminger and Brogan, 1993: 791). As a result it justifies its argument by the direct appeal of the author's own experiences and emotions; the poet makes himself representative, foregrounding himself as a hero figure. The acknowledgement of limitation which invariably follows the desire to speak for a culture stands revealed as a drive towards self-portraiture as well, and this tension 'generates the technical innovations for which these poems are noted; if no single narrative exists to explain a culture, then it follows that . . . discontinuous yet accumulative forms . . . might be useful in tracking a repeatedly engaged, non-guaranteed movement toward an explanatory tale'. This results in 'strikingly tentative arrangements of the shifting, resistant materials of a culture' (Preminger and Brogan, 1993: 791). This 'discontinuous' element is a feature of *The Rough Field* (and 'Nightwalker'). Yet this does not mean that the task of 'synthesizing' the 'various voices and details of a culture or "tribe"' is seen in quite the same ironic light by an Irish poet as it is, say, by a US poet; and a presumed homogeneity of Ireland (both as actual community and potential united nation), as well as a tradition of 'bardic' responsibility deriving to traditions of regionalist modernism can be seen to offset the pressures to discontinuous form.

The idea for *The Rough Field* occurred 'in the early sixties', as Montague explains in the poem's Preface, on a journey from Belfast to Tyrone, 'when I had a kind of vision, in the medieval sense, of my home area, the unhappiness of its historical destiny'. Most of the poem appeared in parts between 1961 and 1971, Montague noting 'I managed to draft the opening and the close but soon realised I did not have the technique for so varied a task. At times during the decade I returned to it when the signs seemed right . . . I never thought of [it] as tethered to some particular set of events' (Montague, 1989: 55). The title of the poem comes from Montague's home townland of Garvaghey, the anglicised form of the Irish *garbh acaidh*, a rough field; its concerns were sketched out in an article entitled 'The Rough Field' in *The Spectator* as early as 1963, and in the later essay 'A Primal Gaeltacht'.[42] For Montague a use of the vestigially textualised County Tyrone countryside – the essay offers a survey of its poetic topoi – pushes poetry beyond the vignettes of rural customs to which Hewitt was limited, drawing from them historical, mythic (and Montague would add, 'racial') resonances to sustain a programme of cultural retrieval and comment on the modern world. Because every 'Irishman' is automatically surrounded and influenced – however unwittingly – by the residue of a Gaelic past, as the name Garvaghey evidences, he has been subconsciously moulded by the 'primal gaeltacht', and by articulating this poetry can, Montague claims, acquire the representative force necessary to epic. Thus, 'A Lost Tradition' speaks of a landscape which is 'a manuscript / We had lost the skill to read'. In this use of 'we', of course, the epic ambition is implicit; and a gesture towards the accommodation of English occurs later in the section in 'Even English': 'Even English in these airts / Took a lawless turn', with names like 'Tullycorker and Tullygluish' 'braid[ing] Scots and Irish'

(Montague, 1995: 33, 38). An earlier verse of 'A Lost Tradition', however, shows the potential limitation of this linguistic accommodation within the 'primal gaeltacht' when it is claimed that 'No rock or ruin, dun or dolmen / But showed memory defying cruelty / Through an image-encrusted name'. 'Cruelty' carries a gaelicising exclusivity rather than an invitation to explore the complexities of the past, and the 'we' clearly does not include Protestants who have no interest in the language (even if they are 'subconsciously' steeped in the names around them). In textualising the countryside Montague renews a politics of language and territory for Irish poetry; moreover, as Thomas Dillon Redshaw argues, 'by reading the plain post-glacial geography of County Tyrone in this syncretic way, the landscape takes on layered dimensions of myth and legend that forecasts the sorts of structured poetic meanings that inform *The Rough Field* more consistently than contemporary fact' (Redshaw, 1974: 40). Redshaw rightly relates the modernistic procedures of the poem to Montague's linguistic-cultural strategy, but also notes on the other hand that 'post-glacial' contains an appeal to the immemorial, a perspective so long, that the simplification of contemporary differences is threatened; 'A Lost Tradition' notably concludes with a vision of the defeat of Gaeldom as 'Ulster's pride, Elizabeth's foemen, / Founder in a Munster bog' at Kinsale in 1601. Nevertheless, the poem generally succeeds in realising Montague's aim to write something more expansive than the lyric in a modernistic form, and should be judged on its handling of the confrontation between modernisation and traditionalism.

The Rough Field follows a narrative of return to a home(land) whose identity has been almost completely eroded by modernisation. Nevertheless the journey from Belfast to Tyrone is also a journey back in time, from a more to a less developed part of Northern Ireland, but also from an area of 'solid British towns, lacking local grace', across the River Bann, the Northern equivalent of the Pale, to the 'beginning of O'Neill', the last Irish chieftain to make a bid for all-Ireland sovereignty before defeat at Kinsale. If Protestant Ulster is established in terms of stereotypes – a 'culture where constraint is all' – the return to collapsed Gaeldom is almost equally so, and is no less disillusioning: 'No Wordsworthian dream enchants me here', the speaker claims, in a bleak landscape which haunts, but cannot be fully returned to: 'all my circling', as he puts it, constituting 'a failure to return' which is historical, personal and linguistic (Montague, 1995: 8–9). The connection with the past and the countryside is seen as now irrevocably broken, except in the inheritance of a 'broken fiddle' found in the house of his aunt. This becomes the occasion of a promise to 'remember my burly godfather'; traditional music emblematises the prodigal's sophisticated cosmopolitan poetry, 'and so succession passes, through strangest hands' (Montague, 1995: 12).

From its outset, then, *The Rough Field* is no less than an epic attempt to read a communal history through a personal one of absence, distanced by migration and education. Technical innovation permits a fluid, open quality which prevents the process becoming too personally insistent. Collage and montage – sixteenth-century woodcuts, depicting Irish customs and the English campaigns against the Irish of the 1580s, typographical oddities, extracts from letters, newspapers, pamphlets, hymns and histories – cut across, expand and qualify the lyric sequence, and the poems themselves often weave together allusions and quotations, often to impressive effect, as in 'The Bread God'.[43] In this, the nineteenth-century novelist William Carleton's descriptions of an open-air mass, a letter from an uncle who is a priest in Australia and hate-mail from Protestant sectarians are interwoven with a sequence of lyrics following memories of massgoing from Montague's childhood, building effectively to a climax in the most virulent of the sectarian pamphlets, followed by a meditative sonnet on an altar rock, the uncle's hope for the future ('perhaps this new man' – O'Neill? – 'will find a way to resolve the old hatreds') and 'An Ulster Prophecy', Montague's own representation of the dividedness of the North, and of Ireland, as a series of folkloric paradoxes. This ends with what the speaker clearly sees as the most unbelievable paradox of all, 'a curlew in flight / surveying / a united Ireland', echoing the earlier circling 'failure to return' (Montague, 1995: 27). The implication is that a dying culture and a divided Ireland cannot be returned to, and provide nowhere for the would-be returnee to ground himself; yet the hankering for a unitary state, psychologically or politically, the plangency which a continuous lyric voice would give, is disrupted not so much by fragmentation as by textual variety.

Weaving between his own past (as in the 'Leaping Fire' section, in which the pious and loving aunt who reared him is memorialised), and the history of Ulster and Northern Ireland (in which the key figure is his father, driven from the new statelet because of his Republicanism in the 1920s), Montague elaborates a number of symbolic images, at once fructive and ominous. There is the 'leaping fire' (of war, but also of domestic fidelity, the hearth at the centre of the older way of life, of the kindling of his own art); the 'severed head' (an allusion to the Celtic habit of decapitating enemies, taken up by the invading English); and, perhaps most potent of all, the 'severed tongue'. The image – used elsewhere in literature to invoke the image of the enslaved and 'tongueless' colonial subject (like Friday in the South African novelist J. M. Coetzee's *Foe*) – is a poignant one for Montague, since it links the extinction of Gaelic to his stammer, induced by a bullying teacher:

> (Dumb,
> bloodied, the severed
> head now chokes to
> speak another tongue –
>
> As in
> a long suppressed dream,
> some stuttering garb-
> led ordeal of my own

> An Irish
> child weeps at school
> repeating its English . . .

> To grow
> a second tongue, as
> harsh a humiliation
> as twice to be born.
> (Montague, 1990: 39)[44]

Tyrone is here offered as the severed and tongueless head of Gaeldom, with Montague its belated and mutilated interpreter; and the attempt to make Tyrone's history symbolise a general crisis of Irish identity is aided by Montague's ability to switch to representations of the Republic (Kearney, 1992: 49).[45]

Montague's ironic critique of the Republic and the 1916 commemorations in section eight, 'A Patriotic Suite', is detailed and shrewd, and stands against the invocation of a simplistic 'race hatred' referred to in section five, 'The Fault' (Montague, 1995: 43). These ten short lyrics constitute perhaps the strongest section of the poem. They begin with the leitmotif of a tin whistle, emblematic of Irish music, symbol both of loss (Irish traditional culture and language) and of Seán Ó Riada's revival of traditional music in the 1960s, in which Montague was involved. Traditional music and Ó Riada are 'that point / where folk and art meet', and the ironically delayed realisation of this Revival goal runs throughout the section: 'The mythic lyre' is now 'shrunk to country size', though once the 'Symbolic depth-charge of music'. As one of the epigraphs of the poem, from Engels, runs: 'The real aims of a revolution, those which are not illusion, are always to be realised after that revolution', and this captures perfectly the ambivalence of the sequence, which is ironic at the expense of the 'real aims' – those of the farmers and professionals who gained from Independence – while at the same time assessing whether there is anything more which modernisation, for all its threat to traditional identity, might offer. In Lucy's words, 'The dream blossoms in revolution and fades into mediocrity while new sorts of freedom begin to push for expression' (Lucy, 1974: 30). Thus, language policy – government hypocrisy and majority indifference towards it – is taken up in part five, while 'The Enterprise', the name given to the Dublin–Belfast express, supplies the title of part six, which looks out over 'Row after row of council cottages' and the docks where a crane symbolically 'tilts into emptiness'. Here another journey to Garvaghey, from Dublin, is being described, and it is almost as oppressive as the one from Belfast. The critique of Lemassian expansionism is clear: 'Here nothing has been planned – / Assembled, yes, casual / And coarse as detritus' (Montague, 1995: 65). This negative take on modernity, resembling Kinsella's in 'Nightwalker', derives from Montague's modernist models. Although Montague is an urban-based, cosmopolitan poet, the negative view of the city in his work, even where it enables the privacy of lovers, reveals a rural bias similar to that of MacDonagh's elaboration of the Irish mode, albeit ironically modified. The tendency to turn passive suffering into spiritual superiority is thus mocked, but not contradicted, in part eight, when it is set against expansion; 'Does fate at last relent / With a trade expansion of 5 per cent?' (Montague, 1995: 66). The implication is that it does not, but this is not endorsed by the poem either.

The new international profile of the Republic, which increased with Patrick Boland becoming the Chairman of the United Nations in 1960, and Conor Cruise O'Brien's appointment as Secretary to the UN General Secretary, is entertainingly charted in this poem, which takes pleasure in an inversion of stereotypes: the 'unsmiling Saxon' is surprised by the 'rational' diplomats of an Ireland now 'prospecting' 'lands beyond / Kipling's setting sun' of the waning British Empire. The Queen, to the shock of Ulster Unionists, 'enters the Vatican' on her first state visit there, but the Vatican ignores Ireland's pleas for the canonisation of Matt Talbot. 'Granted another saint', as Montague sardonically puts it, 'we might shepherd / Another Dark Ages home'. The ambivalence of the new Ireland is clear in the final section; does Ireland have anything more to offer the world other than 'eye-swimming melancholy'? The ironies are uncertain, then; on the one hand, Montague shrewdly sees the survival of traditionalist attitudes together with modernisation, in Thornley's terms (Thornley, 1964). On the other, there is a note – literally, of the tin whistle – of regret, which feeds on a straightforward attack on modernity which is not wholly compatible with the exposure of traditionalist values. The section ends with a juxtaposition of many of these images in the most fragmented, questioning part of the poem. 'While all Europe seeks / New versions of old ways', it seems Ireland seeks an old version of the new way. What is not clear is the extent to which Montague shares in this 'melancholy':

> Sight of the Skelligs at sunset
> restores our Hy-Brasil . . .
> again that note!
> > above a self-drive car.
> (Montague, 1995: 68)

Uncertainty lies behind the ambivalence towards modernisation (an allusion to the 'Gross National Product' asks to be read with the emphasis on 'Gross'), an unwillingness to jettison old values in the face of a few years of material prosperity, but also an unwillingness to cling to them. The vacillation is brilliantly imaged in this section of the poem, which incorporates the contradictions of change with a final image of older national autonomy and new modernity as a 'self-drive' car. Elsewhere, however, the absence of a constructive vision of modernity can mean a lurch towards nostalgia, a vacillation only between two polar opposites, the archaic/traditional and the commercial. In section seven, 'Hymn to the New Omagh Road', this acquires a sectarian dimension; material convenience is rather glibly conflated with Unionism in the form of a vandalistic road-widening scheme in a manner which partially resurrects the terms of 'spiritual empire' (Montague, 1995: 56–9; Mahon,

1973: 136).[46] Something both haphazard and systematic, then, drives *The Rough Field*, its heterogeneity in its first eight sections at least helping to prevent its archaising tendencies from collapsing into idealisation, or its ambiguity towards modernisation becoming republican anticipation. As the Troubles loomed, however, and the temptations of bardic authority beckoned, the balance between modernity and history would be disturbed as Montague attempted to subsume *The Rough Field* to a more consistently 'tribal', racial and mythic aim, and to 'tether' the poem to a very 'particular set of events' indeed.[47]

'Ulster toothpaste', reform and civil rights

> Fifteen years ago it seemed that a group of writers resident in the North of Ireland was emerging to form the basis of a local contemporary literature. But today the group has disintegrated: the wild geese have blown away . . . We have no coherent body of writing, and the Athens of the North has become the Ah-thens of our youth . . . The term 'Ulster Writing' doesn't mean anything any longer. We might as well talk about Ulster toothpaste. (Roy McFadden, 1961)[48]

McFadden's claim that writing in Northern Ireland was meaningless must have seemed a simple statement of the obvious by 1961. W. R. Rodgers had not published a collection since 1951, Hewitt and Robert Greacen since 1948, or McFadden himself since 1947. Not only Regionalism, it seemed, but poetry in Northern Ireland had died, even if Hewitt was still writing, Fiacc had returned to Belfast and Montague had recently received his 'vision' on the road to Garvaghey. Unknown to McFadden, however, a new Northern poetry was already in the offing, one which would show how the literary-cultural scene had been reconfigured by twenty years of post-war reform. In social terms, the changed *zeitgeist* of the 1960s was crucial to the emergence of what would become known as the Belfast 'Group' of Heaney, Simmons, Mahon and Longley. Belfast in this sense was just one of several new regional centres of poetic activity which by the mid-1960s also included Birmingham, Newcastle and Liverpool.[49] All, to some extent, were influenced by the regional modernisation programmes of the Wilson government and by an artistic renewal which included the burgeoning youth culture and counter-culture. Yet in Northern Ireland these stresses were inflected by the conservative and sectarian nature of society, in which Unionist fears and Nationalist expectations had been inordinately sharpened by the Labour victory of 1964.

As with the Republic, any economistic view of reform in the North should be tempered by awareness of the more volatile, if less empirically verifiable political needs which drove it. The post-war years had seen a decline in Northern Ireland's staple manufactures – linen and shipbuilding – employment in which was overwhelmingly Protestant. The Ulster Unionist Party's failure to check the consequent unemployment resulted initially in a fracture in the Unionist cross-class coalition. Working-class defection to the Northern Ireland Labour Party (NILP) in the 1958 election sounded the alarm for the party, which was at first incapable of responding.[50] Unionism was under threat, and liberal currents urging internal reform had emerged in the UUP itself.[51] In 1962 the party lost another Belfast seat to the NILP and in the following year Lord Brookeborough, leader for twenty years, was replaced by Terence O'Neill. The process was reminiscent of de Valera's replacement by Lemass, with the crucial difference that Stormont Northern Ireland would prove far less able to contain change than the Republic. Economic reform imposed by Westminster necessitated socio-political reform, and while Protestant working-class drift was checked at the 1964 election, the threat from without mounted. Like Lemass, O'Neill banked on growth to solve his problems; modernisation through inward investment would produce growth and placate Westminster, while renewing UUP hegemony. And, as in the Republic, it proved perfectly feasible to use the rhetoric of modernisation for mystificatory purposes: 'the ideology of modernisation could function quite simply to defend sectarian activity by defining Nationalist and NILP concern as "reactionary" or "living in the past"', (Bew Gibbon and Patterson, 1996: 138).

The problem was that O'Neill's commitment to reform was weak; if he genuinely believed that prosperity would improve intercommunal relations in the long term, in the short term he was committed more to gesture politics.[52] His policies brought Goodyear, Du Pont and ICI, but left untouched gerrymandering (most blatantly in Derry) and discrimination in housing allocations. At the same time unemployment continued to bear more than twice as heavily on Catholics as on Protestants. Even the gestures were partly undone when the new University of Ulster was sited in 1966 not in Catholic Derry – the logical location – but in Protestant Coleraine, while Northern Ireland's New Town was announced as 'Craigavon', to be located in the Protestant Lagan Valley rather than in a mixed or Catholic area. Thus the East/West, Protestant/Catholic division within 'Ulster' which Regionalism had ignored came to the fore in the 1960s, as a better-educated and emboldened Catholic minority increased the pressure to match reformist words with actions. The process began on a small scale with the formation of the Campaign for Social Justice (CSJ) in 1965.[53] Frustration at continued lack of reform led to the more representative Northern Ireland Civil Rights Association (NICRA) being founded in April 1967. It called for the repeal of the Special Powers Act and the disbandment of the B-Specials, but – as with the CSJ – its aim was to be a mass non-sectarian Movement for full political and civil rights. NICRA, too, was initially frustrated, and turned to public demonstrations and sit-downs, tactics taken from the US black Civil Rights Movement which struck at traditional territorial expressions of Protestant superiority. The determination to test the content of a nominal 'citizenship' and a preparedness to lobby within UK political structures was a change from the passive complaint of the Nationalist

Party in the past and badly wrong-footed the Unionist establishment. Stormont's democratic bluff was called. By the mid-1960s, however, O'Neill's reformist gestures had already aroused not just expectations for real reform, but also the ire of hard-line Loyalists. Within a year or two the Catholic community's expectations had acquired a desperate and mass aspect which meant that their political activity spread rapidly, acquired a broad base and would remain persistent.[54] If modernisation in the South, therefore, had seemed to be bringing the two states together in some ways, divisions remained deep and had begun to widen again.[55]

The Belfast 'Group'

In the context of such change the development of a literary renewal to match that in the Republic was perhaps predictable. Indeed, Michael Longley and Derek Mahon, from Protestant Belfast backgrounds, were students at Trinity College Dublin from 1958 and form something of a bridge between the two centres, both connected with young Trinity poets from the Republic such as Eavan Boland and Brendan Kennelly. Seamus Heaney, destined to be the leading figure, was in the early 1960s introducing himself to the work of Hewitt and 'the glimmering that writing could occur on your own doorstep', as well as encountering poets from the South in the *Miscellany*, contemporary British poetry and, crucially, Kavanagh. In 1963 Heaney met Longley and Mahon in Belfast, and in the same year the Belfast poetry scene was galvanised by the arrival of Philip Hobsbaum as a lecturer at Queen's. Hobsbaum began almost immediately to organise a regular writing group, along the lines of the London 'Group' of which he had been a member.[56]

Hobsbaum's poetic was based on rapprochement between the Hardy tradition of the well-made lyric and the expressivity (though not experimentalism) of a native English modernism. Its effect was to qualify Movement poetics with rawer energies while, at the same time, sanctioning traditional form. The hybrid had a germinating effect in a place where even the tiredest models could receive new energy from a uniquely charged, un-English, fallow 'cultural ecology' (Brown, 1988: 215). Unlike the 1940s, post-war liberalism, prosperity and educational reform generally (but Catholic and working-class articulacy in particular) now enabled the formation of a broader-based literary community, one fusing regional identity, anti-sectarianism, Leavisism with a peculiar interstitial position between the established literary centres of Dublin and London. It is in this combination that the concept of the Belfast Group retains its validity, and Edna Longley's claim that the role of the Group may best be understood by viewing it as a point of aesthetic contact between Belfast, Dublin and London holds good as long as these specific contexts, and the calculated use of the metropolitan connection, is borne in mind (Kirkland, 1996: 77–82). Nor should it be assumed that the London connection was all one-way, simply a cultural neo-colonialism to which Northern poets uncritically succumbed and confirmed by formal conservatism. Even in the less risky early poetry, it is possible to see a healthy caution towards some established identities and an expression of the 'vigorous, slightly distrustful formalist eclecticism' which would lead to work of greater power and originality (Crotty, 1995: 5).

Developments were as swift as they had been halting in the South, aided by concentration in a small geographical area, the dearth of other forms of cultural expression and the sheer unlikelihood of poetic efflorescence. This is not to say, of course, that the energy-dissipating fractiousness of inherited dissent found in the Republic did not have its Northern equivalents – most literary activity involves contention – but it is to recognise the role of the Group poetic in containing centrifugal tendencies. Its activity kick-started the stalled careers of older poets – Greacen, Fiacc and McFadden all benefited from the new sense of the North as a place of literary moment – and the Belfast John Hewitt returned to in 1972 was the hive of poetic activity he had striven (but failed) to create in the 1940s. As a sense of a general style developed, poetic forebears were dusted off and reappraised. MacNeice's re-evaluation as a Northern Irish poet was begun early – Mahon and Malcolm and Edna Longley had written about him in the 1960s – while Kavanagh, via Heaney, became a general model.[57] The house journal of the Northern poets, *The Honest Ulsterman*, was set up in 1968 by James Simmons, its stability aiding the development of successor poets in a way unavailable in the Republic.[58] The permanency of such an individual initiative was mirrored at an institutional level when, in 1970, Michael Longley was appointed first Northern Irish Arts Council Literature and Performing Arts Officer. Crucially, at the earliest stage, poets did not attempt to forge an explicitly national or regional identity, remaining willing to exploit the British link while articulating a sense of apartness (rather as Civil Rights protesters demanded full citizenship rather than separate status). This initial solidarity – one of the most impressive aspects of Northern poetry – would be fundamental to the staying power of its distinctive poetic and would survive, albeit in a modified form, later events. Pre-Troubles origins would thus prove to be crucial in determining the extent to which the Troubles would bear upon and be mediated in poetry after 1969, and it is important to bear this in mind given the different attitudes members and associates of the Group have adopted towards it since (these have to some extent been an index of the shifting fortunes of Northern poetry, its relationship with the poetry of the Republic and the rest of the UK and of the individual writers involved)[59] (Kirkland, 1996: 54–84). As Heaney put it in July 1966, 'the possibility of a cultural life here is the possibility of salvation' or that, in Mahon's words, 'a good poem is the paradigm of a good politics' (Corcoran, 1986: 23; E. Longley, 1986: 185). The point about the power of the myth is demonstrated in the extent to which this statement by Mahon is so much against the grain of his own extremist poetic; on this issue, it is Northern poetic cohesion which overrides personal practice (Kirkland, 1996: 117n.).

'King of the ditchbacks': Seamus Heaney

If Seamus Heaney had not been born, it would have been necessary for Northern Irish poetry to invent him. Catholic, rural, profoundly conscious of responsibility but cautious, his poetry sensuous and learned, he satisfied almost all
of the criteria demanded of an individuated yet communal voice. Heaney's
origins and historical moment meant that *Death of a Naturalist* established his
reputation in precisely those terms of an autochthonous authority unavail-
ingly sought by Hewitt, and with a more complete grasp of English and Irish
poetic traditions than had been available to Kavanagh. This is particularly the
case in the first third of the book, which deals with Heaney's childhood. There,
the terms of his authority are located in characteristically familial, rural and
sensuous fashion in an impressive series of poems: 'Blackberry-Picking',
'Churning Day', 'The Early Purges', 'Follower' and 'Ancestral Photograph',
conveying, in the very unadornedness of their titles, as well as in the 'crackle
and pop of their diction', the immediacy of the poet's involvement with
the land and the rhythms of farming life[60] (Curtis, 1994: 37). 'Digging', the
opening poem, is the first of a series of quasi-anthropological lyrics which take
as their starting point country customs, crafts and trades which act as analogues for writing as they enact a more physical rootedness in the soil from
which the poet has grown. Famously equating pen with spade, the poem not
only asserts a continuity between Heaney and his turf-cutting father and
grandfather but anticipates the theme of a larger communal excavation and
recovery which dominates his *oeuvre*.

This communal dimension is present in the poem's overdetermined
quality; the seemingly gratuitous comparison of pen with a gun, as well as
with a spade ('Between my finger and my thumb / The squat pen rests: snug
as a gun'), indicating a suppressed discomfort at writing from within the stable
tradition of Kavanagh via Wordsworth, Keats, Hopkins, Frost, R. S. Thomas
and Ted Hughes (Heaney, 1966: 13). 'Gun', however, is not just 'One analogy
too many for a short poem', as Corcoran claims, since it gestures towards a
hidden history of oppression and insurgent desire also hinted at in 'Docker' or
the 'living skulls' of potatoes of 'At a Potato Digging' (Heaney, 1966: 32). In
this sense 'Digging' alludes not just to the Irish proverb 'The pen is lighter
carried than the spade', as in Heaney's gloss, but also the English proverb 'the
pen is mightier than the sword', and bears an uncertain relationship to both,
and a similarly overdetermined quality can be seen in many of the poems in
Naturalist, where military metaphors – trout as torpedoes, gun-barrel, ramrod
and tracer bullets, churns as bombs, frogs as grenades – ramify beyond any
ostensible origin in their subjects, bringing Hughes's vitalist reaction against
the Movement together with Nationalist ressentiment (Corcoran, 1986: 45;
Curtis, 1994: 17–18). The point, as the echo of the English proverb in the Irish
one shows, is that the tradition of English nature poetry is not merely a mask
for such grievances. In a 1977 interview with Seamus Deane, Heaney

explained that his first, pre-*Naturalist* poetry had 'faced the Northern sectarian problem. Then this went underground and I became very influenced by
Hughes and one part of my temperament took over: the private County Derry
childhood part of myself rather than the slightly aggravated young Catholic
male part' (Deane, 1977: 66). But this, like Heaney's other later attempts to
disown the 'English' aspects of his writing, simplifies the complex imbrication
of the one with the other. On the other hand, this was more than matched by
some critical responses: if *Death of a Naturalist* was overwhelmingly praised, the
obverse of the dominant, somewhat sentimental reading of Heaney as the
genuine article was a matching stereotype, as in 'his words give us the soil-
reek of Ireland, the colourful violence of his childhood on a farm' (Corcoran,
1986: 45).[61]

The point in noting the complexity of Heaney's reception lies in the fact
that the first collection is varied and uneven, with Movement, Gravesian and
other influences jostling with those more usually noted, and that this is calculated to a degree.[62] Its literariness is not merely unreflective, an instinct
for mimicry subordinated to the 'sensuous', as some critics preferred to see it,
and the knowingness of Heaney's intertextuality can be seen in his placement
of a Wordsworthian dawning sexual awareness (in 'Death of a Naturalist's'
echoes of 'Nutting'), just as the onomatopoeic word-music of 'Churning
Day' verges on, but never quite falls into, Hopkinsesque parody. This is not
to say that Heaney is not attempting to express a very real guilt at growing
away from his roots; it is more that the extent to which such growth is troped
in literary terms should not be underestimated. Insinuating himself within
a late Romantic tradition, Heaney is aware of adult fear that infects that
past even as it tries to preserve it, as in 'Blackberry-Picking's' final, over-
conclusive couplet: 'It wasn't fair / That all the lovely canfuls smelt of
rot. / Each year I hoped they'd keep, knew they would not' (Heaney, 1966:
20).

'Blackberry-Picking' also shows that if English nature poetry is bound up
with buried ressentiment, Heaney's emphasis is less on its current form of
Hughesian violence and phallic assertiveness than on immersion, yielding, dissolution and concealment; threatened by the 'great slime kings' he turns and
runs from them, appalled (Curtis, 1994: 30). The truly distinctive imagery
throughout *Death of a Naturalist* is of rot, overripeness, darkness and ooze and
sucking clabber. On the one hand such imagery embodies the self-immersion
of the pre-conscious child and its essentially tactile perception of the world,
a creaturely understanding which the childhood poems attempt to seize
and 'perfect' before going on to the 'new limits' of an adult poetry, as
'Poem' explains. The bare, declarative title and the fact that this poem is
addressed to the poet's wife indicate that what is being offered is the promise
of a shift from oral-childish to genital-adult sexuality, with a similar promise
being made in aesthetic terms in the guiltily self-aware conclusion of 'Personal
Helicon':

Now, to pry into roots, to finger slime,
To stare, big-eyed Narcissus, into some spring
Is beneath all adult dignity. I rhyme
To see myself, to set the darkness echoing.
(Heaney, 1966: 57)

Following on from 'Poem', this is a (Freudian) rejection of 'childish' masturbatory sexuality. But despite this last word, and the attempted distinction
between 'stare' and 'see', the 'muck' of 'Poem' continues to combine sexual
frisson and political threat in an unavoidable manner, and the next three books
would conspicuously not refrain from 'pry[ing] into roots' (indeed, it becomes
the general plight of the emasculated, infantilised Gaelic bards in 'Ocean's Love
to Ireland' in *North*). But on the other hand the passive, abject connotations
of such imagery also echo the language of Heaney in his role as a communal,
political mouthpiece. In a *New Statesman* article of July 1966, a posture of
ambivalent challenge is troped in precisely these terms: 'A kind of double-
think operates [in Northern Ireland]; something is rotten, but maybe if we
wait it will fester to death.'[63] An apparently childish and escapist immersion
in dark and rot would seem, paradoxically, to be linked with articulation of
the passivity and abjection of the Northern minority, a linkage which will
become most explicit in *North* (1975).

Door into the Dark (1969) picks up, in its title, Heaney's fixation on the
'bruising darkness of instinct and sensation', but extends its range (Curtis,
1994: 13). There are now only a handful of poems of childhood, while the
opening poems – 'Night-Piece', 'Gone' and 'Dream' – set an ominous tone of
self-reproachful exhaustion, absence and nightmare. In a *Listener* article of
1970, Heaney defined his current poetic concerns as 'the blurred and irrational
storehouse of insight and instincts, the hidden core of the self . . . What is faith,
indeed, but a trust in the fog; who is God but the King of the Dark?', adding
that this darkness was not 'a primeval womb which we shall re-enter: it is
something more negative'. The same piece glosses the 'A Lough Neagh
Sequence' in *Door into the Dark* by adverting to statues of St Patrick banishing
the snakes from Ireland found in Irish (Catholic) churches: 'The snakes are
emblems of evil, perhaps . . . But in another way Patrick's staff could be seen
as a spade that's planting a sense of sin in the country . . . Certain life forces
have been paralysed. I know several people in the country who will never eat
eels because of the profound implications of this statue' (Heaney, 1970). The
characteristic mixture of suggestiveness and obfuscation points to the way a
more extensive and expansive use of Irish landscape and location in *Door into
the Dark* is qualified by an air of unease which parallels a growing sureness
about the role of the poet, as *Naturalist*'s writer-analogues of turf-cutter,
ploughman and water diviner are supplemented by a thatcher, eel fishermen
and blacksmith. This sureness is also technical; the best poems achieve a memorable economy beyond the scope of the first collection, although the craftsmen retain their rather antiquarian aspects. This is most marked in 'The Forge',

which sets up a sentimental opposition between the blacksmith beating out 'real iron' and 'flashing' traffic, its nostalgia highlighted by a comparison with poems in which the car becomes an image for contemporary isolation, for journeying 'by remote control', as in 'Elegy for a Still-born Child' (Heaney, 1972: 7, 19). Beyond this, the 'craftsmen' poems hint at a crucial distinction between 'craft' and 'technique' made in the 'Feeling into Words' essay and in the journal *Soundings* in 1974, and point to the importance of a concept of Romantic 'authenticity'.[64]

The best of these craftsmen, for Heaney's purpose, are those whose work comes closest to the traditional notion of 'inspiration'. Thus, the thatcher arrives 'Unexpectedly' and leaves onlookers 'gaping at his Midas touch'. The exemplary instance is given in 'The Diviner' of *Death of a Naturalist*, who possesses a similarly 'unfussed' mastery of his essentially unteachable, innate skill. Heaney's gloss in 'Feeling into Words' explains his significance as a figure for the poet and for a poetic: 'As Sir Philip Sidney notes in his *An Apologie for Poetry*: "Among the Romans a Poet was called Vates, which is as much a *Diviner*" ' (a comparison with the vatic role of the Irish bard is implicit here). Revealingly, what follows is a definition of 'technique' as that which 'allows . . . articulation not necessarily in terms of argument or explication but in terms of its own potential for harmonious self-reproduction' (Heaney, 1980: 47). The seminal excitement has to be granted conditions in which, in Hopkins's words, it 'selves, goes itself', a process in which (as in 'Personal Helicon'), a sexual charge – 'the first alertness or come-hither' – is also present (Heaney, 1980: 48). It points, therefore, to what critics have noted as a trademark Heaney use of what William Empson called the 'self-infolded simile', or self-reflexive image, which as Christopher Ricks has noted is pervasive in recent Northern Irish poetry. From *Death of a Naturalist*'s 'Waterfall' ('The burn drowns steadily in its own downpour') to the more frequent usages in *Door into the Dark* ('Mother's' 'I am a gate for myself'), these ramify throughout the later poetry.[65] Heaney is, as I have argued, aware of the circularity of the trope, which he extended to his themes and structure – 'Follower' and 'A Lough Neagh Sequence' are obvious examples – and, eventually, to collections themselves, in *Wintering Out* and *North*.[66] The 'unknown' or 'dark' quality of such circularity (embodied in the eel's life-cycle, for example) is obviously crucial for Heaney, and can be seen as a strategy for making the abject immersion in the 'clabber' of self and origins a source of power. This reversal can be related, in turn, to the representative character of his writing, which rests upon doing justice to the historically occluded experience of the Northern minority. Most crucial of all is the discovery of a larger structure in which to embody and explore this strategy of reversal and recovery in 'Bogland', the book's final poem. This takes its cue from Theodore Roethke's 'Prairies', and the opposition – in Heaney's inward-delving imagination – of a vertical continuum of Irish history to a horizontal, expansivist one (of the USA, but also of the British Empire). This 'answering Irish myth' is a national self-assertion in which 'Our pioneers keep striking / Inwards and downwards' and in which Heaney becomes a 'pioneer' himself, pulling together in a coherent scheme the more tentative delvings and explorations of 'Digging', 'At a Potato Digging' or 'Bann Clay', but also the water imagery of 'Undine', 'Relic of Memory' and other poems in *Door into the Dark*: the proto-bog poem ends with an unstable, not a stable ground, for identity:

> Every layer they strip
> Seems camped on before.
> The bogholes might be Atlantic seepage.
> The wet centre is bottomless.
>   (Heaney, 1969: 56)

This point is worth stressing, since it discovers a metaphorical equivalent for the Corkeryan notion of Ireland as a 'a quaking sod' and makes the poem (and the bog poems) less secure than it might appear. Nevertheless, the imagery which illustrates the contention that 'the bog [is] the memory of the land-scape', with all its resonance of Jungian racial archetypes, is in some ways less original than might be thought. The central conceit, which proceeds from 'Butter sunk under . . . recovered salty and white' to 'The ground itself is kind, black butter . . . missing its definition', occurs in precisely the sense of Heaney's poem in Robert Farren's *The Course of Irish Verse* of 1948, a book with which he was familiar. Confirming a continuity with neo-Revivalism, the image of butter/bog also points to the way in which Heaney would come to elaborate the image as a central metaphor not only for Irish history, but for his process of writing poems – and specifically those of his poems produced by 'technique' – making the two, in a sense, coterminous. In the essay 'Belfast' (1972) he claims: 'I have always listened for poems, they come sometimes like bodies come out of a bog, almost complete, seeming to have been laid down a long time ago, surfacing with a touch of mystery . . . I think the process is a kind of somnambulist encounter between masculine will and intelligence and femi-nine clusters of image and emotion' (Heaney, 1980: 34). Here the banality of the description – 'with a touch of mystery' – conflicts with the elaborate cov-ering of literary tracks as Heaney naturalises, through the agency of gender, the act of 'true' writing as a necrophiliac version of Keats's famous dictum that 'if Poetry come not as naturally as the Leaves to a tree it had better not come at all'.[67]

Protestant poets? Michael Longley and Derek Mahon

Critical wisdom generally invites us to view the work of Derek Mahon and Michael Longley as complementary, in the sense of offering an opposite iden-tity, to that of Heaney (McDonald, 1997: 81). Behind such a feeling lies the belief that a 'Protestant' culture is, in many ways, a contradiction in terms; Terence Brown has spoken feelingly of Dublin in the 1960s, when 'Most of the lecturers in English at Trinity College exuded an air of Anglo-Irish self-satisfaction giving one to know that a proper relief at having escaped barbarism for civilisation was the only acceptable attitude to provincial origins . . . as the northern crisis rumbled into life, I remember the irritation which *The Irish Times* provoked in me by its patrician, patronising tones as leader article and letter to the editor alike pontificated on all things Northern in the stereotypical terms for which the sobriquet "Black North" is the easiest piece of shorthand' (Brown, 1986: 19). Brown's sense of the polite incomprehension of a literary culture in the North is ratified by Derek Mahon: 'The suburbs of Belfast', as he noted in 1973, 'have a peculiar relationship to the Irish cultural situation inasmuch as they're the final anathema for the traditional Irish imagination'; similarly, 'Whatever we mean by "the Irish situation", the shipyards of Belfast are no less a part of it than a country town in the Gaeltacht' (Cooke, 1973: 10; Mahon, 1972: 14). Turning apparent disadvantage to advantage, Mahon saw the bulk of poetry in the Republic of the time as only slowly recovering from the narcosis of its 'sweet, wild Gaelic twist': 'The Irish, for many years [revered] a poetry which evaded the metaphysical unease in which all poetry of lasting value has its source.'[68] That 'metaphysical unease', of course, describes his own work which, from the outset, delineates the position of one caught between fixed identities but exploiting, rather than being paralysed by, the tensions between them. In a sense, for Mahon, such a liminal positioning is the inheritance of any right-minded Northerner and a sense of the poet as *agent provocateur* goes with the territory. In uncharacteristically blunt fashion, *Night-Crossing*'s 'First Principles' (a poem Mahon chose not to reprint) states 'With pew and with pedestal / I will have no truck', and the poems of that first collection force Irish poetry to address the apparent 'anathema' of his Belfast origins (Mahon, 1968: 33).

They do so, however, less forcefully than this might suggest. 'Glengormley' and 'Spring Vacation' give two sides of the city. The first, suburban, is the Northern Ireland of the post-war growth, a British regional vista of new estates, mod cons and an almost-belief that prosperity has eliminated atavistic hatreds:

> 'Wonders are many and none is more wonderful than man'
> Who has tamed the terrier, trimmed the hedge
> And grasped the principle of the watering-can.
> Clothes-pegs litter the window ledge
> And the long ships lie in clover; washing lines
> Shake out white linen over the chalk thanes.
>
> (Mahon, 1993: 12)

Typically assured, 'Glengormley's' opening is ironic, but unstably so: this is a place where, even in asserting that myth and violent history no longer terrify or inspire, the effort of repression is registered. At one level this repression is seen as good – 'Now we are safe from monsters' – but only in an ironic sense;

the speaker is too displaced from the 'we' who belong to the place to be able to assert safety unironically. At another level, however, the poem signals nostalgia for the repressed past, although it does so – in a further layer of irony – in terms which are clearly overblown: 'No saint or hero, / Landing at night from conspiratorial seas, / Brings dangerous tokens to the new era'. The 1930s' Audenesque glamour of flight and conspiracy the language gestures towards collapses in its own too evident vulnerability. 'By / Necessity, if not choice, I live here too', the speaker concludes, as the saints and heroes are dismissed in bleak acceptance of the plight of their 'new era' counterparts, those 'unreconciled in their metaphysical pain' (Riordan, 1984: 171). 'Glengormley' is charged with the tensions implicit in the pre-Civil Rights period even as it articulates the artistic dilemma of meaningful revolt. In 'The Spring Vacation', on the other hand, Mahon rebukes himself more openly, if still with residual irony, for the kind of indifference displayed in 'Glengormley': 'One part of my mind must learn to know its place', and the 'things that happen in the kitchen houses / And echoing backstreets' should 'engage more than my casual interest, / Exact more interest than my casual pity' (Mahon, 1986: 4). Again, the tendency to flight is being severely scrutinised (the poem is in many senses about surveillance), but the terms in which it is done are 'exacting'; indeed, 'flight' is literalised in *Night-Crossing* in the number of poems using bird-imagery, to illustrate escape from, and yet containment within, the world – 'Canadian Pacific', 'Preface to a Love Poem', 'Bird Sanctuary' and 'Four Walks in the Country Near Saint-Brieuc', in which birds 'watch / The shadowy ingress of mankind'[69] (Mahon, 1993: 16).

Mahon is therefore not simply writing 'about' 'his people' as has been claimed (Shields, 1994: 67). If his home city challenges his detachment, and if he is inclined to 'chastise himself' for desiring escape, he is not, in fact, much concerned with articulating the particular claims of a Belfast culture, nor is he 'despite protestations to the contrary . . . as sure of his place as Heaney' (Riordan, 1984: 170; Kendall, 1994: 111). In rebuking escape, the sense of belonging is redefined, and in Mahon's early work, as Tom Paulin puts it, he returns 'again and again . . . to motifs of silence, exile, utter clear-eyed despair, and versions of the artistic life' (Paulin, 1984: 56). This has both its wryly detached, touristic aspect ('I travel light'), and its *poète maudit* dimension, found in an artistic pantheon of the artistic elect which includes Villon, De Quincey, de Nerval, Van Gogh, Flann O'Brien, Malcolm Lowry, Beckett and Hamsun. All are self-elect outcasts, male (apart from Marilyn Monroe in 'Death of a Film Star') and living on the dangerous edge of things, each marked by madness, crime, and alcoholism or drug abuse. The desperate colour of these lives flares against the inevitability of extinction, when we all 'go plunging into the dark forever'. Tourist, goliard and existential sensibilities play with considerable verve above this darkness although, as Edna Longley argues, the 'humanistic warmth' of Mahon's chief predecessor, MacNeice – whose Anglo-Irish presence is matched by that of the modernist Beckett – has 'largely become vestigial or futile' (E. Longley, 1995: 285). Beside these feral figures are domestic ones whose individualism has shrunk to minor rebellion – 'My Wicked Uncle', 'Grandfather', the speaker of 'Day Trip to Donegal', or the foetus of 'An Unborn Child' who, egocentric in the 'metropolis' of the womb, fails to realise the irony of her demand for freedom:

> I want to see, hear, touch and taste
> These things with which I am to be encumbered.
> Perhaps I needn't worry. Give
> Or take a day or two, my days are numbered.
> (Mahon, 1986: 20)

At the root of this is what Mahon detects, from early on, as something rotten not merely in Northern Ireland, but in modern industrial society *per se*. The *sub specie aeternitatis* perspective of, say, 'Consolations of Philosophy', in which modernist alienation and well-made form are held in tension, is at some distance also from the consolatory or elegiac role of poetry as conceived by Longley or Heaney (Mahon, 1986: 47). For all the element of posturing, outsiderness and irreconcilability are not just a pose, and tend to belie Mahon's more accommodating critical statements. Art is necessarily extreme and isolating even if true revolt is now impossible; or, as Paulin puts it, 'poet and rioter share an occult identity . . . Art [he] implies has nothing to do with liberal ideas of decency' (Paulin, 1984: 56–7). Mahon's is thus a poetry of passively anticipated millenarian futures rather than pasts, those in which apocalypse has already occurred, entropic or posthumous scenarios in worlds which are running down, or have already run down. Paulin exaggerates, but illuminatingly; one of the reasons why Mahon's poetry is so interesting is because it anticipates, long before the general collapse of consensus politics in post-war society, a despair at meliorism, and this despite his personal commitment to a Northern writing community. The abandonment he intuits informs the near-religious pathos he can bring to the Protestant sense of loss. Reading this into the situations of other 'morally ambiguous locations' (Cooke, 1973: 10) – Algeria and South Africa as well as the US Deep South – Mahon therefore prefigures Paulin's later more vigorous attempts to disinter the lost positives of Northern Irish history as a rebuke to the present; the effect is to haunt rather than to scarify, however. It would therefore be 'crass', as Haughton warns, to simply attribute Mahon's uneasy poetic tone to his multiple alienation from Protestant Belfast, Catholic Ireland and England (Corcoran, 1992: 92). Rather, he manipulates and cultivates existing stereotypes to underwrite his extreme ambivalence, forging in the process a self-authoring literary myth (unlike Heaney or Longley, who have little confidence in such a process). As his 1970s' essay 'Poetry in Northern Ireland' claims, 'dissociation' between British, Irish and US traditions is enabling, and he similarly 'dissociates' himself from modernist and well-made traditions by incorporating aspects of both (Mahon, 1970: 89–93). In David Wheatley's words, 'Modernist and cosmopolitan in sympathies, yet rooted and traditional in technique, Mahon provides the ideal test case for the water-tightness of the usual dividing lines in Irish poetry.'[70]

The title of 'Protestant poet' is generally more firmly attached to Michael Longley than to any other Northern Irish poet. Yet this label all too often signifies not the subject matter of his poetry (let alone any ideological content) so much as an assumption that Longley is somehow more 'English' than other poets. Declan Kiberd, for example, claims Auden as an influence on Longley as prelude to a bizarre description of Auden's post-1940s' poetry: '[he] was, along with Philip Larkin, the artist of post-imperial England, a land of anticlimax and antimacassars, evoked with a desperately self-deprecating suburban wit . . . Auden's England was an appropriate model for yet another tradition winding down into self-irony'[71] (Kiberd, 1995: 586). Few familiar with the later Auden's blend of Anglican moralism and camp Horatian lyricism would recognise this assessment. 'Influence', in any case, is not Kiberd's real subject; rather, he is attempting to link Northern Irish Protestant-background poets (Mahon gains a partial exemption) to an essential Englishness via a caricatured Auden in order to evade the difficult task of considering their complex relationship with poetry deemed to be more acceptably 'Irish'. Longley was a consistent anti-modernist, and the poems of his first collection, *No Continuing City* (1969), undoubtedly bear out certain clichés concerning 'English' influence. Movement, Georgian, Elizabethan and Metaphysical sources are clear enough, and homages to other poets – Emily Dickinson, Dr Johnson, John Clare – signal the effects of a traditional university syllabus (although pieces based on classical legend – 'Odyssey', 'Nausicaa', 'Narcissus', 'Persephone' are a reminder that Longley took a joint degree in Classics and English).[72] Even the 'gritty particularity [and] unrhetorical utterance' Hobsbaum looked for at Belfast Group meetings is conspicuous by its absence (M. Longley, 1995b: 40). Nevertheless, misrepresentation and, conversely, vague praise, have been such consistent features of Longley criticism that it is important to attempt to define more clearly his distinctive qualities; to relate what has been seen as blandness to the critical edge indicated in the title of the first collection, *No Continuing City* (1969), drawn from a favoured Presbyterian text and indicating awareness of the shaky foundations of the 'continuing city' of Unionist hegemony.

'A Questionnaire for Walter Mitty' would, at first sight, seem to apply to Longley himself. Mitty 'mix[es] with the doers and the triers / Whose dreaming modulates to enterprise', but never quite joins them, remaining self-confining and small-scale (M. Longley, 1991a: 20). This impression, however, would be false; or, rather, requires a redefinition of what we mean by 'enterprise'. Despite the conventional lyricism of pieces like 'Epithalamion', Longley displays from the first certain traits less assimilable to the reading of him as a rural escapist. Indeed, Stan Smith's dismissal of both Longley and Mahon as 'shell-shocked Georgians' is an (unwittingly) revealing tautology in this sense, given that the Georgians (World War I claiming the lives of Edward Thomas,

Symons, Rosenberg, Owen, Brooke) may be defined, with some precision, as being 'shell-shocked' (S. Smith, 1982: 189). Thomas – about whom Smith and Edna Longley have written – is arguably important to Longley not just because he belongs to an English rural tradition, but because in his career a displaced nativism was forced into poetry by war.[73]

In the most elaborate piece in *No Continuing City*, 'The Hebrides', there is an awareness of poetic flights chastened by the return to Belfast and 'streets where shall conclude / My journey back from flux to poise, from poise / To attitude'. Here, 'poise' and 'attitude' hover around the less complimentary 'pose', with criticism invited (M. Longley, 1991a: 42). This, along with the coastal setting, might recall Mahon if it weren't for the poem's conclusion of a 'vantage point too high above the bay'; the speaker, recognising this, descending, learns to 'covet the privilege / Of vertigo'. Longley, then, uses the sea as a place of Odyssean chance encounter, with littoral and island serving as equivalents of a stranded family origin. For Longley's credentials are not Northern at all, and are called into play precisely because of their part-Jewish Englishness, those of a middle-class boy whose formative years were spent in working-class Belfast. These problematise 'ordinariness' and belonging: in Longley's own words, his upbringing meant he had to re-create himself between school and home as a child, negotiating two cultures, 'twice daily. If that's not being conditioned by Ireland I don't know what is'.[74] This wary sense of outsiderness links, in its familial dimension, with the most overt historical point of reference in Longley's poetry, that of World War I, through his father's participation in the battle of the Somme (ironically meshing with an identity – given the iconic nature of the battle as blood-sacrifice in Loyalist myth – which Longley refuses). Similarly, although Peter McDonald fails to sufficiently stress Longley's non-Ulsterness, he is correct to note that 'There is nothing uniquely "shaky" about Longley's "identity"; instead, Longley is aware of how shaky a concept "identity" is in poetry' (McDonald, 1997: 121).

Like Mahon, then, Longley is a poet aware of his situation not as an 'Ulster' poet in any regional sense, nor as an 'Irish' poet either, but as one who draws on a diverse melange of Irish, British and American formalist models of poetry. More than this, however, he bears out Mahon's claim that 'there was this tremendous interest in [Belfast] in writing poems about particular people and dedicating poems to people, thinking in terms of people rather than abstract groups. This has been our way of talking about politics' (Cooke, 1973: 10). The lack of a 'continuing city' is not tackled by assembling an artistic pantheon in Longley so much as through an eclectic, domesticated, inclusive grouping. *No Continuing City*'s literariness, that is, extends to poems addressed to, or about, an extraordinary range of artists, among them Derek Mahon, Philip Hobsbaum, Solly Lipsitz, Colin Middleton, Eavan Boland, Seamus Heaney, John Harvey and Harry Chambers. The names are exemplary but homely, and point to Longley's tendency to lament the rupture of proper distinctions between public and personal realms, the despoliation of the domestic sphere by violence. The plethora of references is not name-dropping (although it may betray some cultural unease); rather, given the celebratory but insecure tone of many pieces, it reveals Longley's anti-aggrandising stance and commitment to exchange. This has an important literary consequence, since if any one poet embodies the Group's coterie tendency to swap ideas, titles, phrases, verse forms and so on, it is Longley. When Michael Allen notes, 'One senses a great deal of influence and counter-influence between [Longley and Mahon]', he is only hinting at the extent of this and a catalytic role which clearly corresponds to Longley's job as an Arts Council officer.[75] This can be seen most obviously in Paulin's use of the last lines of 'Wounds' in 'Under the Eyes', but 'The Centaurs' suggests Muldoon's poem of the same name, while 'Gathering Mushrooms' links Plath, Mahon's 'A Disused Shed in Co. Wexford' and Muldoon's *Quoof* in a complex intertextual trail. 'Freemartin', described as 'a heifer whose hormones have been overwhelmed in the womb . . . born sterile and, sometimes, sexually malformed' reads very much like a blueprint for another Muldoon collection, *Mules*.[76]

This strategic unassertiveness points to another aspect of Longley's unique role, namely his implicit questioning of a dominant masculinist ethos. An example is the uncollected 'Seahorses', published in 1969:

> The eggs are incubated
> By the male of the species,
> Heraldic the horse's head
> Though his body convulses
> Pumping into the sea sons
> And daughters – his stomach's
> Hundred tiny versions –
> Their death a dignified drift
> And a slow coming to light
> On the shore – an ideal gift
> Or dropped off a charm bracelet.[77]

Only Longley, arguably, would have risked this conceit, with the unsettled 'or' in its final line. More typical is the gentle but grotesque humour with which Longley concerns himself with the issues of paternity and authority, a concern literalised in 'In Memoriam' in the image of his father's testicle sliced by shrapnel:

> That instant I, your most unlikely son,
> In No Man's Land was surely left for dead,
> Blotted out from your far horizon.
> As your voice now is locked inside my head,
> I yet was held secure, waiting my turn.
>   (M. Longley, 1991a: 48)

Autobiographical fact is made to suggest that, for Longley, phallic potency, begetting, existence itself, are chancy, freakish, even risible things. Here, perhaps, is one source for the humility and humour of the poetry.

'The golden half-door': 'Nightwalker', tradition and modernity

Nightwalker and Other Poems – bizarrely hailed recently as 'nothing less than a revivification of contemporary Irish poetry' – lost Kinsella his mainstream audience, in Ireland and abroad, and consigned him to the status of a respected but little understood writer until the 1980s (Jackson, 1995: 13; John, 1996: 97–8). This fall from grace was, in Kinsella's eyes, one which had been pre-pared for in the earlier poetry and was necessary given the fallenness of Irish society, its meretricious rapacity and cultural loss of nerve; and both this descent and his own, in critical esteem as well as in the inner descent into the self the book initiates, are figured in the image of 'falling' which dominates the poetry of the early 1970s. Nevertheless, although Kinsella embodies the discontinuity he finds in a violent Irish history within his work in experimental form, *Nightwalker* shows a continuity from the earlier collections (it is in *Notes for the Land of the Dead* (1973) that the full impact of Pound and William Carlos Williams is registered).[78] Paradoxically, for Kinsella, the only way to do justice to the matter of Ireland he now turned to – myth, family, history, race – was via US poetics and a series of 'singing masters' which included Teilhard de Chardin, Diderot, Mahler, John Scotus Eriugena and, above all, Jung. The causes for change, then, lie in modernisation's intensification of the contra-dictions within Irish culture; asserting an Irish identity involves, ironically, the importing of technique and models in a manner analogous to the import of multinational capital attacked in 'Nightwalker's' most famously splenetic passage:

> Robed in spattered iron she stands
> At the harbour mouth, Productive Investment,
> And beckons the nations through our gold half-door:
> Lend me your wealth, your cunning and your drive,
> Your arrogant refuse. Let my people serve them
> Holy water in our new hotels,
> While native businessmen and managers
> Drift with them chatting over to the window
> To show them our growing city, give them a feeling
> Of what is possible; our labour pool,
> The tax concessions to foreign capital,
> How to get a nice estate though German.
> Even collect some of our better young artists.[79]
>
> (Kinsella, 1996: 77)

As Kinsella explained, the forms of his new poetry were the inevitable conse-quence of a feeling of the limitations of existing Irish poetry and of his contact with US poetry, precipitated by his leaving his Civil Service job to take a post at Carbondale University in Illinois in 1965 ('Nightwalker', set in Dublin on the eve of departure, was written after his arrival there). It shares the pes-simistic hesitancy of his 1966 Modern Languages Association lecture 'The Irish

Writer' (published in 1967). What is interesting, as O'Toole has noted, is the location of the rift in sensibility in language loss rather than in social change, in a line of descent from Irish Ireland (O'Toole, 1988: 15). The opening question posed by 'The Irish Writer' is thus that of the choice of indigenous or imposed languages; though English is 'native' to him, and Kinsella considers including as 'colleagues' fellow-writers in Irish, this has to be rejected because Irish is 'a dead or dying language'; praising Irish poetry he is forced to 'recognise simultaneously [the] great inheritance and [the] great loss' it embodies. Within English-language Irish poetry, which has no tradition, Kinsella finds himself radically isolated: 'So I begin again, and look for the past in myself' (Kinsella, 1967: 9–11). The transposition of the question of cultural solidarity to the past and the self reinforces a sense of weakness of the Irish poetic tradition in English and, beyond it, the 'great cultural blur' of an alien world. Loss outweighs inheritance: 'a full contact with the old tradition', between the 'two entities' of contemporary Irish writing in English and the lost Irish past, 'is, I believe, impossible', the outcome being a more radical isolation (Kinsella, 1967: 10). In a manner confirming Martin's 'inherited dissent' argument (Martin, 1965), Kinsella cites Joyce as the one relevant Irish model for dealing with the conditions imposed on the artist by modernity, notably in his substitution of the city for land as a central term in Irish literature. Joyce, then, becomes 'the true father' to the modern Irish writer, the one who 'makes up all the arrears at once', 'perhaps' standing for 'the Irish tradition . . . as healed – or healing – from its mutilation' (Kinsella, 1967: 14). The language of swift overcoming of 'arrears' resembles that of Montague's claim for overcoming backwardness 'without strain', and the contradiction is evident; even as Kinsella admits the 'diagrammatic' quality of his argument, and denies the value of the 'mere continuity of a tradition' (reflecting the tentativeness of 'perhaps' and 'or'), his definition of a modern Irish poetry seems to hover above an urbanised variant of Corkeryan essentialism, and to rely on the recruiting of Joyce to a unitary ('the') Irish literary tradition.

These contradictory strains are evident in 'Nightwalker' itself. Read against the three variants on 'The Irish Writer' which Kinsella produced between 1967 and 1973, however, the poem can be seen to chart a moment of wavering, the point at which the 'perhaps' and 'or' of his 1966 speech are annulled (Garratt, 1989: 169–71). That is, the variants on the argument show a movement towards the claim that the 'two entities' of contemporary and past Irish writing *can* be joined across the gap of language and cultural loss, and that this can be done by understanding the Irish situation as exemplary. A modern writer, Kinsella had argued in 1966, cannot ever be in all traditions at once, and is thus perforce 'the inheritor of a gapped, discontinuous, polyglot tradition', whether Irish or any other nationality (Kinsella, 1967: 15). Under these circumstances, 'any tradition will do if the function of tradition is to link us, living, with the significant past . . . This is done as well by a broken tradition as a whole one. I am certain that a great part of the significance of my own past, as I try to write my poetry, is that that past *is* mutilated' (Kinsella, 1967: 15). Rejecting 'a' national tradition as *per se* enabling, the Irish experience of discontinuity is made exemplary and the door is left open for the rehabilitation of 'the' national tradition at the level of personal experience in a revised version of the essay published in 1970.[80] It is between these points that Kinsella's attempt to reach back to Gaelic poetry and to explore his own past in experimental modernist form takes shape. From 1967 – that is, in tandem with the *Nightwalker* poems – Kinsella was translating the Old Irish epic *The Táin* (1969), which he rendered in a mixture of prose and modernist verse. As Declan Kiberd has noted, Kinsella's translations attempt to bridge the rift between traditions, and it was through these, arguably, that he managed to hold a different audience (Kiberd, 1995: 587).[81] 'The Divided Mind', an essay of 1973, and the further translations for *An Duanaire* (1980) mark stages in this process of explicit retrieval. The introduction to his *New Oxford Book of Irish Verse* reveals that what Kinsella felt to be at stake was belief in a unitary tradition: 'It should be clear that the . . . tradition is a matter of two major bodies of poetry asking to be understood together as functions of a shared and painful history' (Kinsella, 1986: xxviii). Arguably, then, modernist form is embraced in *Nightwalker* not simply because its modernity, in some mimetic way, will do more justice to the heterogeneity of Lemassian Ireland; it is also because in Kinsella's reading of modernism – as prioritising solitary achievement, rootlessness, fragmentariness and alienation – it appears to accord with the 'essential' Irish condition. His development, that is, reflects an almost Adornoesque sense of the modernist work of art as the sole refuge of the human spirit in the depleted life-world of late capitalism, surviving on terms which ironically curtail its social dimension, and according with a belief that the present era denies a social function to the artist.

Like 'Downstream', 'Nightwalker' follows a nocturnal journey, in which the 'nightwalker' walks from his home to the Dublin suburb of Dun Laoghaire and back again. The gothic announces itself early – 'Monsters of ivy squat in lunar glare' – and, in the original form of the poem, the creation of the moon is imagined, being torn from the earth in 'jets of blood / Petrified in terror, jetted screams' (Kinsella, 1996: 76; 1973b, 86). Distaste for the modern world, symbolised by television and the Apollo moonshots, is the dominant note: the nightwalker's fellow-citizens are observed 'slumped' in the corners of their living rooms, 'Faintly luminous, like grubs'. The poem is at one level a belated Irish version of *The Waste Land*, Eliotic and elitist in its judgement on modernity and the culture industry, with Dublin as a necropolis; thus, the intensity of the references to the sterility of modern life increases through the poem, human chaos contrasting with the order of the night sky. Yet as a Dublin inhabitant himself, the speaker shares its population's insectile existence of waking, eating, commuting, working, passively serving and consuming, in a society founded on violence run by the 'Dragon old men' who dominate Irish politics (Kinsella, 1996: 78). The infection of even the heavens by such violence is figured in an allegory which closes the first of the poem's five sections, as the 'nightwalker' visualises a new constellation in the night sky: 'The Wedding Group: / The Groom, the Best Man, the Fox and their three ladies' (Kinsella, 1996: 78). This plays out a sordid tale of comradely betrayal during the Civil War, and presents an allegory of Irish politics (and cultural politics, since Yeats appears as 'the Player King') after Independence. McCormack reads this as a parable which extends to the rise of Charles Haughey (never named in the poem) in the 1960s as representative of the Republic's new technocracy; Haughey appears on horseback in the second section of the poem 'in hunting pinks' and ascends into the night sky as the new Foxhunter constellation (that is, he represents a further decline from the tragic formation of the state as destroyer of the legacy of de Valera, the 'Fox' of the allegory) (McCormack, 1987: 64). Set against this, as the nightwalker reaches Dun Laoghaire and Joyce's martello tower, is an invocation of the 'Watcher in the tower', 'Father of Authors!' Interspersed with newspaper headlines and memories of school history lessons, this section of the poem partially escapes from the claustrophobic selfhood of part one. In part three, having arrived home, the nightwalker encounters his wife and his love for her. Wife and moon are presented as aspects of the eternal feminine whose Jungian interpretations Kinsella was exploring at the time. Love is a form of trial, as in the earlier poetry, an openness to change which is opposed to the fixities and servilities of Irish life ('A medium in which, from change to change, / Understanding may be gathered') (Kinsella, 1996: 83). But the moon has been sullied by the most extravagant of modern technologies and the final lines find the nightwalker removed, literally, like one of the Apollo astronauts, to the moon. Modern technology has reduced not only human society but the moon, traditional inspiration for the poet, to a mere site of conquest. The nightwalker finds himself looking back, from the 'true desert' of 'the Sea of Disappointment' in which the Apollo 11 mission was scheduled to touch down the following year (the Apollo moonshots, arguably, are what the human 'grubs' are watching on television at the outset of the poem).[82] The alienation from society and self, with which the poem began, can go no further.

'Nightwalker's' ending is intended to underline the fact that it can only be read in a limited sense as a discursive realist-symbolist poem. Allegory, in fact, is its structuring principle, foregrounded in the constellation passage to alert the reader to its general presence, and its use is as crucial to Kinsella's later work as its tentatively 'open' poetics. In particular, it signals a rejection of the realist-symbolist methods of using poetic language, and so a politics rather more subtle than that behind the willing into existence of a unitary literary tradition. Allegory is related to Kinsella's interest, from the beginning, in order and structures, and their relationship to flux or chaos. The psychic delving of 'Nightwalker' and what follows forms a search for order without presupposing or imposing it on the material of experience except insofar as 'the obsession with fact, with specific individual data, wouldn't seem to me to make much sense unless it had some allegorical drive behind it. Experience by itself, however significant, won't do' (Haffenden, 1981: 104). This is a rejection of an empiricist poetics for one concerned with the phenomenology of perception. The 'allegorical', sought for without moral or religious associations, allows for the coexistence of several layers of meaning.[83] McCormack argues that modernisation in the Republic, as well as the state's subsumption within the larger 'economic community' of the EEC and violence in the North, impelled a political-allegorical turn in Kinsella's poetry, one at odds with the compensatory communitarian symbols and elegiac modes resorted to by most Irish writers of the time, with their reliance on 'ever-available pastoral images of the past'. This, in turn, had implications for the very medium of writing, as managerial jargon, advertising idioms and the discourse of an inauthentic politics brought about 'a fundamental alteration of the relationship between language and society which informs (on) Kinsella's writing' (McCormack, 1987: 67).

At one level this reading of Kinsella can be taken to suggest a modernist refurbishing of the identitarian and essentialist concept of the Irish tradition (and, it could be argued, some of McCormack's undoubtedly brilliant formulations contain their own (unstated) prelapsarian idealist assumptions). Kinsella's own critical writings (as finally systematised in *The Dual Tradition* and in his construction of a canon, in English as well as Irish) confirm O'Toole's criticism; the progress from 'The Irish Writer' to its later versions is one of simplification. Yet the poetry itself stands (or, rather, refuses to 'stand'), in its allegorical, 'open' procedures, in opposition to the critical positions adopted. It is possible, then, to see the criticism as making space for a poetry which, in ideological and formal senses, is far more complex and contradictory. The lack of a match between the two has led to notable misinterpretation, and the charges of 'obscurity' and old-style nationalism have been made from critics inside and outside the Republic. Both are often made by the same critics without considering the problem involved; namely, of objecting to poetry both for being too obscure and for not being obscure – or 'oblique' – enough (the question of what such a contradiction signifies is therefore never raised). Less well known, because of the lack of awareness of the experimental strain in Irish poetry, is the response to Kinsella by younger modernist poets in the late 1960s. Here another misinterpretation can be discerned, since the attitude of the New Writers' Press poets to Kinsella was also largely negative, though for different reasons; namely, because it was felt that Kinsella's immersion in issues of identity disqualified him from consideration as a modernist in the fullest sense.

New Writers' Press, *The Lace Curtain* and Geoffrey Squires

The number of journals multiplied in the late 1960s. Augustine Martin had written in 1965 of 'five literary magazines flourishing' whereas 'ten years ago

. . . there was no more than one'; by the late 1960s a plethora had emerged, including James Liddy's *Arena*, Hayden Murphy's *The Holy Door* and *Poetry Broadsheet* (which published concrete poetry, among other experimental contemporary material), the *Irish University Review*, re-energised under the editorship of Lorna Reynolds, and the reborn *Poetry Review* edited by John Jordan (Martin, 1965: 17; Roche, 1996: 71–81). It was, however, still difficult for poets to be published in Ireland in book form, and remained so until the early 1970s, when Gallery Press supplemented Dolmen. Little critical attention has been paid to this ferment of activity in the Republic, and even less to the neo-modernist revival based on poets attached to, or published by, the New Writers' Press, founded in 1967 by Irene and Michael Smith and Trevor Joyce.[84] Yet one issue raised sharply by the Northern poets, in their anti-modernist aspect, is that of this almost diametrically opposed response in the Republic to the strains of modernisation. If the Belfast poets represent the recrudescence of the anti-modernism of Yeats, Hewitt and MacNeice, it is possible to view the group(s) in the South as not so much an opposed response as an equivalent but differently aligned response to the inert 'centre' of Irish poetry – the 'torn halves' of a whole poetic which, in Adorno's phrase, 'do not add up'. Unlike Kinsella and Watters, the NWP poets claimed conscious allegiance with the 1930s' modernists, and the press was founded for the express purpose of publishing the works of Devlin and Coffey. But NWP was catholic in its tastes and soon became an outlet for young poets turned away by Dolmen or British publishers, such as Hutchinson, O'Grady, Durcan and Hartnett, as well as non-Irish poets (including the first European edition of Borges's poetry) (Joyce, 1995: 276). Given what he saw as a dearth of suitably risk-taking young poets in the Republic at the time, Joyce soon joined Smith in writing poetry himself, and it was in its commitment to reviving experimental writing that NWP's chief significance lies.[85] Encouraged by their success, in 1969 Smith and Joyce launched the *Lace Curtain* journal.[86]

Lace Curtain's primary function as NWP's house journal was to publish a wide range of poetry and polemicise against the generality of Irish poetry. In doing so it staked out a distinctive and positive critical position, articulated in Smith's editorials (and elaborated in a long, rather rambling essay, 'Irish Poetry Since Yeats: Notes Towards a Corrected History', published in the *Denver Quarterly* in 1971). Perhaps the crucial critical text carried by the journal, however, was Beckett's essay 'Recent Irish Poetry' of 1934, which *Lace Curtain* republished for the first time in its fourth issue in 1971. Beckett's essay contained blistering attacks on Irish mode poetry which have been cited extensively by cultural and literary critics ever since ('They are the antiquarians, delivering with the altitudinous complacency of the Victorian Gael the Ossianic goods.'). But, of most interest to the NWP poets, were comments with more restricted critical currency which defined the choice for Irish poets as lying between such 'goods' and a recognition 'of the new thing that has happened . . . namely the breakdown of the object, whether current, historical, mythical or spook . . . [a]

rupture of the lines of communication' between subject and object.[87] The *Lace Curtain*'s combativity and exceptionally wide-ranging commitment to translation and an international avant-garde community (*inter alia* of Bachman, Benn, Vallejo, Desnos, Herauld, Machado and Trakl) stemmed from a belief that the modernist crisis of perception had not disappeared; that, if anything, it was now even more acute than it had been in 1934 (attacking the contents of genteel *Dublin Magazine*, James Hogan noted in the *Lace Curtain*'s first issue that 'The sonnet and / or the blue tit cannot pass water . . . in a world where . . . 50% of dairy milk, including probably the dairymaid, is radioactive').[88] It was, therefore, in rather more than merely the spirit of opposition to *The Dublin Magazine*, or of inherited dissent, that the journal's editors strove for a renewal of modernist experiment which seemed to have disappeared.

Smith's acceptance of Kavanagh as well as Beckett indicates his somewhat vaguely defined aesthetic. On the one hand his elision of the differences between the 1930s' modernists (outlined in Chapter 1) allowed him to establish them as an alternative Irish poetic tradition and progenitors of the NWP poets in a way which overlooked the differences between the 1930s' poets themselves and his contemporaries. On the other, a rather manichaean view of contemporary Irish poetry meant that he could not acknowledge the value of work of those poets with a formalist background who, like Kinsella and Mahon, were nevertheless influenced by modernism. The fact that both Kinsella and Mahon appeared in *The Lace Curtain*, however, shows that the vagueness of position also made for an openness which served the journal well; judgements based on individualism and sincerity in poetry rather than a deeper understanding of 'the rupture of the lines of communication' worked for inclusivity. Arguably without such vagueness the journal (and the press) would not have flourished even for as long as they did. As Alex Davis has claimed, Smith's aesthetic mediated the modernisation process in a contradictory fashion. His polemical editorials both pilloried cultural Nationalism and '[refracted] on the level of poetics Lemassian expansionist economics (though not Lemassian nationalism)'.[89] It was, therefore, the sheer heterogeneity of the material presented by *The Lace Curtain* and NWP which, more effectively than Smith's polemics, made the point that identity and the backward look did not necessarily define Irish poetry. Like other poets, whom it fostered, NWP revealed the fissiparous and pluralist responses to modernisation, as new poetic constituencies emerged in the late 1960s in the Republic within which modernisation represented something very different than it did for the older poets with their totalising visions, as it did again for Northern Irish poets.

The point can be made by looking briefly at the work of Geoffrey Squires, a poet who was to be actively involved in the debates on the representation of the Troubles in poetry in the early 1970s. Squires's poetry may usefully be examined here as an example of an adaptation of a radical US modernist poetic to Irish conditions which was rather more successful than the early poetry of Joyce or Smith themselves.[90] Squires's first collection, *Drowned Stones*, was published by NWP in 1975.[91] Organised in six sections, it bears the marks of a close study of Black Mountain poetics, and in particular of Charles Olson's theories of 'open form' or 'composition by field' advanced in his 1950 essay, 'Projective Verse'. For Olson, the modernist subject–object breakdown highlighted by Beckett (as also by Zukovsky in his 'Objectivists' issue of *Poetry* in 1930), was to be tackled by the poet's taking the stance of an object among other objects, rather than imposing him/herself upon the poem's content or materials. The intention was that the work would thereby have 'a seriousness sufficient to cause the thing he makes to try to take its place alongside the things of nature' (Preminger and Brogan, 1993: 977). In *Drowned Stones* these techniques, which include the extensive use of other non-poetic texts and found materials, are deployed to reduce the centrality of the lyric subject which, if not totally dissolved, finds itself displaced as the governing centre of the sequence. The 'speaker' of even those poems which draw on biographical material offers a subjectivity which is deliberately unassertive and displaced. This is signalled in the bracketing of the opening lines in which the 'I' of part one is initially presented in the third person and introduced by a conjunction:

(And all the trouble to learn him, the
strangeness of another, his turnings)

it was good, it was as it should be, we lived
two miles from the town, quite isolated, no
car

didn't get the electric till 1953 and only got
it then because my mother had the good sense to give
the engineer a cup of tea

well he said we might as well take it up the
hill when we're at it

(Squires, 1975: 9)

Here, as Davis puts it, 'The lyric I is, if not dissolved, then displaced as a governing centre of the sequence, such defamiliarisation functioning as the formal correlative of the poem's resistance to the disembodied Cartesian subject' (Goodby and Scully, 1999: 103). The sense of childhood oneness with home is briefly and unsentimentally recalled ('it was as it should be') in a way which indicates its innate conservatism, while location is evoked in a relational sense – distance from town, electricity – and without recourse to evocative proper names. History and modernity are present in the rural electrification programme, but the sense of commentating on event, and of the anecdote in which it is presented, is cut across by the calculated inconsequentiality of the narration and a refusal to draw conclusions or symbolic resonances. The rest of the first section offers a series of disjointed reflections on the subject's place of origin in rural Co. Donegal, a landscape viewed from the point of view of an adult self displaced from a once intimately known locale. Squires accords with William Carlos Williams in fidelity to the sniffing out of particulars by a self always uneasy with its own presence:

> a layer of white sand
> on the bottom, some seaplants
> growing on ledges, where
> they ought to be
> forget how I got here
> (Squires, 1975: 38)

Alongside these minimalist but insistent, faintly charged imagistic fragments, Squires also mixes his other texts: anecdotes, unfinished brief stories, snatches of myth, moving in the other sections of the poem across different landscapes – Iran, France, the USA – and quoting, as it advances, from non-poetic texts which include John Lilly's *Programming and Metaprogramming in the Human Biocomputer* and Lama Anagarika Govinda's *The Way of the White Cloud*. This has the effect of foregrounding one of the poem's chief concerns: that of 'a kind of permanent schizoid dissociation between two realms of reality', in John Lilly's phrase (Squires, 1975: 48). The first realm is 'the public, quantifiable and therefore minimally intelligible but universally legitimate language of official positivism'; the second 'is the relativistic domain of multiple, aesthetic, rich, and morally directed private phenomenologies'. In such a society the 'psychic premium would be on personalities that were flexible, unserious, not characterised towards integration of their being and perceptions, able to withstand a kaleidoscope of relativism by reducing most of it to play'. Such material stresses the multiple nature of the reality observed in the poem, and our partial, shifting knowledge of the object world, perception of that world being relative to the subject's internal, private phenomenology. Rather than existing independently of the human observer, the universe thus has moral and aesthetic significance only in relation to that interior, observing subjectivity. Landscapes for Squires are therefore something the 'I' is outside of, providing sites in which consciousness can become self-consciousness, allowing the mind to reflect on its own landscape. One of the most remarkable aspects of *Drowned Stones*, then, is its solution to the problem of regional/national identity, the way in which it subordinates landscape to the self through, paradoxically, the surrendering of the claims of the 'lyric interference of the individual as ego', in Olson's words (Olson, 1997: 247). In this sense it goes beyond the localism not only of Williams's Paterson and Olson's Gloucester, but – although this has hardly been registered critically – the treatment of territory by Montague, Heaney and so many other Irish poets.

Notes

1 As a poet who emerged in the 1950s, Montague saw in modernisation the chance of a unique contract with modernity and an Irish future 'balanced between the

pastoral and the atomic age', echoing claims he had made thirteen years before in the essay 'Outward Bound' in which the Irishman abroad was described as being 'in a unique position: European but free from the taint of imperialism or racial-prejudice he has a privileged post of observation' (Montague, 1960: 17).

2 False dawns had been heralded before: thus in *Envoy*, in January 1950, similar claims to newly independent poetic identity are asserted along with the opinion that young Irish poets were now taking their nationality more for granted and should 'not [feel] committed to a defence of the "Irishness" of the work' they were reviewing. See Foreword: Mid-Way, *Envoy*, 1:2 (January 1950), 8.

3 The *Miscellany*'s sense of succession is confirmed by a review by John Jordan heralding 'a poetic generation to succeed that of Valentin Iremonger' (Kinsella and Montague, 1962: 116).

4 This had an academic and critical dimension; most poets were aware of critical activity, through the activities of critics such as Donald Davie and Denis Donoghue in Ireland itself, and through their own involvement with academia (the US poet-critics were clearly models for Montague, for example, who had been taught by Blackmur, Ransom and Jarrell in the US in the 1950s, and became a lecturer at UCC in 1973). Mutual regard is reflected in Robin Skelton's essay in *Critical Quarterly* and his *Six Irish Poets* (both 1962) and confirmed in M. L. Rosenthal's inclusion of a section on Irish poetry in *The New Poetry* in 1967, demonstrating Irish reincorporation within the international academic mainstream (Kinsella's *The Pen Shop* (1997) is dedicated to Rosenthal's memory).

5 Kinsella was identified as the leading figure, both abroad and in Ireland; *Another September* (1958) was a British Poetry Book Society Choice, an award he also won in 1960. This was in stark contrast to the lack of non-Irish interest Clarke had lamented in *The Bell* only a decade before, although the lesser honour of a PBS Recommendation for *Nightwalker* in 1968 reflects the extent to which British (and Irish) critics felt that collection to be a disappointment. The *Miscellany* poets' reputations were consolidated in the early 1960s, with Montague's *Poisoned Lands* (1961), Kinsella's *Downstream* (1962) and Murphy's *Sailing to an Island* (1963).

6 The nuclear family became the norm, while use of family planning – in defiance of a papal Encyclical of 1967 – meant shrinking family sizes. Particularly notice-able was the rejuvenation of the population; 'Much was made of the fact (by 1980) that half of the population was . . . under the age of twenty-five' (Gibbons, 1996: 83).

7 In 1965 Lemass became the first Taoiseach to visit Northern Ireland. At this stage, it appeared that his claim that the 'rising tide' of prosperity which would 'lift all boats' held the promise of a fully modern Irish state which would, in turn, lead to the ending of Partition. The naivety of discounting Loyalist ideology was all too apparent; as O'Halloran has argued, the rapprochement symbolised by the famous meeting between O'Neill and Lemass 'involved no proper reassessment of nation-alist attitudes' (or, it might be added, of Unionist ones). It thus avoided the ques-tion of whether the prolonged sacrifices made for self-sufficiency had been justified (O'Halloran, 1987: xviii).

8 A tendency to exaggerate the extent to which Irish Ireland ideology had been over-thrown began early: in 1960 Kavanagh claimed 'The sad notion that Ireland is a spiritual entity is now only propagated by the BBC in England and in the Bronx and in the departments of literature at Princeton, Yale, Harvard and New York Universities' (Kavanagh, 1960: 38).

9 At the beginning of the 1960s the Republic was indubitably a relatively well-developed, capitalist society according to all socio-economic indices, as Liam

Kennedy has shown (L. Kennedy, 1996; Ruane and Todd, 1996). It remained, though, a thoroughly peripheralised economy (Breathnach, 1988).

10 Another reason was a 'remarkable social homogeneity which could contain and resolve . . . conflict without recourse to violence' (F. Tobin, 1984: 154).

11 A Bill allowing the release of proscribed books after twelve years on the banned list was passed in 1967; this freed over 5,000 titles at a stroke.

12 Poets were involved in such developments; Montague, for example, was a founder of Claddagh records in 1960, one of the most important traditional music labels, while Patrick Galvin and James Simmons both recorded LPs. The link between them and the leading composer of his generation – Seán Ó Riada – was very strong.

13 Although there is no space here to attempt an account of 'revisionism', I remark the emergence of a group of historians whose work challenged the dominant Nationalist narratives of Irish history, and that it was significantly enabled by the more critical intellectual climate created by economic reform. See, for an account of some of the debates involved, Boyce and O'Day, 1996, and Ciaran Brady (ed.), *Interpreting Irish History: The Debate on Historical Revisionism* (Dublin, Irish Academic Press, 1994).

14 The basic paradigms include: the 'traumatic' (Irish history as viciously circular and disaster-ridden), to the standard Western model (Hegelian progress through conflict) and local variants, such as the 'Two Nations' theory (in which two distinct cultures co-existed, and could continue to co-exist, in Ireland) and the 'One Nation' theory (in which there was one distinct, Gaelic-Catholic culture which Protestants would eventually join). More radical anti-identitarian positions were, at this stage, hardly to be discerned. In this, as later critics have argued, the 'Two Nations' theory, though preferable to that of 'One Nation', would itself be seen as reinforcing the dubious notion of essential (however mutually respectful) identities.

15 Patrick Galvin, an exact contemporary of Cronin, worked and lived variously in London, Norfolk, Belfast and Spain; similarly, Desmond O'Grady, who had begun a correspondence with Ezra Pound in late 1956 and met and worked with him from 1958, was, by the end of the 1950s, at the centre of a briefly flourishing expatriate poetry scene in Rome (he would later live and work in Greece and Egypt, but was also responsible for establishing a literary festival in Kinsale in the 1960s). Pearse Hutchinson moved to Switzerland in 1951 and lived in Spain for most of the 1960s.

16 'Inherited Dissent: The Dilemma of the Irish Writer' notes the shakiness of the renewal claimed in the *Miscellany* and calls for broader intellectual renewal:

> It has become firmly established in the majority of literate minds that Ireland is a backward, insanitary, inert, despairing country; a people priest-ridden and superstitious, which despises its artists and intellectuals . . . a people soaked in dreams and booze, fixated backwards on the events of Easter week, 1916 . . . helpless in the face of emigration, ignorant of the facts of life, overcome with a Jansenistic fear of sex and the body, bemused with the opium of past splendours – yet in spite of it all, a people friendly, poetic, with a certain gentle unreliable charm. This set of traits cannot be ascribed to the pages of any one writer: they are the cumulative end-product of half a century of writing which was by turns, hostile, embittered and penetrating. Whatever the contemporary social veracity of these portrayals, I do not think that . . . the picture holds good for to-day. (Martin, 1965: 10).

17 See T. Brown, The Counter Revival: Provincialism and Censorship 1930–65, in S. Deane (ed.) 1991: 93: 'In a submerged population, where the provincial mind

senses its own social impotence, definitions of selfhood must perforce involve private feeling, romantic imagination and defeat. A lyric form is an aesthetic acquiescence in the general sense of powerlessness.'

18 See, for example, 'My Last Conversation With Denis Devlin 1959' (O'Grady, 1996: 29).

19 The same 'buckleppin' performance of a limiting and demeaning identity can be seen in Brendan Kennelly's very similar 'Moloney' sequence of the same period.

20 Although the editors of Galvin's poetry make claims for the 'linguistic richness' of his Cork background, what is striking about Galvin's best work in *Heart of Grace* (1959) and *Christ in London* (1960) is its unadorned, spare, ballad-influenced style. In this, Galvin is perhaps truer to his sources that his editors know; his mythicisation of Cork is marked (and can be strikingly effective), but it is the city's febrile cosmopolitanism and Galvin's outsider status rather than 'the Gaelic element . . . permeating all' which best explain his forceful originality. As Galvin himself claimed, 'the establishment was unable to conceive of an urban poet' when he began writing. Hewitt's attack – he singled out 'My Little Red Knife' in a review of *Heart of Grace* as 'particularly revolting' – has more to do with the frankness of Galvin's presentation of sexuality. The poem is representative of his style, and uses a traditional ballad subject animated by variations in line length and metre:

> With my little red knife
> I made her weep
> With my little red knife
> I loved her
> And the wine was heavy in her mouth
> The morning air stood up to shout
> But there wasn't a living soul about
> To see my little red knife. (Galvin, 1996: 111)

The rejection of such raw energies by Hewitt reveals a Northern suspicion of glamorising rebellion, but also the prim introversion of much Irish criticism of the time. See J. Hewitt, *Threshold*, 2:2 (Summer 1958), 73.

21 Richard Kells's review of *Christ in London* underlines the difference between poets in Northern Ireland and the Republic at this time, speaking as it does of 'a collection of ballads that swarms with facile images of killing, bleeding, weeping and so on: facile because they are based on formulae instead of being unique creations'. Kells fails to grasp the extent to which the genre of the ballad is formulaic by definition, and its importance to Galvin as a mode of access to oral tradition and folk culture via such formulae. See R. Kells, *Threshold*, 4:1 (Spring/Summer 1960), 66.

22 This tendency in Kinsella has been noted by Thomas Kilroy: 'Our papish line is dark, angular, blood-boltered. A literature of estrangement, apostasy. Its characteristic subject-matter is repression, sexual and intellectual'. T. Kilroy, *Krino*, 5 (Spring 1988), 157.

23 Fred Botting, *Gothic* (London, Routledge, 1996), 39.

24 'A Country Walk' was Kinsella's own contribution to the *Dolmen Miscellany*. Writing on the *Downstream* collection in the *Poetry Book Society Bulletin* he noted of the three longer poems that they

> were written slowly and more or less together. In each case the single simple idea which gave rise to the poem developed . . . for good or ill – into generalisation and allegory. In 'Old Harry' the theme is guilt and retribution . . . 'A Country Walk' begins in petty agitation and ends in creative calm. The

instrument of inner change is the gradual intrusion of the outer world; the final focal moment, where road and river intersect, is one of total awareness of the self in its physical and metaphysical surroundings. The journey in 'Downstream' is more openly 'meaningful' than that in 'A Country Walk', but a similar process of increasing awareness is involved. During the poem events so arrange themselves as to impose on the traveller an emotional acceptance of the reality of death, and the beginning of a possible under-standing. (T. Kinsella, *Poetry Book Society Bulletin*, 34 (September 1962), 1)

25 'Downstream's' phrasing and imagery closely anticipate that of Kinsella's contri-bution to the Yeats centenary conference in Chicago in 1965:

> It was one thing for Yeats to have foreseen such an upheaval [as World War II] as inevitable . . . It is quite another to have participated in the Second Coming itself, however remotely . . . It was, of course, no news that the human mind was an abyss, and that the will, just as much as the imagina-tion, was capable of every evil. But it was something new that creatures out of Hieronymus Bosch should have materialised in the world, formally inflict-ing and enduring suffering beyond all reason, in obedience to a diabolic logic; it is also something new to have had the orderly but insane holocausts imag-ined by Leonardo da Vinci set loose on the earth . . . The coming to reality of these apparently fantastic images is an inner catastrophe: we have opened up another area of ourselves and found something new that horrifies but that, even more intensely, disappoints. The realization of this disappointment seems to me the most important thing for poetry since Yeats. (Kinsella, 1965: 108)

This passage confirms a sense of guilt, and also Kinsella's deeply moral interpreta-tion of the horrors of the war. While the attempt to grapple with such subjects fits wider trends of the time, it is strengthened by a metaphysical absolutism that sees human existence as a struggle between good and evil, with its realism frequently subordinated to symbolism and allegory.

26 Its figures include 'grief chewers', 'the predatory will', aliens 'Breaking princely houses in their jaws . . . chewing at light', and a grub which 'gropes / Back on itself and begins / To eat its own leaf' (Kinsella, 1996: 56, 59, 73, 75).

27 See Calvin Bedient, quoted in Johnston, 1985: 104: 'Ireland's best living poet has brooded himself to pieces'.

28 P. N. Furbank, New Poetry, *The Listener*, 69:1771 (Thursday 7 March 1963), 435.

29 For a definition of 'the coloniser who refuses', see Albert Memmi, *The Colonizer and the Colonized* (London, Earthscan Publications, 1990), 85–110.

30 The last section of the essay, 'Antidote to Poison', describes the society of the 'harsh coast' as more real than Murphy's own: 'these people . . . we loved . . . better than our own relations . . . They were truly Irish, and that is what my brother and I wanted to be. They seemed sharper, freer, more cunning than we were.' By the end of the essay Murphy relates his decision to seek 'the older, earlier pleasure ground in the treeless hills, on the sea's edge . . . [in] Connemara'. The transfigu-ration is framed by recalling the essay's opening, which tells how Murphy once accidentally swallowed a yew berry while playing in the garden and thought he had been poisoned. In the essay the 'truly Irish' appear as 'the antidote which the poisoning in the pleasure ground needed', the corrective to privilege. But the self-destructive impulse is not total; while garden and Anglo-Irishness figure as 'poison', a guilt at origins, they are also idealised in the form of liberal individuals who refuse to be reduced to the oppressive system to which they belong, such as

the grandmother. Murphy explains that his fear of poison began in Ceylon where it 'was very much associated with a sense of guilt [which was] part of the culture, of imperialism. A sense of guilt on the one hand coupled with a tremendous assurance on the other' (Haffenden, 1981: 144). The second sentence emblematises the ambivalence of Murphy's poetry. His grandmother is gradually transfigured as 'mistress of a beautiful disorder' which must be rejected by the homecoming poet because 'the discipline of the garden had died' and because of his understanding of a colonial past which frees him for a more elemental return to Connemara (R. Murphy, 1963: 240).

31 As Crotty notes, 'The sea which confounds all attempts at mastery may be identified, in one of its aspects at least, with the Gaelic Irish to whom the poet feels bound by ties both of affection and blood' (Crotty, 1995: 149).

32 A. Finlayson, The Problem of 'Culture' in Northern Ireland: A Critique of the Cultural Traditions Group, *The Irish Review*, 20 (Winter/Spring 1997), 83. In social terms, if in the either/or paradigm, there are 'many dimensions to his understanding of faded ancestry, poor gentry, plantation and rectory . . . (there are also) many facets to his vision of people of the other culture, those in between the two and those outside both' (Harmon, 1978: 6, 8–9).

33 Written between 1962 and 1967 as a response to a BBC commission, it was published in 1968. Ironies abound in the circumstances of the poem's composition; it was commissioned for the *Sunday Times*, but the date of its appearance there was changed 'because of the Pope's visit to the Holy Land' (Harmon, 1978: 16). Like *The Battle of Aughrim* and other of Murphy's poems it was broadcast on the BBC Third Programme (in August 1964).

34 The scheme of the poem corresponds to different temporal 'moods', as in a drama. Murphy comments that he had initially planned the poem as a descriptive narrative poem, and that the idea of using dramatic monologues was Ted Hughes's.

35 The book is dedicated to Valentin Iremonger and shows an Ireland simultaneously trapped in the past by poverty and repression and uncertainly embracing a modernising present. The locations switch between a Dublin whose historic centre is being razed by developers and a countryside of drunken futility, dying small towns, flea-pits and grubbed-up hedgerows. The book's most impressive story is 'The Cry', an exploration of Montague's dividedness, whose main character, a journalist now working in London, returns to visit to his parents in Northern Ireland. Here he part-witnesses, and then tries to expose, a beating given by the RUC to a local Catholic man. But he is defeated again and again in his investigation by bluff, fear, resignation and passivity on the part of the RUC and local Catholics; the final humiliation comes as he glances down from his bedroom window into the town square to see the town idiot, Joe Doom, holding up a crudely lettered sign which reads 'Nosy Parker Go home'. The story splits aspects of Montague between the liberal Peter and his republican father (J. Montague, *The Death of a Chieftain* (Dublin, Poolbeg Press, 1978), 58–83).

36 A rousingly patriotic film of 1966, *Mise Éire* (with a lush Mahlerian score by O Riada), was broadcast, as was a specially commissioned TV programme on the Fenian rising of 1866 for which Fallon supplied an appropriately romantic ballad, 'The Young Fenians'. Parades, pageants and thanksgiving services culminated in a ceremony outside the GPO in Dublin, with speeches by de Valera and Lemass – the energetic Taoiseach contrasted with the now-blind, frail President – which was televised to the nation. At the same time, relations with Britain were at a new high point; an Anglo-Irish Free Trade Agreement was signed in time for the celebrations.

37 1966 was also the fiftieth anniversary of the Somme, which Loyalists saw as having

sealed their link with Britain in blood in a manner diametrically opposed to Nationalist blood-sacrifice.

38 Charles Gavan Duffy, *Young Ireland – A Fragment of Irish History, 1840–50* (London, 1880), 153.

39 The occasion of Austin Clarke's *Mnemosyne Lay in Dust* (1966) was his mental breakdown in 1919. Its origins lay in the trauma of the Rising and the youthful psychic misery of sexual continence and religious doubt, but the poem's completion and release were enabled by Clarke's new poetic of the 1950s and the climate of the 1960s (revealingly, it was retitled *Loss of Memory* when it was published in the USA and read in the light of Confessional poetry). Its long gestation over half a century makes it a summation of Clarke's life work, impacting and fusing personal and national histories to an extraordinary degree. Eugene Watters's far less well-known, but equally remarkable *The Week-End of Dermot and Grace* was published in 1964, and republished only once, in 1985, as a special issue of *Poetry Ireland Review* (Watters, 1985). Together with 'Nightwalker' it is the main 1960s' attempt to produce an Irish equivalent of *The Waste Land*, but it tempers Eliot's pessimistic elitism with a Joycean emphasis on the cyclical quality of myth, polyphony and verbal energy.

40 J. Keats, *John Keats: The Complete Poems*, John Barnard (ed.), (Harmondsworth, Penguin, 1987), 442, 450.

41 Thus, 'Sooner or later, if one continues to write poetry, the desire grows to write a long poem or sequence, something more expansive than the lyric . . . while novelists have ransacked the details of twentieth-century life . . . poets have limited themselves, like the castrati of the papal choir, to certain complex, asocial tones. The best relationship many of them can manage with society is chiding, chiliastic' (Montague, 1989: 154). The models Montague draws on are given in his Preface to *The Rough Field*: 'Although living in Berkeley introduced me to the debate on open-form from *Paterson*, through Olson, to Duncan, I was equally drawn to rooted poets like MacDiarmid in *A Drunk Man*' (Montague, 1995: 5).

42 The first essay describes – with an ecumenical gesture to 'John Hewitt [who] once called [Tyrone] "the heart land of Ulster" ' – the 'cold mountainous' terrain of his upbringing, and notes the survival into his lifetime of 'a pre-industrial farming pattern [where] the important thing was "neighbourliness" ', and in which 'the seasonal tasks' rather than 'historical [i.e. sectarian] cleavage' dominated everyday life. Most of the rest of the article is taken up with a description of local customs. Montague is interested in 'the secret life of the countryside', the 'memories of a richer, more resonant past, half-regretted, half-feared', eroded since the war by the 'relentless' rate of change: 'The Rough Field has become part of the twentieth century.' It concludes with a caveat – 'one must avoid seeing all this in a haze of Golden Age nostalgia' – and a vision of mechanised farming set against an image of one of the old women who feature commonly in his work as symbols of continuity, folk wisdom and race memory. 'A Primal Gaeltacht' develops further the earlier essay's interest in place and naming, asserting the relevance of *dinnseanchas* theory to the contemporary poet, rephrasing the problem of wresting cultural identity from the decline of the Irish language and, in the case of Garvaghey, its decline into a 'by-passed and dying place'.

43 It is perhaps worth noting that the woodcuts, which contribute so much to the overall effect of the poem, are not included in the *Collected Poems* of 1995, from which I quote here as the most available edition. They are included in the 1990 Bloodaxe edition.

44 As Quinn notes, this silencing of speech is a source of Montague's writing, since 'it was to become the aphasic's alternative mode of communication, and, therefore, a form of expression originating in deprivation and lovelessness' (Quinn links the taunts of the schoolmistress to maternal abandonment and return to Ireland to be reared by his aunt, although whether it was this which began an 'attract[ion] towards female models of love, nurture, fosterage, plenitude, generosity, security' is more debatable) (Quinn, 1989: 27–8).

45 In this sense, the most objected-to parts of the poem are to some extent balanced by a recognition of internal difference. Thus Richard Kearney, interviewing Montague in 1980, pressed him on the fifth section ('The Fault') in which bardic claims are asserted in uncomplicatedly racial terms and where the language is 'sodden with violent implication'. Montague's answers are notably evasive, justifying the passage in terms of the right to write political poetry by reference to Ritsos and Neruda, begging the question of the comparability of Chile, Greece and Northern Ireland, or of whether Neruda and Ritsos themselves indulged the expression of 'race hatred' in their own work. While Montague is not, of course, endorsing 'race hatred' *per se*, he is, as Kearney attempts to point out, granting it some justification (Hederman and Kearney, 1982: 724–5).

46 Similarly, popular culture is viewed as necessarily debased and inauthentic in 'Roseland', part five of 'A Good Night' (Montague, 1995: 52–3).

47 The distrust of modernity can be glimpsed in Montague's claim that any 'separations' between him and Garvaghey's inhabitants 'are not so much the product of my over-education as of false cultures that have come into their lives. The local singing pubs . . . would often have country and western. The divisions would be inside them, not inside me . . . it is they who are being taken away from what they had, and it is I who am the possessor, and with the older people the guardian, of what had been there' (Montague, 1979: 165).

48 R. McFadden, 'Reflections on Megarrity', *Threshold*, 5:1 (1961), 32.

49 See Edward Lucie-Smith, *British Poetry since 1945* (Harmondsworth, Penguin, 1974), 337. Lucie-Smith's anthology, first published in 1970, noted the growth of groups of poets outside London. He gives a section of his anthology to Belfast poets and correctly cites Belfast as an example of 'the increasing fragmentation of the poetic tradition'. However, he misleadingly defines the poets as 'recognizably post-Movement and neo-Georgian. They owe little to the Dublin tradition of W. B. Yeats, and not much more to the best Irish poet since Yeats, Patrick Kavanagh.'

50 Unemployment was four times the UK average throughout the 1950s: '[T]hroughout the decade unemployment never fell below 5 per cent and averaged 7.4 per cent . . . If it was nothing like the figures for the 1930s, the fact remained that it was now taking place in the context not merely of full employment in the UK but of a relatively better performance by Britain's other regional black spots' (Bew, Gibbon and Patterson, 1996: 117–18). In the election of 1958, the NILP won four Belfast seats.

51 In November 1959 these views were publicly supported by Sir Clarence Graham, Chairman of the UUP's standing committee and by the Attorney General, Brian Maginess, who claimed that 'to broaden our outlook means no weakening of our faith. Toleration is not a sign of weakness but proof of strength' (Barton, 1996: 101).

52 Thus while O'Neill met Lemass and visited a Catholic school, for example, and his stated wish was to 'make Northern Ireland economically stronger and more prosperous . . . and to build bridges between the two traditions within our community', only the first of these was a serious short-term aim (Barton, 1996: 115). It should be borne in mind that Britain's net capital transfer to the North had reached £70 million by 1968; for the argument that the governing principle of the Unionist leadership throughout the 1960s and 1970s was fear of British government intervention, see Bew, Gibbon and Patterson, 1996.

53 The CSJ was middle class, Catholic and focused on the housing allocation issue, and deliberately avoided those issues involving the nature of the state, or which might be seen as republican.

54 Despite the increase in Catholics going on to higher education, statistics show no overall change in the Catholic occupation structure during the 1960s and reveal that an earlier increase in the Catholic middle class was balanced by a rise in numbers in unskilled occupations. Catholics were – and are – more than twice as likely to be unemployed than Protestants, despite their higher emigration rates.

55 Like Lemass, O'Neill was a statist with a belief in central planning; he had also been minister of finance for seven years, had established contact with finance department civil servants from the Republic at World Bank meetings and was 'deeply impressed by the implementation of the Whitaker Report' (Bardon, 1996: 622–3). Both O'Neill and Lemass were progressive, modernising capitalist politicians, committed to attracting investment; to this extent, a degree of optimism about possible convergence seemed warranted.

56 The Belfast 'Group's' meetings were modelled on the tutorials of Leavis with whom Hobsbaum had studied at Cambridge, and continued for three years after he left Belfast in 1966. Dealing with all kinds of writing, these were conducted in a stringently critical spirit which was nevertheless exhilarating for participants, despite dissent from the sometimes inquisitorial atmosphere. Heaney has commented that Hobsbaum was 'a strong believer in the bleeding hunk of experience' (Randall, 1979: 15). Michael Longley's poems were met with 'savage' criticism by Hobsbaum and 'incomprehension' by other Group members who deemed them over-precious (M. Longley, 1995b: 41). Mahon (who never attended a meeting) deemed the Group 'too Leavisite and too contentious' (Scammell, 1991: 4). Nevertheless, Hobsbaum's commitment to his own definition of excellence was unwavering and inspiring, particularly given his belief that it could be found among local writers. Granting them a sense of self-worth and breaking down provincial cultural cringe, he was also instrumental in publicising Heaney, Mahon and Longley during the Belfast Festival of 1965 and guided Heaney towards the publication of his first collection, *Death of a Naturalist* (1966) by Faber, sparking awareness of Northern poetry beyond Northern Ireland. For Heaney, 'what Hobsbaum achieved, whether people like it or not, was to give a generation a sense of themselves, in two ways: it allowed us to get to grips with one another within the group, to move from critical comment to creative friendship at our own pace, and it allowed a small public to think of us as The Group, a single, even singular, phenomenon . . . It's easy to be blasé about all that now, for now, of course, we're genuine parochials. Then we were craven provincials' (Heaney, 1980: 29).

57 A selected poems' volume by John Hewitt, his first book since 1948, was published in 1967. MacNeice was rediscovered and the process of converting him from an English 1930s' poet to a Northern Irish poet began.

58 Editing its first issue, Simmons famously subtitled it 'a handbook for revolution' – a gesture which did not survive a cautionary visit from the Royal Ulster Constabulary – but more significantly chose to include a poem by Hewitt and a picture of Louis MacNeice, recognising the importance of overcoming the earlier divisions of Regionalism (Clyde, 1999: 358).

59 Both Mahon and Heaney have referred to the idea of a 'renaissance' as 'a media event', but given that initial interest came about through an article in the *Observer*, it could be argued that the Group was precisely a 'media event' from the outset (Corcoran, 1992: 7–8; Fallon and Mahon, 1990: xx). Both display a conservative embarrassment which minimises the increasing post-war role of 'journalism' in creating literary events, preferring to maintain a clear distinction between poetry as an elite cultural formation and popular cultural discourses. The point is the way in which, even in denial of its status, the Belfast Group functions, even today, as a powerful literary myth, naturalising an origin for Northern poetry. In this the dual poetic-critical aspect of the Group also needs stressing; a radical regional counter-cultural formation, structurally conservative in its forms, publication methods and conception of the role of poetry, its duality was completely consistent with Leavisite precept.

60 For summaries of the initial critical responses to Heaney's work, see Andrews, 1998: 7–39.

61 More dubiously, another London reviewer claimed that: 'the Faber mantle falls flatteringly on Seamus Heaney . . . here is something like the real thing, mud-caked fingers in Russell Square, a Worzel Gummidge of metaphors'. Quoted in McDonald, 1997: 212.

62 The book is a *Bildungsroman*, running as it does from an initial moment of recall in 'Digging' – 'comes up twenty years away' – through schooldays, intimations of mortality ('An Advancement of Learning', 'Mid-Term Break'), to historical awareness ('For the Commander of the "Eliza"'), the move to the city ('Poor Women in a City Church'), courtship ('Twice Shy'), marriage, work ('The Play Way') and dedication to art ('Personal Helicon').

63 S. Heaney, 'Out of London: Ulster's Troubles', *New Statesman* (1 July 1966), 23.

64 Thus, 'Craft is something that is learned by imitation, a set of available skills . . . But his technique is his poetic personality, his natural accent, not a voice imitated from those poets who have influenced and educated him. Technique matures as the young poet discovers his proper subjects, as he gradually realises that the self is all he has to work towards and out of. Technique can be meticulous with language, it can be reckless, spendthrift, even clumsy – but it must always be authentic' (S. Heaney (ed.), *Soundings 2* (Belfast, Blackstaff Press, 1974), 5).

65 C. Ricks, *The Force of Poetry* (Oxford, Clarendon Press, 1984), 51–4.

66 As Corcoran says in his discussion of 'The Plantation', there is an element of calculation in this 'Janus-faced' quality: 'Both pursuer and pursued, both in control and in surrender, the poet finds himself by losing himself in the language and form of his own poem' (Corcoran, 1998: 22). Like the perfect subordination of the craftsman to his trade, the image of the self-involved poet is of 'technique' in action, his circling figures those of the hermeneutic procedure enjoined on the New Critical reader; the poems exaggerate, to the point of parody, the features of the perfect tutorial poem.

67 J. Keats, *Letters of John Keats*, Robert Gittings (ed.), (Oxford, Oxford University Press, 1985), 70.

68 D. Mahon (ed.) *The Sphere Book of Modern Irish Poetry* (London, Sphere Books, 1972), 12.

69 Interestingly, Mahon refers, in the introduction to his Sphere anthology, to Northern Ireland as 'that once birdless, if still benighted province', thus specifically linking poets and birds.

70 D. Wheatley, *Krino*, 18 (1995), 110.

71 Auden was a model for Irish 1950s' poets precisely because of his mid-Atlantic, un-English, internationalist cultural range. Unless the stagnation of mid-century Irish society is an illusion (and unless Brylcreem was banned) 'anticlimax and antimacassars' would seem to have been as pervasive a fact of life there as in England.

72 See M. Longley, 1995b: 37; 'Herbert . . . is a beneficent influence in my first collection and provides the stanzaic templates for two of its more ambitious poems.' These would presumably be 'A Personal Statement' and 'The Hebrides'.

73 Edward Thomas is also exemplary in his opposition of the natural to the technocratic and life-denying tendencies of modernity and, for Longley, modernism.

'Displacement' is indicated by a taste for metaphysical paradox which goes beyond a question of style: in his Introduction to *Secret Marriages*, a pamphlet of 1968, Longley notes that 'Persephone' and 'Narcissus' 'are all that remains of an attempt to define schizophrenia', even though 'I would be perfectly satisfied of course if the two were read as straight mythological poems.' The 'of course' indicates an habitual modesty which has been too easily accepted by critics, as if it was always obvious what Longley is about. The apparent rejection of history, for example, can equally be read as a refusal to endorse a certain *kind* of history, one predicated on belonging. In this sense, as his best critic Peter McDonald has argued, the Mac-Neicean 'island truancies' of the early poems (visits to Inishmore, the Hebrides, Galapagos, Circe's island) are an attempt to approach 'home' 'without the encoding of tribal claims to certain territories' (McDonald, 1997: 122).

74 'An Outsider Searching for His Home', Eileen Battersby talks to Michael Longley, *The Irish Times*, (11 January 1992), 5.

75 M. Allen, Options: The Poetry of Michael Longley, *Éire-Ireland*, 10:4 (Winter 1975), 129–36.

76 To take the link further: Longley's reference to the freemartin is followed in his Introduction by reference to 'Remembrance Day' in which 'I imagine the possibility of swallows breeding near a battlefield and using blood as well as mud to build their nests', an image which recurs in Muldoon's 'Incantata' in *The Annals of Chile*.

77 'Seahorses', *Threshold* 22 (Summer 1969), 41.

78 See E. Grenan, The American Connection: An Influence on Modern and Contemporary Irish Poetry, in M. Kenneally (ed.), 1995: 28–47.

79 As Eiléan Ní Chuilleanáin claims, the satiric energy of 'Nightwalker' – as opposed to Kavanagh's, or to a lesser extent Clarke's – reveals a generational change: 'While there are ambiguities about identity, the background against which it fails to be defined is viewed with anger rather than despair, with philosophical *Angst* rather than religious resignation' (Ní Chuilleanáin, 1992: 32).

80 Thomas Kinsella, The Irish Writer, in *Davis, Mangan, Ferguson? Tradition and the Irish Writer* (Dublin, Dolmen Press, 1970). In this sense, Kinsella attempts to redeem for the Irish tradition as he sees it what Deane refers to as modernism's 'making a fetish of exile, alienation and dislocation' (Deane, 1983: 58).

81 Heaney, reviewing *The Táin*, reveals the different Northern and Southern expectations for an audience of the time: 'A venture like this indicates a large ambition in a poet, and for Kinsella it represents a stage in his development toward a more public stance, a conscious and explicit relating of the self to the community' (S. Heaney, *The Listener*, 26 March 1970).

82 The 'Sea of Disappointment' echoes the 'disappointment' seen as the condition of the modern writer in Kinsella's address to the Yeats Centenary Conference (*see* n. 25).

83 One way of doing this is to find alternative structures for poetry in science. The French Jesuit priest and palaeontologist, Teilhard de Chardin, writing between the 1930s and 1960s, saw in the evolutionary process some promise of a higher moral order, reconciling Darwinism with Church teachings; Kinsella strips the positivist element from his work, using his ideas as a way of setting the individual within the vast cycle of evolution. Similar scientific, quasi-scientific or philosophical systems, drawn from Renan, Darwin and Jung, are allowed to suggest organisational structures for the fragmentary memories, archetypes and forms Kinsella encounters on his inner quest.

84 The only essay to place the work of the New Writers' Press in context is Trevor Joyce's New Writers' Press: The History of a Project, in P. Coughlan and A. Davis (eds), 1995: 276–306.

85 Joyce makes the point that the republication of Coffey and Devlin was seen as 'a retrospective formality' by the poetic establishment, 'an academic courtesy' which did not involve a consideration of contemporary experimental poetry or the implications of the experimental approach for Irish poetry generally (Joyce, 1998: 22).

86 Comparisons with *The Honest Ulsterman* work to the detriment of the Dublin journal – only six issues ever appeared, while *The Honest Ulsterman* is now in its thirty-second year. Nevertheless, *Lace Curtain* combatively challenged what Smith called the '*Irish literary thing*', while NWP (which went into abeyance, but never wholly vanished) managed to publish over fifty titles between the late 1960s and late 1970s. The project as a whole established, with some panache, a sense that alternatives to mainstream poetry were – however briefly – available in Ireland.

87 *The Lace Curtain*, 4 (Summer 1971), 58.

88 J. Hogan, Deaths and Contacts, *The Lace Curtain*, 1 (Summer 1969), 36.

89 See Davis, 1998: 43: '[Smith's] close identification of modernist artistic production with individualism consorts well with an entrepreneurial spirit deaf to certain self-satisfied shibboleths . . . [although] in attacking the "lovers of Anglo-Irishism in literature", Smith's target is not so much the Irish literary tradition itself as the transformation of that tradition into cultural kitsch. The nostalgic conservatism of those "tenth-rate poets and bombastic shamrock-nationalists" . . . is in this respect, merely the obverse of the "progressive" philistinism of those developers who defaced the Dublin cityscape and the debased taste shown by the enthusiastic audience for Country and Western music. In advocating . . . a poetry that has learned from the example of high modernism, Smith's enterprise, in short, both reflects Ireland's modernisation and challenges it.'

90 For an analysis of Smith's and Joyce's early poetry, see Davis, 1998: 43–5.

91 The first book in a gapped but coherent poetic career which also includes a pamphlet *Sixteen Poems* (published by the *Honest Ulsterman*'s Ulsterman Publications in 1969), *Figures* (1978), *XXI Poems* (1980), *A Long Poem in Three Sections* (published in the *Irish University Review* in 1983), *Landscapes & Silences* (1996) and *This* (1996). For an account of Squires's later poetry, see A. Davis, Geoffrey Squires: From Projective to Phenomenological Verse, in J. Goodby and M. Scully (eds), 1999: 99–107.

Narrow roads to the deep north

The condition of Ulster defeats every liberal device. It nullifies language, repudiates politics. (Bardon, 1996: 827)

The 'Troubles'

In the summer of 1969 the Northern Irish statelet headed by Terence O'Neill effectively lost control of its territory; by 1972, 'after little more than fifty years of devolved power, the British government terminated the existence of an autonomous administration in Northern Ireland' (Bew, Gibbon and Patterson, 1979: 162–206). Civil Rights marches, beginning in August 1968, had led to the brutal suppression by the Royal Ulster Constabulary (RUC) of a march in Derry on 5 October 1968, witnessed around the world on television. This was followed by the first riots in Derry's Bogside area. The result – the British government's insistence that O'Neill make concessions to Catholics – led to yet more marches as the emboldened minority took up NICRA's lead. A Belfast–Derry march, organised by a radical student group, People's Democracy, in January 1969, was ambushed by Loyalist thugs with police collusion at Burntollet (Coogan, 1996: 70–95). As the tempo of events increased, an election was called which significantly increased the power of Nationalist representation at Stormont. Major rioting after the 12 July Apprentice Boys' parade led to major civil disorder, precipitating the entry of British troops into Derry on 14/15 August after the 'Battle of the Bogside', and then to Belfast where Loyalist pogroms of Catholics seemed imminent. The troops were initially deployed to contain the violence until a political solution could be found. As O'Neill fell, caught between pressures from hardliners in the UUP and for reform, he was replaced by Chichester-Clark, who lasted less than two years, during which time the first bombings and shootings started. In 1971 the more hard-line Faulkner took over. Faulkner persuaded the new Conservative government – elected in 1970 – that a tougher approach was necessary. By this time the Army, initially welcomed by the Nationalist population, was being seen increasingly as an alien imposition. Their anger was fuelled by Faulkner's security measures, which targeted Nationalists disproportionately, and included curfews on Catholic areas, roadblocks, intimidatory house searches (17,262 in 1971 alone, for example) and, finally, internment without trial in

August 1971. The brutalities and civilian deaths which inevitably resulted from such measures helped maintain the determination of the minority to resist, or actively oppose, any retreat from what protest had achieved (Lee, 1989: 433–4). Northern Ireland as 'a Protestant state for a Protestant people' was by this stage living on borrowed time, undermined by Unionism's inability to cope with structural change and the unprecedentedly united minority (Cairns and Richards, 1988: 142). Despite the ultimate concession of many Civil Rights demands, the limited effect of reform and the state's heavy-handedness (and police brutality) fuelled the rebirth of the IRA in 1970, which began a military campaign within a year. Loyalist paramilitaries responded in kind. As the tempo of violent confrontation rose, the vicious spiral of retaliatory killings and the political vacuum boosted paramilitaries on both sides. A horrific point of no return was reached on 31 January 1972 – 'Bloody Sunday' – when thirteen peaceful demonstrators, marching against internment, were shot and killed by soldiers of the Parachute Regiment in Derry. Three days afterwards, demonstrators burned down the British Embassy in Dublin. In Britain a Troops Out movement developed, one which had its part in the radical political and industrial movement of the times, but at parliamentary level a bipartisan approach swiftly emerged; there was very little high-level opposition to government (lack of) policy.

The worst period of the Troubles, between 1971 and 1975, also saw the extension of violence to the Republic and the British 'mainland'.[1] Deaths rose from twenty-five in 1970 to 467 in 1972, with bombings increasing from 150 to 1,380 in the same period, and violence remained near this peak until the mid-1970s. With the already distorted democratic political sphere drastically narrowed, conflict polarised along ethnic lines (the Ulster Defence Regiment (UDR), for example, set up to replace the notorious B-Specials as an auxiliary police force in 1970, began with a membership which was 20 per cent Catholic; within one year this figure had dropped to 8 per cent). The social democratic aspect of NICRA and the social revolutionary aspect of People's Democracy were re-routed into sectarianism. Proroguing Stormont in 1972, the government attempted to solve the crisis by replacing it with a Power Sharing Executive in 1973, granting a measure of control over Northern Irish affairs to moderate (Social Democratic and Labour Party – SDLP) Nationalists; and, headed by Faulkner, it began sitting on 1 January 1974 (Bew, Gibbon and Patterson, 1996: 196–9). But if it was too little too late for most Catholics, its proposals for a Council of Ireland proved too much for Loyalists, and it was toppled by the Ulster Workers Council Strike in May (Bardon, 1996: 707–11). From then on, Northern Ireland was governed directly from Westminster.

While economic convergence continued – multinational capital continued to be attracted to the Republic and the North, while the UK and the Republic entered the EEC together in 1972 – fallout from the Troubles was catastrophic; North–South suspicions intensified, relations between Britain and the Republic and with other states were soured. Stereotypes and chauvinisms apparently dead and buried were able to flourish again on both sides of the Irish Sea, and further afield. Moreover, all the anomalies to which British governments had turned a blind eye in Ulster, and the draconian measures required after 1969 (the Emergency Provisions Act of 1973, the Prevention of Terrorism Act of 1974, an armed police force, widespread surveillance, violation of human rights and an extraordinary judicial system of 'supergrasses' and Diplock courts after 1973) – these had their implications for the rest of British society. The Troubles not only tarnished Westminster's cherished self-image as the 'mother of parliaments', but the nature of British society was inevitably warped by the state's response, often making its democratic fabric seem threadbare indeed.[2] In the Republic the Troubles led to a similar, if less drastic questioning of the state (most notably in the Arms Trial of 1970), as well as to restrictions of democratic rights, draining the resources of a country whose security budget was ordinarily minuscule.

1916–22 again?: representation and obliquity

For many among the minority, the key historical parallel with their experience from the mid-1960s was that of 1916–22. Cairns and Richards have noted that 'As the crisis deepened . . . some Nationalists in the North saw the situation as a prelude to unification, and sought vindication in the tropes of the earlier Nationalist revival for a renewed struggle against the metropolitan power and the Unionists, once again identified as its "garrison"' (Cairns and Richards, 1988: 142). If the initial radical-revolutionary language of insurgency should be taken to show that the retreat into sectarianism was not wholly inevitable, the idea of the parallel influenced even those who resisted it; writers who did so nevertheless often saw the Troubles as confirming the circularity and essential murderousness of Irish history.[3] In the North, in particular, the burden of interpretative expectation was placed on their shoulders. On the one hand they seemed peripheral – what was more useless than literature when civil war might be imminent? On the other, given a 'bardic' tradition and the centrality of literature to Nationalist discourse, they seemed natural choices as spokesmen for 'their' communities, intimate with yet detached by their function from the immediacies of the hatreds of their 'people'. Thus, the notion of 'community' – often in a regressive sense – was being strengthened at the time in response to modernisation and the Troubles. An already charged writing was thrust into a situation where oracular pronouncements might be expected, even demanded.[4] As Eve Patten has noted:

> In Ireland, traditional perceptions of the writer as responsible for the registration of public sensibility have long been a source of poetic capital. The literary community continues to prioritize its poets as the primary agents of articulation and critique, a tendency which has been linked both to the legacy of a bardic past and to the twentieth-century inheritance of a

Yeatsian aesthetic grounded in the creative tension between commitment and artistic independence. The personality cult of Seamus Heaney and the critical energy devoted to an Ulster poetic renaissance . . . have meanwhile served to maintain poetry's monopoly on literary / political exchange in a series of landmark volumes. (Patten, 1995: 130)

With poetry embroiled in the political sphere in this way, the question of what a 'public poetry' might look like inevitably arose. Was it the duty of the poet to comply with expectations, to 'comment on', 'engage with' or at least to 'represent' the crisis? More, how could 'the ineffable thing' – violence – be represented (Deane, 1985: 186)?

'Representation' – in its larger philosophical, political and literary senses – could, in many ways, be said to be the unspoken subject of Troubles poetry, and the period immediately after 1968/69 saw a widespread critical debate on the issue; as the poet Geoffrey Squires put it in *The Irish Times* in 1971, 'There is an idea that writing, and poetry in particular, thrives on upheaval and violence, whether in the poet's life, or the life of his times . . . So there is curiosity as to what the troubles in the North will "produce" in the way of new writing, and also, less realistically, as to what influence writers have on events there' (Squires, 1971: 12). Squires shows an awareness that the paradigm structuring expectations combined local and national elements with the still-potent example of Confessional poetry (although this was one which, as we have seen, his own poetry notably did not accept). From a Nationalist perspective, the politicisation of poetry in the previous 'Troubles' of 1916–22 (in the poets of the Rising and, more ambiguously, Yeats) could provide something amounting to a moral example, as it did to some extent in Montague's case. Moreover, the issue of representation was complicated by allegiances to particular styles or traditions of writing, deemed 'Irish' or 'English' (although all were non-modernist; the World War I poems of Thomas MacGreevy were not invoked, for example). At one extreme, as in Padraig Fiacc's anthology *The Wearing of the Black* of 1974, a near-causal link was established between poetic authenticity, even poetic stature, and work which came 'directly' out of the violence.[5] But, overwhelmingly, an explicitly *political* 'public' poetry of the Troubles failed to materialise.[6]

From the start, Heaney, Mahon and Longley refused a reflectionist poetry of the Troubles, with its attendant dangers of appearing to endorse political positions. Effectively, this stressed inseparability of 'style' and 'message', and hence the validity of the 'obliquity' famously assumed to characterise the poetic response to the Troubles. This approach was championed early and strongly by a number of Northern Irish critics.[7] Defending the poets, D. E. S. Maxwell noted in 1973 that 'Much of the present ardour for a "committed" Irish literature recalls the dottiness of 1939 [for a 'war poetry'], even when the respective political assumptions are totally at odds.' In part this was an attack on what Northern writers saw as the incomprehension of their situation by members of the literary establishment in the Republic: as Maxwell noted, '*Hibernia*'s "News in the Arts" has hinted at the necessity of participatory zeal. Recalling Brecht's temporizing in the 1953 Berlin uprising – "the rebellion went down to defeat with the artist sitting by his tale-recorder, inglorious, unbloody, uninvolved" – the columnist adds . . . "A clear message for the artist in Ireland today, North and South" ' (Maxwell, 1973: 91–2). Against this, Maxwell argued for the necessary autonomy of art and the writer's right to permit material to 'ripen' before commitment to print, citing as examples of obliquity Derek Mahon's recognition in some of his love poems of 'metaphors for the Northern situation', and Heaney's observation of 'The Last Mummer': 'I didn't mean this to be a poem about Northern Ireland, but in some ways I think it is'[8] (Maxwell, 1973: 94). Revealingly, however, Maxwell's analysis of poetry goes no further; after these general points, he turns to fiction and drama, in which discursive realist style generally permits a realist aesthetic, albeit one presented in significant rather than meretriciously 'topical' form: 'The local habitation, like Eliot's notorious objective correlative, must have its own autonomous life within the work. It's not authenticated because something exactly the same happened yesterday.' Though this much may be granted, the lack of discussion of poetry's often non-realist modes, compounded by an understandable opposition to *Tendenzliteratur*, leads to a rather lame humanistic conclusion: 'For most people in Northern Ireland life no doubt centres still around work and pleasures. People still read, eat, drink, make love, fall out. It is not sentimental to believe that these are the writer's real subjects' (Maxwell, 1973: 107). For most poets, however, the desire to 'answer to' or 'represent' the communities caught up in the Troubles remained 'a real subject'. If obliquity was a strategy and autonomy a desideratum, the poet could not avoid something of a communally representative status, or the need to explore those beliefs – however reprehensible – held to lie behind the violence, in attempts to 'resolve' and 'appease' them in poetic form.[9]

Such considerations raise, without fully addressing, the twin issues of myth and poetic form in Northern Troubles poetry. In other words, although obliquity was used to express both an avoidance of direct representations of communal politics and, at the same time, immersion and even complicity in the mythicised history behind them, the issue of the extent to which obliquity stems from the fact of communal *inter*-involvement often remains unexplored. The effect is to valorise difference, rather than to challenge sectarian division as immutable. For, as Eamon Hughes has noted, the highly impacted nature of settlement and social patterning in Northern Ireland means that identity there has to be formed 'on terms of intimacy with whatever one chooses to regard as the other', that 'identity does not confront difference; it is constituted by it' (Hughes, 1991: 3–4). Tackling this means tackling the idea of a pre-given, stable and ethnically defined sense of selfhood. In the work of Montague and Heaney, however, insistence on an identity confronting difference confirms the binary terms or 'timeless' divisions, which have dominated cultural debate, rather than undoing them.[10] To some extent, the Protestant-background poets do raise the issue of 'identity . . . on terms of intimacy . . . with the other', although not wholly[11] (Hughes, 1991: 3–4).

These problems are thrown up in two of the most public poetic interventions of the time, the ninth section of Montague's *The Rough Field*, 'A New Siege', and Kinsella's 'A Butcher's Dozen'. Both also raise the issue of the formal consequences of the kinds of choice being made. John Dillon Redshaw offered a different kind of reservation about obliquity in 1974, claiming that it showed an 'unstated agreement with a fundamentally conservative critical ideal . . . which conceives of only the finished poem as poetry'. For Redshaw, the emphasis on 'oblique poise' had been valorised by critics in a way which underwrote 'the already assumed protective postures [and] self-defensive tactics which characterize much of the work of Heaney, Longley, and Mahon, but which ought not to determine a critical view of it'. This meant that 'the position of the Ulster poet is perilous because he is limited to the lyric mode whose traditional dynamics must unfortunately be distorted by experience in order to achieve articulate expression. To equate, however subliminally, all possible poems with the lyric alone, is a limitation' (Redshaw, 1974: 35). Referring to Squires's article, he offered *The Rough Field* as the exemplary text to be set against the domination of lyric with its tendency to select only crises as 'personalisable', and so bypass as legitimate poetic subjects 'the usually undramatic, normal *continua* of plain politics, for instance'. On this basis he expressed the hope for a public poetry which will see 'public matters as a permanent dimension of everyday life, not simply as something that crops up from time to time when things go wrong, or worse than usual', finding it in Montague's 'sequence of sequences' which possesses an 'expansive formality capable of taking in both the intensely personal voice and a wide variety of non-personal social discourse' (Redshaw, 1974: 37).

Redshaw takes 'A New Siege's' penultimate verse as an illustration of the success of Montague's 'expansive formality':

> Lines of loss
>   lines of energy
> always changing
>   always returning
> A TIDE LIFTS
>   THE RELIEF SHIP
> OFF THE MUD
>   OVER THE BOOM
> the rough field
>   of the universe
> growing, changing
>   a net of energies
> crossing patterns
>   weaving towards

a new order
  a new anarchy
always different
  always the same
(Montague, 1995: 73)

This is seen, rightly, in terms of its surges of statement and counterstatement, which move from 'descriptive statements of Natural Law' ('Lines of loss / lines of energy') to allegories for its control ('a tide lifts / the relief ship') 'only to return to the abiding simplicities of Natural Law'. The result is an image of change itself 'suspended in continuity by a conservative vision', yet radically understood in terms of US Black Mountain poetics that 'What does not change / is the will to change' (Redshaw, 1974: 41). This embodies the 'monumentally recidivist stalemate' of Northern Ireland, bringing personal and public discourses together. Nevertheless there are problems with Redshaw's advocacy, and many critics have had difficulties with the conclusion of *The Rough Field*, both with 'A New Siege' and the succeeding, final section, 'The Wild Dog Rose'. Redshaw's claims for the dominance of a formal interest at this point – the challenge being 'more formal and poetic than factual and political' – are debatable (Redshaw, 1974: 38). This is because the poem's conclusion, in its orientation towards the Troubles, marks a distinct swerve from its first eight sections. No longer an open-ended, recuperative modern epic of dispossession and loss, it retrospectively politicises the ethos of passivity and decline it had set out to chart, in accordance with Montague's Introduction to the Summer 1970 issue of *Threshold* ('The Northern Crisis'); 'the flurry of literary activity in recent years was no accident but psychically linked to political change (it even preceded it by a few years) . . . the important thing is not to ignore [the problem of Ulster], as previous generations (with a few honourable exceptions) have tended to do. For the time being to be an Ulster writer is, in a sense, to be a revolutionary writer; old moulds are broken in the North' (Montague, 1970: 1). A teleology is imposed, as the titles show: 'A New Siege' casts the Protestants as a 'garrison', while 'The Wild Dog Rose', part ten, invokes traditional Nationalist-Catholic iconography and a feminised territory. Both confirm, then, the 'old moulds' Montague claims should be 'broken'. Of course, the universalising gestures ('Chicago, Berkeley, Paris') are appropriate to the 'global regionalist' climax of the poem, with its wide historical sweep and urgent contemporary reference, while reported speech, quotations and signs make it a microcosm of the procedures of *The Rough Field* as a whole, with its 'emerging order / of the poem invaded / by cries'. Yet the gap between the abstract theme of change and the concrete one of autobiography – a gap too confidently subsumed in the term 'global regionalism' itself[12] – is revealed by reliance on cliché ('Law and Order's / medieval armour', 'bull-voiced bigotry', etc.), just as the switch in 'A New Siege's' dedication from Mary Holland (in 1970) to Bernadette Devlin (in 1972) indicates something of an opportunist impulse at odds with the requirements of a more nuanced 'public' poetry. In aesthetic-formal terms, it is Montague's refusal to get rid of the lyric ego – that is, his superficial absorption of the Olsonian Black Mountain poetics referred to by Redshaw – which is the problem; the merging of autobiographical subject with that of the nation in a manner characteristic of romantic Nationalism means that a slippage into sectarian stereotypes is always a threat. The poem's refusal of a more radical politics of the subject thus undermines its overt, public political radicalism; ironically, in this sense, its difficulty is that it is not political enough.[13] Devlin herself had claimed at the end of the People's Democracy march from Belfast to Derry in January 1969 that the atmosphere was 'like that of V Day: the war was over and we had won'; yet, as has been noted, what this signified was not 'victory', but rather that 'mobilisation itself was being accounted victory' (Bew, Gibbon and Patterson, 1996: 146–7). This kind of insight into subjective perceptions of the historical moment are absent from 'A New Siege', where fossil rhetorics contradict a thematics of change, fluidity and openness, rendering both inadequate to historical and social complexities. This is not to say that 'A New Siege's' stereotypes are merely 'second-hand images [standing] in for straightforward contempt', or 'identity-rhetoric at its purest' ('straightforward' and 'purest' themselves belong to the mindset attributed to Montague, and *The Rough Field* contains many local instances opposing such rhetoric) (McDonald, 1997: 84–5). Nevertheless, it is around this formal contradiction (which embodies a political one) that *The Rough Field*, for all its major achievement, falters in its epic attempt at representative inclusivity.[14]

The direct link assumed between the poem's present and 1916–22 is clear in Montague's epigraph to 'A New Siege' – 'Once again, it happens . . . / like an old Troubles film, / run for the last time . . .'. Suspended between rhetoric and abstract 'change', the circling image of the whole of *The Rough Field*, which recurs in the 'Epilogue' (appended, in nervously supplementary fashion, outside the poem proper), suggests, in this light, fatalism rather than the outsider's synoptic vision. A consideration of the claims of modernity and tradition concedes that 'only a sentimentalist would wish / to see such degradation again', while remaining frankly nostalgic for 'a world where action had been wrung / through painstaking years to ritual' (the weakly archaic and nostalgic 'wrought' confirming Deane's wish that 'Montague would take a tougher line on loss') (Deane, 1975: 20). That nostalgia had been anticipated in the beautiful but sentimentally Nationalist 'The Wild Dog Rose', in which Montague completes the poem with another Wordsworthian Solitary/*cailleach* figure, recalling (but less critically) 'Like Dolmens Round My Childhood'. Modernisation and traditionalism are too neatly opposed, and correspond too completely to the communities associated with them; thus, although *The Rough Field* asserts an embryonically urban sensibility in Irish poetry on the one hand, its binary divisions confirm a sense of romanticised rural decay and simplistic political interpretations on the other. This is the final impression of the poem, rather than the 'intransigent modernity' some have detected (Matthews, 1997: 118). Northern Ireland – although not the Republic – is ultimately presented as a place 'self-enclosed and static', its unique misery challenged but finally left unscathed by the internationalist invocations. This relative failure can be related to Redshaw's claim for formal radicalism and *The Rough Field*'s status – inaccurately – as 'a *poème fleuve*' (Redshaw, 1974: 45). That is, the strains in the poem's ending(s) relate to the imposition of closure on what was conceived of as an open-ended work, for if the conclusion is not sufficiently political it is not, by the same token, experimental enough either.[15] A sense of 'bardic' responsibility lies behind the arresting of the poem's flow; paradoxically, by turning to directly address the 'crisis', it embraces the lyrical limitations previously refused, doing so in 'tribal' terms and thus foreclosing any openness to mediation between a personal voice and its varied social discourses. Yet it was because of this that *The Rough Field* was to prove so influential. It revealed the contemporary possibilities of history as myth for Irish poetry, renewing the significance of rural landscape (by focusing attention on name rather than place itself), and offering Tyrone's uneven dilapidation and modernisation, as well as Derry's violence, as metonyms for the whole of Ireland and for Ireland as a whole. As Kirkland remarks, this was to be crucial in 'constructing the experience of Northern Ireland through the 1970s as an archetype for the metanarrative of Irish dispossession' (Kirkland, 1996: 75, fns 24 and 51).

At the opposite end of the formal scale from *The Rough Field*, Kinsella's 'A Butcher's Dozen' was written in crude hexametrical couplets. It was published in April 1972, immediately after the Widgery Tribunal Report which exonerated the Parachute Regiment of the British Army from blame for Bloody Sunday. A work less like Kinsella's contemporaneous self-explorations would be hard to imagine, although the continuity between the two has been argued, and the poem has a characteristic gothic-tinged, inward quality.[16] It takes the form of a series of Dantesque encounters with the ghosts of the victims of the 'brutal and stupid massacre', who recount the circumstances of their deaths, condemning the Army, the cover-up and, finally, the Protestant population, before the thirteenth victim concludes with a plea for forgiveness and integrationism. One of the poem's most interesting aspects is that it is a response not so much to the massacre as to Widgery's Report; the occasion is not the crime itself, so much as the hypocritical self-justifications of authority which follow, its contempt for the powerless and its obscene self-legitimations. Heavy ironies and broadsheet forcefulness can thus be seen as a calculated stylistic riposte on behalf of the victims to a sophistical evasion of responsibility, a crude reminder of 'corpses . . . red and raw' which reflects the feelings of anger and futility in the Republic at the time. Yet this aspect – which could have provided the basis for an exploration, say, of the media representation of the event – is overridden by a form whose crudity works to prevent recognition, not of the massacre so much as the complexity of the larger situation to which it is related. Despite integrationist sentiments, and its undoubted 'cauterising' effect, the rhetorical climaxes veer towards the reductively sectarian:[17]

'Take a bunch of stunted shoots,
A tangle of transplanted roots,
Ropes and rifles, feathered nests,
Some dried colonial interests,
A hard unnatural union grown
In a bed of blood and bone,
Tongue of serpent, gut of hog
Spiced with spleen of underdog . . .
Last the choice ingredient: you!'
          (Kinsella, 1979a: 15–16)

Kinsella refers to Britain as 'England', eliding the fundamental political problem (the identification of a million Protestants with the British state) via a Nationalist 'false consciousness' argument (Loyalists as imperial dupes). Given the poem's own linguistic betrayals, however – Loyalists as 'rubbish', 'slops and scraps', 'glum', associated with 'latrines' and 'scribbled magic' – it is hard to discern, with W. J. McCormack, a subtler critique (that at a 'more fundamental level than Nationalist indignation' Kinsella 'registers a complex recognition that politics (in the full Aristotelian sense of the term) is being replaced, or being rewritten, by forces at once more sophisticated and brutal') (McCormack, 1987: 66). 'Complex recognition' is, rather, confused self-revelation. 'A Butcher's Dozen' is the prime example of a deliberately direct intervention into the crisis by a poet – printed, as it was, 'hurriedly, in large quantities, as a cheap pamphlet' for public distribution – but its lapse into essentialism and caricature shows the inability of old-fashioned Nationalism to mediate between a 'rewriting' (the Widgery Report) and its tragic original (Kinsella, 1979a: 9). On the other hand, it is necessary to note that the poem's doggerel echoes various eighteenth-century Irish-language models, and such self-consciousness aligns it with the rest of Kinsella's post-*Nightwalker* work. Nevertheless, the poem's overall effect is to reveal the difficulty, if not impossibility, of a direct 'war poetry', making it a monument to the unworkability of certain historical parallels.

If Kinsella's and Montague's poems tell us something about the tensions between poetic form and a 'public' poetry, they also raise the issue of the formal conservatism of Heaney, Mahon and Longley and the role of myth already mentioned. The strength of the New Critical–Leavisite/Nationalist critical polarity meant that attempts to deal with the crisis in anything approaching a formally expansive, let alone experimental way, was strongly resisted. In the absence of 'expansive' formal means for mediating the Troubles the mythic paradigm, and resistance to it, came to dominate poetry in the early 1970s. In the face of violence the tendency of the 1960s' poets was to see politics not in terms of discourse within the rationalist sphere of civil society, so much as the result of a history available only in mythic, communal terms.[18]

Heaney's 'Feeling into Words' of 1974 is eloquent on the sources of history-as-myth and its dilemmas, and the felt need to 'encompass the perspectives of a humane reason while at the same time granting the religious intensity of the violence its deplorable authenticity and complexity' (Heaney, 1980: 56–7). Heaney's is perhaps the best account of Nationalist history-as-myth, if only because the energy and involvement of his writing hints at identification with 'bankrupt . . . mythologies' insofar as they assume religious-mythic (rather than outright political) forms:

> And when I say religious, I am not thinking simply of the sectarian division. To some extent the enmity can be viewed as a struggle between the cults and devotees of a god and a goddess. There is an indigenous territorial numen . . . call her Mother Ireland, Kathleen Ni Houlihan . . . whatever; and her sovereignty has been temporarily usurped by . . . a new male cult whose founding fathers were Cromwell, William of Orange and Edward Carson, and whose godhead is incarnate in a rex or caesar resident in a palace in London. What we have is the tail-end of a struggle in a province between territorial piety and imperial power . . . [T]his idiom is remote from the agnostic world of economic interest . . . and remote from the political maneouvres of power-sharing; but it is not remote from the bankrupt psychology and mythologies implicit in the terms Irish Catholic and Ulster Protestant. (Heaney, 1980: 57)

Art's necessarily representative function enjoins the poet, for Heaney as for Montague, to reflect or embody his inescapable 'mythos', or inheritance, with all the attendant perils of simplifying a society more complex in historic, social and economic terms than the myth allows. Yet if, for Montague, the route to representative status had been through the quasi-epic, expansive mediation between personal and social discourses, Heaney's lay in an intensification of the traditional lyric's consolatory role and its fixation on identity and groundedness, in pushing it via language politics and myth, towards ellipsis and even the temporary collapse of some of its constituent features, such as metaphor and the lyric 'I'.

Heaney's crorpses: *Wintering Out* and *North*

No poet more completely embodied the encounter between poetry and the Troubles than Heaney, who, in *Wintering Out* (1972), and *North* (1975), not only set many of the terms for Northern Irish, British and Irish poetry for the following decade, but revealed most completely the fantastically impacted nature of the issues – art's relation to violence, gender, colonialism – which the Troubles laid bare. In 'Feeling into Words' Heaney notes how – just two months after the publication of *Door into the Dark* – the 'original heraldic encounter between Protestant yeoman and Catholic rebel' had been 'initiated again' and how, 'From that moment the problem of poetry moved from being simply a matter of achieving the satisfactory verbal icon to being a search for images and symbols adequate to our predicament' (Heaney, 1980: 56). *Wintering Out* essays a realignment of the autonomous poem with the communal artefact, and the book has something of the provisionality we might expect of an immediate reaction, its poems frequently avoiding the epigrammatic or moralising closure of those in the early books (in *North*, as Longley notes, the reaction has become more 'heraldic') (E. Longley, 1986: 160–5). This quality is conveyed in the book's title, drawn from a line in 'Servant Boy'; it describes the rudimentary care given to cattle during winter months when they were left to be tended by boys who were lodged with them. The boy 'wintering out / the back-end of a bad year' has, then, beside his historical aspect (in the Penal Law era) a contemporary resonance. Dispossessed, he is condemned to serve; nevertheless, he maintains his self-respect 'resentful and impenitent', finally bearing 'the warm eggs' of a post-Civil Rights future. The title, then, 'gesture[s] towards the distresses that we are all undergoing in this country at the minute', and while 'comfortless enough' has 'a notion of survival in it' which coincides with a will to survive the present crisis (Corcoran, 1998: 28).

Yet, as the echo of *Richard III*'s 'winter of our discontent' suggests, the title also 'gestures towards' the betweenness of a Northern Catholic/Nationalist-background poet writing within the English lyric tradition. In other words, the various strategies of this volume can be seen in the light of the Corkeryan dilemma which has traditionally faced Irish writers intent on representing the specificity of Irish experience and identity – exacerbated by the repression of that identity in Northern Ireland – but only able to do so in a language and literary tradition perceived as inimical to these: thus, 'I speak and write in English . . . I teach English literature, I publish in London, but the English tradition is not ultimately home' (Heaney, 1980: 34). Heaney's essay 'Belfast' makes it clear that Clarke's solution – of replicating Gaelic prosody in English – held little appeal; despite his own use of *deibidhe* rhyme and some other devices, Heaney finds 'the whole enterprise a bit programmatic'[19] (Heaney, 1980: 36; O'Donoghue, 1994: 29–38). Nevertheless *Wintering Out* does encode its dilemma in linguistic terms, and precisely because of the intimate bond with the English lyric tradition. The exacerbated (post)colonial sense is explored most obviously in the book's historical subjects and through a number of disinherited, liminal and abandoned figures – mummer, servant, abandoned children, *maighdean mara* (mermaid), abandoned mother, missing daughter, infanticide. Unlike the craftsmen and relatives of the first two collections these possess no craft or special skill, and either have no place or role in society or are positioned at its margins. Retrospectively, they politicise the earlier figures, and modify Heaney's earlier, more four-square analogies for the poet. Like the poet in a time of crisis, 'The Last Mummer' – who also relies on a specialised use of language and feels 'trammelled / in the taboos of the country' – negotiates shifting allegiances and is forced to go 'whoring // among the civil tongues' of English (similarly, in a technological age both mummer and poet appear redundant, and there are similarities between the mummer's lost audience, 'charmed in a ring' by 'the luminous screen in the corner', and the zombie-like Dublin populace of 'Nightwalker') (Heaney, 1972: 19). Historical events also contribute to the sense of apartness and a disinheriting inheritance, providing a context for the contemporary crisis; the United Irishmen revolt of 1798 is alluded to in 'Linen Town', along with the destruction of Ulster exports in 'The Wool Trade' (significantly these are both processes in which Protestants and Catholics suffered, although not equally). More central to Heaney's main concerns is 'Bog Oak', a poem which – like 'The Tollund Man' – picks up where 'Bogland' left off; timber discovered in a bog takes the speaker back past the 'moustached / dead' of peasant ancestors, the poem studiedly avoiding hints at 'bog wisdom' or the suggestion of some pre-invasion Gaelic utopia, as it moves to a tentatively ironic vision:

> Perhaps I just make out
> Edmund Spenser,
> dreaming sunlight,
> encroached upon by
>
> geniuses who creep
> 'out of every corner . . .
> towards watercress and carrion.
>   (Heaney, 1972: 15)

Spenser lived in County Cork in the 1580s and 1590s, but the quotation is not from what Heaney sees as the 'dreaming sunlight' of his epic for Elizabeth I, *The Faerie Queene*, but a pamphlet of 1598 taking issue with Elizabeth's Irish policy, *A Veue of the Present State of Ireland* (he felt it should be even more brutal than it was). Spenser is here being used to raise large issues about the relationship of art to violence; the brutal facts of Elizabethan colonial *realpolitik* 'encroach upon' not just his 'dreaming', but our view of him as an escapist, arcadian poet. Spenser is just one of several canonical English literary figures who either endorsed or participated in the Irish plantations (Heaney, 1980: 34–5), and who underline the dilemma of a poet from Heaney's background. This is the cue, in a sense, for the book's linguistic resistance, offered through the occupation of the occupier's own language from within. Thus, the epigraph to 'The Wool Trade', from Stephen Dedalus's bitter reflection after his encounter with the English Dean of Studies, runs: 'How different are the words "home", "Christ", "ale", "master", on his lips and on mine' (Heaney, 1972: 37). This recognition of difference has as part of its point the case made again in 'Traditions', which moves, in its third section, from what has been called the first stage Irishman, Shakespeare's MacMorris in *Henry V*, with his bewildered outcry 'What ish my nation?', to Leopold Bloom, in Joyce's *Ulysses*. Thus, although the 'alliterative' tradition of Shakespeare (and Spenser) has since the sixteenth century 'bulled' and destroyed the 'guttural' Irish one – elegised in 'The Backward Look' – the Irish have the last laugh, since Joyce's great achievement means that 'English is by now not so much an imperial humiliation as a native weapon' (Heaney, 1978: 35). This is not merely the Nationalist obverse of imperial arrogance it might appear; MacMorris's bewilderment is genuine and the Jewish pacifist Bloom is unrepresentative, by any standard definition, of Irishness (although the extent to which Joyce's work lends itself to a traditionalist and thematic literary politics is open to question). These poems, then, point to other, riskier pieces which adopt bolder procedures for insinuating difference within the English tradition.

Though it is a major concern of *Wintering Out* to discover a potential space for Heaney's writing between exclusivist Irish and English traditions, it finds the best way to do so (while remaining faithful to origins) through a linguistic politics which involves neither simply the naming of places, nor just local territorial awareness, but also local dialect. In this, Heaney pushes Montague's idealistic 'primal Gaeltacht' to a higher (or, more accurately, deeper) level. The poems which develop this strategy draw heavily on etymology and linguistics to fortify the claims of the local, viewing the landscape in linguistic terms – of vowel, consonant – and of pronunciation – 'the dislodged / slab of the tongue' (Heaney, 1972: 26). The opening poem, 'Fodder', anticipates this, its first line following directly from and qualifying its title – 'Or, as we said, / *fother*' – in a mocking 'invasion of the imaginative idiom by the critical' which, as O'Donoghue points out, 'is a figure for the supplantation of Standard English by local usage' (Heaney, 1972: 13; O'Donoghue, 1994: 57). (There is also justification for Heaney's practice in the sheer heterogeneity of English-language usage within Northern Ireland.) This use of specialised linguistic knowledge means that learning, a source of guilt in the first two books, is turned against the authority it serves there, a reversal most assertive in 'A New Song', which invokes 'river tongues', from their 'native haunts', to 'flood, with vowelling embrace, / Demesnes staked out in consonants', 'enlist[ing]' English placenames 'as rath and bullaun'; that is, as jointly English- and Irish-origin words (Heaney, 1972: 33).

'A New Song' shows how the decision to use dialectal forms in this way ultimately rests in the territorial form of Heaney's definition of selfhood, and his belief in its self-uttering, authenticating quality. He has claimed 'when we look for the history of our sensibilities I am convinced . . . that it is to . . . the stable element, the land itself, that we must look for continuity' (Heaney, 1980: 149). Yet land, as we have seen, is not only the grounding of the stable self; Heaney is preoccupied with it precisely because it is 'pre-occupied' in another sense, is the ground of sectarian division and of dispossession: 'if this was the country of community it was also the realm of division' (Heaney, 1980: 20). In Heaney, therefore, the rural is often less stable than it appears, fusing an English nature poetry tradition with the notion of the landscape as divided, stolen, waiting to be reclaimed. In 'Toome' the name's original Irish form 'prospects' material from 'a hundred centuries' via the 'musket balls' of 1798 when a United Irishman was hanged in the town. In 'Broagh' however – and for this reason the poem has attracted more attention than any other in the book – the inhabitants of the divided landscape are united briefly against all 'strangers' by their pronunciation of the name:

> Riverbank, the long rigs
> ending in broad docken
> and a canopied pad
> down to the ford.
>
> The garden mould
> bruised easily, the shower
> gathering in your heelmark
> was the black *O*
>
> in *Broagh*,
> its low tattoo . . .
>
> ended almost
> suddenly, like that last
> *gh* the strangers found
> difficult to manage.
>   (Heaney, 1972: 27)

Using dialect words drawn from Irish, Scots and English – 'rigs', 'docken', 'pad', 'boortrees' – the poem concludes with a learned joke; the English equivalent of the Irish fricative is only approximated by the '*gh*', the two ostensibly identical sounds actually having different origins (O'Donoghue, 1994: 63–5). Both Protestants and Catholics in Broagh can manage the shibboleth, uniting them – ironically given the intercommunal violence – against 'strangers', those from outside the locality. Moreover, as McCormack has claimed, the fusing reference and referent – name becoming place – is only the beginning of a process, in 'Toome' as well as 'Broagh', 'in which the classic notions of metaphor and simile are put under enormous pressure, with tenor and vehicle collaborating and masquerading as the other' (McCormack, 1986: 36). In this way, the relationship between 'human subject and poetic place' is undermined in 'Toome', which ends with the subject's survival but within a new pagan, biological realm where – Medusa-like – 'elvers tail my hair', while in 'Broagh' the process is rather one of linguistic synaesthesia, a merging of the senses (the 'black *O*' resembling one of the vowels in Rimbaud's 'Voyelles', 'tattoo' being both visual and audible). The locale, in uttering itself *through* Heaney – and the confusion of the subject gives the poems the appearance of mediumistic incantation – seems to itself resist 'occupation' and the attentions of 'strangers'.[20]

The fusion of speech-as-dialect with landscape and self is both an attempt to extend the schematic yoking of race and place in Montague and Corkery, and an intensification of the 'self-inwoven' aspect of Heaney's work already noted; of what Heaney refers, in profoundly cyclical terms, as 'poetry as revelation of the self to the self, as restoration of the culture to itself; poems as elements of continuity' (Heaney, 1980: 41). 'Gifts of Rain' imagines its figure 'hooped to where he planted', the Moyola river reminding him in the 'absence' of the Irish language to bear witness to 'the shared calling of blood' and 'spell[ing] itself: Moyola / . . . its own score and consort, // bedding the locale / in the utterance' (Heaney, 1972: 25). 'Bedding the locale in the utterance', recalling the 'geniuses' of 'Bog Oak' in the sixteenth-century sense of the word as the spirits of people or places, is what is attempted in 'Toome', 'Broagh' and the third placename poem, 'Anahorish' ('Anahorish' – the 'place of clear water' – indicates, like the 'wells' in 'Fodder', or the references to the Moyola, the extent to which this is a book organised around images of water; these stand as symbols of – Gaelic – pure origin, though this is only implicit, and as symbols of rebirth and territorial reclamation, as in 'A New Song'). Heaney is clearly also drawing on the *dinnseanchas* tradition as Montague had done, although for him division within the landscape has to be registered more consciously. To do so he thematises the clash noted by O'Donoghue in the early work between 'hard' and 'soft' sounds. Just as he tempers, to some degree, the exclusivist aspects of his revamped version of the Irish mode, he is at pains to stress the inclusivist aspect of his division between the 'hard' and the 'soft' linguistically: 'I think of the personal and Irish pieties as vowels, and the literary awareness nourished in English as consonants. My hope is that the poems will be vocables adequate to my whole experience' (Heaney, 1980: 37). 'Vocables' are the result of a quasi-sexual 'mating' of different classes of speech sounds. Typically, Heaney traces an example of a reconciliatory vocable to his own birthplace, Mossbawn, which he notes consists of Scots 'moss', for 'bog', and English 'bawn', a 'fortified house'; the family pronunciation of the last syllable, however, was as 'bán', the Gaelic word for white: 'So might not the thing mean the white moss, the moss of bog-cotton? In the syllables of my home I see a metaphor of the split culture of Ulster' (Heaney, 1980: 35). The procedure would be downplayed in 1990:

> All of this [self-possession grounded on intimacy with a landscape] came most carefully upon its hour in 1972 when political upheavals in Northern Ireland were pressing to the fore all over again old, unfashionable questions about the relationship between poetry, cultural heritage and national allegiance. A few months earlier I had proposed a somewhat oversimplified programme for the poetry I thought I wanted to write. In an attempt to sail between the Scylla of 'the Irish mode' . . . and the Charybdis of a more standardized, New Lines-ish, iambic English, I devised a conceit in which Irish experience was to equal vowels and the English literary tradition was to equal consonants, and my poems were to be 'vocables . . .' It was, admittedly, a fairly Euphuistic conception, but even so, it did signal a genuine stylistic problem, one which has been endemic to Irish writing.
> (P. Fallon, 1990: 13)

The disclaimer, however, is disingenuous; in 1977 he had spoken raptly of the same poems as 'erotic mouth-music by and out of the anglo-saxon tongue' which were at the same time 'faithful to one's own non-English origin' (Deane, 1977: 70). The 'conception' was clearly vital to Heaney, taking as it does the tentative soft/hard sound 'division', extending it to a larger vowel/consonant divide which, in turn, is mapped – at the risk of incoherence – on to a pre-existing, female/male, Ireland/England set of binary divisions. The effect is to profoundly complicate attempts at overcoming stereotypes through the achieved 'vocable' of the individual poem. There are, therefore, many different levels at which the poetry of *Wintering Out* resists anglicisation and simplifies and/or complicates inherited stereotypes in order to make its case (the notion of *The Faerie Queene*, in truth a highly fraught text, as 'dreaming sunlight' is a case of simplification). We might speak, then, of a local impulse to overcome division in *Wintering Out* being opposed, sometimes beyond the point at which it can maintain its detachment, by a principle of polarisation.[21]

North, published three years after *Wintering Out*, remains Heaney's most contentious book, and the one most central to his reputation. Using the 'arte-sian stanza' more consistently than in *Wintering Out*, it develops the earlier book's historical themes and archaeological-etymological approaches at a greater pitch of intensity and system, within the same two-part structure. The most notable difference is *North*'s open treatment of political violence, albeit through the form of an elaborate historical 'myth'. In 1973 Heaney had spoken of wanting to 'take the English lyric and make it eat stuff that it has never eaten before . . . like all the messy and, it would seem, incomprehensible obses-sions in the North, and make it still an English lyric' (Corcoran, 1986: 95). The pressure of the Troubles was primarily responsible for the urge to sound the 'messy . . . incomprehensible obsessions' through which 'his' community was implicated in them, and less obliquely than hitherto; and the extent to which Heaney succumbed to identification with, or approval of, that commu-nity's mythicised history in representing it was, inevitably, a major point of debate when *North* appeared. But the decision to tackle such material was, in the first place, the result of the distance and relative detachment his recent move south had made possible. It was, also, the result of an encounter just after writing 'Bogland' with *The Bog People*, a book by the Danish archaeolo-gist P. V. Glob.[22] Strikingly illustrated with photographs of Iron Age bodies dis-covered preserved in the peat bogs of Jutland, Glob's book argued that these were evidence of ritual sacrifices and inhumations to the fertility goddess Nerthus across Northern Europe (Joyce's brilliant coinage in *Finnegans Wake*, 'crorpse', might be applied as a description of their presumed function of ensuring agricultural fertility). Glob's book had a profound impact on Heaney. It confirmed 'Bogland' as an important symbolic insight into the nature of Irish history and identity, but also allowed the construction of a historical myth by which recent violence might be placed and understood within a larger frame. Some structure of this sort was clearly crucial to any exploration, but it could be argued that this one particularly suited Heaney's ritualistic and anti-modern tendencies.[23] Re-reading the myth-steeped work of Geoffrey Hill and David Jones, as well as *The Rough Field*, Heaney used Glob as the pre-text for an overarching historical myth in which the Troubles could be viewed as the most recent instalment of recurring cycles of Northern violence – Viking, English and Irish – over two millennia.

North undoubtedly does succeed in invoking 'messy . . . obsessions' in poems in which voyeurism, necrophilia, blood-sacrifice and hopeless abjection feature powerfully. As if to contain such transgressive material, however, the binary structure of the collection is elaborate, even rigid. The pair of prefatory dedication poems, which link family, love and rural community in an idealised vision of childhood and communal, seasonal 'calendar customs', are separated from the main text. The poems show what has been violated by the Troubles but also – through their archaic vocabulary and nostalgic ruralism – by education and modernity. Further distance is achieved by an internal 'frame' of 'Antaeus' and 'Hercules and Antaeus' in part one. Antaeus and Hercules embody, in an almost programmatic sense, the sensuous–instinctive and discursive–rationalist binarism within Heaney's work. While Hercules represents rational comprehension of atavism – in the name of which *North* is conceived – he also triumphs over it, and so over those territorial energies which the Antaean side of Heaney regards as his source of strength. Both poems can be read as allegories of colonisation, in which hopes for native renewal have become a consolatory myth, 'pap for the dispossessed'. They also trace an internal division, in which the rational is seen cutting across the deepest springs of inspiration. Together they embody Heaney's dilemma in *North*; how to represent a mythicised communal history, constituted by (and contributing to) the violence, and by doing so to move away from its mystifications via their fuller comprehension – while at the same time discovering his own unavoidable complicity with those myths and mystifications.

If Herculean rationality is inextricably immersed in Antaean knowing, the path to release, for Heaney, can only be through the unconscious of national and self understanding. He can proceed either 'lightly as pampooties / over the skull-capped ground' or, in the 'bog poems', through the 'slime kingdoms' of the 'insatiable bride', and these alternatives represent the stylistic procedures of the book's parts, which are more obviously complementary than in *Wintering Out* (Heaney, 1975: 24, 41). Three sequence-poems examine the components of the tripartite myth of *North* in turn, subjecting the familiar etymological terms to yield up their separate contributions to a national, or rather tribal, identity. 'Funeral Rites' focuses on 'Irish' (i.e. Northern Catholic) passivity and death-obsession; 'Viking Dublin: Trial Pieces' on Nordic violence and settlement-making; and 'Bone Dreams' on the quasi-sexual dimension of the colonial relation with the English (Heaney eroticises a pre-Reformation England in order to be able to reverse this by sexually possessing 'her' Pennine 'spine', 'Maiden Castle', and so on; although this has been seen as a love poem to England it is, rather, a seduction couched in anti-colonial, and strikingly sexist, terms). Heaney here says farewell to the etymological poem in appealing to (feminised) England to 'come back past / philology and kennings' to a memory which is pre-linguistic, geological rather than archaeological: 'I am screes / on her escarpments' (Heaney, 1975: 29). That the poems are to be read as tracing an actual history of conflict and conquest is confirmed by the appearance of 'North', the title poem, between 'Funeral Rites' and 'Viking Dublin: Trial Pieces', the Viking raids postdating Celtic settlement but preceding the Vikings' founding of Dublin. The structure unravels somewhat in the poems which follow 'Kinship', and the discursive mode of part two is heralded in 'Ocean's Love to Ireland' and 'Act of Union', which take up the imperialism-as-rape trope, and the more transparent 'Aisling' and 'The Betrothal of Cavehill'. The most disturbing and convincing historical presences in part one are undoubtedly the Vikings, since the Irish and English figures tend towards stereotypes of passive religiosity and active imperial predation. Given this, it is no surprise that 'Viking Dublin: Trial Pieces' is the historical poem in which Heaney is most self-critical, accusing himself – in an anticipation of 'Exposure' – of being 'Hamlet . . . skull-handler, parablist, / smeller of rot // in the state'. Interestingly Viking raids and Heaney's own quest are fused in the title poem, in which voices of 'violence and epiphany' are identified with poetry in 'the longship's swimming tongue' (Heaney, 1975: 23, 19).

If, overall, it is highly doubtful whether the 'myth' of Northern violence offered as a kind of explanation for the Troubles convinces (except as an arresting analogy for the intimacy of violence and poetry of 'North'), the dubiousness of 'coming to consciousness / by jumping in graves', receives notable expression in the six 'bog poems' at the heart of part one.[24] These had been anticipated by *Wintering Out*'s 'The Tollund Man', a piece which linked Glob's bog bodies to the Troubles, and also to an earlier Black and Tan atrocity:

> Tell-tale skin and teeth
> Flecking the sleepers
> Of four young brothers, trailed
> For miles along the lines.
> (Heaney, 1972: 48)

The poem concludes by imagining a pilgrimage to Aarhus where the Tollund man is on display in the 'old man-killing parishes'. In a sense, the *North* 'bog poems' – 'Come to the Bower', 'Bog Queen', 'The Grauballe Man', 'Punishment', 'Strange Fruit' and 'Kinship' – fulfil this vow. The six-part 'Kinship', the last of them, perhaps has the most in common with the placename poems of *Wintering Out*, in that – concerned with Heaney's own 'kinning' with the bog – it develops the reading of place as language, the bog as 'hieroglyphic peat'. Both bog and the self of the poet are involuted, self-infolded, made up of the 'ferments of husk and leaf', recycling vegetation or language (the leaves pun is implicit) (Heaney, 1975: 40, 43). Noting its allusiveness, Corcoran observes 'This bog is . . . already almost a poem'; and for Heaney another of its attractions is therefore its nature as a primal, self-originating source of identity and meaning, of the kind sought in 'Anahorish' (Corcoran, 1986: 103). This is most obvious in section four's opening line 'This centre holds', a rewriting of Yeats's 'the centre cannot hold' of 'The Second Coming'. The language of *Wintering Out* – 'This is the vowel of earth / dreaming its root' – is again on display, but now with a more gloomy emphasis on the 'rot' of its sources. The final image subjects the notion of the self of the speaker to some questioning, as if the letter 'I' of the lyric subject was literally being bent in growing 'out of all this / like a weeping willow / inclined to / the appetites of gravity' (Heaney, 1975: 43). The speaker enters the land as language is collapsed into it, tracing an inability to achieve full selfhood. The visible aspect of 'weeping', as opposed to the hidden subtext of the bog, is what will be revealed in part two. In the meantime, as well as developing these issues of language and, tentatively, of identity, 'Kinship' also addresses its bog-buried sources in more detail. Section six returns us to *North*'s myth of violence, asking Tacitus, the Roman commentator on the Nerthus cult in his *Germania* to read – like Heaney in Aarhus – 'the inhumed faces' of the victims of current atrocity, and, in some of the most controversial lines he has written, to

> report us fairly,
> how we slaughter
> for the common good
>
> and shave the heads
> of the notorious,
> how the goddess swallows
> our love and terror.
>   (Heaney, 1975: 45)

'Us' may be the Northern population as a whole – like the 'our' of 'our predicament' – but like that usage it also bears with specific weight on the IRA and the complicity of the minority in countenancing its campaign of violence. The gender and sexual aspects of this already noted can be seen in the image of women whose heads are shaved for sleeping with British soldiers, and in the last lines of the poem, with their overtones of fellatio and castration. The first image forms the basis of 'Punishment'; as Edna Longley has pointed out, 'As women cannot be "bridegrooms", Heaney must find them a different place in the "archetypal" pattern', his solution being to present the female bog bodies as adulteresses (E. Longley, 1986: 153). 'Punishment' deals with one of them, the Windeby bog girl of Glob's account, opening with a confusion of speaking self and victim – 'I can feel the tug / of the halter at the nape / of her neck . . .' – before the speaker distances himself to admit that he too would have cast 'the stones of silence'. The self-indictment is clear; he is the divided 'I'

> who would connive
> in civilized outrage
> yet understand the exact
> and tribal, intimate revenge.
>   (Heaney, 1975: 38)

This distancing and dumbness has its aesthetic dimension, too, as 'The Grauballe Man' shows. What the poem foregrounds is its 'poeticisation' of its object. Like the juices of the bog, the poetic process – or, rather, poetic language defined as essentially metaphoric – insistently tropes the brute facts of the murdered man's body; in succession his wrists are 'like bog oak', his heel a 'basalt egg', his instep 'a swan's foot', and so on. The poem matches Glob's own aestheticising impulse: 'The majestic head [that of the Windeby girl, who features in 'Punishment'] astonishes the beholder and rivets his attention. Dark in hue, *the head is still full of life and more beautiful than the best portraits of the world's greatest artists, since it is the man himself we see*'[25] (my emphasis). Glob's claim appears to be a *reductio ad absurdum* of realism, but it is actually a form of aestheticism; the dead man is appreciated not for his 'realism' at all, but as a set of conventional abstractions – 'majestic', 'full of life', 'beautiful', 'the world's greatest artists'. *The Bog People* is scarcely an objective work of archaeology, as this shows, and suggests a source for Heaney's pitting of 'reality' against art in his poems. After trying to comprehend the body through simile and metaphor, therefore, 'The Grauballe Man' interrupts itself with the question 'Who will say "corpse" / to his vivid cast?' before moving to a conclusion in which the artwork-like 'perfected' image of the man in his memory is 'hung in the scales / with beauty and atrocity'. The 'scales' of the poem finally kick, in its final lines, in favour of the 'actual weight / of each hooded victim, slashed and dumped', rebuking the aestheticising tendencies Heaney finds in himself (Heaney, 1975: 38). As this summary suggests, however, the poem is a little too schematic to be wholly convincing. 'Strange Fruit' makes a better job of self-confrontation.[26] It begins in the simile-ridden style of 'The Grauballe Man', but then turns, as if to apologise to the girl; as Heaney put it in an interview, 'the voice that came in when I revised [it] was a rebuke to the literary quality of that reverent emotion', so that she ends up 'outstaring axe / And beatification' (Haffenden, 1981: 67; Heaney, 1975: 39). Yet despite such apologias, the 'bog poems' – and others in part one, like 'Ocean's Love to Ireland' – attracted considerable critical flak. If reception outside Ireland was overwhelmingly positive, within it reactions were far more mixed. Attacks largely centred on the aestheticising representation of violence and Heaney's refusal to condemn it, most stingingly in Ciaran Carson's *Honest Ulsterman* review.[27]

A more important weakness of *North* is its use of gender stereotypes. Like Montague, Heaney as a Northern minority male poet (reliant on a Nationalist historical narrative) inclines towards such stereotypes, simultaneously asserting through them a masculine self *vis-à-vis* Britain as imperial aggressor and a feminine self *vis-à-vis* the Marian sensibility which colours his politics. Sexual and sectarian stereotypes are invariably fused; thus Heaney tropes Protestantism as masculine and sexless ('Our Father' is a 'between chaps sort of thing') while Catholicism is innately feminine and sexual, the 'something faintly amorous' in the Hail Mary' (Haffenden, 1981: 61; Allison, 1992: 113).

'The Tollund Man' – like 'Undine', in which phallic male labour 'liberates' the passive female – reveals the sexual charge the sacrificial aspect of the bog sacrifices held for Heaney; 'She tightened her torc on him / And opened her fen, / Those dark juices working / Him to a saint's kept body' (Heaney, 1972: 47). Moreover, the passage quoted earlier from 'Feeling into Words' makes clear not only the gender categories in which Heaney viewed the Irish/English struggle, but also his linkage of them to an older typology of the Mother Goddess, 'the goddess of the ground who needed new bridegrooms each winter to bed with her in her sacred place, in the bog'. As Jonathan Allison remarks, the bog is genitalised, not simply gendered; 'In the Nordic fertility sacrifice, which Heaney views as continuous with Celtic decapitation rituals and which he uses as a metaphor for Irish republican martyrdom, we may read an image of castration in the act of copulation, as the young male corpse becomes absorbed in the vagina of the goddess' (Allison, 1992: 110). The 'black maw / Of the peat' is a *vagina dentata* courted, in the necrophiliac 'Come to the Bower', by the poet-bridegroom: digging becomes a phallic, penetrative act, a cultural retrieval but fraught with the perils of castration (Heaney, 1975: 31). In 'Ocean's Love to Ireland' and 'Act of Union', as Patricia Coughlan has shown, Heaney recycles older representations of the feminine as passive, deter-mined by biological function and deprived of speaking voice, individuality and agency (Coughlan, 1991: 99–107). In the first, literary potency is made equiv-alent to possession of the 'ruined maid' of national territory; without their poetic equivalent of Viagra, Irish bards – in accordance with the sovereignty myth – 'sink like Onan', reduced to a masturbatory relationship with their muse (Heaney, 1975: 47). The ritual and cyclical tendencies of *North*, in Coughlan's reading, lead to, and stem from, gendered fetishisation, determin-istic closure, and the deployment of the scopic male gaze which objectivises and itemises women as Other, with the gender implications of *North* of a piece with the backward-looking traditionalism of Heaney's work generally. In this connection the use of 'strange', noted earlier, might be taken as revealing a degree of blindness on Heaney's part to his own procedures, a sense in which the mystifier is mystified by his aesthetic instincts. Heaney is a poet who cannot, in certain important and central aspects, deal with the contemporary or with female agency, the two frequently seen as aspects of each other (the dearth of love poetry in the first four collections an indication of the degree to which the maternal – woman defined in biological terms – subsumes the individual female figure). Yet conceding this does not fully explain the force of the bog poems (or, for that matter, of other poems in *North*, or elsewhere). On the other hand it is not enough to simply argue, as Michael Parker does, that in *North* Heaney is critical of himself and 'his community' (Parker, 1993: 151). Rather, some explanation of the power of the poems to disturb may be glimpsed in the book's contradictions. In this sense a poem like 'Bog Queen', like 'Strange Fruit', can better be seen as a moment of self-awareness in a debate which is finally overwhelmed by the strength of Catholic-Nationalist abjection.

For Allison 'Bog Queen' is crucial because it links the carefully established devotional relation with the land – hitherto accepted by the reader – to necrophilia and self-disgust. Confronted with the inadequacy of that relationship, from this point on the reader is forced to perceive the consciousness of the speaker of the poem as standing 'slightly to one side' of the seductions of self-immolation attacked by Carson and Longley and so implying criticism of it (Allison, 1992: 113).[28] Much here, of course, relies on how 'implicit' is taken (ironically, some of those who argue against an explicit political poetry find Heaney, on this point, not explicit enough). The sequence Allison traces supports his claims, but *North* later reverts to the stereotypes and complicities which had been put into question. Nevertheless, the endless recycling process within part one, the insistent collapsing of difference, the subjection of the self as 'grist to some ancient mill', significantly reworks a similar movement in Montague ('all my circling a failure to return') and Yeats (the centrifugal gyring of 'The Second Coming' reversed, its apocalyptic tone become abject). The anxiety or 'ambivalence' perceived by the speaker in his apologias is contradicted in notorious local cases ('I, too . . .'), but suffuses *North* as a whole, which is most insecure precisely when it is most assertive, and vice versa. The very notion of 'bog poems' reflects this: 'bog', after all, is precisely a sign of abjection, of the Irish generally (in colonial discourse) and the rural specifically (in urban Irish sensibility), where it connotes 'backwardness' (as in 'bogtrotters', 'bogmen', or, for British troops stationed in Northern Ireland, 'bog-wogs'). It is a short distance from comments such as that in *The Times* in 1963 – 'Irish industry has developed at a pace quite out of keeping with the traditional bogland lethargy' – to outright denigration.[29] The bog poems are predicated on a daring, if conservative, recuperation of a stereotype; yet the final outcome, given Heaney's mythical approach, is his immersion in the backwardness it represents. Accepting a scapegoat status, the identity of his speaker is crushed under the burden of multiple signification it has to bear, and the habitual excessiveness of Heaney's claim to unified, transcendent, self-present subjecthood grounded in a specific place – always suspect – is foregrounded and made vulnerable.[30]

So little history?

Yes, the Catholics: there is no equivalent Protestant voice. (C. C. O'Brien, 1975: 23–4)

Assessment of Protestant poetry has been based on the assumption that 'The contemporary northern Protestant's sense of history is . . . markedly similar to that of the Catholic nationalist' (Brown, 1988: 226). Both schemas claim a kind of Protestant historical amnesia: 'We have so little history / We must remember who we are' (Paulin, 1983: 29). Since there can be no such thing as a *lack* of history in any absolute temporal sense, this indicates a belief that the history there is not worth looking at. The belief stems partly from the fact that Irish history has been so consistently viewed in quasi-literary terms, and the North was relatively unproductive of literature before the 1960s. To the extent that this has changed over the last thirty years, in the North as well as the South, this is no longer the case, with Tom Paulin, especially, exploring Protestant histories and iconographies (masonic ritual, European Protestantism, Paisleyism, United Irishmen, etc.). But this exploration has been on the basis of that history as a counter, or mirror image, to Nationalist history. In this sense it follows Hewitt, uncovering more than him, but not in a fundamentally different manner. As David Miller has argued, Loyalism's asymmetrical relationship to the British state, through contractarianism, made it a peculiarly autonomous and threatened form of communal identity (Miller, 1978). The experience of Loyalists, since 1968, has – despite occasional reversals – been that of continuing erosion of self-esteem and control, seen in terms of abandonment by Westminster and gradual forced union with the Republic. As Kirkland notes, this is mediated to some extent in the poetry of James Simmons, in which the trope of marriage (with its personal origins in Lawrentian attitudes to sexuality, divorce and middle-age disillusion) mediates this process by presenting it as 'a clash of irreconcilable force between himself and the exotic other which leaves room only for the possibility of betrayal' (Kirkland, 1996: 67). Through the plebeian democratic ethos of his poetry, Simmons associates modernism with Catholicism (both are ritualistic and elitist) and women, and all three with a treacherous Republic. Thus, an insouciant detachment from the Troubles (described by him as a kind of 'blister' on a 'collective backside' on which Northerners must sit) shifts towards endorsement of the status quo (Simmons, 1974: 9). It is in the poignant ballads 'Claudy' and 'The Ballad of Gerry Kelly: Newsagent' that Simmons is at his best precisely because the impersonality of the genre prevents the use of the marriage/relationship trope. The first of these lists a small town's inhabitants at their daily activities before a particularly horrific bomb blast:

> For an old lady's legs are ripped off, and the head
> Of a man's hanging open, and still he's not dead.
> He is screaming for mercy, and his son stands and stares
> And stares, and then suddenly, quick, disappears.

> And Christ, little Kathleen Aiken is dead,
> And Mrs McLaughlin is pierced through the head.
> Meanwhile to Dungiven the killers have gone,
> And they're finding it hard to get through on the phone.
>   (Simmons, 1986: 125–6)

Stylistic details, such as the mimicking of the redundancy of ballad language, as well as its spareness – 'his son stands and stares / And stares' – contribute to the overwhelming effect. Such a poem can, however, by its very nature, only be written very rarely; and Simmons's later attempts to deal directly with the Troubles, such as 'From the Irish' and 'For a Dead Policeman', founder on the moralistic strain which, as part of his pugnacious libertarianism, had been present in his writing from the beginning.[31]

Derek Mahon

Simmons's consistent secularism and individualism highlight both the Protestant-background poet's opportunity for querying mythic and archetypal histories and, at the same time, show a shallowness and failure to empathise with lived communal experience which others felt only myth could furnish. Detachment has, of course, been read as disconnection from history. Yet Longley and Mahon, as already suggested, displace anxiety into an exploration respectively of natural and cultural forms, drawing on the more uneasy aspects of their predecessors – Hewitt, MacNeice and Beckett – to find appropriate, but non-appropriative means for dealing with the Troubles. In 1970 Derek Mahon left Northern Ireland to work in London. *Ecclesiastes*, a pamphlet which appeared that year, hints at the intensity of his need to escape in the self-directed violence of its title poem:

> God, you could grow to love it, God-fearing, God-
>   chosen purist little puritan that,
> for all your wiles and smiles, you are (the
>   dank churches, the empty streets,
> the shipyard silence, the tied-up swings)
>   (Mahon, 1990: 28)

The speaker mocks the tribal bardic urge by ironically urging himself to succumb to it: 'Bury that red / bandana, stick and guitar . . . Your people await you . . . God, you could do it, God / help you, stand on the corner stiff / with rhetoric, promising nothing under the sun.' This is a far cry from the plangent, abject relationship between Heaney and his 'people', and its destructive aspect can be seen in its full intensity in 'Matthew V. 29–30', from *The Snow Party* (1975). This remarkable *tour de force* takes the phrase 'If thine eye offend thee pluck it out' to elaborate a relentless and blackly comic attempt to eliminate the 'offence' of humanity itself; compliance leads from minor self-mutilation (removal of ear, nose, tongue, toes) to 'a prolonged course / of lobotomy and vivisection' and 'Paraffin for the records' of the offending self, then to 'deletion of . . . many people . . .' and finally of the entire universe out of which the self had been constituted. 'Only then', as the last line sardonically observes, 'was I fit for human society' (Mahon, 1986: 69–71). If millenarianism (his community's and Mahon's own) is sent up, so too is the impurity of the lyric 'I', tainted with selfhood, in a way which recalls the radical suspicion of self and tradition among earlier Anglo-Irish writers such as Beckett, Elizabeth Bowen and MacNeice. There is in Mahon's work a tension between this suspicion and the reassurances of discursive, empirical poetics:

as he puts it of Jaccottet, 'he is not greatly troubled by the disjunction between the signifying word and the thing signified; language is a given and suffices for his purpose, the lyrical apprehension of a given world' (Mahon, 1998: 11). Although language's 'givenness' wins out at the level of style in Mahon, it is always under pressure, signalled in his interest – unique among the Belfast poets – in modernism. In more general terms this means that Mahon sub-scribes to the general liberal-humanist definition of the poem and its embod-iment in shapely form of art's transcendence of discord. In 'Poetry in Northern Ireland' in 1970, Mahon had argued that 'The poets themselves have taken no part in political events, but they have contributed to that possible life, or to the possibility of the possible life; for the act of writing is itself political in the fullest sense. A good poem is a paradigm of good politics – of people talking to each other, with honest subtlety, at a profound level.' Yet the isolationism and apocalyptic, *sub specie aeternitatis* stance of these poems implies a critique of post-war consensualism and Western consumerism which verges on anti-humanism and is resolutely unconsoling. As Crotty puts it, 'The apocalyp-tic perspectives of "Lives" and "An Image from Beckett" derive from late twentieth-century conditions beyond the reach of MacNeice's humanism' (Crotty, 1995: 253). It is the tension between these positions, as Mahon was increasingly drawn to contemplate the maelstrom of the North, which pro-duced the exceptionally finely balanced poetry of *Lives* (1972) and *The Snow Party*, poetry which fastidiously distances itself from the mundane world of sectarian horrors even as it finds itself increasingly complicit in them.

The difference between such an understanding of history and that of Montague or Heaney can be traced, briefly, in one of those poems which reveals the kind of intertextual debate which has been a constitutive feature of Northern Irish poetry. The poem 'Lives' is affectionately but slyly dedicated to Heaney, and critiques the archaeological paradigm behind 'Bogland' and its successors in a short trimeter measure which itself mimics the 'artesian' qua-trains of *Wintering Out*. The poem's single voice details a series of bizarrely diverse incarnations which add up to (by refusing to add up) a mischievous alternative to the 'plants' forming any 'nubbed treasure'. It opens with a Heaney-like find:

> First time out
> I was a torc of gold
> And wept tears of the sun.
>> (Mahon, 1990: 36)

But the abruptly irreverent opening line signals what will follow. The voice becomes that of Elpenor's oar from Ithaca,[32] 'a bump of clay // In a Navajo rug', 'a stone in Tibet', 'A tongue of bark / At the heart of Africa' and, finally, an anthropologist. A random series of events encountered by the voice – an electric shock in Tucson, the outbreak of World War I – add to the sense of arbitrariness. The eclectic mixture of (non-Irish) belief systems, narratives and cultures prevents a single historical narrative, and provides stimuli to the mobile imagination rather than hermeneutical props for ontological ground-edness.[33] This range implicitly identifies nationalisms as Eurocentric and tele-ological, rejecting precisely the linear 'artesian' narrowness Heaney prized, and for this reason the archaeologist-as-poet is discarded in favour of the anthro-pologist as a more appropriate model. Anthropologists may study living as well as dead cultures, and are – as the study of human beings go – relativists. Nev-ertheless, Mahon ironises this figure too in the final lines. Incarnating the plu-ralist desire to know other 'lives', the anthropologist nevertheless carries with him 'credit card, dictaphone, / Army surplus boots / And a whole boatload / Of photographic equipment', paraphernalia which ultimately prevents him from entering what he studies, symbolising his presumptiveness. The self is problematised, this time through excess rather than lack of possibility ('I know too much / To be anything any more'), but the main point is to counter imposed, pre-existing meanings; and the ending attacks both those who (like Mahon himself) are tempted to appropriate the identity of the anthropologist, and those (like Heaney) who would inhabit history:

> And if in the distant
>
> Future someone
> Thinks he has once been me
> As I am today,
>
> Let him revise
> His insolent ontology
> And teach himself to pray.
> (Mahon, 1990: 37–8)

A series of poems build on the conceit of 'Lives's' speaking objects to mock the presumption of humanity from a still more detached point of view. For Mahon, objects, particularly worn ones, speak – 'Homage to Malcolm Lowry' opens 'For gear your typewriter and an old rugby boot' – and speak against all human constructions (Mahon, 1990: 56). 'The Apotheosis of Tins' is set in a sewer outlet on a beach and speaks on behalf of 'the terminal democracy / of hatbox and crab, / of hock and Windowlene' (Mahon, 1986: 74). The dis-interested 'tins' and other *disjecta* of the title seem, as O'Neill puts it, 'to have read Keats, *Hamlet*, and perhaps, a dash of Kant', as they soliloquise: 'deprived of use, we are safe now / from the historical nightmare' (O'Neill, 1999: 216). What has been discarded by humanity is safe from its constructions and is at liberty to 'resist your patronage, your reflective leisure'. Anti-utilitarianism has obvious relevance to Mahon's perception of his background, whose more philistine aspects confirm his interest in *l'art brut* as much as *l'art pour l'art*. At the same time, however, their desire to discover 'saintly / devotion' lingers on in tension with their effacement, 'self-knowledge' poised against the desire for a 'pre-lapsarian metaphor' (Mahon, 1990: 45). The wittiest and most energetic of these testings of anthropocentrism, 'The Mute Phenomena', is a version of the final sonnet in de Nerval's sequence *Les Chimères*, translated by Mahon in more orthodox fashion in 1982. The original – with its epigraph 'Everything feels!' – alludes to the Pythagorean belief in the 'sympathy' possessed by all seemingly inanimate objects. Behind the rewritten version lies Mahon's knowledge of more recent French literature, influenced by existentialism and phenomenology, however. These contexts, not yet critically explored, can be seen in the resemblances between Mahon's practice and those of French writers of the 1950s and 1960s such as Alain Robbe-Grillet. For Robbe-Grillet, the leading figure of the *nouveau roman*, metaphor is to be seen as a fundamentally deceptive and sentimental device which forces the reader to draw comparisons between the human and the non-human which have no basis in reality. In his early novel *Les Gommes*, for example, the central character, Wallas, is a special agent sent to solve a crime who gradually realises that the real culprit is himself, since, as a human being, he is continually guilty of imposing symbols and meanings on objects. Mahon's poem is playfully utopian in a way alien to Robbe-Grillet; but it is nevertheless a short step from the assumptions behind such a novel and 'The Mute Phenomena's' brick wall which 'resents your politics and bad draughtsmanship' and the 'ideal society', conceived in a lost hubcap, 'which will replace our own' (Mahon, 1990: 64).

The historical nightmare and stony identities of tin cans and hubcaps are not so easily evaded for human beings, however, and their desire to escape through renunciation can at best be only temporary. The title opening poem of *The Snow Party*, 'Afterlives', shows Mahon's further absorption of the Troubles in his third volume. The poem, dedicated to Simmons, shares something of the dedicatee's own sexist and plebeian truculence – 'What middle-class cunts we are / To imagine . . . That our privileged ideals / Are divine wisdom' – and, in its expletives (later gentrified to 'middle-class twits'), speaks of the suppressions of class and gender involved in the construction of the intensely masculine selfhood of the Northern poets. A sense that he has not 'lived [the Troubles] bomb by bomb', contributes the speaker's sense of posthumous existence (Mahon, 1990: 50–1); and the word 'afterlife' is also to be found in 'Leaves' (chiming with 'Lives') later in the book, in which – in a variation on the Virgilian epic simile for the hordes of dead – autumn leaves in 'the heaven / Of lost futures' symbolise 'The lives we might have led / [Which] have found their own fulfilment' (Mahon, 1990: 52). The anguished difficulty of retaining a residual sense of attachment to 'my own' is allegorised in 'The Last of the Fire Kings', in which the fire king/poet – the priest of the sacred grove presented in the opening pages of Fraser's *The Golden Bough*, fused with Celtic fire festivals – expresses a yearning to be 'Through with history'. The fire king himself, as communal expectation requires, has reigned for five years, awaiting the potential usurper he must fight, while his mind is

Perfecting my cold dream
Of a place out of time,
A palace of porcelain

Where the frugivorous
Inheritors recline
In their rich fabrics
Far from the sea.
  (Mahon, 1990: 59)

The desire to be 'free from history' or 'out of time' leads, the passage initially implies, to the ivory tower of artistic transcendence. Such withdrawal is relished, but also mocked (in the polysyllabic and obscure 'frugivorous' and the alliteration on 'p'), for the fire king is in Belfast, not at all 'far from the sea'. Although wanting to end the 'barbarous cycle' by killing himself – so breaking that cyclical, traumatic history Mahon elsewhere accepts as distinctively Irish – this will not be allowed by the 'fire-loving / People, rightly perhaps'. 'Rightly perhaps' indicates both wavering attachment and guilt at not inhabiting, like them, 'a world of / Sirens, bin-lids / And bricked-up windows'; who is he, in other words, to 'release them / From the ancient curse'? To succumb will be to 'die their creature and be thankful'. There appears to be little ground between subservience and the vatic role Mahon refuses.

The inhuman 'cold dream' of perfection of the work rather than the life glances sideways at the chilly, exquisite tableau of 'The Snow Party' itself, whose seventeenth-century Japanese source – Basho's aptly titled *The Narrow Road to the Deep North* – suggests the haiku as one source for Mahon's trimeters. It uses Basho's account of a tea ceremony held while snow is falling to juxtapose oriental civility and culture with its apparent opposite. As the china 'tinkles', elsewhere ('hygienically cordoned off in their own stanzas', as Kendall points out), 'they are burning / Witches and heretics / In the boiling squares' and 'Thousands have died since dawn / In the service / Of barbarous kings' (Mahon, 1990: 57; Kendall, 1994: 109). While this suggests an anti-Orientalism – barbarous Europe and civilised Japan – which follows the anti-Eurocentric pattern of 'Lives', the last verse implies a more general comment on the way artistic withdrawal shades into irresponsibility:

But there is silence
In the houses of Nagoya
And the hills of Ise.

Moreover the Irish dimension of the implied rebuke to such a 'cold dream' has already been made clear in the middle section of the poem, where the reiteration of 'falling' snow unmistakably echoes the closing cadences of Joyce's 'The Dead', which centre on Gabriel Conroy's failure to comprehend his society (and to love). The 'silence' is both necessary for aesthetic contemplation and creation ('the mind moves upon silence', in Yeats's phrase), and partakes of the culpable silence of those who do not speak out in times of persecution. A despairing silence may oppose burning, boiling and killing, but in acknowledging its ineffectuality it becomes complicit with them; in the words of Brecht's 'An die Angeboren' (translated by Mahon in *The Hunt by Night*), 'What sort of times are these / When idle chat is treated / As wicked nonsense, / Implying as it does / Avoidance of other topics?' (Mahon, 1982: 18). The insight of the poem, then, is that the apparent conflict between art and historical nightmare is, horrifyingly, no conflict at all; as the seventh of Walter Benjamin's 'Theses on the Philosophy of History' puts it, 'There is no document of civilization which is not also a document of barbarism.' For Benjamin, it is not only that the artwork is, like history, appropriated by the victors, but that implicit in all art in class societies is the expropriated labour which permits the leisure and patronage necessary for its creation; thus, 'the cultural treasures [the historical materialist] surveys have an origin which he cannot contemplate without horror' (Benjamin, 1979: 258).[34]

Mahon's most admired individual poem – and one which has been treated as a summation of the work of the 1960s' generation of Northern poets and as the 'culmination of this phase of Mahon's career' – is the last piece in *The Snow Party*, 'A Disused Shed in Co. Wexford' (Riordan, 1984: 175). Dedicated to J. G. Farrell, whose novel *Troubles* (1970) – set in the Civil War of 1922–23 – ends with the burning-down of a hotel, the poem imagines a shed full of mushrooms abandoned, and then discovered half a century later in the present of the Northern Irish Troubles. The poem could thus be said to conflate the fate of the Anglo-Irish caste and the larger Protestant population in the Free State and the Republic – some burnt-out, but generally well-treated, though subject to slow attrition through emigration and intermarriage since the 1920s – with that of Protestants in Northern Ireland. Yet to say as much is to simplify the poem which conspicuously does not begin with this subject, but – in keeping with its epigraph ('Let them not forget us, the weak souls among the asphodels', from Seferis) – with a proposition and a series of abandoned, depopulated waste locations familiar from the rest of the collection:

> Even now there are places where a thought might grow –
> Peruvian mines, worked out and abandoned
> To a slow clock of condensation . . .
> Indian compounds where the wind dances
> And a door bangs with diminished confidence . . .
>
> (Mahon, 1986: 79)

As the poem homes in on the shed where 'A thousand mushrooms crowd to one keyhole' '[wait] for us in a foetor / Of vegetable sweat', this proposition remains hanging over the poem like a question; what might the 'thought' be? Marvellously atmospheric, but haunted by its own initial query, the poem proceeds via a mixture of descriptive and hinted-at allegorical modes, the latter particularly in evidence in the fourth verse:

Those nearest the door grow strong –
'Elbow room! Elbow room!'
The rest, dim in a twilight of crumbling
Utensils and broken flower-pots, groaning
For their deliverance, have been so long
Expectant that there is left only the posture.

One way of interpreting this is that the shed, as the self-isolated ('dim' and locked) statelet of Northern Ireland, contains two kinds of 'mushrooms', the Protestants who assertively monopolise most of what little light there is ('"Elbow room! Elbow room!"') and the Catholics, defined by their supplicant, abject 'posture'. This possible allegory of sectarianism, however, is countered by the poem's presentation of their common plight, and by the far broader vistas of human suffering it will open out to in its final verse (although on the other hand it should caution us against seeing the mushrooms as being there only to be metamorphosed into 'representatives of the lost, suffering and victimised throughout history') (O'Neill, 1999: 217). Edna Longley, for example, has remarked that Mahon 'takes a predominantly religious view of history', and the 'expropriated mycologist' of the third verse certainly echoes the 'ruined millionaire' of Eliot's *Four Quartets,* while the poem generally presents what she calls 'a split poetic psyche' divided between the mushrooms and the 'god'-like narrator who opens the shed (E. Longley, 1995: 296). This emphasis on the religious aspect of Mahon's poetry is in keeping with Longley's earlier reading of 'A Disused Shed', in which the poem (and poetry) itself is offered in quasi-religious form against the depredations of history. Given the references to 'a half-century in the dark' and 'the flash-bulb firing-squad we wake them with' in the penultimate verse, and the direct historical reference of the last verse, it is unsurprising, however, that most critics have seen the poem as a turn towards the history which Mahon could be said to distance himself from in his first three collections:

They are begging us, you see, in their wordless way,
To do something, to speak on their behalf
Or at least not to close the door again.
Lost people of Treblinka and Pompeii!
'Save us, save us,' they seem to say,
'Let the god not abandon us
Who have come so far in darkness and in pain.
We too had our lives to live.
You with your light meter and relaxed itinerary,
Let not our naïve labours have been in vain!'
(Mahon, 1986: 80)

For Seamus Deane, the 'sad and terrifying scene' which 'the cracking lock / And creak of hinges' reveals is the release of the mushroom/people 'into, not from, history'. As he puts it, Mahon in this poem seems to 'invert his usual procedure: the lost lives are not lived after history, but before it' (Deane, 1985:

163). This claim is in accordance with Deane's more general one that at this point of his career, Mahon is no longer a poet who wishes to be 'through with history', but one who wishes to encounter it more directly (and by 'history' Deane intends a specifically Nationalist-inflected Irish history). If this is more persuasive than Longley's attempt to cordon the poem off as a self-subsistent artefact whose function is to resist history, it is nevertheless a somewhat narrow reading which does not fully account for the last verse's invocation of 'Treblinka and Pompeii', clearly chosen as examples of natural and human cat-astrophes respectively, or for the mushrooms' veiled atomic symbolism. The apocalyptic dimensions of Mahon's poetry, already noted, are present in 'A Disused Shed' also. In this sense, Maurice Riordan's psychological slant on Deane's reading – that 'the disused shed is also a version of Plato's cave and the loss expressed is metaphysical' – has some force. Riordan's claim that the mushrooms represent 'all that is suppressed in consciousness', however, while suggestive (there is undeniably a confrontation between the civilised 'we' and the denied, atavistic life of the mushrooms), still does not explain the mute pleading of the mushrooms, the apparent disproportion of the reference (par-ticularly to Treblinka) or the pathos of the conclusion (Riordan, 1984: 176). Similarly, the pun on 'light meter' – the poet's, and that of the tourist and 'flash-bulb firing squad' of the media discovering Northern Ireland – impli-cates the poet-narrator with the mushrooms themselves, of course, and shows the speaker to be unresolvedly 'trapped between complicity and an outright *non serviam* – like the poem itself', while the poem also offers at one level a version of the Protestant historical pathos found in pieces such as 'Nostalgias' (Kendall, 1994: 108). But perhaps what all of these readings miss, in their attempt to specify 'A Disused Shed's' 'meaning' is its resistance to a singular interpretation. More radically than a phrase like 'richly ambiguous' would suggest, 'A Disused Shed' finds its significance in Mahon's writing as a poem of great formal accomplishment which holds together disjunctive, competing and ultimately unresolvable realist, allegorical and symbolic modes of writing. The strain of this is most evident in the 'risk' of the line about Treblinka and Pompeii, whose exclamation mark 'admits that this line is violently, almost involuntarily, yoking together heterogeneous things'; the events are incom-mensurate, not mere illustrations of disaster, as most critics assume (O'Neill, 1999: 217). This may lie behind an understanding of the 'thought' which has hovered above the poem from its first line; that in its freedom to open up the horrors of history, the poem highlights its inadequacy to 'represent' its victims. The mushrooms may wish 'us' to 'speak on their behalf', but the narrator does not do so; rather, he 'ventriloquises their own "wordless" speech' (O'Neill, 1999: 218). The danger the poem faces is that of arrogating the suffering of the mute victims of history in the process of attempting to speak for them. 'A Disused Shed' mocks the idea that history can be transcended in poetry while at the same time – like 'Lives' but at a greater pitch of despair – it recognises past events not as 'a history' but as narrative.

Michael Longley's Troubles

The circumspection of Longley's attitude to the Troubles is well known and explains the lack of the interest in larger historical and mythic frameworks of specifically Irish provenance in his work.[35] Nevertheless, if the imagination is autonomous and essentially non-political – 'the imagination has a life of its own, a life that has to be saved: if it isn't everything else will be lost' – the poet unavoidably 'responds to tragic events in his own community' and would be 'a poor artist if he did not seek to endorse that response imaginatively' (Kirkland, 1996: 57; M. Longley, 1995b: 73). The contradiction between these two points is bridged by the word 'imaginatively', and it is the quality of invention in Longley's best poems which give them their distinctive quality, making for a tendency to go off at the 'splintering tangent of the ricochet' which cuts across the generally even sensibility of the poet and his adherence to well-made forms (M. Longley, 1991a: 87).

This can be seen in 'Wounds', where an elegy for his father, a 'belated casualty' of World War I, leads to a vision of the unimaginable – No Man's Land as 'a landscape of dead buttocks' – or in the mixed modes of 'Wreaths' (from *The Echo Gate*), three poems whose subjects are given in terms of their jobs (M. Longley, 1991a: 86, 148–9). All are elegies for the Troubles dead, and each involves a violation of the domestic. Thus, in 'Civil Servant', 'someone' walks in and shoots the man cooking breakfast: 'A bullet entered his mouth and pierced his skull, / The books he had read, the music he could play.' After his body has been removed, his grieving widow takes 'a hammer and chisel' and '[removes] the black keys from his piano'. The connection between 'the music he could play' and this apparently irrational gesture is resonant, but in a disturbing, not consolatory way. If it suggests the violence of loss, is it also a comment on discordance (black notes being sharps and flats), or on the black-and-white, binary distinctions made so lethally manifest in the killing? The poem offers no explanation, but like the others it makes the larger point that the first step towards the killing was the dehumanising reduction of the man to his official function (M. Longley, 1991a: 48). Even more disturbing is the third poem, 'The Linen Workers' – about a massacre of a busload of factory workers – which begins with a seemingly bizarre meditation on Christ's teeth:

> Christ's teeth ascended with him into heaven:
> Through a cavity in one of his molars
> The wind whistles: he is fastened for ever
> By his exposed canines to a wintry sky.
> (M. Longley, 1991a: 149)

There is present here a buried image of the way in which people are fastened to sectarian identities – the 'canine' working somewhat as 'the weasel's tooth' in Yeats's 'Nineteen Hundred and Nineteen' as a metonym for vicious infighting – which are themselves, like the 'cavity', hollow. Through the insistence on sectarian division, Christ (and Christianity) are themselves 'fastened', crucified even, to the 'wintry' atavisms of the North. The conceit is elaborated further in the second verse, in which Christ's smile reminds the speaker of his father's false teeth: 'they wore bubbles, / And, outside of his body, a deadly grin'. 'Deadly', like 'canine' keeps the as yet unmentioned slaughter lurking beneath the surface of the poem. This breaks in abruptly in the opening line of the next – 'When they massacred the ten linen workers . . .' – drawing the estranging images into the vortex of the imagined massacre with its bodies falling and, falling from them, 'spectacles, / Wallets, small change, and a set of dentures: / Blood, food particles, the bread, the wine'. The 'bread' and 'wine' refer back, bitterly rather than in any consolatory way, to the Christ in whose name, ostensibly, the massacre has been conducted, or the religious sanction given by some to the actions of paramilitary groupings ('Christ's teeth' perhaps echoing the archaic blasphemous exclamation 'God's teeth!'). In the final verse, Longley returns to his father's death and how, attending to his body in order to 'bury [him] once again', he must give the corpse its spectacles, small change, 'And into his dead mouth slip the set of teeth'. The reported journalistic detail of the false teeth fallen on the road is seen as the trigger of the poem and its oblique meditation on the roots of the Northern crisis. Longley's need to 'endorse' 'imaginatively' his 'response' to a public event has overcome his fear of being 'an interloper, a voyeur' by the fact that the public horror has invaded the private grief in the form of the false teeth. The intrusion provides what could be the only possible sanction for addressing a public event.

North and South

The Northern virus inevitably infected the Southern body politic. The wonder is that it infected it so little for so long. (Lee, 1989: 458)

The Republic to which Heaney moved in August 1972 after receiving death threats (and followed by the jeering of a Paisleyite newspaper) was one in which the optimism generated by modernisation was beginning to sour. Crisis gradually impinged on the Southern state, although to a limited degree and against much resistance. The government of the Republic had, in August 1969, deployed troops along the border as rioting in Belfast reached its height, and 3,500 families (3,000 of them Catholic) were driven from their homes in the (then) greatest population displacement in Europe of the post-war period. But although Jack Lynch had ambiguously declared that 'we will not stand by', the Republic never intended to do more than offer succour to the expected flood of refugees. As Brown notes, 'It was clear throughout the 1970s that the majority of the population of the Republic did not wish the Northern crisis and the avowed republican nationalism of the state's traditional ideology to interfere with the economic progress of the country' (Brown, 1985: 281). Nevertheless, the Troubles were seen to some extent as a return of the Republic's own repressed atavisms and a disturbing reminder of the violent origins of the state, and voices were raised both in favour of 'the struggle' in the North, as well as against the Republic's own previous unwillingness to confront the logic of its irredentist claims on the province in Articles 2 and 3 of the 1937 Constitution. The nightmarish intensity of the debate this generated is well caught in Paul Durcan's 'Ireland, 1972', which offers the traditional trope of the nation as family in shocking, lethally dysfunctional terms:

> Next to the grave of my beloved grandmother
> The grave of my first love murdered by my brother.
>   (Durcan, 1995: 61)

The ambivalence of the response in the South was writ large in the 1970 Arms Trial case, in which two leading ministers – Noel Blayney and Charles Haughey – were sacked by Lynch on suspicion of having chanelled funds to the IRA, and then tried and acquitted by the courts. The survival of this episode by the government indicated the fundamental stability of the state; as Haughey's later political success would show, he was hardly damaged by this association in the eyes of the electorate. Nor should hindsight be allowed to conceal the fact that it took almost a decade for most to be convinced, North and South, that the Troubles were not some temporary manifestation of violence (in the North itself, hopes for a positive social transformation continued to linger through the early 1970s) (McCormack, 1986: 14).[36]

In mediating these, those poets who had emerged from the relative optimism of the 1960s produced a poetry very different from that which might have been expected following the epic labours of the *Miscellany* poets. The chief characteristic of the new situation was the fragmentariness it induced in the still-recovering poetry scene in the Republic. While *The Rough Field*, that is, provided a model for some poets of the uses of mythic history, it was least influential in the Republic and among the youngest poets. This had negative, but also positive, aspects; not all poets, *pace* McCormack, turned to ruralism. On the one hand, experimental poetry was a casualty of fragmentation and the renewed involution and focus on identity and community; New Writers' Press, and – to some extent – the poets associated with it, lapsed, as Trevor Joyce has put it, 'into a long sleep from the mid-1970s through the mid-1990s, troubled by occasional bursts of REM' (Gilonis, 1998: 22). On the other hand there was a positive response, insofar as fragmentation released a wide number of voices hitherto suppressed not only by official discourses of Irishness, but overshadowed by attempts to 'represent' the modernising nation in epic form. These voices, whose distinctive experience had been suppressed or annexed by Nationalism (though some of them emerge vociferously in Clarke's satires), included the population of the Gaeltacht areas, the working class and city dwellers generally, women and the young. The greatest contrast with

Northern Irish poetry of the period is, then, the lack of a universalising tone, or aesthetic 'centre', which could 'hold' or – given the experimental development of Kinsella and the re-orientation towards the North by Montague in his post-*Rough Field* work – of a dominant figure (such as Heaney furnished for Northern poets even after his move South). As Montague himself put it in 1974, 'One's general impression of the younger poets is of a competing multiplicity of styles, from which only a few names separate themselves' (Montague, 1989: 125). But by way of compensation, as it were, there emerged, for the first time since the 1930s, Irish women poets of achievement.

One clear result of the Troubles was a switch in external attention from the *Miscellany*-generation poets (this compounded by Kinsella's stylistic 'turn') to those in the North. The imbalance in reception – partly because Northern Ireland was news, partly because of the sheer excellence of Heaney, Mahon, Longley and their successors – cast something of a shadow over the already tense debates on identity which the Troubles had opened up. As Eiléan Ní Chuilleanáin has written, 'The Republic seemed, in spite of its territorial claims on the six Northern counties, its inheritance of a long literary tradition which embraced the whole island, its very considerable influence on both cultural and political events in the North and its excellent, and interesting writers, to belong on the sidelines, culturally and politically' (Ní Chuilleanáin, 1992: 26). The Northern poets' influence on those in the Republic was thus resisted by older poets there, and more enthusiastically accepted by younger ones, and it is from this period that the dismissal of the idea of 'Group' as a 'journalistic phenomenon' originates (encouraged, to some extent, by some of the Northern poets themselves). In formal terms, only Eavan Boland can be regarded as having affinities with the Northerners' attachment to the well-made lyric (although this would resurface in still younger poets in the Republic later in the decade). Ní Chuilleanáin, however, registers the South's detachment of itself from Northern atavisms in her comment that 'In Northern Ireland, with its weighty inherited problem of colonialism, it is possible, as it has been for Irish Nationalist poets over the centuries, to blame Britain or the past for the deformities of the present. Heaney's poems of prehistoric ritual killings . . . may be seen as strategies to avoid the asking of certain harsh questions close to home, the ascription of particular blame, in a way which seems more possible in the North than the Republic' (Ní Chuilleanáin, 1992: 34). This identifies the stronger satiric and public scope of poetry in the Republic in the 1970s – as in the case of Durcan – without indicting the obliquity of Northern writing.

While there was a dispersal of Northern poets, the paradoxical effect of the Troubles on them was to confirm the aesthetic of the well-made, of craft, of the pre-1968/69 Group, sharpening the distinctiveness of their situation and preserving their air of cohesiveness (indeed, it could be argued that violence ensured that Northern poetry *increased* its autonomy). While considerable interchange between the different poetries occurred, the different experience of the Troubles served to confirm a sense of divergent trajectories, and the patronising tone of some Southern critics can be seen counterpointing a Northern brashness, even rudeness.[37] On the other hand, the attacks on the perceived insularity and mediocrity of Dublin literary life from the North were constant.[38] Behind some of these attacks from the North was the attempt at self-assertion against the belief that, in the words of another Southern critic, 'Ulsterness, willy-nilly, means Irishness; and it is the poets, generation on generation, who have rediscovered and declared this truth in different ways' (Lucy, 1977: 18). The continuing weakness of the poetic infrastructure in the Republic, and the difficulty of being published (as compared with the seeming ease of Northern poets in attracting London publishers), have also to be taken into account. Boland and Durcan – rough contemporaries of the Belfast poets – published first collections in 1967, but their second books did not appear until 1975.

Eavan Boland

The lack of poetry by women in Ireland stems historically from a number of factors: an intensely patriarchal public and private ethos, intensified by religious patriarchy and Nationalist and Loyalist hypermasculinist constructions of subjectivity, in which women's choice was 'between Virgin Nun or Conjugal Rights' (Kelly, 1988: 23); large families (bearing particularly on Catholic women, given the opposition of the Church to contraception and abortion); lack of social provision, meaning that women were attached to the roles of carers for disabled and elderly family members; and a tradition of male writing about women in which religious and Nationalist iconography and tradition combined to represent them as passive, emblematic of territory, archetypal, to be spoken for, rather than speaking their own individuated subjectivity. In addition to this, as feminist critics have noted, poetry is the most elite of the literary arts and has traditionally been the last to yield a place to women writers. It is in the context of all of these barriers that the career of Eavan Boland has to be seen as exemplary for Irish women poets from the 1960s onwards, when women poets appeared together with a broader movement for women's rights in Ireland, as in the rest of the Western world. Boland's exemplary status is partly due to the fact that her career so closely parallels this general movement, the way in which her writing moved hesitantly towards self-definition. In describing the difficulty of starting a literary career in Dublin in the 1960s in *Object Lessons*, it is therefore the admission of her initial ignorance which is as important as her gradual understanding of the terms of her exclusion: 'I know now that I began writing in a country where the word woman and the word poet were almost magnetically opposed. One word was used to invoke collective nurture, the other to sketch out self-reflective individualism' (Boland, 1996: xi). The subtitle of that book – 'The Life of the Woman and the Poet in Our Time' – indicates both the size of the task and the earnest literalness with which she tried to link 'the Woman' and 'the Poet' which had previously been kept apart by custom.

Boland's earliest work, collected in *New Territory* of 1967, seems, despite its title, anything but 'new' in the 'territory' it covers. Disabled by her status and attempting to 'write like a man', her apprenticeship was prolonged by her first impulse to 'write male poems'. A peremptory Yeatsian tone appears both imitative and compensatory for a felt lack of power; mythological subject bespeak a disconnection, almost a willed isolation from the stresses of mod- ernisation and the crumbling of older identity discourses in the Republic of the time. For all that, Boland's account of these years in her autobiographical *Objects Lessons* (1996) is a moving one, and there are hints in these artificial and decorous pieces of the strains involved in suppression. In the best account of her early work, Derek Mahon has pointed to the hieratic and legendary properties of the poems, exemplified in a piece like 'The Flight of the Earls':

> Now in the middle ages see
> The legendary boy of king and queen:
> A peacock of all chivalry
> He dies at twenty on some battle-green
> And ever since
> The good Black Prince
> Rides to the land of might-have-been.
>   (Boland, 1995: 6)

'Kings, princes, courtiers and "sycophants" throng these pages; women are few and far between', as Mahon puts it, and this is true enough. But the presence of such figures arguably hints at an interest in negotiations of power which would later take more overt and specifically feminist forms; indeed, sympa- thetic though he is, Mahon unwittingly identifies the problem faced by Boland when he observes that 'I now realise that she was struggling to assert herself in what she correctly perceived as a male-dominated literary culture. Was it, for her, a necessary struggle? She had only to look at a door and it flew open' (Mahon, 1996: 106). The question of the second, and the chivalry of the final sentence, reveal only too well the difficulty of having doors opened for one, rather than being allowed to open them oneself. Nevertheless, if the longest poem in the collection, 'The Winning of Etain', has for its heroine a figure who neither thinks nor acts on her own behalf, two poems – 'From the Painting Back from Market by Chardin' and 'Athene's Song' – sound a 'proleptically "feminist" note', one which is returned to – albeit still in a muted key – in her next collection, *The War Horse* (1975) (Mahon, 1996: 107).

This book shows a distinct shift in Boland's strategies and aims, and marks the point at which she moves from a historiography 'still male-oriented and Plutarchan' (Mahon, 1996: 108). A nascent feminism is crossed with an aware- ness of the contemporary triggered by the Northern crisis, and the title poem is a revealing, if not wholly successful attempt, to deal with the intrusion of Northern violence into the life of the Republic. 'My first political poem' as

Boland put it, it takes as its ostensible subject a horse 'loosed from its daily tether / In the tinker camp' near the suburb in which she lives, having moved from the city and the literary world to a domestic existence (Boland, 1996: 179). The horse, part mythic, part real, causes damage to hedges and garden flowers as it wanders by.[39]

> He stumbles on like a rumour of war, huge,
> Threatening; neighbours use the subterfuge
>
> Of curtains; he stumbles on down our short street . . .
> Thankfully passing us. I pause, wait,
>
> Then to breathe relief lean on the sill
> And for a second only my blood is still
>
> With atavism. That rose he smashed frays
> Ribboned across our hedge, recalling days
>
> Of burned countryside, illicit braid:
> A cause ruined before, a world betrayed.
>
> (Boland, 1975: 9)

The vocabulary ('rose', 'volunteer', 'war', 'maimed', 'blown', 'corpses', 'mutilated', 'ribboned' – recalling the 'Ribbonmen') hint at the guilty conscience of Nationalists in the Republic over the 'betrayed' 'cause' of national unity now manifest in Northern violence. The rather obvious symbols of the Republic's impotence and hand-washing attitudes can be seen as 'reminders of bloodlettings past and present that will not respect artificial barriers erected by forced forgetting and negotiated borders'; as Kevin Reilly argues, they are 'various psychological ploys' Southerners use 'to maintain a wall between themselves and . . . violence'. [40] The pervasive and blatant symbolism tends to smother the poem, betraying an unease which is its author's rather than the guilt which is its nominal subject. Yet the suburban location points to the more novel aspects of the book. Boland has said of the horse itself, 'it was far more difficult to make myself the political subject of my own poems than to see . . . the possibilities in front of me', and pointed out that with her move to Dundrum and family after 1970, she became a kind of non-person for the Dublin literary world; yet bringing that world, however tangentially, into the poem shows how her displacement beyond the metropolitan centre and, even more, as a married woman and mother, would gradually be turned into a resource, a point from which to apply pressure on the narrow complacency of the poetic mainstream (Boland, 1996: 179). By foregrounding elements accounted 'unpoetic' by the tradition which she wished to enter, Boland broke with it to some degree, forcing it to incorporate her. The final section of *The War Horse* shows Boland developing this realisation, containing as it does the modest yet defiantly titled 'Ode to Suburbia', as well as 'Naoise at Four' and 'Suburban Woman'. These poems look forward to the suburban domestic and child- and woman-centred poetry which would follow (as if anticipating one political outcome of related developments in the social sphere, 'The Laws of Love' is dedicated to Mary Robinson). Despite its limitations, *The War Horse* marks an advance for Boland, pushing beyond an earlier suppression of female identity.

Paul Durcan: media, orality, modernity

The stiltedness of Boland's earliest poetry throws into relief the changes in cultural production taking place in the Republic, as elsewhere, in the 1960s and 1970s. As Steven Connor has noted, in cultural terms, the period since World War II has seen an explosion of cultural forms – TV, video, performance art, heritage, and so on – which have 'fundamentally readjusted the relations between art, culture and society . . . the assumption that cultural representation primarily reflected or expressed those [new] relations of power has given way to an intimation of the power of culture itself to construct and transform such relations of power' (Connor, 1996: 2). This multiplication of cultural forms took place in a very short space of time in the Republic, and no poet has registered the implications of such change more keenly than Paul Durcan.[41]

In Durcan it could be said that the heterogeneity and 'not-caringness' of Kavanagh's later poetry – which, as we saw, could veer into the wholly slapdash – are adjusted in the light of the technological and information revolutions of the 1960s. Poetry, then, functions as a visionary, even 'spiritual' power, but is at the same time wholly aware of, and unantagonistic to, an information-saturated public sphere (despite Durcan's having taken an Archaeology degree at University College Cork, there is none of the archaeologising tendency found in other poets of the time in his work). In the eight years between *Endsville* and *O Westport in the Light of Asia Minor*, Durcan found his characteristic style, emerging as a radically naive but self-questioning narrator who mixed literal and phantasmagoric event in suspiciously deadpan discursive narratives.[42] Some, in an (almost) straightforward, recognisably lyric mode, suggest the essential continuity with Kavanagh; thus, 'They Say the Butterfly Is the Hardest Stroke' invites us to intuit a Zen-like correspondence between its title and the poem itself, but is clearly a 'statement' – albeit in the form of a non-statement – in a way most of the later poems avoid:

> From coves below the cliffs of the years
> I have dipped into *Ulysses*,
> *A Vagrant*, *Tarry Flynn* –
> But for no more than ten minutes or a page;
> For no more than to keep in touch
> With minds kindred in their romance with silence.
> I have not 'met' God, I have not 'read'
> David Gascoyne, James Joyce or Patrick Kavanagh:
> I believe in them.
> Of the song of him with the world in his care
> I am content to know the air.
>
> (Durcan, 1995: 48)

The fact that Durcan *had* 'met' Kavanagh is not the point here (although it suggests that he is quite capable of manipulating details in ways ostensibly at odds with his apparent frankness); what is at stake is poetry as a form of faith rather than of works, or 'reading'. Such 'reading', viewed in a merely quantitative sense – of 'completing' or somehow 'dealing' with a text merely by reading it through from cover to cover – is opposed by the poem, which is fundamentally anti-academic and anti-ratiocinative. Text – words – are here abolished; it is the 'air', or music (or spirit) which is important.

Durcan's interest in other media than print, then, is linked to an interest in what is potentially positive within the new mass culture, and to a general attitude to modernisation which is concerned with the possibility of wresting a radical modernity from its complacent materialism (O'Toole, 1988: 35). One rather crude way of illustrating this is in his use of television. In Kinsella's 'Nightwalker', television is a form of late capitalist anaesthesia, watched by the half-dead 'grubs' who make up the population of Dublin as necropolis. Durcan is aware of the negative influence of television as passive cultural consumption, and *Teresa's Bar* (1976) includes the satirical 'Wife Who Smashed Television Gets Jail'. Here it is not the medium as such but its abuse which is the issue, since for Durcan, television acts – like the printing press, photography and cinema in the past – not simply as a new medium, but to change the already existing art forms and the relationship between them. Marshall McLuhan's notion of the 'global village' (which can be contrasted with Montague's more roots-centred 'global regionalism') is relevant here; even more pertinent, in their application to Ireland, are the ideas of Walter J. Ong who held that television broke down, for the first time, the barriers between print and oral tradition.[43] This positive attitude towards oral literature and its utopian linkage to the mass media is clear in Durcan's work as a whole. In this sense, his style represents an acceptance of the polyphonic, near-schizophrenic babel of images and voices through which contemporary society understands itself, his poetry attempting some form of literary equivalent. The displacement from the literary, in turn, effects an undermining of certain aspects of the authority of the speaking voice; we can take the utterances of a Durcan poem *seriously*, that is, while their redundancies, repetitions, clumsinesses make it impossible to take them as *authoritative*.

There are limits to Durcan's ability to manage the disconcerting melange of registers and properties which his poems incorporate, however, given his spiritual-moralist stance, essentially negative attitude to form (that is, form as interference with utterance) and linguistic utopianism. 'In Memory: The Miami Showband – Massacred 31 July 1975' is one of Durcan's poems from the darkest days of the Troubles, and involves an encounter with 'a patriotic (sic) / Versifier', who 'whines into my face: "You must take one side / Or the other, or you're but a fucking romantic."' The awfulness of the event here pulls the enraged tenderness of the vision into the inchoate, either/or register of the 'fellow-poet' who defends sectarian bloodshed:

His mouth gapes like a cave in ice;
It is a whine in the crotch of whose fear
Is fondled a dream-gun blood-smeared;
It is in war – not poetry or music –
That men find their niche, their glory-hole
(Durcan, 1993: 45)

The tenuousness of the progression – 'a whine in the crotch of whose fear /
Is fondled' – matches the search, but fails to find an insight which is conclusive; similarly, the generalisation – do *all* men 'find their niche' in war? –
goes against the redemptive and humanist grain of the poem's spirit, setting
the artist aside from the rest of humanity as a member of an elect (a tendency
which may be linked to Crotty's astute comment that 'The twin and perhaps
contradictory assumptions that poetry is a sacred calling and that it should be
accessible to everybody lie at the heart of Durcan's work' (Crotty, 1995: 286)).
The performance aspect is crucial here, since too much rests on the ultima-
tism of the final resonant line: 'You made music, and that was all: You were
realists / And beautiful were your feet.' The killers are simply 'racists', the
political dimension to murder transposed to a moral plane, the musicians
become apolitical: they 'made music, and that was all'. Being 'content to know
the air' only of 'the song of him with the world in his care' may seem, on this
occasion, inadequate to the circumstances of the poem.

Munster poets and the hidden Corkery

Although Durcan is primarily a Dublin poet, his residence in Cork during the
1970s can be taken to highlight the fact that in too many accounts of poetry
in the Republic, the capital is taken to stand for the entire country. Cork, the
Republic's second city, has been consistently overlooked. Yet the city and its
hinterland – the province of Munster, possessing the most substantial Gaeltacht
areas – played a crucial role in poetry after 1970. If urbanism, cosmopolitanism
and liberal exploration characterised most young Dublin-based poets of the
1960s' there were among them a number of writers less committed to exploring the processes of change. The Munster origins of Michael Hartnett and
Eiléan Ní Chuilleanáin inclined them to a reworking of elements of 'traditional'
Irish culture and of the Irish language in a way which echoes, albeit more
faintly, the neo-regionalism of the Northern poets. The paradigm for the work
of these writers was Corkery's *The Hidden Ireland*, the dominant text in the cultural politics of the Free State, which took Munster as a model for the rest of
Ireland.[44] In an article of 1969 (published in book form in 1988), the historian
Louis Cullen revealed that the success of Corkery's arguments in this key text
rested more on assertion of cultural continuity than on documentation. In
Hartnett's and Ní Chuilleanáin's work, however, there is a limited application

of Corkery's mythic history to reassert an occluded regional identity in the face of the forces of modernisation. While Hartnett's work, like Montague's, pores over 'shards' of a lost culture, Ní Chuilleanáin's incorporates the very notion of lostness, of secrecy itself, within its procedures, running them together with the silencings typically encountered by a woman poet. Both of these poets, as well as the younger Thomas McCarthy later in the decade, can be seen as trying in a more general sense to achieve a reconfiguration of the balance of international and local elements in Irish poetry as well as countering Dublin's literary dominance in exploring the resources of an alternative topography, history and culture. The interest of all three in translation, history, myth and international themes (evidenced in McCarthy's Paris, but also in Hartnett's Lorca translations and Ní Chuilleanáin's use of classical legend) prevents a reading of this regionalism as merely a form of Kavanagh's parochialism. Similarly, neither of the two older poets, acutely conscious of the fragmentariness of the cultures they knew, were attracted to the more wholesale cultural renovations of Montague and Kinsella. Scepticism and a sense of hiddenness or absence distinguishes their poetry, and while it contains elements of 'the backward look' – particularly in Hartnett – it is too ghostly and vestigial to simply be regarded as nostalgic.[45]

Michael Hartnett: 'a language fit to sell pigs in'

The early poetry of Michael Hartnett, brought up in Newcastle West, Co. Limerick, near an Irish-speaking area (although for him Irish had been 'merely another school subject'), was marked by its precocity and preciosity, a mixture of song-like clarity and free verse abstraction, by rural themes and international allegiances typical of the 1960s generation. The heterogeneity to some extent reflected uncertain thematic and formal purposes. By the early 1970s, however, Hartnett had found the focus which had eluded his early work. Central to this process had been translation; versions from Chinese, translations of seventeenth- and eighteenth-century Irish poetry and of a number of Lorca's *Gypsy Ballads*, published in 1972, show a growing technical ability and clarity. In the latter, Hartnett scores a major achievement in creating an equivalent of Lorca's own sophisticated form of the folk ballad and lyric in his own musical idiom. This – with its dense yet subtle assonance, consonance, internal rhyme and strict metrical faithfulness – owes something to Clarke's attempts to realise the 'Irish mode', but with a lightness of touch which suits the original perfectly, making it one of the very best English translations. Beyond the technical and tonal success, however, Lorca's vividly stylised treatment of gypsy life, together with Irish Gaelic poetry, can be seen as reinforcing Hartnett's belief in the fitness of cultural and linguistic dispossession as a subject, sharpened by life in Dublin. In this sense, the road from Granada to

Córdoba became part of the route to Hartnett's most impressive English-language poetry collection, *A Farewell to English* (1975).

Hartnett's cultural retrieval is not at all straightforward; anticlerical, it draws on what the Revival writers (for their own reasons) had seen as the essentially 'pagan' quality of the Irish peasantry. Thus, Mrs Halpin in 'Mrs Halpin and the Lightning' is scared of thunder because 'these were the ancient Irish gods / she had deserted for the sake of Christ'. Hartnett himself has gone on record asserting the continuance of pre-Christian superstitions, superstitions he deploys in some of his poems as instances of a form of nature worship. 'Death of an Irishwoman' represents the simplicity of his work at its most powerful. Plangently direct, it mourns an old woman defined by her loneliness, ignorance ('she thought the world was flat') and pagan stubbornness, and gestures towards a slow rural tragedy of ageing and isolation in the West, granting deprivation and inutility a lyric valedictory power:

> But sentenced in the end
> To eat thin diminishing porridge
> In a stone cold kitchen
> She clenched her brittle hands
> Around a world
> She could not understand.
> I loved her from the day she died.
> She was a summer dance at the crossroads.
> She was a cardgame where a nose was broken.
> She was a song that nobody sings.
> She was a house ransacked by soldiers.
> She was a language seldom spoken.
> She was a child's purse, full of useless things.
>
> (Hartnett, 1991: 76)

The woman is recognisably kin to the *cailleach*, and carries its symbolic freight (she could be taken as nationally representative, like the crone of 'The Wild Dog Rose'). The image of a 'house ransacked by soldiers' may be an allusion to house searches in the North at the time, while a language 'seldom spoken' certainly refers to the Irish language and claims for its centrality in Irish culture. Even the 'summer dance at the crossroads' might refer to de Valera's 1943 Patrick's Day Speech. But the poem in no way insists on this, unlike Montague's, and its force derives rather from the continuation beyond death of the old woman not as a subject so much as a list of material but abstract items blankly itemised without commentary or judgement. Where Montague strains to generalise from personal experience to tribal representation, Hartnett – by modulating into folk-song-like repetition – succeeds in achieving, precisely by giving up on, an approximation to impersonal and folkloric, though not bardic, speech.[46] 'Irishwoman' (in its focus on the living force of the person after death) can be related, albeit in its suitably shrunken mode, to Lorca's *duende*, a form of artistic possession which John Berger has related to cultural supersession under the impact of modernisation and proximity to death.[47] The anti-modern strain is clear, the incoherence of the old culture signalled in the woman's break-up into abruptly but lovingly listed effects.

Other poems more blatantly rework a Corkeryan anti-Anglo-Irish strain. 'A Visit to Castletown House' recounts a Paul Tortelier concert of harpsichord music; A Big House poem, it mimics Yeats's 'Ancestral Houses' but opposes the Yeatsian elision of the passage of 'violence' into 'sweetness' and his apotheosis of Ascendancy culture the speaker has seen:

> Black figures dancing on the lawn,
> Eviction, Droit de Seigneur, Broken Bones:
> And heard the crack of ligaments being torn
> And smelled the clinging blood upon the stones.
> (Hartnett, 1991: 74)

A Farewell to English was not only a collection of poetry, but a literal farewell to Hartnett's first language, and it requires consideration as an intervention into the language politics of the time. In 1974, the year before publication, Hartnett (reading with the Irish poet Mairtín Ó Direáin at the Peacock Theatre in Dublin) had publicly announced his decision to henceforth write poetry only in Irish, a gesture of solidarity, as he put it, with a dying language. He would keep his silence in English for ten years. The announcement followed a decision by the Fine Gael–Labour government not to make a pass grade compulsory in Leaving Certificate exams and, as Hartnett has explained, was bound up in the general political situation of the time:

> It had to do with . . . the attitude of the government of the time – a coalition government containing Conor Cruise O'Brien *et al.* Irish was an embarrassing language to have – you couldn't trade with it in Brussels. I wanted to make a stand . . . [young Irish-language poets] were doing much the same without making any sort of pompous and public stand. (O'Driscoll, 1987: 20)

The kind of difficulties involved in giving up writing in one's first language can be seen to mark not only the *Farewell* collection, but all of Hartnett's subsequent writing. In *Farewell* there is a tension between the cruder, programmatic aspects of the decision – which in some ways was a self-mutilation, for Hartnett's three books in Irish would contain no poetry as good as his best in English – and the ambivalence and reservations surrounding such a drastic step. Thus, in 'A Visit to Croom 1745', Hartnett's insistence on the brutal realities of eighteenth-century peasant life offsets the quest of the speaker who, in cadences which resemble those of T. S. Eliot's magi, seeks the eighteenth-century 'court' of poets which flourished at Sean O'Tuama's inn in Croom, Hartnett's birthplace. The irony, as Kerrigan has pointed out, is that although this is the year of the Scottish Jacobite rising, those he finds in the court 'talk broken English of an English king': the Irish, crushed by the Penal Laws, did not rise in support of the Pretender (Hartnett, 1991: 77).

The most dubious aspects of *Farewell*, and its weakest poetry, can be found in its title sequence which elaborates the rationale for renouncing English. The seven-section sequence is strongest in its consideration of the position of Hartnett's Irish-speaking home area, and opens in a pub, linking it to 'A Visit to Croom 1745'. Concrete imagery – 'She cut the froth from glasses with a knife / and hammered golden whiskies on the bar' – and the savouring of Irish words, vie with abstract statement: 'I sunk my hands into tradition / sifting the centuries for words'. The speaker is 'flung back / on the gravel of Anglo-Saxon', contrasted with the 'dark slate' of Irish, which is imagined as descending in an avalanche 'on the cogs', damaging 'the wheels, clogging / the intricate machine' (Hartnett, 1991: 78). Unspecified, the machine resembles that of 'Staghorn Whistle' earlier in the book used for 'conveying / messages for morons' (Hartnett, 1991: 65). Just as there it contrasts with the primal vision conjured up by the whistle, so here it underwrites a simplistic judgement on those in thrall to modernity, while 'Anglo-Saxon' as a racial term shows the degree of Hartnett's indebtedness to Irish Ireland ideologies (in the third section of the poem, post-Yeatsian poets are seen as 'commis-chefs' under 'Chef Yeats' concocting 'the Anglo-Irish stew' from 'a simple Anglo-Saxon stock', where 'stock' is racial as well as culinary) (Hartnett, 1991: 80). As the sequence moves from Croom into crude cultural summary, Hartnett's line becomes shorter, less open to subtle variation. At its most basic, the relationship between Britain and Ireland is presented as that between a 'brimming Irish sow / who would allow / any syphilitic boar / to make her hind end sore' and an 'English boar', a scenario similar to that in Heaney's 'Act of Union' (Hartnett, 1991: 81). The last two sections attack, conventionally enough, the bureaucratic conformism of the new state (summed up as 'the noble art / of writing forms in triplicate'), and – equally conventionally – offer a definition of the poet as a 'rebel' fully in accord with the inherited dissent stereotype: 'Poets with progress / make no peace or pact' (Hartnett, 1991: 82). Irish has become, in an uncritically gendered manner

> the conscience of our leaders,
> the memory of a mother-rape they will
> not face . . . our final sign that
> we are human and therefore not a herd.
> (Hartnett, 1991: 83)

The effect is of a desperate burning of bridges and a pessimism which, as Hartnett admitted, was justified. The last section reaches an appropriately exhausted lyricism

> I have made my choice
> and leave with little weeping:
> I have come with meagre voice
> to court the language of my people.
> (Hartnett, 1991: 84)

In typing Irish poetry in English as essentially un-Irish, reaching back beyond Lemass's decoupling of modernisation and anglicisation, Hartnett offers a reactionary vision. Yet if 'A Farewell's' crudeness serves as a reminder of the unevenness of modernisation and the survival of Irish Ireland ideologies in the culture of the Republic, the renunciation of linguistic colonialism, drawing on the Gaelic substratum of folkloric belief and the Gaeltacht areas, serves as a reminder of the tensions within the Republic rather than of a quarrel with Britain. The problem, as Ciaran Carson puts it, lies not so much in the 'farewell' but 'saying cheerio to the Saxon in such a half-assed way', lending the book an impression of hasty assembly and poetry 'confused, derivative, lyrical, hysterical, posturing, and on occasions, exact'[48] (Carson, 1975a: 187). More remarkable as an expression of what Hartnett himself has referred to in terms of self-division, is the contemporary 'Cúlú Íde' / 'The Retreat of Ita Cagney'. A poem concerning a widow who bears a child out of wedlock and is perse-cuted, set in an unspecified time, it was written simultaneously in Irish and English, in the transitional period following the poems of *Farewell*. 'I would sit down and write a few lines of the poem unthinkingly . . . but I'd come back to it and see that it was half in English and half in Irish, or a mixture' (Cadogan, 1997a: 6). Hartnett has claimed that '[it] almost broke my heart and indeed my mind to write, because both languages became so intermeshed. One is not a translation of the other. They are two versions of the one poem; but what the original language is, I don't know' (O'Driscoll, 1987: 21). As an expres-sion of the linguistic schizophrenia awoken by the perceived threats to tradi-tional Irish identity and culture in the late 1960s and early 1970s Hartnett's description of his predicament could hardly be bettered.

Thomas Kinsella: life after *Nightwalker*[49]

a man's life's no more than to say 'one'
(Shakespeare, *Hamlet*, V.ii.74)

Fragmentation, the turn to 'authentic' Irish and mythic sources – the condi-tions of the new poetry in the Republic – can be seen in a very different form in Kinsella's development following the exertions of the *Nightwalker* volume. Refusing to publish in journals, where his poems were surrounded by extra-neous material, he set up the Peppercanister Press (in collaboration with Dolmen), and embarked upon an open-ended series of poems in modernist form. The first of these, 'Notes From the Land of the Dead' appeared in the Dolmen-published *New Poems 1973*. In the same year the first Peppercanister pamphlet – *Fifteen Dead* – appeared. The sequence was taken up again in *One* (1974) and developed through *A Technical Supplement* (1976), *Song of the Night and Other Poems* (1978) and *The Messenger* (1978). A break occurred with *An Duanaire* (1980) – Kinsella's translation interest continuing to parallel his own poetry – before *Songs of the Psyche* (1985) and nine more titles.[50] This list – albeit of short, pamphlet-length collections – suggests the immense persistence of Kinsella's effort and his brooding presence within contemporary Irish poetry, as well as the difficulty in doing critical justice to his achievement.

In ways which recall both Heaney and Montague, the poetry from 'Notes' onwards shifts to face inwards towards psychic, familial and racial depths, fusing personal and archetypal material and drawing on a variety of intertexts (among them Jung, Diderot, Teilhard de Chardin and Mahler). Yet the radicalism of Kinsella's polyphonic, numerological and allegorical use of his material produces very different effects from those of his contemporaries, as the poetic self is deconstructed only to rise through various layers of the (collective) unconscious to elegy, anatomy, history and social satire. The distrust of a unitary self sets Kinsella apart from the more stable lyric voice preferred by most other poets, and while his essentialist material is similar, it is rendered in ways both more blatant and more ghostly than theirs, phantasmagoric and provisional rather than 'realist'. This very immateriality of presentation has its obliquely political significance, since the foregrounded, overtly structured quality of the esoteric material challenges official discourses in literature and public life at a time when both were attracted to kitsch-ruralist Irishness. It is this political dimension which has been overlooked in Kinsella criticism, which tends – like Heaney's, and because of the powerful critical presences of both poets – towards the hagiographic or the dismissive.

In line with a rejection of imposed order, a desire to let 'delicate, distinct tissue begin to form' of its own accord, Kinsella remarks of 'Notes' that 'What I'm trying to do . . . [is] start almost before consciousness and let the dawning of individuation control what will happen', to get Irish mythic material into the poetry by dramatising it through incidents in his early life.[51] The most important source here, and for all of the later poetry, is the work of Jung.[52] Despite the dubiously essentialist nature of Jungian theories – which assume racial and gender identities as givens – Kinsella attempts a radical exploration of selfhood and becoming through the processes and structures (such as individuation, the collective unconscious and archetypes) which they outline (Jackson, 1995: 87–90; McCormack, 1987: 68–70). In doing so, he consistently mixes discourses – the scientific and the poetic are the commonest kinds – and deploys a series of images, some familiar from his earlier work: those of the quest-journey; consumption (and blood-sacrifice); the Triple Goddess archetype; the spiral or serpentine image (often the uroboros, or tail-swallowing serpent); and the drop, or fall.

'Notes', in essaying the basic trajectory of the quest, is one of the fullest expositions of the whole sequence although, as with the other books, the interrelatedness of its parts, their refusal to stand alone, make quotation and excerption almost impossible. Its three-part structure – an introduction, followed by 'an egg of being', 'a single drop' and 'nightnothing' – is divided into a series of childhood encounters and incidents, and treatments of material from

Irish myth, suggestive of alignments between these, and progress from personal individuation to a larger cultural and national form of individuation. Thus, the untitled introduction sets the scene of the poet as alchemist-mage preparing to drop into the self, 'getting quietly ready / to go down quietly out of my mind' (Kinsella, 1973a: 9; Broder, 1979: 89). Down in the layered self, negotiating what will become a characteristic landscape of origins biological and psychic – 'endless broken shells', 'red protein eyes' – the poem's quest ends 'on the / count of / O', the 'O' not a letter but a large, hand-drawn, incomplete oval (Kinsella, 1973a: 10–12). This is zero, the nothing of beginning, but also an 'egg of being' from which all will start. Within each poem, the same imagery of descent into the Jungian abyss and quest for individuation – through journey, cauldron, prize (of the 'egg of being') – recurs in different forms. The egg appears in the first poem, 'Hen Woman', in which the young Kinsella watches his grandmother rush from her cottage to pick up a hen about to lay an egg. 'A mutter of thunder', as in *Finnegans Wake*, announces a fall, as the egg hangs and then drops to the grating below, smashing uselessly (but recalling the grating against which the poet in the introduction had broken 'in a distress of gilt and silver / scattered in a million droplets') (Kinsella, 1973a: 15). As 'Hen Woman' puts it, reflexively turning on (or swallowing, uroboros-like) Kinsella's intertextual procedure:

> I feed upon it still, as you see;
> there is no end to that which,
> not understood, may yet be noted
> and hoarded . . . in the yolk of one's being, so to speak
> there to undergo its (quite animal) growth
> (Kinsella, 1973a: 16)

The old woman's cry of indifference – 'It's all the one. / There's plenty more where that came from!' – and the child's answering 'Hen to pan! / It was a simple world' seem to indicate an anecdotal-symbolic close with an easily extractable moral (indeed, Edna Longley speculates that the poem 'owes something to an intelligent reading of Seamus Heaney'): nature is fertile, eggs are laid and (usually) get cooked and eaten (Kinsella, 1973a: 17; E. Longley, 1975: 135). But *'Hen to pan'* is an alchemical formula in Greek, meaning 'one in all', whose symbol according to Jung is the uroboros (John, 1996: 127). Similarly, the seemingly incidental detail of a dung-beetle struggling at the boy's feet with 'a ball of dung bigger than its body' suggests the scarab, the ancient Egyptian symbol of rebirth, acting as another reminder of the poem's allegorical level of meaning, one which resists the urge to symbolic closure.

As Brian John points out, the poems which follow chart a similar path, one which is anything but 'simple' (John, 1996: 128). 'A Hand of Solo', set in the boy's grandmother's shop, and referring to a card game played by 'real' people – 'Jack Rat', 'The Boss', 'Angus', 'Uncle Matty', the grandmother –

commingles childhood memory with archetypes drawn from the collective unconscious according to Jung, as the grandmother acquires mythic significance. The transformation occurs when the child approaches her and is given a pomegranate:

> Strings of jet beads wreathed her neck
> And hissed on the black taffeta
> And crept on my hair.
> '. . . You'd think I had three heads!'
>   . . . Her stale abyss . . .
>   (Kinsella, 1973a: 19–20)

The child's fear connects with myth – three heads (of the Triple Goddess, or Cerberus), hissing Medusan snakes, the abyss of the underworld – and identifies his grandmother with Hecate (the pomegranate, Proserpine's fruit, having already established one connection between personal memory and Greek myth). The dependence on female agency for utterance has already been signalled in an opening lyrical section – 'Woman throat song / help my head / back to you sweet' – and the poem ends with the child 'driving' his tongue, sexually, into the fruit (imaging the rape of Proserpine), his throat flooded with juice/blood and initiating him into mysteries which will later enable his song (Kinsella, 1973a: 18, 20). There are dead-ends and frustrations; 'The High Road', as its title suggests, is about disappointment, since the boy finds no archetypal womb or rebirth in the local 'Robber's Den' into which he climbs (Kinsella, 1973a: 21–3). Yet 'low' roads need to be taken to reach the underworld and undergo testing and individuation. This occurs again in 'Ancestor', the dying grandmother he is sent in to kiss giving off a 'smell, musky and queer', 'Her profile against the curtains . . . old, and dark like a hunting bird's' drawing him once more to the 'abyss' (Kinsella, 1973a: 24). Generally there is a combination of vividly realised local imagery and incident with larger mythological-quest structures, linking Kinsella's past to his induction into his vocation as poet.[53]

The second section of 'Notes', 'a single drop', now aligns the abyss with the land of the dead, or unconscious, and with Irish myth. 'Nuchal' (subtitled '*a fragment*'), the first piece, takes, as its title suggests, the form of an incomplete narrative from a larger record. The text used by Kinsella is the old Irish *Lebor Gabála Érenn* (*The Book of the Takings* (i.e. the invasions) *of Ireland*), in which Nuchal is named as the source of the four rivers of Eden, presided over by a maternal figure, source of creation. Having evoked the *Lebor Gabála Érenn*, which will become a key text in the later work, Kinsella uses it more heavily in 'Survivor', in which the speaker fuses with Fintan, a mythological survivor of the early stages of the first, antediluvian 'taking' of Ireland by the mainly female expedition of Cessair, who fled as 'thieves' from the Eden of 'Nuchal'. The expedition consisted of three men and fifty women, but with the death of two of the men Fintan was left to satisfy the sexual appetite of all the women. He escaped both women and the Flood by hiding in a cave, and his endurance and explorations in another 'land of the dead', as Ireland becomes, make him emblematic of Kinsella's general themes. In the process of the Flood, sickness and death which he witnesses, the figure of the Great (beautiful) Mother becomes the Terrible (hag-like) Mother, in accordance with Jung's categorisation of the forms of the Triple Goddess and resembling the Irish hag, or *cailleach*. Finally seeking death, Fintan encounters her:

> There is nothing here for sustenance.
>   Unbroken sleep were best.
> Hair. Claws. Grey.
>   Naked. Wretch. Wither.
>   (Kinsella, 1973a: 38)

'Wither'/whither is a typically Kinsellan pun, both hidden and blatant; at the verge of death, Fintan points the onward path of the sequence. In 'night-nothing', the last section of 'Notes', the poem returns from the personal and archetypal past to the recent past. Parts of this section recall Kinsella's horrified fascination with the Holocaust.[54] Others echo, in contemporary Dublin, scenes from the previous sections.[55] The fragmentary self ('I.I.I . . .' in 'Ely Place') draws on the earlier material to suggest past inheritance, and an essential continuity of Irish experience (Kinsella, 1973a: 46). The notations of place in the poems of this section are the 'notes' by which the modern world may be interpreted, and the last poem, 'Good Night', closes with the dissolution of the self in the abyss of sleep to the sound of one of Dublin's underground rivers, the Camac: 'Camacamacamac . . .' There are no conclusions – 'Good Night' comes from the 'gulf' – and no 'truths, or any certainties' (Kinsella, 1973a: 53). Yet, at the same time, there is a fractured, drowsily disconnected assertion that snake-like 'monsters' live and feed 'in us', an acceptance of unconscious depths which may be horrific or benign, but which, if individuation is to occur, cannot be ignored (Jackson, 1995: 109).

Ciaran Carson's New Estate

If Kinsella's post-*Nightwalker* work suggests similarities with the excavational activities of Heaney's poetry of the early 1970s which both poets might wish to disavow, Ciaran Carson's scathing 1975 review of *North* signalled the gap emerging between the 1960s' Northern poets and those poets, roughly a decade younger, who emerged in the late 1960s and early 1970s (Carson, 1975b: 183–6). His own first collection, *The New Estate*, appeared the year after the attack, and was what reviewers like to call an accomplished debut. Yet after a further pamphlet, *The Lost Explorer*, in 1978, Carson's poetic development was put on hold for a decade. It is now impossible to separate this early poetry from the extraordinary impact of his second collection, *The Irish for No* (1987), but certain continuities may be discerned.[56] Carson's Belfast upbring-

ing is present in *New Estate*, but so too is an interest in traditional Celtic culture
(there are translations of early Welsh as well as Irish lyrics), a reminder that
his parents spoke Irish at home. There is a Heaney-like concern with craft –
in 'Linen', 'Beleek', 'The Casting of the Bell' – combined with poems about
more humdrum domestic chores, such as house-painting and chimney-sweep-
ing. Although there are a set of personal and distinctive concerns, then, their
chief characteristic is conformity to the generic tone of Northern Irish poetry
of the time; the poems are well-made, formal, avoid overt emotion and offer
lyric closure, albeit in a slightly offbeat way, revealing the difficulty of manoeu-
vring in an increasingly congested space. Nevertheless, although Carson
claimed in 1990 that the book 'now appears too "accomplished" – . . . not
taking too many risks . . . it's too reserved', there are aspects which raise it
above the ruck. Carson's humour is already apparent, and elements of a critique of Heaneyesque notions of mythic history appear in 'The Insular Celts';
a poem, as Carson has pointed out, which 'speaks very much in inverted
commas', its voice that of 'a proud and foolish Celt' who makes a virtue of his
insularity (Brandes, 1990: 80). Its imagery and procedures quietly spoof those
of Heaney and Montague:

> They will come back to the warm earth
> And call it by possessive names –
> Thorned rose, love, woman and mother;
>
> To hard hills of stone they will give
> The words for breast; to meadowland,
> The soft gutturals of rivers,
>
> Tongues of water . . .
>   (Carson, 1988b: 11)

The difficulty is that the poem remains wholly reliant on what it is negating
to escape the terms of the argument generated by its targets. Put another way,
Heaney, like Antaeus, cannot be challenged successfully on his own terrain.
Only a radically new style – one in which the critique of myth is implicit
in anti-lyricism, in foregrounded commercial detritus, in the bricky streets
and alleys of Belfast – would enable Carson to break free of the older poet's
gravitational power.

Paul Muldoon: 'Your answers to our questions'

Another anxiety of influence to be overcome would be that of Paul Muldoon,
the most precocious, influential and charismatic poet of his generation, who
by 1987 would have published five collections and (in terms of his influence
on other poets at least) be vying with Heaney for the position of leading Irish
poet. The similarities between Muldoon and Heaney are marked; both had
rural Catholic backgrounds, following the scholarship route to Queen's University, where Heaney was Muldoon's tutor for a time. Muldoon's early poems,

in *Knowing My Place* (1971) and *New Weather* (1973), are, superficially at least, Heaneyesque, featuring *dinnseanchas*, folklore and rural customs, rural imagery and the father–son relationship central to *Death of a Naturalist*. *New Weather* appeared with Faber in 1973 at Heaney's recommendation, and on the back of his own burgeoning reputation. But while there are similarities, the differences were apparent from the outset, and most fundamentally in Muldoon's attitude to poetry's function, expressed in his treatment of place, language, religion, sexuality and myth. As Claire Wills has pointed out, while Heaney has made radical poetic use of his rural inheritance, his discussions of poetry, like the poems themselves, are couched in terms of balance and resolution, of integration above the disintegrative forces of the Troubles (Wills, 1998: 21). Muldoon, however, is resistant to claims for poetry's moral or social force; and Heaney's typical vocabulary in the discussion of poetry – redress, succour, solace and so on – is dismissed by Muldoon who clearly suspects the religious freightage of such terms. Muldoon's rejection of religion is much more thoroughgoing than Heaney's – one result, it may be, of a 1960s', rather than 1950s', adolescence – and his development as a writer in the period of the Troubles means that he does not share, to the same degree, the civil rights sense of communal responsibility which marks his predecessors. His poetry is more prepared – indeed, insists on – discordance as a fact of existence. This is not to say, however, that Muldoon is somehow less 'political' than Heaney; indeed, there is little if anything in Heaney's work as forthright as 'Meeting the British', in which genocide is practised against the Native Americans by giving them 'six fish-hooks / And two blankets embroidered with smallpox' (Muldoon 1987: 16). Nevertheless, this is a rare example, and charges of flippancy and aloofness have regularly marked Muldoon's critical reception. To understand these, perhaps, it is necessary to grasp how Muldoon deliberately sets out to subvert other Heaneyesque qualities, such as local attachment and territorial piety, a faith in self-presencing through language, and the idea of sexuality as defined by familial and communal structures.

This can be seen partly in terms of literary influence. While Heaney has acknowledged Robert Frost as a poet who endorses the modern pastoral, Muldoon is far more indebted to Frost's epistemological scepticism and narrative trickery, his appeal lying in his 'apparently simple, almost naive, tone of voice and use of language, underneath which all kinds of complex things are happening . . . his mischievous, sly, multi-layered quality under the surface' (Haffenden, 1981: 133–4). This points also to Muldoon's greater interest in narrative – summed up in 'The Country Club's' quotation of Frost, 'all the fun's in how you say a thing'. Individualism, or a kind of strategic irresponsibility (often in the persona of Byronic philanderer as opposed to Heaney's Wordsworthian celebrator), is opposed to the portentousness of lyric utterance with the weight of history upon its shoulders and accompanying bardic role: 'Most of the world is centred / About ourselves', as the title poem of *New Weather* puts it. If one poem in *New Weather* sums up Muldoon's suspicion of this role it is 'The Hedgehog', which refuses communal expectations in a humorous but memorably determined way. Typically it begins not with the subject of its title but with an intermediary, the snail:

> The snail moves like a
> Hovercraft, held up by a
> Rubber cushion of itself,
> Sharing its secret
>
> With the hedgehog. The hedgehog
> Shares its secret with no one.
>   (Muldoon, 1973: 36)

Secrecy is suggested by the hesitancy of the verse, enacted in line breaks on the indefinite pronoun, while that secrecy – analogous to the uncanny manner of locomotion of both creatures – is one which the poem will suggest is linked to knowledge of violence and consequent refusal of public co-option (both creatures are defined by their protective, defensive coverings). Their reserve is contested by a suspiciously cajoling collective voice, requesting the hedgehog to 'come out / Of yourself and we will love you . . . We want / Your answers to our questions'. The hedgehog's silence gradually exposes the obtuse, possessive and threatening aspect of that 'we', which wonders what the hedgehog hides, and why it 'distrusts' questioners, forgetting

>   the god
> Under this crown of thorns.
> We forget that never again
> Will a god trust in the world.

The final shift from hedgehog to Christ is swift, shocking and faintly grotesque, the creature revealed as an image of the artist refusing a bardic role. A humbler form of the demiurge of Joyce's *A Portrait of the Artist as a Young Man*, Muldoon's hedgehog conflates artist and god, but in a take-it-or-leave-it, rather than imperious manner; if the artist is a god, he resembles the *dieu caché* of Jansenism, who leaves his creation bereft by withdrawing from it. Romantic conceptions of both artist and god are subjected, by assured self-effacement, to a powerfully ironic scrutiny.

Muldoon's withdrawn, ironic, individualism shapes his style and treatment of his material. Thus, while several poems in *New Weather* have rural settings, there is no attempt to represent these in the vividly lush terms of *Death of a Naturalist*; and, although speaking of the value of having a knowable locale out of which to write – Muldoon claims that his home town of the Moy, Co. Armagh, has functioned in his work like Faulkner's Yoknapatawpha – locale functions primarily to be 'changed by the creative process', the Moy becoming Marengo, for example, in 'Paris'. *New Weather*'s *dinnseannchas* do not offer a readable landscape; indeed they are cryptic to the point of hermeticism, the lyric identity they bespeak unsure, shifting and provisional. Similarly the methods of the *seannachie* (traditional storyteller) in 'Seanchas' rebuke those listeners who '[Think] [them]selves superior' to his inconclusive narrative technique, since his region may have 'Nothing. And no heroes people this landscape / Through which he sees us off' (Muldoon, 1973: 34). Rather than the amplitude of 'Anahorish', or 'Broagh', then, names tend to slide towards the emblematic or allegorical in Muldoon, to be the occasions for metamorphic transformation, or suggestive of parallel realms. Heaney, in a sympathetic early review, wrote of the 'hermetic tendency' he felt this could lead to, citing 'At Martha's Deli', a poem in which we encounter characters named 'Will' and 'Faith', and which asks (at one level) to be read as a parable; acknowledging this, Muldoon has recorded a taste for writing which was 'emblematic in an almost Jonsonian way' (Heaney, 1980: 213; Kendall, 1996: 59). Many early poems – 'The Radio Horse', 'Blowing Eggs', 'Dancers at the Moy' – while thematically about failure, absence and loss, also hint at the belief in the inadequacy of language which lies, as Benjamin has argued, behind allegory, although in playful rather than abject, Heaneyesque fashion. Similarly, Muldoon's extensive use of cliché – in line with his antagonism to Romantic notions of originality – points to the way in which dead language may be revived, linking the limitations of language to social constraints and remetaphorising the jaded trope by taking it literally; in 'Vespers', for example, we learn of a 'defunct window', that 'the frost has designs on it' (Muldoon, 1973: 27).

In terms of his use of figurative language, rather than reaching for a single concluding symbol Muldoon prefers what he calls the 'conceit' – that is, a single metaphor extended throughout the course of a poem, as in 'The Centaurs' in *Mules* (1977). This disorientatingly blurs the imperial figures of William of Orange, Cortes and Saul into their mounts, deflating them within the mundane context of a backstreet and a milkman's cart, but simultaneously celebrating the transformative powers of the imagination. The notion of the conceit as the driving force of the poem resembles Muldoon's interest in 'structures which can be fixed like mirrors at angles to each other – it relates to narrative form – so that new images can emerge . . . mischief is possible' (Haffenden, 1981: 136). In this sense Muldoon's allegiance to the Group poetic is detectable in his claim that 'poems should be intact', or integral, but can be seen also as under pressure from the beginning by the narrative/allegoric urge generated by sceptical, unrooted and 'single, if dislocated personality'. This is perhaps most evident in Muldoon's reconfiguration of Heaney's familial confinement of sex (and reproduction) and erotic attachment to the land. For Muldoon, poetry does not recover the preoccupied land through subversive inhabitation of the English tradition; language is always already loss, a falling short, and it is the fact of loss, not the thing lost, which is evoked in 'Blowing Eggs'. Poetry thus becomes not recovery but deception, 'the start of the underhand', and in cultural terms this means a break with Catholic familial and communal structures (Muldoon, 1973: 14). 'The Upriver Incident', 'Cuckoo Corn' and 'Skeffington's Daughter' in *New Weather* are about the violence inherent in these structures; in the latter, a father forces his daughter to have an abortion, and the conceit of the medieval instrument of torture which impaled the bodies and faces of its victims encloses a tale of a girl 'Leaving backstreet and foetus / Behind her' so that she might again be taken for 'that clever, / Careful virgin. // Not one to lose face' (Muldoon, 1973: 45). Gender, as William A. Wilson has shown, plays a crucial role in the early poetry and its semantic uncertainties and deconstructive game-playing, finding in 'Identities' a recurring narrative situation in which the poet-speaker 'meets a woman who offers him a liberating union through the offices of stolen papers, of words. This proposal, which seems to fail inevitably, is made in the context of the absent father, the embodiment of a past dispensation, whose origins the poet then searches for' (Wilson, 1987: 318). Innocence, as *New Weather*'s opening poem 'The Electric Orchard' puts it, cannot be verbalised once it has gone, but neither can the process of loss itself: 'None could describe / Electrocution, falling, the age of innocence' (Muldoon, 1973: 12).

Of course, there is a danger of schematism in such explanations, as Muldoon himself has noted, and in *Mules*' 'The Mixed Marriage' he mocks even as he offers just such a 'diagrammatic' representation in autobiographical terms. The poem (whose title's usual meaning in a Northern Irish context is a marriage between a Protestant and a Catholic) sketches the polarities of an upbringing by a schoolteacher mother and rural labourer father in quasi-*Sons and Lovers* mode. The mother is linked with rationalism, light, learning and piety ('She had read one volume of Proust . . . She opened *The Acts of the Apostles, / Aesop's Fables, Gulliver's Travels.*'), the father with darkness, 'the land he would never own' and oral tradition (Muldoon, 1977: 42). The product of this mistress–servant relationship, the poet-to-be acts as a go-between or third term, although he finally remains with his father as his mother goes 'upstairs' at night while the father 'dim[s] the light' before telling tales of hunting and faction fights. The poem's above / below realms rehearse the metaphysical dimension of *Mules*, the relation between sky and earth, the material here-and-now and the religious-transcendent taken up in the title poem. This opens with a question – 'Should they not have the best of both worlds?' – and proceeds to test it, in Muldoon's characteristically quasi-allegorical mode (Muldoon, 1977: 52). Thus, donkey and horse represent Protestant/earthly and Catholic/heavenly alternatives respectively (the donkey is borrowed from 'Parsons', a Protestant neighbour, the mare is 'ours'). Yet the mare's 'feet of clay gave the lie' to this identification of horse with the heavens, and the cross on the donkey recalls its divine role in bearing Christ. The image of the mule allows Muldoon to think about what poetry does, not in terms of obligation to society but as something stubbornly preordained (Wills, 1998: 44, 48–9). Mules are genetic dead-ends, a place where different strains meet and cancel out unfruitfully and are, therefore, fit emblems for Northern Irish society, paralysed by sectarian division. The overcoming of these opposites in the act of coupling is hinted at, in homoerotic terms, by the description of 'Sam

Parsons and my quick father / Tense for the punch below their belts'. But the word 'mule' echoes 'Muldoon', and parallels between animal and poet are also there to be drawn. For as well as being proverbially obstinate, a genetic dead-end, mules are also one-offs whose very nature denies the trammels of offspring, family, tradition and inheritance, a symbol of autonomy, fated to childlessness as the poet is to poetry, both mediating between earth and the sky, the material and the heavenly, as in the poem's final image:

> We might yet claim that it sprang from earth
> Were it not for the afterbirth
> Trailed from it like some fine, silk parachute,
> That we would know from what heights it fell.
>   (Muldoon, 1977: 52)

The mule is seen as a kind of fallen angel (it does not '[spring] from earth' like Heaney's Antaeus) and so although Muldoon continues his distancing of self from the Troubles, he offers a quirkily hybrid quality which mediates between different and opposing states and whose inbetweenness can provide (poetic) insight. Miscegenation, although it is not offered as a 'solution' to paralysis and sterility, does suggest that sexuality may be an oppositional force.[57]

Nevertheless, the aesthetic heterosis of Muldoon's miscegenated poetic cannot translate into a solution to the problems involved in political hybridity. 'Should they not have the best of both worlds?' is a reasonable enough expectation, but reasonableness is lost in the political reality of the realisation that the newly born mule was 'neither one thing nor the other'. A tension therefore arises between poetic idiom and the political heterogeneity that idiom accounts for, as Muldoon seeks identity defined by similarity rather than by difference. Politically, in Northern Ireland, people remain firmly 'one thing or the other', or are forced to remain so, even if Muldoon can 'have the best of both worlds', imaginatively transforming mule-like contingencies. In political terms, hybridity remains irreducible, containing conflict and crisis, and in this sense 'Mules' can be seen as a poem about misplaced optimism as well as about the nature of the poet. Hybrid identity has a potential which is negated by the sense of a necessary estrangement from either 'side'. Something of this is suggested, in typically playful fashion, in 'Lunch With Pancho Villa', the poem which opens the collection. One way of approaching this poem is suggested by the critic Andrew Waterman's criticism of Muldoon which appeared around the time of *Mules*:

> My hostility is not of course to rural themes ... but where Wordsworth, Hardy, Frost, Lawrence, wring eternal verities from such things Muldoon places his details and dialect-words in the knowing spirit of the flower-arranger ... these apparently authentic recognisable renderings prove simulacra merely, like the 1975 facsimile-Georgian housefronts artfully inlaid into old Dublin streets.[58]

Waterman is careful to make it clear that he is not being anti-rural or -main-stream, but 'wring' betrays a sense that rural pieties are felt to be at the end of their tether. Muldoon's 'knowing spirit' is implicitly identified as the leading voice of a transformation of the Northern poetic, and the terms in which he is dismissed – 'simulacra', 'facsimile', 'artful' – reveal the organicist basis of the critique. Interestingly, 'Lunch with Pancho Villa' features precisely the kind of 'facsimile' Waterman objects to – 'That suburban street, the door, the yard – / All made up as I went along' – and at the same time raises the viability of traditional ruralism in poetry (Muldoon, 1977: 12). It is both a sly defence of the rural and a blatant 'simulacra', describing what the speaker admits in its second part is a wholly fictive meeting between himself and a 'celebrated pamphleteer', the 'Pancho Villa' figure of the title. The pamphleteer receives the poet-speaker in his home and rebukes him for his work's concentration on 'stars and horses, pigs and trees', exhorting him to write about what is 'true' and 'near to home' – 'people getting killed, left, right and centre' (Muldoon, 1977: 11). It is the debate over poetry's 'representative' responsibilities with which I started this chapter but figured not in terms of tribal affiliation versus imaginative freedom so much as an internal debate within a poet who has already made his mind up about the priority of the claims of his art. He is told to 'Just look around you. / People are getting themselves killed / Left, right and centre / While you do what? Write rondeaux?' (*Mules*, as Kendall notes, is full of poems precisely about 'stars and horses, pigs and trees'). The question, like the poem's opening line – 'Is it really a revolution, though?' – anticipates Muldoon's repudiation of 'pamphleteering': 'if we were living in a banana republic and being truly, monstrously oppressed, one can imagine pamphleteering, but not in Northern Ireland . . . The society is much too complex' (Haffenden, 1981: 137). In this sense it is wrong, I think, to claim that the poem is partly about making the rural relevant to an urban revolution which has ignored the fact that the campaign against the British state by militant Republicanism stems ultimately from 'sectarian struggles over land' (this would be to reduce it to little more than an aide-memoire for the IRA) (Wills, 1998: 45). Nevertheless it is correct to see Muldoon dramatising his self-division; he is both Pancho Villa and the 'rural' poet. In the second part the 'invention' of the first is admitted, along with doubt about the speaker's attitude to the revolutionary:

> Of course I gave it all away
> With those preposterous titles.
> *The Bloody Rose? The Dream and the Drums?* . . .
> Or was I desperately wishing
> To have been their co-author . . . ?
> (Muldoon, 1977: 12)

Muldoon here does not so much reject 'Pancho Villa' as recognise, while being unable to accept, the partial truths he and the poet-speaker represent. This is clear at the end, when the speaker distances himself from his earlier persona, wondering what he should say to a 'callow youth' of a young writer about to visit him, who will 'be rambling on, no doubt, / About pigs and trees, stars and horses'. 'Lunch with Pancho Villa' thus establishes the theme of poetic responsibility in a time of violence in Muldoon's work, but by acknowledging the complexity of the society in which it occurs through its playful self-reflexivity.

Notes

1 1974, the worst year for violence outside the North, was the year of the Birmingham pub bombings by the IRA and of the Loyalist car bombs in Monaghan and Dublin which killed thirty-three people.

2 The European Court indictment of the British government for torture, while revelations concerning the unlawful convictions of the Birmingham Six, the Guildford Four and others all show just how state forces and the judiciary were prepared at times to connive in the miscarriage of justice.

3 Seamus Heaney, for example, dropped the vaguely irredentist 'Requiem for the Croppies' from his poetry readings after 1970, but would articulate in *North* an Irish identity defined, fatalistically, in terms of its innate violence.

4 Thus John Montague, for example, would ally *The Rough Field* to the cause of the Northern minority, reading outside Armagh Women's Prison in 1971 as part of a protest against the imprisonment of Bernadette Devlin. Lines by Hewitt would be quoted by the Taoiseach, Jack Lynch, in illustration of the need for the population of the Republic to understand the 'national minority', Unionist tradition on the island of Ireland (Liddy, 1979: 125).

5 Thus: 'the poets in this collection are concerned with the continuing war that being Irish means; the centuries old cycle of division, hatred and violence. Each of them, like every Irishman, is Cain and Abel, the killer and his brother victim . . . the poetry they write is urgent, necessary, always fine, and sometimes great' (Fiacc, 1974: dustcover).

6 This could be a matter of regret for critics like Seamus Deane. Thus, the overwhelmingly positive response to *North* beyond the province was partly the result of a feeling that Heaney's previous volume, *Wintering Out*, had been a let-down (the *TLS* reviewer, for example, regretted a lack of Troubles material: 'the bog oak, turf-banks and cobblestones prevail, and no one is plucking up the latter to throw them at anyone'). See Corcoran, 1986: 71. The objection persisted into the 1980s and 1990s – by critics as distinct in their ideological positions as Andrew Waterman, Desmond Fennell and Declan Kiberd – that the poets had evaded their appointment with history.

7 See Harry Chambers, *Fortnight*, 81 (1974), 12: it has become a cliché that 'the [Northern Irish] poets incline towards an oblique confrontation of their situation'. Obliquity, as a literary strategy, can be shown to have deep roots in the social fabric of Northern Irish life: as Rosemary Harris, in a pioneering study of life in Ulster had discovered, the intimacy and closeness of the different communities in the North had led to the development of elaborate and subtle codes of (superficial) courtesy to allow accommodation and avoid conflict, argument, or even simply giving offence. These allowed people to live as neighbours for some purposes and as 'strangers' for others, and their circumspection and elaborate care fed linguistic habits of tact and indirection. (See Rosemary Harris, *Prejudice and Tolerance in Ulster*,

1972, cited in J. Whyte, 1996: 9–11.) This limited conflict and fostered the ap-
preciation of nuance; on the negative side, it permitted the survival of 'deep suspicions and extraordinary stereotypes', and fed a sense of uncertainty and evasiveness, as the title of Heaney's (un-oblique) 'Whatever You Say, Say Nothing'
shows, or as alluded to in Mahon's 'The Spring Vacation' with its 'humorous formulae' and 'hidden menace in the knowing nod' (Mahon, 1986: 4).

 8 Eavan Boland, 'The Northern Writer's Crisis of Conscience', interviews, *Irish Times*
(12, 13, 14 August 1970). Cited in D. E. S. Maxwell, 1973: 93.

 9 The tension can be seen in Deane's claim on the one hand that 'There is very little
to be gained from directing the argument any further towards the sterile debating
points about the writer and his relationship / duties / attitudes to society', and on
the other that, regrettably, there were no poets for whom a collective politics was
'a mode of the imagination' (Deane, 1975: 9).

10 One example of the institutionalisation of this perception of immutable ethnic division came in the 1970s' 'The Planter and the Gael' tour, involving John Montague
and John Hewitt. Although a ground-breaking attempt at cross-community
cultural politics, it was recognised even at the time that it constituted a dubious
confirmation of division and stereotypes. See Kirkland, 1996: 64.

11 Such an approach only became widespread with the second generation of Northern Irish poets, from the mid-1970s, and involved also a break with the notion of
Northern Ireland as a place wholly self-enclosed, static and 'finished' in social
terms, impervious to differences of class and gender, set apart and unique in what
Hughes calls its 'cherished self-pity'.

12 For example: in 1967, the Irish American Cultural Institute began a series of
regular awards to Irish composers, painters and writers; recipients included Hartnett in 1975 and Montague in 1976. The terms of the award citation for Montague
are revealing, perhaps, of the expectations which lay behind the award, Montague
being judged worthy by virtue of his functioning as 'an international relay station
. . . transmitting outward and inward poetic and humanistic forms' but 'without
the least diminution of his identity as an Irish writer'. Here the identitarian grounds
for judging Irish writing according (ultimately) to its thematic Irishness are made
clear.

13 For an examination of the fusing of the individual subject with that of the nation
in romantic Nationalism, see David Lloyd, *Nationalism and Minor Literature: James
Clarence Mangan and the Emergence of Irish Cultural Nationalism* (Berkeley, University
of California Press, 1987).

14 See, for example, Derek Mahon, review of *The Rough Field*, *Malahat Review*, 27 (July
1973), 132–7.

15 Gerald Dawe notes, somewhat acerbically, 'the insistently moral ambience of
[Montague's] work which sees the autobiographical and cultural as one and the
same recurrent imaginative project: the poet as oracle, invoker of powers', claiming that 'in this regard [he] is very much more a traditionalist than he would have
us believe' (Corcoran, 1992: 29).

16 It also characteristically takes the form of a journey ('I went with Anger at my heel
/ Through Bogside of the bitter zeal'), and Northern sectarian hatreds are the overt
manifestations of the 'mutilation' and 'discontinuities' noted by Kinsella elsewhere.
Although 'A Butcher's Dozen' in some senses deviates from the main thrust of
Notes from the Land of the Dead and the Peppercanister poem-pamphlet sequence
which developed directly from it, it is part of a larger detour which included twin
elegies for Seán Ó Riada ('A Selected Life', published July 1972, and 'Vertical Man'
of August 1973) and an elegy for John F. Kennedy on the tenth anniversary of his
assassination ('The Good Fight', published November 1973). As Kinsella recognised

by later issuing the elegies and 'A Butcher's Dozen' together as *Fifteen Dead* (in 1979), these very public deaths coincide with and comment upon the more abstract and hermetic material of a private and visionary 'land of the dead', and serve as a reminder of the political thrust of the apparently obscure poetry which would follow it. On the other hand the continuity between 'A Butcher's Dozen' and this work can be overemphasised, eliding its obvious weaknesses.

17 Denis O'Driscoll notes: 'It remains the stuff of politics, of letters to the newspaper, and is neither revelatory, healing, nor very well written' (D. O'Driscoll, Public Vices and Private Voices, *Hibernia* (21 June 1979)).

18 Deane's comment – 'when myth enters [Heaney's] poetry [in *Wintering Out*] so too does history' – shows, in this sense, an awareness denied to Heaney's *TLS* reviewer (Deane, 1985: 179). It is this mythic access to communal feeling which Conor Cruise O'Brien describes as 'the thing itself' in his review of *North* (C. C. O'Brien, 1975: 404). The use in poetry of myth – in the sense of a history which the writer knows to be a selective naturalising of sectarian division – would lead in the late 1970s to considerable discussion of the legitimacy of its use (although agreement on the existence in the first place of such communal histories was considerable). For Wills the real difference between the two groups of critics is not over whether or not 'communities' adhere to mythic histories; it is that while one set – Deane, Montague, Heaney – wants the door on such atavisms opened, the myths to be aired and their force to be acknowledged, another – Foster, Longley – wants it kept closed. (Effectively, each impugns the motives for the others' preference – namely, the accusation of conforming with, even abetting, violence on the one hand, on the other of wishing the effects of systematic repression to be concealed and shut away.) The relationship between history and myth and between the poet and his putative 'community' thus became crucial to critical interpretations of the poetry, since although the poets may not ostensibly subscribe to a mythicised history, they nevertheless define themselves in terms of a social responsibility to bear witness to their community in crisis (Wills, 1993: 27–37).

19 More forcefully, in his *Crane Bag* interview of 1977 by Deane, Heaney notes that 'Discussion of what tradition means has moved from a sort of linguistic nostalgia, a puerile discourse about assonance, metres and so on, to a consideration of the politics and anthropology of our condition' (Deane, 1977: 64).

20 In 'Oracle', the poem following 'Broagh', the second person subject of the poem actually becomes 'lobe and larynx / of the mossy places'. Again, this echoes Corkery's claim that 'all the Gaels – were one, it may be maintained, with the very landscape itself.' See Corkery, 1979: 56. On the other hand it is necessary to note that 'Broagh' itself may be read as critiquing the other placename poems; thus, a Derridean reading of the poem would see in its 'mark' (the 'heelmark'), a print, or trace, a sign of writtenness at odds with the poem's charateristically Heaneyesque obsession with the oral/aural properties of the signifier. As a trace, it marks the absence of the marker/writer, and thus tellingly illustrates the poem's inability to locate the presence of place and, by extension, the poet's (desired) self-presence. In this respect, 'Broagh' makes explicit what the other placename poems occlude, namely the speaker's dis-placement.

21 This, of course, can be related to Heaney's uncertain sense of gender, communal and class identity, taken up in the more domestic and personal poems of part two, often relating to marriage, developed as a trope – in the figure of the ring, or circle – as emblematic of wholeness, but also of sacrifice and mutilation. (Part two gives the biographical context of politicisation in referring to a sabbatical year in California in 1970–71 where he discovered that 'poetry was a force, almost a mode of power, certainly a mode of resistance' – and, more important perhaps, the way in

which primitivism could be harnessed to that power.) Berkeley, like the rest of the USA, was politically charged by the anti-Vietnam War protests and the radicalised Black and Chicano minorities. The poets of the Bay Area – Snyder, Bly, Duncan – were rejecting dominant East Coast ironic idioms in favour of myth-influenced forms of writing, and primitivism was in the air (it was from these poets, as well as William Carlos Williams, that Heaney developed the 'artesian' stanza used in *Wintering Out* and *North*). Heaney's interpretation of this – 'the whole movement was back to a kind of reality I had known in my childhood' – shows that if he came to understand that poetry could be political, he did so by aligning it with the contradictory Irish experiences of modernisation and a Wordsworthian poetic. The journeying trope identified by Brown as destabilising the 'well-made' lyric is extended in the journey to the US and there is a memorable image of Heaney's sense of entrapment, stranded on 'a scurf of winkles and cockles' and 'Unable to move without crunching / Acres of their crisp delicate turrets' (Heaney, 1972: 77; Brown, 1988: 215–18). The pessimistic, downbeat note of the end of *Wintering Out* anticipates the fact that it was to be Heaney's last book to be written in Northern Ireland. Unable, on return from the USA, to settle down in Belfast, in August 1972 – under threat of physical violence – Heaney moved to the Republic, 'pursued by the catcalls of the Paisleyite *Protestant Telegraph* as it bade farewell to "the well-known Papist propagandist"' (Corcoran, 1992: 173).

22 P. V. Glob, *The Bog People: Iron-Age Man Preserved*, transl. Rupert Bruce-Mitford (London, Faber and Faber, 1969).

23 As he noted in 1977, '[my] energies quickened more when contemplating a victim, strangely, from 2,000 years ago than they did from contemplating a man at the end of the road being swept into a plastic bag . . . there is something terrible about that, but somehow language, words, didn't live in the way I think they have to live in a poem when they were hovering over that kind of horror and pity. They just became inert' (Corcoran, 1986: 96).

24 'Bog' is an unstable signifier which has been used for different, often contradictory purposes in different contexts. First and foremost, as a metonym of Ireland itself, it has given rise to a number of derogatory stereotypes. Typically, Irish Ireland writers tried to invert this image; Higgins and Colum both wrote of the quintessential 'bog wisdom' enshrined in the heart of the peasant, while Farren used the metaphor of bog butter to characterise Colum's mind, in an image later taken up by Heaney in 'Bogland'. But the negative image of the bog is given a profounder critical force by an anti-Irish Ireland writer, Peadar O'Donnell, in his 1929 novel, *Adrigoole*. O'Donnell's novel is about a republican family victimised by Free State neighbours after the Civil War; in it, the main character – before being driven mad – ponders continuously on the need for the Donegal native to go 'out into the world sometime or deeper into the bog', the bog which 'sucks an' sucks at any strong life above it'. For O'Donnell, as a Marxist writer, the bog represented isolation, backwardness and 'rural idiocy'. See J. M. Cahalan, *The Irish Novel* (Dublin, Gill and Macmillan, 1988), 192–3.

25 Glob, *The Bog People*, 36.

26 As McCormack notes, the title of the poem is that of a lyric by Langston Hughes, the black US poet, which deals with lynchings of Blacks in the Southern USA; as a Blues song, it was given wide circulation by Bessie Smith (McCormack, 1986: 53). This allusion is being juxtaposed with what Heaney sees as the pastoral and complacently decorative role of fruit in the English pastoral; 'gourd' appears to echo Keats's 'To Autumn' ('to plump the gourd and swell the hazel-shells').

27 In 'Escaped from the Massacre?', Carson complained that Heaney as an individual had succumbed to external pressures to acquire 'the status of myth, of institution',

and that this had infected his poetry; '[he] seems to have moved – unwillingly, perhaps – from being a writer with the gift of precision, to become the laureate of violence – a mythmaker, an anthropologist of ritual killing . . . in the last resort, a mystifier' (Carson, 1975b: 183). He noted the elision of historical and social differences in Heaney's Northern myth, its displacing of violence from the socio-political sphere to that of the foreordained: 'it is as if he is saying, suffering like this is natural . . . removed to the realm of sex, death and inevitability'. The passive aspect of the treatment of violence was linked to ritualistic tendencies, 'like a mystery of the Catholic Church' (Carson, 1975b: 184–5). Edna Longley would follow a similar anti-ritualist line, attacking *North*'s 'homogenisation', and substitution of 'announcements' ('I push back . . .', 'I step through . . .') for 'genuine prospecting', dubbing it 'a book of martyrs rather than tragic protagonists'. Longley perceptively noted that Heaney's 'passivity' had a strategic function, and also that there is a problem in *North* in distinguishing between voluntary and involuntary martyrdom which raises awkward political questions. Like Carson, she also overlooked Heaney's own uncertainties and self-mockery. To claim that the final part of 'Kinship', for example, 'defines the battlefield in astonishingly introverted Catholic and Nationalist terms' is to ignore its black humour:

> Our mother ground
> is sour with the blood
> of her faithful,
>
> they lie gargling
> in her sacred heart
> as the legions stare
> from the ramparts.

The 'legions' here are those of the British Army, who, like the Roman legions, in the words of Tacitus, 'make a desolation and call it peace'; but they are also those of the Legion of Mary (while 'gargling' is hardly compatible with the dignity of the 'sacred heart') (E. Longley, 1986: 154).

28 Allison adds: 'By so arranging the poems of *North* that the association of earth, grave, womb, vagina and corpse manifests itself gradually, by thus seducing the reader into sensual complicity, by displacing intimacy to . . . archaeologically significant icons – Heaney shapes a context in which revulsion might understandably be shared, and convincingly links revulsion and fascinated devotion. Moreover . . . 'Bog Queen' . . . turns the relation from male certainty, allowing Heaney not only to cast doubt on his speaker's enthusiasms but also to endow his characteristic ambivalences with political significance . . . Heaney . . . conveys the profound ambivalence at the heart of that bond [with the land] – a sexual ambivalence that figures itself in necrophilia, a self-conscious ambivalence which perceives an implicit insatiable violence in its hope to deflect blame.'

29 Denis Ireland, Fog in the Irish Sea, *Threshold*, 5:1 (Spring/Summer 1961), 50.

30 The crisis of surplus signification the bog poems enact, while smothering difference, also overwhelms Heaney's own basic distinction of authentic from the inauthentic. This can be seen in 'Feeling into Words', in which – quoting Wordsworth on the 'hiding places' of poetic 'power' – poetry is defined, with characteristic circularity, as 'revelation of the self to the self'. Piling clause upon clause in an attempt to bring closure to the definition, Heaney here refers to 'poems as elements of continuity, with the aura and authenticity of archaeological finds, where the buried shard has an importance that is not diminished by the importance of the buried city; poetry as a dig, *a dig for finds that end up being plants*' (my emphasis) (Heaney, 1980: 41). 'Plants' nicely labels the unconscious sleights of hand by which

pathologies (and also ideologies) operate; answers already decided on, identities already fixed, are placed as if to seem 'natural' discoveries, tokens of authenticity. The swerve from 'finds' as authentic discovery to 'finds' as 'plants', manufactured evidence, a falsification of discovery and pure origin, is revealing in a way Heaney does not intend: 'finds' cannot 'end up' as 'plants' – if they were 'planted' in the first place they cannot be 'found' in the authentic sense. It allows, that is, a self-deceiving, even criminal dimension to the archaeological method (you only truly 'find' what you're already looking for). Heaney's lack of a full awareness of his own procedures perhaps emerges in his interview with James Randall: 'I'm very angry with a couple of snotty remarks by people who . . . speak as if the bog images were picked up for convenience instead of being . . . a deeply felt part of my own life, a revelation to me' (Randall, 1979: 19). On the one hand this confirms suspicions of Heaney's naive faith in the self-present self – the self, being always different from the self it contemplates, can never truly confirm that 'self' – and the conviction that the authentic 'finds' in his work are actually inauthentic 'plants'. Yet it also points to a self-division, to the strain of suppressing difference, and to the genuine complexity and tentativeness of the best of this poetry. Elsewhere, Heaney has discussed his work in terms of two main types, the inspirational and the laboured-for. The first kind – not just the bog poems – he has likened to 'finds' in a bog. 'I have always listened for poems, they come sometimes like bodies come out of a bog, almost complete, seeming to have been laid down a long time ago, surfacing with a touch of mystery' (Heaney, 1980: 34). One way of describing this is by recourse to feminist theory; Julia Kristeva's concept of the subject in process – that is, of unitary subjectivity as an inherently unstable effect of language – is peculiarly appropriate. Chris Weedon, in *Feminist Practice and Poststructuralist Theory* (Oxford, Basil Blackwell, 1989), 88–9, offers a succinct account of Kristeva's theories in this regard. Additionally, given the fluidity of subjectivity in Irish society, we might recall that Heaney's own apparently stable origins and sense of selfhood are just that. The characterisation by radical critics of Heaney as 'bourgeois', while it takes in the more consolatory aspects of the poetry, is lazily inadequate to the volatile state out of which it emerges. (David Lloyd's thoroughgoing assault on Heaney, for example, in 'Pap for the Dispossessed': Seamus Heaney and the Poetics of Identity, links *North* to a general tendency to succumb to a communal Nationalist 'politics of identity' and subordinate ethics to aesthetics, burying real difference – of gender, class, place – in an illusory racial unity constituted by an essential Irish predilection for violence: 'in locating the source of violence beyond even sectarian division, Heaney renders it symbolic of a fundamental identity of the Irish race, as "authentic" '. For Lloyd, the agonising of the observer in 'Punishment' is fake, incompletely radical, its artful voyeurism 'smuggled back in as the unspoken and unacknowledged condition for the understanding of the "exactness" of . . . "revenge" '. As I argue, there is justice in this charge, but it has to be qualified by admitting Heaney's own perturbed awareness of the inadequacy of his own sense of 'identity'.) (Lloyd, 1993: 31.) In fact, 'bourgeois' as a label ironically echoes that of conservative critics, such as Tony Curtis, who describes Heaney in indiscriminate fashion as 'a Catholic and born into the tribe of Éire and the Falls Road' (Curtis, 1994: 101). As McCormack comments, 'the notable aspect of Heaney's poetry is that "bourgeois subject" remains still a highly charged and historically problematic category in the social conjuncture from which he writes' (McCormack, 1986: 77). Awareness of such a dimension brings the issue of 'community', so prevalent in Heaney criticism, under scrutiny, as divisions of class and national identity are exposed. (See Fionnuala O'Connor, 1993, for details of the complex internal differentiation of the Northern Catholic community.) Heaney may well desire the tribal homogeneity Curtis perceives, but his writing nevertheless represents an 'improper' socio-literary miscegenation, one embodying the mixed angst and dissatisfaction of a rising fraction of the Catholic rural middle class, granted a voice but still disempowered; nor can history and class be discounted by appeals to the ancient basis of a rural society 'more thoroughly overturned, altered and renovated than any other in the British Isles' (McCormack, 1986: 77). *North* does not merely construct a (conscious) myth to explore the history apparently subscribed to by 'those who do the killing' on the republican side (so eliding the historic and social specificity of IRA violence); it also reveals the degree to which Heaney was able to represent a notional communal allegiance before succumbing to it. In this sense the book's most lasting effect may have been the turning point in the development of successor poets who were enabled to break not only with his subject matter, but also with Heaney's lyric procedures.

31 The second of these, based on the Gaelic 'Lament for Art O'Leary', has been claimed by Edna Longley as 'question[ing] or broaden[ing] Irish martyrology by proclaiming an RUC man as worthy of lamentation as O'Leary', but what might be more worth questioning is the whole issue of 'martyrology'; certainly, the poem's granite-jawed upstanding caricature comes nowhere near fulfilling his deconstructive role (Simmons, 1986: 21).

32 The reference to Elpenor's oar, like Eiléan Ní Chuilleanáin's in 'The Second Voyage' (discussed in Chapter 4), may owe something to Pound's use of it in the *Cantos'* own archaeology of the dead, and thus indicate something of his tangential use of modernist motifs.

33 Lines in an earlier version of the poem in *The Lace Curtain* – 'An end to the / Grindstone, the alchemical / Stone and the / Stone of destiny' – stress the oscillation between anti-mythic and humanist urges; on the one hand they acknowledge the kind of preference shown in 'The Spring Vacation' for 'wet / Stone' whose 'material, mineral reality [outfaces] the human scenes played before it' (McDonald, 1997: 90); on the other they echo Yeats's 'stone in the midst of all' as an image for fixed beliefs that fossilise the spirit in 'Easter, 1916'. See *The Lace Curtain*, 5 (Spring 1974), 80–1.

34 As Joris Duytschaever has pointed out, there are 'affinities between Benjamin and Mahon in terms of utopian and messianic impulses and potentialities' (Joris Duytschaever, History in the Poetry of Derek Mahon, in Joris Duytschaever and Geert Lernout (eds), *History and Violence in Anglo-Irish Literature* (Amsterdam, Rodopi, 1988), 100).

Although Edna Longley has read such work as an assertion that the value of poetry resides in its standing above the fray, embodying in its formal perfection the separateness of the artifactual world in which political conflict is redeemed, Mahon's practice puts this notion under severe scrutiny; similarly, it seems to me, John Constable offers only a partial truth when he claims that 'What [Mahon] confronts in the second volume is "the human heart", and he knows there is no escaping it.' See J. Constable, Derek Mahon's Development, *Agenda*, 22:3–4 (Autumn/Winter 1984/5), 110.

35 As he writes, 'I find offensive the notion that what we inadequately call "the Troubles" might provide inspiration for artists: and that in some weird *quid pro quo* the arts might provide solace for grief and anguish. Twenty years ago [in 1970] I wrote in *Causeway*: "Too many critics seem to expect a harvest of paintings, poems, plays and novels to drop from the twisted branches of civil discord"' (M. Longley, 1995a: 73).

36 The Troubles gave an important boost to 'revisionism' in general. Anti-Partitionist forms of Nationalism now came to be seen, at least officially, as tarnished. The most important figure in the controversy – as a man of letters and as a government minister in the Fine Gael–Labour coalition of the early 1970s – was Conor Cruise O'Brien. O'Brien's attacks on lazy assumptions about Northern Ireland as simultaneously a place of the utmost barbarity and belonging to the Republic were tonic; never before had someone in such a position of authority – he was Minister of Telegraph and Posts – spoken out so boldly (although O'Brien damaged his case later in the decade by adopting a position from which the whole history of the Southern state, and 1916–1922 itself, could be seen as a mistake). A member himself of a family prominent in Nationalist politics, O'Brien argued that Unionists were not only not the prisoners of a 'false consciousness', but were wholly justified in defending their right to separatism against a Republic which they saw as illiberal, theocratic and economically backward (Brown, 1985: 283–6). As Heaney noted, despite his exaggerations, O'Brien was therefore responsible in the 1970s for bringing about 'some kind of clarity in Southerners' thinking about the Protestant community in the North' (Brown, 1985: 286). Similarly, if with more restraint, Francis Shaw's attack on the cult of Patrick Pearse, 'The Canon of Irish History: A Challenge', which had been suppressed in 1966, appeared in 1972, attacking Pearse's equation of revolutionary self-sacrifice with the crucifixion, Nationalist martyrology and the proclamation of Irish history as 'seven centuries of solid and unbroken military resistance' (Brown, 1985: 287–8). Nevertheless, the growing sectarian dimension of the conflict helped to preserve the post-Civil War configuration of politics in the Republic. Thus, if the Troubles encouraged revisionist attitudes, they also confirmed existing structures. One effect of this could be seen in a throwback to cultural formations associated with the birth of the state – perhaps by way of compensation in a non-political sphere – in a new ruralism and communitarianism, part of what W. J. McCormack has called the 'depoliticization' of Southern society: 'Faced with expanding violence in the 1970s, and that intricately involved with the spread of increasingly impersonalised modes of living . . . the Irish imagination for the most part opted for an older, more cohesive community. It braced itself for the shock of the new by elegising and simultaneously inventing an interior order which spoke of "a more humane architectural proportion", "more supportive parish structures", "the greater warmth of the pre-nuclear family". In this, of course, it relied on ever-available pastoral images of the past' (Gibbons, 1996: 3; McCormack, 1987: 67).

37 In two articles on Northern poetry published in 1978 and 1979, for example, the US-based poet-critic from the Republic James Liddy discussed 'Ulster Poets and the Catholic Muse' and 'Ulster Poets and the Protestant Muse' in terms which showed how little understanding had developed in the previous decade. Thus, Heaney's 'careful stanza making' is seen as wholly in 'the British tradition'. For Liddy, while their 'closeness to catastrophe which could be called genocidal . . . animates most Northern Irish [poets] of the minority' (Liddy speaks elsewhere of 'native poets'), McFadden's concern for sectarianism is genuine but weaker than theirs 'because he *must* be less secure in his feelings' (my emphasis) (Liddy, 1978: 134, 127, 129).

38 In *The Honest Ulsterman* in February 1972, for example, the columnist Jude the Obscure wrote of the 'misogyny and its sentimental male friendships', 'alcoholism', 'snobbery', 'churchiness' and 'the traits [of] a homosexual community' of the Dublin literary scene, an attack which points to the gender stereotypes – the Republic as soft, female, backward-looking, the North as male, rugged, progressive – which often underlay Northern criticism. John Jordan's reply in *Hibernia* in June of the same year calls attention to its implicit sectarianism: 'Mr Foley and "Jude" . . . will not help themselves by seeing Dublin as the great Popish ulcer in the body politic'. See J. Jordan, Northern Lights, *Hibernia* (23 June 1972), 10.

39 In some ways 'The War Horse' asks the same questions as Mahon's 'Glengormley'; '[W]hy should we care', it asks about 'a rose which now will never climb / The stone of our house . . . a volunteer', about a crocus – 'one of the screamless dead' – since 'we' are safe, 'our unformed fear / Of fierce commitment gone'? (Boland, 1980b: 9).

40 Kevin P. Reilly, *Éire-Ireland*, 15:3 (1980), 122.

41 The visual in Durcan's poetry – its increasing concern with film, painting and photography, noted by Kathleen McCracken – is of a piece with the belief that language in Ireland has been abused 'and by poets as much as gunmen or churchmen', a belief which, while it pushes his poetry away from formal containment (with a vengeance, some would argue), prevents the search for modernist-influenced alternatives, seen as elitist (C. Tóbín, 1996: 34). Style and stance are bound together by the notion that poetry is in competition with, and shaped by, the mass media, and that performance is of its essence.

42 Non sequiturs, banal or lame endings, overheard conversation, lists ('The Hat Factory' lists thirty-eight different kinds of hat in its central passage, for example), ballad-like refrains, deliberate archaism, mixed metaphor, snatches of nonsense verse and digression punctuate the narrative surface, making generalisable 'messages' or subjects hard to extract. This style, or stance, has scarcely changed during Durcan's career, and the later work is embryonically present in *O Westport*; the quasi-surreal satire of 'The Limerickman that Went to the Bad', the divorce poems in lyrics to his wife Nessa, *Daddy, Daddy* in 'Poem for My Father', sexual politics in 'Pulpit Bishop Sickness, AD 1973' and the critique of militant Republicanism in 'The Night They Murdered Boyle Somerville.'

43 See, for example, Walter J. Ong, *The Presence of the Word: Some Prolegomena for Cultural and Religious History* (New Haven/Ladon, Yale University Press, 1967).

44 'Hidden Ireland(s)' is, as John Kerrigan has pointed out, a motif loosely resorted to by critics whenever they wish to advert to any previously unrepresented aspect of Irish life, but in its Corkeryan origins it refers specifically to the Penal Law period and Corkery's claim in *The Hidden Ireland* (1924) that the Munster Gaelic population had kept faith with their culture, paying secret homage to the dispossessed Catholic nobility and maintaining a bardic tradition through Courts of Poetry, held in aristocratic Big Houses, or in inns. The book's obvious flaws – its lack of empirical evidence, its blatant retrospectively Nationalistic spirit – made it a sign for all that was self-deluding in Irish Ireland ideology, and it was the subject of L. M. Cullen's 'The Hidden Ireland: reassessment of a concept', *Studia Hibernica*, 9 (1969; repr. 1988). But its continuing resonance has to be seen in the light not just of neo-Corkeryanism – the poets in question cite Corkery's influence but are, in other ways, cultural pluralists – but also of material and linguistic-political factors.

45 The material context for neo-Corkeryan attitudes lies in the unevenness of the modernisation process in the 1960s, which left behind many parts of rural Ireland – notably in the West and South West – and signalled the end of the small-farm economy which had been prevalent in the impoverished Gaeltacht areas. Cork was disadvantaged and declined relative to Dublin in the same period. In the 1970s, however, it emerged as an alternative poetic centre, with young poets grouped around the older figures of Montague, Seán Lucy and Sean Ó Tuama. The further decline of Irish, exacerbated by modernisation and the growing crisis of identity which accompanied it, gave impetus to the exploration of a regional identity. There is, of course, an ironic dimension to the adoption of an aesthetic of 'hiddenness' or of Munster, since between Corkery's influence and that aesthetic lay precisely the failure of the state for which he was an ideologue to secure an assured future

for the Irish language (Kerrigan, 1998: 79). By the late 1960s a 'civil rights' movement had begun in the Gaeltacht areas and was engaging in direct action. The
political campaign for investment, employment and adequate media resources
(Irish-medium radio and TV stations) had a strong youth involvement, and fed
into the assertiveness of the poetic efflorescence at University College Cork, and
the group of Irish-language poets based around the journal *Innti* who studied there
in the early 1970s. Inherited ideas of 'hiddenness' (or isolation) which John
Kerrigan has claimed 'enriched the way [English-language] Munster poets think
about where they come from' were accentuated by more than simply the persistence of Irish, however; difference or 'hiddenness' was foregrounded by them as
a deliberate tactic.

46 It is likely that this is one of the poems Hartnett referred to in 1986: 'I've noticed
in many of my poems that when I want to build up the character of a person I
don't catalogue them or their physical attributes as such but rather their belongings'. In this case, the woman's 'belongings' are a set of memories (O'Driscoll, 1987:
18).

47 John Berger, *Success and Failure of Picasso* (London, Writers and Readers Publishing
Cooperative, 1980).

48 A more sustained creative use of the tension between the claims of residual traditional culture and modernity is found in Hartnett's translation work, in which (in
quality and quantity) he has been second only to Kinsella among poets of the
period. Translations of 'The Hag of Beare' (1969), *Ó Bruadair* (1985) and *Haicéad*
(1993) serve Hartnett's vision of a betrayed Irish culture and his identification with
the poets of a traumatised seventeenth-century Gaelic culture in much the same
way as Feiritéar and Ó Rathaille in Kinsella.

49 While the latest (1996) version of Kinsella's pre 'Notes From the Land of the Dead'
poems is used in discussions of the work before this point, the section which
follows refers to the 1973 text (slightly revised from the 1972 Cuala Press version).
Kinsella's always heavy and incessant revision is judged, in the latest version, to
have gravely weakened the early versions of the poems in question, sacrificing
many of their more complex effects. Thus, the subdivisions of the sequence into
three parts have now been removed, while the invocation ('hesitate, cease to exist,
glitter again') no longer ends with 'the count of O', and the conclusion of 'Hen
Woman' has been altered.

50 Details of the extent and complexity of Kinsella's post-*Nightwalker* publication
history are given in Dawe, 1995: 204–15.

51 Daniel O'Hara, An Interview with Thomas Kinsella, *Contemporary Poetry: A Journal
of Criticism*, 4:1 (1981), 7–8.

52 In Jungian psychology, the unconscious is ultimately communal and taps into a
collective, racial unconscious which generates powerful archetypes. These may be
accessed through psychic self-exploration, as well as via art and religion. The ancestry of the psyche 'goes back many millions of years', while 'the unconscious corresponds to the mythic language of the dead, the land of the ancestors'. See C. G.
Jung, *Memories, Dreams, Reflections*, transl. Richard Winston and Clara Winston (New
York, Pantheon, 1973), 191; also Jolande Jacobi, *Complex/Archetype/Symbol in the
Psychology of C. G. Jung*, transl. Ralph Mannheim (London, Routledge and Kegan
Paul, 1959), 59–62. Jung further proposes that individuation, a fully realised sense
of self, can only be attained by accessing that realm: inner peace and contentment
depend largely on whether or not the historical family which is inherent in the
individual can be harmonised with the transient conditions of the present. He does
so in specifically gendered terms; the male achieves individuation by finding his
anima which will complete the self (Jung is notably more sketchy on the role of
the female equivalent, the animus).

53 Crucial to the open-ended form of the poem, Kinsella has stated that order should be 'elicited' rather than imposed and rejected the notion that the structures he discovers are willed; speaking of the alchemical tropes of *New Poems 1973*, for example, he has claimed that 'I don't think [they] came about just because one is interested in Jung, it's just that when you get to a certain area that's what you find' (Cadogan, 1997a: 5).

54 In the radically fragmented 'All is Emptiness and I Must Spin' the disintegrative effects of such knowledge on the self are the historical equivalent of the zero which becomes 'an egg of being' in the introductory poem (Kinsella, 1973a: 44–5).

55 Thus, 'Ely Place' features the speaker apparently arbitrarily jabbing a penknife into 'her throat, / her spirting gullet!', recalling 'Sacrifice' in 'a single drop', which features a ritual sacrifice which is offered as an image of self-sacrifice in love (Kinsella, 1973a: 46–7, 41–2).

56 As Kathleen McCracken's excellent essay on Carson puts it 'Their republication in 1988 made "reading back" a confirmation of certain continuities and departures.' McCracken finds many such 'continuities', but notes the formal discontinuity between their structural conservatism and the later long-line poetry with its multiply plotted textures (McCracken, 1995: 369).

57 Elsewhere in the book – in 'De Secretis Mulierum', 'Largesse' and 'Cider' – Muldoon tries to establish a libertine persona, albeit one undercut and qualified. In 'The Girls in the Poolroom', macho pretence is mocked by Emily: 'I asked her once, "Are you asleep?"/She said, "I am. I am." ' At the same time the lines 'How could I help / But make men of them?' points to the theme of androgyny and anal (non-reproductive, hence non-familial) sex which runs throughout the work (Muldoon, 1977: 31).

58 A. Waterman, Ulsterectomy, *Hibernia*, 43:17 (26 April 1979), 17.

Opening up the field

> The politicising of women's issues in Ireland coincided with their
> poeticising, and they became poetic subjects in both Gaelic and English.
> (Ní Chuilleanáin, 1992: 37)

Timorous liberalism, inherited boundaries

The issues of language, place, identity and myth broached by Heaney and
Montague continued to dominate poetry in the late 1970s and early 1980s;
but, as in the case of Carson and Muldoon, they were being increasingly
queried by younger poets, while neo-modernist experimentalists like Squires
treated such issues altogether differently. This trend can be discerned in the
South as well as the North, and may be read in the light of the larger social
and political developments of the time. In the Republic these stemmed from
the fallout from the 1974–75 and 1979–81 economic crises, which marked
an end to the Lemassian boom, as well as the gradual realisation of the permanence and full implications of the Troubles.[1] A different economic, social
and political dynamic came into play, of coping with contraction and the re-
emergence of atavistic forces after only a brief acquaintance with expansion
and convergence. Although prosperity increased, albeit more gradually, a sense
of disillusion mounted. Slowdown, inflation and rising budget deficits brought
rising unemployment – from 7.9 per cent to 12.5 per cent between 1974 and
1978. The mid-1970s' Fine Gael–Labour coalition had been ousted by Fianna
Fáil in the 1977 election, in which Fianna Fáil gained their largest share of the
vote since 1938. Preaching austerity, but borrowing heavily to preserve their
populist base, Fianna Fáil were in turn ousted in 1982 by Fine Gael and Labour
which moved to carry out neo-liberal policies, in line with developments in
the UK, USA and elsewhere in the capitalist world. (In Northern Ireland, on
the other hand, while it was part of the British state, attempts to placate and
mollify insurgent fractions of society meant that the province was, ironically,
in many ways protected from the ravages of Thatcherite policies on the 'mainland'.) In social and political terms, the mid-1970s marked the end of the
bloodiest phase of the Troubles and the beginning of moves towards their
'Ulsterisation' (the RUC/UDR rather than Army policing of the Troubles)
(Coogan, 1996: 289). At roughly the same time the IRA moved to embrace

the idea of a 'long war'; that is, abandoning the aim of the direct overthrow of British control in favour of a strategy of making Northern Ireland impossible to stabilise, thereby draining the resources and morale of the Westminster government over an extended period. In the political area, Direct Rule from Westminster remained, although local government was reformed. The relationship between all three states involved was a complex one. The Troubles tarnished the democratic structures and drained the resources of the Republic. Similarly, through a growing rapprochement between the British and Irish governments, the Protestant majority's sense of being wanted by and/or belonging to Britain was threatened in the North. This rapprochement – always a fear of Loyalists – was boosted by the hunger strikes by IRA prisoners in the Maze prison in 1980–81, and the subsequent deaths of ten of them, which brought the IRA, in the form of its political wing, Sinn Féin, into electoral politics. Initially this met with striking success (although forced on them by the actions of the hunger strikers, the IRA could rationalise this as part of a 'long war' strategy, to be conducted with – in Martin McGuinness's words – 'a ballot box in one hand and an armalite in the other'). As Sinn Féin made substantial inroads into the moderate Nationalist support of the SDLP, so the British and Irish governments sought to contain them, aided by the SDLP. It was as part of an attempt to head off the forces of Republicanism, therefore, that the negotiations began which would culminate in the Anglo-Irish Agreement of November 1985. Not the least of the ironies of the period was the fact that it was the notoriously intransigent government of Margaret Thatcher (whose cabinet was the target of an audacious IRA bomb attack in 1984) and a nominally republican Fianna Fáil government led by Charles Haughey which signed the Agreement.

It was not economic change alone, of course, which impelled the social realignments which literature mediated. In the 1970s, and again – less successfully – after 1982, the leader of Fine Gael, Garret FitzGerald, had 'sought to replace the crumbled hegemonic consensus, built around a de facto Catholic state, with a pluralist consensus embracing Catholic and Protestant religious traditions equally' (Lee, 1993: 653). FitzGerald's aim was, in effect, to extend economic modernisation into the social sphere, albeit in a gradual manner favourable to the interests of big business. What has been called 'timorous liberalism' (as well as the more bullish anti-nationalism of Conor Cruise O'Brien) spread and consolidated itself in the Republic during the 1970s, based on the growth of the middle class and motivated by a number of factors – the desire to modernise the country in line with Europe, increased international economic competition, the continuing secularisation of society and the implicit critique perceived in the continuing rejection of the Republic by Northern Protestants. For all this the Republic remained a deeply conservative society, one suffused with the values of Catholicism, Nationalism and ruralism, although less stridently so than in the past, and its newly internationalised economy and culture ensured that it would not escape the effects of the general shift towards reaction in the advanced capitalist nations. Moreover, reaction to social liberalisation and the Northern crisis had begun, by the mid-1970s, to encourage a powerful traditionalist response.

In literary terms, a complex interaction, varying all the way from charged stand-off to gratefully accepted influence, prevailed between the Republic and Northern Ireland in the late 1970s and 1980s. On the one hand, the traditional claim – as if according to Articles 2 and 3 of a poetic Constitution – was that Northern Irish poetry was part of a broader, Irish, tradition: thus, Seán Lucy could write in *Hibernia* in 1977 that 'Ulsterness . . . means Irishness', despite – or perhaps in defiance of – the fact that the Troubles had had the effect of sealing off the border between North and South, in intellectual as well as social affairs, shrouding Belfast literary affairs from the view of the Dublin literary would (Lucy, 1977; C. Tóbín, 1996: 104–5). Most notoriously, and following the unwillingness of Northern poets themselves to be seen as no more than the creations of hype, Thomas Kinsella dismissed the idea of a separate Northern poetry as a 'journalistic entity' (Kinsella, 1986: xxx). On the other hand, younger poets and critics, aware of the inflammatory potential of such claims and embarrassed by them, could deny the links between Northern and Southern poetries altogether. In the introduction to his anthology *The Inherited Boundaries*, also published in 1986 – and the first Dolmen anthology since the 1962 *Miscellany* – Sebastian Barry claimed that 'the story of Northern Irish poetry is a fine story . . . but no part of our own' (S. Barry, 1986: 14). Neither position, of course, is entirely satisfactory; indeed, both show the persistence of binary approaches to the issue. Lucy and Kinsella fail to respect, that is, the specificity of the achievement of the Belfast Group poets and their successors, annexing it to a wider 'Irish' tradition which seemed suspiciously totalising and continuous (in Kinsella's case this meant actively excluding Longley, Muldoon and others, while – arguably – accepting Mahon partly on the basis of his expressions of sympathy for Nationalism). On the other hand, as Terence Brown has noted, 'In writing such a passage Barry is in fact indicating how much a part of the Republic's story the Northern thing has been. It has induced respect with a slightly envious sense of being overlooked; a determination to make that neglect good and a factitious, reactive, and not very convincing partitionism' (Brown, 1986: 22). Between partitionism and annexation-dismissal, the subtler interactions and differences between the separate but linked bodies of poetry tend to be lost. Nevertheless, Barry's diminishing of the importance of antagonism towards Britain, and resultant focus on internal difference within the Republic, does reflect a genuine and continuing shift of sensibility on the part of a generation of poets born in the 1950s. In his words, 'The great feeling, growing up then, through the sixties and seventies, was that the Republic was run by jobbers and gombeenmen, who could not be taken seriously, and much less admired . . . The English had been intolerable as a crust (and they were, doubtless) – now an intolerable cupidity was to take their place' (S. Barry, 1986: 18). The cultural agenda offered is not that of dealing with stagnation or the stresses of change, nor even the Troubles, but 'intolerable cupidity', Western consumerism and complacency.

Seamus Heaney: from *Field Work* to Sweeneyspeak

Aspects of the traditionalist response are exemplified in the post-*North* work of Seamus Heaney. Following the mixed critical reception of *North*, Heaney broke with its mythic intensities – as signalled in its last poem 'Exposure' – a break discussed in an interview with James Randall in 1979. There, he expressed the desire for a more public poetic language, for a return to the iambic norm and a less dense style, to return to a 'rhythmic contract' with the reader and 'to . . . use the first person singular to mean *me* and in my lifetime'[2] (Randall, 1979: 16, 20). *Field Work* (1979) bears out the wish to return to the quotidian in its discarding of the myth Heaney had elaborately constructed. The variety of the collection – pastoral, elegy, translation, lyric, love (or marriage) poem, translation – reflects this, and in a lusher style than *North*. In certain ways this represents a return to the early poetry, and a rural-pastoral sonnet sequence – 'Glanmore Sonnets' – lies at the heart of the book. Nevertheless, the dominant tone is set by the Troubles. Stripped of mythic structure, now seen implicitly as inadequate to comprehension of the violence, the poetry sorrowfully examines its cost in openly personal terms, while at the same time attempting a different kind of public address, one drawn largely from the poetry of Robert Lowell. If this can have its drawbacks – as Corcoran has pointed out, the poems are full of Lowellian oracular questions and adjectival 'runs' – it does, to some extent, allow Heaney to deflect the self-centredness of a more purely personal subject matter into a larger communal drama, at the same time as he tentatively raises the possibility of disengaging from it, and from his spokesman's role (Corcoran, 1998: 84). Alongside Lowell, Dante is a major influence, shaping the book by bringing together the senses of the poet in 'exile' and as transformer of personal grief into permanent art, of midlife reassessment and as inquisitor of the dead. Yet, at the same time, *Field Work* is also, in its embrace of traditional verse forms, a reappraisal of the English lyric tradition, and a number of figures from it – Wyatt, Wordsworth, Lawrence – feature. Put simplistically, the tension which runs through the collection is that 'between song and suffering' (Parker, 1993: 153).

Elegy is traditionally a genre in which public and private grief can be aired – think of *Lycidas* and *Adonais* – and Heaney's elegies are both for specific individuals killed in the Troubles, and for Ireland itself, conceived in unitary terms in 'Sibyl', which concludes with the line (mournfully echoing *The Tempest*) 'Our island is full of comfortless noises' (Heaney, 1979: 13). Those mourned include a university friend, a drinking companion, a cousin, and artists such as Seán Ó Riada and Francis Ledwidge, the Ulster Catholic poet killed fighting in the British Army in World War I. If Ledwidge is an example of sectarian 'strains' which 'criss-cross in useless equilibrium', Heaney's hope is clearly that such strains do not cancel out in *Field Work* (Heaney, 1979: 60). Nevertheless, influences, traditions and Heaney's own uncertainties concerning the violence he is now distanced from, jostle uneasily in the book and continually conflict with its rich style and lyric poise. For *Field Work* wavers 'timorously' (to use Seamus Deane's adjective) at the beginning of a gesture of revolt against an anxious, duty-laden earlier self in its opening poem 'Oysters', whose speaker asks to be 'quickened into verb, [the] pure verb' of the writing life, while at the same time feeling afraid to accept the 'glut of privilege' which the oysters, symbolising the aesthetic, represent. The poem expresses a mixture of guilt at detachment, anger at feeling that guilt, and a new desire to be free from the burden of community. These are not easily escaped: he is finally 'angry that my trust could not repose / In the clear light, like poetry or freedom / Leaning in from the sea' (Heaney, 1979: 11).

The unease, while pervasive, is directly dramatised only occasionally; in the first of the 'Glanmore Sonnets' early rural pieties seem to be reasserted unproblematically:

> My lea is deeply tilled
> Old ploughsocks gorge the subsoil of each sense
> And I am quickened with a redolence
> Of the fundamental dark unblown rose.
> (Heaney, 1979: 33)

The 'fundamental dark unblown rose' is the roisín dubh ('little dark rose') of Nationalist song, here expressed by the earth itself. Heaney's attachment to his territorial metaphor holds back, as it were, the desire to repose his 'trust' in the maritime light 'leaning in' of 'Oysters', and it is this, rather than the conflict with an 'English tradition', which is at the heart of the problem raised by *Field Work*. Nostalgic attachment shows again in the elegy for Ó Riada; Heaney alludes to the fusion of European art and Irish traditional music (mentioned in Montague's 'A Patriotic Suite'), but his image for Ó Riada's conducting style – 'like a drover with an ashplant / herding them south' – is deliberately archaic, and the composer is, uncomplicatedly, *'our* jacobite' (my emphasis) (Heaney, 1979: 30). This has its political ramifications, since there is a sense in which the entire volume, suffused as it is with liturgical imagery and visionary, ghostly presences, is one long backward-gazing *aisling*: 'After a Killing's' 'Who's sorry for our trouble?' uses an Irish idiom, but is also close to the 'cherished self-pity' identified by Eamon Hughes (Heaney, 1979: 12). Rather differently, 'Leavings' juxtaposes Will Brangwen and Thomas Cromwell, architect of the dissolution of the monasteries, in a pastoral scenario which suggests a continuity between Ireland (defined in religious and sectarian terms) and a pre-imperial England made bereft by the Reformation: 'I rode down England . . . down from Ely's Lady Chapel, / the sweet tenor latin / forever banished, / the sumptuous windows' (Heaney, 1979: 57). The poem echoes Heaney's essay of the time, 'Englands of the Mind', in which Ted Hughes, Geoffrey Hill and Philip

Larkin are presented as the laureates of a 'diminished', post-imperial England in order, arguably, to release his sympathies (although Hughes subscribes, like Heaney, to the idea of a fall from worship of the earth mother in the sixteenth century). Certainly, the liturgical aspects of the book – specifically a Catholic, rather than pagan form of ritual, as in *North* – suffuse the collection. Melodic ease and rural nostalgia combine with the most quietist of artistic credos in the last verse of the much anthologised 'The Harvest Bow': '*The end of art is peace* / Could be the motto of this frail device / That I have pinned up on our deal dresser' (Heaney, 1979: 58). The attempt to isolate the claim – from Coventry Patmore – by italicising it does not make this less anodyne. On the other hand, some of the poems in the book break from its complacencies. 'The Badgers', while echoing a generally Nationalist tone, disturbingly senses a complicity with those who carry out the killings, while in the powerful and moving 'Triptych' Heaney turns (albeit momentarily) on greed in the Republic: 'My people think money / And talk weather' (Heaney, 1979: 13). The book's analysis of a mounting crisis of conscience is posed sharply in its most discussed piece, 'Casualty'. At one level this is a palinode, or apology poem, for 'Punishment' and 'Kinship'. Heaney claims identity with a drinking acquaintance who was blown up in a bar after breaking a curfew imposed on Northern Catholics by the IRA, as they planned a revenge attack after Bloody Sunday. The description of the funeral of the Bloody Sunday victims carries in 'swaddling' overtones of constriction and infantilism: 'The common funeral / Unrolled its swaddling band, / Lapped, tightening / Till we were braced and bound' (Heaney, 1979: 22). Parker objects to this interpretation, highlighting the associations of 'swaddling' with the newborn (and, it might be added, with the Christ child) (Parker, 1994: 163). More important, perhaps, is the poem's use of 'tightening', the verb ambivalently used of Nerthus's garotting of her sacrificial victims. This *North*-like ambivalence can be seen in the poem's central question: 'How culpable was he / That night when he broke / Our tribe's complicity?' But the real question here is whether a genuine dilemma is being posed: why, in other words, the poem doesn't consider the answer 'not guilty at all'? Does tribal 'complicity' carry sufficient opprobrium, given its context of an indiscriminate revenge bombing? Heaney's solidarity with his acquaintance is undermined by a damaging equivocation insofar as it can only fully be expressed at the end of the poem at the level of lonely 'beyondness' in the consolatory and cliched image of fishing-as-writing. *Field Work*, for all its virtuosity – it is arguably Heaney's most lyrically appealing volume – is a more elaborate representation of the rural-territorial as site and origin of Irishness. The overarching myth of *North* is replaced by new influences, but the non-Irish influences are frequently overborne by lushly elegiac hand-wringing and a too purely Nationalist self-absorption.[3]

If Heaney had abandoned the notion of an overarching myth of Northern violence, he had clearly not, in *Field Work*, abandoned Nationalist mythic-historical narratives. The issues raised by Heaney's use of myth were widely debated in the late 1970s, however, and provided the impetus for new thinking on cultural matters. This was most marked in the journal *The Crane Bag*, established by Richard Kearney and Mark Patrick Hederman in 1977, which ran until 1985. *The Crane Bag* was a wide-ranging cultural journal which, although it carried no original literature as such, dealt with the issues being aired in poetry and drama at the time. In itself, *The Crane Bag* marked a new sophistication of cultural debate, posited on the emergence of a self-sustaining intellectual class in the wake of the expansion of higher education in the Republic and the growth of literary, cultural and Irish studies generally, within Ireland and beyond.[4] Some of the reasons why it was felt that myth was important have already been touched upon; it provided, it was felt, access to the atavism fuelling the Troubles at a level below which mere 'rationalism' could not reach. In a number of influential essays, Kearney attacked older versions of myth, particularly the martyrological aspects which feature so heavily in *Field Work* (although there was no direct attack on Heaney), countering them by proposing that myth could be saved for the purposes of cultural analysis and literary activity by laying stress on its utopian and liberatory aspect, one enabling a move forward beyond its atavistic versions. In this sense, at the heart of *The Crane Bag*'s idea of itself and its function was the concept of what its editors termed 'the fifth province', a calculated challenge to the Nationalist notion of the four provinces (or 'Four Green Fields'), separated by Partition but inevitably to be reunited in the projected integral nation of Ireland. Given a putative origin in the legendary 'Mide/Meath' (or 'middle' province of the annals), the fifth province was described by Hederman as 'the secret centre . . . the place where all oppositions were resolved', one which – like *The Crane Bag* itself – was 'a no-man's land, a neutral ground, where all things can detach themselves from all partisan and prejudiced connection' (Hederman, 1985: 110). This Platonic/idealist standing back from division offered, it was felt, a way of opening up a space in which atavistic myths could be reconsidered in a more objective fashion than hitherto, and where – in particular – the impasse of Northern Ireland could be rethought in cultural terms which might pave the way for future political initiatives.

The imagining of a neutral space, however Platonic, fed into political developments, as I shall show, since – like the Celtic Revival of the turn of the century – its ultimate aim was the preparation of the ground from which the idea of a secular republic, one acceptable to Unionists, might emerge. The limitations of this are dealt with later; but it is important to note that such developments were matched in Heaney's poetry by a turn away from reliance on the mythic histories underlying *Field Work* after the late 1970s, a turn which issued in his translation of the Middle Irish poem *Buile Suibhne* as *Sweeney Astray* (1983) and the poetry of *Station Island* (1984).[5] An indication of Heaney's aims in *Station Island* may be found in 'Widgeon', a poem dedicated to, and imitative of, Paul Muldoon:

It had been badly shot.
While he was plucking it
He found, he says, the voice box –

Like a flute stop
In the broken windpipe –

And blew upon it
Unexpectedly
His own small widgeon cries.
(Heaney, 1984: 48)

The ventriloquism – in both senses – and uncertain tone of the poem ('He found, he says') register the entry of a qualitatively different and refreshing level of irony into Heaney's poetry, one which bears on a debate between responsibility and a desire to assert the autonomy of the artist.[6] 'Station Island' is a record of residual faith going through the motions of 'Habit's afterlife' (Heaney, 1984: 67), although it is not his first attempt at a sequence based on the idea of penitential exercises, having been preceded by *Stations* in the early 1970s. But whereas those were anecdotal prose fragments, 'Station Island' is more obviously a spiritual autobiography. Its twelve sections – short of the fourteen stations of the cross – narrate encounters with a teacher, a school-friend, a first love, the murdered cousin of 'At Lough Beg' in *Field Work* and his literary mentors Carleton, Kavanagh and Joyce. The overall effect is of con-fessional self-questioning. This can be indirect, as in the Carleton section, in which what Corcoran calls the insistent pressure of the Troubles in the poem is taken up by the 'turncoat' Carleton and leads to the speaker engaging in a parody of Heaney's early style and immersion in ooze: 'the melt of shells cor-rupting, / old jampots in a drain clogged up with mud' (Corcoran, 1986: 166–7; Heaney, 1984: 66). It can also be direct, as in section IX, in which the narra-tor has a nightmare: 'All seemed to run to waste / As down a swirl of mucky, glittering flood / Strange polyp floated like a huge corrupt / Magnolia bloom, surreal as a shed breast, / My softly awash and blanching self-disgust' (Heaney, 1984: 85). Heaney is directly reproached, too, by the ghost of Colum McCartney, for his having 'whitewashed [the] ugliness' of his death in *Field Work* (Heaney, 1984: 83); and the general effect is of repentance for '[sleep-walking]', in section IX, 'with connivance and mistrust', and self-disgust for having been so communally 'biddable' (Heaney, 1984: 85) – a critique, that is, of immersion in the atavistic delusions of his community as embodied in history-as-myth. Given Heaney's attachments to place and origins, these are strong words, and reveal in the concluding image of a 'stone swirled under a cascade' the desire of the poem as a whole to be '[ground] down to a differ-ent core' of being (Heaney, 1984: 86). Yet 'Station Island' as a whole suffers from its episodic and basically lyric structure. The poem's 'penance' section – a translation of St John of the Cross – confirms an obsession with purity of origins, water and cleansing, but perhaps least satisfactory is the final section – an encounter with Joyce – which confirms a sense of evasion as well as self-questioning. That is, although Joyce confirms Heaney's need for a break with community – 'Let go, let fly, forget. / You've listened long enough. Now strike your note' – that 'note', in the closing lines, is defined in all too familiar terms. Joyce's 'advice' is generalised, apparently 'radical' but blandly innocuous: to 'Keep at a tangent / When they make the circle wide', 'fill the element / With signatures on your own frequency' is no more than what Heaney had been doing since *Door into the Dark* (Heaney, 1984: 93–4).

Yet the Heaneyspeak of the weaker parts of 'Station Island' is followed in the third section of the book by Sweeneyspeak. In his translation of *Buile Suibhne*, the eighth-century account of the bird-man King Sweeney, Heaney had noted – following Graves – how Sweeney could serve as a 'figure of the artist, displaced, guilty', migrant, scared and exiled from community. The Sweeney poems in *Station Island* – titled 'Sweeney Redivivus' – show Heaney adopting a Sweeney mask, as well as that of the medieval monk transcribing the original Sweeney poem, to disturbing and powerful effect. Sweeney here, for Corcoran, 'is, above all, the name for a restless dissatisfaction with the work already done, a fear of repetition, an anxiety about too casual an assimilation and acclaim, a deep suspicion of one's reputation and excellence', and the hesitant use of a 'bare wire' language elsewhere becomes consistent in these poems, as does the rejection of the comforts of community (Corcoran, 1986, 180). Thus, in 'Alerted', the 'bark of the vixen in heat' breaks 'the ice of demure / and exemplary stars' – perhaps the too-anthologisable lyrics of *Field Work* – and leaves him 'alerted, disappointed' with the darkness and intimacy of his previous position 'under my old clandestine / pre-Copernican night' (Heaney, 1984: 106). Heaney's agonised internalisation of community expectation is effectively externalised in 'The First Kingdom', again using properties taken from the original, and setting personal reputation in the frame of bitter realisation:

> And if my rights to it all came only
> By their acclamation, what was it worth?
> I blew hot and blew cold.
> They were two-faced and accommodating.
> And seed, breed and generation still
> They are holding on, every bit
> As pious and exacting and demeaned.
> (Heaney, 1984: 101)

There is in the refusal of stylistic consolation – of music, imagery and metaphor – a force in these poems which works against too easy attachments. 'The First Flight', one of the most impressive pieces in the sequence, images the escape Heaney feels he now must make, rebuking the earlier 'sleepwalking' self and acknowledging that he 'was mired in attachment' as he announces a need to '[master] new rungs of the air' (Heaney, 1984: 102–3).

Revisionisms: Derek Mahon's *The Hunt by Night*

The impasse of *The Snow Party*, perceptible in its perfect but fragile balance between aestheticism and history, continued, with increasing signs of exhaustion, to haunt Mahon's poetry for over a decade. Like Heaney, if less successfully, Mahon attempted to break out of this impasse, and *Poems 1962–78* included new lyrics which showed him stretching to write a more studiedly inconsequential sort of poetry.[7] Mahon's impulse to revise his work is well known and has been charted at length by Peter Denman; it might be linked to the uneasiness and self-punishing streak already noted, as also to a gradual acceptance of Irish nationalism, as reflected in the positive attitude to his work by Kinsella, otherwise hostile to Northern Irish poetry.[8] 'Courtyards in Delft' is based on Pieter de Hooch's series of paintings of Delft courtyards, works which exemplify the Dutch Golden Age middle-class world of honest cleanliness, order and thrift. Paying tribute to 'oblique light on the trite', the 'immaculate masonry', it initially seems a homage in the spirit of 'Glengormley'. Even if there is no 'spinet-playing emblematic of / The harmonies and disharmonies of love', or 'the dirty dog, the fiery gin' of contemporary low-life genre paintings by Jan Steen, the poem insists that 'this is life too', cherishable for its 'vividly mnemonic' 'verifiable fact[s]'. The fourth, final stanza, however, propels us from simple naturalistic fidelity to a disturbing implication of this world, and the poet himself, in imperial predation:

> I lived there as a boy and know the coal
> Glittering in its shed, late-afternoon
> Lambency informing the deal table,
> The ceiling cradled in a radiant spoon.
> I must be lying low in a room there,
> A strange child with a taste for verse,
> While my hard-nosed companions dream of war
> On parched veldt and fields of rain-swept gorse.
>   (Mahon, 1981: 21)

'Veldt' and 'gorse' metonymically project an analogy between Protestantism and imperialism, Britain and the Netherlands, Northern Ireland and South Africa, back across the poem. The poem dramatises Mahon's at-home-ness and alienation in a way familiar from earlier work, and implicitly critiques the implication of his own poetry – 'the chaste / Perfection of the thing and the thing made' – in an order where cleanliness is next to godliness is next to imperialism. Yet in *The Hunt by Night* a year later, the poem had acquired an additional stanza:

> For the pale light of that provincial town
> Will spread itself, like ink or oil,
> Over the not yet accurate linen
> Map of the world which occupies one wall

And punish nature in the name of God.
If only, now, the Maenads, as of right,
Came smashing crockery, with fire and sword,
We could sleep easier in our beds at night.
(Mahon, 1982: 10)

This stanza remained in *The Faber Book of Contemporary Irish Poetry* (1986) and *The Penguin Book of Contemporary Irish Poetry* (1990), the latter edited by Mahon himself. In his *Selected Poems* of the same year, however, it had disappeared.[9]

Most critics have debated the two versions of the poem according to whether the additional stanza makes too explicit and self-punishing what was guiltily suggestive, a 'gloss', or 'rather over-explanatory stanza' (E. Longley, 1986: 203). In a Leavisite/New Critical sense, the purpose of the poem – any poem – is to achieve rich and ironic ambiguity and 'tension', productive of proper balance, and this is best served by hinting at, rather than spelling out, the violence inherent in the 'morally ambiguous position' Mahon explores. Paradoxically, however, the 'over-explanatory' surplus of material is intended precisely to purify the poem, to make clearer the link between culture and violence, critiquing the aesthetic even as the poem embodies it in typically shapely form. Like all of Mahon's best poems, then, this one asks questions about its own perfection as an aesthetic object, although in doing so it has to invoke the violence it would oppose. The point is the form this excess and violence takes, in the sense both of the content of the stanza and of the stanza itself. Typically 'Courtyards' enacts Mahon's oscillation between consolatory humanist and anti-humanist millenarian stances, but it is notable that it does so through the eruption of the mythic and poet-dismembering Maenads into the poem's rationally reflective space. The Maenads are a pagan rebuke to what has been done in 'the name of [a Christian] God', but they are also examples of the female presences almost always suppressed in Mahon's highly mas-culinist work. They are, that is, not just transmogrified versions of the 'wives / Of artisans' but represent the return of the repressed in a much broader sense. They are *female* figures of retribution (sources include Rimbaud's 'Bacchantes des banlieues' and Shelley's 'fierce Maenads', but also – risibly – plate-smashers at the end of an evening in a Greek restaurant). As in 'Afterlives' – although in a figural way – a crisis in representation brings about violence gen-dered as female.[10] More than this, the fifth stanza asks to be read as an example of what Jacques Derrida has called a *supplement*; that preface, appendix, repe-tition, footnote, etc., which, apparently dispensable and merely additive (according to Western ways of thinking), actually turns out to reveal a lack at the heart of the seemingly self-sufficient 'main' text, and thus to be a 'sup-plement' to it in quite a different way. The supplementary stanza points to a lack at the heart of Mahon's writing – female figures as invisible domestics, the barely seen wife/muse – which, in *The Hunt by Night*, begins to be redressed at a thematic level at least. To link the incipient postmodern play of the final stanza to 'The Hunt by Night' means registering Mahon's fear that the disruptive elements – the Maenads, the plate-smashing – risk dissolving the exclusory drive for authentication in playfulness.

Field Day, Tom Paulin and literary politics

Despite the attempt to align culture with politics in *The Crane Bag*, Kearney was alone among its many contributors in making a submission – based on the 'fifth province' concept – to the New Ireland Forum, which began meeting in 1983 to discuss ways forward from the impasse of the Northern crisis (although the journal was wound down partly because of the threat to its grant posed by its interest in matters deemed non-literary by the Arts Council). The *Report* of the Forum, however, was to reveal the difficulty of moving beyond division, and of old-fashioned perceptions of the North in the Republic. A bland assertion of the distinct rights of 'two traditions' on the island of Ireland did not gloss over the fact that, for its framers, the Nationalist tradition was the senior tradition and that at the heart of the problem was Unionism's need to find an accommodation within it. There was in particular a 'refusal to face up to the full implications of a consensus policy . . . [it was] . . . a monument to the evasions and ambiguities which have been a hallmark of Irish nationalism to date' (O'Halloran, 1987: xviii). Southern Nationalists had internalised the 'elasticity of geographic vision by which Britain had claimed/disclaimed Ireland before Independence, applying it to Northern Ireland . . . Liberating Ulster meant, for republicans, the restoration of the past as they perceived it, as well as of the territory of the island.' If this problem never became paralysing in the heterogeneous forum of *The Crane Bag*, there are reasons for believing that it impeded the effectiveness of the most significant offshoot of the journal, the Field Day collective, which was formed in 1980.[11]

It is worth considering Field Day's implications for poetry in the 1980s, and in particular that of Paulin, one of its members. Paulin's career as an academic in the English university system, as a memorably vituperative critic, essayist and anthologist, and as a poet of seemingly direct political statement, complicate a reading of his first three collections – *A State of Justice* (1977), *The Strange Museum* (1980) and *Liberty Tree* (1983) – in placing them within the debate over Northern Irish poetry occurring in England in the late 1970s and early 1980s, as well as in specifically Irish ones. In one way, Paulin's earliest work can be seen as embedded deep within an English provincial, empiricist lyrical poetry of urban and suburban decay, of littoral disenchantments (Paulin studied at Hull University) and general impoverished bleakness stemming from Hardy via Larkin. In formal terms, too, these poems are faithful to such a tradition, although their factuality is offset by an Audenesque attraction to abstractions – such as 'state' and 'justice'. Their peculiar mixture of dourness and idealism derives from acceptance of the absolute failure of the Northern Irish state, and they are notable for their attempts to explore, in a far more explicit manner than Longley or Mahon, the history and psyche of what the titles of two poems refer to as a 'cadaver politic', or a 'lost province' (Paulin, 1977: 16; Paulin, 1980: 16). Paulin does accommodate, to some extent, the 'bereft sensibility' of the older poets (as well as of MacNeice) in poems such as 'Iniskeel Parish Church' (Paulin, 1977: 15), and there is a recognition of the sheerly sensual appeal of the aesthetic (debated in 'The Garden of Self-Delight' and 'Man with Hookah'), as well as the elegiac (as in 'Seaside House') and even the tenderly erotic ('Newness') (Paulin, 1980: 40–1, 49–50; Paulin, 1977: 39, 36). But the overwhelming sense in these poems is one of histori-cal determinism underpinned by a Calvinist sense of repression and political impasse (Robinson, 1988: 105). The history of collusion between state and sectarianism is illustrated in 'Settlers', set at the time of the Ulster Covenant and gun-running by the Ulster Volunteer Force in 1912, in which the cross-class basis of Loyalism is revealed; likewise, the psycho-sexual implica-tions of masochistic religious and political relationships are stressed in 'Still Century':

> The hard captains of industry
> Held the province in firm control . . .
>
> A crowd moves along the Shankill,
> And lamps shine in the dull
>
> Streets where a fierce religion
> Prays to the names of power . . .
>
>   . . . They are tied
> To the shade of a bearded god,
>
> Their dream of happiness is his smile
> And his skilful way with the hardest rod.
>   (Paulin, 1980: 10)

As Alan Robinson has pointed out, these poems are – for all their concentra-tion on 'the long lulled pause / Before history happens' – intent on counter-ing Catholic-Nationalist rural mythic narratives (a link between racial myth and Nazism is made obliquely in 'Thinking of Iceland', for example) with a radically disaffected urban Protestant attempt at historical exploration, if not explanation (Paulin, 1977: 11). Against a fetishisation of 'the backward look', Paulin posits – albeit only tentatively – 'an order that's unaggressively civil-ian', where 'the Law is glimpsed' only 'on occasional traffic duties' in the post-war suburban setting of a housing estate (similar to Mahon's Glengormley) in 'A New Society' (Paulin, 1977: 19). Yet this opposition of Jacobinism to Jacobitism is scarcely the endorsement of a Whig historiography, in which Protestantism is innately progressive, Catholicism innately reactionary. Paulin's sense of the fragility of this 'order' is – in the social sense – much more pro-nounced than Mahon's, aware that the price of apparent social stability in Northern Ireland is 'the angers / Of Leviathan', the state set over Hobbes's 'state of nature' now run amok (Paulin, 1980: 16). Indeed, as in the work of Heaney and Montague, the extremism of the deterministic binarism involved can give rise to the feeling that Paulin somehow condones, or at least only passively records, an ineluctable cyclical violence, as in the 'controversial' 'Under the Eyes', in which Belfast's 'retributions work like clockwork / Along murdering miles of terrace-houses', and which concludes with the brutally memorable image of 'a Judge / Shot in his hallway before his daughter . . . A rain of turds; a pair of eyes; the sky and tears'[12] (Paulin, 1977: 9).

Where Paulin's poetry registers the moment of Field Day, however, is in its attempt to escape this sense of present determinism, and a merely passive Protestant dissent, through a historical recovery of the radical origins of Ulster Presbyterianism in the eighteenth-century republican Enlightenment tradition embodied in the United Ulstermen of the 1790s and the 1798 Rising. This use of his own historical myth, albeit one in which the constructedness of history is foregrounded, is itself, arguably, a reflection of a perception of the absolute nature of impasse of the Troubles in a period when they were acquiring permanent and institutional form. For Paulin, the effort of rethinking the moment of Catholic and Protestant unity in this rebellion against British dominance is worth the risk of idealisation, and can be seen as his own historically located version of the rather vaguer fifth province concept as outlined by Kearney and Field Day. As he put it in his Field Day pamphlet of 1984 (which reveals the linguistic dimension of his project), it is part of a search for 'An [Irish] identity which has as yet no formal or institutional existence' (Paulin, 1984: 17). By returning to this moment of maximum historical awareness and transformative possibility, the hope is that it will be possible to ascertain how 'a plain / Presbyterian grace' can 'sour, then harden, / As a free strenuous spirit changes / To a servile defiance that whines and shrieks / For the bondage of the letter' (Paulin, 1983: 16).

This is the narrative of historical decline (or fall) explored in *Liberty Tree*, Paulin's most coherent and brilliant collection to date, which takes as its emblem the trees planted by republican clubs (in Britain as well as Ireland) in anticipation of the spread of revolution from Republican France in the 1790s. Its icons – Tone, Porter, Biggar, McCracken, Hope – many of them halfforgotten, are announced in 'Under Creon', the book's opening poem (as, later, their '[endurance] of posterity without a monument' is considered in 'Father of History') (Paulin, 1983: 32). 'Under Creon' – 'Creon' here representing the British state – takes as its point of departure a view of 'Rhododendrons growing wild below a mountain', the 'mountain' being that above Belfast where the United Irishmen took their 'Jacobin oath'. The smothering rhododendron is an 'imperial shrub' in which he has 'searched out gaps', seeking a local substitute which can '[sing] / dissenting green', and which will prove to be the juniper bush (commonly used as a 'liberty tree'). The seven-page 'Book of Juniper', first published separately in 1981, explores this idea most fully, but in a more extreme elliptical and anagogical manner. Eight short untitled sections leap between Ireland, 'a Roman spa / in Austro-Hungaria' and Mandelstam ('the leavening priest of the Word') exiled in Voronezh in a kind of 'pilgrimage in search of a national identity'. This begins in the early Christian period ('the original liturgy / on a bare island'), but – as Robinson claims

– refuses the comfort of the eucharistic 'yeasty word' for that of the juniper
('an in-the-beginning . . . *juniperus*') (Robinson, 1988: 120; Paulin, 1983: 23).
The following sections are metamorphoses of the juniper – invoked in its
leaves, berries (a 'nordic grape'), scent and humble persistence – and its sym-
bolisation of promised republican liberty where 'The subtle arts are still to
happen' (Paulin, 1983: 23). The final passage evokes 1798 (with perhaps a
sideways glance at Dunsinane Wood in *Macbeth*), reimagining the doomed
French invasion of 1798 transposed to a utopian imaginative plane in which
the juniper, fifth-province-like, reconciles trees and plants emblematic of
Ireland, North and South, Scotland and England:

> and I imagine
> that a swelling army is marching
> from Memory Harbour and Killala
> carrying branches
> of green juniper . . .
>
> now dream
> of that sweet
> equal republic
> where the juniper
> talks to the oak,
> the thistle,
> the bandaged elm,
> and the jolly jolly chestnut.
> (Paulin, 1983: 27)

The pathos of the vision, of course, acquires its force by being contrasted, else-
where, with images of the current fallen state of the North. For example, 'Of
Difference Does it Make' (the reader automatically supplies the 'Not a jot')
centres on the fact that the only Bill sponsored by a non-Unionist member of
Stormont to be passed in the fifty-one years of its existence was the Wild Birds
Act of 1931. Paulin makes a political point about the repressive monolith of
Unionist rule, but also inflects the Northern Irish tradition of nature poetry, as
found in Hewitt and Longley; even the ornithological, in Northern Ireland, can
be seen as having been politicised by the regime, if only because it was the
one thing which was not felt to threaten its interests (Paulin, 1983: 51). Generally, however, these poems are far more abrasive, and draw heavily on the
Ulster demotic and dialect Paulin uses throughout the book. 'Off the Back of
the Lorry' juxtaposes 'two rednecks troughing / in a gleamy diner', 'Paisley
putting pen to paper / in Crumlin jail' and Elvis 'during the last / diapered
days' to form a kind of Deep South/Loyalist dual vision described as 'a sort of
prod baroque / I must return to / like my own boke' (Paulin, 1983: 33). Similarly, there is satire directed at the Secretary of State for Northern Ireland ('Call
him Sir Peregrine Falkland'), Conor Cruise O'Brien ('a batty style / and slack
o'whoozy emotion') and such representative imaginary Ulster characters as
'Professor "Deeko" Kerr' (Paulin, 1983: 69, 47). Most bitterly, 'Desertmartin'

focuses a disaffection with Protestant culture, which he sees as having declined to one 'of twigs and bird-shit / Waving a gaudy flag it loves and curses' – on a small town which became a byword for 'ethnic cleansing' in the 1922 Troubles.[13]

The mordancy of Paulin's attack on elements of Loyalist culture tended to obscure the wide range of subject matter encompassed by the book, as well as the fascination (borne out in his selection of political prose for the *Field Day Anthology*) and even outraged sympathy which Paulin felt for 'the Big Man [and] his wee people' (Paulin, 1983: 16). It was inevitably singled out for attack in reviews and criticism, most notably by Edna Longley. For Longley, Paulin's use of Ulster dialect was 'a talking-down to people whose own talk ("dunchered") he misappropriates in order to despise them'.[14] More seriously, in aesthetic terms, those poems – such as 'Martello' – which mixed a critical or non-poetic lexis with more traditional vocabulary were dismissed as 'intellectual bullying of [their] subject matter'. Longley ignored the fact that similar stylistic processes were to be seen at work in the 'bare wire' style of Heaney, as also in the violent material of Muldoon's *Quoof*, or that the use of a mixture of different 'discourses', and free verse, had less to do with a systematic ideological project of 'bullying' poetry as a form of 'discourse' than with the pragmatic poetic need of a second-generation Northern Irish poet to escape what he saw as 'That kitsch lumber room . . . stacked / with a parnassian dialect' (although arguably, Longley's attack, while couched in anti-critical theory terms, deliberately mistook its target in order to head off the threat to the integralist aesthetic of Northern poetry as she had defined it which Paulin's poetry seemed to pose) (E. Longley, 1986: 197).[15] Longley was on surer ground when she attacked Field Day in terms of Paulin's poetry as 'writing Protestants out of history unless [they were] prepared to go back and start again in 1798' (E. Longley, 1986: 192). On the other hand, however, it was precisely the stylistic devices which disrupted the seamless assertion of this in Paulin's poetry – open forms, parataxis, different linguistic registers and dialect – which were ruled out of court by Longley.[16]

Longley's attack is interesting because, matching her attacks on Field Day, it raises the issue not only of the contexts in which Paulin's poetry was received, but also the broader terms in which Northern Irish poetry and criticism in the early 1980s was responding to the challenge of new modes of critical practice within British academia, and the increasing attention being paid in Britain to Northern Irish poets. As has often been pointed out, the irony of the situation is that Paulin, while involved with Field Day (and an idealist but nevertheless neo-Nationalist cultural agenda), was also deeply involved in the resistance to precisely the kind of 'levelling' or Cultural Studies approaches to English Literature in Britain which Longley had detected in his poetry (Kirkland, 1996: 102–9). While *Liberty Tree* shows signs of accommodating such theoretical languages, it does so empirically, that is as quotation, or for the purposes of impressionistic critique.[17] Nor is there an attempt to problematise a somewhat naive faith in the oral and in plain-speaking expressivity, as his introduction to *The Faber Book of Vernacular Verse* shows (Paulin, 1990: ix–xxii). Like Longley, Paulin has remained committed to a belief in the primacy of the aesthetic, though in a more radical and democratic sense, attempting to carve out a 'protected territory for the aesthetic within Ulster', albeit one based on an ideal 1798 republican Protestantism (Kirkland, 1996: 107). As well as attacking, and then coming to a rapprochement with, post-structuralism, this involved Paulin in the polemical activity – against canonical English authors as well as the literary culture of the South, and the Southern state generally – for which he has become well known (indeed, not only does this activity reveal more of an implication in Englishness than he cares to admit, but also the extent to which he is in danger of becoming the stage Ulsterman he sometimes depicts in his poetry).[18] The area of agreement between Paulin and Longley, however unacknowledged, points to a Northern Irish set of critical premises which might be inflected along different political-sectarian lines, but which shared similar Leavisite ground and (ultimately) a faith in the unitary lyric subject.[19]

Outside history: including the excluded

'Judging . . . by the pamphlets here in front of me', Eavan Boland would write in a review of the first set of Field Day pamphlets in 1983, 'this is green nationalism and a divided culture.'[20] Boland's comment showed that Field Day was not only distinctive in its 'apartness', but in some ways badly out of touch with developments in the Republic. Moreover, there was a certain aptness in this sentiment being articulated by the leading women's poet of the Republic, given that Field Day's final project, the *Field Day Anthology* (1991), would be universally censured for its lack of female representation. By that time, a generation of women writers, critics and intellectuals had established themselves in the South, making impossible the masculinist assumptions of the past. Although Field Day had committed itself to re-examining old stereotypes, it was therefore in the Republic, arguably, that the best chance of re-examining the oldest and most central stereotypes of all was possible. In this sense, the much maligned lack of coherence in the South provided an alternative to the ultimately totalising strategies of the Derry group, and nowhere more so than in the emergent women's (and urban and political) poetry which appeared in the 1980s. While the breakdown of insularity had aided secularist currents in the 1970s, modernisation could not simply be equated with reform in the Republic, and international developments had also been closely observed by Catholic fundamentalists. The growth of new right pressure groups in the USA was noted in the Republic where the right feared the threat to the authority of Church and family and availed themselves of networks and modern technologies to spread their influence. More generally there was no major realignment of politics along class lines in the Republic, as radicals had believed would naturally occur as a result of industrialisation in the 1960s and 1970s; a 'normal' European political configuration notably did not emerge.[21] By the 1980s, this passive, deterministic stance could be seen as having endorsed a failure to challenge the clerical and Nationalist consensus. FitzGerald's 'constitutional crusade' in the 1980s, which attempted such a challenge, was in some ways a brave course, but it suffered a major blow in his mismanagement of the 1986 Divorce Referendum, which the right won. There was a general unwillingness by politicians to say much about the extent to which the Church's social power was rooted in its large degree of control in crucial areas of health, education and welfare. This authority bore down with particular weight on women.

The backdrop to the new prominence of women's poetry in the 1980s was the newly established, small but effective and vociferous women's movement in the Republic which had managed to make its mark on the statute book, but whose achievements now came under traditionalist fire. A joining of forces may be seen in the conjunction of government legalisation of (limited) access to contraception in 1979 and the visit in the same year to Ireland of Pope John Paul II. His address made clear the terrain over which the struggle would be waged: 'May Irish mothers, young women and girls', he pleaded, 'not listen to those who tell them that working at a secular job, succeeding in a secular profession, is more important than the vocation of giving life and caring for this life as a mother' (Haberstroh, 1996: 14–15). It was in the aftermath of his visit that the Pro-Life Amendment Campaign (PLAC) was set up, a group which 'provided a rallying point for a variety of mentalities resentful at recent social changes' (Lee, 1993: 653). Abortion was already illegal under Irish law and opposed by the vast majority of the population (despite public silence on the 4,000 Irish women a year who travelled to the UK for them); PLAC, however, demanded a pre-emptive amendment to the Constitution which would make it constitutionally impossible for pro-abortion legislation to be passed at a future date. For this a referendum was necessary. PLAC campaigned until one was held in 1983, when the amendment was passed by a two to one margin. However, the victory was a pyrrhic one; only 55 per cent of the electorate voted, and the majority – given the massive campaign in favour – was hardly overwhelming. The vote also revealed a sharp division between Dublin opinion and that of the rest of the country.[22] In effect, the campaign was a traditionalist 'cleansing ritual', an attack to head off what was perceived as a growing tide of godless materialism. As Tom Garvin has argued, this reaction can be seen as 'the latest battles in a long, and partly symbolic, political and moral war against external secularist forces and the Anglo-American world' (Garvin, 1988: 5). By focusing on the control of women and women's bodies it appealed to traditionalist conceptions of national identity in which female purity, Mariology and the 'mother' Ireland trope were central.

The challenge of women's writing and the whole issue of gender – so pervasive and yet so occluded in Irish poetry – thus became central in the 1980s and increasingly unignorable for the male-dominated literary establishment. This was not simply the issue of representation of women in Irish poetry, or the lack of women poets, however. For what was at stake was not merely an addition of positive representations or the odd female voice. Rather, looking back across the half century, it is possible to see a much more pervasive and deep-rooted displacement activity occurring, whereby the structuring provided by religion for writing was relocated – as the authority of the Church waned – in myth (owing some of its appeal to the centrality of Mariology in Irish Catholicism). This, in turn, was rooted in essentialist notions of gender. In Kavanagh, Fallon, Watters, Montague, Kinsella and Heaney we find a whole-sale resort to stereotypical gender models and archetypes. These offered the basis for a reinscription of the religious hunger for significance via the tropes of female submissiveness in the achievement of masculine individuation and of kingly/bardic marriage to the female territory and the 'threefold goddess' of mythology (classical as well as Irish). There was some (indirect) resistance to this – notably by Clarke, who explicitly politicised the position of women in Irish society – but, given the dearth of women writing poetry, his was a voice easily ignored. The emergence of women poets, then, chal-lenges perhaps *the* major basis on which much Irish poetry is founded. As Wills has pointed out, 'the representation of the Irish land as a woman stolen, raped, pos- sessed by the alien invader is not merely one mythic narrative among many, but, in a literary context, it is *the* myth, its permutations so various and ubiquitous it can be hard to recognise them for what they are'[23] (Wills, 1993: 57).

There was, predictably, opposition to women claiming a place in the poetry mainstream.[24] As Boland (and, to a lesser extent, Ní Chuilleanáin) became more prominent, however, women's poetry flourished. In the early 1980s, for example, the Dublin-based Women's Education Bureau set up writing groups specifically for women writers, an initiative that spread to the rest of the country.[25] This was a question first and foremost of other women poets – Roz Cowman, Paula Meehan, Nuala Ní Dhomhnaill, Rita Ann Higgins, Sara Berkeley and Medbh McGuckian. But anthologies of women's writing also appeared for the first time, together with feminist historical, sociological and critical works and several women's publishers and reading networks.[26] It was not a straightforward process; the continuing exclusion of women from the canon of Irish poetry is illustrated by the fact that Sebastian Barry, in *The Inher-ited Boundaries*, could not understand 'by what parsimony or freak of nature . . . no woman poet was born [in the 1950s] in the Republic' (Barry, 1986: 29), while Kinsella's 1986 *The New Oxford Book of Irish Verse* included not a single poem by a woman. A. A. Kelly's *The Pillars of the House*, published in 1987, was the first anthology of women's poetry to be published in over half a century. This was also the case in criticism: Garratt in 1986 did not discuss one woman poet, while Johnston in 1985 had devoted just over three pages out of 292 to what he called 'a feminine viewpoint'[27] (Johnston, 1985: 260).

Eavan Boland: owning her image

Eavan Boland was the poet who most overtly reflected these advances and the contesting of them. In her collections of the early 1980s – *In Her Own Image* (1980) and *Night Feed* (1982) – the domestic vein opened up in *The War Horse* was given in turn a more radical and more flexible edge, while she would broaden her vision to explore the place of women within Irish history in *The Journey* (1986), *Outside History* (1990) and *In a Time of Violence* (1994), a vision elaborated in a number of critical pieces, which included the pamphlet *A Kind of Scar* in 1989 (published, appropriately, by Arlen House, the first Irish women's press, which Boland had helped to found). This historical interest is already implicit in her 1980's 'Witching' – 'I will / reverse / their arson, // make / a pyre / of my haunch . . . / I'll singe / a page / of history / for these my sisters', punning on 'sing(e)' – and it is possible to judge Boland's work throughout the 1980s as a pioneering attempt to establish women's voices unignorably within the mainstream of Irish poetry (Boland, 1980: 29–30).

In Her Own Image marks the turning point in Boland's career. Its ten poems are written in a deliberately unsophisticated, forceful style and are calculated to upset cherished stereotypes. The gentility of the earlier work is overthrown in what Dawe has called a 'coming-out, an expression of the need to be heard and not just seen', as Boland deals with taboo subjects (all related to women's bodies as objects of adornment, male possession and violence), including anorexia, masturbation, menstruation and mastectomy (Dawe, 1992: 174). Short, irregularly broken lines predominate, vocabulary and syntax are simplified, rhythms are punchy, rhymes obvious and frequent. Behind the aggressive drive is Plath and the clipped trimeters of 'Lady Lazarus'. 'Mastectomy' is typical:

> My ears heard
> their words.
> I didn't believe them.
>
> No, even through my tears
> They couldn't deceive me.
> Even so
>
> I could see
> through them
> to the years . . .
> (Boland, 1980: 19)

It is not merely the loss of the breast which is the subject here, but the attitude of 'them' – the male 'specialist' and 'surgeon' – to that loss. This is conditioned by male hatred of their infant dependence on the mother, while the appetite for mutilation finds an analogy in the masculine propensity for war (surgeons, like soldiers, are 'bladed men'). The breast thus becomes a looted town, reduced from a 'blue-veined / white-domed / home / of wonder' to 'a brute site': those who will operate on her, the speaker concludes, will claim 'the true booty' (Boland, 1980: 19–21). The way women are viewed and view themselves is tackled in 'Exhibitionist' and 'Making Up', in an attempt to reverse the direction of the male scopic gaze which objectifies women, and which is internalised by the victims of patriarchy.[28] 'Making Up' is about the way women make themselves acceptable to the male gaze, rejecting the process in the claim that 'Myths / are made by men' (Boland, 1980: 31–5, 36–8). Indeed, all the poems in *In Her Own Image* address this need to resist the ways in which the male lyric labels and idealises women, forcing it to confront in very specific terms a female physicality it was content to ignore by mythologising.

The theme of 'Making Up' is also that of 'Tirade for the Mimic Muse', the book's opening attack on the conventional relationship of women to, rather than their representations in, poetry. The argument is with women poets' acceptance of hand-me-down consolations and complicities:

> I've caught you out. You slut. You fat trout
> So here you are fumed in candle-stink.
> Its yellow balm exhumes you for the glass.
> How you arch and pout in it!
> How you poach your face in it!
> Anyone would think you were a whore –
> An ageing out-of-work kind-hearted tart.
> I know you for the ruthless bitch you are:
> Our criminal, our tricoteuse, our Muse –
> Our muse of mimic art.
>
> (Boland, 1980: 9)

The 'mimic muse' offers a poetry which is reflective only; beneath the cosmetic mask there is a 'dead millennium' of female underachievement and a deliberate ignorance of the realities of being a woman – ageing, domestic labour, childbearing, objectification by men and patriarchy, and male violence. Boland turns against her former willingness to wait 'on [her] trashy whim', forcing her to look in a mirror which reflects not the made-up face but one (the poem itself) which reveals these realities. Nevertheless, there are disturbing signs even in this opening piece which signal ways in which her polemic can embarrass Boland. The invective of the first verse, for example, is almost entirely in the idiom of misogynistic disdain. Yet the poem, by its very nature, eschews the ironies which might signal that the speaker is herself caught up in the sexism which has produced the 'mimic muse'. While the 'tirade', then, is effective as a message, its lack of linguistic subtlety undermines that message. This is a general problem in Boland's work; when Neil Corcoran claims, for example, that 'The Dublin suburb, the place of the woman and of the "lethal / rapine of routine", thus gets into Irish poetry in a memorable way', he too easily accepts that Boland, simply by virtue of being a woman writer, has managed to negotiate the disjunction between the two levels of suffering represented by 'lethal / rapine' on the one hand, and mere 'routine' on the other (Corcoran, 1997: 118). The glibness which can result derives from a desire to '[urge] the poem too forcibly to its chosen theme', as Dawe puts it, although it is of course a result of the programmatic urgencies which drive the work (Dawe, 1992: 178).[29]

In this light it is noteworthy that the title poem and its companion piece, 'In His Own Image', are perhaps the most impressive. The first movingly deals with a child victim of male violence and brings something of Boland's gift for surfaces and adornments to its shocking subject: 'Let her wear amethyst thumbprints, / a family heirloom, a sort of burial necklace' (Boland, 1980: 13). The other poem raises the issue of the relationship of adornment, or art, to violence in a different way. Here, the irony missing in some other pieces is brought to bear with powerful effect. The speaker, after lovingly listing domestic details, breaks off to ask herself:

> How could I go on
> With such meagre proofs of myself?
> I woke day after day.
> Day after day I was gone
> From the self I had last night.
> > (Boland, 1980: 14)

A drunk husband's violence supplies the lack of self-definition the woman has ironically conceded – 'Now I see / that all I needed / was a hand / to mould my mouth' – and he becomes an artist who 'creates' his wife in beating her: 'What a perfectionist! / His are a sculptor's hands: / they summon / form from the void . . . I am a new woman'. This gives a wholly different view of the agonising over the art–violence relationship as explored by Mahon, for example, and points the way to poems which consider the relationship between the male artist and female subjects and the notion of an ungendered (but actually male-dominated) art which they presuppose.

In Her Own Image reflects, in its moments of uncertainty, the debates between liberalism and separatism in Irish feminism (and the tension which arises when a liberal feminist poet explores separatist sentiments). Boland's characteristic liberal feminism reasserts itself in *Night Feed*, which explores more fully the domestic themes of the third section of *The War Horse*, asserting the legitimacy of the suburban and domestic, private female experience as poetic subject as a challenge to masculine tradition. In the collections which follow this, however, Boland broadens this assertion to include the reinscription of women's experience within the historical record. Perhaps her best-known poem in this vein is 'Mise Éire', which takes its title from the traditional self-identification of the beautiful visionary maidens, or *aislingi*, of eighteenth-century Jacobite poetry. The title means 'I am Ireland', which had in turn been used by Patrick Pearse, leader of the 1916 Rising, as the title of a poem he wrote on the eve of his execution by the British, and by Ó Riada for his music for the 1966 film of the same name. Boland's *aisling* is a single emigrant woman facing poverty and prostitution in England or the USA. Far from bemoaning her fate, however, she is presented as exercising choice:

> No. I won't go back.
> My roots are brutal:
> I am the woman –
> a sloven's mix
> of silk at the wrists,
> a sort of dove-strut
> in the precincts of the garrison – . . .

> I am the woman
> in the gansy-coat
> on board the 'Mary Belle',
> in the huddling cold

> holding her half-dead baby to her . . .
> 　　　　(Boland, 1995: 102)

In the words of *A Kind of Scar*, what is attempted here is the alignment of 'the truths of womanhood and the defeats of a nation' (Boland, 1989: 20). Being marginalised as a 'woman poet in a national tradition', for Boland, confers advantages of 'a quick critical sense' and an eye to the possibilities of subversion. At the same time, it is clear that Boland's aim is not the overthrow of the existing Irish poetic tradition; far from it. 'Mise Éire's' aim, rather, is to make the figure of the woman more representative, and in a complexly human rather than demeaningly emblematic way, of the nation's history. In this sense, Boland's writing can be associated with what Elaine Showalter calls the gynocritical, that is, the attempt of women writers to establish themselves within an existing canon – or to establish a female canon in imitation of the male-dominated one – rather than challenging the canon, or notion of a canon, in any absolute way. There are, of course, dangers in such approach, namely of female experience merely bolstering established stereotypes of femaleness and of the nation by adding verisimilitude to them. In other words, there may be what Edna Longley has perceived in Boland's work as a failure to interrogate the notion of the nation in traditionally conceived terms.[30] A similar limitation – although it would be wrong to overstress it – may be discerned in the straightforwardness of Boland's publicising of the private and domestic in her poetry. One danger of this, clearly, is that it may tend, counter to its intention, to reinforce a patriarchal view that women write best, and most appropriately, about domestic ('minor') subject matter. Another danger relates to the extent to which Irish women's private experience is already, as Wills and Loftus point out, at the centre of public debate in Ireland. If women's bodies and spaces, that is, are already a part of public discourse as promoted by the Church and state, representing traditionally 'private' experience in a realist manner can carry only a limited subversive charge (Wills, 1993: 50). Yet, for all this,

Boland's discovery of female experience as a value in itself was a major break-through in Irish poetry: '[she] set down a new pattern for other women to follow. Coloured by the silence of emptied homes and the straying horses which seemed to have escaped from Parnassian halting-sites, her years in sub-urbia had cohered . . . Gone was the Trinity seminar, the elaborate scaffolding of academic relationships, the Glass Kings of the male enterprise' (McCarthy, 1998: 183–8).

From the borderlands: Eiléan Ní Chuilleanáin

The other leading woman poet of her generation presents a very different attempt to deal with the male-dominated tradition. Eiléan Ní Chuilleanáin's opposition to social constraints is notable for the absence of an overt or a *staged* confrontation with patriarchy, offering subversion of that tradition in an occluded manner, and making a strategy of hiddenness in a manner connected to her Cork and Munster origins. Ní Chuilleanáin has noted of her family back-ground – privileged like that of Boland – that although 'It was suggested that Ireland was somehow an egalitarian society . . . the behaviour and perfor-mance of women hardly entered into that idea' (Ní Chuilleanáin, 1982: 614). While Boland offers obscure ancestors in *Object Lessons* to offset the celebrity of her parents, Ní Chuilleanáin – from an equally well-known Nationalist family – has felt compelled to make her heredity subtle and her treatment of Irish history 'oblique and problematic', with her ambivalence ('I felt free; but also threatened') pointing to her exploitation of the unthinkability of a woman's poetry in a subversive rather than confrontational manner. Her first two collections, *Acts and Monuments* (1972) and *Site of Ambush* (1975), show her working influences and material similar to Boland's – women's experience, traditional stereotypes, the Elizabethan lyric – in a way which buries a growing awareness of the difficulties of a woman writer more deeply and disturbingly in the texture of her writing. It is for this reason, perhaps, that she has attracted less attention.

'The Lady's Tower' is a good example of the direction of Ní Chuilleanáin's indirection, rewriting as it does the Yeatsian symbol of the tower from a spe-cifically female point of view: 'Hollow my high tower leans / Back to the cliff; my thatch / Converses with spread sky'. Unlike Yeats's, however, this tower is ruined; the woman is a witch, perhaps the female equivalent of Yeats's mage. The emphasis, as in so many of Ní Chuilleanáin's poems, is less on the struc-ture than on its process of dissolution, usually by water:

> I hear the stream change pace, glance from the stove
> To see the punt is now floating freely . . .
>
> Opening the kitchen door
> The quarry brambles miss my hair
> Sprung so high their fruit wastes.
> (Ní Chuilleanáin, 1986: 11)

It is as if the Lady of Shalott had survived the journey to Camelot, recovered from her fixation on Lancelot, undergone consciousness-raising with a women's group and decided to retire to her now dilapidated tower to become the local wise woman. The subtlety of Ní Chuilleanáin's verse, typically unobtrusive, can also be seen in these lines; the final line here exchanges an iamb for a trochee, throwing the stress on 'Sprung' and enacting the movement of the swishing bramble missing her hair as she opens the door. In the tower itself, the magic is unobtrusive; Sorcerer's Apprentice-like, 'my broom chases down treads ... the yellow duster glides / Over shelves, around knobs'. Again, like Boland, the domestic is being introduced to Irish poetry – indeed, to the heart of one of its fortresses – but in an uncanny and playful, rather than serious or realist, manner. Similarly, when she deals more directly with women's experience of men – as in 'Wash', about a widow ridding herself of the taint of her husband, of male possession – the event is presented in a more enigmatic, even parabolic manner than in, say, 'In His Image':

> Women and world not yet
> Clean as the cat
> Leaping to the windowsill with a fish in her teeth;
> Her flat curious eyes reflect the squalid room,
> She begins to wash the water from the fish.
> (Ní Chuilleanáin, 1986: 67)

Ní Chuilleanáin's introduction to *Irish Women: Image and Achievement* (1985), an academic text, provides a useful way into *The Second Voyage* (1977; rev. edn 1986) and *The Rose-Geranium* (1981), particularly in its focus on the place of women in social terms. A sense of class privilege and the 'unbalanced' nature of the Republic reveal a view of the effectiveness of women's writing more deeply conditioned by an awareness of social contexts than Boland's. This at first might seem paradoxical, given Boland's pioneer status and the difference between her clear style, with its consistently anti-patriarchal stance, and Ní Chuilleanáin's opaque ruminations. Indeed, it could be said that one of the distinctions between her and Boland is that Boland self-consciously offers herself as a national, as opposed to a regional or local, voice. Nevertheless, Ní Chuilleanáin subscribes to what is in some ways a more complex understanding the dialectical relationship between the social image of women and the images of the world devised by women themselves in the process of their self-liberation: 'The image created by woman herself may supersede the one presented to her by history and society, but she remains a member of society, an interpreter of history, and thus can never ultimately separate herself from a historical image of the feminine' (Ní Chuilleanáin, 1985: 1). If her poetry seems to pose the issue of emancipation less radically than Boland's, her criticism shows this to be the result of the greater emphasis she places on sociological and material contexts – 'the social matrix' – as opposed to the agonistic struggle of the individual woman poet (while Boland sees the issue of her position as a writer exclusively in gender and national terms, for Ní Chuilleanáin both categories are complicated by class and political categories).[31] The consequences of this awareness of, and insistence on, the paradoxical and incomplete nature of reform can be seen readily enough in the poetry, for while Boland's work is full of objects and references to an external social reality, its habitual subservience to an argument and thrall to surfaces and appearances make it paradoxically more weightless and abstract than Ní Chuilleanáin's. Despite the shadowiness of the properties of Ní Chuilleanáin's poems, their more vaguely defined figures, buildings and landscapes, its nuanced social awareness informs a phenomenological sense of the speaker's contingent dependence on, and interaction with, the outside world. Hers is a poetry of provisional rather than fixed selfhood and in this sense is experimental, despite its ostensible modesty, in a way Boland's is not. Thus, Ní Chuilleanáin's awareness of just how thorough is the interpenetration of self and society lends an almost somnambulant quality to some of her work, a lack of easily extractable viewpoints and conclusions which has been mistaken for a lack of urgency.

Geraldine Meaney has argued that Irish women poets have availed themselves of Richard Kearney's utopian reading of myth because Irish history has offered them 'little except exclusion and denial' (Meaney, 1995: 100). While not rejecting this claim – Ní Chuilleanáin is not for those who want 'to wallow a meretricious Irishness' – it presupposes an absolute exclusion which Ní Chuilleanáin herself does not feel (J. W. Foster, 1978: 150). Rather, her adoption of myth is better seen as part of a general trend in Irish poetry, a bending of it to female goals. 'Odysseus Meets the Ghosts of the Women' and 'The Second Voyage' are companion poems in which Ní Chuilleanáin reworks the explanatory power of classical myth in just this way. The first piece, based on Odysseus' visit to Hades, echoes a theme which haunts Greek tragedy – the overthrow of matriarchal society. Here, as in the epic, the ghosts of the women – even 'Anticleia / His own mother' – ignore Odysseus as they make for the pit of blood drained from the ram he has sacrificed. The need for restitution, for a return to the physical world, perhaps parallels that of the struggle for an ending to ghostly status, a recognition within the patriarchal order. Odysseus, hero though he is, cannot bear their clamour: 'he fled / For the long ship, the evening sea / Persephone's poplars / And her dark willow trees' (Ní Chuilleanáin, 1986: 25). The 'willow trees' recur in 'The Second Voyage' which follows, although the poem begins with Odysseus at sea (in both senses). He is attempting to discipline the ocean, gendered as female (although the episode draws on Odysseus' dispute with Poseidon); the inventiveness of the language here – '[he] saw / The ruffled foreheads of the waves / Crocodiling and mincing past: he rammed / The oar between their jaws' – redeems the rather tired trope. Similarly, Odysseus' thoughts use Irish idioms:

> If there was a single
> Streak of decency in these waves now, they'd be ridged
> Pocked and dented with the battering they've had,
> And we could name them as Adam named the beasts . . .
>   . . . these
> Have less character than sheep and need more patience.
>   (Ní Chuilleanáin, 1986: 26)

The identification of Odysseus with Adam's role in naming the creation, and the sea's unruly, disruptive resistance to 'battering', verbal or physical, shows the ocean to be a threat to masculinity. Crucially, the identification of Odysseus with naming and the feminine with disruptive otherness, structures the rest of the poem's narrative. For when Odysseus thinks of escaping the threat the Siren-like sea poses, he considers 'park[ing]' his ship and walking inland with an oar: 'I'll face the rising ground and walk away / From tidal waters, up riverbeds'. Odysseus would like to seek a non-tidal – that is, non-moon-influenced, hence non-female and subordinate form of water, for which the recognition of the oar as an oar would be the test: he would go 'Over gaps in the silent hills' – the land does not talk back, like the sea – until he meets a farmer who takes the oar for a winnowing fan:

> There I will stand still
> And I'll plant you for a gatepost or a hitching-post
> And leave you as a tidemark. I can go back
> And organise my house then.
>   (Ní Chuilleanáin, 1986: 26)

Even as Odysseus considers this possible escape, however, it is noticeable that it is undermined by its contradictions. In order to regain his power (which includes the Adamic one of giving things their proper names) he will have to find someone who will misname his oar; worse, the phallic oar will have to be confused with a fan – that is, not just the agricultural implement but something which, in the more usual meaning of the word, is an object of female adornment. 'At the edge of signification' between the ocean and the land where language ought to be stable, sexual identity, as Meaney puts it, 'becomes blurred' (Meaney, 1995: 110). Unmanned, Odysseus realises to his dismay that 'the profound / Unfenced valleys of the ocean still held him; / He had only the oar to make them keep their distance'. Still 'at sea' he attempts to summon up images of inland water which represent conventional, 'civilised' (from a male point of view) femininity, but fails: the sea is inescapable:

> He considered the water-lilies, and thought about fountains
> Spraying as wide as willows in empty squares,
> The sugarstick of water clattering into the kettle,
> The flat lakes bisecting the rushes. He remembered spiders and frogs

Housekeeping at the roadside in brown trickles floored with mud,
Horsetroughs, the black canal, pale swans at dark:
His face grew damp with tears that tasted
Like his own sweat or the insults of the sea.

(Ní Chuilleanáin, 1986: 27)

There are incidental ironies here – the 'empty squares', the 'housekeeping'
frogs – which show that, even in this more restricted attempt to impose his
will on the sea, Odysseus' imaginings thwart themselves, and we might also
note the echo of Matthew 6:28 ('Consider the lilies of the field, how they
grow: they toil not, neither do they spin'), which recalls Christ's message of
trusting to providence rather than human (social, male) provision. The 'second
voyage' of the poem's title is non-Homeric, being the invention of Dante in
Canto XXIV of the *Inferno*; whereas in English, the most famous use of this
version is Tennyson's 'Ulysses'. Both have Odysseus leaving Ithaca after his
homecoming from Troy, setting out again on a quest for knowledge beyond
the edge of the known world. In Tennyson's version Odysseus' masculine dissatisfaction with domestic dullness is marked ('Matched with an aged wife, I
mete and dole / Unequal laws unto a savage race').[32] Ní Chuilleanáin reverses
this, but not in a mechanical or predictable way: faced with female insubor-
dination and desire, Odysseus in her poem is prepared to settle for domestic-
ity and reject the ocean, but finds he cannot do so. There is in this an implicit
critique of certain kinds of valorisation of the domestic, and specifically of the
kind found in Boland. To claim, as Meaney does, that Ní Chuilleanáin 'follows
Dante's Ulysses beyond the Mediterranean parameters of the first voyage, into
an uncharted Atlantic and over the edge of the known world' is therefore
to misread the poem; her point is rather to show that male attempts to reject
the female as a precondition of the quest for truth and intellectual virtue are
self-defeating[33] (Meaney, 1995: 111).

In its subtle, multiply signifying intentions 'The Second Voyage' is typical
of the texture of much of Ní Chuilleanáin's subsequent poetry. The *Cork*
sequence, also published in 1977 (and collected in *The Rose-Geranium*), has as
a possible motivation 'the impulse to work out new relationships with place
by going against the grain of a loco-descriptive project', as John Kerrigan has
pointed out (Kerrigan, 1998: 88). In this it would seem to be a continuation
of the kind of interior/exterior mapping attempted in 'Site of Ambush' (Ní
Chuilleanáin, 1986: 14–21). The thirteen short poems also chart 'sites', this
time in her native city, which take advantage of Cork's maze-like network of
lanes, alleys, courts and disused spaces to embody her own explorations of
hiddenness. Specific locations are identifiable. Part one visualises the enis-
landed state of the city 'with its hooked / Clamps of bridges holding it down'.
Part two opens 'In the graveyards of the city'. Some pieces are titled – part six
is 'A Gentleman's Bedroom' and part thirteen, 'Sandstone', alludes to the kind
of rock on which north Cork is built. But these are not clues to a topography
or itinerary, and the poems pay more attention to the deliquescent, blowsy

furniture of the city – peeling housefronts, crumbling statues, windows and rooms seen through windows, half-flooded cellars, shops, the River Lee. Proper names are rare; this is a ghost town. More, the city is perceived as a psychological matrix (one of the quester's alter egos is of a minotaur trapped in his labyrinth), the 'I' merely a device to enable narrative until, as Kerrigan notes, 'the absences which might define location' have been catalogued.[34] The continual urge to gaze into interiors, to avoid guidebook description, is part of the desire to show that 'what is characteristic about Cork is not what makes it distinctive but what makes it mysterious', such that 'We could be in any city', but that the very fact of inscrutability is paradoxically what makes Cork Cork and nowhere else. The attention to walls, mirrors, windows, doors, the play of shadow and light is, of course, reminiscent of a complex of images which feminist criticism has specialised in interrogating. An opaque geography of interiors, and of ingress and egress has, as studies of women's writing have shown, traditionally been a way of coding a specifically female experience of constraint, access and confinement. Although 'The Rose-Geranium' sequence of three years later blends various sites – the US, Dublin and Italy as well as Cork – it, too, typically finds its speaker looking 'beyond the open window', gazing at 'my decaying brick wall', 'strok[ing] the pane revealing the garden', noting 'high broken doors', and with a similar sense of transparent confinement to that of the 'Cork' poems (Ní Chuilleanáin, 1981: 10–22).

Medbh McGuckian

If Ní Chuilleanáin's poetry has been seen as opaque, Medbh McGuckian's flaunts an obscurity without parallel among mainstream Irish poets. The fact that her severest critics have been her male Northern Irish contemporaries – James Simmons has deemed her work a 'confidence trick', while Patrick Williams's review of *On Ballycastle Beach* was entitled 'Spare That Tree!' – may be connected to this, indicating a link between style and her status as the only Northern woman poet of achievement of the last thirty years.[35] Faced with an almost entirely male poetic culture, McGuckian has arguably pushed its limitedly oblique strategies deep into the stylistic realm as a way of opposing its discursivity in order to create a space in which she can write without being overwhelmed by precedent. Evoking 'obscure' sources – Dylan Thomas, Hart Crane, Wallace Stevens – as well as Sylvia Plath and Emily Dickinson, McGuckian's poems thus deploy a battery of devices – periphrasis, inverted sentence order, ambiguously referring pronouns – within sinuous but confident syntactical structures, in a manner simultaneously alluring and evasive. As 'Slips', one of the more straightforward poems in *The Flower Master* (1982), suggests, McGuckian may see herself as a manifestation of the repressed or 'unconscious' of Northern poetry, and her approach has certainly been viewed as 'continuous with that slippage of language associated by Freud with subconscious revelation, slips of the tongue and slips of the pen' (Corcoran, 1993: 223):

I see my grandmother's death as a piece of ice,
My mother's slimness restored to her,
My own key slotted in your door –

Tricks you might guess from this unfastened button,
A pen mislaid, a word misread,
My hair coming down in the middle of a conversation.
                                        (McGuckian, 1982: 21)

But while such a poem is characteristically elusive in its final meaning, it nevertheless points to what McGuckian shares with other Irish women poets; the 'word misread' may be those of an ignored or suppressed women's poetry, and the references to grandmother and mother echo the desire of many women poets to speak for foremothers in celebrating a non-masculine line of descent. On the other hand, the sexual innuendo of 'My own key slotted in your door' indicates the complications McGuckian brings to a straightforward poetics of female self-assertion, since if (as seems likely) the addressee is male, the vulnerability, even abandon, of the final image, is surely complicated.

For although McGuckian's poetry is overwhelmingly 'feminine' – in its concern with domestic space, imagery of the female body and its processes, and unembarrassed use of traditional gender stereotypes – it is not intended to confront (as with Boland) so much as to subvert, intrigue, even seduce ('the last thing I would want to be is provocative') (K. Smith, 1986: 16). Thus, a qualified acceptance of feminism (McGuckian's poetry has proved the most amenable of any Irish poet to readings in terms of a radical French feminist *écriture féminine*) has been accompanied by claims that she 'writes for men'[36] (Robinson, 1988: 202; K. Smith, 1986: 15). *The Flower Master* reveals the tactical use of stereotypes in its title; flowers are traditionally gendered as female in patriarchal iconography, and the word 'anthology' means, literally a bunch of flowers, but in gathering her own McGuckian is simultaneously picker and picked.[37] The usual concerns of women's poetry in English – writing in a male-dominated tradition, speaking for a little recognised subjectivity, the perception of women's poetry by literary establishments as 'minor' – operate here, but complicated by the gendered freight – Ireland as woman, Virgin Mary as asexual role model – stemming from a Northern Catholic and Nationalist inheritance. Rather than articulating a clear ideological position, or recuperating lost histories like Boland, McGuckian's 'flower master', a Japanese flower arranger in the title poem, is also the poet engaged in 'womanly' gardening and 'none other than ... Baudelaire, whose *Fleurs du mal* ghost this text' (Docherty, 1992: 193). The speaker 'gently [strokes] the necks of daffodils' to 'make them throw their heads back to the sun', adopting a male role of cultivating female subservience (although elsewhere flowers may be masculine and phallic, as in the 'helmet'/glans of 'The Orchid House'), while at the same time the 'black container' of the last verse is the female genitalia, and the poem an address to a male lover whose penis ('a special guest') is soon to be welcomed 'to the / Tea ceremony, must stoop to our low doorway, / Our fontanelle, the trout's dimpled feet' (McGuckian, 1982: 26, 35).[38] The position of the speaker is fluid; authoritative and submissive, poet and lover, s/he invites a number of interpretations, none of which entirely fixes the poem's meaning. The provisionality of identity is linked to McGuckian's interest in the liminal – between sea and shore in 'The Heiress', childhood and womanhood in 'Eavesdropper' – and to the crossing of boundaries (windows and doors feature extensively) which may include that which divides Ireland.

'Tulips' shows just how versatile McGuckian's flower imagery can be in the exploration of these themes. It opens with the hesitant adolescent realisation of sexuality and moves through a consideration of the tulips' resistance to male penetration by rain (gendered as male), but their succumbing to (similarly male) 'sunny absences'. In a sense, this is a version of the old story about the storm and the sun attempting to get the traveller to remove his coat, but McGuckian complicates matters with literary tropes. The tulips are described as 'like all governesses', apparently reserved, but then too 'easily / Carried away'. It is precisely the 'independence' of the flowers that has led them 'to this grocery of soul', a generosity exploited by men. This is 'gross' in the physical sense, but also echoes the Mrs Grose of Henry James's *The Turn of the Screw*, a novella centring on a governess who may well have been seduced by her employer. But this is by no means straightforward; women like James's governess are victimisable because they can imagine a freer existence which may be achieved through men, 'a kind / Of twinness'. Being thwarted may produce 'ballets of revenge' against their exploiters, as the tulips/women are 'sacrificed to plot'; but the poem's claim is that, despite this inequality, the male manipulation, or 'artistry of light', is actually a 'lovelessness [of] a deeper sort / Of illness than the womanliness / Of tulips with their bee-dark hearts' (McGuckian, 1982: 10). The poem itself is a 'ballet of revenge', but of a very subtle kind, and it is in this sense typical of the way McGuckian's other apparently jaded imagery – of domestic space, houses, gardens, fruit (particularly the Eve-tempting apple), moon, planets, weather, colours – may serve to bend patriarchal restraint towards creative empowerment. This is the case in 'The Seed-Picture', another paradigmatic piece, with its single (female) parent refusal of a submissive role, and discovery in an apparently lowly artistic activity of 'a creative outlet in which to fabricate a new, independent identity'. The poem's speaker represses a freer self under a 'sky resolved to a cloud the length of a man', but the final lines articulate the resentment of abandonment in their list of seeds ('black rape / For the pupils, millet / For the vicious beige circle underneath'), and gesture towards a new self through the portrait in the surround of 'pearl barley' which 'catches light, makes women / Feel their age, and sigh for liberation' (Robinson, 1988: 203; E. Longley, 1994: 246; McGuckian, 1982: 23).

The kind of marital crisis inferred in 'The Seed-Picture' takes centre stage in *Venus and the Rain* (1984). Male assumptions are again challenged in 'Culprits', and 'my own manless law' is asserted in 'Star', but the prevailing tone is of a complex interrogation of the departed husband and of the self (McGuckian, 1984: 28, 45). In 'To the Nightingale' he is addressed in resigned despair ('you were still half in love with me'), while painful memories break through in 'On Not Being Your Lover', and the moment of departure is recalled in the bitterly titled 'Epithalamium' ('Your childhood must have been standing / On its head, when you said "Don't / Call me darling" – that empty, spearshaped / Word') (McGuckian, 1984: 13, 16, 17). A wide range of emotional states are articulated as the speakers of the poems attempt, as Robinson puts it, to '[avoid] both emotive self-dramatisation and ugly recrimination', to balance independence with sorrowful attachment in 'my un-freedom' (Robinson, 1988: 206; McGuckian, 1984: 16). The speakers frequently engage in a kind of double bluff, considering the possibility of growing assertive in order to avoid 'Going over to your camp', or imagining another alter ego in 'The Sitting' as someone who 'prefers / My sea-studies' to the (interior, domestic, confined) portrait the speaker is trying to paint (McGuckian, 1984: 15). Elsewhere McGuckian ventriloquises male speakers – Swift in 'Vanessa's Bower', for example – and dramatises the way her own diffidence is erased by such patriarchal voices in 'Pain Tells You What to Wear'. Nevertheless, the tendency of the poems – as in 'Aviary', where the (female) speaker's 'degree of falsehood' is asserted by the man in the opening line – is to imagine rebeginning the relationship, or to placate the male:

> And if you feel uncertain
> Whether my pendant foliage mitigates the damage
> Done by snow, yet any wild bird would envy you
> This aviary, whenever you free all the birds in me.
> (McGuckian, 1984: 21)

The usual stereotype – woman as bird in a cage – is eroticised here to counter the male desire for flight. Such tactics of refusal of aggression, openness and so on, have been seen as quiescence, a biologically essentialist emphasis on the woman as nurturing as opposed to the male as aggressive and dominant. One response to this has been to draw a link between McGuckian's practices and the theories of Luce Irigaray and Hélène Cixous; Eileen Cahill, for example, sees the poetry as unproblematically fitting their definitions of *écriture feminine*, '[sinning] against the laws of logic, congruity, grammar, causality, linear structure, and unity', adopting a 'middle voice' and '[interrogating] oppositions' (Cahill, 1994: 265–6). Yet even apart from the rather tired notion of the 'middle voice', it seems clear that the one thing McGuckian's poetry refuses to do is 'interrogate', and that this is a large part of its point. A more rewarding approach lies in noting the difference between McGuckian's use of 'feminine' material and the archetypal female motifs which Boland and Ní Dhomhnaill have attempted to reclaim, in their poetry, from their limiting Catholic Nationalist contexts. For Clair Wills, for example, the strength of the attachment of such female mythic material to its ideological surrounds works to foil Boland, given her basically discursive poetic, despite her attempt to impart a radical inflection to it; conversely McGuckian, thanks to her opacity and secrecy, prevents the kind of familiarity which allows patriarchal reappropriation. Thus, 'by figuring sex and childbirth in language which seeks to veil rather than represent she emphasises the integral relation between sexuality and the public sphere, the ways in which the female body is already inscribed in public life' (Wills, 1993: 69). By 'public life', Wills means official debates on contraception, abortion and divorce in the 1980s, as well as traditional Nationalist genderings of the nation as female (although the two areas are inextricably linked), and she makes the point in order to give McGuckian's poetry its political dimension: reprivatising women's experience is, in the Irish Catholic context, a gesture of dissent. Accurate though this is, it relies on a distinction between 'private' and 'public' spheres which Wills herself admits is difficult to sustain (particularly in an Irish context in which they are relatively undifferentiated), and her attempts to read specifically political meanings into individual poems are often wrenched and disablingly reliant on McGuckian's own claims about the poems' occasions[39] (Wills, 1995: 381). On the other hand, the claim that 'instead of intimacy we are confronted with secrecy', to the extent that McGuckian's use of stereotypes of femininity can only be conceived on the level of parody, is highly suggestive, and points to the later work's concern with etymologies and 'stolen' or palimpsestic texts.

Paul Durcan

If any single male poet could be said to have satirised the failures of 'timorous liberalism' in the Republic and registered the importance of the women's movement it was Paul Durcan. To merely list the headline-like titles of some poems – 'The Average Nazi Family is Alive and Well and Living in Ireland', 'Archbishop of Kerry to Have an Abortion' and 'Margaret Thatcher Joins the IRA' – is to trace a mocking, semi-surreal social history of the times. Thus, Durcan mocks the eclectic soulless materialism of Ireland in the 1980s via an account of architectural styles in 'The Haulier's Wife Meets Jesus on the Road Near Moone':

> We live in a Georgian, Tudor, Classical Greek,
> Moorish, Spanish Hacienda, Regency Period,
> Ranch-House, Three-Storey Bungalow
> On the edge of town:
> "Poor Joe's Row" –
> The townspeople call it –
> But our real address is "Ronald Reagan Hill"
> > (Durcan, 1985: 4)

Behind the anti-authoritarianism is an awareness of gender roles and constructions; sexual freedom continues to be, therefore, a prime concern.[40] 'Fat Molly', for example, from *Sam's Cross* (1978), invents a foster-mother female equivalent of the eighth-century scribes at Kells who teaches him 'the art of passionate kissing: / From minuscule kisses to majuscule / On lips, breasts, neck, shoulders, lips / And the enwrapping of tongue around tongue . . . Like all great education it was perfectly useless' (Durcan, 1993: 38–9). More subversively, in 'Making Love Outside Áras an Uachtaráin', the narrator recalls making love with a girl outside the presidential mansion, and imagines de Valera interrupting them with murderous intent:

I see him now in the heat-haze of the day
Blindly stalking us down;
And levelling his ancient rifle, he says 'Stop
Making love outside Áras an Uachtaráin.'
(Durcan, 1993: 41)

A more broadly historical fantasy is conjured up in 'Backside to the Wind', which imagines an Ireland with a French, rather than British, colonial past, thoroughly gallicised (rather than imperfectly gaelicised) as a result. Implicitly mocking the restraints of British culture, the poem moves from the fourteen-year-old speaker at Killala Bay, humorously noting that 'Wine would be the staple drink of the people / A staple diet of potatoes and wine', via 'worker priests' and an Irish Rimbaud, to the 'asphyxiating' present reality of 'Anglo-American mores', pollution and the return of mass emigration:

And yet I have no choice but to leave, to leave,
And yet there is nowhere I more yearn to live
Than in my own wild countryside,
Backside to the wind.
(Durcan, 1993: 36)

Less straightforward are the semi-surreal narratives, such as 'For My Lord Tennyson, I Will Lay Down My Life', which (with unwonted brevity) brings the literary vocation, Durcan's history of depression and – perhaps – the violence of the North into a single weirdly compelling focus:

Here at the Mont St Michel of my master,
At the horn of beaches outside Locksley Hall,
On the farthest and coldest shore,
In the June day under pain of night,
I keep it in my mind to say,
As his assassins make for me,
The pair of them revolving nearer and nearer
(And yet, between breaths, farther and farther),
Make it say:
'For My Lord Tennyson I Shall Lay Down My Life.'

I say that – as nearer and nearer they goosestep:
Vanity and *Gloom* not far behind.
'For My Lord Tennyson I Shall Lay Down My Life.'
(Durcan, 1993: 66)

Durcan's poetry in the 1980s caught the *zeitgeist*, thumbing its nose at authority in a way which was less possible in a public sphere which had become both
more complicated and offering reduced options for dissent, his 'womanism'
and opposition to the IRA aiding acceptance (though this is not to diminish
the bravery of the positions adopted in his work) (C. Tóbín, 1996: 168). Attacks
on the IRA and the South's tolerance, or ignorance, of its violence, informed
the reception of his work in the North; a 1982 *Selected Poems* from Blackstaff,
with a Foreword by Edna Longley, was a turning point in Durcan's popularity,
sanctioning him as one of the (few) acceptable faces of poetry in the Republic there (somewhat oddly, considered in formal terms). This in turn consolidated Durcan's reputation in the Republic and abroad.[41] Reception aside,
however, his poetry clearly reflected the way in which, by the 1980s, following the shifts in Northern politics, arguments in favour of internal social change
in the Republic had become inextricably bound up with or subsumed in the
larger debate on the relations between North and South.

This dual awareness of the interrelatedness of the Irish situations clearly
lay behind the greater coherence of the collections he published in the 1980s.
While maintaining his comic-satiric edge, the books trace marital breakdown
in *The Berlin Wall Café* (1985), develop what might be called an East European
option in *Going Home to Russia* (1987) and explore his relationship to his father
in *Daddy, Daddy* (1990). If the first section of *The Berlin Wall Café* deals with a
number of typical Durcan themes – Church, problematisations of gender and
sexuality – the heart of the book, and 'test' of its author's 'feminism', as it
were, is the second section's rending sequence of poems concerning his broken
marriage. Retracing episodes from courtship and married life, the poems accept
the wife's view of his inadequacy, taking her side in an attempt to achieve self-
understanding. The basic charges are those of neglect, self-absorption, possessiveness and male self-pity and immaturity (in 'The Turkish Carpet', the
speaker confesses 'I clutched despair to my breast / And with brutality kissed
it – Sweet Despair –') (Durcan, 1985: 56). In 'The Pieta's Over' – the title's
excruciating pun a literal one, since 'excruciating' means 'from the cross' – the
wife tells 'my dear, droll husband' that 'it is time for you to get down off my
knees / And learn to walk on your own two feet'. The 'sacredness' of the poet's
calling, conflated with that of men generally, is mockingly admonished – 'A
man cannot be a messiah forever, / Messiahing about in his wife's lap' – and
the theme of arrested male emotional development is a major theme of the
sequence (Durcan, 1985: 52). Men's reliance on women, and their insistence
that women nevertheless present themselves as similarly arrested, is the
subject of 'The Day My Wife Purchased Herself a Handgun': 'If it's one thing
a wife must not do it's to grow up: / A man will endure anything – except a
grown-up woman' (Durcan, 1985: 51). Durcan's characteristic idealisation of
his wife – 'You – incarnate coincidence of the beautiful and the true' – is offset
by extremist imagery drawn from Nazism (Durcan, 1985: 59). 'The Jewish
Bride', for example, takes a painting (by Rembrandt) as its point of departure,

seeing the wife as 'A Jewish Bride who has survived the death camp, /Free at last of my swastika eyes' (Durcan, 1985: 38). This view of possessiveness as innately masculine and fascistic recurs in the last poem, 'The Vision of St Hubert', which begins 'I decided to hunt down my wife: / Gauleiters of revenge revved up in my veins' (Durcan, 1985: 69). It ends with another risky pun (this time on the poet's name), as his resolve for revenge breaks down in the final lines:

> I got down off my high horse and knelt at her feet . . .
> Promising her never again to seek her out,
> Never again in this city to darken her doorway,
> To woo her only and always in the eternity of my loss:
> Let us now praise famous women – and their children.
>
> (Durcan, 1985: 70)

There are, of course, many objections to be raised about Durcan's references to Nazism, as there are to his persistent idealisation of women.[42] Sean O'Brien has noted that '[Durcan's] courtliness is an extension of the franchise, not a revision of the theology' (that is, of the women in his poems as inversions of Cathleen Ní Houlihan, and as versions of the Virgin Mary) (S. O'Brien, 1998: 108). Both aspects of the work can be read as tendentious, glib and self-dramatising, disproportionate to the events being discussed, although it should be noted that O'Brien's is a specifically English response to an Irish poet (he elsewhere shows his awareness that certain satirical attacks by Durcan would, in the English context, be 'to state the merely obvious', but does not allow that to qualify his criticism of Durcan's treatment of gender). The problems O'Brien identifies may have some bearing on the non-Irish tenor of Durcan's next two collections. Thus, *The Berlin Wall Café* relocates the same concerns to the still-divided Berlin. It traces the speaker's failure as a husband to a visit there in 1980, when 'all I could talk about was the Berlin Wall'. What is rebuked here is the coincidence, in the male imagination, of idealisation of the woman and male self-importance, and the way the two are functions of each other. In the fantasy of the poem, the wife 'escapes' from West Berlin into East Berlin 'where you are free of me / And of the Show Biz of the Free Democracies', a conclusion which points to the larger transposition of 'home' to a different one-party state than Hitler's – the then-crumbling Soviet Union – in the book which followed (Durcan, 1985: 60).

Thomas McCarthy

The few discussions of the poetry of Thomas McCarthy are notable for agreement on the fact of the work's occasional 'prettifying aestheticism' (Crotty, 1995: 390; Naiden, 1991: 111). Nevertheless, the poetry's unique concern with a specific politics, which exists in a dialectical interplay with such 'aestheticism', means that it cannot be regarded in isolation. As 'Professor Bachelard' puts it, 'he unearthed the seed of all poems / with the new "sentimental method"'.[43] (McCarthy, 1981: 55). Thus, while much has been made of the inseparability of private and public spheres as the distinctive feature of second-generation Northern Irish poetry, little has been said of its centrality to McCarthy's work (it is absolutely wrong – and says much about the US reception of Irish poetry – to claim, as James Naiden does, that 'Politics is an important element . . . although only in an observational sense') (Naiden, 1991: 105). 'State Funeral', in which television blurs private memory and the family unit with a public ceremony, is exemplary in this regard. As McCarthy has claimed:

> it was a mistake actually to believe that there was one section of the poetry that was private and the other section that was public because I'm hardly ever out of the public and the public domain is hardly ever out of my private life. Sometimes I will describe a personal experience through something that's totally political and sometimes I will use a political metaphor to describe something private . . . the two are inextricably linked (Geden, 1996: 5).

Such claims echo those of the women's movement of the time: 'the personal is political', and in an account of the formative period for his writing, 'Five Summer Afternoons', reading, flower scents, weather and writing fuse with 'the years of the first Coalition of my memory, the years of the murdered British ambassador, the humiliated and later vindicated President Ó Dálaigh' (McCarthy, 1991: 8). Yet it is the degree to which the two interfuse and the attentiveness to the minute specifics of a particular party at a given historical period – Fianna Fáil between the 1930s and the 1970s – which mean that McCarthy – unlike the older Boland, Hartnett, Durcan and Ní Chuilleanáin – treats not so much the political (although that is present) as politics itself.

Ironically for a poet deemed sentimental, McCarthy is in this sense by some way the most consistently *political* poet now writing in the Republic. On the one hand, his comments about current politics are more outspoken, radical and specific than those of his contemporaries (and this willingness to address recent history also extends to his fiction);[44] on the other, his poetry anatomises the populist mixture of crusade and clientelism which marks Fianna Fáil as a party. It is therefore no coincidence that he emerged as a poet at precisely the moment when, as he has noted, Fianna Fáil seemed to recapture its electoral dominance in the 'Bloomsday Election of 1977 that swept [it] back to power with an almost bizarre majority', the party polling its highest-ever vote.[45] The point is – as defeat in 1982 showed – that this triumph conspicuously did not break the post-1948 pattern of pendulum politics; and, like McCarthy's own poetry – consciously nostalgic for de Valeran 'austere grandeur' yet at the same time distancing it with scrupulous irony – victory proved to be a *simulacrum* of past power, of the de Valeran hegemony which was mutating into a qualitatively different politics (and a different Fianna Fáil) by the end of the 1960s.[46] Although the son of a Fianna Fáil activist, and a party worker in his own right as an adolescent, in McCarthy's later chronicling of the party's past 'his now detached attitude to Republicanism', as Kerrigan puts it, 'was never far from the scepticism which makes for intelligent political verse' (Kerrigan, 1998: 81). Thus, while it is true to say that McCarthy uses Fianna Fáil in his poetry because it accesses his childhood, and while his insistent localism – it is the Party in the West Waterford area of his birthplace, Cappoquin, which features in the poetry – ties it to the Munster-derived 'hidden Ireland' trope in Hartnett and Ní Chuilleanáin, his work also has a broader significance.

The First Convention (1977) initiates a series of poems on de Valera and mid-century politics, as well as on a number of father substitutes for McCarthy's own 'weak' father. Although these have something of the tone of Montague's overview of the Republic of 1966 in 'A Patriotic Suite', the tone is less caustic and more that of the insider, and displays a completely different – that is, anti-mythical – attitude to politics than that found in, say, Heaney. There is ideal-isation in the de Valera sequence – which runs from 'State Funeral' through *The Sorrow Garden* (1981) in 'De Valera's Childhood', 'Returning to De Valera's Cottage' and 'De Valera's Youth', 'De Valera, Lindbergh and Mr Cooper's Book of Poems' – but also a keen postcolonial awareness:

> Lloyd George was wary of his
> fox-like comings and goings:
>
> 'all that is truly dark
> and furtive and violent in
>
> the Irish mind' was what
> he thought. He should have
>
> known that such an animal
> existed only in colonial
>
> thought.
>   (McCarthy, 1981: 15–16)

McCarthy's presentation of de Valera is positive – his emergence from a deprived background is sympathetically sketched – but inflected by a revisionism which, nevertheless, in its more anti-Nationalist aspects, McCarthy rejects; to return to de Valera's childhood, for example, is to return to the childhood of the nation, but also to childishness, or political naivety, with de Valera himself 'a great child' (McCarthy, 1981: 17). The death of de Valera becomes, in *The Sorrow Garden*, bound up with the death of McCarthy's father and of 1940s' and 1950s' Ireland. In this historical sense, McCarthy extends the necessarily narrow focus of one of his chief influences, Austin Clarke, in a poem like 'A Neutral State, 1944', with its benign yet critical image of an Ireland without a blackout, 'the soft glow / of De Valera's Ireland, and her bog neutrality' (McCarthy, 1981: 39).

Such a mixture of political-historical exactitude and ambivalence is characteristic of McCarthy's self-effacing and unagonising Nationalism, one which undercuts 'tribal' stances. It is a poetry which aligns itself, in its sense of literary and political tradition, with non-masculinist attitudes while attempting to counter the simplifications of revisionism and an overeager embrace of Europe and abandonment of the Irish past: thus, in *The Sorrow Garden*, 'The Wisdom of A.E.' faces 'The Provincial Writer's Diary', to the discomfiture of Corkery's attempt to interpret the British presence as 'explaining all misery'[47] (McCarthy, 1981: 42–3). Nevertheless, Heaney and Montague are presences in the poetry, and in some senses McCarthy's work negotiates its own space between theirs.[48]

The Non-Aligned Storyteller (1984) is perhaps the one collection by a poet of McCarthy's generation in the Republic which can stand comparison with the achievement of his Northern contemporaries, and reveals an ability to relate the Northern Troubles to the political crises of the Republic in one of its most impressive poems, 'Counting the Dead on the Radio, 1972'. 'The dead', of course, are those of Bloody Sunday. What distinguishes McCarthy's treatment is not so much a lack of the force of 'A Butcher's Dozen'; the second section of the poem conflates powerfully enough the speaker's brother's killing of a rabbit ('the muffled thuds and grunts / of its torture, its boy-inflicted wounds') with the report of the massacre on the radio ('Adolescent soldiers / have gone wild'), and its satirical edge is as sharp as Kinsella's:

> Lemon rind sticks to my mother's throat.
> She throws up in an effort to understand. I say
> *Mama, a whole regiment has been attacked*
> *by a Catholic priest waving a blood-stained*
> *handkerchief. That's what the radio says.*

Rather, it is what has preceded this which gives it such force; a series of eerie, almost surreal allusions to ballot-rigging in the Republic and the trustworthiness of news broadcasts mediated through the figure of the speaker's father:

> Who has been making midnight phone calls?
> Who has been canvassing in the name of the dead?
> My father has left for the city, running scared:
> he wants no part in this. He has left
> his number but says we should only trust
> the *News* . . .
> Fatherless, the radio has plenty to say.
> (McCarthy, 1984: 28–9)

Likewise, in a series of poems on Fianna Fáil – 'The President's Men', 'The Chairman's Widow', 'Folklore of the Party', 'Party Shrine', and so on – there is a more critical treatment of the self-mythologising side of the political culture McCarthy knows so intimately, but also an exhaustion of it as a subject. Emigration, which returned to 1950s' levels in the 1980s, lies behind the volume's title poem, whose speaker is the photographer of the life of a dying town. There is a sense, then, in McCarthy's poetry of the 1980s, of a more ruthless line being taken with Nationalism and of its being offset by a greater international interest.[49] This ruthlessness is perhaps most evident in transposed forms, most notably in poems about the fate of European Jewry – far more tactfully treated than in Durcan's Nazi imagery – which has its local aspect; the Jewish population driven out of Limerick in 1904 settled in Cork, which is the only Irish city to have had a Jewish Lord Mayor. Behind this pessimism, McCarthy's political radicalism has increased – *Seven Winters in Paris* (1989) is based on flight from a Republic in which 'Two referenda' have been lost and the death of 'Garrett Parnell' and his 'timorous liberalism' (McCarthy, 1989: 11). It is possible to detect in this a loss of faith in the power of historical understanding to offset the depradations of modernisation and of the lack of any alternative coherent national narrative, but McCarthy is also too unillusioned to invoke a hidden Ireland (*Seven Winters* is notable for the lack of local reference).[50]

Free State and Soviet: Michael O'Loughlin

The years in which McCarthy's poetry first appeared – the late 1970s – were, in the Republic, those in which the Lemassian *Wirtschaftswunder* lost impetus. Unemployment rose again, from 116,000 in 1977 to 160,000 in 1982, public borrowing spiralled, and the debt per capita became one of the highest in the developed world. Blame for the crisis was, predictably, placed on the supposed profligacy of the public sector and the greed of workers. In the face of the attacks – on the semi-state industries, welfare provision and so on which followed – and the general reactionary climate of the time, there developed a widespread political and labour opposition, in tandem with campaigns for the defence of women's and other rights. Most notably these occurred in a series of demonstrations – some of the biggest in the history of the state – against the unequal tax burden, which fell disproportionately on the shoulders of workers as opposed to farmers (the Pay As You Earn (PAYE) tax scheme being dubbed 'Pay All You Earn' as a result).[51] Michael O'Loughlin's 'Snapshot: PAYE March' shows the emergence, in the face of such unrest, of a distinctly Brechtian sensibility in marked contrast to the radical but rural Nationalist focus of McCarthy:

> two hundred thousand marchers
> jamming up O'Connell Street
>
> spilling like blackberry jam
> into the side streets and alleys
>
> Kelly's Larkin rising above them
> as if he grew out of their shoulders
>
> while Parnell, O'Connell and Father Matthew
> stand about in awkward poses
>
> like discarded cardboard props
> from a long-forgotten movie.
>
> (O'Loughlin, 1980: 40)

In O'Loughlin's poem the monuments of conventional Nationalism, whose statues punctuate Dublin's main thoroughfare, are revealed as irrelevant, while Larkin – the famous trade union leader and champion of the Dublin poor – suddenly comes into his own. The collection from which it comes, *Stalingrad: The Street Dictionary* (1980), was published by the new Raven Arts Press, a small publishing house dedicated to representing a Dublin previously omitted from literature, that of the giant northside working-class estates, afflicted now by endemic unemployment, drug-use and violence (and in one sense another 'hidden Ireland').[52] *Stalingrad*'s title maps a city symbolising the failure of the major revolution of the twentieth century on to the geography of Dublin, epicentre of an Irish revolution seen as failing not in the Nationalist sense of incomplete unity but from the point of view of the working class victimised and marginalised within the new state. The valorisation of failure is read in terms of this excluded class perspective in the title poem, 'Stalingrad' – 'I was born to the stink of whiskey and failure' – which superficially resembles the miserablism of an O'Grady or a Fiacc, while undermining the resemblance in the radical historical analogy it proposes (O'Loughlin, 1980: 9). Elsewhere in the collection fragments of family and personal history, the blues, and trips to the West of Ireland centre around a narrative of European travel – conflating migrant worker and bohemian poet in order to look back from East Berlin on a Dublin in which the working class have been made exiles within their own city, relocated to brutally functional estates which are a far cry from the suburbs of Eavan Boland:

> I was standing in Rosa-Luxembourg Platz
> Looking down Karl-Marx Allee
> The streets don't lie
> Truth is concrete
> The worst slums in Europe
> Bear the names of our liberators.
>   (O'Loughlin, 1980: 10)

The lines point to the way redevelopment was directed by ministers from rural areas antipathetic to Dublin, and by architects whose previous experience consisted of designing churches and cowsheds, part of a government policy by which the city was administered, policed and schooled by largely rural personnel. The disparity between the immense catastrophe of Stalinism and the limited deprivations of de Valeran Ireland are acknowledged, but in a way which compels reviewing 1916–22 in the context of the post-World War I wave of revolution, the authors of the Easter Rising figured as heralds of the Bolsheviks:

> Here it was hunger, there it was murder,
> De Valera, Stalin, Free State and Soviet,
> The grotesque reality of an aborted ideal
> Where we talked like kings in a palace of dreams
> And lived like dogs in the ruins of the city.
>   (O'Loughlin, 1980: 12)

Rejection of Nationalist Ireland is complete, but the desire for revolution is tinged by the ambivalent knowledge of the 'seductive and brutal . . . choral cathedral of Lenin' (O'Loughlin, 1980: 42). The 'dead hand of Church and State / Squeez[es] out our souls / through the holes in a tin whistle', but Stalinism is clearly no alternative and the worst knowledge, in 'The City' (a version of Cavafy), is that escape is limited (O'Loughlin, 1980: 44). Defeatism alternates with qualified hope, but concludes with an image of a cab driver who 'drives hundreds of miles' every week to 'end up back where he started'. As the speaker himself is taxied back to Finglas he realises a shared destiny of journeying and entrapment. 'Taxi-Metre' offers an explanation for the crudity of the book itself (the taxi-driver 'fill[s] his dictionary with words like this: / Fuck, and bastard, and bollocks'), and narrator and driver also share 'a secret language of hate', swearing together, as they '[scan] the darkness for something to save us / From ending up back where we started' (O'Loughlin, 1980: 45).

Atlantic Blues (1982) suggests a modification of *Stalingrad*'s anger, pointing to the emergence of a cooler, more ironic style which coincided with O'Loughlin's move to Amsterdam and the collection *Diary of a Silence* (1985). Its longest poem, 'Limerick, 1919', is one of his most successful, centring as it does on a near-forgotten but, for Irish socialists, talismanic episode from the Anglo-Irish War. In 1919, rebelling against a curfew imposed by British troops, the Limerick Workers' Council declared a General Strike and ran the city for almost two weeks, overcoming military occupation and bypassing the Nationalist terms on which the war was being waged. The Limerick 'soviet' was perhaps the best example of workers' control anywhere in the then Great Britain, and O'Loughlin mourns it as a lost possibility and a potential hope for the future. O'Loughlin's claim that 'History cannot be stolen, only hidden' is provocatively couched in terms which mimic Corkery's, and the poem draws effectively on European socialist poetic tradition (from Mayakovsky to Enszensburger): 'The factories found their speech / based on the iron grammar / Of machines and bricks and sweat'. Even as this smacks of translationese, it rewrites the usual pietistic terms in which translation is considered in the Irish poetic tradition, and the poem powerfully offers Limerick, 'A rusted hatchet town . . . A far-flung valve of Empire . . . Dumped like a sack of anthracite / At the side of the unheeding river' as an image of an Ireland bereft by its lack of a socialist politics and vision (O'Loughlin, 1982: 9–13).[53]

Paul Muldoon: immrama, hunger strikers and sonnets

Muldoon has referred to his poetry as 'whimful', a coinage possibly connected to *Why Brownlee Left*'s 'Whim', whose protagonists encounter over a disputed translation of an Irish legend; as the male speaker puts it to the female reader '*Cu Chulainn and the Birds of Appetite?* / More like *How Cu Chulainn Got His End*', a pass which means that 'once he got stuck into her he got stuck / Full stop'.

The comic-brutal dogknotting sees them having to be 'manhandled onto a stretcher / Like the last of an endangered species', and appropriately introduces the mixture of violence, perverse sexuality and delicacy which characterises both *Brownlee* (1980) and *Quoof* (1983) (Muldoon, 1980: 7).[54] In 'October, 1950' Muldoon's own conception is the subject:

> Whatever it is, it all comes down to this;
> My father's cock
> Between my mother's thighs.
> Might he have forgotten to wind the clock?
> (Muldoon, 1980: 9)

Origins here, are literary – *Tristram Shandy* is a Muldoon *ur*-text – and crudely biological, and the relish of language which follows the opening hardly offsets the uncertainty (conception in a 'room' or 'an open field') and determinism of the last line: 'Whatever it is, it leaves me in the dark'. Origins and fate now seem less to do with a 'mulish' mixed ancestry than a destiny rooted in historical contingency, although in 'History' the ironically all-encompassing scope of the title raises the issue of how such contingency might be defined. Asking 'Where and when exactly did we first have sex?' – a question the poem cannot answer (although it guesses at the room 'where MacNeice wrote "Snow", / Or the room where they say he wrote "Snow"') – leads to the realisation that if we cannot be sure of such an important event in our personal lives, we can hardly be sure of the origins of any 'historical' event (Muldoon, 1980: 27). Attempts to escape, through understanding, become returns, a fate which awaits so many of the protagonists of the poems in *Brownlee*.

Such uncertainty is also political. In 'The Boundary Commission', in a village divided by the border between Northern Ireland and the Republic, the speaker remarks 'how a shower of rain / Had stopped so cleanly across Golightly's lane / It might have been a wall of glass / That had toppled over' (Muldoon, 1980: 15). The boundary is in one sense an arbitrary line drawn on a map and imposed upon social realities which cannot be so easily divided (the framers of the boundary, particularly for Catholics, were accused of making a division which penned the maximum number of Catholics capable of being dominated by a Protestant majority within the northern statelet). Arbitrariness, here, has a political rationale. Nevertheless, while this is recognised, the conclusion points to the difficulty, if not impossibility, of beginning from such origins in a reconsideration of Partition (as a republican would insist). Instead, the speaker – carefully framed by the opening italics and representation in the third person – wonders 'which side, if any, he should be on' (Muldoon, 1980: 15). Recognising historical injustice, the poem refuses to see this as soluble by any return to a 'pure' originary state.

Uncertainty concerning the past problematises attempts to understand the present or guess the future, and in this sense the past can and does exercise a deterministic grip over the present, but in ways which make outcomes difficult to predict. 'Anseo' seems a clear case of predictability, however. Joseph Mary Plunkett Ward, its central figure, is beaten for persistent absence at registration (at which the children call out 'anseo', the Irish for 'here, here and now, / All present and correct'), and gradually comes to anticipate and collude in his punishment, arriving with 'a sally-rod' for the master to use on him (Muldoon, 1980: 20). Muldoon here, typically, literalises a cliché – to make a rod for one's back – since, in the final verse, Ward has grown up to be an IRA 'Commandant' (a rod for society's back) who has his volunteers call out 'anseo' at morning parade. Worrying this determinism, however, is the fact that Ward's preparations for his beatings eventually reach the point where he brings to class an elaborate cane, its 'twist of red and yellow lacquers . . . so delicately wrought / That he had engraved his initials on it'. Clearly in excess of the poem's linkage of Ward's masochistic collusion to republican marty- rology, this raises the possibility that the poet and the IRA man are both artists, glancing at the aestheticisation of violence of *North*, rejecting art as con- solation and raising the issue of art's inherent amorality. Muldoon avoids simplification, while at the same time making some specific political points. As he has noted '['Anseo'] is about a very complex society indeed' (Haffenden, 1981: 137). Brutal directness and the most cautious indirection meet again in 'Ireland':

> The Volkswagen parked in the gap,
> But gently ticking over.
> You wonder if it's lovers
> And not men hurrying back
> Across two fields and a river.
> (Muldoon, 1980: 19)

Like the Volkswagen itself, this poem may be a booby trap to a certain kind of reviewer. Thus Michael Kane indicted the poem for its 'comprehensive title' and 'political bad taste', underscoring the way the comprehensiveness is part of the poem's affront to Nationalist piety (Kane, 1981: 51). Every detail con- tributes: 'Volkswagen', literally, 'people's car', hints at its creation by Hitlerian *fiat* (and the IRA's claim to be a 'vehicle' for the will of an Irish 'people'); the ticking comes from Heaney's 'A Constable Calls', but qualifies that poem's por- tentousness; the 'two fields and a river' ironically echo the Nationalist ballads 'Four Green Fields' and 'Only Our Rivers'. Even the 'gap' the car is parked in may be an allusion to the political vacuum in Northern Irish politics filled by the paramilitaries. 'Ireland' justifies its title by the fact that, while 'about' Northern Ireland, it is clearly set in the Republic and considers the blind eyes sometimes turned there to the IRA's activities as well as the North. Although the poem shows Muldoon's recourse to MacNeiceian allegory, a reader's response is more a bruised wonderment at a society, or rather societies, in which, as Kendall puts it, 'either . . . lovers in a parked car are more unusual, and therefore more worthy of mention, than terrorists returning to their getaway vehicle; or [in which] people have become so sensitized to political violence that they suspect it even in the inconsequentialities of everyday life' (Kendall, 1996: 78–9).

If there is difficulty in pinning down origins and determining the effects of the past, by the same token a space for imagining alternatives is conceivable. In *Brownlee* an escape from preordained roles is imagined; as O'Donoghue notes, 'the recurrent theme of leaving/parting . . . bears heavily on the Northern Ireland context, where the matter of rootlessness and belonging, the temptation to be "up and off", has been bitterly contentious from MacNeice and Kavanagh to any of the contemporary poets' (O'Donoghue, 1995: 409). Muldoon clearly places himself in this tradition of pitting programmatic against random behaviour, 'that sense of idealism, be it in terms of romantic views of women, or ideal societies or revolutionary politics', claiming that 'One of the ways in which we are most ourselves is that we imagine ourselves to be going somewhere else . . . that our home is somewhere else,' and the sonnet 'Immrama' derives from Muldoon's father's attempt to emigrate to Australia with a friend in the 1930s; for Muldoon this 'underlines the arbitrary nature of so many of the decisions we take . . . I would speculate on my father's having led an entirely different life' (Haffenden, 1981: 139). Often the evasion of destiny is not so clear-cut, or is more ambiguous, as in the paradigmatic title poem. This avoids answering 'why' Brownlee 'left' partly by suggesting that his name already contains his end (the 'brown lea' in which his abandoned horses are discovered),[55] as well as the more conventional explanations of sociology (emigration) or folklore (kidnap by the *sidhe*):

> . . . the last rig unbroken, his pair of black
> Horses, like man and wife,
> Shifting their weight from foot to
> Foot, and gazing into the future.
> (Muldoon, 1980: 22)

While the emblematic naming of *Mules* suggested the (limited) allegorical usages defined in MacNeice's terms, in *Brownlee* this takes on a more complex function reminiscent of his definition of parable proper. This influence is most apparent in the concluding long narrative poem 'Immram', which draws on the Old Irish form of *immram*, or 'rowing around' travel tale, a genre including (happily for Muldoon) the *Immram Mael Duin*. Muldoon's spirited rewriting of this text – in which the hero goes in quest of his father's murderer but eventually, in a spirit of Christian reconciliation, forgives him – takes the form of Chandleresque *film noir* gumshoe narrative. The search in Muldoon's version is for the father himself (he turns out to have been another kind of 'mule', a cocaine-smuggler), rather than his killer, which problematises the idea that 'solutions' may be discovered or uncovered, or wrongs fully righted, thus making its (very oblique) political point. The same kind of critique of essence

is implicit in the shaping of the material; local details from the original reappear in almost unrecognisable form (thus a black cat becomes a black blues
musician, a magic door becomes a hotel's revolving door, the Atlantic Ocean
becomes a 'pool' hall and 'that old Deep Water Baptist Mission', and so on).
The protagonist in this deliberately digressive narrative encounters a series of
emblematically named characters – Lieutenant Brendan O'Leary, Redpath,
James Earl Caulfield III, Foster, and finally a Howard Hughes 'hermit' figure
– as he uncovers corruption, violence, sexual brutality and drug-running. As
Muldoon has explained, however, a large part of the poem's meaning is its
pastiching, parodic style, which dramatises the concerns of the rest of the book
(determinism, for example, becomes 'Your old man was an ass-hole. / That
makes an ass-hole out of you'), as well as dramatising his own evasiveness
and its potentially lethal consequences:

> They came bearing down on me out of nowhere.
> A Buick and a Chevrolet.
> They were heading towards a grand slam.
> Salami on rye. I was the salami.
> (Muldoon, 1980: 40)

Nevertheless, there is a keenly satiric edge to the poem, at the expense of other
texts (one target is Tennyson's 'dreadful' version of the original), of family and
authority (and hence tradition), religion (sent up via Californian surf culture)
and the whole notion of arriving at true origins (the parents in the poem prove
'false', and the protagonist arrives 'back, like any other pilgrim', where he
began in 'Foster's pool-room'.

Quoof is the most radical of all Muldoon's deconstructions of Heaneyesque
pieties and, with *Madoc*, the darkest of any of his books. In *Quoof*, the violence
of the Troubles comes home to roost, overshadowed as it is by the IRA blanket
protests in the Maze Prison, followed by the hunger strikes of 1980–81 over
political status, during which ten Republican prisoners died. As we might
expect, loss, violence, dismemberment and death figure centrally; bomb alerts
sound, hands are severed, and people are blown to smithereens. Predatory violence extends to poems dealing with relationships, which run the gamut from
the offhand and sour ('Aisling') to those of violent and brutal sex ('Blewits')
and cannibalism. The volatility of the historical moment is matched by an
increased emphasis on metamorphosis and shape-shifting evidenced in earlier
poems like 'Centaurs'. This is partly by way of an extension of Muldoon's interest in Native American culture to shamanism; the book's epigraph comes from
Knud Rasmussen's anthropological study *The Netsilik Eskimos* which tells the
tale of a female shaman who makes herself a penis with a willow-branch and
a husky from a shit-stained lump of snow. This is a reminder that androgyny
is another favourite theme; in 'The Unicorn Defends Himself', the speaker
awakes to find himself the ambiguous middle term in a sexual sandwich,
'between two bodies, true, / one wire-haired and one smooth' (Muldoon,

1983: 34). The naive 'true' should not distract from the fact that the location is of a piece with an habitual refusal to take sides, particularly when those 'sides' take conventional forms.

As Muldoon put it in his *Poetry Book Society Bulletin* note, *Quoof* is intended at one level to 'purge myself of the hourly kennings of the news bulletins', to treat language of certain public, official kinds as linguistic constipation which must occasionally be dealt with by drastic means. Likewise, the shamanic dimension has contemporary resonance, as the secular equivalent of a shaman's trance, induced by hallucinogenic drugs, keeps cropping up. Indeed, the central section of the long concluding poem 'The More a Man Has, the More a Man Wants' is an *aisling* vision produced by LSD. This aspect of the work is meant to remind us of the extent to which Muldoon is, in some ways, a typical product of late 1960s' youth counter-culture (and he has claimed that 'the world is hallucinogenic') (Keller, 1994: 24). On a deeper level, one of the chief functions of drug references is that the distortions of reality they produce match the political and psychic phantasmagoria of the Troubles. In addition, there is the implied connection between the shaman and the poet; here, as in earlier connections between revolutionaries and terrorists and the poet, Muldoon suggests a comparison of himself with another extreme, asocial figure. Most provocatively of all, the images of women in *Quoof* are presented almost invariably in sexual, and often extremely disturbing, terms; one is seduced to be 'fist-fucked' and disembowelled, another tarred and feathered, yet another presented as the dominatrix figure of pornography, complete with 'whip', 'thigh-length boot' and 'hackled gulp of semen'[56] (Muldoon, 1983: 23).

Several of these elements run together in 'Gathering Mushrooms', a title which alludes to Mahon's 'A Disused Shed in Co. Wexford', but also to Muldoon's father's one-time occupation as a mushroom-grower, and mushrooms (revealingly 'between', neither plant nor animal according to biological taxonomy) recur as a motif – usually in a poisonous or hallucinogenic capacity – throughout. In its original publication, 'Gathering Mushrooms' was dedicated to Ciaran Carson, and in narrative terms it moves from a memory of the backyard of the childhood home to student high jinks 'fifteen years on . . . thinking only of psilocybin', as the speaker and his companion '[trip] through Barnett's fair demesne'. Psilocybin blends the mundane world of Muldoon's father with a legendary figure 'who has opened the Gates of Troy', an 'ancient warrior' as well as a Heaney-like craftsman who will 'glance back from under his peaked cap / without breaking rhythm'. By the penultimate verse it is the narrator, however, who is wholly changed in what is the first of the book's many transformations of human beings into animals: 'my head had grown into the head of a horse'. The Muldoon-horse – kin to the Trojan Horse, but also the totemic horse of the Celts – speaks the final verse.[57] After the previous verse's shimmering sunset '[deepening] through cinnamon / to aubergine' and a 'green-gold dragon', this proves to be an utterly sobering and minimalist appeal for support for the Republican cause on behalf of the Maze blanketmen:

> *Come back to us.*
> *However cold and raw, your feet*
> *Were always meant*
> *To negotiate terms with bare cement . . .*
>   (Muldoon, 1983: 7–9)

Muldoon's monitory alter ego provides a chastening moment after what has gone before. Yet the point is not simply to rebuke escapism; however much sympathy Muldoon may be showing in allowing the appeal, the one thing the metamorphic poet cannot afford to do is 'wait' within the stasis of an unalterable and frozen ideology. What *Quoof* does from this point on is move through Muldoon's childhood to the historic moment of the book's writing. This is perhaps the result of a return to the source of his lack of the identitarianism demanded by the voice of 'Gathering Mushrooms', an exploration of the roots of the absence of 'roots', as it were. This may suggest a coherence which the collection is at some pains to deny, and it is, of course, far more than just an 'answer' to the ventriloquised, horse-sense ('straight from the horse's mouth') of the blanketman, and involves recovery of the poet's extraordinary 'hallucinogenic' imagination, the sexual and artistic desires which structure and restructure the self, trapping as well as liberating it.

This imagination is at work in 'Trance', in which the horse of 'Gathering Mushrooms' reappears as a Christmas present the three-year-old discovers hidden up the chimney. The image is subjected to transfiguration – 'A wind out of Siberia' whistles round the house, bringing with it more 'voices', this time of nomadic tribes beyond the Urals ingesting mushrooms (and drinking the urine of those who have eaten them) (Muldoon, 1983: 10).[58] But this remarkable juxtaposition is offset by the facing poem in which the image is entrapment; again three years old, the speaker '[plunges]' his arm into a glass jar for the last piece of rock:

> I would have given my right arm to have known then
> how Eglish itself was wedged between
> ecclesia and église.
>
> The Eglish sky was its own stained-glass vault
> and my right arm was sleeved in glass
> that has yet to shatter.
>   (Muldoon, 1983: 11)

The place the child lives is 'wedged' between two words meaning 'church' and is like a church, 'its own stained-glass vault'. 'Vault' has its more sinister connotations (the church is a repressive and deathly institution), and the 'cloverock' the child is reaching for in the glass jar suggests division, of the self as well as of a sectarian society (it echoes the Methodist hymn 'Rock of Ages', which is implored to 'cleft for me', although things which are cloven are reputedly devilish too). Yet the childhood memory also protects the adult self; unlike so much else in the book, the glass has 'yet to shatter'. That 'yet to' is part, however, of the forward-looking aspect of the book and most famously recurs in its title poem, 'Quoof', which also turns on the difficulty of communicating the familial – 'our family word / for the hot water bottle' – an act which proceeds to adulthood and sexual boasting, as the speaker tells how he has 'taken it into so many lovely heads / or laid it between us like a sword' (Muldoon, 1983: 17).

The focus on the familial and the body, however, should not obscure the fact that *Quoof* is intensely concerned with the hallucinogenic historical realities of Northern Ireland. The body and the family are thus politicised in a manner which recalls (even as it works to different ends) the tactics of the blanketmen and hunger strikers; as Allen Feldman has noticed, one of the prime aims of Republican prisoners involved in these protests was precisely the different politicisation of their imprisoned bodies, which they offered as equivalents for the colonised body of Ireland.[59] The obsessive interest in bodies and bodily fragmentation and emblematisation in *Quoof*, particularly in its concluding long poem, 'The More a Man Has, the More a Man Wants' (whose central section is an *aisling* set in such a prison), can clearly be related to this strategy, although for Muldoon such an 'emblematisation' is not intended to assert an originary identity but rather to challenge constrictive notions of origin at the level of family, sexuality, religion and politics. In the most virtuosic display of his miscegenatory and hybrid poetic to that point, 'The More a Man Has' offers the tale of Gallogly, a terrorist on the run in Northern Ireland, crossed with that of an Apache or 'Oglala Sioux' Indian, with whom he merges explosively at its conclusion when he literally 'kicks the bucket', one packed with 'fertilizer / and a heady brew / of sugar'[60] (Muldoon, 1983: 63).

If Muldoon has been dismissed as a postmodern trickster, this is largely because he has been read within a highly charged set of cultural coordinates which a poem like 'The More a Man Has' is attempting to destroy. Thus, a depoliticised English reading can be found in Tim Kendall's interpretation of 'A Trifle' which misses, as Sean O'Brien has pointed out, the fact that the 'trifle' bears the same colours as the Union Flag and, at one level at least, stands for 'the tit of imperial subsidy' to Northern Ireland by Westminster (S. O'Brien, 1998: 172). Neil Corcoran confesses that he misses the point of 'Yggdrasil', and it is true that Muldoon embeds his literary-political source quite deeply.[61] Yet while concealed, it is also, typically, blatant through an echo of one of the most notorious lines in Irish poetry, Yeats's version in 'Under Ben Bulben' of the Young Irelander John Mitchel's plea 'Give us war in our time, O Lord!' The tree the speaker climbs in the poem is both the world-tree of Norse mythology (and Heaney's 'Nerthus'), and also of Frost's 'Climbing Birches'; his desire on reaching the top is to answer his watchers 'with my tonsure' – the sign of a scribe, and of his separation as an artist from society. But this is followed by the realisation that he is being led not away from the 'legend' his people 'yearn for', but towards it. The 'paper . . . spiked on the top' reads:

> *It may not be today*
> *or tomorrow, but sooner or later*
> *the Russians will water*
> *their horses on the shores of Lough Erne*
> *and Lough Neagh.*
> (Muldoon, 1983: 27)

The baffling horses – why *Russian*? – show not simply a 'trickster' spirit at work, but an obliquely devastating reference to Mitchel's *Jail Journal* and his inversion of the prayer 'Give us peace in our time, O Lord' to praise Russia, Britain's adversary in the Crimean War: 'Czar, I bless thee. I kiss the hem of thy garment. I drink to thy health and longevity. Give us war in our time, O Lord!'[62] As I have noted, Yeats echoes the same dubious appeal to assert that 'violence' is required for even the 'wisest man' to 'accomplish fate' (Yeats, 1989: 450). The full force of the reference, however, appears later in Mitchel's memoir, when he relates how, after the outbreak of the war, he visited the Russian ambassador in Washington to persuade him to back a Russian invasion of Ireland. Muldoon, characteristically, projects an apparently bizarre fantasy from firm historical facts. The fact that the first lines of the verse echo the republican 'our day will come', together with the italics, show this to be another message from the blanketman of 'Gathering Mushrooms'. But most spectacularly in *Quoof* it is the sonnet itself – exploded, starved, reassembled and finally dismissed with a 'Huh' – which presents Muldoon's politics as a politics of form.[63]

'Little boat of the language': Nuala Ní Dhomhnaill

Ní file ach filíocht í an bheann [Woman is not poet but poetry]
(Seán Ó Riordáin, quoted in Ní Dhomhnaill, 1992b: 23–4)

If the career of Michael Hartnett showed that Irish- and English-language poetries could be seen, as late as 1975, as requiring an either/or choice, the generation of younger Irish-language poets grouped around the journal *Innti* were to show – as Hartnett himself has acknowledged – that a series of barriers between the two could be bridged. Along with Muldoon, Hartnett was to be the most prolific translator of the outstanding poet to emerge from the ferment in Cork in the early 1970s, Nuala Ní Dhomhnaill.[64] Isolationism was broken by the *Innti* poets who brought the internationalist energies of the new youth culture to Irish poetry, forcing it to engage with non-Gaeltacht and non-Irish issues and endowing it with a more contemporary idiom.[65] The key figure in this process was Michael Davitt, the *Innti* editor, whose urban attitudes and contemporary concerns opened up new contexts to the poetry at precisely the time when these could be best exploited. Soon after cutting the umbilical link with the Gaeltacht, in a kind of reversal, 'Ní Dhomhnaill was able to see the vitality of beliefs enshrined in its folklore' (Denman, 1992: 253). That is, the stance made available a new assessment of the resources of tradition; and in this, Ní Dhomhnaill's gender was also to prove vital, as she became, with her second collection (*Féar Suaithinseach*, of 1984), the most visible Irish-language poet, and one of the best known in the country. That visibility has been magnified by Ní Dhomhnaill's rejection of separatist attitudes, summed up in 'Ceist na Teangan'/'The Language Issue', which speaks of '[placing] my hope on the water/in this little boat / of the language', as Moses was set adrift on the Nile

> only to have it borne hither and thither,
> not knowing where it might end up;
> in the lap, perhaps,
> of some Pharaoh's daughter.
> (Ní Dhomhnaill, 1994: 155 transl. Paul Muldoon)

This strategy of risk has been extensively pursued in a dual-language *Rogha Dánta/Selected Poems* (1986), *Pharaoh's Daughter* (1990) and *The Astrakhan Cloak* (1992a), as she has actively sought a wider audience for her work, recruiting the cream of English-language poets as translators.[66] The effect has been to broaden the dialogue between the poetries of Ireland's two languages as no other poet has done, breaking with the fears of compromise and dilution which inhibited earlier Irish-language poets.

It is this symbiotic relationship with English which makes Ní Dhomhnaill so important to English-language poetry, complicating as it does the previously uneasy relationship of poets such as Heaney, Montague, Kinsella and others to the Irish tradition. By breaking with that tradition the *Innti* poets paradoxically enabled a healthier, less guilty relationship to develop, one which could eschew a purely excavatory approach to Irish poetic texts.[67] This was particularly the case with Ní Dhomhnaill given her gender and the fact that the role of women in Irish-language poetry had been so marginal to it up to that point, despite the fact that one of the leading figures of the 1950s' generation had been a woman, Máire Mhac an tSaoi. Ní Dhomhnaill's luck was to appear at a time which enabled her 'alliance of feminism and folklore', one leavened by extensive experience of life abroad and foreign culture (she is married to a Turkish geologist and lived in Turkey in the 1970s before returning to Ireland and publishing her first collection, *An Dealg Droighin/The Thorn of the Blackthorn*, in 1981). Nevertheless, this 'alliance' is by no means straightforward, although it impinges upon the same sorts of issues – of stereotypes, female poetic identity, feminist politics – found in the work of her English-language contemporaries.

These issues are dramatised in Ní Dhomhnaill's first book in a series of poems which reshape the folk tradition through the Munster fertility goddess Mór; similarly, the title poem of the second book is subtitled 'Fianaise an chailín i ngreim "Anorexia"' ('Evidence of the girl anorexic'), referring to Ní

Dhomhnaill's own affliction with the disease, and the poem specifically deals with the male treatment of this (largely) female illness. Central to the collection is a group of poems headed 'Bean an Leasa', which can be glossed (roughly) as 'the woman from the fairy ring'. In Denman's words, the figure develops as 'a mixture of witch, enchantress, child-taker, weird sister and doppelganger'. This distinctly menacing presence functions as a vehicle for reshaping folk tradition by subjecting it to a modern social and political awareness. In 'An Crann' (translated by Muldoon as 'As for the Quince'), this figure intrudes to hack down a tree in a suburban back garden with a Black & Decker.[68] Reporting her husband's response to the creature when she returns ('Why didn't you stop her? / What would she think / if I took a Black & Decker / round to her place / and cut down a quince-tree / belonging to her?'), the housewife is made to suffer – 'I could barely lift a finger / till Wednesday' – while the tree itself appears 'safe and sound / and still somehow holding its ground' (Ní Dhomhnaill, 1994: 36–9). The effect is to make a point about the ability of buried folkloric belief to disrupt a humdrum suburban existence, as well as about the fate of women content to merely echo a male judgement. In *Feis/Festival* (1993), Ní Dhomhnaill's third collection, the themes of the earlier work are extended as the earth mother (Mór) is brought into line with contemporary personal experience of a life in middle-class Dublin, and does so in line with the sexual connotations of its title (from the Old Irish 'fo-aid', 'sleeping with') (Denman, 1992: 254; Welch, 1996: 392). In the collaboration with Muldoon, *The Astrakhan Cloak*, a selection of poems from *Feis* rearranged by Muldoon himself, draws on the connections between Ní Dhomhnaill's work and the vanishings and voyagings of his own earlier work; this is particularly evident in 'Immram'/'The Voyage', a fourteen-poem sequence which uses the medieval journey poem as a source and which fuses the heavenly cities of the Bible with those of Celtic mythology such as Hy-Breasil. The degree of latitude Ní Dhomhnaill allows her translators in reshaping her work has been criticised, but it is perhaps best seen as a mark of her confidence and a sign of her desire that translations of her work should have validity in the host language.[69]

At the most obvious level, the feminist allegiances of Ní Dhomhnaill's work are apparent in the inversion of the usual casting of woman as muse and as national territory. This can fuse with the frankly sexual energies of the poetry already noted, as in 'Oileán'/'Island': 'Your nude body is an ocean / asprawl on the ocean bed. How / beautiful your limbs' (Ní Dhomhnaill, 1994: 40–3). On the other hand, as in the Mór sequence of *The Thorn of the Blackthorn*, male presumption is rebuked, when the hero Cú Chulainn is demoted in favour of female figures from the Ulster Cycle such as Queen Medb. These mortal women are complemented by, and are presented as avatars of, the Great Queen, who – as Mór and Badb – may display positive and negative powers. Thus, in 'Agallamh Na Mór-Riona Le Cú Chulainn'/'The Great Queen Speaks. Cú Chulainn Listens', the Queen promises revenge on the hero for his rejection of her; these, as Haberstroh notes, are couched in the language ('you gave me the back of your hand') of contemporary abuse of women at the hands of men (Haberstroh, 1996: 170). She also warns Cú Chulainn that by rejecting her positive aspect he has delivered himself to her deathly aspect, that of Badb, figured as a carrion-crow who feeds off the dead of battle. Ní Dhomhnaill's purpose is not simply to attack the traditional male warrior-myth, however; in restoring the goddesses to their active forms in her poetry, she is concerned to articulate the darker sides of the female psyche, as in 'Breith Anabai Thar Lear'/'Miscarriage Abroad', in which autobiographical details – the speaker's loss, and her jealousy at 'my best friend's new born child' – are aligned with the Great Queen's malign aspect. In similarly subversive fashion, Ní Dhomhnaill is concerned to challenge the denial of the flesh and patriarchal oppressiveness of the Christianity which overwhelmed pagan and folkloric beliefs.[70] The monitory aspect of such female reimagining can be traced in what might be called the ecological aspect of the work; abuse of the earth, and earth mother, will lead to the kind of retribution meted out to Cú Chulainn, but on a planetary basis, as war and environmental degradation.

So much might suggest the dangers of Ní Dhomhnaill's procedure from a feminist point of view; that is, the extent to which she essentialises a conception of the female as archaic to set against an equally essentialised 'masculine' modernity. It is necessary, however, not to assume that all figurings of the nation as female are equally reactionary in contemporary poetry, particularly in those of women poets. The problems of using stereotypes lie in the readiness with which, even in their transformed versions, they reinscribe themselves within an ahistorical, essentialist schema. Replacing the sexless, marginalised figures of myth with more sexually and socially active versions may still leave us with figures who, while energetically debunking older assumptions, nevertheless enter the socio-political realm only via their sons and husbands. The sovereignty goddess (the Great Queen) has as her primary mythic function the conferring of power upon the tribal chieftain who symbolically mates with her to ensure agricultural fertility and clan prosperity; and certainly the use of ancient Irish female archetypes by woman poets has been read as expressive of some 'genuine' voice of female experience, that is of woman as eternal feminine or *ewig weibliche*. In Wills's words, what is at work here is the acceptance of myth as origin, rather than as a tactic or vehicle for engaging with contemporary constructions of gender.

That myth also has its literary and racial dimension, and in her Introduction to *Rogha Dánta* Máire Mhac an tSaoi claims that 'the literary tradition to which [Ní Dhomhnaill] adheres is unique, in that it goes back unbroken to the origins of our Indo-European culture'. This simplistic myth of origin is both programmatically anti-modern ('the sadism and Satanism of our present rootless and drifting mass-culture') and concerned to make of Ní Dhomhnaill herself the figure for a patently reactionary solution to the fall into history: 'she is Mór, the Mór-Rionn, Medb . . . Our Lady of Ballinspittle before the event . . . We hosts of the detribalised are immeasurably in her debt; she has restored to us something of our lost wholeness' (Ní Dhomhnaill, 1993: 9–11). This clearly attempts to wrench Ní Dhomhnaill into a pre-women's movement, Catholic outlook which her work does not bear out.[71] Yet at the same time, it reveals the difficulties of using such material, and Ní Dhomhnaill herself is sufficiently ambivalent on the issue to allow interpretations like these to flourish. In her essay 'What Foremothers?' of 1992 (in which she attacked the US/British poet Anne Stevenson's claim that the contemporary Irish woman poet is enabled by her literary tradition), Ní Dhomhnaill displays a belief in the 'myth of sovereignty envisaged as a woman' being 'shockingly alive in the collective psyche' (Ní Dhomhnaill, 1992b: 27). Yet while dismissing the 'unholy alliance of Marxist–Freudian reductionist intellectuals [who] seek to deny it', she asserts that 'We ourselves are constructed by the construct' (Ní Dhomhnaill, 1992b: 27–8). Ní Dhomhnaill's point is, in fact, readily assimilable to certain 'Marxist–Freudian' positions; namely that images and myths of the kind she refers to have material force and cannot simply be regarded as epiphenomena (Ní Dhomhnaill, 1992b: 28). Likewise, her attacks on the state and on the Church are forthright, and directly at variance with Mhac an tSaoi's allusion to the moving statue at Ballinspittle (which gives the impression that Ní Dhomhnaill's countenancing of the power of myth lends ideological support to the folk piety the events represented).[72] For Ní Dhomhnaill, indeed, the hyperrationalistic denial of the power of images of Mother Ireland can lead to the terroristic activities of women such as Máiréad Farrell, one of the IRA active service group gunned down in Gibraltar by the SAS in 1988 (Ní Dhomhnaill, 1992b: 29–30; Coogan, 1996: 343–4).

In many ways, this attitude to myth recalls that of Heaney; its grip on the communal imagination is accepted and explored, with varying degrees of critical stringency, even as its most obviously malign (supposed) effects are deplored. Yet the force of Ní Dhomhnaill's poetry stems from its very different response to such acceptance; rather than archaeology and elegy, she offers the hybrid destabilising of traditionalist poetic norms, oral and folkloric material (rather than an established textual canon of myth and legend) and overt female sexuality. Like McGuckian, Ní Dhomhnaill accepts feminism insofar as it is heterogeneous and capable of serving tactical needs, although her engagement with contemporary political and social realities is less oblique. Her attempts to set folk material at a critical angle to the contemporary world can be seen most disturbingly in 'An Bhatrail'/'The Battering', from her third collection, which needs to be read in the light of one of the *causes célèbres* of the 1980s' backlash against women, the infamous 'Kerry Babies' case. In May 1984 a schoolgirl, Joanna Hayes, confessed under police interrogation to killing an infant who had been found with stab wounds on a nearby beach. Hayes was later found innocent – the baby was not hers – but in the process she did confess to concealing the (natural) death of her own baby at around the same time, and its burial on the family farm. A few months later another teenager,

Ann Lovet, was found dead outside a church in Co. Longford, having given birth there, alone, to a dead child. Both incidents, and the furore which surrounded them, highlighted the fact that, as Eiléan Ní Chuilleanáin put it, 'the political debates and showdowns of the period [in the Republic] were not about terrorism or law and order but about abortion and divorce' (Ní Chuilleanáin, 1992: 34). A tribunal into the Hayes incident was set up to find out how the police had persuaded her to confess. Yet its inquiries were sensationalised, both inside the tribunal and in daily press reportage. Police argued that Hayes had had twins with different DNA through superfecundation and disposed of them separately. Press accounts presented a witch-hunting profile of her as a child murderess. At this point, it could be argued, pagan/medieval folkloric belief systems could be seen to be informing modern concepts of reality in a way resembling that of a Ní Dhomhnaill poem. The Hayes case was of great interest to Ní Dhomhnaill, and 'The Battering' echoes it in the links it draws between folklore and modern life:

> I only just made it home from the fort last night with my child
> from the fairy fort.
> He was crawling with red lice and jiggers
> and his skin was so red and raw
> I've spent all day putting hot poultices on his bottom
> and salving him with *Sudocrem*
> from stem to stern.
>   (Ní Dhomhnaill, 1992a: 25)

The speaker goes on to recount how she had saved her son just in time from the creatures in the *lios* ('fairy fort') and of how she had to perform various manoeuvres (catching him by his left arm, pulling him across a 'lank of undyed wool' and so on) to free him. She is now guarding him ('so far so good') against being substituted for a changeling, which she swears she would kill and 'bury out the field'. It is in this final stanza that the parallels with the Hayes case come through most forcefully as the speaker confesses that, having killed any changeling

> There's no way I could take it anywhere next
> or near the hospital.
> As things stand,
> I'll have more than enough trouble
> trying to convince them that it wasn't me
> who gave my little laddie this last battering.
>   (Ní Dhomhnaill, 1992a: 25)

The reference to a child-burial alludes to the folk practice of crediting the places where dead unbaptised (or stillborn) infants were buried with special power. These resemble the *lios*, which are linked in turn with the lore of dead children, infanticide and demonised female figures. One way of reading the poem, then, is as the speaker's rationalisation of having beaten her baby son by blaming the violence on to the supernatural inhabitants of the *lios*. Yet the child-burial links the speaker not with Hayes as such, but with the persona constructed for her by the press and police at the tribunal. The poem shows its speaker to be both in a poor psychological state and also suspiciously conversant with folkloric practices, in accordance with the tribunal's description of Hayes. Yet if 'The Battering' mediates the Hayes case, Ní Dhomnhaill is arguably also doing something more than simply equating folkloric images of maternity with a part of the modern female psyche. By drawing parallels between the innocent Hayes and the persona ascribed to her, it is also implied that the demonic aspect of the female psyche may not be part of the female psychological make-up at all, but rather a collective projection of patriarchal attitudes to women. In this reading 'The Battering' reveals a folkloric female unconscious, but removes it from the poem's speaker in order to turn it back against a society which needs to believe in the existence of demonic female infanticide. At this further level the poem becomes a critique of the hyperrational denial of the folkloric, exposing its grip on a society which prides itself on being free of such beliefs. To this extent, Ní Dhomhnaill's 'archaising' practices undercut a reactionary modernity which stigmatises rural/'backward' populations in gender terms. Folkloric belief circulates invisibly in a climate of fear at Irish identity being seen as 'backward' by those forces symbolising a desired modernity, leading to the internal stigmatising of those associated with traditional belief systems as 'savage'. It is for precisely this reason, as Ní Dhomhnaill seems to argue elsewhere, that myth and folklore remain living resources, not anachronisms, for Irish poets.

Notes

1 The larger backdrop to these national and local changes was the unpropitious one of slump, followed by monetarist, neo-liberal assault on the post-war consensus from the mid-1970s onwards. During the 1980s, however, a new cold war tended to put the problems of Ireland, from the point of view of the UK and USA – key players in any peace process – into the shade.

2 The stance was an attempt to guarantee that the poetry was 'intended as communication as well as self-communication', re-entering the mainstream of the English tradition after trying to rough it up (Corcoran, 1986: 127).

3 It is inaccurate, therefore, to locate the problem of *Field Work* in a conflict between 'an undeniably English literary style and the act of bearing witness for a dispossessed agricultural Catholic and Irish community' (Wills, 1993: 34). The collection is all too faithful to the simplistic ideas of 'bearing witness' and of a 'dispossessed community'; it asserts a nationalism steeped in the masochistic ethic of triumph through 'enduring most', most famously elaborated by the hunger striking Lord Mayor of Cork, Terence MacSwiney, in 1920 (R. F. Foster, 1989: 499).

4 For an acerbically brilliant, if brief, discussion of *The Crane Bag*, see *The Crane Bag* (1977–85), in McCormack, 1986: 48–52.

5 Soon after *Field Work*, Heaney wrote of wishing to drop the 'Keatsian woolliness' of its style in favour of 'writing a bare wire', and both *Station Island* and *Sweeney Astray* move beyond its ambivalent resentment at obligation and notions of

endurance to an emphasis on the isolated but autonomous artist (Corcoran, 1998: 110). The responsibilities entailed by freedom nevertheless continued to haunt Heaney, but are explored in the first section of the book in oppositional artist-figures, such as Chekhov who 'thought to squeeze / His slave's blood out' (in 'Chekhov on Sakhalin'), in poems which distance themselves from the involved 'I' of lyric ('Making Strange', the 'Shelf Life' sequence) and in a number of more problematic explorations of personal history ('The King of the Ditchbacks').

6 *Station Island*'s main work, the twelve-part 'Station Island' sequence, follows an internal debate which poems such as 'Widgeon' intimate is sporadic, if powerful at a number of points. The poem's title refers to St Patrick's Purgatory, a place of penance on an island in Lough Derg in Donegal, where penitents fast and for three days traverse the 'stations' of the cross, and the first, introductory section, conjures up the figure of Sweeney who appears in all three sections of the book. Here, in the first of a series of visionary (Dantesque) encounters, he is the 'sabbath-breaker', Simon Sweeney, recalled from childhood journeys to school and church, who, as a traveller (or tinker), represents an un-pious, unassimilated section of society. His advice to Heaney – 'Stay clear of all processions!' – is a direct rebuke to the poet's sense of communal responsibility, and sets the tone for what follows.

7 Critics were ambivalent regarding this work, which included the appropriately titled 'Light Music' sequence. Moreover, while some saw *Courtyards in Delft* (1981) and *The Hunt by Night* (1982) as a return to form after such dalliances, others found an exhausted aestheticism or signs of simplification and decline (Riordan, 1984: 176; Constable, 1984: 115). Certainly, Mahon dried up as a poet in the 1980s, moving into TV adaptations, film scripts and translations (gaps in his reviewing output and a poem like 'At St Patrick's' also indicate bouts of physical and psychological breakdown). Between 1982 and *The Hudson Letter* (1995) there appeared only a pamphlet, *Antarctica* (1985), whose brevity and title say much for a sense of arrest. An attempt to resist this is detectable in *Courtyards in Delft* and *The Hunt by Night*. On the one hand the title poem of the latter, although seen as fanciful and lightweight by some, pushes the 'tourist' aspect of Mahon's writing to a certain extreme, falling as it does between a modernist vision of history as alienation and an incipient, never-quite-realised postmodern one in which history is not 'the great / Adventure we suppose', but instead 'some elaborate / Spectacle put on for fun / And not for food'. On the other, the revisions to the title poem of the former show a felt awareness of a lack in the earlier poetry.

8 See P. Denman, 'Know the One? Insolent Ontology and Mahon's Revisions', *Irish University Review*, 24:1 (Spring/Summer 1994), 27–37. Mahon is one of only two contemporary Northern poets to be included in Kinsella's *New Oxford Book of Irish Verse* of 1986.

9 There, the fourth verse now included something of the lost fifth one, concluding 'While my hard-nosed companions dream of fire / And sword upon parched veldt and fields of rain-swept gorse' ('fire and sword' incorporating something of the apocalyptic flavour of the deleted verse). At one level the additional verse's explicit spelling-out of the desire for punishment can be linked to Mahon's Nationalism. Given the complexity of the verse, however, it would be too easy to put the change down simply to this. Another alternative is to ask whether the change is, like Heaney's 'Widgeon', a reflection of the general shift in sensibility among younger Northern poets. But why should a shift towards greater subtlety be registered by what seems to be a lack of it? In the first version there is a tension between commitment to overt 'verifiable fact' as an aesthetic principle and implicit analogy, or parable, of the sort noted in 'A Disused Shed in Co. Wexford'. This hints at the kind of bourgeois-bohemian antagonism which is the theme of so many poems

from 'Glengormley' on, as well as some pertinent art-historical ones. By moving indoors the poem has recourse to a different pictoral language; as Mahon's second stanza suggests, there are elements in Dutch Golden Age interiors of an 'emblematic' iconography of narrative moralities seemingly at odds with the empiricism of 'verifiable fact'. Nevertheless such interiors are still primarily concerned with representation and stem from a 'visual culture,' as Svetlana Alpers has argued, as opposed to Italianate High Renaissance and Baroque humanist culture which focuses on the nude and relies on text and narrative. (See Svetlana Alpers, *The Art of Describing* (Harmondsworth, Penguin, 1989).) For Edna Longley the poem is a case of 'excluded lust, chaos and ruin' and the pressures to rebel which bourgeois existence may engender, a generalisation from bohemian disdain to anti-imperialist critique. Certainly, the violent obverse of Protestant mercantilism and its cleanliness and work ethics is a target. (See Longley's brief but suggestive discussion of this poem in E. Longley, 1994: 243–4.) But the new stanza does not simply say this again in plainer terms. At the level of imagery the inoffensive light of the first stanza, 'glittering' and 'lambent' by the fourth, is ironised in stanza five, where its 'paleness' grows threatening, destructive, an Enlightenment rationality whose companion is empire, utilitarian measure and exploitation. If the map, like Protestant Ulster, is backed by 'linen', the light spreads 'like ink or oil', twin liquids which fuel ideological and economic domination over 'nature' (which is the 'natural' inhabitants of expropriated territories and also the colonisers' own human nature, both 'punished . . . in the name of God'). With four stanzas, it is possible to read the poem as endorsing the claim (as made by Longley) that 'the [fourth] stanza's proto-poet signifies how this way of life, this way of art might incubate its opposite: a Munch, a Mahon'. The fifth stanza endorses this, but only in the limited, artist-as-rebel sense; what it also makes clear is the more difficult truth that the dreaming poet and the 'companions' who 'dream of war' are only super-ficially antagonists, products of a division of labour within the same capitalist society, aligning the poet with the specialists of Weber's *The Protestant Ethic and the Spirit of Capitalism*, and implicating art itself in violence, as in 'The Snow Party'.

10 Arthur Rimbaud 'Villes I,' *Les Illuminations*, in Wallace Fowlie (ed. and transl.), *Rimbaud: Complete Works, Selected Letters* (Chicago, University of Chicago Press, 1975), 240. Mahon has of course translated Rimbaud's 'Le Bateau ivre'.

11 The overlap can be seen in the fact that the fifth in Field Day's pamphlet series was Kearney's 'Myth and Motherland'. Field Day's founders and board members included Heaney, Paulin and Deane, as critic-poets, the dramatist Brian Friel, the singer David Hammond and Stephen Rea, a leading Irish actor. It attempted to establish a counter-hegemonic cultural space and, eventually, to reassess the Northern crisis as postcolonial, within the Republic as well as the North. In this, it deliberately conflicted with both traditional Nationalist attitudes in the North and the Republic, and the developing liberalism of the Southern Euro-oriented middle classes (although it found allies in the Republic, like the critic Declan Kiberd, and further afield). The focus of the group, reflecting its attempt to displace critical attitudes into different moulds, was the marginalised city of Derry, 'a symbolic city in the minds of the unionist and the nationalist people', according to Deane (Kirkland, 1996: 132). In a sense, it could be said that the fifth province concept was both the non-hegemonic space of Field Day's various activities and Derry itself: a place severed from the North and the South, origin of revolt in 1968, the one place, if anywhere in Ireland, where it was felt a programmatic rethinking of old paradigms might begin. Ostensibly, in its founding project – the staging of Friel's play *Translations* at Derry's Guildhall in 1980 – Field Day was part of a revival of regional theatre in Ireland, and the main organisational activity of the group was the annual

staging and touring of plays as part of this movement. Field Day soon branched out into print, however, as part of its aim of cultural renewal, issuing five sets of three pamphlets between 1983 and 1988, and culminating with *The Field Day Anthology of Irish Literature*, a 1,500-page three-volume epic compilation, in 1991. Field Day's significance has been extensively debated over the last two decades by, among others, Kirkland, McCormack, Edna Longley, Richards and the board members themselves.

12 At the same time, as O'Donoghue has pointed out, Paulin's political imagination was never confined merely to Ireland; 'States', the opening poem of *A State of Justice*, is pointedly plural and establishes 'an Audenesque *paysage moralisé*, concerned with general problems of affiliation and political restlessness' (O'Donoghue, 1992: 174). Likewise, there are already in these first two collections examples of his drawing on Eastern Europe for analogies with the Northern crisis, most impressively in 'The Other Voice', in which Trotsky and Mandelstam represent the fate of different kinds of idealism in the aftermath of the Russian Revolution. As O'Donoghue notes, 'The most successful, and most anthologised, poem in the book, "Anastasia McLaughlin", explicitly marries the Russian and Irish experiences, making one historical event the matrix of another (like a medieval typologist).' In these poems Paulin extends the kinds of analogies drawn by Mahon with the US Deep South/Algeria in an extension of his 'morally ambiguous' locations which were to become common in the work of others – Heaney, McGuckian, Durcan – in the 1980s.

13 'After the IRA had killed three policemen and burned a mill in Desertmartin, seven Catholics were murdered in reprisal and following the burning of some of their businesses and homes, all the Catholic residents of this Co. Londonderry town were driven out' (Bardon, 1996: 491).

14 Even Seamus Deane noted in his review of *Liberty Tree* that Paulin 'sees Unionism as nothing more than a cargo cult, made up of Union Jack umbrellas, orange sashes, B Specials'. See S. Deane, 'Black Mountain Jacobin', *The Honest Ulsterman* (Winter 1983), 49.

15 Similarly, as Longley would have known, Paulin's definition of Northern poetry as 'kitsch' had not prevented him from praising, in lavish terms, the work of Hewitt, Michael Longley, Heaney, Mahon and Muldoon. This particular interpretation of the 'kitsch' reference comes from Deane's review of *Liberty Tree*, not from Paulin himself. Longley, in Kirkland's words, reads *Liberty Tree* 'not as poetry afflicted by bad politics but as politics itself' (Kirkland, 1996: 194).

16 A more stringent (if still not wholly satisfactory) critique of Paulin's diction is offered by Edward Larrissey:

> Dialect words . . . are a sub-category of the same concern [poetry of the empiricist moment: of the vivid capturing of things seen]: an enlargement of the vocabulary of urbane diction, but sanctioned by the dictionary, and all in the service of exactness. In so far as this [use of dialect words] is a linguistic exoticism, as it clearly is for most of Paulin's readers, it is still safely a matter of precision with individual nouns, verbs and adjectives . . . It is far more acceptable than the kind of exoticism that involves rhetoric or 'abstract nouns': that of John Ashbery, for instance, whose poetry, says Paulin, 'is littered with clichés and lumps of junk diction'. It never occurs to him that all of Ashbery's poems operate within invisible quotation marks, and cannot be seen in terms of the empiricist's idea of language as a nicely-wiped window on the world. They are, rather, pieces of studied interpretation which make knowing use of cliché and banality.

Larrissey underestimates the disruptive effect of Paulin's diction, but correctly identifies his basically empiricist poetic, as well as his fundamental miscomprehension of modernism and postmodernism. See Edward Larrissey, 'Things, Description, and Metaphor in Contemporary British and Irish Poetry', *The Yearbook of English Studies: British Poetry Since 1945 Special Number*, 17, C. J. Rawson (ed.) (London, MHRA 1987), 224.

17 Paulin is as unsympathetic to the work of Irish modernists such as MacGreevy as Longley and, despite Kirkland's assertion that '*Liberty Tree* refuses to privilege the potential of the aesthetic over competing and quotidian historical discourse', the collection pointedly concludes with a utopian lyric voice in 'To the Linen Hall'.

18 See McDonald, who quotes Paulin's observation that 'Otherness . . . can reduce the writer to an entertainer, a media clown', and his comment that this 'is not without its possible relevance to the poet's own media-friendly excursions into stereotypes of the Northern Irish Protestant identity' (McDonald, 1997: 107).

19 It is notable, in the period of the establishment of Field Day and the emergence of Paulin as a polemicist, that Northern Irish poetry was canonised in Motion and Morrison's *Penguin Book of Contemporary British Poetry* (1982). The debates around the anthology were complex, revealing as they did the attempts by metropolitan critics to come to terms not just with Heaney and the 1960s' poets, but the newer figures, including Paulin. There was a degree of resentment at the fact that a quarter of the poets selected were Northern Irish; Michael Hulse, for example, in a review redolent of the terminology of the Prevention of Terrorism Act, complained about the 'fool's licences' being extended to backward-looking, 'mystical' and rural Irish poets. (See M. Hulse, 'An Occasion for Shrieking?', *Critical Quarterly*, 25:3 (1983), 61.) There was a point to be made here about the relationship between ruralist modes and modernisation, but it was generally overlooked. Nevertheless, the Penguin book could be said to set the seal on the triumph of the Northern poets as an insurgent formation within British poetry, for all that Heaney famously demurred at his inclusion in the first Field Day pamphlet, 'An Open Letter' (1983). (Heaney took issue with the word 'British' in the book's title; what is most striking is the poem's mildness and its rather narrow Nationalist symbolic lexicon.) For Motion and Morrison, Heaney played the role of founding uncle, if not father, in the creation of a post-1960s' 'ludic' and narrative sensibility in British poetry. Since this was far better as a description of Muldoon, it revealed just how important the incorporation of Heaney within a redefinition of British poetry had become. Field Day's polemical activities, as this shows, were tied up in the process by which Heaney, and through him Northern poetry generally, was becoming the subject of a 'personality cult', and by which Northern poetry was becoming central to a British poetry in the process of change. Field Day, like Paulin, was – in the words of Friel – partly about getting through to Protestants, and its polemical activities would, after attempting to challenge inherited binaries ('civilian and barbarian', in Deane's pamphlet, for instance), widen their remit to include Protestant voices. But its essentially unitary stance – on language, culture, encapsulated in the concept of the fifth province – meant that it was ultimately to fail. For Longley, this was proof that Field Day's 'locus' was reactionary, 'a visionary Derry awaiting Jacobite restoration' (E. Longley, 1992b: 21). Yet Field Day's reaching out to international contexts reinvigorated cultural debate, even as it was restricted by its broadly neo-Nationalist agenda. Its 'complete cultural ideal', in Paulin's phrase, was at root Nationalist inclusivism, but – as in Heaney's placename poems – an idealist, linguistically centred one. The tension between history and myth remained central and can be traced back to Deane's contributions to *The Crane Bag*. Similarly, although Field Day commissioned pamphlets by Protestants which problematised notions of a monolithic Protestant community, it rejected two commissioned plays which attempted a similar goal. See Shaun Richards, 'To Bind the Northern to the Southern Stars: Field Day in Derry and Dublin', *The Irish Review*, 4 (Spring 1988), 52–8; also 'Field Day's Fifth Province: Avenue or Impasse?' in E. Hughes (ed.), 1991: 139–50.

20 Eavan Boland, 'Poets and Pamphlets', *The Irish Times* (1 October 1983), 12. The publication in 1983 of three pamphlets established the terms of the debate, and were followed by twelve more, in four batches, over five years to 1988. By the mid-1980s Field Day's work had set the terms for the current debate in Irish criticism. The first batch of three pamphlets was concerned with language; the second with notions of tradition, myth and history; the third with the Protestant experience; and the fourth with legal-repressive apparatuses. The final batch, having moved from a synchronic consideration of language towards a limited consideration of history, came from critics outside Ireland altogether: Jameson, Said and Eagleton. With these heavyweight critics, however, the promising earlier move towards historical analysis veered off in a totalising, abstract and almost purely postcolonial direction. (See K. Barry, Far Foreign Field Days, *The Irish Review*, 6 (Spring 1989), 102–4.) The need for such critics to lend authority to the project was in itself, of course, significant. Nevertheless a major virtue of the Field Day pamphlets was that they could contradict each other. If W. J. McCormack was largely correct in predicting that 'despite an air of iconoclasm . . . the company's principal achievement . . . will turn out to be a reformulation for the late twentieth century of an aesthetic already implicit in Yeats', Seamus Deane was correct to claim that Field Day had been able to 'expose the history and function of [the idea that culture alone could capture a universal notion or essence] and to characterise its disfiguring effects' (McCormack, 1986: 58; Deane, 1990: 7).

21 Writing in 1980, Paul Bew, Peter Gibbon and Henry Patterson stated that 'urbanization and modernization have relegated the national question to the margin of Irish politics', in P. Bew, P. Gibbon and H. Patterson, Some Aspects of Nationalism and Socialism in Ireland: 1968–78, in Austen Morgan and Bob Purdie (eds), *Ireland: Divided Nation, Divided Class* (London, Ink Links, 1980), 160. Luke Gibbons, on the other hand, argues that the cultural-political backlash of the 1980s was a *result*, rather than a reaction against, modernisation. The left in the Republic had relied naively on modernisation theory's assertion of a teleological relationship between industrialisation and working-class consciousness to explain the progressive impact that multinational capitalism would have on traditional political allegiances. The conflict between modernisation and 'traditional' Irish values and landscape could be seen in what seemed to be the almost schizophrenic way the country was advertised abroad; by, on the one hand by Bord Fáilte (Ireland as unspoilt rural landscapes), and on the other by the Irish Development Agency (Ireland as 'the most profitable Industrial Location in Europe'). As Gibbons points out, 'the most striking feature of the IDA promotional material' is that it 'magically reconciles' these images in slogans which combine rural beauty with investment incentives (Gibbons, 1996: 82–93).

22 See Tom Garvin: '[I]n a sense the rise of liberal Dublin amounted to an attempted reversal of the cultural consequences of the independence of 1922, and was clearly seen as such. One commentator, Desmond Fennell . . . sees the rise of the liberals as being a stage in the reprovincialisation of Ireland, a process which is turning the Republic back into a mere province of the United Kingdom. The process of making the dreary 1950s an object of ideological nostalgia is well under way. In fact, in the 1950s, Ireland was far more obsessed with London and with Britain generally than it ever has been since' (Garvin, 1988: 5).

23 As Wills's language suggests, the representations she is talking about are inflected by the process of English colonisation in Ireland, traceable in a progressive idealisation of Irish womanhood from the seventeenth century onwards, with the various allegorical identifications of Ireland with female figures – Shan Van Vocht, Cathleen Ní Houlihan or Mother Éire – serving to imprison Irish women as pure and passive, and to type the entire Irish nation as 'feminine' or (by reversal) 'masculine' and warlike. Wills adds 'The motherland trope . . . is like a pin which connects sexual stereotyping with political and cultural domination of the Irish – thus the ways in which the poets are radical in terms of sexual and gender politics bear on issues of imperialism, and definitions of national identity' (Wills, 1993: 56).

24 In Boland's words, '[around 1980] I began writing poems which were perceived as sub-Plath . . . The result was that I was excluded, in some significant ways, from what was the so-called discourse at that time' (Consalvo, 1993: 112).

25 Poetry which tackled hitherto taboo subjects was a sign of the growing confidence of women poets at the beginning of the decade. Boland's *In Her Own Image* (1980), discussed in Chapter 4, was the most prominent of these, but Eithne Strong's *FLESH . . . The Greatest Sin* (1980), seen as 'a female equivalent to *The Great Hunger'*, was equally frank about the subject of female sexuality, while Mary Dorcey's *Kindling* (1982) was the first collection of avowedly lesbian poetry to appear in Ireland. All are examples of what Alicia Ostriker has called the 'release of anatomy' which marks a crucial stage in the advance of women's poetries: 'One of the ways we recognise a poetess – which is to say a woman poet locked into sentimentality by her inhibitions – is that she steers clear of anatomical references. As womanly inhibition declines, we grow aware of its sources in dualistic ideology, gender polarisation and the dread of female sexuality. One of the ways we recognise that a woman has taken some kind of jump is that her muted parts begin to explain themselves' (Haberstroh, 1996: 92).

26 See, for example, Ní Chuilleanáin, 1985; Hooley, 1985; Kelly, 1987; Smythe, 1989b. These cultural and literary anthologies and collections were also matched in the 1980s by individual studies of women's role in the making of the nation and in Irish history generally. Women's presses set up in the 1980s included Attic Press, Arlen Press and Salmon Press (the latter was specifically founded to publish women poets).

27 Although Johnston has, to some extent, amended his omissions in the Afterword to the second edition of *Irish Poetry after Joyce* (1995). The tendency persists, however; recent studies by Kirkland (1996) and McDonald (1997) find no space for McGuckian in their analyses of Northern Irish poetry, while Matthews (1997) confines women's poetry to a subsection of his Introduction.

28 Thus, the speaker of 'Exhibitionist' performs a parodic striptease in her suburban bedroom, mocking the conventions of pornography in order to break out of the 'gimmickry / of sex' into her own 'aesthetic' of autonomy. At the same time she aims revengefully to 'imprison' the male lust which gawps after her 'light that is // unyielding / frigid / constellate' (Boland, 1980: 31–5).

29 In 'Menses' the freedom of the speaker's mind as her body is subjected to the pull of the moon and menstruation is imagined in contrast with the 'ruffian growths' of weeds in her garden. These are envied as being 'to themselves' a 'christening' and 'marriage bed' – that is, subsisting without male agency – and imagined as 'street-walkers, / lesbians, / nuns. / I am not one of them.' The problem here is the stereotypical nature of alternatives being proposed. Again, the potential irony in her later admission that she will later 'moan, / for him [her husband] between the sheets' (the radical feminist contention that marriage is merely a legalised version of being a 'street-walker') is undercut by the polemical nature of the piece,

which would seem to eschew this kind of subtlety (Boland, 1980: 25–7). More to the point, there are no other images of autonomous womanhood. The appeal of the image ('ruffian growths' and 'riff-raff') seems here to have overridden the larger argument; indeed, it might seem that the impingement of class on female solidarity, which Boland elsewhere denies, makes itself felt at the poem's expense.

30 E. Longley, 'From Cathleen to Anorexia: The Breakdown of Irelands', *A Dozen Lips* (Dublin, Attic Press, 1994), 177, 180.

31 One example of this can be seen in Ní Chuilleanáin's assessment of the vulnerability of the gains made by women in the 1970s to attacks in the 1980s. As she explains, advance was partly the outcome of the increase in the marriage rate in the 1960s and after. As a result of this, appeals made on behalf of women's rights were justified through an appeal to the Constitution's declared aim of supporting the institution of marriage and the integrity of the family. What was elsewhere posed as the improvement of women *per se* was often, in the Republic, justified in conservative and patriarchal terms (hence the focus of groups like PLAC on the Constitution) (Ní Chuilleanáin, 1985: 7).

32 J. D. Jump (ed.) *Tennyson: In Memoriam, Maud and Other Poems* (London, Dent, 1985), 44.

33 In making these claims Meaney is extending the useful points she makes about the use of water imagery in Ní Chuilleanáin (as in the claim that for Odysseus 'fear of drowning is a half-welcomed fear of losing identity').

34 As Kerrigan notes, 'even then his/her nature, which shares a transparent elusiveness with its setting, slips from the maleness of the minotaur to the (equally horned) soft-bellied femininity of the slug' (Kerrigan, 1998: 88).

35 P. Williams, *The Honest Ulsterman*, 86 (Spring/Summer 1989), 49–52.

36 McGuckian gives her reasons as being that women are 'much more knowing . . . I'm very simple and more like a man than a woman', 'I feel the male mind is cleaner or sharper – or more receptive to what I have to say' (K. Smith, 1986: 15, 16).

37 Typically, McGuckian herself has said, 'I don't like flowers, or rather I don't know or understand them. They're totally alien creatures . . . They're like women – I'm terrified of women, but fascinated at a distance' (K. Smith, 1986: 18).

38 The 'special guest' is also the child which it is hoped will be conceived at such a 'ceremony' (which has its overtones both of Mahon's Japan and of *Alice in Wonderland*), with 'fontanelle' and 'trout' blending together female and male genitals, foetus and lovers.

39 It could be argued that, if McGuckian's practices are to be aligned with any strand of feminist theory, they have most in common with the ideas of Julia Kristeva. Kristeva stresses the need for female self-assertion and the necessary use of the phrase 'we are women' in the immediate political arena as a slogan for women's demands. But she controversially refuses to define woman as an essential being, arguing that woman as such is unrepresentable; that the belief that one is a woman is nearly as absurd and obscurantist as the belief that one is a man. The claim reflects the attempt to avoid radical feminist essentialism (of the kind associated with Cixous and Irigaray), and the ambivalence resembles McGuckian's. Elsewhere in her work, Kristeva posits a distinction between the symbolic order and the pre-speech 'semiotic' order, within which the child exists before inculcation into linguistic and patriarchal discursivity; one implication of this is that the attempt to define women in language self-defeatingly inscribes them within patriarchy, measuring woman against man in terms of lack and deficiency. Nevertheless, it should be stressed that Kristeva does not, by way of contrast, denote the semiotic as essentially female; rather, it is ungendered. Its important to writing is its persistence as

a form of energy capable of disrupting the Symbolic Order, a disruption Kristeva traces in a series of key modernist texts. Such avant-garde activity is linked to women's discomfort and difficulty with patriarchal language – what, in 'Women's Time', Kristeva calls 'noun + verb; topic-comment; beginning-ending' – in order to suggest a link between earlier modernist practice and the contemporary situation of women at a time in which their estrangement from language has 'begun to dissipate' and allow them to make a connection with the subversive energies of the semiotic. Again, as in McGuckian, Kristeva's writings do not deny the necessity of the symbolic; poetry of the kind McGuckian writes is disruptive of its codes, but accepts that the semiotic and symbolic are interdependent processes; what is undermined is a binary mode of thinking, not male (or female) identity as such, however provisional these may be.

40 As Gerald Dawe has noted, 'Durcan has seen how central to Irish life is the relationship between family life, sexuality and authority . . . many men [submit] in their roles as father and husband, to the mind-forged manacles of convention. In contrast, women represent and embody freedom, rebelling against the feeble conspiracies of male fantasies by living in much closer harmony with their true selves' (Dawe, 1992: 182–3).

41 The extent to which Durcan is at odds with society has been exaggerated, for example by Peter McDonald in a review of *Going Home to Russia* which sourly notes, of a poem on Solzhenitsyn, that 'The prospects of Durcan's receiving such a recall from a repentant Ireland seem as remote as the Russian Glasnost they would presuppose' (McDonald, 1988: 107). However, while Durcan's relationship with the Republic is not unproblematic, he clearly understands, and cultivates, his audience there.

42 The equation of the IRA with Nazism is perhaps the most tendentious aspect of this in Durcan's poetry. Thus in 'The Feast of St Bridget, Friday the First of February 1985', on the IRA shooting of the driver of a bus full of schoolchildren – which opens 'Don't suppose Derrylin will ever be as prestigious as Auschwitz' – the issue is not whether the crime is not despicable and vile (it is) but its linkage to the far greater enormity of the Holocaust, and consequent evasion of historical and political specifics (Durcan, 1995: 28). Nevertheless, such usages must in turn be seen in the context of the belated and incomplete understanding of Nazism in Ireland after World War II discussed elsewhere in this book; in this sense, it can also be read as part of Durcan's purpose of provoking historical awareness (in the later 'Fjord', for example, Durcan addresses his father: 'Look into your Irish heart, you will find a German U-boat, / A periscope in the rain and a swastika in the sky') (Durcan, 1990: 106). In the context of gender relations, there is the gynocidal psychic formation posited in Klaus Theweleit's study of Freikorps psychology, *Male Fantasies*, by which the 'fascist fantasy' 'springs from a dread that (perhaps) lies in the heart of all men, a dread of engulfment by the "other", which is the mother, the sea or even the moist embrace of love . . . [one] implicit in the daily relationships of men and women'. On the other hand it should be noted that Barbara Ehrenreich, in her Foreword to this work, insists that 'It would be a perverse reading of *Male Fantasies*, and a most slovenly syllogism, which leaps to conclude that "all men are fascists" or that fascism and misogyny are somehow "the same thing" . . . The problem is not that any comparison "trivializes" the Holocaust (we need comparisons if we are to inch our way up to some comprehension of the "unthinkable"), but that we need to preserve the singularity of the horrors we seek to understand.' See K. Theweleit, *Male Fantasies: Women, Floods, Bodies, History* (Oxford, Polity Press, 1987), xv. Whether or not these answer to a sense of disparity in Durcan's usages, the sense in which it may be taken as either a sign of or a substitute for the seriousness of his self-examination points back to the problem of the opposition between openness and sacredness in his poetry. For a brilliant discussion of the tendentiousness of the use of Nazi imagery in Sylvia Plath's poetry (and thus linked to Durcan's *Daddy, Daddy*), see Jacqueline Rose, *The Haunting of Sylvia Plath* (Cambridge, Mass., Harvard University Press, 1992).

43 McCarthy himself has commented: 'I do think the more soft-focus poems in . . . *The First Convention* and *The Sorrow Garden* are complete avoidances really of my father and the impact he had on me.' This reinforces the general point; as he adds, '. . . sometimes I blame Fianna Fáil for things I should blame my father for . . . people . . . are surprised that I have more admiration for the Party than appears in the poems. It's because the Party is loaded with guilt that should be my father's' (Geden, 1996: 7).

44 McCarthy has written two of a trilogy of novels concerning power politics in the years since Independence. *Without Power*, for example, opens with the preparations in Fianna Fáil for the 1973 election, in the aftermath of EEC membership, the outbreak of the Troubles and the Arms Trial. Among the subjects treated, and in specific political terms rather than generalities, are the rise of the IRA and the emergence of Conor Cruise O'Brien.

45 Thomas McCarthy, 'Five Summer Afternoons', *Éire-Ireland*, 26:1 (Spring 1991), 8.

46 As David Thornley noted at the time: 'Thirty years ago this was a Party of republicanism, language revival, economic protection: today it is a Party of realism, talks with Captain O'Neill, growth, planning, free trade' (quoted in McCarthy, 1998: 24).

47 Just as Fallon, for example, had used the gentle mysticism of AE as a counter to Yeatsian phallocentrism, so McCarthy, in 'The Wisdom of A.E.', praises him as 'the first to live by the eternal Feminine . . . his deepest vision was that feminine thought / And lack of a killing view' (McCarthy, 1981: 42). McCarthy remembers a preference for AE over Yeats at university 'because I preferred . . . his quiet mysticism to Yeats's political mysticism' (Geden, 1996: 1). Although the essentialism is questionable, McCarthy does not go on from this to elaborate a myth of the feminine in his work, unlike Fallon, Heaney or Montague.

48 Montague had moved to Cork to teach at UCC, where McCarthy studied, in 1973, and was a major influence on younger poets in the city, particularly in his internationalist stance. However, a transference of allegiances occurred from the *Miscellany* poets to the Belfast Group poets in the mid-1970s. McCarthy has written of the effect of the death of Seán Ó Riada in 1971 that it 'had a stunning effect on many of the poets [such as Montague] who were advancing into middle age. They identified with him completely . . . so that they were momentarily drawn into the world of elegy and disappointment . . . A gap opened up between ourselves and our elders. We wanted leaders who would feed us imaginatively and technically. We turned elsewhere, mainly to Ulster poetry, to learn technique' (McCarthy, 1991: 11). 'Ulster poetry was at its zenith' and – McCarthy characteristically blurs literary and socio-economic registers – 'The star of Heaney was rising at this time . . . it was like the rising tide of Lemass's economic programme.' The young poets tried to emulate the Northerners by forming a Hobsbaum-style poetry workshop at UCC; without an 'authority figure', however, this 'soon began to fall apart', confirming a general point about the isolation of writers in the Republic and the inability of a diffuse literary scene to generate a poetic critical mass (McCarthy, 1991: 14). In this sense, Barry's claim that 'it would be tricky to detect [Heaney's] influence on the younger poets of the South' ignores not just his sanction to ruralist-pastoral modes, but also a formal licence (S. Barry, 1986: 21).

49 Although McCarthy opposes what he calls the 'politbureau' of the EU, a

Francophile dimension – not always convincingly – asserts itself in *Seven Winters in Paris* (1989) (Geden, 1996: 4).

50 John Kerrigan's claim for the continuing importance of the local in McCarthy's work – while it has a general force – to this extent misses the anger of his later poetry of the 1980s: 'Wary of full-blown Republicanism because of violence in the North, and troubled by the homogenising globalism which was sweeping McDonald's and Apple Computer Inc. into Munster, many sought "the type of anchoring provided by a sense of place". This resembles the place-centredness found in the poetry of . . . McCarthy – a globally-aware particularity rather different from old-fashioned regionalism. If their localising is influenced by the legacy of Irish Irelandism, it also represents at the level of text-production that specialised reinforcement of the local within a global economy which geographers call glocalisation' (Kerrigan, 1998: 82).

51 By 1995 the PAYE sector contributed 87 per cent of all income tax, with farmers contributing just 1.7 per cent.

52 Run by Dermot Bolger, Raven's authors – among them Ferdia MacAnna, Paula Meehan and Roddy Doyle – were associated with a new writing which asked to be read as 'Dublin's answer to American dirty realism – a kind of "Dirty Dublin Poetic realism"' (MacAnna, 1991: 29). It is in this aggressive urban countercurrent, defined in Bolger's *Invisible Cities: The New Dubliners* (1988), that O'Loughlin can be placed, with his Finglas provenance and punk-influenced poetic. The back-cover blurb of *Stalingrad* encapsulates the Raven Arts rejection of traditionalism: 'It was once said of a book of contemporary Irish poetry that it was a sign made in the name of a tradition. This book is a two fingered salute shoved in the face of that tradition'. The 'book' in question was *The Rough Field*, and the reviewer Heaney; and it is against such reverent and self-congratulatory pieties that such poetry, however crudely, defines itself. (The book's epigraph, from John Berger's *Ways of Seeing*, crystallises its argument – 'Every tradition forbids the asking of certain questions about what has really happened to you'.)

53 One of the most interesting aspects of O'Loughlin's poetry is the way in which it was read. Seamus Deane, for example, praised the force of *Stalingrad*, and Deane's own poetry of impoverished Derry shares concerns with those of O'Loughlin's Finglas (back cover of *Atlantic Blues*). Nevertheless the anti-mythic drive, the absence of Nationalist imperatives and overt socialism of O'Loughlin sit awkwardly beside Deane's elision of socialism within a revived Nationalism and reveal a North–South division over the legacy of 1916. It is precisely a mark of O'Loughlin's originality that – however briefly – his poetry problematises the relationship between myth and politics which preoccupied *Crane Bag* and Field Day at the time by raising the issue of class.

54 If *Mules* marked a major advance for Muldoon, *Why Brownlee Left* can be seen as consolidating it, while *Quoof* (1983) has become one of those collections which Michael Hofmann has deemed 'more like a new religion than a book of poems' (Hofmann, 1990: 18). Against the background of the institutionalisation of the Troubles and the blanket protests and Hunger Strikes, both collections incorporate more of the violence of the crisis than their predecessors, while marking also a technical leap for Muldoon in the evolution of a form of long narrative poem – in 'Immram' and 'The More a Man Has, the More a Man Wants' – which goes beyond the lyric sequence or collage methods of Montague and Heaney and takes the notion of creative and parodic 'translation' to new heights.

55 It might also be argued that this is a typically negative, Muldoonian twist to the 'self-involved simile'; rather than confirming self-groundedness, the trope in his hands is a form of word-play which leads to self-erasure.

56 Perhaps most disturbingly, the title poem hints that we read the objectification of women involved back into the poet's childhood (as Wills notes, one of *Quoof*'s most disturbing aspects is its juxtaposition of apparently wistful, even nostalgic childhood poems – centred particularly on Muldoon's father – cheek by jowl with violent ones) (Wills, 1998: 87).

57 Talking horses recur in *Madoc*; they also recall Swift's Houyhnhnms and the 'Stoned Horse' of Ed Dorn's postmodern, surrealised Western epic poem *Gunslinger* (1975), who smokes enormous joints known as Tampico Bombers. Indeed, Dorn's poem has points of contact with a number of Muldoon's. As in 'Immram', the quest of the eponymous central character is for a Howard Hughes-like figure. The drug-influenced narrative of 'The More a Man Has' recalls *Gunslinger*'s division into books devoted respectively to marijuana, LSD and cocaine (twice); more profoundly, Dorn's book uses drugs as a means for troping the psychological problems of the USA during the Vietnam War, just as Muldoon's does for the Troubles. A major aim of *Gunslinger* is to force the reader to question received linguistic and literary habits (recalling Muldoon's desire to 'purge' himself of media-speak). In addition, the philosophical concerns of Dorn's work are echoed in *Madoc*; if Muldoon's poem queries Western metaphysical narratives, *Gunslinger* alludes to Heidegger (announced in the greeting 'Hi! Digger'), Lévi-Strauss, Parmenides and others as it plays with, and deconstructs, Cartesian rationalism. Muldoon has claimed to have read *Gunslinger*, 'though I don't remember it well' (Keller, 1994: 21). The point here is not that *Gunslinger* is some kind of Muldoon *ur*-text, since there are radical differences between it and his work; rather, it is to note other US influences on him than those usually adduced (Frost, Chandler) and the critical failure to note them. See E. Dorn, *Gunslinger* (Durham and London, Duke University Press, 1989).

58 Behind the Father Christmas tale is said to lie the red and white colour of the fly agaric mushroom the nomads eat, and the way that those living in tents erected during the seasonal migrations following the reindeer herds entered their makeshift turf-built dwellings through the smoke hole in the roof.

59 Feldman notes (1991: 227):

> The Blanketmen saw their passage through the disciplinary machinery of the prison as a journey to the inner truth of the British state. The prison system for them encapsulated a wider colonial power which had imprinted discourses of domination upon their bodies. There was a semantic and historical equivalence between the colonization of Ireland and the colonization of the Blanketmen's bodies. In their view, they had lived through a reenactment of the relation of domination that characterized Britain's historical relationship to Ireland. And they had reversed the historical trajectory . . . The history of their passage through discipline and punishment had to be externalized and dramatized beyond prison space. This could only be accomplished through the exiting of emblematic bodies from that place and the resultant release of historical codes.

60 As in 'Immram', Muldoon is again parodically rewriting or 'translating' an original, Radin's translation of the Winnebago Native American Trickster myth, this time mixed with an even wider variety of heterogeneous material – *Alice in Wonderland*, Edgar Allan Poe, Jung, *Kidnapped*, Chuck Berry, Yogi Bear and many others. The poem is metamorphic in the most basic sense – Gallogly changes into a bear and a mole among other creatures – and violence operates at a cartoon-like level (after being shot in the chest with a double-barrelled shotgun, at one point, Gallogly manages to recover). The poem is written in forty-nine fourteen-line stanzas, or 'crumbled sonnets' as they have been called, and so represents a meta-morphosis of constraint at the formalist level too, even mimicking at one point a hunger striker's wasted body in a verse of one-word lines.

61 Corcoran claims that 'The reader's delight is all in the trickery. These poems run rings around us, wrong foot us and outwit us; they invite us, and entice us, to catch up with them . . . I have read and re-read "Yggdrasil" to the point of memorizing it . . . and I have my ideas about how its fluid images may be thought to maintain some vague congruity, but I have no confidence whatever that this would correspond with what anyone else might construct from the poem' (The Shy Trickster, *Times Literary Supplement*, 28 October 1983, 1180).

62 John Mitchel, *Jail Journal* (London, Sphere Books, 1983), 342.

63 Muldoon's fetishisation of the sonnet form was of a piece with the nature of his transformation of the confining strategies inherited from his predecessors. Like a number of the trapped figures in *Brownlee* and *Quoof*, Muldoon's use of the sonnet echoes the attempt to escape from, and the inevitability of repeating, the past. Although, in one sense, nothing so exemplifies the faith in 'ancient packing' valorised by Edna Longley, in another it shows how Muldoon deployed the sonnet and the sonnet-sequence as a battering ram against that inheritance, breaking with form through form by intensifying, rather than relaxing, formal constraints. The claim that the political message of 'The More a Man Has' 'remains, above all, its metamorphic medium' sidesteps the historical issues involved in those of form ('above all' revealingly rendering the 'metamorphic' autotelic and limiting its subversive charge) (Longley, 1986: 210). There is an almost mathematical progression in the incidence of sonnets in Muldoon's work, which builds to a high point in the early 1980s; *Mules* has sixteen (of forty poems); *Why Brownlee Left* has nine (of twenty-seven); *Quoof* fifteen (also of twenty-seven), together with the forty-nine 'imploded' sonnets of 'The More a Man Has'; and *Meeting the British* seven (of twenty-three). So pervasive are they that other lyric forms appear, in context, to be trace particles produced by Muldoon's bombardment of the sonnet form. One reason for this is certainly the traditionally erotic-political content of the sonnet in its Petrarchan origins. The sonnet found definitive form in Sidney's *Astrophel and Stella* of 1591, which inaugurated a decade in which it was the dominant lyric form in English. The same decade of the 1590s was also that of the Nine Years War, bloodily conducted by the English against O'Neill and the Irish population in Ulster. This was followed by more thorough plantation than anywhere else in Ireland, laying the basis for the unique strength of the crown's presence there. It is in this historical coincidence that one source of Muldoon's choice of form surely lies. Yet although this recalls Heaney's allusions to Spenser, Sir John Davies and Raleigh, Muldoon is not interested simply in highlighting, in a humanistic way, the 'contradiction' between imperial aggression and the civility of Elizabethan lyric. Rather, in a more radical sense, he deconstructs that tradition at its most intimate formal level, availing himself of the way the themes of the sixteenth-century sonnet coincide with his own attack on religious and familial definitions of sexuality.

English Petrarchanism was a self-centred masculine discourse adapted to the pursuit of patronage and in negotiating the power struggles of the Elizabethan court. The fetishisation and figurative dismemberment of the woman/patron addressee, the self-torturing obsession with the 'icy fire' of love, were, as Stephen Greenblatt, Gary Waller and others have argued, nearly always sublimated rhetorical strategies in a struggle for personal advancement. If Heaney sought to appeal to integration within the English tradition in the 'Glanmore Sonnets', Muldoon – cutting eroticism free from land-love and Mariology – sets up a tension between strict erotic decorum and an often brutal sexual content in destabilising literary-political norms. Androgyny and sexual role reversal mimic those found in Shakespeare's *Sonnets*, for example, and various poems (not always sonnets) detail more deviant and deadly sexual practices. In the fragmented sonnet 'from *Last Poems*' Muldoon pushes Petrarchan tropes of dismemberment and erotic cannibalism to comic-horror extremes when the speaker proposes to eat his ex-lover's womb 'like the last beetroot in the pickle jar', together with 'my own lightly-broiled heart on the side' (Muldoon, 1983: 31). Such perverse sexuality prevents easy assimilation to the English tradition and continues Muldoon's pursuit of a poetry which is not centrally concerned with consolation.

This carries a cost of course. As the debates around 'Aisling' in particular have shown, the dubious sexual politics of the Elizabethan sonnet – a male discourse which silences as it idealises women – carries over into Muldoon's poetry. Nevertheless in his use, and implosion, of the sonnet, Muldoon is also politicising form in a manner which is implicit in that metamorphic form which critics insist is the true political (i.e. 'evasive') content of his poetry. For if 'we find the impress of history in the literary work precisely as literary, not as some superior form of documentation', as Terry Eagleton has argued, it is surely not the least of the ironies of *Quoof* that its critics have generally failed to recognise the way in which the supremely arbitrary and (seemingly) anachronistic, continually collapsing yet always-re-adaptable sonnet formally metaphorises the state – in both senses – of Northern Ireland after 1968/69 (Goodby, 1994; Eagleton, 1992: 5).

64 The outstanding Irish poets of the previous revival of Irish-language poetry in the 1950s had, as Ní Dhomhnaill put it, 'dragged Irish poetry kicking and screaming into the 20th century', but their work had remained set, physically and imaginatively, in Ireland itself. There was virtually no interaction between them and English-language Irish poets (as Kinsella had noted in 1965), and little exchange with poetry abroad (Ní Dhomhnaill, 1992b: 25). As Peter Denman has noted, 'they found their resource in the sense of a linguistic community rather than of a literary community' (Denman, 1992: 252).

65 As Dermot Bolger has pointed out, one of the principal reasons why younger, urban poets matched Irish-language poetry's isolationism with their own rejection was because, before the 1970s and 1980s, the language was seen as one of officialdom and tokenism, deployed to 'hem us within an idea of nationhood which simply could not contain the Ireland of concrete and dual carriageways (which is as Irish as turf and boreens) that was the reality before our eyes' (Bolger, 1986: 10).

66 Ní Dhomhnaill's translators include Seamus Heaney, John Montague, Derek Mahon, Michael Longley, Ciaran Carson, Medbh McGuckian and Eiléan Ní Chuilleanáin as well as Hartnett and Muldoon.

67 It is noticeable that pre-*Innti* poets engaging in translation from Irish did not tackle twentieth-century material; Kinsella's *The Táin*, Hartnett's 'The Hag of Beare' and Heaney's *Sweeney Astray*, for example, returned to the more or less distant past, invariably lending the poet's efforts a dated aspect.

68 The rendering of what Hartnett translates as simply 'The Tree' as a quince tree is one among several intertextual jokes played by Muldoon (presumably with Ní Dhomhnaill's consent); it seems to be a reference to 'the quince-tree I forgot to mention' from 'Lunch with Pancho Villa' in *Mules*.

69 Brion Nic Dhiarmada, in a review in the *Irish Literary Supplement*, notes Muldoon as a 'promising' choice of translator in *The Astrakhan Cloak*, but adds:

In his previous contacts with Ní Dhomhnaill's work, Muldoon didn't so much translate the poems as re-imagine them. That same tendency is also much in evidence in this collection. Indeed the title of the present volume could serve as a benchmark for Muldoon's style of translation in general. The reader will search in vain for a poem of that name, or its Irish equivalent, in the work of Ní Dhomhnaill. It comes in fact from Muldoon's version of a line from the poem 'Deora Duibhshléibhe'/'Dora Dooley.' Ní Dhomhnaill's 'faoi chlóca uaithne' which translates literally as 'under a green cloak,' becomes, in Muldoon's poem, 'with the cloak of green astrakhan' from which he takes the book's title [and] which also serves as a pun on the Irish word 'aistriúchán,' which of course means 'translation'! (Quoted in Haber-stroh, 1996: 189–90)

The mixture of different registers and discourses in Ní Dhomhnaill's poetry makes the translator's task a difficult one, however s/he approaches it: as Angela Bourke notes of Michael Hartnett's translations in *Rogha Dánta/Selected Poems*,

in . . . poems which refer back and forth from Early Irish saga to modern feminism, or from the Sphinx to an Irish Purgatory legend, he follows less surely, so that in 'Cú Chulainn I,' the distinctive 'womanness' of the poet's voice and the withering tolerance of the original are all but lost . . . In other cases a straightforward idea in the original becomes obscure in translation. In ['Cú Chulainn I'] Cú Chulainn in Irish is told he has a chip on his shoulder. In English, however, he mysteriously 'lacks a lump' on it, and in another poem of the same series, where the Great Queen taunts him with his fear of her vagina dentata, she mentions 'cíor mhaith . . . chun do mheilte' (a good set of teeth to grind you), but Hartnett takes *cíor*, a row of teeth, to refer to a comb. (Angela Bourke, Rich, Colorful and Sensuous, *Irish Literary Supplement* (Spring 1989), 18.

As this shows, it is not only linguistic competence but also the gender (and generation) of Ní Dhomhnaill's translators which can affect the perception of her work in English, and point to the dangers inherent in the strategy of extensive translation.

70 In 'An Cuaiteoir'/'The Visitor', the speaker (a contemporary woman but linked with the Great Queen) is transformed by Christ's embrace from sensually welcoming woman into the Virgin Mary. What women are condemned for is their sensuality, which is suppressed in the process of turning them into the asexual handmaiden and helpmeet symbolised (but in unattainable fashion) by the Virgin. Ní Dhomhnaill also frames the Christian creation and virgin birth myths within those of Irish folklore and mythology in order to reimagine creation in female, as well as male, terms.

71 Similarly, the comment of another contemporary woman Irish-language poet, Biddy Jenkinson, on Mhac an tSaoi's claim that to write poetry in Irish is a sort of ancestor worship enabling the word to 'survive the shipwreck of the way of life from which it sprung' points up the difference between the sea-change in attitudes on this issue among Irish women poets of the different generations: 'We are marginalised by a comfortable monoglot community that would prefer we went away rather than hassle about rights' (Denman, 1992: 258).

72 Ní Dhomhnaill's attitude to the use of myth has much in common with Richard Kearney's reading of myth as either atavistic or utopian; of the former she notes that 'in the absence of direction by a responsible intelligentsia, this permeability of

the collective ego-boundaries can be manoeuvred and choreographed to very dubious purposes. The moving statues are a case in point. So too is the recent procession through the streets of Dublin of the image of Our Lady of Guadaloupe, on which, or so it was widely noised abroad, rose petals descended, (Presumably from whatever level of the stratosphere that Heaven keeps them conveniently frozen)' (Ní Dhomhnaill, 1992b: 29).

Out of Ireland?

Twilights, ceasefires, Celtic tigers

In 1988 the Northern Irish critic Tom Clyde published an essay entitled 'An Ulster Twilight?' in the journal *Krino*. Claiming that 'We are seeing the dying days of that remarkable twenty-year period of intense poetic activity in the North of Ireland' – sealed by the death of John Hewitt and the departure of Muldoon for the USA the year before – Clyde gloomily detected important poetic activity in the North in the work of Medbh McGuckian alone. Speaking positively of what he calls its 'many different traditions', his definition of Northern Irish poetry is nevertheless a residential one. Contradictorily, however, Clyde's essay later attacks precisely the 'atavistic' and 'bardic' appeal found in Montague's *The Rough Field* and Heaney's *North* as in some way responsible for the poetic decline he deplores.[1] The point is not that Clyde was wrong about 'dying days' (although he writes just a few months before the appearance of Ciaran Carson's *The Irish for No*, the most spectacular poetic resurrection since Clarke's in 1955), but the incompatibility of 'different traditions' with a definition of the 'Irish' poet by location. For – as Irish history all too strikingly illustrates – one major, if unexplored 'tradition' in Irish writing has been of *dis*location, of diaspora and (in older terminology) emigrant writing.[2] Moreover, the latest diasporic trends – augmented by the return of mass emigration in the 1980s and accelerated by economic globalisation in the 1990s – have arguably reconfigured the terms on which poets relate to Ireland, either beyond or from within it. This in turn has meant that the poetry of recent years has shared in the general proliferation of diasporic and axial modes of cultural production thriving on multi-locatedness and challenging traditional notions of allegiance, identity and belonging.[3] At the same time, the way in which this has affected poets like Heaney, Longley and Mahon has been limited. Indeed, although Clyde's point may seem unfair to Heaney, whose post-*North* poetry shows a shift away from the archaeological tropes and rootedness of the early work, there is an important sense in which it holds good. For despite Heaney's turn to a poetry of air and light in *The Haw Lantern* (1987) and *Seeing Things* (1991), it can be argued with some justice that he nevertheless renews in this work the vatic claim of the poet to moral authority, albeit now as outsider (rather than as communal speaker). This is made particularly clear in his critical writing in *The Government of the Tongue* (1988) and *The Redress of Poetry* (1995) in which the assuaging power of art is force-fully asserted and, as Edna Longley suggests, the communal may be insinuated in disguised form as a kind of priestly-aesthetic authority (E. Longley, 1992a: 69). Heaney's assertion of the moral claims of the poet is partly conveyed by drawing analogies between Eastern Europe and Ireland (and through the use of Eastern European poetic parabolic strategies), and in the criticism through an invocation of Mandelstam as exemplary.[4] Likewise, Michael Longley's work – remarkably renewed in 1991 with *Gorse Fires* after a twelve-year silence – draws on analogies with Homeric legend and the Holocaust, while Derek Mahon's similarly self-renewing *The Hudson Letter* (1995) is set in the USA and concerns itself with the condition of homelessness. To a large extent these geographical (and to some extent historical) displacements have thus served to extend, rather than break with, the core concerns – of responsibility, home, alienation, community – which marked their earlier work. For younger poets, however, an already existing scepticism towards such terms within the Irish context permitted a fuller acceptance of displacement, which informed the aesthetic stances and formal strategies of their poetry in correspondingly more radical fashion. 'Globalisation', of course, tends to be defined in terms of 'globalisation from above' – more of the same commercial products everywhere, the dominance of corporate culture and of English (usually American English) as a world language. Yet it is possible to discern, in the work of writers and cultural agents working between cultures, the emergence of what might be called a 'globalisation from below' which resists these trends, one whose driving force is culture-crossing by individuals and grassroots networks and which – in its creative and non-defensive acceptance of the permeability of cultures – is to be distinguished from earlier attempts to square the circle of the local and the international defined as 'global regionalism' or 'glocalisation'.[5]

The dispersals and redefinitions, together with the economic, social and political changes in Ireland during the 1990s and earlier, ultimately demand to be read within the context of the globalisation of politics and economies. Changes in the North have been largely political, and have followed in the wake of the Anglo-Irish Agreement of 1985. The decision in 1987 by the Unionist parties to work against the Agreement politically – after opposing it until then through a campaign of civil disobedience – as well as the continuing containment of republican violence by the British state, led to the agonisingly drawn-out peace process. This involved the Downing Street Declaration of 1993 by the British and Irish governments, and the subsequent Framework Documents of 1995. The first was 'a document of considerable originality and sophistication', formalising the lack of a 'selfish strategic or economic interest' in Northern Ireland by the British government; the general tenor of both, in a modification of earlier discussions between John Hume, the SDLP leader, and Gerry Adams of Sinn Féin, was that the British government would increase its role as a 'facilitator' not for Irish unity as such but for an 'agreed'

Ireland, that is, one conditional on majority consent in the North (Bew, Gibbon and Patterson, 1996: 229). The moves led to the IRA ceasefires of 1994 (broken in 1996) and 1997 and, finally, to the Good Friday Agreement of 1998. During the period, the operations of the British state were coming under increased scrutiny – with the Stalker Inquiry into an alleged 'shoot-to-kill' policy, for example, raising enormous suspicion in Britain concerning the operations of state forces and a subsequent cover-up – resulting in the overturning of notable miscarriages of justice, including the convictions of the Guildford Four and the Birmingham Six. In a sense, these events also reflected an increased British flexibility and self-scrutiny on the larger issues surrounding the North. At the same time, the election of David Trimble as leader of the Ulster Unionist Party in 1995 saw the birth of a more proactive, articulate Unionism.[6]

The Good Friday Agreement itself was notable for its involvement of US mediation and political change in the Republic as well as in Northern Ireland, since perhaps the most crucial precondition for Unionist acceptance of the proposed devolved assembly was the elimination of Articles 2 and 3 of the 1937 Constitution claiming jurisdiction over the six Northern counties. The ceasefire and attempts to construct a new civil order in the North were related, in the larger scale of things, to a blurring of ideological oppositions internationally which followed the end of the cold war in 1989–91. (This blurring had its effects on other long-standing internecine conflicts such as those in Palestine and Southern Africa.) In the Republic a partial recovery of the project of liberalising society can be discerned throughout the 1990s, symbolised most tellingly by the election of Mary Robinson, the Republic's first woman President, in 1990.[7] The general tendency towards secularisation which had begun under Lemass was resumed, leading to the legalisation of divorce in a (barely won) referendum in 1996 and to some relaxation of other restrictions. At the same time, a series of child and sex abuse scandals shook the Church and undermined its authority. Paradoxically, one result of such changes has been the outflanking of those poets whose work relied in the 1970s and 1980s on attacking the Church and official discourses on Irishness (which included a sense of national denial concerning responsibility for the North). Paul Durcan's *Going Home to Russia* (1987) for example – predicated on the notion that while the largest totalitarian regime on the planet was opening itself up to reform the Republic remained locked in its own form of authoritarianism – would seem curiously dated within just a few years of its publication; this may be one reason why Durcan's most recent work (from *Daddy, Daddy* onwards) returns to Ireland and a personal past, abandoning such analogies.[8]

If the semi-solution to the Troubles was in part due to their being approached in an international framework, the Republic over the same period confirmed its orientation towards the European Union and transnational capital. A spectacular expansion of the economy from the early 1990s seemed to justify this outward-looking stance, and led to the application of the term

'Celtic Tiger' by analogy with the economies of the Far East and Pacific Rim. Between 1994 and 1997, for example, export growth at 15.3 per cent was the third highest in the twenty-nine-member OECD, making the Republic the third largest (non-oil) exporter on a per capita basis in the world and the eleventh most competitive economy globally by 1998, ahead of both the UK and Japan.[9] 'Celtic Tiger' demands cautious appraisal, however, in the light of the fact that it first entered the public domain on 31 August 1994, the same day – uncoincidentally – as the IRA ceasefire. Ireland as 'Celtic Tiger' can be taken to signify, among other things, a new metaphor around which a national consensus, of the kind sought in the 1980s by FitzGerald, could be constructed on grounds favourable to the state and business interests. It is important to bear this in mind, since the economic growth referred to has been of a very specific kind and has had limited beneficial effects as far as a majority of the population are concerned. Although, as in the 1960s, economic growth slowed the mass emigration, it also revealed the Republic to be increasingly an assembly economy exploited by transnational corporations for its cheap skilled labour, low corporation tax and proximity to the European heartland. Statistics show a reality of vulnerable development, low wages and continuing poor social provision and reliance on emigration.[10]

The changes associated with shifts in the general cultural climate since the 1960s have been described as falling broadly within the area of the postmodern. In artistic terms the postmodern is variously taken to signify a (non-linear) shift from a concern with depth and authenticity to surface and playfulness, from structure to eclecticism, from parody to pastiche and from epistemology to ontology among other things, although the defining elements are fiercely disputed and apply differently (and with different aesthetic and political implications) to different cultural forms (architecture as opposed to film, for example) and different national cultures.[11] In identifying 'the postmodern' here, the intention is not to endorse its claims as a cultural mode of production distinct from that of modernism (which postmodernism's advocates homogenise and travesty); rather, the more modest aim is to identify it as a prevailing metadiscourse which has academic currency as a period marker.[12] Within such a limited definition of its usefulness, however, it is worth noting the renewed emphasis within postmodern discourses on local cultures. The interstitial nature of Irish culture – the result of very partial involvement in the grand narratives of the Enlightenment and the industrial revolution – complicates any straightforward postmodern reading of the Irish situation.[13] One of the ways that this has been mediated in the Irish context can be seen in the recent burgeoning of postcolonial readings of Irish culture. Certainly, the moments of the postmodern and the postcolonial can be said to coincide. In Irish Studies, however, the latter is frequently mobilised merely to reinscribe those older paradigms (of Nationalism, Unionism, etc.) which the former would deconstruct. The problems of such accounts lie chiefly in their reductiveness; of comparing Irish literature to that, say, of decolonising Africa, as totally conditioned by the struggle against colonialism and decolonisation.[14] This is not to suggest that postcolonial paradigms are wholly inapplicable, of course. As Colin Graham has recently shown, postcolonial theory can usefully fragment and disintegrate the monologism of cultural affiliation through concepts such as mimicry and hybridity 'out of a recognition of the claustrophobic intensity of the relationship between Ireland and Britain'.[15] This, in turn, bears on the legitimacy of models drawn from English, Irish and other literary traditions (visible in a debate on canonical issues in the 'anthology wars'), and in continuing uncertainties over the use of the English language in Irish poetry.[16]

The institutional background to such debates is also worth noting, since the quantitative increase in the rate and volume of international cultural traffic over the period, and the political initiatives in Northern Ireland, suggest that qualitatively different strategies for negotiating the gap between the global and the local have emerged. In Northern Ireland, on the one hand, since the mid-1980s, the Northern Ireland Office has 'gone cultural', developing through a Central Community Relations Unit a series of initiatives such as the 'Varieties of Irishness' conference of 1989, and attempting to promote the 'two cultures' deemed to exist in the province on a footing of parity and mutual respect (Alan Finlayson has argued that this has unwittingly endorsed the exclusivist aspects of those cultures it aims to bring together by refusing to interrogate the notion of cultural identity as such)[17] (Finlayson, 1997; McDonald, 1997: 1–4). In the Republic, conversely, there has been a move away from fixed notions of Irish culture to some registration of new possibilities. (Perhaps the best symbol of this in the 1990s was Irish soccer. Once seen as a non-Irish sport, the success of the Republic's international team – half-Irish and half-English and with an English manager for most of the 1990s – was taken to represent the acceptance of a more plural definition of Irishness.) At government level there has been a *laissez-faire*, non-directional approach to Irish cultural matters since the 1960s (Ruane and Todd, 1996: 237). Beyond this, the formulation of a 'new nationalism' voiced in the Forum for a New Ireland of 1983–84 has taken more concrete form in the idea of a 'migrant nation' through the overcoming of the stigma of emigration produced by increased national self-confidence in the Republic. As Richard Kearney puts it, 'If over seventy million people in the world today claim to be of Irish descent, it is evident that this [migrant] definition of nationality . . . extends far beyond the borders of a state or territory. Irish-Americans, Irish-Australians or Irish-Britons, for example, can affirm a strong sense of national allegiance to their "land of origin" even though they may be three or four generations from that land and frequently of mixed ethnicity . . . Mary Robinson [appealed to this sense] when she came to office in 1992–3' (Kearney, 1997: 5). Recent poetry reveals these forces at work, with, at the very least, renewed attempts to expand or even jettison paradigms forged in the struggles for cultural self-definition of the previous *fin de siècle* period.

Postcolonial Paulin

One of the most provocative applications of the term 'postcolonial' has been to Loyalists by John Wilson Foster. Foster's claim, in 'The Critical Condition of Ulster', an essay written on the eve of the Anglo-Irish Agreement, was that the condition of Northern Protestants within their state differed in significant respects from that of the coloniser as outlined by a postcolonial theorist like Albert Memmi; that is, that they had never been able to feel secure in their privileges: 'Irredentism was a constitutional fact and often more than that. The Ulster Protestant, feeling the perpetual threat of being taken over, already experiences in some sense, and exhibits the symptoms of, *the condition of being colonised*. His (sic) legendary intransigence is the anticipation of a calamity' (J. W. Foster, 1991: 271). This argument – while it fails to define the stark difference between settler and colonial experiences of being 'colonised' – hints at complexities in the Protestant position which have too often been overlooked. This ressentiment, for which Foster perhaps acts as something of an apologist, is complexly and imaginatively explored (rather than simply accepted) in Tom Paulin's *Fivemiletown* (1987).[18] The book explores what it is to have a hyper-British identity and yet hate the English, to possess a frontier-state sense of loyalty now chronically out of kilter with a more liberal and multicultural parent society. Although the Anglo-Irish Agreement signed on 15 November 1985 contained clauses guaranteeing the right of a majority in the North to determine which state they would belong to, it made provision for an Intergovernmental Conference, headed by the British secretary of state and the Republic's foreign minister designed to promote cross-border cooperation and was instituted without consultation with the Unionist parties in a move to break the impasse they had imposed on negotiations which had begun after the New Ireland Forum of 1983–84. The sense of betrayal at lack of consultation was memorably expressed in the speech to Parliament by the Official Unionist MP Harold McCusker twelve days afterwards: 'I went to Hillsborough on the Friday morning . . . I stood outside . . . not waving a Union flag – I doubt whether I will ever wave one again – not singing hymns, saying prayers or protesting, but like a dog and asked the Government to put in my hand the document that sold my birthright . . . I felt desolate because as I stood in the cold outside Hillsborough castle everything that I held dear turned to ashes in my mouth' (Bardon, 1996: 757). McCusker's shock, alienation and self-pity is echoed in 'An Ulster Unionist Walks the Streets of London' ('I waited outside the gate-lodge / waited like a dog / in my own province'), which imagines its speaker walking through London 'like a half-foreigner / among the London Irish. / What does it feel like? / I wanted to ask them – / what does it feel like / to be a child of that nation?' (Paulin, 1987: 42). The political predicament of Unionists is further probed and articulated in 'The Defenestration of Hillsborough' and 'The Red Handshake'; in the latter, the speaker considers seeking Protestant identity by scraping the earth 'from off that ridge

where the Third Force / melted out of *The Tain*', only to discover the parodically name 'Bowden Beggs' wrapped in black plastic 'and breathing, "Mind,
it can get no worse"' (Paulin, 1987: 4). Apocalyptic response, pathetic anticlimax and dour vernacular understatedness come together as Paulin juggles
stereotypes, emphasising the importance to Protestant identity and politics of
personal testimony and biblical analogy (thus, the title of a piece like 'The
House of Jacob from a People of Strange Language' refers to the notion of
Ulster Protestants as the lost tribe of Israel).

In extending the nexus of references generally taken to make up an Ulster
Protestant sense of identity, Paulin both casts his net beyond Northern Ireland
(far more widely than a comparably mythicising poet of Nationalist background, such as Heaney), and personalises the exploration of Protestant identity, often in a specifically sexual manner. The formal properties of many of
the poems – unpunctuated, irregularly lined – are more disrupted and spare
than in *Liberty Tree* (and it is perhaps significant that while Paulin, like Heaney,
McGuckian, Durcan and others, is fascinated by Eastern European poetry, it is
at least as much as a confirmation of directness of style as of moral authority).[19] The very extremism and range of *Fivemiletown* shows Paulin to be dramatising what he sees as the lack of Protestant mythology and history. In *Ireland
and the English Crisis*, Paulin had noted that 'The community possesses very
little in the way of an indigenous cultural tradition of its own . . . the result is
an unusually fragmented culture . . . A provincialism of the most disabling
kind' (Paulin, 1984: 17). The identitarianism lurking behind 'community', 'tradition', 'culture' and 'provincialism' reveals an assumption that Loyalism is an
impoverished Nationalism, and within identitarian categories – but the decision to be made in reading the poetry is the extent to which such sentimental and idealist conceptions are offset by its formal disruptiveness.

For Paulin, the Anglo-Irish Agreement poses Ulster Unionists with the
choice (also dramatised in his play *The Hillsborough Script* of 1987), of 'either
to jump or get pushed', as the close of 'The Defenestration of Hillsborough'
puts it (Paulin, 1987: 54). Again, this is a reworking of the words of a Unionist politician, and his reference to the Defenestration of Prague in 1618 which
began the Thirty Years War (between Catholic and Protestant powers), and
Paulin returns to the phrase 'We've been put out on the window-ledge' in his
introduction to his second collection of essays, *Minotaur* (1992: 16). The poems
of *Fivemiletown* suggest the way in which this larger European context is incul-
cated through a Northern Irish education, with its emphasis on a Protestant
history. Paulin notes in *Minotaur* that 'I studied the . . . Thirty Years War within
the Northern Irish system of state education . . . with hindsight I can see that
the school syllabus was designed to reinforce a Protestant identity and to sub-
merge the Catholic population of the province within those values', and the
poems also draw on other manifestations of a distinct Protestant inheritance
in 'Jefferson's Virginia', 'Symbolum' (a version of a poem on the Masons
by Goethe), and versions of poems by North European outsider writers,

Strindberg ('From Landsflykt') and Heine ('Chucking it Away') (Paulin, 1992: 16). Any critique thus implicates Paulin himself, and complicates the investigation of identity, particularly at the level of sexual allegory at which several of the poems operate. 'Waftage: An Irregular Ode' takes an adolescent sexual encounter which ends when the narrator buys as a gift 'this tin / of panties coloured / like the Union Jack'. '[Slinging]' these 'in the bin', the girlfriend rejects the speaker in terms which partake of the British distaste for Ulster Protestants:

> 'I just can't stand you.
> No one can.
> Your breath stinks
> and your taste
> it's simply foul –
> like that accent . . .'
>   (Paulin, 1987: 7–8)

At this point the narrator – presenting himself unconvincingly as 'real cool' – 'chucked her'. The predicament mirrors that of the Unionist politicians – to be pushed or to jump? – and, while mocking him, the poem presents the betrayed speaker as one who does 'jump' from the window-ledge he finds himself on. As McDonald notes, 'the loyalist mind, presented with a fait accompli as its political future from London and Dublin, has either to leap into new thinking or be forced there. Paulin differs from British and Irish politicians in seeing this act as something different from obeisance or humiliation . . . One side pushes, the other defiantly jumps: something similar happens in "Sure I'm a Cheat Aren't We All?"'[20]

Throughout *Fivemiletown* Paulin messily complicates the relationship between the political and the personal, between Protestantism's claim to a monopoly on Enlightenment rationalism and its irrational obstinacy. Indeed, in excavating the mythic aspects of Protestant identity he finds fewer signs of civility than in *Liberty Tree*, with its idealist vision of 1798 and the United Irishmen. Protestantism's claim to establish a sphere where private pleasure might flourish without being subject to the demands of the familial and tribal is considered in 'Now For the Orange Card' which begins as a conceit on the similarity between the British Safety sign on a condom packet (thus linking Protestantism with sexual pleasure disjoined from pregnancy and family). Yet its description as 'a french letter – / enlightened, protestant, / and *juste*' declines swiftly into a recognition of the brutality of male power over women ('a signet ring / on a butcher's finger') which provokes a decision to 'go down into the ground / like Achilles'.[21] Contraception is associated with the death of the 'natural', as it would be in Catholic teaching, Wills points out, and Achilles is seen as a 'pushy jerk'. The admission at the end of the poem – 'what nature is / and what's natural, / I can never tell just now' – indicates the larger confusion in *Fivemiletown* of the desire for the 'natural' and a commitment to the political and public[22] (Paulin, 1987: 10–11; Wills, 1993: 145). This is figured in the discovery of the energy of Dissenting traditions in their extreme paramilitary or Paisleyite aspects rather than in the 'weary orthodoxies and permanent nay-saying' of the Unionist establishment. It also points to those conflicts in Paulin's work generated by his simultaneous valorisation of oral energies and witnessing, and the desire to debunk romanticism with its dangerous yearnings for authenticity and rootedness (S. O'Brien, 1998: 185–6).

These conflicts receive their most thorough examination in *Fivemiletown*'s long concluding poem, 'The Caravans on Lüneberg Heath' which, like *The Book of Juniper*, brings together historical fragments and scraps of narrative in order to shed light on the Northern Irish present. The main figure representative of linguistic 'rootedness' here is Heidegger, captured after World War II, but still ambiguously justifying his support for Nazism. Heidegger is the main subject of the second half of the poem. The first half, in opposition to Heidegger's racial advocacy of the German language, presents the figures gathered around the poet Simon Dach, who established during the Thirty Years War a poetic group (the 'cucumber lodge') which met in a bower (or 'pumpkin hut') in his friend Heinrich Albert's Königsberg garden. Dach's poem of 1641, 'Lament Over the Final Demise and Ruination of the Musical "Pumpkin Hut" and the Little Garden' commemorates the destruction of bower and garden by the expansion of Königsberg. Dach is mediated for Paulin partly through Günter Grass's novel *The Meeting at Telgte*, set in 1647, which fictionalises an encounter between Dach, Albert and other German writers. *The Meeting at Telgte* is itself an analogue, or allegory, for the post-World War II formation of German Leftist writers, the Gruppe 47, formed to deal with the difficulties of recreating German literature in the aftermath of Nazism and under the shadow of the impending division of the country by Stalinism and the Allies. A number of Paulin's interests are thrown into sharp relief by this conjunction of events – the role of writers at a time of war, the innate superiority (or otherwise) of one language over another, the need to purify official and literary languages of the accretions of authoritarian abuse among them – and the parallels between the 'thirty years war' of the Troubles ('x years of blood and shit') and those of the seventeenth century (and the period between 1914 and 1945) hardly need labouring (Paulin, 1987: 55). Parts two and four of 'Caravans' rework Dach's poem in a way which stresses the original's refusal to place art at the service of Nationalist renewal; particularly important to Paulin is the fact that Dach's 'pumpkin hut' was a structure which blurred the distinction between culture and nature and, in its transience, did not set itself up as an aesthetic structure (or 'dwelling' in Heideggerian terminology). Heidegger, who aimed at precisely this mobilisation of art and romantic valorisation of the aesthetic, is described, stubbornly unrepentant, in part five. This modulates into the voice of a Paulinesque persona observing the surrender of German forces on Lüneberg Heath in April 1945, and the final section returns – with the line 'now I can get born again' – to the educational contexts of earlier poems. Here, in a 'onestorey partitioned / tacked out of hardboard /

and scrap fuselage' school, the speaker sees links with the main body of the poem (the school houses are named after Northern Irish generals, such as Montgomery and Alanbrooke who fought in World War II), while at the same time offering a parallel between the 'pumpkin hut' and the ramshackle building in which classes take place (Paulin, 1987: 65). The final lines seem to suggest that 'Tommy's wee collection / of aesthetic judgements' is contained by the place where he was 'kitted out' as a 'blue British citizen' – 'Tommy' remains implicated in the despised community from which he originates. At the same time the final comic-phallic gesture links Paulin with the pleasuring, impermanent ideal of Dach and other artists (such as Jackson Pollock) celebrated in the book:

> ... and if you ask my opinion now
> I'll tell you about our musical *Kürbishütte*
> then hand you a cucumber
> and say it doesn't exist
> (Paulin, 1987: 66)

'That's another story': Carson redivivus

> The city is a map of the city.
> (Carson, 1988b: 32; 1990: 69)

The most radical transformation of the Northern Irish poetry scene of the late 1980s occurred with the reappearance of Ciaran Carson. In *The Irish for No* (1987), Carson expanded the thematics of Northern Irish poetry by making Belfast insistently the centre of a powerful body of work, a move consolidated by the even more city-centred *Belfast Confetti* in 1989. Both books showed just how far Carson had transformed his work in reaction against Heaney and in response to the intimidating example of Muldoon. Yet if the urban subject matter was most immediately gripping, even more important were the ways in which thematics (of the city, but also of narrative, memory and language) fed a formal development beyond the dominant lyric, over which Carson had shown a somewhat disaffected mastery in *The New Estate*. The most striking feature of the poetry was the use of a long line, one matching the apparently rambling and inconsequential narratives of many of the poems.[23] Above all, the shape of poem such a line produces is immediately, and visibly, at odds with the usual shapeliness of the lyric surrounded and demarcated by the white space of the page, as *The Irish for No*'s opening poem, 'Dresden', proclaims:

> Horse Boyle was called Horse Boyle because of his brother
>   Mule;
> Though why Mule was Mule is anybody's guess. I
>   stayed there once,
> Or rather, I nearly stayed there once. But that's another story.
> (Carson, 1988a: 11)

'Dresden's' opening lines also declare the methods – calculated self-interruption and self-correction, digression and parenthesis, contradiction and taletelling – by which Carson's longer poems proceed, as the narrator sets up a Russian-doll-like set of interlocking story-lines, to return, devastatingly, to Horse's past as a rear-gunner on the bombing raid on Dresden, the remembered (or almost remembered) 'thousand tinkling echoes' of smashed china 'between the rapid desultory thunderclaps' of the falling bombs, and the last image of the two brothers living in isolated squalor in their 'decrepit caravan' (Carson, 1988a: 15, 11). Within the framing narrative is Horse's tale of Flynn who, carrying a bomb across the border on a bus for the IRA, gives himself up to the policeman who gets on board because his bike has a puncture. Flynn's acquisition of 'the best of Irish' during his thirteen years imprisonment ('He had thirteen words for a cow in heat') is a reminder that Carson, though raised in Belfast, has Irish as a first language, but is wholly unsentimental about a tongue which the modern world has, to some degree, passed by. As Douglas Dunn notes, the power of the poem lies in the reader's realisation of how the narrative climax has been prepared; when the information about Horse's past is delivered, the poem's own 'thousand tinkling echoes' of anticipation – 'the watchdog tin cans, the shop bell, digging in a gravel pit, all start falling, ringing and chinking. It becomes a story of broken objects and a broken man, of life at the edge of life, achieved with masterly discretion.'[24] As this suggests, too, 'Dresden' underlines the fact that the majority of the poems in *The Irish for No* are largely about trapped and damaged lives, its subjects including madness, bombings, shootings, forced emigration and internment.[25]

What offsets this bleakness is the linguistic texture of the poetry (although flat and unpoetic it is precise to a degree), its humour, and the sheer momentum and curiosity of the narrative voice. Like the 'baroque pyramids of empty baked bean tins' surrounding the caravan, the long narrative poems, which make up the first and third of the book's three sections, seem to teeter vertiginously between different memories and narratives (Carson, 1988a: 11). Yet they are rigorously manipulated by a voice which does not so much reject the lyric 'I' as the intensity of its self-involvement. It is a voice which implies, in its inclusiveness – about apparently minor details such as brand names, disfigured shop signs, pop songs – that 'literature is just another element in a universe of discourse' (Ormsby, 1991: 6). 'Calvin Klein's *Obsession*' shows that the arbitrary associations and filmic fades which memory generates – and which, in 'Dresden', for example, move the reader from falling tin cans, via their similarity to the sound of a shop bell, to memories of a specific shop – may, in Carson's hands, generate an inner, ruminative narrative on the workings of memory without losing any power to hold our attention. Such associationism puts both narrative and the coherent self to some degree of risk – 'There is no final way of telling a story' as Carson claims (Brandes, 1990: 84). Further, it shows not merely the exploitation but the internalisation of an understanding that there can never be a single authoritative meaning of a text, only different readings, since meanings circulate endlessly between the ideological and the textual. Ideology in its most obvious sense is ever-present in Carson's poems. 'Dresden's' tale of Flynn – the IRA man who surrenders to a police-man who has boarded the bus he is on merely because his bicycle has a punc-ture – shows that Carson uses politics thematically at least (and, as the Allies' destruction of the strategically unimportant German city shows, this cuts in a number of directions). But it is also present more pervasively in the way he treats other texts, a treatment of a piece with the anti-lyric and demotic thrust of his style and choice of the second-hand, marginalised and discarded as poetic subjects. Thus, Carson's critique of Heaney, for example, begun in his review of *North*, is renewed in the collection's title poem, which hinges on the fact that there is no 'Irish for no' (nor is there for 'yes'). Negation is achieved through repetition and a negative qualifier ('Did you do that?' 'I did not do that').[26] This makes Irish incapable of denial as straightforwardly as in English, a fact germane to Carson's digressive procedures, and makes the phrase a sum-mation of the conditional, provisional nature of experience as he perceives it.[27] The poem opens with a line from Keats's 'Ode to a Nightingale' – 'Was it a vision or a waking dream?' – but goes on to set a number of distinctly un-Romantic scenes from Belfast life against Keatsian escapism, concluding with a real, rather than a wished-for and rejected, death:

> What's all this to the Belfast business-man who drilled
> Thirteen holes in his head with a Black & Decker? It was just
>   a normal morning
> When they came.
>
> (Carson, 1988a: 50)

The literary context of this final vivid scene, however, pointedly charges a certain kind of writing with inattention to such horrors; the 'they' open a 'door into the dark: / *The murmurous haunt of flies on summer eves*. Empty jam-jars. / Mish-mash. Hotch-potch.' Heaney – via his Keatsian style – and even Mahon (the door is that of a shed), are, it is suggested, too concerned with plenitude and aesthetic closure in their poetry to acknowledge the harsh realities of the Troubles or the Belfast landscape in which they are (largely) fought out (Corcoran, 1993: 208). There is a certain crudity in this kind of rebuttal (a later poem, in another direct rebuke – to Heaney's 'The Toome Road' – will have armoured cars driving along on 'heavy Heaney tyres'). Nevertheless, it serves to underscore crucial differences of approach not merely to subject matter but to language, and directly opposes the notion of poetry as consola-tory, or as conveying 'government'.[28]

'Smithfield Market', in *The Irish for No*, concludes with the image of 'a map of Belfast / In the ruins' of the bombed market, where 'Something, many-toothed, elaborate, stirred briefly in the labyrinth' (Carson, 1988a: 37). A sense of enclosure dominates in *Belfast Confetti*, which takes up the impossibility of mapping the city: the phrase 'the city is a map of the city', used twice in his work, means, as Carson has pointed out, that the city itself is unmappable. Only Belfast is adequate to Belfast, and maps of the city, as 'Turn Again' and 'Revised Version' suggest, are inaccurate as soon as they are conceived.[29] Not only can certain things not be shown (military sites, for example), but by definition they do not map the present. Like memory, in fact, they are arbitrary yet persistent, a source of fascination but untrustworthy. As O'Brien claims, perhaps the nearest one may come to possessing the totality of the city is, paradoxically, to be lost in its labyrinths (and, simultaneously, in the labyrinths of one's memories of the city), a point made in the epigraph to the collection, from Walter Benjamin's *A Berlin Childhood Around the Turn of the Century* (S. O'Brien, 1998: 189). Maps are a form of the past continuing through to a changed present, a disparity which may be a source of creativity and of danger. (In this regard, the essay 'Walking in the City' by the cultural theorist Michel de Certeau can be read as a development of Benjamin's comments in a manner which illuminates certain of Carson's practices.)[30]

Thus, not to have the right map in Belfast can lead to the terrifying encounter of 'Question Time', in which the speaker is accosted by republican paramilitaries and quizzed concerning the layout of streets which no longer exist: 'The map is pieced together bit by bit. I am this map which they examine, checking it for error, hesitation, accuracy . . . Eventually I pass the test. I am frisked again, this time in a regretful habitual gesture. *A dreadful mistake*, I hear one of them saying, *has been made*, and I get the feeling he is speaking in quotation marks, as if this is a bad police B-movie and he is mocking it, and me, and him' (Carson, 1990: 63). This is the 'many-toothed' minotaur lurking in 'Smithfield Market', although the unmappable contingency of the city is also its source of energy and attraction. *Belfast Confetti* reveals a Joycean relish of city life, yet rather than paralysis – the attempts of the Falls Road Club of Adelaide in 'Schoolboys and Idlers of Pompeii' recalling Joyce's claim that Dublin could be reconstructed from *Ulysses*[31] – Belfast is revealed again and again as a site of continual change and imaginative possibility ('Perpetual motion, the scaffolding of shopping lists, or the collapsing city') (Carson, 1988a: 33). Such novelistic discursivity sets Carson's Belfast off from that of other Northern Irish poets; rather than seen as sterile, as ambiguous home, or as take-off point for the imagination, Belfast is a process – informing narrative and character in the longer poems – a flow of destruction, alteration, rebuilding, albeit one largely shaped by bombings, military requirements, brutalist town planning and a sectarian redivision of territory.[32]

If Belfast is embodied metamorphic energy, then the 'confetti' of the title refers to the detritus or by-products of that metamorphosis; as Meir points out, the word 'comes in different guises in different places in the volume: as snow, spattered blood, bullet holes, rioters' halfbricks; or, in a telling irony, as the very words of the poems themselves' (Meir, 1991: 8). In similar fashion, the book itself is made up out of heterogeneous materials. Although it maintains the tripartite structure of *The Irish for No*, it complicates this by interspersing the long and short poems with haiku and prose pieces, as well as quotations from the 1678 *Ordinance of the Corporation of Belfast*, a versified pastiche of John Ruskin's prose style and other non-literary texts (although not as in the juxtaposed, collage effects of *The Rough Field*; rather, poetry and personal history merge with local history and etymology in 'Brick' and 'Farset' in the manner of the 'indeterminate slabbery semi-fluid' sleech upon which the city is built). Even more than in *The Irish for No*, the various parts of *Belfast Confetti* rely for their meaning on their intertextual status: separated from the other poems in the book, they inevitably lose some narrative resonance (again, the intricate resistance to excerptibility is a gesture against the tradition of the free-standing lyric).

The postmodernity of Carson's city lies in the way its variousness – produced through the spectator-inhabitant – exceeds explanation. If its processual energies 'can rebuff any ready-made moral explanation – though Carson is, implicitly, a moralist at every turn' – then it cannot be grasped by a single image, statement or consciousness (S. O'Brien, 1998: 191). The attempt to do so can lead only to pessimistic or utopian simplification. The darker aspects of Carson's work can perhaps be seen asserting themselves in his more recent work, in which there has been a shift from location and narrative to language. Always present, as a poem like 'Belfast Confetti' illustrates, *First Language* (1993) is a collection in which Belfast as a physical presence has all but disappeared (revealingly, 'The Ballad of HMS *Belfast*' is a poem named for a ship moored in the Thames). Carson 'is thrown back on himself and the balance between things and words falls more heavily on the latter' in 'a book invaded by crisis' (S. O'Brien, 1998: 193). If the emphasis is on narrative units in *The Irish for No* and *Belfast Confetti*, in *First Language* and *Opera Etcetera* (1996) the unit of focus is the phrase, word or even individual letter (the latter collection includes three sequences; one based on the letters of the alphabet, the other on their international call sign equivalents – 'Alpha', 'Bravo', 'Charlie', and so on – and one on Latin tags). Another way of putting this is to note that the sense of the arbitrariness between signifier and signified which was always there in Carson's poetry – and which problematised the alignment of form and story in his narratives in its denial of causality – becomes more or less predominant. It is a shift confirmed in Carson's remarkable prose work on traditional music of 1996, *Last Night's Fun*, which lays great emphasis on the arbitrariness of the process of naming of tunes. Additionally, 'first language' can refer to Irish – Carson's first language as a child – or it can pose a larger question about the reliance of the memory he is so obsessed with elsewhere on language. Do we remember things through or in language? Does the experience come before the words which name it, or not: 'first, language' or the event?

The style and forms of *First Language* therefore mark a change from its predecessors. The long line is deployed frequently in couplets and, making use of poetry's most common arbitrary form, rhyme is used extensively for the first time. The foregrounding of linguistic play, the interpellation of poetic language between event and representation at the expense of any 'plot' which this produces, is clear in 'Grass':[33]

> We'd done a deal of blow, and dealt a hand or two of Brag,
> Which bit by bit became a bloody Patience, except no one
> Seemed to twig which hand was which, or who was who or whom
> Or what was ace or deuce.

> Hardly any shock, when in the general boggledybotch, the budgie
> Unlatched himself from out the room, and what he cheeped and Canterburied
> Wasn't Gospel – which hardly gave a fiddler's, since the flats were on the bias
> Or on the juice.

> > (Carson, 1994: 16)

Poetic form is now more assertively foregrounded than previously, and the style illustrated by 'Grass' conforms to a general trope which organises the collection, that of the diversity of language itself. With a picture of the Tower of Babel on the cover, the collection alludes to a mythic site of the loss of a common language and speech and the fall (or release) into 'the freedom and imprisonment of language and translation' (Horton, 1995: 85). 'Babel', as Horton notes, 'is analogous to the imperialist desire to dominate and colonise', but the multiplicity of language contains the possibility of confusion and discord as well as of plurality and free-play; at one point, in 'Correspondences', Carson rhymes 'Parable' and 'babble' as if to make this point.[34] The book itself may have a 'meaning', but this is prevented from settling into anything as definite as can be found in the earlier books by the verbal exuberance, itself thematised as drunkenness and drug-induced states (as in 'Grass'), most obviously in the translation of Rimbaud's 'Le bateau ivre' (Baudelaire, Ovid and others feature among the several translations in the book, although the 'translation' Carson is interested in is less that between languages as of translation itself as an ontological condition). The risk taken in *First Language* and *Opera Etcetera* is that involved in a brave move beyond the communal and local material of the earlier collections to an investigation of the principles which underlay them.

Negotiating Americas: Paul Muldoon

One area of Irish literary experience minimised in Declan Kiberd's *Inventing Ireland* – that between Ireland and the USA – features largely in the work of Muldoon after *Quoof*. *Meeting the British* (1987), *Madoc* (1990), the libretto *Shining Brow* (1993) and *Hay* (1998) all have US themes, while *The Annals of Chile* (1994a) develops the Latin American connections of 'Lunch with Pancho Villa' and the Brazilian/Argentinian destinations imagined in *Why Brownlee Left*. Focusing on Irish-American traffic, this work is implicitly critical of taking the Anglo-Irish relationship as solely constitutive of Irish identity. One of the things Muldoon accomplishes in *Meeting the British* is to remind us that 'the huge importance of America in Irish culture cannot be accommodated within an Anglo-Irish paradigm' (O'Toole, 1996: 15). The work considers personal and artistic relocation, how Muldoon was to remake himself as a poet in the USA, and how the past and the present might be kept in creative relationship with each other. This was is in keeping with Muldoon's sensitivity to the fluidity of cultural traffic between Ireland and the USA (and within postmodern culture generally). In fact the inappropriateness of the traditional notion of 'exile' is one he attacked when it was applied to him by Seamus Deane (Muldoon, 1994b: 36). But, as the title poem of *Meeting the British* and 'Madoc – A Mystery' from *Madoc* make clear, this does not preclude a critique of colonialism. Similarly, the intensely literary character of the work – '7, Middagh Street', 'Madoc – A Mystery' and *Shining Brow* present artists (among them Yeats, Auden, MacNeice, Coleridge, Southey and Frank Lloyd Wright) – is not merely thematic, since all are central to problems of literary politics, including those of Romanticism, modernism and postmodernism, which are part of Muldoon's negotiation of the relationship between his own poetry and the USA.[35] On the other hand, the literariness of *Meeting the British* in particular has led to its being seen as a failure by a significant number of Muldoon's critics (Kendall, 1996: 146–7).

If the impermanent address of '7, Middagh Street' is a consciously partial, literary entry into the USA, *Madoc* (1990) contains in its title poem what is by common consent the most complex poem in modern Irish literature.[36] The longest of Muldoon's long poems – 246 of the book's 257 pages of poetry – 'Madoc – A Mystery' is the apotheosis of two strains in his previous work, that of the culture and fate of the Native Americans and that of the imagined or alternative existence. In order to avoid the fate Muldoon himself gleefully foresaw for academic expositors of the work, only a fraction of what happens in 'Madoc' can be suggested here. That said, it is clearly a poem about writing a poem in (and about) the USA, and it pays its dues to Muldoon's new place of residence. Massively ambitious, it is a historiographical metafiction with similarities to the postmodern narratives of John Barth, Thomas Pynchon or Umberto Eco. (Though there are resemblances to US postmodern poems like Dorn's *Gunslinger*, 'Madoc' is less radical stylistically, adhering to conventional syntax and plot even as it disrupts linearity and signals its own fictionality, as in '[Collingwood]': 'An even more distressing thought . . . How might Coleridge have stolen a pirogue, when there was none to steal?')[37] (Muldoon, 1990: 218.)

The origins of 'Madoc' lie in Muldoon's editing of Byron in the late 1980s, work which led him to consider the literary politics of Romanticism. Byron's dispute with Robert Southey pointed Muldoon towards Southey's epic poem *Madoc* of 1805 which provided the pre-text for a 'remake' (Muldoon, 1990: 3). Behind 'Madoc' lay the plan, mooted by Southey and Coleridge in the mid-1790s, to found a utopian ('Pantisocratic') community in the USA. The poem projects what might have happened if the pair had managed to cross the Atlantic, interweaving the fictional narrative with the history of the young

Republic, as it addresses the legend treated by Southey's epic (this derives from Welsh *immram* concerning a group of settlers, led by Prince Madoc, who fled civil war in Wales in the twelfth century to sail to America, where they became 'white Indians'). At the same time 'Madoc' is a parody of that Romantic genre, the long philosophical poem; each of its 233 short sections is supertitled with the name of a Western philosopher, from '[Thales]' to '[Hawking]', setting up a metanarrative above (or to the side of) the main 'story'.[38] The stylistic heterogeneity is also far greater than anything encountered in Muldoon's earlier work. Extracts (and pastiches) from various texts – including Byron's *The Vision of Judgement*, Thomas Moore's and Coleridge's poetry, Southey's journals, letters and histories (such as that of the Lewis and Clark expedition across North America) – shape, and vie for attention with, the story of the poem. The reader may follow the various characters in this tale, but at the same time 'Madoc' teases and frustrates, and not merely by stylistic means or the elision of narrative connections. In addition it foregrounds the reader's search for coherence; thus, a sub-narrative involves the fate of a 'teeny-weeny key' which, it is hinted, might solve the obscurities of the poem[39] (Muldoon, 1990: 117). Outside of this, and further complicating it, is a science fiction framing narrative set in a future shaped by the effects of Southey and Coleridge's venture, concerning the fate of South, a descendant of Southey's, who is wounded and captured as he attempts to make off with a sheet of paper bearing the motto 'Croatan' from a plant belonging to the 'Unitel' corporation.[40] 'Croatan' is another possible 'key'; it is the word which was found branded on a piece of wood when Raleigh returned in 1586 to discover that the colony he had established at Roanoake in Virginia had vanished, an event alluded to in 'Promises, Promises' in *Why Brownlee Left*. In 'Madoc' it is the word South steals from Unitel and which he is discovered to have glossed 'in sympathetic ink: / C[*oleridge*] RO[*bert Southey The S*[ATAN[*ic School*]', a reference to Southey's attack on Byron which, the poem suggests, is more appropriate to the colonialism of Coleridge and Southey. Later still the word is glossed (in '[Harman]') as 'Not "CROATAN", not "CROATOAN", but "CROTONA"' (Muldoon, 1990: 258). 'Crotona', as critics have pointed out, is the name of Pythagoras' western place of exile, and may refer also to the croton tree which produces an oil formerly used as a purgative (and so linked to the purgative role Muldoon claimed for 'The More a Man Has', as well as being something 'Madoc' is keen to perform on romanticised European–US fictions concerning Native Americans).[41] As Michael Hofmann notes, 'the poem is too full of solutions: no body, no motive, but stacks of clues'; its overdetermination is part of its theme (Hofmann, 1990: 18). The main point is the way such 'keys' or clues are seized on by the reader not only because of the complexities of the Coleridge–Southey story but also because of the unsettlingly different kinds of congruence between this and the metanarrative constituted by the supertitles.

At the outset of the poem the dying South is hitched up to a futuristic device called 'a retinagraph' 'So that, though it may seem somewhat improbable, / all that follows' – that is, the Southey/Coleridge section of the poem – 'Flickers and flows / from the back of his right eyeball' (Muldoon, 1990: 20). What 'flickers' from South's disintegrating retina is an increasingly disintegrated and gapped account of the Pantisocrats and their companions. It opens in 1795 with them trekking up the Susquehannah Valley towards – appropriately given Muldoon's comment that this can be read as a poem 'about the failure of Ireland, as a state' – the town of Ulster. At this point ('[Aenisidemus]') their guide, Cinnamond, and Sara Fricker (Coleridge's fiancée) disappear, followed by Bucephalus, the talking horse, a colt and a pack-horse. Coleridge and Southey split up to track them down, diverging along what '[Parmenides]' has called 'the fork in the trail / where the Way of Seeming and the Way of Truth / diverge' (Muldoon, 1990: 21). As the poem proceeds, the relevance of the Madoc legend – and its anti-colonial, as well as Romantic-political edge – becomes increasingly apparent. The legend first appeared in print during the reign of Elizabeth I, and was used as a means of establishing a British claim upon North America prior to that of the Spanish and Portuguese. As Gwyn A. Williams has remarked, 'whatever his original provenance and character, Madoc first effectively entered history as an instrument of imperial conflict. His story was henceforth to follow the ebb and flow of imperialism, trade rivalry and colonial settlement with hypnotic precision' (G. A. Williams, 1979: 67). 'Welsh' or 'white' Indians, it was argued, proved the existence of a pre-Columbian British settlement, and spurious etymologies – among other evidence – were established to justify the validity of a territorial claim.[42] (Thus, 'penguin' a Native American word, was construed as deriving from the Welsh 'pen gwyn', or 'white head', by Sir George Peckham in his *True Reporte* of 1583. As 'Madoc' sardonically observes (in '[Whitehead]', an excellent example of the way a philosopher's name glances off the poem's story): 'Southey wakes in a cold sweat; / penguins don't have white heads'[43] Muldoon, 1990: 195.) The search for 'white Indians' – variously identified with the actual tribes of the Modocs and Mandans – and the Madoc legend were thus established as part of a colonising discourse. By the 1790s it had re-emerged to be deployed in the imperial rivalry between Britain, France, Spain and the USA in the region of the Upper Missouri. As '[Anaxagoras]' has it, 'In the light of the X Y Z affair / America and France are limbering up for war' (Muldoon, 1990: 24). (This is not to say that Muldoon does not amuse himself in planting clues which suggest that the Madoc legend may, after all, be true; echoes of Madoc's name – in words such as 'Médoc', 'mattock' and 'Monadcnoc' – crop up throughout the text. Yet their deeply embedded, almost arbitrary appearance suggests that, even if the legend were true, the 'white Indians' have been assimilated almost completely within the native population.) By the 1790s, however, the legend had acquired radical political force for Welsh republicans under the influence of the French Revolution; one of them – John Evans – features in 'Madoc'.

The very different fates of Muldoon's Coleridge and Southey are to be read against this background, since Southey's *Madoc* was written specifically as a corrective to the radical guise the legend had assumed.[44] Two kinds of colonial outcome are being dramatised. Coleridge, adrift in the wilderness, develops from a transcendentalist dreamer to an assimilationist – albeit ironically at certain points – who embraces Native American culture.[45] Following the political apostasy scorned by Byron, Southey declines from being a representative of self-control (by comparison with Coleridge) into violent irrationalism, and becomes a colonist of the worst kind as he constructs a citadel, 'Southeyopolis', and oppresses the indigenous population. Coleridge, in pursuit of Sara (and laudanum), has witnessed a white woman being initiated (sexually) into a native tribe and, as Kendall notes, 'seems to accept her disappearance from the narrative'[46] (Kendall, 1995: 238). His further adventures link him to shamanistic and (appropriately given his addiction) drug-induced visionary practices, as he moves between tribes and drugs in a shape-shifting quest which turns up hints of the almost imperceptible traces of Madoc's descendants. Southey on the other hand eventually provokes a revolt against his rule; deserted and reduced to a pathetic figure, Southeyopolis is finally overrun by the Cayugas and he is hacked to death (although it is worth noting that Southey's attachment to Bucephalus is emphasised as a redeeming feature). The genocide committed against the Native Americans is recorded in the latter stages of the poem, symbolised, as McCurry points out, by the iambic leitmotif of drum beats – 'De dum, de dum, de dum, de dum, de dum' – which gradually modulates as the narrative progresses to be replaced by the Christian 'Te Deum. Te Deum. Te Deum. Te Deum. Te Deum' (McCurry, 1992: 103; Muldoon, 1990: 26, 105). Thus, in '[Camus]', 'the Mandan villages are ravaged by smallpox', recalling the germ warfare practised against the Ottawa Indians in 'Meeting the British', while in '[Nozick]'s' ghastly pun, 'The Modocs, led by Captain Jack, are systematically hunted down on the laver-breads of Oregon' (Muldoon, 1990: 246, 259).

Ultimately the greatest stylistic achievement of 'Madoc' is its combination of a 'postmodern' sense of play and scepticism with a savage critique of Western imperialism and its metaphysical foundations. The notion that Western 'grand narratives' are inevitably terroristic is, of course, a favourite one of postmodern theorists. However, there are important qualifications to any assessment of 'Madoc' as a poem which simply illustrates this thesis, one which relates to Muldoon's specifically Irish inflection of the postmodern (apart from the thematic one by which British colonisation of Ireland is associated with the Madoc legend and its function in the colonisation of America). In 'Lunch with Pancho Villa' the speaker, opposing the ideologue, had claimed that 'there's no such book, as far as I know, / As *How it Happened Here*' (Muldoon, 1977: 12–13). The terms resemble those of Wittgenstein, who argued that it is impossible to construct a private language, a code accessible only to the individual subject her/himself since language is irremediably social and the description of our private sensations is 'parasitic upon the existence of a public language'. As in 'Quoof' – which is precisely about the way a 'private' language is always already fallen into the 'irremediably public'[47] – '[Wittgenstein]' makes public Sara Fricker's 'private' language, 'Now your stumparumper is a connoisorrow / who has lost his raspectabilberry' (Muldoon, 1990: 219). The dualism of 'Madoc' mimics precisely the parallel but disconnected system proposed by Wittgenstein, mocking attempts to prioritise either public or private language in a simultaneously witty and agonised manner. Both poetry and philosophy in the poem converge on the problematics of the relationship between language and reality. It could be argued that in 'Madoc' Muldoon turns such insights against the Romantic presumption that philosophy, poetry, language and reality are organically linked, and against the notion of the philosopher-poet. In this process Byron is crucial. The Romantic poet who most completely collapsed the distinction between poetry and personality, Byron was also Romanticism's chief ironist, and is the chief source of Muldoon's own particular brand in 'Madoc'. Byronic irony cuts the ground from under Romanticism's rooted certainties of the self, belonging and so on, but at the same time it is scarcely apolitical. In its critical aspect 'Madoc's' irony works against the politics of disillusion implicit in its philosophical dimension, a disillusion which asks how we can ever change the world if the causal link of world to word is broken. To say as much is not to question the disenchantment which lies beneath the enchanting linguistic surfaces of the poem, of course. It is, though, to acknowledge that it simultaneously critiques imperialism and permits the deconstruction of the postmodern means by which it does so (while spoofing those naive postmodernisms which are unaware that the postmodern itself already contains the means for its own deconstruction). The poem thereby operates politically, interrogating its own radical intertextuality to dialectically transform both the textualisation of history and the historicisation of text.

In its Irish political dimension, 'Madoc's' imperialist critique occurs in a manner destructive of both imperial claims and the residual Nationalist and essentialist pieties lurking behind Field Day-influenced definitions of the postcolonial. This point is made by Edna Longley in her reading of the poem, which traces what she sees as its Irish literary politics. However, in doing so she perversely inverts the terms of the attack on Unionism represented by 'Southeyopolis', viewing the citadel perversely as 'mainly a failed literary construction, with Seamus Heaney (and perhaps Field Day) implicated' (E. Longley, 1994: 57). While not denying the one-to-one correspondences between figures in the contemporary Irish literary political scene in the poem (Heaney as Southey to Muldoon's Coleridge, for example), Richard Kirkland sees it more in terms of a dramatisation of tensions between Muldoon's desired marginal, adversarial status and his near-inevitable assimilation within the 'New-Critical institution' represented by those such as Longley (and, inevitably, Kirkland himself). In this reading it is Unitel which is comparable to the Field Day venture, being 'the once emergent and now dominant hegemonic formation' in the poem's imagined future. At the same time, this 'arrangement' is, for Kirkland, revealed by the poem as 'unable to contain all the insurgent elements that constitute it at any one time', among which Muldoon's own poem must – presumably – be counted (Kirkland, 1996: 169). (Certainly, the Troubles and their influence on cultural debates can be discerned in a poem in which 'Geckoes armed with Zens' oppose 'Cayugas' with 'Lasabers'; company or state forces versus South – suggesting the 'south' of Ireland – and his guerrilla band.) Ultimately, however, Kirkland's ingenuity seems too reductively reliant – like Longley's literalness – on a belief that 'Madoc' shares his own fixation on the significance of Field Day.[48] 'Madoc's' final lines observe that 'It will all be over, de dum / in next to no time – / long before "The fluted cypresses / rear'd up their living obelisks" / has sent a shiver, de dum, de dum, / through Unitel, its iridescent Dome', apparently in reference to South's failure. But South's cry – 'The fluted cypresses / rear'd up their living obelisks' – is pointedly a tribal one lifted from a bad poem by the execrable Southey, and to wholly conflate this with Muldoon's acceptance of failure is surely wrong (Muldoon, 1990: 257). 'Madoc' is predicated on Muldoon's successful escape from the politics of the 'Geckoes' and 'Cayugas' through his move to the USA, nor is his particular postcolonial inflection of the postmodern aesthetic detachable from it. The disintegration of the lyric 'I' of South's narrating 'eye' is charted to the point of collapse and death, but within the poem that point is notably not represented. A revolutionary self of sorts survives, having successfully evaded the limitations of the 'I' of the Northern Irish lyric, as equally its complete dissolution as required by more intransigent versions of the postmodern.[49]

'Comes the experiment . . .': neo-modernism and the avant-garde

In the informational universe, communication starts with resistance.[50]

In '[Pascal]' in 'Madoc', Thomas Jefferson demonstrates a polygraph he has invented. Like the poem itself, the instrument duplicates writing which runs 'parallel to the parallel / realm to which it is itself the only clue' (Muldoon, 1990: 96). Such a 'parallel realm' might serve as an image for the world of Irish neo-modernist poetry which has intermittently shadowed mainstream poetry since the 1950s.[51] The separation between these 'realms' is noticeably greater, at an institutional level, in Ireland than in either Britain or the USA, with their relationship characterised not so much by polemic as by ignorance and outright dismissal. Yet at the same time, arguably, the gap between the practices of some 'mainstream' poets and certain neo-modernists is narrower than elsewhere. (It could be argued that the post-*Nightwalker* work of Thomas Kinsella forms a kind of bridge between a more or less acceptable modernism in Irish poetry, and the more radical submerged strains; neo-modernists would distinguish themselves from him, however, on the basis that despite stylistic similarities, their work specifically rejects the issues of family, nation and tradition by which Kinsella is engrossed.) Thus, while the conservatism of much Irish poetry is undeniable – and, in a small and congested literary culture based on identitarian cultural politics, contributes to the stigmatising of experimentalism – it is noticeable that Irish neo-modernists have not adopted the most radical stances and practices of the international neo-avant-garde, and that there may be specifically 'Irish' reasons for this. Although neo-modernist poets have been aware of such developments – particularly in the USA, and since the 1960s – there has been no reciprocal attention until very recently. Ignored by Irish mainstream outlets and establishments, the likes of Maurice Scully, Randolph Healy and Catherine Walsh failed to make much impact on experimental poetries outside Ireland in the 1980s. Lingering ignorance is visible in Iain Sinclair's recent anthology of British neo-modernist poetry, *Conductors of Chaos*, in which Irish poetry, monolithically conceived, serves as a whipping boy for much that is deemed to be wrong with British mainstream poetry: 'Ireland, a swamp of corrupt decisions, is reduced to package for export. Bog and bomb and blarney: a heap of glittering similes burnished for westward transit.'[52] Irish poetry is reduced to Heaney (and a caricatured Heaney at that) in an attempt to skewer depoliticising trends in Britain. Sinclair thus shows no awareness of the experimentalism which emerged after the decline of the New Writers' Press group (NWP) in the late 1970s. This took the form of two Dublin-based journals, *the Belle* (1978–80) and *the Beau* (1981–84), edited by Maurice Scully, and a (brief) experimental poetry scene in the city which also included Billy Mills and Randolph Healy. This continued, in diasporic mode, through the 1980s, during which time Catherine Walsh emerged and associated herself with the group.[53] By the early 1990s, a new gathering of energies was perceptible with the return to Ireland of Walsh and Mills and in new work by Scully. Additionally, the early 1990s saw renewed activity on the part of Trevor Joyce and Geoffrey Squires of the NWP poets. A chance convergence between older and younger poets at the 'Assembling Alternatives' experimental poetry conference in New Hampshire in 1996 produced the beginnings of a more general and organised neo-modernist poetry in the Republic, one which has found an academic-critical focus in an annual conference at UCC since 1997, and a growing awareness of the poetry abroad.

Ironically, given the belatedness of these developments, it is precisely these poets who are most aware in their work of the new information technologies and the effects of globalisation and postmodernism, while also resisting the more tendentious varieties of postcolonialism. While claiming affiliation with Coffey and (in Scully's case) Watters, all owe something to US examples, with a general commitment to 'a poetry of process' rather than a 'poetry of product'; in Scully's words, 'poetry (space) "is an activity / not a body of reading" ' (Mills, 1998: 27; Scully, 1994: 10). Thus, Randolph Healy's work emphasises the mind's inability to make sense of a world far too vast for 'the suburbia of the psyche' to grasp it and order it ('Any statement is too rich in meaning for us to be able to test all of its consequences') (Scully, 1983: 11). Healy's work as a scientist led him to an exploration of the logical sentence, most impressively in 'Colonies of Belief', a poem which moves from flatly establishing a principle of difference in quasi-scientific terms to the inevitability of power structures emerging from difference, and finally succumbing to the narrowing of viewpoints which power brings. Forgetting the complexity of the world 'They see everything from a point of view; / stay indoors discussing themselves; / allow no checks of their comfort'. Only in the final lines does the language acquire any affective charge as those with power 'calculate / theorems in axiomatic systems and / call it truth . . . swagger, dominate, / dabble, destroy, dream, exploit and die out' (Goodby and Scully, 1999: 5). After the dry scrupulousness of what went before, the conclusion is charged with an almost elegiac power for the cyclical growth and decay of all sentient life and systems; the lines could apply equally to imperial power or overweeningly self-assured aesthetic stances. The implied critique of a poetry which assumes mastery over contingent flux is foregrounded more forcefully in the work of Scully which, as Alex Davis has noted, 'takes to an extreme point the preoccupation with information, its materiality, its transmission and reception, that marks the work of the Irish neo-avant-garde' (Davis, 1998: 47). Scully's expressionism – in which random sense-impressions, mock-pedagogical voices, collage fragments and lyrical interludes can switch within the same line or syntactic unit – is at the other end of the emotional spectrum from Healy's amused coolness, and is more obviously a continuation of the avant-garde assault on art as institution. Sceptical about language and literature he is, like Healy, convinced of the need to realise the inability of poetry to do justice to the world: 'The world is extremely complex and the most complex poem the mind can conceive and execute is extremely simple in the world. A poem is beautiful to the degree it records an apt humility in the face of complexity it sees but fails to transmit, doubting its presumption in the light of that' (Scully, 1983: 10). Nevertheless, Scully's recent poetry – like Healy's – has moved from such statements of principles to a richer exploration of their implications. By engaging with the problematics of the literary system, indeed, it could be argued that Scully's work problematises the 'mainstream'/marginal divide in a way which would not interest, say, a US L=A=N=G=U=A=G=E poet.

'Lines in Fall': Trevor Joyce

Scully's critique of what he calls 'the Gem School' of poetry resembles that of a less Heraclitean poet, Trevor Joyce (Scully, 1994: 10). Citing Joan Retallack's conversations with John Cage, Joyce has asserted that poetry must avoid 'imitating the images of beauty with which [poets] are already familiar' since, paradoxically, 'The degree to which our desire to possess beauty leads us to imitate its image rather than its processes . . . makes experience of beauty harder to come by within the fluid circumstances of everyday life'[54] (Joyce, 1998: 24). Such an approach, Joyce claims, flows inescapably from the condition of the artist in the late twentieth century; the dilemma facing mainstream 'poetry of expression' is that, arriving at the point of being 'aware of things, events, experiences . . . with which it recognizes itself as incommensurable', it can do little more than '[state] forcibly the horror of its own privileged futility to intervene, to do more than merely observe, record and move on'. Expressive art is brought to the end of its tether, for Joyce, in the face of 'the horror' which is unavoidable in an age of informational excess (Cage's 'fluid circumstances of everyday life').[55] The formal implications of this stem from mainstream poetry's felt need to 'speak on behalf' of suffering being thwarted by an essentially expressive or communicative attitude to language and form (discursive syntax and pre-given formal procedures). The result is a conflict between the attempt to avoid arrogating such suffering and the conventionality of the vehicles in which expression occurs[56] (Gilonis, 1998: 19). The argument is, in effect, that dominant poetic attitudes to form and language are in fact not 'expressive' *enough* to deal with contemporary realities. Resistance to media manipulation and the language of advertising, that 'unassailable praise-poetry of our time', can only come about by foregrounding the constructedness of the voice of the poem and its artefactual and artificial nature. There is agreement here with the US critic Marjorie Perloff, who has argued that opposition to 'information overload' and the crisis it creates for poetry can be brought about through the disruption of instrumental discourse – conventional language habits in which language is a means to an end – rather than through liberal railing and regret.[57] Joyce's understanding of the predicament of poetry can be related to the 'Celtic Tiger' phenomenon, given its reliance on microelectronics and information technology, from computer assembly to software systems testing and telesales, and its effective abandonment of the 'normal' European model of socio-economic development (he is himself a Business Systems Analyst for Apple Inc., which has its main European plant in Cork).[58] This 'mutant' modernisation, as Luke Gibbons has shown, has had major implications for the relationship towards the Irish past and national identity, tending to invoke the past even more intensely than had previously been the case, but in the manner of postmodern simulacra. IDA publicity material, for example, could juxtapose computers and dolmens, proclaiming as it did so that 'Missing the Industrial Revolution was the best thing that ever happened to the Irish'. Such 'neo-traditionalism' could '[abolish] not only continuity', which Lemassian reformers had been keen to assert, 'but history itself'.[59]

Joyce's *stone floods* (1995) and *Syzygy* (1998) explore some of the implications of the issues outlined above in an impressively varied manner. The first book is a collection of lyric pieces which, as its oxymoronic title suggests, explores tensions between an early allegiance to aestheticism and an openness derived from the examples of Coffey, Beckett and Chinese writing. The result is a series of poems which dramatise a thematics of control and transgression, of stasis and movement. 'The Turlough', for example, refers to the geological feature which provides a basis for the title ('turloughs' are seasonal lakes in limestone country, unmarked on maps, whose sources are often untraceable):

It is raining elsewhere
Vertical floods reverse
stone floods
the karst domain
each sink turns source
Rocks bring forth fruit elsewhere
(Joyce, 1995: 10)

Joyce uses the geological feature as the point of departure for a meditation on the ways in which the past can irrupt into the present; in which, for example, buried psychic matter can emerge within the conscious mind, or the night sky is always the 'past', the light of stars already old in an expanding universe. Informing this is the theory that the expansion of universe (and of time) will eventually reach a limit and then reverse. The red shift detected by astronomers will become blue, or – in a typical pun – 'in a blue shift / Venus meets Mars' (Joyce, 1995: 11). Such vast perspectives are common in Joyce, as in much earlier modernist poetry; so, too, is his cosmopolitanism, the use of distant historical periods and cultures as a means of relativising our views of contemporary Western society. Poems on the lost Central Asian civilisation of the Tocharians ('Tocharian Music'), ancient China ('Cold Course'), or derived from a wide range of sources – Jorge Manrique, Meng Chiao, the Gnostic writings unearthed at Nag Hammadi – are present not simply as 'window dressing', as Robert Archambeau notes, but as a means of interrogating the basic concepts of flux and fixity (Archambeau, 1998: 11). 'The Turlough' raises questions concerning the linearity of time and the boundary fixed between past, present and future. Likewise, other poems repeatedly turn on, or try to dwell in, liminal states between states. Lack of punctuation, shifting subject positions, paronomasia and parataxis, although not radically disjunctive in effect, allow the exploitation of syntactical and lexical ambiguity, breaking down barriers and crossing thresholds at the linguistic level in a manner which reinforces thematic interests. In 'The Opening', for example, a 'you' is addressed in the first two verses who appears to inhabit a different world to that of the speaker, the 'you' able to cross boundaries the speaker cannot (going through a wall 'in which there is no door / but you have opened it'). That 'you', however, is by virtue of this very ability, under threat, '[stumbling]' and '[dropping] through' a 'floor in which there is no chasm'. In the final verse a failure of intersubjective intercourse between the 'I' of the speaker and the 'you' is registered, the speaker shutting the book the 'you' opened in the first verse (which is stone floods itself), and frozen in the stasis of the final couplet's repetition: 'I look to the night / which has begun to fall / which will not be long now' (Joyce, 1995: 7). It is worth noting in the light of this poem – which has clear personal and psychological aspects – that Joyce does not eschew the personal in his writing, or a lyric closure familiar in more mainstream poetry. Nevertheless 'The Opening' problematises the speaking self of lyric to the extent that it cannot presume to speak 'on behalf of', '[charting] the collapse

and the reinforcement of boundaries, the reaching for and frustration of communication in a highly ambivalent fashion . . . boundedness is linked to being,
but at the price of a dissatisfied longing for a breaching of the enclosed self,
an opening associated with danger' (Davis, 1998: 46).

Stone floods anticipates *Syzygy* in 'Chimaera' which, like 'The Turlough',
draws on the Japanese renga form 'which uses systematic ambiguity to chain
together a series of brief stanzas every one of which hinges both forward and
backward'. 'Chimaera' is a composite made up of lines taken from Lovelace,
Aloysius Bertrand and the Book of Lieh Tze. The scheme is not rigidly adhered
to – as Joyce puts it, 'there is interference on all channels' – but the general
theme, or argument of the poem can be glossed as a colloquy between the
three voices which interpenetrate, dramatising their different attitudes towards
the boundaries of selfhood (Joyce, 1995: 51):

> A moth bred out of moonlight I disturbed
> From the dark folds where it lay hid
>
> A naked thing that seems no man may cheat
> And love like any jack
> Another dressed may prove a beast
> (Joyce, 1995: 26)

Overall, the poem plays Lovelace's self-confidence against Bertrand's neurotic
obsession with breakdown and Lieh Tze's utter lack of difficulty with boundaries or the transformations which blur them (much of the poem is to do with
bestial metamorphosis). 'No voice wins', as Joyce puts it: 'Although I feel the
third to be the strongest, it does not have the last word, and even if it were
to prevail, that would merely leave it prey to an ultimate annihilation.'[60] In
Syzygy, however, the principle of recombining texts is taken much further, to
a point where they defy easy synopsis. The book contains two poems, 'The
Drift' and 'The Net'. As Nate Dorward points out, 'Fragments of three quotations are threaded forward and backward through a set of 12 poems called
"The Drift".'[61] This is the fifth verse:

> when the thieving
> that was well advanced faltered
> the imperial presence surveyed
> the ordered territories
> and declared in measured words
> nothing there is savage any more
> intelligence and griefs are tamed
> rage is reduced in parks
> only perhaps along the furthest bounds
> may be some dirt a little ghost
> and these are even as we speak contained
> in three quart jugs
> (Joyce, 1998: 7)

Here the fragmented quotations reappear according to the scheme within a structure which permits the reader to follow a narrative (here the standardisation of measure under the first Emperor of China, glossed in Joyce's notes to the poem, is to the fore).[62] Joyce's combinations use a structure derived from a palindromic canon by Guillaume de Machaut and a computer spreadsheet program. These twelve poems, however 'are then pulverized and rearranged as "The Net", a set of twenty-four three-line stanzas. "The Drift's" sober and precise lyrics deal with inhuman environments (outer space, the desert, the sea) and the processes of time; "The Net" is altogether denser',[63] reworking the interstitial thematic material of 'The Drift' and placing the three found phrases at either end of the poem, with a governing line – on flux and change – as the centre around which the variations wheel

> courses ghosts disclose from high
> there is nothing finished or not yet begun
> creak what soft amends rage but even these lost their
>
> stars from elsewhere . . .
>
> (Joyce, 1998: 12)

The result is a work which contrasts the strictest of structural procedures and (Cage-like) aleatory material with the intensely personal concern for the processes of order/disorder and states of liminality found in *stone floods*, but in a far more complex manner. Intensive reworking and patterning produce an intricate and ludic consideration of temporality and decay with a density which corresponds (while it does not pretend to match) the saturation of contemporary life by media and information technologies. In J. C. C. Mays's words, 'it is a word-game driven by moral meaning', while the nullity implied in the overlap of the elements of the syzygy – the point at the centre of the poem where 'nothing is finished or not yet begun' – means that 'At the heart of . . . the poem there is . . . nothing . . . the core [it] contains vanishes while it drives [the constituent parts]' (Mays, 1998: 59). Although it would hardly please either poet, Joyce's use of palindromic structure to generate variety within repetition – and his technical ingenuity in the development from lyric to large structure – irresistibly recalls the Muldoon of 'Yarrow'.

'Out of bondage, almost': Catherine Walsh

If Trevor Joyce's neo-modernism – in its reluctance to wholly abandon traditional lyric registers and its concern with generative formal systems – exploits a tension between symbolist modes and avant-garde aleatory practices, that of Catherine Walsh belongs more completely in the latter category. The youngest of the neo-modernist poets, her work has a number of sources. As with Joyce and other Irish experimental poets, Coffey is clearly far more important than Devlin; but Walsh combines this with other and varied sources, among them Austin Clarke (valued for his use of assonance), Emily Dickinson and the US

Objectivist poet Lorine Niedecker. The interest in reworking the material of past cultures evident in Joyce is, with Walsh, displaced in favour of a more demotic, present-tense and fragmentary poetics of indeterminacy in which the difficulties of linguistic communication itself are foregrounded. As she has said in interview, 'The kinds of misunderstandings that crop up are as much a part of our lives and are as important as the understandings' (Skelt, 1991: 184). Autobiographical material is refracted through the broken surfaces of a spatially dispersed text, with the information reaching the reader often cautious or incomplete. It is no coincidence that all of Walsh's books to date – *Making Tents* (1987), *Short Stories* (1989), *Pitch* (1994) and *idir eatortha* (1996) – begin with a personal sense of dislocation, of being in transit, not belonging. In this sense they challenge what she sees as the dilemma facing Irish poets of definition within or against an Irish tradition, or traditions. In her words, 'You need to be incorporated into the tradition to be an Irish writer and you exist as an Irish writer on those terms or you might as well not exist', adding that 'you are only supported if you are part of that tradition . . . that must celebrate above all else your sense of Irishness and your sense of being part of an ongoing linear tradition of Irish writers, writing out of bondage, almost'. It is this 'inherited dissent' paradigm which Walsh rejects, one which has a specific form for the Irish woman poet since, as Joyce notes, 'she is an Irish woman writer who sidesteps the ball and chain of conservative form [and] self-consciously "radical" thematics which has been represented for far too long as the only proper model for women poets in this country' (Gilonis, 1998: 25).

The title of *Making Tents* signals this (punning on 'make intense' or 'making tense', as well as the setting up of temporary homes), as does its prefatory poem 'Nearly Nowhere', the only piece in the book, apart from the closing 'Modalities', to be titled. The book's contexts are those of migrancy and the necessary provisionality of the attempt to make the self at home in the world and in language. The poetry counterpoints Imagistic observation and meditation, modernist wordplay and disorientating repetition in the style of Gertrude Stein:

> Repeat the changes change the
> repeats the change repeats the
> repeat changes change it repeat
> change it.
> (Walsh, 1996: 71)

Walsh's experience as a teacher of English in Barcelona also features as a version of linguistic unease; one piece opens with comments from a Spanish primer ('and the student or scholar who / is unaware of the significance / of diacritical marks') and ends with conversation drifting up a ventilation shaft 'during the siesta', 'snatched and strange / I understand nothing' (Walsh, 1996: 79; Archambeau, 1998: 15). But Irish contexts also recur. The following fragment, for example, conflates a childhood memory with 'a family "myth" concerning the Black and Tans (Irish history) and the actual song of the wood pigeon, represented as a kind of visual map' (Mills, 1998: 35):

```
                take two cows
        Taffy            take two
    wood pigeons              across the river
            in the orchard
            ka      cu      coo
        khaki            kacu
                (Walsh, 1996: 80)
```

Another piece which lists places in a childhood landscape – 'Dan's yard / The mill field / The bog / The big field / The L field / The murdering field / The relics' – is typical of the way in which the affective charges of place and name are purged in order to separate contemplation of place from a mythos of belonging or rootedness, the poem's conclusion ('more or less / everything / still / in the same place') suggesting that while the named landscape (and by implication its social context) has scarcely changed, the speaker has, and in a way which may provoke 'harsh words'[64] (Walsh, 1996: 76).

After *Making Tents*, Walsh's writing became more fractured. *Short Stories* mixes unattributed quotes, material on the shifting of the polar ice caps, dictionary definitions, natural history and occasional historical references (to Pliny's Rome and Manetho, who 'in about 280 B.C. / divided history . . . his source material was incomplete –') (Walsh, 1989: 14). The aim seems to be to disrupt 'The constant temptation to indulge in anecdotal narratives'. This is followed by a series of short paragraphs on making a hand-to-mouth existence in Spain, the illogicality of roads and routes ('encompassing previous cartography, erring, avoiding, changing the stratification of the provenance of faith'), concluding, aptly, with the image of migratory birds spiralling upwards over Gibraltar before crossing the sea to Africa (Walsh, 1989: 19–20). The appropriation of external material within this text is deliberately unattributed and unglossed, and points to the ways in which the next two books ('collections', by this stage of Walsh's career, hardly seems the right word) will mix different source materials and languages – Irish, Spanish, Dublin slang – in order to explore the role of information, with the various registers, languages and narrative material presented in spatial layouts which multiply the number of sequential readings available. *Pitch* orchestrates itself as if inviting the reader to construct any number of alternative readings from what is offered:

```
        unless      less important
        time        now
        stood       element of
        still       confrontation
        less        her only joy
        time
```

```
I used to read her        stood        'never rescind' they said
well                      still        collectively denying any
                                       oh well
                                            (Walsh, 1994: 11)
```

This rupturing of the verse-flow is also often the occasion for refrains, chants and musical effects, and overall *Pitch* is a richer work than the earlier books, moving as it does through a range of locations (rural and urban), materials and styles, from pure modernist lyric ('o glad snow / morning of light / less wish / you were here') to encounters with social deprivation ('Old Mrs Rudd in a one room flat on James' Street / going home later squeamish not able to eat till the smell / warm sliced cheese run through the wild grounds work/house St. Kevin's')[65] (Walsh, 1994: 26). In both cases, Walsh avoids potential difficulties; that, for example, in labouring to break free of conventions the lyric can be caught in poeticisms and mere stream of consciousness reportage (her ear for Dublin speech and use of enjambement ensures challenge and reward for the attentive reader). What is presented throughout is what Walsh calls a 'stratification / of experience' which leaves 'no narrative' in the singular sense 'easy in the mind', a poetic which tentatively celebrates indeterminacy in calling for the breaking of interpretative limits in 'the endless strata / of conceptual errors' (Walsh, 1994: 36; 1996: 22). Behind this lies an interest which she shares with the modernist avant-garde in the communal possibilities of poetry, although the fragmentation of her work reveals doubt as to whether this can be accomplished.

Idir eatortha (meaning 'between worlds') continues the interest in unbelonging, but lends itself even less to description (or quotation) than previous books. This, indeed, is part of the point. The poem at one level is a score (Walsh's own readings of her work involve mimicry, pace- and timbre-shifts and so on, rather than being mere recitals), complete with cues ('[horrified]', '[singing]'), and seems to demand more its enactment than the usual private, readerly encounter with a text. Yet, as elsewhere, the stress is on the plethora and confusions of linguistic-informational material – 'prestige is a brand name too', as the poem notes – and this can only be fully realised by close (re)reading; performance can only ever realise one version of the text (Walsh, 1996: 49). Nevertheless, the book is noticeably concerned with a variety of transient urban soundscapes, offering disconnected shards of overheard speech and sound effects which may add up to a narrative (there are references back to earlier work; the nausea at the squalor in which Mrs Rudd of *Pitch* lives, for example):

'they do but they don't'

'the council, The Council. The Local Borough Council.
No corpo and county here. no craic
The greetings . . .'

'here's a likely looking pair

[politely, respectfully]

[shovelling sounds]

[accelerating footsteps
female voice]

'I don't know George, drunk'
'this time of the morning dear? don't know'
'well, Irish, Scottish perhaps'

(Walsh, 1996: 39)

Throughout the work there is an uninsistent political dimension which is partly thematic – material on the demolition of working-class *barrancas* in Barcelona before the 1992 Olympic Games, for example, in *Pitch* – but this chiefly flows from a democratic immersion in the various competing discourses which surround the modern subject and the distortions to which Walsh subjects ordinary speech. These foreground the paradoxical difficulties of communication in an age which pours more of its energy into the dissemination of information than any before it. Walsh's poetry, rather than simply ironically framing such competing 'language games and phrase regimes', mimics their superabundance in order to question them and, through them, the 'opacity of the post-contemporary world' (Davis, 1998: 48). These ideological occasions may have their gender aspect – although again this is not insistent – and it is one which can be related to the kinds of issues raised by Irish women's poetry generally. Walsh seems unconcerned with the kind of gender politics of the sort found in Boland or in the parodic 'femininity' of McGuckian; an unspecifically gendered modern subjectivity seems to be under scrutiny in her work. However, it would be possible to argue that the kinds of issues raised by the work of other contemporary female neomodernists in the USA and Britain – Lyn Hejinian and Denise Riley, for example – are very much at stake in Walsh. Yet Walsh's status as an Irish woman poet has led to a lack of critical engagement with her work by feminist avant-garde theorists. That is, it could be argued that the complexity of the balance between private and public spheres, expressivist and exteriorised voice, allowed to British/US women experimentalists cannot be discerned by a criticism which still relies on the primacy of a Nationalist paradigm when it comes to Irish poetry. Thus, Clair Wills claims that 'despite their many differences, both political and aesthetic, [Irish women poets] have tried to find ways in which they can work to some extent within the Gaelic or native Irish tradition, rather than simply rejecting it outright, *since to reject it would involve accepting some sort of place within an English tradition – more particularly the English tradition of the well-made Movement lyric, with its aesthetic of "privacy"'* (my emphasis) (Wills, 1993: 53). Even allowing for the fact that Irish circumstances demand a more complex involvement with nationality than obtains for British and US poets, this would seem to deny to Irish women poets the kinds of stylistic latitude allowed to their counterparts elsewhere.

Such considerations lead to the question of how, precisely, the vexed issue of identity might be said to bear on Irish neo-modernist poetry. As Romana Huk has argued, reservations concerning the more extreme anti-identitarian positions adopted by US poetry inform the work of Irish neo-modernists.[66] Pointing to the post-imperial lack of a desire to conceptualise the nation in British and US neo-modernist poetries, Huk notes that in Ireland the nation as a concept still has force, with assumptions about its moribund status less clear-cut. Given the link drawn by neo-modernists between the integral self and the nation state, what this implies is that in the Irish context there is still room for a less suspicious concept of individual subjectivity for equivalent Irish poets; or, rather, that there is still the possibility for these writers to pose, in a meaningful way, the opposition between individualism and the reduction of selfhood into language effect. The subject, in the Irish context, can be viewed as retaining historical specificity rather than needing to be 'democratically' dissolved into the 'writing pool' of L=A=N=G=U=A=G=E poetry. It is for these reasons, Huk claims, that Irish poets appear to be under less pressure from homogenising forces and to engage with mainstream writing even as they reject it.[67] Contemporary neo-modernist Irish poets are more rigorously excluded from the official poetry world in Ireland than in the USA or the UK (where a Bernstein or a Prynne can occasionally be published or reviewed in mainstream journals) and are consequently more isolated.[68] This may be because, unlike British poetry, there does not exist in Ireland – unless Kinsella is taken as its representative – a bridging group which Ian Gregson has called 'retromodernists' (among whom he includes Edwin Morgan, Roy Fisher and Christopher Middleton). These poets, while committed to a modernist anti-realism nevertheless maintain, as Gregson puts it, 'a fraught nostalgia both for epistemological assurance and ontological authenticity' (Gregson, 1996: 127). Yet trace elements of Irish speech and locations, stripped of appeals to self-authentication, punctuate the work of Irish neo-modernists, as Joyce and Walsh show, while modernist precedent and cosmopolitanism consistently influence 'mainstream' poetry, particularly in the Republic. With Northern Irish poets such as McGuckian, Muldoon and Carson, the strongly rooted New Critical and metrically conservative inheritance resists similar influences to produce more ingenious experimental forms than are found in the Republic (a comparison between the treatment of the sonnet in Kennelly's *Cromwell* and Muldoon's *Quoof*, as Edna Longley notes, illustrates the point) (E. Longley, 1994: 196–200). Both Northern and Southern mainstream responses, while less sceptical of expressivism and linguistic discursivity than neo-modernist work, are contiguous with it in mediating uneven (but accelerated) modernisation and Irish interstitiality. As a result, 'mainstream' and experimental poetries appear more separated than in the US or Britain at the same time as the potential for blurring the boundaries between them seems greater.

Splenditello: Ian Duhig

If Irishness in the 1990s has been increasingly defined according to the notion of the 'migrant nation' and diaspora, how are those poets who developed almost wholly outside Ireland, or who were not born in Ireland, to be defined? The issue of the acceptance of poets ruled out of consideration as Irish by long-standing identity-tests is raised sharply not only by Muldoon, whose work – while increasingly 'American' – maintains its explicit Irish dimension, or by neo-modernists consciously affiliated to an internationalist poetic. Equally awkward for traditional conceptions of literary belonging may be those poets of Irish provenance living in England such as Maurice Riordan, Fergus Allen, Matthew Sweeney and Ian Duhig, all four of whom are included in Patrick Crotty's *Modern Irish Poetry* (1995), an anthology reflecting the shifts of definition which have taken place in the 1990s.[69]

In Duhig's first collection, the history which is excluded from Sweeney's spare lyric poetry erupts centre stage and in near-bewildering, baroque profusion. Among its subjects are Bismarck, a Bulgarian Madame Sosostris on the eve of World War I, Baron Corvo, Annie Pleydell, Apollinaire's English governess, an anonymous eighth-century Irish scribe, Jean Valtin, Frank Harris, James but also William Joyce ('Lord Haw-Haw'), a Mexican transsexual in 1919, Edgar Allan Poe in the Bowery, Cecil Rhodes, a French plantation owner in Toussaint L'Ouverture's Haiti, the slum landlord Rachman and the seventeenth-entury Italian lesbian nun Benedetta Carlini. As Crotty has noted, one of Duhig's purposes is to 'seek out the brutalities behind the euphemisms of history', but the manner in which this is achieved is far from the pious 'exposure' of iniquity for the edification of the *bien-pensant*, even as it is calculated to correct official histories. Offsetting a pessimistic revelation of oppression is a near-amoral delight in the grotesque and absurd, conveyed in a mixture of verbal delicacy and exquisitely calculated crudity which intensifies, rather than distracts from, the strangeness and shock of the material. Combining energy, linguistic relish and a preference for simile and synecdoche rather than metaphor – take, for example, 'I said he played the spinet / like a lobster trying to escape its pot' – the distinguishing feature is a wit which refuses to concede any ground to the precious or self-preening (Duhig, 1991: 44). Thus, 'The Irish Slave' takes as its subject the capture, by Barbary Corsairs, of virtually the entire population of the Irish fishing village of Baltimore in 1698. Its speaker traces the opulence of the Ottoman court to which he has been sold, leading the reader inexorably towards his current situation, summed up in the opening line of the final verse:

> Castration has been a good career move.
> I will learn to call the nightingales bulbuls
> I could be drinking my mother's badger tea;
> The Kizlar is preparing my sherbet.
>
> (Duhig, 1991: 15)

This is both hilarious, ruefully self-consoling and jarringly anachronistic ('career move') in a way calculated to disrupt a reading of the poem as historical tourism. Since the speaker was destined for 'the priest's black frock', enforced celibacy was his fate in any case; at least in Istanbul, it is implied, the 'years of forgiving the sins of children / and women while men diced in the church porch' have been avoided. Duhig has a considerable gift for symbolic closure (consider the 'raw vision of Emma Goldman / who'd sell herself for the price of a revolver' in 'On the Trail'), and for poignant effect ('From the Plague Journal' movingly relates the after-effects of the Hiroshima bomb), but his blackly energising humour attends the most mundane or dreadful circumstances. The danger lies, for English critics, in mistaking Duhig's virtuosity in monologue and burlesque as mere entertainment, attempting to pigeonhole it with the sterile exoticism that is sometimes mistaken for imagination, or to resurrect a stage Irish stereotype in order to fend off the substantial challenge the poems offer.[70] The near-savagery of Duhig's humour is amply illustrated by 'Fundamentals', whose speaker is a Livingstone-like missionary haranguing African tribespeople. He concludes his sermon in a manner which is simultaneously uproarious and chilling:

> From today, I want you to remember just three simple things:
> our God is different from your God, our God is better than your God
> and my wife doesn't like it when you watch her go to the toilet.
> Grasp them and you have grasped the fundamentals of salvation.
> Baptisms start at sundown but before then, as arranged,
> how to strip, clean and re-sight a bolt-action Martini-Henry.
>
> (Duhig, 1991, 10)

The poem's effectiveness lies in its refusal to condemn; arrogance, obsession with propriety (and property) and subservience of religion to imperial power-broking are presented in devastatingly comic form precisely because moralising and lyric plangency are so robustly (though not unsubtly) refused. More virtuosically, 'Nineteen Hundred and Nineteen' offers a transsexual speaker in the Mexican Revolution 'dismissed from Tlaltizapa for changing sex'; looking for an alternative role he writes to a series of famous figures – Mangonistas, Lenin, Freud – and finally Yeats: 'Dear Willie, how's the Vision? // Mine's double, ha-ha. Shit. Willie, I'm finished / in Mexico – it's full of bigots. Ireland can't be worse. / I'll work. Your brother paints – I'll hold his ladders. The one about this year – / change it round – it'll do for Ireland.' The final verse suggests that Yeats has accepted the deal (and taken the title of his/her/Duhig's poem for his own use), but also that the speaker is again adrift, 'frowned on' by 'Michael Robartes', a Crazy Jane-like 'drunken madwoman in red skirts, publicly disputing with the bishop'. Duhig's aim here is not merely to send up Western canonical figures from a non-Eurocentric viewpoint ('He wrote to Freud . . . No Mexican has ever heard of the sexual revolution'), but also to raise the issue of national and sexual identity in a genuinely

provocative way (Duhig, 1991: 45). Mexican revolutionary groups have a tradition – repeated in Chiapas today – of support from transsexuals, while Yeats
famously wrote of the androgynous nature of his imagination (one effect of
the poem is to problematise also narrow conceptions of Irishness, both by
drawing links with Mexico's civil war, and by mocking conservative readings
of Yeats's work).

A use of Irishness in Duhig's work (reflected also in an interest in ballad
forms, traditional music and tale-telling) takes the form of radical cultural and
historical displacement. London-Irish identity becomes an asset, a source of
superiority – a reminder, perhaps, of his membership of that generation of
second-generation English Irish who were prime movers in punk and new
wave music from the mid-1970s (John Lydon and Elvis Costello – *né* Declan
McManus – being the prime examples). Implicitly claiming a difference from
the Irish poets of his generation, Duhig – partly tongue in cheek – has noted:
'We were unbelievably arrogant in the early 70s as London Irish. For us,
culchies began at Shepherd's Bush . . . if we were patronising to our parents
and elders, we treated the English with colonial contempt . . . if other London
Irish writers were honest with themselves, they would agree that we secretly
despised the English' (Redmond, 1995: 26–7). Refusing 'marginal', let alone
victim status, Duhig's is a gleefully anarchic acceptance of multiple anomalousness. The epigraphs to *The Bradford Count* – Hugh of St Victor's 'The man
who loves his homeland is a beginner; he to whom every soil is as his own is
strong; but he is perfect for whom the entire world is a foreign country' and
Brecht's ' "You are impertinent", they said to me. / "I'm not impertinent", I
said: "I'm lost" ' – indicate the sharpness of the angle of attack (Duhig, 1991:
5). The saint's sense of homelessness is religious. In juxtaposition with the
politicised bewilderment of Brecht, however, the effect is of an assault not just
on rootedness, but also on any non-estranged, liberal or merely casual
pluralism.

In *The Mersey Goldfish* (1995) and *Nominies* (1998), the sheer exuberance
of the first book is muted by greater thematic and structural consistency. *The
Mersey Goldfish* utilises Duhig's name, whose root in Irish ('dubh', meaning
black or dark), is more commonly anglicised as Duffy. A 'Mersey goldfish',
however, is Scouse slang for human sewage floating in the Mersey, and the
book explores shit (also present in its sense as hashish), origins and blackness
in typically provocative and disturbing ways. Its etymologies are very much in
the vein of recent Northern Irish poetry, though their scatological aspect could
be seen as an attempt to create a very different kind of 'Bog Poem' from those
of Heaney (they also recall Brecht's malodorous challenge: 'If the palace of
culture stinks, is that not because it is built out of dogshit?'). More significantly, the introduction of 'blackness' to a discussion of origins casts a new
light on the terms within which such debates are conducted in Ireland, as
British (and US) racialism complicates Irish sectarian categories.[71] *The Mersey
Goldfish* manages to encompass, among others, the Nationalist use of 'black' to

describe Northern Protestants (as in 'the black North', but since turned by dis-affected Loyalists against the RUC), the Royal Black Institution (a Protestant Israelist sect), Malcolm X's Baconian beliefs, James II (known to Gaelic Ireland as Séamus na Caca, or James the Shit), John Wilkins, inventor of a mechan-ical bowels for ships' toilets, and the Jesuit 'blackrobes' (as the Native Amer-icans called them). 'A Repeat', for example, builds itself around 'an episode of Sesame Street' and features the letter K (at one level, the book is a children's primer). It is set in Berlin at the time of the wave of violent racism following German reunification, and its occasion is a confrontation with a shopkeeper who slams and locks her door against the speaker and the (black, Scottish) poet Jackie *Kay* with a key that 'scrabbles KKK' (Duhig, 1995: 16). The typi-cally Rabelaisian riposte, literally sweet revenge, has both poets messily noshing cakes outside the shopkeeper's window. From this it is a short step to a poem on Rudolf Höss, nicknamed 'schwarze Paula' by Hitler. Yet this most tainted source of blackness offers the strongest of home truths. Recalling his Alexandria birthplace, Höss notes 'You English would hate it, you'd hate the "wogs"' (Duhig, 1995: 32). English racism is to the fore in 'Gyron's Submis-sion', in the voice of the black character from Jarry's *Ubu Roi* play-cycle, but equally important are nineteenth-century theories asserting the African prove-nance of the 'archipelagical indigenes' of Britain and Ireland, according to which 'the traces of our black ancestry / . . . are existent in a hundred sur-names', surnames such as 'Duhig'. The poet acquires racial blackness, although this could only seem spuriously appropriative were the imposture not so bla-tantly a debunking of a poetics of identity and linguistic essentialism. The poem sends up the illogicality of such procedures (at one point Gyron 'proves' Ubu's claim on the British throne by arguing 'two *U*s there mean you're doubly upper-class') (Duhig, 1995: 31). This is of a piece with the deeper linguistic and personal uncertainties of the book, which, however, is clear that exposing the illogical attribution of essential qualities to words by no means overcomes connotations which may all too easily be transferred to racial (or political) Others.[72] The way such racial and political procedures are coded is a theme of *The Mersey Goldfish*, but a major point is the lack of secrecy such codes often afford, and it is suggested that if language has any inherent quality it is duplic-itousness. Many ciphers, as 'The Muck Island Box' shows, are only made to be broken. Duhig has said that 'some of my poems are puzzles or a kind of idiot cabbala', that is, offered because of the way they can be seen through. 'There is a fantasy abroad', he adds, 'that the principle function of language is to communicate. In many circumstances the purpose of language is to excom-municate' (Redmond, 1995: 30). If there is an attitude to history to be drawn from this, however, it is not a doomy but ultimately comforting determinism; history may not be a plot, but it is made up of many miscegenated plots, the extent of which – like language itself – exceeds the comprehension of any single individual.

Nominies, Duhig's most recent collection, takes the hybridity of his work a stage further, immersing itself more in British regional folklore and north-ern English literary tradition, while developing the primer and song/ballad aspects of *The Mersey Goldfish* in making the lore of children central to its struc-ture (the work of Iona and Peter Opie is an important source; 'nominies' is a Yorkshire word for children's chants). The book follows a fourfold structure derived from the opening title poem, which is based, to some degree, on Walter Calverley's infanticide, the subject of the play *A Yorkshire Tragedy*, attributed to Thomas Middleton. Following children's beliefs (as in the April Fool's Day pranks) that the turning point of the day is noon – as opposed to the adult reckoning in which midnight is the point of change – the book follows an oppositional pattern in which children's lore undermines adult wisdom. It also draws on Duhig's experience as a worker in hostels for the homeless, setting the life-histories of the inmates of one to ballad tunes heard from a pub next door (from which the inmates and hostel workers were themselves barred). Like the earlier collections, *Nominies* concerns itself with the experience of those excluded from society and with few or no rights – children, the home-less, conscripts, slaves, Native Americans. To put it like this implies a moral-ism which the poetry opposes as it explores humour, song, charms and game-playing as forms of resisting, and reversing, existing power structures. The collection reflects the banal heartlessness, the institutionalised cynicism of the last years of John Major's Tory government, at the same time as it is driven by the relish of language and love of the grotesque which pervades the earlier work. Duhig's taste for the grotesque has more than a merely debunking func-tion, particularly in combination with the ventriloquism and monologue of which he is also fond. Dramatic form is inherently decentring, often staging without conceding authority to the usual power relations which inform com-munication and interpretation (as Isobel Armstrong has argued, it was the political mode of a post-revolutionary situation for Browning). On the other hand the grotesque arrives where a fantastic, ludic intellectual complexity and the energy of a disruptive libido are forced to live together within a single style. By its concentration on extremes, on incongruities, the grotesque acts as cul-tural critique; its very fragmentariness, hybridity and intensity foreground the problematic nature of the sign, a strategy at the heart of Duhig's work. It is deeply historical because, as Armstrong puts it, 'the Grotesque's perception of incompleteness extends to modernity and historicises that'.[73]

The end of an era?

The point at which Ian Duhig emerged in Britain in the early 1990s can be seen to shed some light back on the opening concerns of this chapter with a migrant postmodern-influenced Irish poetry. For this moment, it might be said, marks the point at which the new energy of hitherto marginal poetic areas (i.e. 'regional', Scottish, working-class, black and women's poetry) which had developed in the 1980s became central in British poetry, and a critical interest in the overlap between neo-modernist and 'mainstream' poetries was articulated. The anthology which marked this turn was *The New Poetry*, which, while rather programmatically valorising the 'marginal', can be linked with the critical shift and a general 'estranging of the mainstream' (Gregson, 1996: 238). While the process of 'estranging' has been exaggerated, it would be accurate to say that the notion of an English tradition, against which Irish poetry variously defined itself, or which it ambiguously embraced in order to rework it, has radically altered in the 1990s. This has important implications for Irish poetry, particularly the 'middle generation' of Irish poets, North and South, of which Heaney is the leading figure. David Kennedy quotes Heaney's conclusion to his essay 'Englands of the Mind', which argues that 'English poets are being forced to explore not just the matter of England but what is the matter with England', a sentence which expresses the postcolonial ressentiment so finely balanced in Heaney's own poetry. However, as Kennedy rightly notes, Heaney's comment 'assumes a consensus about England, the matter of England and the English language, but even as Heaney was writing consensus was being irrevocably eroded and would be followed by polarisation and fragmentation' (D. Kennedy, 1996: 77).

Heaney's assumptions underline the point about the more or less thematic response of his generation of poets to broader trends in Irish society in its international contexts in the 1980s and 1990s. These – the ceasefire and complex negotiations of entrenched positions in the North, the various interpretations of the migrant nation in the Republic, and the effects of the postmodern and globalisation – suggest that a broader redefinition of Irish poetry has been taking place. Within this redefinition it will become increasingly urgent to locate Irish poetries in their historical moments. To uncover lost or suppressed genealogies is not merely to add texts to a canon whose main interpretations have already been settled for posterity. To the contrary, it is to suggest that those interpretations themselves are equally part of a history of cultural production and interpretation. If older, conservative critical formations can be related to isolation and provincialism (but also be read in terms of local resistance to marginalisation by metropolitan literary centres), then a more recent criticism also requires historicisation. In other words, this bifurcation of critical discourses (between older and newer paradigms) needs to itself be read as a mediation of the split to be observed in social, political and economic spheres in an Ireland positioned between developed and underdeveloped, metropolitan and marginalised conditions. The 1990s have shown that Ireland's cherished uniqueness is not wholly exceptional (this being one reason why Eastern European – or Algerian or South African – analogies appeal to writers). But this does not mean that Irish situations can be unproblematically subsumed within a 'backward' versus 'advanced' paradigm. Notions such as 'regressive modernisation' (what Marx called the law of combined and uneven development) have to be subject to an awareness of historical specificities. If Ireland is to be thought of as unique at all it is as a result of its position between the

USA and Britain, but this too is as inadequate as the notion of uniqueness – predicated on an 'essential' transhistorical identity – which is challenged by an increasing fluidity of those relationships.

Within a new international framework, the new (and often violent) nationalisms which have erupted since the fall of the Stalinist states have been taken to confirm the legitimacy of national aspiration, but also to reinforce doubts that nationalism can take wholly benign forms. Such debates are at present particularly important in Ireland, North and South. The Northern Ireland peace deal is at the moment of writing (July 1999) balanced on a knife-edge, while in the Republic there is a fear of an ever-more rootless polity which has severed significant links with its past and traditions by participation in the Good Friday Agreement. Jettisoning national 'identity' is seen by many in these circumstances as succumbing to an internationalism which is never neutral, dominated as it is by (increasingly) US culture and the 'New World Order'. It is clear, therefore, that to cling to older configurations of Irish identity set within the frame of a rapidly dissolving Anglo-Irish antagonism is to remain fixated on outdated colonial models; how 'post' does 'postcolonial' have to be before it ceases to be a – or the – primary determinant in the way Irish writing is read, and reads itself? Similar considerations apply to the emergence of women's poetry, in which the simple assertion of the right to speak or to belong to 'a' tradition now seems inadequate. Cross-fertilisation between the Republic and the North has increased in the 1980s and 1990s as political entrenchments have seemed increasingly irrelevant (and under the influence of historiography, sociology, women's studies and other disciplines which, before the 1960s, had been set in traditional moulds). Nevertheless, the polarisation of the debates over Irish writing's postcoloniality and/or postmodernity points to an unresolved legacy. And if, at an institutional level, poetry in Ireland seems far healthier than it was twenty, let alone thirty, years ago, with the burgeoning number of literary festivals, journals, presses, workshops, reading circuits and academic attention to contemporary writing (although several of these show signs of having reached saturation point) – a crisis of generational transmission shows signs of reappearing. This is not simply to make the case that a perceived lack of outstanding younger poets, North and South, is a reflection of the commodification of literary culture. As an alternative to the isolationism of the poets of the 1950s and 1960s, as well as the programmatic reaction to modernisation of their immediate successors, the attention poetry is receiving can only be seen as a positive development. Nevertheless, the gap between sophisticated academic discussion of Irish poetry and the tendency towards bland criticism and reviewing suggests that the reaction against an earlier acerbity may have gone too far.

The situation in the Republic, while interestingly fluid, still suffers from the lack of the focus which continues to bind together and give cohesion to the work of the best Northern Irish poets. No single historical moment has galvanised poetry in the Republic; modernisation is a process, but Burntollet and

Bloody Sunday were events. The basis for Northern prominence, laid before the Troubles, is rooted partly in the fact that, as Carol Rumens has noted, 'the community is small and close-knit, and perceives itself as such even when scattered by emigration. There is some degree of dialogue between Northern Irish and British poets, more productive than between Southern Irish and American, because prosodic and linguistic variations are small enough to change hands as live usable currency. But undoubtedly the *real* dialogue is between the Northern Irish themselves – a bardic clan with its own semi-secret language of reference and allusion . . . the habit of mutual close-reading and hard-criticism has never disappeared' (Rumens, 1997: 28). Diasporic redefinitions of Irishness, while problematic – promoting double-edged promises of prosperity and frequently glossing the brutal agendas of transnational capital – hold real prospects for the new millennium for both poetries. Having established an international presence within the English-speaking world, it would seem unlikely that Irish poets will forego an exploration of their interstitial situations for a relapse into older modes, in terms either of identity, tradition or continuity (or the mirror-image 'discontinuity' substitute for it). In this sense the concluding lines of Garratt's 1989 edition of *Modern Irish Poetry* gesture towards a notion of change which is inadequate in its refusal of history: 'if it no longer resembles Yeats's right rose tree, the tradition nonetheless seems assured of some kind of continuity, its trunk apparently weathered and hard enough to survive even its own isolation' (Garratt, 1989: 275). There is, for Irish poetry now, no 'isolation', and any organic metaphor is profoundly misplaced. What the best poets of the last decade acknowledge is that reality in and out of Ireland is not only too complex for any single writer or work of literature to encompass, but that the very incomprehension it enforces, incorporated and yet resisted by poetry, may provide the most urgent source of creativity in the twenty-first century.

Notes

1 For Clyde, Northern poets now realise that

> they can no longer perform that 'bardic' function within one nation or tribe which was previously claimed or assumed. There emerges a growing realisation that we have no longer 'one nation' (temporarily sundered), nor even 'two traditions', but many different traditions, overlapping and inconsistent. We are now heading into a post-revolutionary period reminiscent of the 40's and 50's, when the disillusionment which sets in when a national myth has been created and found wanting once again requires the demythologising energy of an O'Faolain and a *Bell*. (Clyde, 1988: 95–6)

2 As Bernard O'Donoghue puts it, 'Nobody would now say that Dublin cannot be evoked or represented from Paris or Trieste' (O'Donoghue, 1995: 404).

3 In the work of Michael O'Loughlin, an Irish poet living outside Ireland from the mid-1980s, these processes can be seen at work. A qualitative change in the level of cultural exchange has further eroded the notion of 'exile' and there is, in the poetry of Muldoon particularly, a singular lack of that lyric confinement and sense

of separation from the dynamics of Irish culture which limited the poetry of a Patrick Galvin or a Pearse Hutchinson in the 1950s. O'Loughlin's later poetry centres around his encounter with Europe, often defined in terms of his residence in Amsterdam. *The Diary of a Silence* (1985) marks an abrupt break with the stridencies of his first two collections and an attempt to understand Ireland in the context of a more ironic perspective informed by European writing (it is revealing that 'new and selected poems', *Another Nation* (1996), includes only eleven early poems). *Diary of a Silence* charts the interaction between Ireland and the continent in both directions – 'Frank Ryan Dead in Dresden' and 'Heinrich Böll in Ireland' – traced back to a habit of listening to the radio in bed as a child 'Ear pressed to the heart of Europe / Softly thundering distant music, / Slurred insomniac lullabies / For complex children' (O'Loughlin, 1985a: 52). The book is concerned to represent the 'shards' which bulk so large in the poetry of Montague and Heaney as those of post-war Europe, and the new poems of *Another Nation* develop the theme of 1980s' emigration, Dublin as 'an emptiness' with a 'lack of sustaining tradition' (O'Loughlin, 1991: 7). Against this, though in response to it, O'Loughlin offers, in an article of 1991 – 'Meridian – Dublin and Amsterdam' – the Dutch city as 'the centre I had dreamed of in the suburbs of Dublin: a boring, perfectly satisfactory utopia' (O'Loughlin, 1991: 11). What Amsterdam linked was the notion of the suburb as 'the true cultural capital of our time', decentred, passively opposed to authority, and the social democratic tradition. Behind the Amsterdam suburb of Betondorp he finds the philosophy which is 'the hidden creed of modern Europe', an 'idea of social answerability', a place explicitly designed to allow people 'to live full, healthy lives'. In the new post-cold war European order O'Loughlin expects the status of national capitals to decline, and that of suburbs – 'the cutting edges of the empire, the frontier posts' – to rise. The overcoming of the national cultures resurrected in the aftermath of World War II means a move from 'the suburbs of silence' to a 'new Europe' which may as well take place in post-Nationalist Ireland as elsewhere.

4 The turn to Eastern Europe as a source of analogues for the Irish condition can be seen as continuing the momentum of *Station Island* and *Sweeney Astray* towards 'a new kind of self-reliance . . . a recognition that the self is interesting not as an example', as it was expressed in *Preoccupations*, 'but as an exception', that is free of communal obligations and able to 'issue, as well as receive, instruction' (Corcoran, 1987: 127). *The Haw Lantern* confirmed the taste for chastening confrontations and allegory of *Station Island*, with the titles of a number of poems – 'From the Canton of Expectation', 'From the Land of the Unspoken', 'Parable Island' – echoing those of poems by poets such as Zbigniew Herbert and Czeslaw Milosz. In Heaney's criticism, Mandelstam was reaffirmed as the exemplary figure signalled first in the reference to 'inner émigré' and 'tristia' in 'Exposure'. Opening with 'Alphabets', about the acquisition of writing and languages, and closing with 'The Riddle', the collection signals also an increased concern with etymology, and willingness to remain in a state of uncertainty consonant with the resolution to dispense with miring 'attachment'. As Steven Matthews has argued, in Heaney's later poetry the hesitancy about the role of poetry which weakened pieces such as 'Casualty' becomes 'an opportunity in itself', albeit at the cost of some forcefulness (Matthews, 1997: 172). The counterbalancing claim for moral authority present in the poetry is emphasised in *The Government of the Tongue* (1988), whose title signifies both repression and the right to vatic power earned by writers under such governance. In Heaney's words, 'The poetic art is credited with an authority of its own. As readers we submit to the jurisdiction of achieved form, even though that form is achieved not by dint of the moral and ethical exercise of mind but by what we call inspira-

tion' (Heaney, 1989: 92). McDonald notes that 'Authority is something that moves from the poem to the poet . . . but the argument is by its nature essentially unanswerable' (McDonald, 1995: 176).

In *The Haw Lantern*, but even more in *Seeing Things*, an imagery of transcendence, broken syntax, offhandedness and occasionally abstract allegorical language signals the shift from communal attachment and the '[crediting of] marvels', while maintaining individual authority: 'Do not waver / Into language. Do not waver in it' (Heaney, 1991: 56). The stress on the aesthetic, self-delighting dimension of art and simultaneously its power to assuage is finely balanced between scrupulousness and a self-parodic 'insistence on having things both ways' (S. O'Brien, 1998: 95). A self-secure identity is underwritten by the appeal to exemplary figures, which in turn validates Heaney's own poetic practice in which experience (now individual rather than representative) is prized above meaning (the main focus of recent anti-foundationalist critical discourse). Heaney's admiration for the resistance of the poet under dictatorship is that of someone who wishes to be similarly situated where the authenticity of voice in 'the fully exposed poem' is unchallengeable, something which what he calls 'the postmodern age' will not allow, but it also hints at the complexity of the postcolonial situation of the North. This, of course, is by no means to dismiss the originality of works such as the 'Squarings' sequence of forty-eight twelve-line near-sonnets of *Seeing Things*, in which Heaney successfully manages to present 'the image of the visionary experience as a transgression of the threshold (or *limen*) of normal perception', evoking mortality through the 'implicit sublimity' of this world and an insistence that 'there is no next-time-round' (Robinson, 1992: 52; Heaney, 1991: 55). These are virtuosic as well as visionary works, notations which work against the urge to create a free-standing lyric by being inconclusive and reliant on their position in the sequence, qualifying the big music and rhetoric of earlier work. The dangers of self-parody are real, however, and *The Spirit Level* (1997), Heaney's first post-Nobel collection, tends to recapitulate over-insistently the various phases of the career. The award of the Nobel Prize identifies one of Heaney's chief problems in this later poetry; namely, how to avoid the dilemmas of a self-consciously 'outsider' poet laden with honours and attention.

5 Investigations of cultural 'globalisation from below' are at an early stage, and many of the most obvious examples of those involved – from Turkish-German to black and Southern Asian British writers – are non-Irish (though see n. 3 above). Nevertheless, certain general responses to increased 'globalisation from above' link these with Irish writers who live abroad or negotiate between two (or more) cultures. As the rubric for the 'Inter-links: Transnational Imagination, Translation and Cultural Policy' conference statement puts it, as 'identities grow more plural and flexible . . . Voices of 'minorities' become major – the 'margins' become central to cultural change.' For further details and methodology, see the 'Axial Writing' research project of the ESRC Transnational Communities Programme at http://www.transcomm.ox.ac.uk

6 As Bew, Gibbon and Patterson note, Trimble's short-term objective was not to win over Catholics – a 'highly utopian project' – but to restore the party's fortunes by making it 'more attractive to intelligent Protestants after the more passive leadership of James Molyneaux and the setbacks of the post-1985 period' (Bew, Gibbon and Patterson, 1996: 235).

7 Robinson's election was even more notable given her past as a civil rights lawyer and feminist with a record of activity on censorship, women's and Travellers' rights. Her incumbency was marked by an expansion of the scope of a largely symbolic position. Visits to famine-stricken areas of Africa, to West Belfast and to Bucking-

ham Palace demonstrated a willingness to break out of the usual confines of the post, as did her embrace of the concept of the 'migrant nation' (that the 'Irish nation' included all those of Irish descent worldwide). Her election compelled all political parties to rethink their positions on women's issues and to increase the number of female candidates at elections.

8 One of the poets quoted by Mary Robinson in her inauguration speech was Paul Durcan; and the international political context and influence of change can be seen at work in *Going Home to Russia* (1987). Going abroad is a 'going home', a 'Goodbye to the conscientious politicians of Ireland / Who believe in the Right of the Few to Free Speech / But not in the Right of the Many to Work and Health, / Housing, Transport, Education, Art' (Durcan, 1991: 66). Durcan is anti-political, however, rather than proposing a different politics, and the poem shows that his 'understanding of materialism is not itself materialist: in place of economics he has morality, and in place of politics he has hope' (S. O'Brien, 1998: 106). The journey to Russia is thus a return to an ideal Ireland which never was and/or which will be. The sequence involves a Russian muse/lover, Svetka, an anti-Cathleen Ni Houlihan who, typically, exposes male shortcomings and presumptions, at the same time as Durcan's persona adopts Russian qualities, pleading, for example, for Solzhenitsyn's return: 'Alexander Isayevich, we have served our sentence: / Have mercy on us and, if you please, come home' (Durcan, 1991: 76). Yevtushenko's 'Zima Junction' becomes 'Trauma Junction', 'The Girl With the Keys to Pearse's Cottage' becomes 'The Woman with the Keys to Stalin's House' as Durcan proceeds, via Pasternak's grave and a homage to Mandelstam, to a discovery of the grave of John Field, the Irish classical composer, who died miserably in Moscow in 1837.

Throughout this, the notion, as Richard Kearney puts it, of Durcan feeling 'a foreigner in his native land and a native in a foreign land' is strong. Kearney's advocacy of the utopian potential of myth is read into Durcan's imaginings: 'His utopian images stem from a basic ambiguity towards homelands. As he puts it in one poem . . . "Should there be anyone in the world who has not got mixed feelings?"' (Kearney, 1992: 53–4). With more *parti pris*, McDonald claims the sequence 'finally opts for a complete relocation of "home" (among the most dangerous, and certainly one of the most common words in Irish poetry) in the secular, utterly different world of the Soviet Union', and 'exchang[es] (in the imagination at least) a closed and controlled society for one of more substantial freedom . . . the poetry's trip to Russia is a kind of principled self-exile' (McDonald, 1988: 106–7). *Going Home to Russia*, however, is probably best seen as the logical conclusion in a developing displacement of Ireland which can be charted from the 1970s onwards. This displacement also involves a partial invocation to his much loved and feared father, a High Court judge and Fine Gael stalwart, who became the chief subject of *Daddy, Daddy*. This returns to consider Ireland again, using the father as another means for coming to terms with a society which may, at last, be on the verge of the kind of radical self-assessment the poetry has consistently demanded. There is risk involved in dealing with this personal link to paternal and state authority since the position as visionary outsider is complicated by affection. But the title sequence – one in a long and, as Maurice Elliott has argued, complex, seven-part volume – is perhaps Durcan's most coherent to date, structured as it is around the trope of a 'marriage' between son and father, a secret divorce, followed by a second marriage before the father's death (Elliott, 1992). The provocation of the work is signalled by its indebtedness to Plath's famous 'Daddy', and the characterisation of Judge Durcan (and, by implication, neutral Ireland) as 'Fascist' recalls Plath's poem and the Nazi imagery of earlier work. What saves the poem from the failures of those poems is the precision of its sentiment – the father buying his son a copy of the

Beatles' *Sergeant Pepper* album, the salvaging of the pyjamas he died in for the poet to wear, a radio warbling down the ward from the deathbed. Here, refraining from the social critique to which his poetry is in many ways fundamentally unsuited, Durcan achieves a significant triumph.

9 Likewise, the average annual growth rate of the economy in the same period was at 8.9 per cent compared to an EU average of 2.4 per cent, and the Republic was the only developed country to feature among the world's twenty fastest-growing economies forecast for 1999. While the UK remained the major trading partner, the proportion of Irish exports to the UK had declined from 55 per cent in 1973 to 25 per cent by 1998, and the USA had become the major investor, underlining the new European and international orientation of the country. (Revealingly, also, official government sources of information stress the link between diaspora and emigrant experience, giving 'an ease at working and interacting with other cultures', and economic success.) See the website Economic Data Ireland at http://www.irish-trade.ie

10 See the website 'The Celtic Tiger . . . who's doing the roaring?' at http://flag.black-ened.net/revolt/ws98/ws53__tiger. html As this points out, economic growth has relied on increased exploitation rates: 'The annual index of wage costs has dropped from 87.9 in 1990 to 72.1 in 1995, while output per person rose from 145.4 in 1990 to 214.1 in 1995.' The site also underlines the fragility of the phenomenon; the economist Denis O'Hearn is quoted as saying: 'it is barely an exaggeration . . . to say that the difference . . . boils down to a few US corporations in computers and pharmaceuticals'. It notes that ten large transnational corporations in 1994 accounted for 75 per cent of all value added to goods in the manufacturing sector, with manufacturing itself accounting for 40 per cent of economic growth.

11 Lyotard's essay 'Defining the Postmodern' succinctly identifies three basic grounds for the claim that we live in a postmodern era: that the ideas of progress, rationalism and objectivity which underwrote Western modernity are no longer applicable, largely through their discounting of cultural difference; that there is a lack of confidence in the superiority and distinctiveness of 'high' from 'low' art; and that it is no longer possible to separate the real from the copy, or simulacrum, in a reality shaped and saturated by technology, particularly communications technologies. See Simon During (ed.), *The Cultural Studies Reader* (London, Routledge, 1993), 170–3.

12 For a lucid and persuasive critique of the claims of postmodernism and its supersession of modernism, see Callinicos, 1989.

13 The notion of the postmodern as the lat(est) cultural manifestation of capitalist society can clearly be related to certain economic and social developments in Ireland. Similarly, reaction to postmodernism's anti-foundationalism can be traced in the cultural-political debates of the 1980s and 1990s already glanced at, and it is arguable that the increased academicisation of poetry itself is a postmodern phenomenon. More significantly, postmodernism's levelling of distinctions between margins and centres, its anti-authoritarianism and (implicit) sanction of the local has marked recent cultural and intellectual trends. Such complications can be read, of course, as another chapter in a debate over modernising Irish culture which stretches back to the 1950s. Contemporary manifestations of this, in postmodern guise, may be seen in the debates on myth (which Richard Kearney has attempted to define in postmodern, utopian, non-atavistic form), in speculations about the narrative of Irish history (fragmented and so possibly anticipatory of postmodern discontinuity) and in postcolonialism in cultural criticism (although not, of course, in 'revisionist' historiography) which took its cue from the international critical

trend boosted by Edward Said's massively influential *Orientalism* (1979) (Wills, 1993: 107–8; Kearney, 1992: 41–63).

14 Thus, Anne McClintock is guilty of postcolonial criticism's general lack of discrimination with regard to Ireland when she claims that 'Currently China keeps its colonial grip on Tibet's throat, as does Indonesia on East Timor, Israel on the Occupied Territories and the West Bank, and Britain on Northern Ireland. Since 1915, South Africa has kept its colonial boot on Namibia's soil . . . None of these countries can, with justice, be called "post-colonial"' (A. McClintock, The Angel of Progress: Pitfalls of the Term 'Post-colonialism', in Patrick Williams and Laura Chrisman (eds), *Colonial Discourse and Post-Colonial Theory: A Reader* (Hemel Hempstead, Harvester/Wheatsheaf, 1993), 295. While the validity of 'post' is correctly challenged here, the ranking of the suffering of the Nationalist community in Northern Ireland with that of the East Timorese or Namibians shows the kind of revolutionary defeatism (and kowtowing to militant Republicanism) which has marked the writings of many British Left academics on Ireland.

Perhaps the most thoroughgoing critical application of the postcolonial paradigm can be found in Declan Kiberd's history of modern Irish literature, *Inventing Ireland* (1995). Chief among the problems created by a systematic recourse to a postcolonial reading is the eliding of writing which does not fit the thesis; as Fintan O'Toole points out, 'most of the literature written by Protestants in Ireland after the partition of the island in 1920 is either ignored or mentioned only in passing', as is much contemporary writing from the Republic (which focuses on divisions and splits within Ireland) and work 'produced by Irish writers in England', while the book as a whole is undertheorised (O'Toole, 1996). The result is that if he accepts a certain degree of pluralism, Kiberd ironically often endorses a thematic and locational definition of Irishness little different from that of critics, like Clyde, on the other side of the ideological fence. This said, postcolonial theory is generally confused by the complexity of Irish writing; if, in some accounts, Northern Ireland can be compared with Namibia, in the standard introduction to the subject, *The Empire Writes Back*, Irish literature is excluded from discussion on the grounds of insufficient 'postcoloniality' (Ashcroft, Griffiths and Tiffin, 1989: 8). Kiberd's omissions thus reflect the very real problems of definition which afflict postcolonialism almost as much as postmodernism in an Irish context(s), as well as his Nationalist agenda; and *The Empire Writes Back* reveals the gap between national self-perception and external perceptions of Irish identity, in this case from a non-UK or US perspective (for a change). In this sense, some attacks on the homogenising effects of the term 'postcolonial' have themselves fallen into the trap of presenting postcolonial experience in a monolithic way. More recently, in the 1990s, Luke Gibbons and David Lloyd have used the notions of 'allegory' and 'adulteration', respectively, to bring a more sophisticated Bhabha- and Bakhtin-influenced methodology to describe the 'modular histories' of Irish postcolonialism (or decolonisation), arguing that 'Analyses unproblematically transposed from Western models of tradition and modernisation to Irish history fail to engage with what is specific about its decolonising formations – namely, the lack of secure traditions and the politically charged nature of the discourses of modernity' (Smyth, 1998: 34). Kiberd's own comment that *The Empire Writes Back* 'passes over the Irish case very swiftly, perhaps because the authors find these white Europeans too strange an instance to justify their sustained attention' is disingenuous; even a cursory reading shows that there is no 'perhaps' about the 'passing over' and Ashcroft *et al.* are quite specific in their reasons for the denial of postcolonial status to Irish literature (Kiberd, 1995: 4–5). Drawing on Max Dorsinville's exploration of the ways in which 'dominated' cultures may themselves 'dominate' internal subcultures (thus, white

Australian literature is 'dominated' and hence postcolonial in relation to British literature, but 'dominating' and hence itself colonial in regard to Aboriginal literature), they argue that while it is possible to claim that Irish (like Scottish or Welsh) societies were the victims of English expansion, 'their subsequent complicity in the British imperial enterprise makes it difficult for colonized people to accept their identity as post-colonial', although adding that Dorsinville's model does enable 'an interpretation of British literary history as a process of hierarchical interchange in internal and external group relationships' (Ashcroft, Griffiths and Tiffin, 1989: 33). See, for example, MacLaughlin: '[Irish emigrants to the USA] played a significant role in clearing native Americans from the interior [and] they were among the chief benefactors of white colonialist expansion . . . Irish involvement in bitter "race wars" against native and black Americans is a forgotten chapter in current debates on Ireland's internationalist and anti-colonial legacy' (MacLaughlin, 1994: 5).

15 C. Graham, 'Liminal Spaces': Post-Colonial Theories and Irish Culture, *The Irish Review*, 16 (Autumn/Winter 1994), 29–43.

16 Elements of this can be seen in the debate over the attitudes of writers to the use of the English language, which has been a major pillar in the cultural politics and writing of Heaney, Montague, Hartnett and the Field Day project. In what might be called the Dean of Studies Syndrome, the alienness of English to a putative Irish reality is configured in terms of a basic postcolonial model of abrogation and appropriation, taking sanction from the famous encounter between the Dean of Studies and Stephen Dedalus in *A Portrait of the Artist as a Young Man*. As has been argued, the interpretation faces the problems of both naively assuming that Stephen's position is Joyce's own, and ignoring Joyce's own heterodox and anti-essentialist approach to the issue of language in his writings. The result is the elevation of the language issue to the status of a master trope for the postcolonial linguistic condition, avoiding more detailed consideration of material and historical evidence – the question being to what extent, precisely, English in Ireland should now be considered imposed or 'unnatural'?

17 A more general criticism of the therapeutic state-directed sponsorship of culture can be found in Muldoon's *The Prince of the Quotidian*, which notes 'the casuistry / by which pianists and painters and poets are proof / that all's not rotten in the state: / amid the cheers and cries of "bravo" / I hear the howls of seven dead / at a crossroads between Omagh and long Cookstown' (Muldoon, 1994b: 35).

18 Paulin has claimed that 'the Irish writer who publishes in Britain has a neo-colonial identity', and if this overrides differences, it also identifies the question of a radically estranged Protestant identity. As in *Liberty Tree*, Paulin's relationship to this identity is, as McDonald has put it, 'inside and outside at once, trying to speak with the accent of the community he anatomizes, while also subjecting that community to a scrutiny complicit with the hostility felt towards it by its historic enemies' (McDonald, 1997: 102–3). It emphasises the divisions within Unionist and Loyalist ideologies as well as Protestant Republicanism and dissent, continuing the themes of *Liberty Tree*, but with a more pessimistic inflection. In this sense, *Fivemiletown* is one of the very few literary works to treat seriously the relatively unexplored issues raised in David Miller's analysis of the complexities of the Ulster Protestant contractarian identity (Miller, 1978).

19 See Paulin's essays on Herbert, Holub and Rózewicz, each of which concludes with a gesture to stylistic qualities – 'lucidity', 'craft', 'like a diagram of a self-destruct mechanism' (Paulin, 1993: 210, 224, 232).

20 P. McDonald, Jump or Get Pushed, *The Irish Review*, 4 (Spring 1998), 95.

21 Robinson reads this optimistically as an 'oblique celebration of erotic love as an underground act', but in doing so seems to conflate Paulin's Achilles (who

enters Hades because he is dead) with Aeneas (who visits it in order to return) (Robinson, 1988: 121–2).

22 As Wills puts it, 'Privacy is embraced but at the same time seen as collusive in the reactionary desire to separate public from private life and thereby render politics opaque' (Wills, 1993: 139).

23 Carson notes that one of the reasons for abandoning poetry for eleven years was its mandarin aloofness by comparison with traditional music and its culture. He notes that a handbook on traditional music he wrote, published in 1986, provided a way back into poetry. As he has claimed, perhaps somewhat fancifully, 'The way the long line moves is not unlike the movement of a reel. The basic 8-bar unit of the reel – which can be further divided into smaller units, 2 or 4 or whatever – corresponds roughly to the length of, and stresses within, the poetry line' (Brandes, 1990: 82). This technical development owed something to the US poet C. K. Williams, while the oral style had its sources in the crime fiction of George V. Higgins and the procedures of the *seannachie*, or traditional Irish storyteller, as well as to the improvisatory phrasing of Irish traditional music (Carson is Traditional Arts Officer for the Arts Council of Northern Ireland and plays the flute and tin whistle).

24 Douglas Dunn, The Poetry Says Yes, *Irish Literary Supplement* (Fall 1988), 38.

25 The most complex and longest of such tales-within-tales poems is 'Queen's Gambit' in *Belfast Confetti*. As Kathleen McCracken points out, in the best account so far of the poem, it 'consists of no less than five narrative strands', giving different versions of tales involving the ambush of a British Army patrol by republicans and a raid by 'Ordinary Decent Criminals' which become mixed up with each other (McCracken, 1995: 366–7).

26 As McCracken notes, this too has its ideological or political dimension, since 'whereas in English one can make an unequivocal statement for or against a united Ireland, in Irish such an expression will be necessarily ambiguous' (McCracken, 1995: 368).

27 In this sense, Sean O'Brien's claim for *First Language* (1993) that 'the sense that Carson is writing English as if it were Irish is especially strong in this book' can also be applied to its two predecessors (S. O'Brien, 1998: 193).

28 This is perhaps even more evident in part two, the central section of the book, which is set in what will become the territory of Carson's next collection. A series of short poems (of nine long lines), it ranges over the 'no man's land between reality and nightmare' of inner Belfast (Welch, 1996: 84); indeed, the first of them, 'Belfast Confetti', provides the next book's title at the same time as it dissolves the distinctions between writing and 'reality':

> Suddenly as the riot squad moved in, it was raining
>   exclamation marks,
> Nuts, bolts, nails, car-keys. A fount of broken type. And the
>   explosion
> Itself – an asterisk on the map. This hyphenated line, a burst of
>   rapid fire . . .
> I was trying to complete a sentence in my head, but it kept
>   stuttering,
> All the alleyways and side-streets blocked with stops and
>   colons.
>   . . . What is
> My name? Where am I coming from? Where am I going?
>   A fusillade of question-marks.
>
>   (Carson, 1988a: 31)

In these pieces the grimy energy and detritus of the inner city the speaker knows 'like the back of my hand, except / My hand is cut off at the wrist' are writ large; like the bombed Grand Central Hotel in 'Night Patrol' this is a form of lyric which has had its 'Victorian creamy façade' 'tossed off / To show the inner-city tubing: cables, sewers, a snarl of Portakabins, / Soft porn shops and carry-outs' (Carson, 1988a: 34).

29 The always already belatedness of mapping is linked to Carson's emphasis on the instantaneity of traditional music (infinite variation within finite conventions) and the ability of music to '[defeat] time by its mnemonic' (Carson, 1996a: 197).

30 Presenting an ideal for the city against the theories of planners, architects and bureaucrats, de Certeau rejects the 'voyeur's', or bird's-eye view for that of a pedestrian; walking in the city has its own 'rhetoric', by which the walker individuates and makes ambiguous the 'legible' order imposed by planners 'a little like the way waking life is displaced and ambiguated by dreaming'. Such walkers are 'practitioners of the city . . . below the thresholds at which [official] visibility begins', their practices organising the city, composing 'a manifold story that has neither author nor spectator, shaped out of fragments of trajectories and alterations of spaces: in relation to representations, it remains daily and indefinitely other'. In doing so, for de Certeau, practitioners temporarily evade and subvert the classifications of power, and he traces what he calls 'the chorus of idle footsteps' to arrive at a theory of interaction with the spaces and 'leftovers' of the city which asserts the primacy of the imagination to reconfigure and narrativise these in a form of resistance: 'Things extra and other (details and excesses coming from elsewhere) insert themselves into the accepted framework, the imposed order.' This is immensely suggestive in the context of Carson's work, although it has to be stressed that the malignity of Belfast – its state of war and siege – imparts a darker edge to de Certeau's utopian proposals. In particular, Carson's concern with surveillance goes beyond anything in the de Certeau essay. See de Certeau, 1984: 151–60.

31 The expatriates, unlike Carson himself, are fixated on the past of Belfast: 'Running back the film of the mind's eye, the alphabet soup of demolition sorts itself into phrases, names, buildings, as if, on the last day, not only bodies are resurrected whole and perfect, but each brick, each stone, finds its proper place again' (Carson, 1990: 54).

32 The increasing geographical segregation of working-class Belfast has been a particular feature of the city; Neil Jarman notes that 60,000 people, or 12 per cent of the population, had to move house between 1969 and 1976, most of them within the city. See N. Jarman, Intersecting Belfast, in Brian Bender (ed.), *Landscape: Politics and Perspectives* (Oxford, Berg Press, 1987), 109. Simultaneously, in the words of the Belfast novelist Glenn Patterson: 'The city was changing day by day, its buildings were being erased, its roads rerouted, its territorial boundaries redrawn. While there can be no ignoring the destabilising effects, social and psychological, of all this (I choose the words deliberately) deconstruction and revision, it nevertheless contains within it a certain liberating potential. In particular it resists the closure of traditional interpretations in which one unchanging territory is endlessly contested by two mutually exclusive tribes: the old politics of one thing or the other. Identity becomes dynamic rather than birth-given and static. Concepts like flux and exchange replace the language of original states.' See G. Patterson, I am a Northern Irish Novelist, in I. A. Bell (ed.), *Peripheral Visions: Images of Nationhood in Contemporary British Fiction* (Cardiff, University of Wales Press, 1995), 151.

33 As O'Brien notes, 'In ['Grass'] a group is betrayed by an informer, a "fact" elicited from a glut of doubletalk and euphemism which sounds at least as hell-bent on perpetuating itself as the speaker is on exacting revenge. The poem provokes the

question of how anything anyone involved in whatever this lot are up to could possibly be a secret for longer than five minutes, given their inherent mouthiness – which returns us to the absurdist figures of earlier narrative poems' (S. O'Brien, 1998: 193).

34 P. McDonald, Difficulties with Form, *The Irish Review*, 16 (Autumn/Winter 1994), 130.

35 *Meeting the British* concerns itself with the ambiguities of trade and exchange, sexual as well as cultural and economic ('intercourse', in all its senses, might be the best word). In 'Profumo', his mother's injunction – 'Away and read Masefield's *Cargoes*' – is the basis for a querying of the exoticism which often conceals the inequalities of trade, explored throughout the book. At the same time, the theme of openness (or closedness) to exchange makes this Muldoon's most personal collection to date, and nowhere more so than in 'The Soap-Pig', an elegy for the BBC producer Michael Heffernan which, for the first time in his work, presents in a 'realistic' manner Muldoon's own life and loves. This prepares the way for the more thorough unravelling of a personal past, previously suppressed and disguised, in *The Prince of the Quotidian* (1994), *The Annals of Chile* (1994) and *Hay* (1998). '7, Middagh Street', the long concluding poem of *Meeting the British*, is set in 1940 at a time of personal and historical endings and beginnings for its various characters, Carson McCullers, Chester Kallman, Benjamin Britten, Gypsy Rose Lee, Auden, Salvador Dali and Louis MacNeice, as well as Yeats (who had died the year before), who lurks as a ghostly presence to be celebrated and mocked. These bear on Muldoon's own move to the USA in 1987 and his marriage to an American, Jean Hanff Korelitz, as well as the pull of origins against both an unstable bohemian artistic tradition and the urge to flight from events where engagement of the more obvious sort might be demanded (World War II, Spain, Northern Ireland). The poem insists on haphazardness, contingency and juxtaposition, its 'ventriloquised' monologues arranged in a way suggestive both of the arbitrary linkage of the historical figures involved, and of circularity or entrapment, through its use of the corona form (a corona is a variation of the Renaissance sonnet-sequence in which each poem begins with, or 'exchanges', the final line of its predecessor. Positions on the relationship between art and politics are also exchanged, and modified in the process, between the poem's parts. In 'Wystan', we get a moralist version of what seems like Muldoon's own aversion to political commitment in poetry, while 'Salvador', in aestheticist mode, reprocesses 'The Boundary Commission' with an Anarchist whose taxi 'carried two flags, / Spanish and Catalan. Which side was I on? / Not one, or both, or none'. Although Muldoon shares traits with both, neither position is fully endorsed. As elsewhere in Muldoon, the authority of MacNeice is called for; the final section, 'Louis', opposes Auden's claim that 'poetry makes nothing happen', describing him as 'a stylite / waiting for hostilities / to cease, a Dutch master / intent only on painting an oyster' (Muldoon, 1987: 56). Nevertheless, art is consistently connected with the inevitable betrayal of, or to, origins. In the final sonnet-section of 'Louis', MacNeice, 'after drinking all night in a Sands Street shebeen', leaves for home by 'the back door of Muldoon's', only to be accosted by a 'one-eyed foreman' from Harland and Woolf who challenges MacNeice's humanism by calling him a 'Fenian', tribal origins rearing their ugly cyclopean head. 'Louis', then, embodies the impossibility of leaving origins fully behind; he is said to be incapable of concluding the corona by '[caulking] a seam / on the quinquereme of Nineveh', as the poem becomes an interrupted circular set of deliberations rather than a linear narrative (Muldoon, 1987: 60).

36 See, for example, the amused exasperation of Michael Hofmann's observation that

'One often feels tempted to throw the whole thing at a computer and say: "Here, you do it"' (Hofmann, 1990: 18).

37 Appropriately, one of the major sources for 'Madoc' is Gore Vidal's fictionalisation of the federalist conspiracies against Jefferson and the politics of the young Republic in *Burr*.

38 The bracketing suggests the separation of mind and body in Western philosophical and religious thought (compared with the holistic views of the Native Americans' belief in 'Manitou', or the Great Spirit, and its presence within the land). The 'mind' of the poem is thus separate from the 'body' of its text.

39 Apart from the 'teeny-weeny key', and a 'pearwood box', there is a 'valise' in the possession of Southey. When the Pantisocrats split up, Coleridge gets this. Later he deems it 'the lesser of two evils' to present it to Handsome Lake, the shaman (Muldoon, 1990: 118). It then disappears until in '[Meinong]', seventy pages later, Southey opens his writing desk in which there is a 'pearwood box' and 'Inside . . . – hold on a minute – / is an exact replica / of the valise. / Its very contents are identical' (Muldoon, 1990: 188). Or are they? The last couplet notes: 'All except for a dog-eared letter in cuttle- / ink addressed by Coleridge to "my dearest Cottle"'. The letter turns up again soon after in '[Whitehead]'. It reads: 'My Dearest Cottle, I am fearful that Southey will begin to rely too much on *story & event* in his poems to the neglect of those *lofty imaginings* that are peculiar to, & definitive of, the POET.' The letter, a critical comment on poems like Southey's dogmatic *Madoc*, is also an auto-critique within Muldoon's poem, reminding the reader of its separation of '*story & event*' and Romantic philosophical '*lofty imaginings*' between the story of Coleridge and Southey and the metanarrative of the supertitles. If this seems like wheels within wheels, then it is part of the point about the endless circularity, the continual recycling of culture, which 'Madoc' is trying to make. Later still, Handsome Lake (in '[Ortega]') 'takes a firm hold / of the handle of his valise' (which contains the letter) 'and sets out on an inner / journey along the path covered with grass' (Muldoon, 1990: 212). By '[Putnam]' the by-now 'otherworldly valise' is back in Southey's possession and the cycle seems to have come full circle. Or has it? A return to the poem's opening reveals that South, too, has 'a valise'. This might be yet another circle – the futuristic narrative encircles that of the Pantisocrats. Yet the valise actually first appeared *outside* the poem in one of the seven short poems which make up part one of the collection *Madoc*, 'A Briefcase'. The briefcase/valise of this poem contains 'the first inkling' of the long poem 'Madoc' (which is anything but a 'brief case'); and the speaker of the poem, a version of Muldoon, is afraid to put the briefcase and poem down 'for fear it might slink into a culvert / and strike out along East River / for the sea. By which I mean the "open sea"' (Muldoon, 1990: 12). So the 'mystery' of the poem's subtitle keeps escaping the circles constructed to contain it, Russian doll-like, and keeps being apprehended by the poet. 'Madoc', that is, continually resists the intertextuality which would keep it confined to language, striking out for 'reality' (or history) – the 'open sea' – which is placed in quotation marks as if to remind us, ironically, that it is impossible to be sure that 'reality' exists 'out there' anyway. This, presumably, is one reason why 'The Briefcase' is addressed to Seamus Heaney, a poet who, unlike Muldoon, does believe that words have a sovereign, magical power to represent things 'out there'.

40 Unitel is capped with an 'iridescent Dome' which recalls that of Xanadu in Coleridge's 'Kubla Khan'.

41 See Edna Longley, Way down upon the Susquehannah, *The Irish Times* (3 November 1991), 22.

42 If, in *Madoc*, Muldoon is arguing again against the establishing of pure origins, a further irony within the poem is that the Mandans (or Modocs), as Welsh, are

already more British than the British (since the Welsh were the 'original' inhabitants of the island of Britain).

43 Language, as Muldoon has noted, was a 'weapon of colonisation'. Interview with Blake Morrison, *The Independent on Sunday* (28 October 1990), 37. Part of the process of disinheriting Native Americans was the appropriation and destruction of their languages. Muldoon fills the volume therefore with words from these in commemoration and celebration, reminding us of the native presence even as the colonisers destroy it. Jacqueline McCurry lists, among others, squantum, kinnikinnick, manitou, mackinaw, wannigan, sachems, sagamore, mugwump, punk, cougar, raccoon, coyote, tomahawk, wigwam, quamash, caucus, powwow, skunk, woodchuck, hickory, lacrosse, calumet, beaver, buffalo, gopher, Tammany, kayak, pirogue, hammock, toboggan, canoe (McCurry, 1992: 103).

44 Southey's epic – conservative and Christian – specifically justified the imperial 'civilising' mission in the Americas, by conflating all Native American religious systems with the bloody rituals of the Aztecs.

45 As Richard Holmes, Coleridge's biographer, notes: 'it is not impossible to imagine Coleridge, in some alternative life, flourishing among these original Susquehannah pioneers, and making his own distinctive contribution to the history of the Wild West' (R. Holmes, *Early Visions* (London, Penguin, 1989), 90). A letter of 1804 by Coleridge on the subject of the philosopher-poet anticipates Holmes's description: 'But yet you will agree, that a great poet must be, implicite if not explicite, a profound metaphysician. He may not have it in logical coherence, in his Brain & Tongue; but he must have it by Tact: for all sounds, & forms of human nature he must have the ear of a wild Arab listening in the silent desert – the eye of a North American Indian tracing the footsteps of an enemy upon the leaves that strew the forest' (*ibid.*, 326). This 'profound metaphysician' aspect of Coleridge's thinking is, of course, mocked by 'Madoc'. So, too, are any Romantic beliefs in the essential purity of Native American culture. Their paradoxically 'British' aspect is apparent in '[Aquinas]', in which Coleridge anticlimactically meets Thayendenaga after a mystical passage 'Up a spiral staircase with precisely two hundred and thirty-three steps, each conjured from the living rock' and 'Through the hoopless hoop of a black rainbow': 'He offers Coleridge tea and scones, / pres- / erves and clotted cream' (Muldoon, 1990: 64). Thayendenaga, it turns out, is half-Scottish. In this sense it is the British (or Europeans) who deny hybridity, categorising Native Americans as 'Indians' (as they did by naming them 'Red Indians', in error, on first encountering them), rather than recognising their diversity.

46 As Kendall also notes, while all the other historical figures in the poem die at their predetermined times in 'real' history, Sara's – in 1845 – is passed over, suggesting her absorption into the Native Indian population.

47 A. Callinicos, *Marxism and Philosophy* (Oxford, Oxford University Press, 1989), 22–3.

48 Again, it is worth noting that *Gunslinger* has its version of 'the institution', namely *rob art*, taken from Howard Hughes's middle name, and alluding to what Dorn sees as US capitalism's role in destroying the artistic impulse.

49 It is impossible to do justice to the full range of Muldoon's work since *Meeting the British*, work which surely establishes him as the most inventive Irish poet now writing. The libretto *Shining Brow*, written after *Madoc*, and based on the life of Frank Lloyd Wright, marks a stylistic shift from his poetry of the 1980s in its reliance on repetition (again, as in 'Madoc', it is possible to see Muldoon evolving forms which have an affinity with those of modernist and neo-modernist experimental writing – and critiquing any notion of the 'integral' design – while at the same time maintaining a connection with the traditional, discursive and lyric inheritance of Northern Irish poetry; it is no coincidence that Wright, the main subject of the piece, is subjected to a critique of the modernist artist as exploiter of 'primitive' cultures

and as 'charismatic character' and 'self-publicist') (Keller, 1994: 7). Welshness stands in for Celticism ('shining brow' translates Taliesin, the Welsh poet), as in 'Madoc', and *Shining Brow* also extends and simultaneously bids farewell to the Native American thematics of the work; Wright's idealisation of Native American culture – 'The Hopi, the Huron, the Hunkapapa Sioux / might have taught the Greeks and Romans / a lesson in harmony' – is a comment on Muldoon's own extensive usage and, to some extent, a self-rebuke (Muldoon, 1993: 67).

In *The Annals of Chile* Muldoon returns to his earliest Irish locations in a gesture of final farewell (Wills notes that the poem arose from a visit to Ireland in the spring of 1992) (Wills, 1998: 167). As in the early lyrics, 'The Moy is as exotic as it is familiar', and the trigger for the Latin American concerns of the book (which include a translation from Vallejo and references to Neruda, as well as Bernardo O'Higgins, the Irish-descended governor of Chile) is Muldoon's elaboration of visions of the continent from pampas-grass which grew around the house in his childhood (S. O'Brien, 1998: 173). 'Yarrow', the collection's long poem, is 'set' in three time periods – the present, the early 1970s and the early 1960s – and draws heavily on the extravagant imaginative life and exotic reading of Muldoon as a boy. It jumps between them, just as the narrator of the poem's present flicks between the channels on his TV and video recorder, in a fantastically complicated weave. Technically it represents a move beyond even the mutations of sonnet form and the collage structure of 'Madoc'; 'Yarrow' takes twelve off-rhymed poems of twelve, nine or six lines as its templates (each based on sestina form), generating ninety rhyme words in a poem of over a thousand lines; each time a poem is repeated, as with the conventional setina, the rhyme scheme is changed, with the variations themselves forming a pattern, although this at times may be broken. Overall, as Wills notes, 'After the central poem, which rhymes with the first, the sequence reproduces the exact order of all the preceding seventy-five poem forms in reverse, ending with a variation on the first poem' (Wills, 1998: 180). The elaborateness of the work does not disguise the fact that it is a poem of reparation to Muldoon's mother, a circling around what the poet himself has called 'a deep-seated hurt', in which the curative powers of yarrow signify something of the intention to assuage and uncover pain. Yet the final image – of a shipwreck in which nutmeg, or sweetener, for Muldoon's dying mother's porridge is lost – is a mark of the poem's ultimate failure to accomplish its aim. As this brief description suggests, 'Yarrow' is the best example of what Declan Kiberd has called the 'awesome symmetry of [Muldoon's] arrangements' and – given the comparative modesty of the structures of *Hay* (1998) – may represent their high point (Kiberd, 1995: 611).

50 John Wilkinson, 'Too-Close Reading: Poetry and Schizophrenia', *The Gig*, 1 (November 1998), 49.

51 'Neo-modernist' is used here to distinguish poets such as Trevor Joyce, Maurice Scully and Catherine Walsh, discussed here, from the 'postmodern' aspects of those deriving from, but to some extent challenging, mainstream poetry, such as Carson and Muldoon. Like 'postmodernist', 'neo-modernist' is a vague term which smacks of critical convenience as much as it usefully describes the actual variety of the poetic practices it gestures towards. Nevertheless, in nominating a difference in the sources of the work of these different groupings of poets, the terms may have some diagnostic serviceability. Ian Gregson, using the term 'retro-modernist' where 'neo-modernist' is used here, attempts a basic definition. Gregson notes, on the one hand, that 'retro-modernists' are 'profoundly unlike 'anti-modernists' – such as Larkin – in their anti-realism: 'their poems do not characteristically construct a reliable sense of the poet's personality authoritatively describing and commenting on self-consciously familiar slices of life'. On the other hand, he points out, his 'retro-

modernists' – he cites Edwin Morgan, Christopher Middleton and Roy Fisher – do not push their anti-realism to the point of 'a playful celebration of the impossibility of ever fully apprehending the real', as does a postmodernist proper such as John Ashbery. Rather, they maintain 'a fraught nostalgia both for epistemological assurance and ontological authenticity. Larkin and Ashbery both make assumptions, though of an opposite kind; for these retro-modernists, by contrast, the nature of the real is always in question and the experimental forms of their writing are evolved in an attempt to grasp it while simultaneously acknowledging its elusiveness' (Gregson, 1996: 127–8). For neither grouping of poets discussed here is such a distinction binding; the 'postmodernism' of Muldoon and Carson is more bound to discursivity and the real than in Ashbery, while it cannot be said that there is anything as strong as an urge to 'grasp' reality in the work particularly of Walsh or Scully (although in Joyce, the influence of such modernist concerns are stronger). Despite certain limitations, however, Gregson's argument provides one way of conceptualising some basic differences and possible lines of critical enquiry. For a more detailed and equally useful discussion of these issues in their British contexts, see 'Just the Facts, Just the': A RoughGuide to British Postmodernism, in D. Kennedy, 1996. For some of the related issues raised by postmodernism, the avant-garde and L=A=N=G=U=A=G=E poetry in the USA, see Bob Perelman, *The Marginalization of Poetry: Language Writing and Literary History* (Princeton, Princeton University Press, 1996).

52 I. Sinclair, *The Conductors of Chaos* (London, Picador, 1996), xiii.

53 In 1985, as Scully withdrew from publishing, hardPressed Poetry was begun by Billy Mills, joined a year later by Catherine Walsh, although both left to work abroad in the late 1980s.

54 It is worth noting that Ciaran Carson's concern to distinguish between 'art' and 'traditional' musics, at the expense of the former, is couched in terms which resemble those of Joyce. In *Irish Traditional Music*, the handbook which he has said paved the way for the stylistic breakthrough of *The Irish for No*, Carson cites Cage to make a point similar to that made by Joyce: 'When we separate music from life what we get is art (a compendium of masterpieces). With contemporary music, when it is actually contemporary, we have no time to make that separation (which protects us from living) and so contemporary music is not so much art as it is life and anyone making it no sooner finishes one of it than he begins making another just as people keep on washing dishes, brushing their teeth, getting sleepy, and so on' (Carson, 1986: 8–9). It is necessary, perhaps, to distinguish also between this position and that of Paulin's later insistence on the 'NOW' of poetry, which valorises the instant but in a rather naively authenticist way. Carson's poetry stands, in relation to Cage's words, somewhere between Paulin's and Joyce's practices.

55 As Joyce puts it, 'Remember that this information overload is not emotionally or linguistically neutral. Images of suffering, the irreducible experience of real pain, are pressed on us by media which demand our outraged response, but leave that response, once elicited, without possibility of external effect. So, these poems turn from images of war, famine, disease, "bulk dead", the whole spectrum of human wretchedness, to a language in which all positive terms have been appropriated by advertising, the unassailable praise-poetry of our time.' It is worth noting that Joyce does not dismiss the mainstream poets he refers to, Mahon (or Boland), as being 'bad in some essential way'. Rather, they face the problem 'they are too proper . . . they exclude too much . . . they are depressingly predictable and fundamentally joyless', imitating the images of beauty with which they are already familiar and 'nudging them occasionally towards the mess that is the world, only

through a sense of guilt . . . at perpetrating such works of beauty in such a foul environment' (Gilonis, 1998: 24).

56 In this sense, the very mastery of conventional language and poetic forms is precisely what generates the unease of such poetry for Joyce, since '[I]t puts us in the same position to the resources of language as technological mastery has enabled industry to adopt in relation to the resources of the natural world', and 'we do not listen to our slaves' (Gilonis, 1998: 24).

57 M. Perloff, *Radical Artifice: Writing Poetry in the Age of Media* (Chicago, Chicago University Press, 1991), 205.

58 Nearly one-third of PCs sold in Europe are now made in Ireland, and pharmaceuticals, telemarketing and financial services – all highly communications technology-reliant – follow a similar pattern. As Economic Data Ireland claims, 'At 37% the high technology share of exports [from the Republic] is three times the EU average'; to take one example, the Intel plant north of Dublin makes Pentium II processors for all of Europe. See Economic Data Ireland and 'Celtic tiger may be in for a pounding' at wysiwyg://10/http://www.snh.com.au/news/9812/30/world/world6.html Again, it is not 'backwardness' which is the dominant feature of Irish development so much as the disparity between underdevelopment and the most cutting-edge contemporary technologies. (Official acceptance of this disparity can be seen in the decision by the IDA in 1983 to shift its emphasis from job creation to wealth creation, abandoning the Lemassian strategy by which investment and industrialisation would modernise the whole of Irish society. In effect, this reflected that the goal of thoroughgoing industrial modernisation on the West European model had not, and would not, come about, and marked an acceptance of the Republic's status as peripheral).

59 In Gibbons's words, 'This is saying, in effect, that a "post-industrial" revolution in an electronic age need no longer be encumbered by a vision of social progress' (Gibbons, 1996: 91). Gibbons is somewhat overeager to refute the standard equation of modernisation with social progress (his pessimism can seem a more intellectually sophisticated version of Desmond Fennell's thesis that liberalism represents reprovincialisation); if neo-traditionalism helped refurbish social control, this did not go uncontested, while the work of neo-modernist poets suggested some ways in which the positive potential of modernity might be harnessed to social self-awareness.

60 Personal letter to the author, May 1995.

61 The three 'found' lines are: 'and then there is this sound the red noise of bones', from Neruda; part of a folk curse ('when the thieving sea will fit in three quart jugs'); 'we suffer an exposure to the tune of several millions', from the financial pages of a newspaper.

62 Other glosses refer to some of the recurrent themes of the piece(s); the fish – a salmon – as symbolic of the principle of life, and a concern with debris and its status.

63 N. Dorward, 'In the Net', *The Gig*, 1 (November 1998), 58.

64 As Alex Davis has claimed, the Walsh 'fields' poem is opposed to, say, 'Anahorish', where, in the aural properties of the signifier, it is claimed that the signified can be conjured up. Heaney's poem is contradictory – its adjectives ('soft', etc.) actually supplement the name, which is revealed as being inadequate to itself as a signified. For Walsh – despite her interest in musical effects in her poetry – everything (words and objects) are more or less in the same place, pointing to the inevitably supplementary nature of all writing.

65 One model for Walsh's treatment of Dublin may be Roy Fisher's seminal *City* (1961), which is set in/deals with, his native Birmingham. It is a poem in which as David Kennedy puts it 'documentary realism accesses hallucinatory fiction [and]

the grounded self gives up its identity' (D. Kennedy, 1996: 103). Walsh's poems, like Fisher's (in such later works as *Furnace* as well as *City*), offer a model of representation without a dominant subjectivity – and hence the urge to moralise – dramatising doubts about where the self ends and its environment begins.

66 'American readers' of Walsh, as Mills has pointed out, 'assume that the L=A=N=G=U=A=G=E writers must have been formative for her . . . Walsh's attitude to the relationship between language and world is profoundly different to theirs' (Mills, 1998: 34). Elaborating this, it might be said that the 'mind', however 'stratified' in Walsh is never wholly expunged from her poetry, bearing the afterimage of the individual ego, as in the work – to differing degrees – of other Irish neo-modernists. This may explains Walsh's wariness with regard to L=A=N=G=U=A=G=E poetry which, in one influential variety, seeks the total dissolution of the 'I' within the field of language. On the other hand Walsh's interest in the communicability of ideas, however distorted by transmission from one context to another, also prevents identification with the alternative L=A=N=G=U=A=G=E poetry of, for instance, Bruce Andrews, in which all utterances are so intimately coded that they escape intersubjective understanding.

67 These ideas were presented by Huk at 'Make It New (Again)', the Third Cork Conference of Alternative Poetry & Performance Art, 25 April 1999, in the paper 'On foreign-national locations of the place and/or non-place of the(ir) unpronounceable idir eatortha: Returns of nationalism in/as disguise undisguised, or: Ironies inherent in current inscriptions of Irish experiment in the Anglo-American tradition'. Since published in *the Journal*, 2 (1999), 65–77.

68 Crossovers between mainstream and marginalised poetries occur, albeit with something of a time lag, in both the USA and Britain; thus Bloodaxe, now the largest poetry publisher in Britain, has recently published the collected poems of J. H. Prynne.

69 The problems raised by their inclusion require some consideration here. Sweeney and Duhig, in particular, given their status in a British poetry scene, blur the boundaries between British and Irish poetries in ways different from those offered by past 'exile' poets, from Coffey to Galvin. Tom Paulin shares something of the peculiar position they occupy, but in Paulin's case there is, arguably, a willed (Northern) Irishness which these poets clearly do not share (as well as a greater awareness of the potential dangers of stereotyping 'Englishness'). In Sweeney's case, the main stylistic allegiances are from the USA, and signal the way in which Irish poets have generally been more open to American example than their British counterparts. Nevertheless, there is a low-key quality to much of the poetry which suggests that at some level he has also assimilated an English reticence along with an American sense of estrangement, dislocation and violence, espousing a demotic miniaturism and urbanism. For Duhig, a near-obsessive formalism recalling the Northern Irish poets plays against a delight in the grotesque and a verbal ferocity which owes something to an Irish taste for storytelling and oral culture, but also to Browning and the English northern tradition which includes Ted Hughes and Tony Harrison. Duhig, despite an expressed dislike for Geoffrey Hill's work, has a similar interest in lavishness and ritual; as Kennedy notes, 'there is, perhaps, an echo in all of this [interest in historical marginalia] of Geoffrey Hill's idea of the past commanding our "belated witness" – and Duhig's language is similarly fortified, muscular and strange . . . – but he is vulgarly comic where Hill is pompous, and energetically curious where Hill's learned grandiloquence can appear as aristocratic hauteur' (D. Kennedy, Historical Vulgarities, *Times Literary Supplement* (19 October 1991), 42).

70 This kind of English misreading of *The Bradford Count* can be found in Adam Thorpe's review: '[He] remains content with shards . . . He is mainly drawn to the

darker corners of the Catholic past, to boils and saddle-girths and St Sepulchre's Without and his own Irish origins probably explain the almost obsessive and balefully funny sifting of these choice parts . . . Where he avoids indulgence, Duhig manipulates the material impressively.' The point here is that Thorpe, even when impressed by Duhig, sees him in thematic and wholly expressivist terms (terms which Duhig's range of material is designed to question). Nor does Thorpe notice that miscegenation and the energies of the grotesque are aimed precisely at undermining categories such as 'Irish origins' and 'Catholic past' (A. Thorpe, *Observer* (20 October 1991), 24).

71 Thus, in interview with John Redmond, Duhig notes 'Dubh for me is interesting because in English "black man" means "the devil" and fascists are wheeling out the old codes in England (Column 88 used to refer to H. H. or Heil Hitler; the new Column 18 works the same device) and "black" prefixes an army of insults. It does so in Ireland too but with a different slew. However, in Irish a man of colour is not black (*dubh*) but blue (*gorm*) and for a while I liked to fancy the Irish were less racist, even to their language, than the English. But I asked a tinker. Know the word *nigéar*?' (Redmond, 1995: 31). The question of the sources of Duhig's poetry is one which has been significantly misrepresented by Tim Kendall. In a review of *The Mersey Goldfish*, Kendall claims that the poetry '[crossed] Browning's dramatic monologue with a free-wheeling slanginess derived from Muldoon' (T. Kendall, 'Parlour Tricks', *Poetry Review*, 85: 4 (Winter 1995–96), 87). This misses the fact that while Duhig is indeed indebted to Browning's gnarled style and harnessing of the energies of the grotesque, his 'monologues' are rarely 'dramatic' in the Browningesque sense of including an unidentified interlocutor whose function is to destabilise readerly interpretation. Similarly, Muldoon's 'slanginess' is very different from Duhig's use of the vernacular, one deriving – as Neil Reeve has noted – from 'a vigorous and highly sophisticated oral culture of pubs, streets and football terraces, combative bandinage and self-satirising verbal identity' which has its specifically English (London and Yorkshire) contexts. (See N. H. Reeve, *Irish Studies Review*, 7: 1 (April 1999), 129). When Kendall goes on to deprecate Duhig's 'pedantic' use of allusion in contrast to 'the allusive genius of Eliot or Muldoon' he misses the point of Duhig's calculated philistinism, which is deliberately intended to disrupt the seamless meshing of allusion with poetic discursivity, as well as engaging in invidious comparison rather than criticism. More bizarrely, he finds 'Nineteen Hundred and Nineteen' 'slavishly indebted' to Saul Bellow's *Herzog*, in the apparent belief that Bellow has patented the 'epistolary idea' he takes (wrongly) to be the structuring principle behind the poem. The larger critical point to be made relates to a very English valorisation of Muldoon and its empiricist 'influence'-hunting methods.

72 The politics of the McCarthy witch-hunts are 'black', for example; 'Roll Call' details the case of the blacklisted writer Dalton Trumbo, used by Kirk Douglas as the scriptwriter for *Spartacus*. It opens with Trumbo suffering from writer's block: 'he can see no end, / no gesture enacting its testament . . . what was it again that *testa* meant?' Pondering the meaning of 'testa' (head') gives him his cue: in imagination he cuts to the scene of the rebellion's last stand. Crassus, the Roman commander, offers mercy to those who will identify their leader, then 'Focus on Kirk's heroic face' as he announces 'I am Spartacus'

> . . . but his neighbour roars in stereo
> 'HE LIES. I, I AM SPARTACUS,'
> then the next man's 'IT IS I' and the next
> 'I', 'I', 'I', 'I', 'I AM SPARTACUS.'
> (Duhig, 1995: 39)

The conclusion is movingly effective, since Trumbo finds the perfect conclusion to the revolt, but also dramatises a utopian, compensatory solidarity against the blacklisting; this scene is his 'testament'. But at the same time, we have learned that Douglas's use of Trumbo is an open secret in the studio. This doesn't make it any the less courageous, but it does multiply the ironies. Trumbo changes his name to 'Sam Jacks', but the man who has accepted the blacklist, Samuel Goldwyn (*né* Goldfish) has already changed his own name from a Jewish to an Anglo-Saxon one.

73 I. Armstrong, *Victorian Poetry: Poetry, Poetics and Politics* (London, Routledge, 1996), 288, 291.

Select bibliography

Primary texts

Boland, E. (1973), The Tribal Poet: John Montague, *The Irish Times*, 20 March, 10
——(1975), *The War Horse*, Dublin, Arlen House
——(1980), *In Her Own Image*, Dublin, Arlen House
——(1982), *Night Feed*, Dublin, Arlen House
——(1989), *Selected Poems*, Manchester, Carcanet Press
——(1990), *Outside History*, Manchester, Carcanet Press
——(1994), *In a Time of Violence*, Manchester, Carcanet Press
——(1995), *Collected Poems*, Manchester, Carcanet Press
——(1996), *Object Lessons: The Life of the Woman and the Poet in Our Time*, London, Vintage Press
Carson, C. (1975a), Au Revoir: review of *A Farewell to English*, *The Honest Ulsterman*, 50, 187–9
——(1975b), Escaped from the Massacre?: review of *North*, *The Honest Ulsterman*, 50, 183–6
——(1976 repr. 1988b), *The New Estate and Other Poems*, Oldcastle, Gallery Press
——(1986), *Irish Traditional Music*, Belfast, Appletree Press
——(1987 repr. 1988a), *The Irish for No*, Newcastle upon Tyne, Bloodaxe Books
——(1989 repr. 1990), *Belfast Confetti*, Newcastle upon Tyne, Bloodaxe Books
——(1993 repr. 1994), *First Language*, Oldcastle, Gallery Press
——(1996a), *Last Night's Fun: A Book About Irish Traditional Music*, London, Jonathan Cape
——(1996b), *Opera Etcetera*, Newcastle upon Tyne, Bloodaxe Books
——(1997), *The Star Factory*, London, Granta Books
Clarke, A. (1974), *Collected Poems*, ed. L. Miller, Dublin, Dolmen Press
——(1976), *Selected Poems*, ed. T. Kinsella, Dublin, Dolmen Press
——(1991), *Selected Poems*, ed. H. Maxton, Dublin, Lilliput Press
Coffey, B. (1991), *Poems and Versions 1929–1990*, Dublin, Dedalus Press
Cronin, A. (1956), A Massacre of Authors, *Encounter*, 6:31, 25–32
——(1980), *R.M.S. Titanic*, Dublin, Raven Arts Press
——(1982), *New & Selected Poems*, Manchester, Carcanet Press
——(1989), *The End of the Modern World*, Dublin, Raven Arts Press
Devlin, D. (1989), *Collected Poems of Denis Devlin*, ed. J. C. C. Mays, Dublin, Dedalus Press
Duhig, I. (1991), *The Bradford Count*, Newcastle upon Tyne, Bloodaxe Books
——(1995), *The Mersey Goldfish*, Newcastle upon Tyne, Bloodaxe Books
——(1998), *Nominies*, Newcastle upon Tyne, Bloodaxe Books
Durcan, P. (1975 repr. 1995), *O Westport in the Light of Asia Minor*, London, Harvill Press
——(1985 repr. 1995), *The Berlin Wall Café*, Belfast, Blackstaff Press

——(1987 repr. 1991), *Going Home to Russia*, Belfast, Blackstaff Press

——(1990), *Daddy, Daddy*, Belfast, Blackstaff Press

——(1993), *A Snail in My Prime: New and Selected Poems*, Belfast, Blackstaff Press

Fallon, P. (1990), *Collected Poems*, Manchester / Loughcrew, Carcanet Press / Dolmen Press

Galvin, P. (1996), *New and Selected Poems*, ed. G. Delanty and R. Welch, Cork, Cork University Press

Hartnett, M. (1975 repr. 1991), *A Farewell to English*, Dublin, Gallery Press

——(1985), *O Bruadair: Selected Poems of Dáibhí O Bruadair*, Dublin, Gallery Press

——(1987), *A Necklace of Wrens*, Dublin, Gallery Press

——(1994), *Selected and New Poems*, Dublin, Gallery Press

Healy, R. (1983–4), Logic as a Starting Point for Poetry, *the Beau*, 3, 10–12

——(1987), *Arbor Vitae*, Bray, Wild Honey Press

——(1996), *Rana, Rana!*, Bray, Wild Honey Press

——(1997), *Flame*, Bray, Wild Honey Press

Heaney, S. (1966), *Death of a Naturalist*, London, Faber and Faber

——(1969), *Door into the Dark*, London, Faber and Faber

——(1970), King of the Dark, *The Listener*, February, 181–2

——(1972), *Wintering Out*, London, Faber and Faber

——(1975), *North*, London, Faber and Faber

——(1978), The Interesting Case of John Alphonsus Mulrennan, *Planet*, 41, 34–7

——(1979), *Field Work*, London, Faber and Faber

——(1980), *Preoccupations: Selected Prose 1968–1978*, London, Faber and Faber

——(1983a), *An Open Letter*, Derry, Field Day Theatre Company

——(1983b), *Sweeney Astray*, London, Faber and Faber

——(1984), *Station Island*, London, Faber and Faber

——(1987), *The Haw Lantern*, London, Faber and Faber

——(1988 repr. 1989), *The Government of the Tongue: The 1986 T. S. Eliot Memorial Lectures and Other Critical Writings*, London, Faber and Faber

——(1991), *Seeing Things*, London, Faber and Faber

——(1995), *Crediting Poetry*, Oldcastle, Gallery Press

——(1997), *The Spirit Level*, London, Faber and Faber

Hewitt, J. (1981 repr. 1991), *The Selected John Hewitt*, ed. A. Warner, Belfast, Blackstaff Press

——(1987), *Ancestral Voices: The Selected Prose of John Hewitt*, ed. T. Clyde, Belfast, Blackstaff Press

——(1992), *The Collected Poems of John Hewitt*, ed. F. Ormsby, Belfast, Blackstaff Press

Hutchinson, P. (1982), *Selected Poems*, Dublin, Gallery Press

——(1990), *The Soul that Kissed the Body*, Oldcastle, Gallery Press

Iremonger, V. (1951), The Young Writer and *The Bell* 2, *The Bell*, 17:7, 12–18

——(1988), *Sandymount, Dublin: New and Selected Poems*, Dublin, Dedalus Press

Joyce, T. (1973), *Pentahedron*, Dublin, New Writers' Press

——(1976), *The Poems of Sweeny Peregrine*, Dublin, New Writers' Press

——(1995), *stone floods*, Dublin, New Writers' Press

——(1998), *Syzygy*, Bray, Wild Honey Press

Kavanagh, P. (1960), *Come Dance With Kitty Stobling and Other Poems*, London, Longman

——(1972 repr. 1992), *Patrick Kavanagh: The Complete Poems*, ed. Peter Kavanagh, Newbridge, Goldsmith Press

——(1973), *Collected Pruse*, London, Martin Brian and O'Keeffe

——(1996), *Patrick Kavanagh: Selected Poems*, ed. A. Quinn, Harmondsworth, Penguin Books

Kennelly, B. (1969), *Selected Poems*, Dublin, Allen Figgis Ltd

Kinsella, T. (1965), Poetry Since Yeats: An Exchange of Views, *Tri-Quarterly*, 4, 100–11
——(1967), The Irish Writer, *Éire-Ireland*, 2:2, 8–15
——(1973a), *New Poems 1973*, Dublin, Dolmen Press
——(1973b), *Selected Poems 1956–1968*, Dublin, Dolmen Press
——(1974), The Poetic Career of Austin Clarke, *Irish University Review*, 4:1, 123–30
——(1979a), *Fifteen Dead*, Dublin, Dolmen Press
——(1979b), *One and Other Poems*, Dublin, Dolmen Press
——(1988), *Blood and Family*, Oxford, Oxford University Press
——(1994), *From Centre City*, Oxford, Oxford University Press
——(1995), *The Dual Tradition*, Manchester, Carcanet Press
——(1996), *Collected Poems 1956–1994*, Oxford, Oxford University Press
Longley, M. (1968), *Secret Marriages*, Manchester, Phoenix Pamphlet Poets Press
——(1973), *An Exploded View: Poems 1968–72*, London, Victor Gollancz
——(1991a), *Poems 1963–83*, London, Secker and Warburg
——(1991b repr. 1993), *Gorse Fires*, London, Secker and Warburg
——(1995a), *The Ghost Orchid*, London, Jonathan Cape
——(1995b), *Tuppenny Stung: Autobiographical Chapters*, Belfast, Lagan Press
McCarthy, T. (1981), *The Sorrow Garden*, London, Anvil Press
——(1984), *The Non-Aligned Storyteller*, London, Anvil Press
——(1989), *Seven Winters in Paris*, London, Anvil Press
——(1991), Five Summer Afternoons, *Éire-Ireland*, 26:1, 7–18
——(1998), *Gardens of Remembrance*, Dublin, New Island Books
McFadden, R. (1996a), *Collected Poems 1943–1995*, Belfast, Lagan Press
——(1996b), 'One Who Stayed': An Interview with Roy McFadden, by Sarah Ferris, *Irish Studies Review*, 17, 21–4
MacGreevy, T. (1991), *Collected Poems of Thomas MacGreevy*, ed. S. Schreibman, Dublin, Anna Livia Press
——(1998), *Thomas MacGreevy Hypertext Chronology*: http://www.ucd.ie/~cosei/-index.html
McGuckian, M. (1982), *The Flower Master*, Oxford, Oxford University Press
——(1984), *Venus and the Rain*, Oxford, Oxford University Press
——(1988), *On Ballycastle Beach*, Oxford, Oxford University Press
——(1992), *Marconi's Cottage*, Newcastle upon Tyne, Bloodaxe Press
——(1994), *Captain Lavender*, Oldcastle, Gallery Press
——(1998), *Shelmailer*, Oldcastle, Gallery Press
MacNeice, L. (1965), *Varieties of Parable*, London, Cambridge University Press
——(1979), *Collected Poems*, ed. E. Dobbs, London, Faber and Faber
——(1987), *Selected Literary Criticism of Louis MacNeice*, ed. A. Heuser, Oxford, Clarendon Press
Mahon, D. (1968), *Night-Crossing*, London, Oxford University Press
——(1970), Poetry in Northern Ireland, *Twentieth Century Studies*, 4, 89–93
——(1973), Review of *The Rough Field*, *The Malahat Review*, 27, 132–7
——(1981), *Courtyards in Delft*, Dublin, Gallery Press
——(1982), *The Hunt by Night*, Oxford, Oxford University Press
——(1985), *Antarctica*, Dublin, Gallery Press
——(1986), *Poems 1962–1978*, Oxford, Oxford University Press
——(1990 repr. 1993), *Selected Poems*, Harmondsworth, Penguin Books
——(1995), *The Hudson Letter*, Oldcastle, Gallery Press
——(1996), *Journalism: Selected Prose 1970–1995*, Oldcastle, Gallery Press
——(1997), *The Yellow Book*, Oldcastle, Gallery Press
——(1998), *Words in the Air: A Selection of Poems by Philippe Jaccottet*, Oldcastle, Gallery Press

Mills, B. (1998), Other Places: 4 Irish Poets, in H. Gilonis (ed.), 27–36
Montague, J. (1957), The First Week in Lent – A Political Snapshot, *Threshold*, 1:2, 70–1
——(1960), Outward Bound, *Threshold*, 4:2, 68–74
——(1963), The Rough Field, *The Spectator*, 26 April, 531
——(1964 repr. 1978), *Death of a Chieftain*, Swords, Poolbeg Press
——(1970), Foreword, *Threshold: The Northern Crisis*, 23, 1
——(1972 repr. 1990), *The Rough Field*, Newcastle upon Tyne, Bloodaxe Press
——(1979), Global Regionalism: Interview with John Montague, *Literary Review*, 22:2, 153–74
——(1989), *The Figure in the Cave and Other Essays*, ed. A. Quinn, Dublin, Lilliput Press
——(1995), *Collected Poems*, Dublin, Gallery Press
Muldoon, P. (1973), *New Weather*, London, Faber and Faber
——(1977), *Mules*, London, Faber and Faber
——(1980), *Why Brownlee Left*, London, Faber and Faber
——(1983), *Quoof*, London, Faber and Faber
——(1987), *Meeting the British*, London, Faber and Faber
——(1990), *Madoc*, London, Faber and Faber
——(1993), *Shining Brow*, London, Faber and Faber
——(1994a), *The Annals of Chile*, London, Faber and Faber
——(1994b), *The Prince of the Quotidian*, Oldcastle, Gallery Press
——(1998), *Hay*, London, Faber and Faber
Murphy, R. (1955), Three Modern Poets, *The Listener*, 54:1384, 8 September, 373–5
——(1963), The Pleasure Ground, *The Listener*, 70, 15 August, 237, 240
——(1968), *The Battle of Aughrim and The God Who Eats Corn*, London, Faber and Faber
——(1985), *New Selected Poems*, London, Faber and Faber
Ní Chuilleanáin, E. (1978), Drawing Lines, *Cyphers*, 10, 47–51
——(1980 repr. 1982), Woman as Writer: The Social Matrix, in M. Hederman and R. Kearney (eds), 1982, 614–18
——(1981), *The Rose-Geranium*, Dublin, Gallery Press
——(1985), (ed.) *Irish Women: Image and Achievement*, Dublin, Arlen House
——(rev. edn 1986), *The Second Voyage*, Dublin, Gallery Press
——(1989), *The Magdalene Sermon*, Dublin, Gallery Press
——(1992), Borderlands of Irish Poetry, in E. Andrews (ed.), 25–40
——(1994), *The Brazen Serpent*, Dublin, Gallery Press
Ní Dhomhnaill, N. (1986 repr. 1993), *Selected Poems: Rogha Dánta*, transl. M. Hartnett, Dublin, New Island Books/Raven Arts Press
——(1990 repr. 1994), *Pharaoh's Daughter*, Oldcastle, Gallery Press
——(1992a), *The Astrakhan Cloak*, Oldcastle, Gallery Press
——(1992b), What Foremothers?, *Poetry Ireland Review*, 36, 18–31
O'Grady, D. (1979), *The Headgear of the Tribe: Selected Poems*, ed. P. Fallon, Dublin, Gallery Press
——(1996), *The Road Taken: Poems 1956–96*, Salzburg, University of Salzburg Press
O'Loughlin, M. (1980), *Stalingrad: The Street Dictionary*, Dublin, Raven Arts Press
——(1982), *Atlantic Blues*, Dublin, Raven Arts Press
——(1985a), *The Diary of a Silence*, Dublin, Raven Arts Press
——(1985b), *Patrick Kavanagh and the Discourse of Contemporary Irish Poetry*, Dublin, Raven Arts Press
——(1991), Meridian – Dublin and Amsterdam, *The Irish Review*, 10, 7–13
——(1996), *Another Nation: New and Selected Poems*, Dublin, New Island Books
Paulin, T. (1977), *A State of Justice*, London, Faber and Faber
——(1980), *The Strange Museum*, London, Faber and Faber
——(1983), *Liberty Tree*, London, Faber and Faber

——(1984), *Ireland and the English Crisis*, Newcastle upon Tyne, Bloodaxe Books

——(1987), *Fivemiletown*, London, Faber and Faber

——(1990), *The Faber Book of Vernacular Verse*, London, Faber and Faber

——(1992 repr. 1993), *Minotaur: Poetry and the Nation State*, London, Faber and Faber

Scully, M. (1983), As I Like It, *the Beau*, 3, 10

——(1987), *Five Freedoms of Movement*, Newcastle upon Tyne, Galloping Dog Press

——(1994), *The Basic Colours: A Watchman's Log*, Durham, Pig Press

——(1997a), *Interlude*, Bray, Wild Honey Press

——(1997b), *Postlude*, Bray, Wild Honey Press

——(1997c), *Prelude*, Bray, Wild Honey Press

——(1998a), *Steps*, London / Saxmundham, Reality Street Editions

——(1998b), *Zulu Dynamite*, London, Form Books

Simmons, J. (1986), *Poems 1956–1986*, ed. E. Longley, Newcastle upon Tyne, Bloodaxe Books

Squires, G. (1969), *Sixteen Poems*, Portrush, Ulsterman Publications

——(1971), Public Poetry, *The Irish Times*, 30 March, 12

——(1975), *Drowned Stones*, Dublin, New Writers' Press

——(1978), *Figures*, Belfast, Ulsterman Publications

——(1980), *XXI Poems*, London, Menard Press

——(1996), *Landscapes & Silences: A Sequence*, Dublin, New Writers' Press

Walsh, C. (1987), *Making Tents*, Dublin, hardPressed Poetry

——(1989), *Short Stories*, Twickenham/Wakefield, North and South

——(1994), *Pitch*, Durham, Pig Press

——(1996), *idir eatortha & Making Tents*, Dublin, hardPressed Poetry

Watters, E. (1964 repr. 1985), *The Week-End of Dermot and Grace*, in R. A. Kelly and C. Ellis (eds) *Poetry Ireland Review*, 13

Yeats, W. B. (1989), *Yeats's Poems*, ed. A. Norman Jeffares and W. Gould, London, Macmillan

Selected anthologies

Barry, S. (1986), (ed.) *The Inherited Boundaries*, Dublin, Dolmen Press

Bolger, D. (1986), (ed.) *The Bright Wave: An Tonn Gheal*, Dublin, Raven Arts Press

——(1988), (ed.) *Invisible Cities: The New Dubliners*, Dublin, Raven Arts Press

Crotty, P. (1995), (ed.) *Modern Irish Poetry: An Anthology*, Belfast, Blackstaff Press

Dawe, G. (1982), (ed.) *The Younger Irish Poets*, Belfast, Blackstaff Press

Fallon, P. and Mahon, D. (1990), (eds) *The Penguin Book of Contemporary Irish Poetry*, Harmondsworth, Penguin Books

Fiacc, P. (1974), (ed.) *The Wearing of the Black: An Anthology of Contemporary Ulster Poetry*, Belfast, Blackstaff Press

Garrity, D. (1948), (ed.) *New Irish Poets*, New York, Devin-Adair Company

Greacen, R. and Iremonger, V. (1949), (eds) *Contemporary Irish Poetry*, London, Faber and Faber

Harmon, M. (1979), (ed.) *Irish Poetry After Yeats: Seven Poets*, Dublin, Wolfhound Press

Hooley, R. (1985), (ed.) *The Female Line: Northern Irish Women Writers*, Belfast, Northern Ireland Women's Rights Movement

Kelly, A. A. (1987 repr. 1988), (ed.) *Pillars of the House: An Anthology of Verse by Irish Women*, Dublin, Wolfhound Press

Kinsella, T. (1986), (ed.) *The New Oxford Book of Irish Verse*, Oxford, Oxford University Press

Kinsella, T. and Montague, J. (1962), *The Dolmen Miscellany of Irish Writing*, Dublin, Dolmen Press

MacDonagh, D. and Robinson, L. (1958), (eds) *The Oxford Book of Irish Verse*, Oxford, Clarendon Press

Mahon, D. (1972), (ed.) *The Sphere Book of Modern Irish Poetry*, London, Sphere Books

Montague, J. (1974), (ed.) *The Faber Book of Irish Verse*, London, Faber and Faber

Muldoon, P. (1986), (ed.) *The Faber Book of Contemporary Irish Poetry*, London, Faber and Faber

Ormsby, F. (1990), (ed.) *Poets from the North of Ireland*, Belfast, Blackstaff Press

Simmons, J. (1974), (ed.) *Ten Irish Poets: An Anthology*, Manchester, Carcanet Press

Smythe, A. (1989b), (ed.) *Wildish Things: An Anthology of New Irish Women's Writing*, Dublin, Attic Press

Books and articles

Allison, J. (1992), Acts of Union: Seamus Heaney's Tropes of Sex and Marriage, *Éire-Ireland*, 27:4, 106–21

Andrews, E. (1992), (ed.) *Contemporary Irish Poetry: A Collection of Critical Essays*, London, Macmillan

——(1998), *The Poetry of Seamus Heaney*, Cambridge, Icon Books

Archambeau, R. (1998), *Another Ireland: An Essay*, Bray, Wild Honey Press

Ashcroft, B. Griffiths, G. and Tiffin, H. (1989), *The Empire Writes Back: Theory and Practice in Post-colonial Literatures*, London, Routledge

Bardon, J. (1992 repr. 1996), *A History of Ulster*, Belfast, Blackstaff Press

Barry, K. (1996), Critical Notes on Post-Colonial Aesthetics, *Irish Studies Review*, 14, 2–11

Barthes, R. (1989), *Mythologies*, London, Paladin Press

Barton, B. (1996), *A Pocket History of Ulster*, Dublin, O'Brien Press

Bell, D. (1991), Cultural Studies in Ireland and the Postmodern Debate, *Irish Journal of Sociology*, 1, 83–95

Benjamin, W. (1979), *Illuminations*, London, Fontana

Bew, P., Gibbon, P. and Patterson, H. (1979), *The British State and the Ulster Crisis: 1921–72*, Manchester, Manchester University Press

——(1996), *Northern Ireland 1921–96: Political Forces and Social Classes*, London, Serif Press

Bew, P., Hazelkorn, E. and Patterson, H. (1989), *The Dynamics of Irish Politics*, London, Lawrence and Wishart

Bew, P. and Patterson, H. (1982), *Seán Lemass and the Making of Modern Ireland 1945–66*, Dublin, Gill and Macmillan

Bohman, K. S. (1994), An Interview with Medbh McGuckian, *The Irish Review*, 16, 95–108

Boyce, D. G. and O'Day, A. (1996), (eds) *The Making of Modern Irish History: Revisionism and the Revisionist Controversy*, London, Routledge

Bradley, A. (1988), Literature and Culture in the North of Ireland, in M. Kennedy (ed.), 36–72

Brandes, R. (1990), Ciaran Carson Interviewed by Rand Brandes, *The Irish Review*, 8, 77–90

Breathnach, P. (1988), Uneven Development and Capitalist Peripheralisation: The Case of Ireland, *Antipode*, 20:2, 122–41

Brennan, R. (1995), Contemporary Irish Poetry: An Overview, in M. Kenneally (ed.), 1–27

Broder, P. F. (1979), Breaking the Shell of Solitude: Some Poems of Thomas Kinsella, *Éire-Ireland*, 14:2, 80–92

Brown, T. (1975), *Northern Voices: Poets from Ulster*, Dublin, Gill and Macmillan

——(1985), *Ireland: A Social and Cultural History 1922–85*, London, Fontana Press

——(1986), Poetry and Partition: A Personal View, *Krino*, 2, 17–23

——(1988), *Ireland's Literature: Selected Essays*, Mullingar, Lilliput Press

Brown, T. and Grene, N. (1989), (eds) *Tradition and Influence in Anglo-Irish Literature*, London, Macmillan

Bruce, S. (1992), *The Red Hand: Protestant Paramilitaries in Northern Ireland*, Oxford, Oxford University Press

Butler, H. (1986), *Escape from the Anthill*, Mullingar, Lilliput Press

Cadogan, A. (1997a), Interview with Michael Hartnett (unpublished)

——(1997b), Interview with Thomas Kinsella (unpublished)

Cahill, E. (1994), 'Because I Never Garden': Medbh McGuckian's Solitary Way, *Irish University Review*, 24:2, 264–71

Cairns, D. and Richards, S. (1988), *Writing Ireland: Colonialism, Nationalism and Culture*, Manchester, Manchester University Press

Callinicos, A. (1989), *Against Postmodernism: A Marxist Critique*, Cambridge, Polity Press

Carlson, J. (1990), *Banned in Ireland: Censorship and the Irish Writer*, London, Routledge

Clyde, T. (1988), An Ulster Twilight: Poetry in the North of Ireland, *Krino*, 5, 95–102

——(1999), *HU*: A Contemporary 'Little Magazine' in its Contexts, in H. Klein, S. Coelsch-Foisner and W. Görtschacher (eds) *Poetry Now: Contemporary British and Irish Poetry in the Making*, Tübingen, Stauffenburg Verlag, 355–63

Cohen, R. (1997), *Global Diasporas: An Introduction*, London, UCL Press Limited

Connor, S. (1996), *The English Novel in History: 1950–95*, London, Routledge

Consalvo, D. M. (1993), In Common Usage: Eavan Boland's Poetic Voice, *Éire-Ireland*, 28:2, 148–61

Constable, J. (1984), Derek Mahon's Development, *Agenda*, 22:3–4, 107–18

Coogan, T. P. (1995 repr. 1996), *The Troubles: Ireland's Ordeal 1966–96 and the Search for Peace*, London, Arrow Books

Cooke, H. (1973), Harriet Cooke Talks to the Poet Derek Mahon, *The Irish Times*, 17 January, 10

Cooney, S. (1967), Austin Clarke's 'Celebration': A Commentary, *Éire-Ireland*, 2:3, 16–26

Corcoran, N. (1983), The Blessings of Onan: Austin Clarke's *Mnemosyne Lay in Dust*, *Irish University Review*, 13:1, 43–53

——(1986), *A Student's Guide to Seamus Heaney*, London, Faber and Faber

——(1987), Seamus Heaney and the Art of the Exemplary, in C. J. Rawson (ed.) *The Yearbook of English Studies: British Poetry Since 1945 Special Number*, 17, 117–27

——(1992), (ed.) *The Chosen Ground: Essays on the Contemporary Poetry of Northern Ireland*, Bridgend, Seren Books

——(1993), *English Poetry Since 1940*, Harlow, Longman

——(1997), *After Yeats and Joyce: Reading Modern Irish Literature*, Oxford, Oxford University Press

——(1998), *The Poetry of Seamus Heaney: A Critical Study*, London, Faber and Faber

Corkery, D. (1924 repr. 1979), *The Hidden Ireland: A Study of Gaelic Munster in the Eighteenth Century*, Dublin, Gill and Macmillan

——(1931), *Synge and Anglo-Irish Literature*, Cork, Cork University Press

Coughlan, P. (1991), 'Bog Queens': The Representation of Women in the Poetry of John Montague and Seamus Heaney, in D. Cairns and T. O'Brien Johnson (eds) *Gender in Irish Writing*, Milton Keynes, Open University Press, 88–111

Coughlan, P. and Davis, A. (1995), (eds) *Modernism and Ireland: The Poetry of the 1930s*, Cork, Cork University Press

Crotty, P. (1990), Vocal Variations, *The Irish Review*, 9, 104

——(1997), Cunning Ampersands, *The Irish Review*, 20, 136–43

Cullen, L. (1988), *The Hidden Ireland: Reassessment of a Concept*, Dublin, Lilliput Press

Curtis, T. (1994), (ed.) *The Art of Seamus Heaney*, Bridgend, Seren Books

Davie, D. (1975), Austin Clarke and Padraic Fallon, in D. Dunn (ed.), 37–58

Davis, A. (1995), 'Foreign and Credible': Denis Devlin's Modernism, *Éire-Ireland*, 30:2, 131–47

——(1996), Irish Poetic Modernisms: A Reappraisal, *Critical Survey*, 8:2, 186–97

——(1997), Denis Devlin: Aestheticism and the Avant-Garde, *Colby Quarterly*, 33:4, 305–19

——(1998), 'No Narrative Easy in the Mind': Modernism, the Avant-Garde and Irish Poetry, in H. Gilonis (ed.), 37–50

Dawe, G. (1989), An Absence of Influence: Three Modernist Poets, in T. Brown and N. Grene (eds), 119–42

——(1992), The Suburban Night: On Eavan Boland, Paul Durcan and Thomas McCarthy, in E. Andrews (ed.), 168–93

——(1995), Poetry as Example: Kinsella's Peppercanister Poems, in M. Kenneally (ed.), 204–15

Deane, S. (1975), Irish Poetry and Irish Nationalism, in D. Dunn (ed.), 4–22

——(1977 repr. 1982), Happy and at Home: Interview with Seamus Heaney, in M. Hederman and R. Kearney (eds), 1982, 66–72

——(1983), *Civilians and Barbarians*, Derry, Field Day Theatre Company

——(1985), *Celtic Revivals: Essays in Modern Irish Literature 1880–1980*, London, Faber and Faber

——(1986), *A Short History of Irish Literature*, London, Hutchinson

——(1990), (ed.) *Nationalism, Colonialism and Literature*, Minneapolis, University of Minnesota Press

——(1991), (ed.) *The Field Day Anthology of Irish Writing*, 3 vols, Derry, Field Day Theatre Company

De Certeau, M. (1984 repr. 1990), Walking in the City, in S. During (1990) (ed.), *The Cultural Studies Reader*, London, Routledge

Delanty, G. (1994), Circles Radiating: The Poetry of Patrick Galvin, *Éire-Ireland*, 29:1, 141–50

Denman, P. (1989), Austin Clarke: Tradition, Memory and Our Lot, in T. Brown and N. Grene (eds), 63–78

——(1992), Rude Gestures? Contemporary Women's Poetry in Irish, *Colby Quarterly*, 28:4, 251–9

Docherty, T. (1992), Initiations, Tempers, Seductions: Postmodern McGuckian, in N. Corcoran (ed.), 191–210

Dorgan, T. (1996), (ed.) *Irish Poetry Since Kavanagh*, Dublin, Four Courts Press

Dunn, D. (1975), (ed.) *Two Decades of Irish Writing: A Critical Survey*, Cheadle Hulme, Carcanet

Eagleton, T. (1981 repr. 1992), *Walter Benjamin or Towards a Revolutionary Criticism*, London, Verso

Elliott, M. (1992), Paul Durcan – Duarchain, in E. Andrews (ed.), 304–28

Fallon, B. (1998), *An Age of Innocence: Irish Culture 1930–1960*, Dublin, Gill and Macmillan

Farren, R. (1948), *The Course of Irish Verse in English*, London, Sheed and Ward Ltd

Feldman, A. (1991), *Formations of Violence: The Narrative of the Body and Political Terror in Northern Ireland*, Chicago, University of Chicago Press

Finlayson, A. (1997), The Problem of 'Culture' in Northern Ireland: A Critique of the Cultural Traditions Group, *The Irish Review*, 20, 76–88

Foster, J. W. (1978), Review of *The Second Voyage* by Eiléan Ní Chuilleanáin, *Éire-Ireland*, 13:4, 147–51

——(1991), *Colonial Consequences: Essays in Irish Literature and Culture*, Dublin, Lilliput Press

Foster, R. F. (1989), *Modern Ireland 1600–1972*, Harmondsworth, Penguin Books

Garratt, R. F. (1986 rev. 1989), *Modern Irish Poetry: Tradition and Continuity from Yeats to Heaney*, Berkeley, University of California Press

Garvin, T. (1988), The Politics of Denial and of Cultural Defence: The Referenda of 1983 and 1986 in Context, *The Irish Review*, 3, 1–7

Geden, M. (1996), unpublished interview with Thomas McCarthy in part fulfilment of M.A. dissertation for Department of English UCC, 9/12/1996

Gibbon, P. (1975), *The Origins of Ulster Unionism: The Formation of Popular Protestant Politics and Ideology in Nineteenth Century Ireland*, Manchester University Press, Manchester

Gibbons, L. (1996), *Transformations in Irish Culture*, Cork, Cork University Press

Gilonis, H. (1998), (ed.) *For the Birds: Proceedings of the First Cork Conference on New and Experimental Irish Poetry (26 April 1997)*, Sutton, Mainstream Poetry Press / Dublin, hardPressed Poetry

——(1999), Introduction to Trevor Joyce, paper delivered at the Sub Voicive Poetry Conference, London, 29 January, british-poets@mailbase.ac.uk

Goodby, J. (1994), Hermeneutic Hermeticism: Paul Muldoon and the Northern Irish Poetic, in C. C. Barfoot (ed.) *In Black and Gold: Contiguous Traditions in Post-War British and Irish Poetry*, Amsterdam, Rodopi Press, 137–68

——(1996), 'A Rising Tide': Irish Poetry in the 60s, in T. Dorgan (ed.), 116–35

Goodby, J. and Scully, M. (1999), (eds), *Colonies of Belief: Irish Modernism, Angel Exhaust*, 17

Gramsci, A. (1971 repr. 1996), *Selections from the Prison Notebooks of Antonio Gramsci*, ed. and transl. Q. Hoare and G. N. Smith, London, Lawrence and Wishart

Gray, K. M. (1994), The Attic Lips: Feminist Pamphleteering for the New Ireland, *Éire-Ireland*, 29:1, 105–22

Gregson, I. (1996), *Contemporary Poetry and Postmodernism: Dialogue and Estrangement*, London, Macmillan

Haberstroh, P. B. (1996), *Women Creating Women: Contemporary Irish Women Poets*, Syracuse, Syracuse University Press

Haffenden, J. (1981), *Viewpoints: Poets in Conversation*, London, Faber and Faber

Hancock, T. (1994), Identity Problems in Paul Muldoon's 'The More a Man Has, the More a Man Wants', *The Honest Ulsterman*, 97, 57–64

Harmon, M. (1973), New Voices in the Fifties, in S. Lucy (ed.), *Irish Poets in English*, Cork, Mercier Books, 185–207

——(1978), (ed.) *Richard Murphy: Poet of Two Traditions*, Dublin, Wolfhound Press

——(1989), *Austin Clarke: A Critical Introduction*, Dublin, Wolfhound Press

Hawthorn, J. (1996), *Cunning Passages: New Historicism, Cultural Materialism and Marxism in the Contemporary Literary Debate*, London, Arnold

Hederman, M. P. (1985), Poetry and the Fifth Province, *The Crane Bag: Contemporary Cultural Debate*, 9:2, 110–19

Hederman, M. and Kearney, R. (1982), (eds) *The Crane Bag Book of Irish Studies (1977–1981)*, Dublin, Blackwater Press

Hofmann, M. (1990), Muldoon – A Mystery, *London Review of Books*, 20 December, 18–19

Horton, P. (1995), First Language, *The Honest Ulsterman*, 99, 85–6

Hughes, E. (1991), (ed.), Introduction, in *Culture and Politics in Northern Ireland*, Milton Keynes, Open University Press

Hutchinson, P. (1997), Pearse Hutchinson Interviewed: Drowning in the Aesthetic, *Poetry Ireland Review*, 52, 22–33

Jackson, T. H. (1995), *The Whole Matter: The Poetic Evolution of Thomas Kinsella*, Dublin, Lilliput Press

Jameson, F. (1988), Periodizing the 60s, in *The Ideologies of Theory: Essays 1971–1986. Volume 2: The Syntax of History*, London, Routledge, 178–208

John, B. (1996), *Reading the Ground: The Poetry of Thomas Kinsella*, Washington D.C., Catholic University of America Press

Johnston, D. (1985, rev. edn 1995), *Irish Poetry after Joyce*, Notre Dame, University of Notre Dame Press

Kane, M. (1981), Review of *Why Brownlee Left*, *Cyphers*, 15, 49–51

Kearney, R. (1988), *Transitions: Narratives in Modern Irish Culture*, Dublin, Wolfhound Press

——(1992), Myth and Modernity in Irish Poetry, in E. Andrews (ed.), 41–62

——(1997), *Postnationalist Ireland: Politics, Culture, Philosophy*, London, Routledge

Keller, L. (1994), A Conversation with Paul Muldoon, *Contemporary Literature*, 35:1, 4–32

Kendall, T. (1994), 'Leavetakings and Homecomings': Derek Mahon's Belfast, *Éire-Ireland*, 29:4, 101–16

——(1995), 'Parallel to the Parallel Realm': Paul Muldoon's *Madoc: A Mystery*, *Irish University Review*, 25:2, 232–41

——(1996), *Paul Muldoon*, Seren Books, Bridgend

Kenneally, M. (1995), (ed.) *Poetry in Contemporary Irish Literature*, Gerrards Cross, Colin Smythe

Kennedy, D. (1996), *new relations: the refashioning of british poetry 1980–1994*, Bridgend, Seren Books

Kennedy, L. (1996), *Colonialism, Religion and Nationalism in Ireland*, Belfast, Institute of Irish Studies

Kennedy, M. (1988), (ed.) *Cultural Contexts and Literary Idioms in Contemporary Irish Literature*, Gerrards Cross, Colin Smythe

Kerrigan, J. (1998), Hidden Ireland: Eiléan Ní Chuilleanáin and Munster Poetry, *Critical Quarterly*, 40:4, 76–106

Kiberd, D. (1995), *Inventing Ireland: The Literature of the Modern Nation*, London, Jonathan Cape

Kirkland, R. (1996), *Literature and Culture in Northern Ireland Since 1965: Moments of Danger*, Harlow, Longman

Lee, J. J. (1989 repr. 1993), *Ireland: 1912–1985*, Cambridge, Cambridge University Press

Leerssen, J. (1998), 1798: The Recurrence of Violence and Two Conceptualizations of History, *The Irish Review*, 22, 37–45

Liddy, J. (1978), Ulster Poets and the Catholic Muse, *Éire-Ireland*, 13:4, 126–37

——(1979), Ulster Poets and the Protestant Muse, *Éire-Ireland*, 14:2, 118–27

Lloyd, D. (1987), *Nationalism and Minor Literature: James Clarence Mangan and the Emergence of Irish Cultural Nationalism*, Berkeley, University of California Press

——(1993), *Anomalous States: Irish Writing and the Post-Colonial Moment*, Dublin, Lilliput Press

Loftus, R. (1964), *Nationalism in Modern Irish Poetry*, Madison, University of Wisconsin Press

Longley, E. (1975), 'Searching the Darkness': Richard Murphy, Thomas Kinsella, John Montague and James Simmons, in D. Dunn (ed.), 118–53

——(1986), *Poetry in the Wars*, Newcastle upon Tyne, Bloodaxe

——(1988), *Louis MacNeice: A Study*, London, Faber and Faber

——(1992a), The Aesthetic and the Territorial, in E. Andrews (ed.), 63–85

——(1992b), Belfast Diary, *London Review of Books*, 14:1, 21

——(1994), *The Living Stream: Literature and Revisionism in Ireland*, Newcastle upon Tyne, Bloodaxe Press

——(1995), Derek Mahon: Extreme Religion of Art, in Kenneally (ed.), 280–303

Lucy, S. (1974), John Montague's *The Rough Field*: An Introductory Note, *Studies*, 63, 29–30

——(1977), Irish Writing: A New Criticism, *Hibernia*, 1 April, 18

Lyons, F. S. L. (1973, 2nd edn 1985), *Ireland Since the Famine*, London, Fontana

MacAnna, F. (1991), The Dublin Renaissance: An Essay on Modern Dublin and Dublin Writers, *The Irish Review*, 10, 14–30

McCormack, W. J. (1986), *The Battle of the Books*, Dublin, Lilliput Press

——(1987), Politics or Community: Crux of Thomas Kinsella's Aesthetic Development, *Tracks: Thomas Kinsella Special Issue*, Dublin, Dedalus Press, 61–77

——(1994), *From Burke to Beckett: Ascendancy, Tradition and Betrayal in Literary History*, Cork, Cork University Press

McCracken, K. (1995), Ciaran Carson: Unravelling the Conditional, Mapping the Provisional, in M. Kenneally (ed.), 356–72

McCurry, J. (1992), 'S'Crap': Colonialism Indicted in the Poetry of Paul Muldoon, *Éire-Ireland*, 27:3, 92–109

McDonald, P. (1988), Home and Away, *The Irish Review*, 4, 106–9

——(1995), Seamus Heaney as Critic, in M. Kenneally (ed.), 174–89

——(1997), *Mistaken Identities: Poetry and Northern Ireland*, Oxford, Clarendon Press

McIvor, P. K. (1983), Regionalism in Ulster: An Historical Perspective, *Irish University Review*, 13:2, 180–8

MacLaughlin, J. (1994), *Ireland: The Emigrant Nursery and the World Economy*, Cork, Cork University Press

Martin, A. (1965), Inherited Dissent: The Dilemma of the Irish Writer, *Studies*, 54, 1–20

Matthews, S. (1997), *Irish Poetry: Politics, History, Negotiation. The Evolving Debate, 1969 to the Present*, Basingstoke, Macmillan

Maxwell, D. E. S. (1973), Imagining the North: Violence and the Writers, *Éire-Ireland*, 8:2, 91–107

Mays, J. C. C. (1976 repr. 1999), A Poem by Denis Devlin with Some Questions and Conclusions, in J. Goodby and M. Scully (eds), 1999, 81–7

——(1998), Drift into Net Back to Drift, *the Journal*, 1, 58–60

Meaney, G. (1995), History Gasps: Myth in Contemporary Irish Women's Poetry, in M. Kenneally (ed.), 99–113

Meir, C. (1991), Review of *Belfast Confetti*, *The Linenhall Review*, 8:1, 8–11

Miller, D. W. (1978), *Queen's Rebels: Ulster Loyalism in Historical Perspective*, Dublin, Gill and Macmillan

Mitchell, A. and Ó Snogaigh, P. (1985), *Irish Political Documents 1916–1949*, Dublin, Irish Academic Press

Muri, A. (1999), McGuckian Bibliography http://www.lights.com/~muri/mmbiblio.html

Murphy, S. (1997), Obliquity in the Poetry of Paul Muldoon and Medbh McGuckian, *Éire-Ireland*, 31:3/4, 76–101

Naiden, J. (1991), 'Orphaned Like Us': Memory in the Poetry of Thomas McCarthy, *Éire-Ireland*, 24:2, 104–19

Nash, C. (1993), Remapping and Renaming: New Cartographies of Identity, Gender and Landscape in Ireland, *Feminist Review*, 44, 39–57

O'Brien, C. C. (1975), A Slow North-east Wind, *The Listener*, 94, 25 September, 404–5

O'Brien, S. (1998), *The Deregulated Muse*, Newcastle upon Tyne, Bloodaxe Books

O Conner, L. (1998), The 'War of the Womb': Folklore and Nuala Ní Dhomhnaill, in B. Stewart (ed.) *That Other World: The Supernatural and the Fantastic in Irish Literature and its Contents*, Gerrards Cross, Colin Smythe

O'Connor, F. (1993), *In Search of a State: Catholics in Northern Ireland*, Belfast, Blackstaff Press

O'Donoghue, B. (1992), Involved Imaginings, in N. Corcoran (ed.), 171–88

——(1994), *Seamus Heaney and the Language of Poetry*, Hemel Hempstead, Harvester / Wheatsheaf

——(1995), 'The Half-Said Thing to Them is Dearest': Paul Muldoon, in M. Kenneally (ed.), 400–18

O'Driscoll, D. (1987), An Interview with Michael Hartnett, *Poetry Ireland Review*, 20, 16–21

O'Halloran, C. (1987), *Partition and the Limits of Irish Nationalism: An Ideology under Stress*, Dublin, Gill and Macmillan

Olson, C. (1997), *Collected Prose*, Berkeley and Los Angeles, University of California Press

O'Neill, M. (1999), 'Holding Nature up to Art': The Poetry of Derek Mahon, in H. Klein, S. Coelsch-Foisner and W. Görtschacher, (eds) *Poetry Now: Contemporary British and Irish Poetry in the Making*, Tübingen, Stauffenburg Verlag, 215–23

Ormsby, F. (1991), Ciaran Carson Interviewed by Frank Ormsby, *The Linenhall Review*, 8:1, 5–8

O Seaghdha, B. (1990), Ulster Regionalism: The Unpleasant Facts, *The Irish Review*, 8, 54–61

O'Toole, F. (1988), Island of Saints and Silicon: Literature and Social Change in Contemporary Ireland, in M. Kennedy (ed.), 11–35

——(1996), Sins of Omission, review of *Inventing Ireland*, *Observer Review*, 7 January, 15

Parker, M. (1993 repr. 1994), *Seamus Heaney: The Making of the Poet*, Dublin, Gill and Macmillan

Patten, E. (1995), Fiction in Conflict: Northern Ireland's Prodigal Novelists, in I. A. Bell (ed.) *Peripheral Visions: Images of Nationhood in Contemporary British Fiction*, Cardiff, University of Wales Press, 128–48

Preminger, A. and Brogan, T. V. F. (1993), (eds) *The New Princeton Encyclopaedia of Poetry and Poetics*, Princeton, Princeton University Press

Quinn, A. (1989), 'The Well-Beloved': Montague and the Muse, in A. Quinn (ed.) *Irish University Review: John Montague Special Issue*, 19:1, 27–43

——(1991), *Patrick Kavanagh: Born-Again Romantic*, Dublin, Gill and Macmillan

——(1992), Speaking the Unspoken: The Poetry of Mary Dorcey, *Colby Quarterly*, 28:4, 227–38

Randall, J. (1979), An Interview with Seamus Heaney, *Ploughshares*, 5:3, 7–22

Redmond, J. (1995), Interview with Ian Duhig, *Thumbscrew*, 3, 25–32

Redshaw, T. D. (1974), John Montague's *The Rough Field*: Topos and Texne, *Studies*, 63:1, 31–46

Riordan, M. (1984), An Urbane Perspective: The Poetry of Derek Mahon, in M. Harmon (ed.) *The Irish Writer and the City*, Gerrards Cross, Colin Smythe, 169–79

——(1985), Eros and History: On Contemporary Irish Poetry, *The Crane Bag*, 9, 49–55

Robinson, A. (1988), *Instabilities in Contemporary British Poetry*, London, Macmillan

——(1992), Seamus Heaney's *Seeing Things*: Familiar Compound Ghosts, *Anglistentag*, 14, 46–56

Roche, A. (1996), Platforms: The Journals, the Publishers, in T. Dorgan (ed.), 71–81

Rosenthal, M. L. (1967), *The New Poets: American and British Poets Since World War Two*, Oxford, Oxford University Press

Roulston, S. (1983), Past Tense, Present Tension: Protestant Poetry and Ulster History, *Éire-Ireland*, 18:3, 100–23

Ruane, J. and Todd, J. (1996), *The Dynamics of Conflict in Northern Ireland: Power, Conflict and Emancipation*, Cambridge, Cambridge University Press

Rumens, C. (1997), Taig-Tickling and Prod-Picking: Some Northern Irish Poets and their Critics, *Thumbscrew*, 7, 20–8

Ryan, J. (1975), *Remembering How We Stood: Bohemian Dublin at the Mid-Century*, Dublin, Gill and Macmillan

Said, E. (1991), *Orientalism*, Harmondsworth, Penguin Books

Scammell, W. (1991), Interview with Derek Mahon, *Poetry Review*, 81:2, 2–6

Schirmer, G. A. (1995), (ed.) *Reviews and Essays of Austin Clarke*, Gerrards Cross, Colin Smythe

Sergeant, H. (1953), Ulster Regionalism, *Rann*, 20, 3–7

Sheehy, M. (1968), *Is Ireland Dying? Culture and the Church in Modern Ireland*, London, Hollis and Carter

Shields, K. (1994), Derek Mahon's Poetry of Belonging, *Irish University Review: Derek Mahon Special Issue*, 24:1, 67–79

Skelt, P. (1991), (ed.) *Prospect into Breath: Interviews with North and South Writers*, Twickenham and Wakefield, North and South Press

Skelton, R. (1969), The Poetry of Thomas Kinsella, *Éire-Ireland*, 4:1, 86–108

Smith, K. (1986), Interview with Medbh McGuckian, *Gown Literary Supplement*, 15–18

Smith, M. (1971), Irish Poetry Since Yeats: Towards a Corrected History, *Denver Quarterly*, 5, 1–26

Smith, S. (1982), *Inviolable Voice: History and Twentieth Century Poetry*, Dublin, Gill and Macmillan

——(1995a), The Language of Displacement in Contemporary Irish Poetry, in M. Kenneally (ed.), 61–83

——(1995b) 'Precarious Guest': The Poetry of Denis Devlin, in P. Coughlan and A. Davis (eds), 232–48

Smyth, G. (1998), *Decolonisation and Criticism: The Construction of Irish Literature*, London, Pluto Press

Smythe, A. (1989a) The Floozie in the Jacuzzi: Intersextextual Inserts, *The Irish Review*, 6, 7–24

Stewart, B. (1998), Inside Nationalism: A Meditation upon *Inventing Ireland*, *Irish Studies Review*, 6:1, 5–16

Thornley, D. (1964), Ireland: The End of An Era?, *Studies*, 53, 1–17

Tóbín, C. (1996), (ed.) *The Kilfenora Teaboy: A Study of Paul Durcan*, Dublin, New Island Books

Tobin, F. (1984), *The Best of Decades: Ireland in the Nineteen Sixties*, Dublin, Gill and Macmillan

Walsh, C. (1975), Arts and Studies: Caroline Walsh Talked to Valentin Iremonger, *The Irish Times*, 22 October, 10

Warner, A. (1973), *Clay is the Word: Patrick Kavanagh 1904–1967*, Dublin, Dolmen Press

Welch, R. (1996), (ed.) *The Oxford Companion to Irish Literature*, Oxford, Clarendon Press

Whyte, J. (1996), *Interpreting Northern Ireland*, Oxford, Clarendon Press

Williams, G. A. (1979), *Madoc: The Making of a Myth*, London, Eyre Methuen

Williams, P. and Chrisman, C. (1993), *Colonial Discourse and Post-colonial Theory: A Reader*, Hemel Hempstead, Harvester / Wheatsheaf

Wills, C. (1993), *Improprieties: Politics and Sexuality in Northern Irish Poetry*, Oxford, Clarendon Press

——(1995), Voices from the Nursery: Medbh McGuckian's Plantation, in M. Kenneally (ed.), 373–99

——(1998), *Reading Paul Muldoon*, Newcastle upon Tyne, Bloodaxe Press

Wilson, W. A. (1987), Paul Muldoon and the Poetics of Sexual Difference, *Contemporary Literature*, 28:3, 317–31

Index

Note: n. after a page reference indicates a note number on that page.